THE ROOTS

OF

THE MODERN

AMERICAN

EMPIRE

THE ROOTS
OF
THE MODERN
AMERICAN
EMPIRE

A Study of the Growth
and Shaping of
Social Consciousness in a
Marketplace Society

BY

WILLIAM APPLEMAN WILLIAMS

Vintage Books
A Division of Random House
New York

Library of Congress Catalog Card Number: 77-85619
Manufactured in the United States of America

First Vintage Books Edition, October 1970

FOR

William Best Hesseltine

AND

Harvey Goldberg

With deeply affectionate

gratitude for their friendship,

and with

great respect for their

wisdom and courage

PREFACE

In the practical as in the theoretic life, the man whose acquisitions stick is the man who is always achieving and advancing, whilst his neighbors, spending most of their time in relearning what they once knew but have forgotten, simply hold their own.

William James, *Psychology*, 1892

A man must have a certain amount of intelligent ignorance to get anywhere.

Charles Francis Kettering, 1946

Notes on the Relevance of History,
and for an Autobiography
of This Book

"THE TROUBLE is that something's gone wrong. It should be turnin' out great. We've just gone off the road someplace. That's what we've got to find out—where we've gone off the road. Then—"

"Hell, it's not that. You're just wrong. It's a new ball game, and you just don't get it yet. Yesterday's dead, and every day-before-yesterday's dead. Forget it. Slip it. Bury it. If you'll do that, then . . ."

That exchange, scribbled down even as I added my own remarks, occurred in my office in the fall of 1967 between two highly intelligent and engaged students who were discussing the troubles and tensions of the nation and the university. I fired my words into theirs:

"You're both wrong. Nothin's gone wrong—at least not in that sense. Yesterday's not dead or gone. We're just meeting it head-on for the first time in a hundred years."

All three of us were arguing about the relevance of a knowledge of American history to the enormous task of making sense out of our contemporary predicament, and to the work of formulating and acting on positive and creative alternatives to that unhappy situation. The crucial aspect of that conversation, typical of many I've had with students since 1964, is that the initiative was with the man who was saying that history is irrelevant. Carried to its extreme, that argument denies the value of any indirect or vicarious experience. And it is advanced in that form more often than many parents (or professors) either know or care to admit. In most cases, however, even the extremists are launching their own fear on the wings of wild rhetoric in the desperate hope that it will be shot down.

For the truth of the matter is that not even the young extremists want to have to make every mistake over again. What they want is some relevant history. It is a fair question. It is a reasonable demand. And it is a very clear need.

I

I am not at all sure that this book fully meets the demand, or wholly satisfies the need. But I am confident that it speaks to the question.

There are several themes in the argument that a knowledge of history is at best incidental to our contemporary crises. Many of them are advanced by people who defend, rather than criticize, the status quo. This is particularly true of the assertion that nothing can be done about what happened in the past, and that no useful purpose is served by discussing those aspects of the matter. "It doesn't make any difference how we got into the difficulty," runs that refrain. "We can't do anything about that, and we have to see it through." The underlying nature of that argument is very similar to the one made by the critics. "It doesn't make any difference how we got into the mess we're in," the opposition says, "except maybe to blame the right people, because we can't do anything about that. The important thing is to change it all."

The one approach ignores the distinct probability that seeing through the predicament without understanding it will do nothing but sustain and compound the inherent difficulties of the problem. The other misses the similar probability that the effort to change the situation without comprehending it will merely recreate it in a different form.

A more sophisticated version of the argument that the past is largely irrelevant takes the form of pointing out the great differences between the contemporary scene and American society during the eighteenth or nineteenth centuries. Those who advocate that approach grant the possibility (and value) of learning by example, but hold that the illustration has to be comparable in all fundamental respects. Thus they maintain that it is impossible for a highly centralized industrial political economy, governed by an elite from the upper class, to learn anything significant or actionable from a society that was largely agricultural, that was still operating on the assumptions of the classical free marketplace, and that, in social and political matters, was freer and more open.

Cast in that form, the assertion that history is irrelevant becomes more plausible. One has to penetrate deeper into the issues, for example, to establish the value of a modern corporation executive knowing anything about nineteenth-century agriculture in Minnesota and the Dakotas. Yet even there the case for irrelevancy is by no means as obvious as appearances seem to suggest. One of the striking problems confronting the modern executive, for example, is created by the way the organization and the operation of the corporation destroy the old social and economic ecology without creating a new balance based on a community of association, interest, and mutual responsibility. That was precisely what happened, however, when consolidated capital from outside the region moved into the Red River Valley and created the huge bonanza grain farms of the late 1870s and early 1880s. The approach ultimately failed because its economies of scale proved insufficiently rewarding over a period of time, because it provoked serious political opposition, and because it failed to generate the development of a society (let alone a community).

Those are the very troubles that confront the modern corporation as it moves through the second half of the twentieth century, and those difficulties have been intensified and extended because the leaders of the corporation economy have failed to anticipate or recognize them. Knowledge of the past might not have produced prompt and perfect solutions, but it would have alerted the latter-day executives to the unfavorable probabilities. And such awareness could have provided them, in the person of James Jerome Hill of the Great Northern Railroad, with the example of a corporation leader who did learn from the weaknesses and the failure of the bonanza farms, and who applied that lesson for the benefit of his own corporation and for the rest of the people in the region.

Hill did not become a utopian, or even a reformer in the usual sense of that term, but he did recognize and act on the necessity of dealing with the needs of the agricultural society in which he operated. He realized that all corporations would go the way of the bonanza farms unless they became more relevant and responsive to the requirements of the rest of society. Hill's performance makes the additional point that people are more likely to learn from the past, and to act creatively on that knowledge, if they assume that history is relevant. The attitude that history is incidental reinforces the propensity that we humans seem to have against learning in any other way than being burned. Hill did believe he could learn from the experience of other people, and the experience of other people, after all, is the essence of history.

The relevance of history becomes particularly strong in connection with attitudes, ideas, and patterns of behavior—with social consciousness and its consequences. In certain respects, at least, those phenomena evolve in a way that is similar to the cycle of metamorphosis in insects. Not only do attitudes and ideas go through various stages of development in which they appear as distinct things, but the later forms are apt to appear so different from the earlier ones that it is quite possible to conclude that they have no relationship with each other. Such confusion often leads people to believe they are acting on quite different assumptions, and following a wholly different logic, than is actually the case. When their expectations are not fulfilled, therefore, they are prone to explain the discrepancy by pointing to other factors, including other individuals and nations, instead of reexamining their own outlook. It is often difficult to change one's attitude and behavior even when the need for such action is understood, and hence the failure to do so when one lacks that understanding should not be considered strange or incomprehensible.

II

Historians, being human, have been known to overlook the particular relevancy of a certain part of history. In a very real sense, moreover, this book is a product of my own discovery that I had made just that mistake. I was very slow in realizing that the ideas and actions of Americans between 1860 and 1893 played a primary part in the development and acceptance of the foreign policy that the United States followed after 1893. I was slow, furthermore, not only in the sense that it took me a considerable amount of time to grasp the precise nature of the connection, but I was slow in recognizing the insights and other indicators that I saw but whose full meaning I initially failed to grasp.

Anyone who studies American history in a serious way quickly realizes that the United States has a record of sustained expansion beyond the limits that it occupied at any given moment in time. As often happens in such cases, however, that central theme in the nation's history has often been taken for granted and therefore slighted. No major historian placed expansion at the center of his explanation and interpretation of American history until 1893, when Frederick Jackson Turner argued that expansion was the key factor in accounting for America's past prosperity, democracy, and general well-being.

Turner richly deserved the fame and influence that his synthesis brought him; but it is fascinating, as well as important, to realize that very little of the acclaim was based upon the recognition and acceptance of the primary importance of *expansion* in his argument. Instead of talking about expansion, the vast majority of historians, along with other academics and nonacademic intellectuals, used the term *frontier* in discussing and debating Turner's analysis. And his argument quickly became known as the Frontier Thesis.

The term *frontier*, however, is static rather than dynamic, and that characteristic of the word provides an accurate indicator of the way historians (and others) responded to Turner's idea. There was very little study of the expansionist thrust that acquired the sequence of frontiers. Most of the research and the arguments were focused on the question of whether or not a specific frontier situation actually produced political and social democracy, or on the issue of how much economic benefit accrued from a particular frontier. The subject of expansion was vaporized in the heat of those quarrels.

Those relatively narrow limits imposed upon the debate about Turner's thesis also reinforced two general tendencies that restricted the discussion of his argument to the past. Since he was a historian, and had offered his idea as an explanation of the seventeenth, eighteenth, and nineteenth centuries, most people thought of it within that framework. That propensity was strengthened, moreover, by the closing out of continental expansion. There was no obvious spur to apply Turner's thesis to twentieth-century American history because the United States did not acquire another huge territorial slice of the Western Hemisphere. There was hardly any thought, for that matter, of testing Turner's hypothesis by examining it in the light of a long period without such territorial expansion.

That approach might have been suggested by the increasing consolidation and centralization of economic and political power, and by the question of whether or not those developments were primarily due to the inherent nature of the process of industrialization. Instead, the reaction was to dismiss the relevance of Turner's thesis because of the seemingly obvious vast differences between an agrarian and an industrial society. And the problems of writing the history of even the major episodes of twentieth-century American development rapidly became so broad and complex that historians working in that area concentrated their attention and energy on the immediate and specific issues that attracted their curiosity and interest.

The historians who came into professional maturity during and after World War II were inclined to be concerned with questions involving wars, postwar eras, and the crises connected with the cold war and the place of the Negro in American society. That was certainly my own orientation, and it prompted me to undertake a study of American policy toward the Bolshevik Revolution and the Soviet Union. I was operating on an avowed argument that the study of history was relevant to our own time.

One of my criteria for relevance, however, was limited, and limiting, in important respects. I was thinking in terms of a very short period of time. The powerful minds of teachers like Fred Harvey Harrington and Paul Farmer, and the confrontation with human reality that comes from sustained research in primary-source materials, quickly disabused me of the idea that American - Russian relations could be understood in terms of the thirty years between 1917 and 1947. As a result, I extended my research and tried to place the cold war in the perspective of the long sweep of Russian - American involvement.

III

That additional work indirectly led me to an initial insight into the broader significance of Turner's analysis and interpretation of American history. For, in doing research into American - Russian relations at the turn of the twentieth century, I discovered that important Americans had given very serious attention to the expansionist theme in Turner's thesis. The most dramatic instances involved major intellectual and political leaders such as Brooks Adams, Theodore Roosevelt, and Woodrow Wilson. Adams independently developed his own, and even broader, version of the frontier-expansionist thesis, and probably did so before Turner. Roosevelt responded to the work of both men, while Wilson was more directly influenced by Turner's formulation of the idea.

It quickly became apparent, moreover, that Adams, Roosevelt, and Wilson applied the frontier-expansionist thesis to the problems of late nineteenth- and twentieth-century American diplomacy. They thought about American relations with the rest of the world in terms of the continuing need to expand in order to sustain the dynamic relationship between expansion, prosperity, democracy, and domestic well-being (and order), and they acted on that conception of the world. In their view, the new frontiers would be supplied by the continued overseas expansion of the American marketplace, and they formulated their foreign policies in order to create and maintain the momentum required to achieve that broad objective. They dealt with the more narrow and specific political and strategic (meaning military) aspects of foreign policy within the framework (and limits) created by that underlying evaluation of the American political economy.

It also became clear, however, that such intellectual and political leaders approached economic problems with an explicit awareness and acceptance of the classical marketplace outlook and attitudes. So did the businessmen, particularly those who controlled large firms, and those who involved themselves actively in making economic policy for an entire industry or for the integrated economic system. The record of their thought and policy recommendations made it apparent that they operated on a conviction, created by practical experience, received wisdom, and continuing analysis (which in many cases had become an article of faith), that the system of entrepreneurial capitalism could function successfully only if the marketplace constantly expanded.

At that point, during the winter of 1952-1953, I saw four options for further research and study. I could investigate the sources, and the developing nature, of the idea that capitalism could not sustain itself without an expanding marketplace. That would ultimately lead, I realized, to the question of what marketplace expansion meant—directly and indirectly—in terms of foreign policy and relations with other societies. And, probably sooner rather than later, that would bring me to the problem of the relationship between the frontier thesis and the theory of marketplace expansion under capitalism. Those three alternatives, I concluded, were interrelated regardless of which one was chosen as a starting point. On the other hand, I could proceed along a different route by trying to discover whether or not the frontier thesis and the theory of capitalist expansion exercised any influence on American foreign relations prior to 1893, the year in which Adams and Turner published their explicit statements of the frontier thesis.

If I had taken that road, I would have explicitly begun work on a book dealing with the period covered in this volume. That strategy of intellectual inquiry struck me, however, as being too frontal and crude. I sensed that I might well march right up the hill and right back down again without realizing that I had merely taken a swim in the moat instead of capturing the castle. That skepticism was well founded, even though I was not particularly articulate about it at the time. When I finally began to ask that question, I discovered that the answers were hard to come by, and I realized that I would very probably have missed a good part of the story at that stage in my efforts as a historian. For one thing, I would have concentrated far too much on urban businessmen, and on politicians and others with a formal intellectual conception of the frontier and marketplace theses.

At that point in my work, in any event, it made more sense to ask the question about influence in connection with the period after the frontier-expansionist thesis had become known as an explicit, well-formulated idea. And, as I admitted to myself in my stronger moments, that decision was no doubt influenced by my great excitement in discovering that important leaders had seen and acted on the expansionist theme in Turner's interpretation. As a result, I chose to approach the larger questions by studying the role of the frontier thesis in the making of twentieth-century foreign policy.

Once again, however, I pushed open another intellectual door more or less by accident. I was fortunate enough to be teaching in a school (the University of Oregon) with an enrollment small enough to make it possible to carry on a more or less open discussion as an integral part of undergraduate lecture courses. I began, in order to facilitate and focus that kind of dialogue, to reproduce and distribute documents that were not generally available in published form. Some of the students caught the spirit of that approach, and a kind of competition developed in reading the standard documents with more care and penetration, as well as in finding data that had not been used in connection with foreign relations.

I gradually realized, in the course of that sustained intellectual inquiry, and in conversations with my colleague Orde S. Pinckney, that many Americans had thought in terms of, and had acted on, the central ideas of Turner's frontier thesis long before Turner had been born. And they had used such supposedly twentieth-century concepts and phrases as "the safety valve" in discussing the usefulness or necessity of expansion in solving America's problems. At the same time, I learned much about early capitalist thought and policy from that dialogue, and from my colleague Robert Campbell, an unusually intelligent economist who is also a great teacher and a warm and generous human being. That process gave me a growing appreciation of the nature and significance of mercantilism as the precursor (and shaper) of laissez-faire capitalism.

Looking back, I can see that my excitement and enthusiasm probably carried me along too fast. The inherently interrelated and reinforcing activities of research, solitary reflection, debate and argument with student and faculty colleagues, and writing, became a chain reaction. And the momentum increased when I moved to the University of Wisconsin and reentered the high-energy intellectual atmosphere created by colleagues like William Best Hesseltine, Merrill Jensen, George Mosse, Merle Curti, and Harvey Goldberg, and by the students in my classes and seminars.

The articles and books that I produced during those years could usefully have been less cryptic and more polished. I realize now that I was writing, at least unconsciously, for and to a group of people that formed a vital part of my intellectual life as the data and the ideas were integrated into analyses and interpretations. They were, in effect though not in intent, the primary audience for such works as "The Frontier Thesis and American Foreign Policy" (1955), "The Age of Mercantilism: An Interpretation of the American Political Economy, 1763-1825" (1958), *The Tragedy of American Diplomacy* (1959; revised and enlarged edition, 1962), and *The Contours of American History* (1962).

I V

As I carried on that research and writing, and as I discussed and thought about the information I gathered, I increasingly comprehended the relationships between the period before 1893 and the years of the twentieth century. *I came to see that the expansionist outlook that was en-*

tertained and acted upon by metropolitan American leaders during
and after the 1890s was actually a crystallization in industrial form
of an outlook that had been developed in agricultural terms by the
agrarian majority of the country between 1860 and 1893.

As I gradually understood that connection, and outlined and developed it in various lectures, articles, and books, I gained a full appreciation of my debt to Nancy O'Connor, an intelligent, insightful,
and personable young woman who had taken an active part in my
courses and seminar at the University of Oregon. She had chosen,
in defining the subject of her master's thesis, to take the intellectual
option of asking the direct question about the pre-1893 influence of
the idea that capitalism required continuous market expansion. In
confronting that issue, she saw and outlined some aspects of the agricultural influence on foreign policy. Her thesis (and our conversations
about it), operating in my mind after 1955 as an unobtrusive tutor,
unquestionably helped me recognize the significance and meaning
of the data that I thereafter found in my research.

Other students made contributions to my education after I moved
to the University of Wisconsin and began (in 1959 - 1960) to deal directly with the role of agriculture in the evolution of modern American
foreign policy. Some of the assistance, as with that provided by Henry
Berger, Lloyd Gardner, Walter LaFeber, Tom McCormick, and Marty
Sklar, consisted of ideas offered in freewheeling discussions of the
subject, and of information they found in the course of their independent and often unrelated research.

Other help was more specific and formal, and grew out of the interest and excitement that the subject generated among a number of
younger graduate students at Wisconsin. I had never organized my
seminar around my own research projects, or around a narrow idea
or theme. I recognized the advantages and rewards of that approach,
but decided against it on the grounds that it cramped the curiosity and
the imagination of the students, that it overpersonalized the intellectual process around the professor, and that it inhibited my own functioning as a writer because of the ethical problems connected with the
authorship of books written on the basis of group research.

In the beginning, moreover, my seminar was wholly concerned
with twentieth-century history. But two students, James McHale and
Mrs. Brady Hughes, insisted on exploring the influence of agriculture
on American foreign policy after 1933. I reluctantly acquiesced, caught
as I was between millstones of my own choosing. Their research not
only made it clear that the agriculturalists continued to influence policy after the political economy had become thoroughly industrialized, but it provoked a number of other students to persevere in their
preference for working on various aspects of the question in the nineteenth century.

Their assault came at a time when I was ready to surrender. I was intellectually sated as a historian, at least for the time, with the problems of the twentieth century; and I was weary from the years of hard labor involved in directing a graduate seminar that often carried more than thirty students—meaning it had to be taught in two or three sections. The upshot was that the seminar was oriented to the nineteenth century, and that I gained much from the research and thought of the students. In particular, I was educated in important ways by Edward Crapol, James L. Erlenborn, Patrick J. Hearden, Gerald Markowitz, Gary Pennanen, Stanley Remsberg, Michael Roe, John Rollins, Howard Schonberger, and Tom Terrill. They extended my factual knowledge of the foreign policy activities of the livestock raisers and the meat processors, the flour millers, the railroad managers, the agricultural implement manufacturers, the cotton textile manufacturers, and various political leaders and other government officials of the period. More importantly, they applied their active minds to the problem and gave generously of their ideas (including criticism).

Many students in my undergraduate and graduate lecture courses also contributed to my fund of facts and ideas. They often discovered significant documents, and their generally unfettered minds often caught aspects of the problem that the rest of us overlooked in concentrating too narrowly on a particular theme. David Allmendinger was particularly helpful and stimulating during the first year that I suggested the topic to my lecture courses as a subject they might care to explore in their research papers.

V

A good part of my own research was carried on in the extensive resources of the Wisconsin State Historical Society, and I thereby increased my already extensive debt to Ruth Davis and Josephine Harper. They are unique in their abilities to save time and effort in finding materials already known, and in suggesting other sources that might be missed without their knowledge and insight. Their friendly remarks— which usually opened with a disarming "What about . . .?" or "Have you thought of . . .?" or "Did you look at . . .?"—often made me feel the fool but usually left me much better informed. And I owe special appreciation to Emory M. Pittenger, who gave me unrestricted freedom to roam the extensive and rewarding periodical and document sections of the Agricultural Library; to Mrs. Lucile Kellar, who helped me find the relevant materials in the huge McCormick Collection; and to Esther Nelson, who guided my foraging in the Historical Society's magnificent collection of newspapers.

Other knowledgeable and generous men and women helped me wherever I worked throughout the country. Helen Finneran, for example, led me expertly (and with warmth and wit) into and through the confusing records of the Department of Agriculture deposited in the National Archives. Her colleague Buford Rowland, the archivist of the records of the Congress, helped me find some of the most stimulating and rewarding documents that I read during the entire seven years of my research on this subject. And, as has been my experience with all men trained by William Hesseltine, he extended my understanding of those documents by giving me the benefit of his own knowledge and thought.

Halfway across the continent, the staffs of the historical societies in such places as Chicago, Minnesota, Iowa, and Nebraska offered their own special contributions. I am especially grateful to the members of the staff in Nebraska. They first granted me access to, and then gave me tips on using, the collections that were withdrawn from general use (for service purposes) at the time I arrived. And when I reached the Library of Western History at the University of Wyoming, Gene M. Gressley graciously permitted me to wander at will through the vitally important materials he has found and assembled. He made my stay in Laramie particularly fruitful and enjoyable. At the end of the long trek, in the new and unusually attractive building of the Oregon Historical Society, my old friend Thomas Vaughn likewise pointed me toward collections that proved unexpectedly rewarding.

Very little of that extensive research would have been possible if I had been required to operate within the limits of my normal resources. No historian can teach to earn his regular salary and at the same time carry through a major research project. He must find some source of funds which enable him to purchase free time. I had five benefactors. Victor Rabinowitz and the board of directors of the Louis M. Rabinowitz Foundation gave me rare support, and I take especial pleasure in thanking them publicly for their confidence, patience, and generosity. They not only helped me, but also extended grants to several students in my seminars.

I also received assistance from the Social Science Research Council, the American Philosophical Society, and the American Council of Learned Societies. Those organizations were especially kind in defraying the high cost of traveling back and forth, and up and down, across the vast reaches of the United States. And the research committee of the Graduate School of the University of Wisconsin extended indirect financial aid.

My greatest obligation is to the men and women who helped and encouraged me as I labored to make sense of all the data I assembled. I feel particularly indebted to several colleagues and friends. Lloyd Gardner and Warren Susman gave me a boost at the outset, when the

task seemed almost insurmountable. Mort Rothstein gave generously
of his extensive knowledge of the nineteenth-century marketplace.
And Lee Benson and Al Bogue offered stimulating comments based
on their own work in the period.

I offer special thanks to a scholar whom I saw only a few times. A
good many years ago, as I was just beginning to explore the effects
and influences of the frontier thesis, James C. Malin of the University
of Kansas gave freely to me from the vast resources of his unconven-
tional and unusually fertile mind. It was an act of human generosity
and kindness that I gratefully treasure, and the kind of incitement to
intellectual exploration that can keep a young historian going for the
rest of his career.

Several other men helped me in connection with specific aspects
of this project. Henry Borzo of Drake University opened my eyes to
the way the search for overseas markets led the agrarians to initiate
the risky strategy of combining business with humanitarian aid that
became so characteristic of twentieth-century American foreign policy. Lewis Gould of the University of Texas forced me to think more
incisively about the relationship between the federal government
and its dependent and subject territories. And Hans Ulrich-Wehler
of Germany kept me digging for more information about the European
reaction to American exports, and offered me imaginative suggestions
about the relationship between the thoughts of the farmers and the
ideas of urban leaders.

V I

Perhaps I owe my greatest obligation, however, to the dirt farmers
whom I have known as members of my family, or as close friends and
teachers. While I was neither born nor reared on a farm, there was always a farm on one or both sides of my family from the time that southwestern Iowa was settled during and after the Civil War until the end of
World War II. Many of my close childhood friends came from families that lived on farms, or that derived their income directly from
the land or from industries closely associated with agriculture. And
the cities that I had come to know and like by the time I was finishing
high school—Omaha, Des Moines, and Chicago—were centers of
interpenetration between agriculture and industrialism.

As a result, and indirectly as well as directly, I learned a considerable amount about the history and the life of the farmer, and about
his relationships with the rest of society, long before I had the slightest intention of being a historian. One of the standard stories told in
my family, for example, concerned a shrewd bargain that the farmers

of the area had driven in negotiations with the Rock Island Railroad. The company had been undecided whether to run its mainline tracks through Atlantic (where I was later born), or through a town named Lewis about six miles to the south. At that time, shortly after the Civil War, both settlements were about the same size, and a strong case was made that the surveys indicated a lower grade with fewer curves along the route through Lewis.

That was later proved correct, and perhaps the men of Atlantic knew it was true at the time. But the farmers and other businessmen who had created the settlement in Atlantic (and named it on the flip of a coin because the location was thought to be halfway between the two oceans) overcame science with an appeal to avarice. The land they had claimed and cropped was unusually fertile: even then its reputation was widely known, and in subsequent years the soil and produce from the region always ranked at or near the top in international competitions.

Even without such formal confirmation, the farmers of Atlantic knew their land was a powerful instrument of progress as they defined that elusive phenomenon. They offered the railroad a substantial number of acres of the rich soil in return for an agreement to lay the main line through Atlantic. And then, in a low key, almost as supplicants, they asked the Rock Island to designate Atlantic as a mandatory stop for every train—passenger as well as freight—that used the line through the town. And when the directors agreed, the settlers drew the contract so well and tightly that the Supreme Court repeatedly upheld it when the corporation tried to break the provisions.

Having obtained their railroad, the founders of Atlantic plotted the town by plowing a furrow straight south from the spot they selected for the depot. They named that trace Chestnut Street, and then ran several parallel channels (also named for trees) exactly 300 feet on both sides of it. Finally, they crossed those with similarly spaced (but numbered) furrows running east and west. In such fashion, the farmers scratched their town into the land. And, given their hard bargain with the Rock Island, the combination of the fecundity of the soil and their energy gradually transformed those intersecting furrows into the major agricultural and merchandising center between Des Moines and Omaha. For many years, even during the Great Depression of the 1930s, Atlantic boasted the highest rate of turnover in retail goods in the United States.

But anyone who grew up in Iowa during the Depression learned very quickly (and well) about the deep and direct relationship between the fluctuations of the business cycle and the conditions of life for the farmer. Hence it came as no staggering surprise to me that many of the erstwhile Republicans in the area voted for Franklin Delano Roosevelt in 1932, or that one of my grandfathers had been an early (and effective) Democrat. Nor was there any great difficulty in understanding why there had been an Atlantic chapter of both the Grange and the Northern Farmers' Alliance during the latter half of the nineteenth century. The father of one of my close friends put the matter very simply in lecturing us about the campaign of 1936: "Politics is as necessary to us farmers as markets, fertilizer, and rain."

One also came to know the life of the farmer. Sometimes it was from a distant relative who had been driven off the land by the economic whip of the marketplace, and who, when he came to "stay awhile," searched for the will to move on in reminiscences about how much harder it had been growing up as a child in a sod house on the frontier. Many times it was from seeing the hundred differences between one's own home in town and the home of one's close relative on the farm. And, finally, as one grew a bit older, the lesson was learned through a full day's work in the field; and then, afterward, in seeing, through the wild shadows flung across the barnyard by a swinging, hand-carried kerosene lamp, the desperate fear and fatigue in the very soul of an uncle as he scuffed his field shoes clean with a worn corn cob. And, sometimes, to see his deep frustration at not having the corn to feed the pigs, erupt in an angry outburst during a conversation with his wife or children—or myself.

One likewise observed that, weary as they were, the farmers read newspapers and magazines and books, and then talked about what they had learned. And the talking led to explanations, and the explanations on to different policies, and the policies to action. It also became clear that the marketplace could thwart the best efforts of such men. As when the town's corn canning factory, long the largest in the world, went bankrupt and never reopened. Or when the fertilizer plant managed to survive only through the desperate, almost fanatic, will of its founder—and the dedication of his employees.

Finally, one learned early and at first hand how the farm was tied into the world marketplace. The connection was made through exports. As in the case of my grandfather, who exported his beloved and prize-winning hunting dogs to England and France, and to Germany and even Russia, until the Great Depression destroyed his market—and nearly destroyed him. Or as with the fathers of two good friends, brothers who built a great name and a vast business breeding magnificent draft horses and beautiful Angus cattle for the farmers of the world.

Many men have written of the thrill of watching and helping a circus train unload as the first light of the coming day gradually dimmed the torches and lamps. And a joy it was. But that exhilaration was no greater than the headiness that came from being part of a crew that moved those great work horses and shining cattle into the stock cars that stood poised to carry them on their way to Australia, Latin America, or Europe. Particularly when one knew that he could ride at least as far as Omaha or Kansas City or Chicago in return for feeding and watering the precious cargo.

VII

That kind of export-dominated relationship with the world political economy has produced several different responses by the American farmer. One such posture has been associated with those few and short interludes when the capitalist system has functioned with some meaningful approximation to the forecasts of its innovators and the promises of its advocates. During those delightful moments of history, the American farmer manifested a relaxed acceptance of the rest of the world and a willingness to live and let live. He revealed an understanding of the inherent, as well as the explicit, limits on any effort by the United States to control or change the rest of mankind. Having learned the danger, as well as the futility, of assaulting nature in that sense, he applied the wisdom he had learned in dealing with his land and his animals to his relationships with other peoples.

That outlook has provided the basis for the farmer's reaction against various efforts by the United States to reform, remake, or control large portions of the globe. His opposition to such attempts to manipulate nature have prompted him to concentrate on riding his own fenceline while trying to restore impersonal, or at any rate unpersonalized, marketplace relations with other nations. That was largely the case, for example, between 1903 and 1914, and between 1920 and 1939. And, during the Korean War, many farmers in Iowa became particularly militant opponents of the American decision to cross the 38th parallel in an effort to unify Korea as an American ward.

But there have also been times when the farmer's export-dominated relationship with the world marketplace led him to develop and advocate a vigorously assertive and expansionist foreign policy, or to support such a policy formulated by others. And, since he actively and causally related his freedom in the marketplace with his personal political and social freedom, the farmer was strongly inclined to defend and justify such expansionism on the grounds that it extended the freedom of all men. Opening the foreigner's marketplace, he often argued, would open the foreigner's society for the foreigner. American farmers evolved and agitated just such a militantly expansionist foreign policy between 1860 and 1893. That policy played a major causal role in the advent of American imperialism after 1893, and continued to exert a pervasive influence on American thinking about foreign affairs throughout the twentieth century.

So we return to the relevance of history. American farmers, acting

at a time when they composed the great majority of the nation's population, were crucial actors in developing an outlook that has carried
our contemporary industrialized system to a major crisis in foreign
affairs. If we can understand that history as a prelude to accepting
it, and accept it as a prelude to changing those ideas and policies, then
we nonagrarians who compose the great majority of today's America
can give the other (largely agrarian) peoples of the world a chance
to make their own history by acting on our own responsibility to make
our own history. If that be isolationism, then the time has come to make
the most of it.

CONTENTS

INTRODUCTION

*Our people are decided in the opinion that it is neces-
sary for us to take a share in the occupation of the
ocean, and their established habits induce them to require that the sea be kept open to them, and that line of
policy be pursued which will render the use of that
element as great as possible to them. . . . But what will
be the consequence? Frequent wars without a doubt
. . . Our commerce on the ocean and in other countries
must be paid for by frequent war.*

Thomas Jefferson to John Jay, August 23, 1785

*Acquiescence in the practice and pretensions of the British
Govt is forbidden by every view that can be taken of
the subject. . . . It would recolonize our commerce by
subjecting it to a foreign Authority.*

President James Madison, January 8, 1812

*Illinois wants a market for her agricultural productions;
she wants the market of the world. Ten counties of
that state could supply all the home market. We want
a foreign market for our produce, which is now rotting in our granaries.*

Senator Sidney Breeze, July 21, 1846

*I ask every citizen in the great basin between the Rocky
Mountains and the Alleghenies . . . to tell me whether
he is ever willing to sanction a line of policy that may
isolate us from the markets of the world, and make
us dependent provinces upon the powers that thus
choose to isolate us?*

Senator Stephen A. Douglas, 1861

*We believe that this country has been run quite long
enough under the direction of New England. . . . We
fetch and carry, and bark, and roll over, and fight other
dogs precisely as and when we are bidden by our New
England Master.*

Chicago *Times*, November 16, 1865

*Cheap transportation is vital to our prosperity. . . . The
West must remain an exporting and an importing country to an enormous and increasing extent. . . . We to-
day are sold, soul and body, in bonds to Europe, and
if not there to our cities.*

Remarks of Illinois Farmers
in Convention Assembled,
March 1872

*It is clear that much the most important factor in main-
taining the commercial prosperity of the United States
during the recent past has been its agricultural industry. It is further clear that if the commercial prosperity of the country is to be maintained in the future it
must continue to find abroad a market for its surplus
agricultural products.*

Editorial in *Bradstreet's*, January 19, 1884

*The prosperity of the nation depends upon the prosper-
ity of the agricultural people, and, further, the pros-*

*perity of the farmers depends upon their ability to sell
their surplus to foreign nations. . . . Therefore we demand that your honorable bodies remove as many
as possible of the barriers of commerce. . . . [And lower
the] high rates of internal freight.*

> Petition from The Farmers of
> Minnehaha County, Minnesota,
> to the Congress, March 1890

*A silver standard, too, would make us the trading cen-
ter of all the silver-using countries of the world, and
these countries contain far more than one-half of the
world's population. . . . Why not reverse the proposition and say that Europe must resume the use of silver
in order to trade with us? . . . Are we an English colony or an independent people?*

> William Jennings Bryan, 1893

*I believe, gentlemen, that the time has come for the United
States as a great nation to take its place as one of the
great commercial nations of the world.*

> Populist leader Jerry Simpson, 1894

*The most striking fact about the whole thing is that the
number of our people to-day wholly dependent on foreign markets is larger than the number of those employed in the protected industries.*

> Populist Tom Watson, in
> *People's Party Campaign Book*, 1894

*If we had the principal trade of India, China, Japan, and
South America, which we would have with silver re-
monetized . . . our virtual monopoly of the trade of
those countries that now supply Europe with many articles would put these articles under the control of our
traders and we would fix the price to Europe.*

> William "Coin" Harvey, 1895

*We need these points of departure such as the Philippines
in every ocean and as outposts for the protection of
our commerce. The commerce of America must be extended. . . . Our duty requires us to stand for liberty
everywhere. . . . We will take a hand in the correction
of the evil.*

> Editorial in *The Western Rural*, 1898

A

Survey of the Territory

I

THE EXPANSIONIST, imperial foreign policy adopted by the United States at the end of the nineteenth century was largely formulated in industrial terms by men who were leaders and spokesmen of that part of the political economy. They were primarily concerned with obtaining markets for surplus manufactured goods and venture capital, and with acquiring reliable access to cheap raw materials needed by the American industrial system. That industrial orientation of American foreign policy became increasingly clear during the twentieth century as American leaders struggled to build and maintain an international system that would satisfy the interrelated economic, ideological, and security needs and desires of the United States as they defined those objectives.

When the policy was crystallized in the latter years of the 1890s, and to an increasing degree in subsequent decades, the dynamics of the policy-making process centered in a relatively small group of economic, political, and intellectual leaders who characterized American interests and needs in those industrial-financial terms. Part of that centralization of power and authority was due to the inherent nature of government, particularly in a social system as large and as geographically extended as American society. Part of it was explained by the additionally inside, quasi-secret, and administrative character of foreign policy decisions in any government. Neither the majority itself nor a legislative assembly can handle policy matters on a routine basis.

4

In the underlying sense, however, it was the result of the consolidation and centralization that accompanied the maturation of modern industrial capitalism in the United States, and which provided the industrial-financial leaders with their power base.

All of those factors have led historians to emphasize the industrial nature of the policy, and to stress the role of the small group of top policy makers. And, because of their power, authority, and influence in the political economy, those men have enjoyed and exercised a significant degree of sustained, unchallenged initiative. They have, of course, been subjected to pressures from various organized interest groups; and they have encountered resistance from other branches of the government, and from occasional upwellings of public feeling and opinion. Those forces have caused delays and shifts of emphasis in implementing the broad policy adopted at the turn of the century, but they have not produced major changes in the nature of the policy or a serious weakening of the power wielded by the leadership elite. In a great majority of instances, moreover, the more general opposition to one or another aspect of the policy developed around a dissident faction of the leaders. Such was the case, for example, in connection with the defeat of President Woodrow Wilson's effort to establish the League of Nations on the basis of America's policy and power.

Much later, the opposition to the Vietnam war manifested some characteristics which suggested that movement might develop as an exception to the general pattern of criticism of American foreign relations in the twentieth century. It is possible that the resolution of the war could involve, or lead into, a reevaluation and change of the imperial policy first codified during the 1890s. Even if that possibility becomes reality, however, it is apparent that the origins of the opposition to the war involved members of the policy-making elite as well as outside critics. But it would also be clear under such circumstances that widespread support had developed for a more far-reaching shift in outlook and policy.

Whatever may happen in connection with the Vietnam war, the historical evidence makes it apparent that precisely such an involvement of the majority of the adult population played a vital part in the evolution and adoption of the imperial policy at the end of the nineteenth century. American imperialism was not forced on the majority by a domestic elite, any more than it was imposed on the country by outside forces or foreign nations. That presents what appears to be a paradox. For, on the one hand, the majority of the American people from 1865 to 1900 was associated with the agricultural part of the political economy. Yet, on the other hand, the policy itself was formulated in industrial terms by leaders of that section of the system.

II

The paradox is apparent rather than real. The resolution begins with a knowledge of the seventeenth-century colonists who produced a surplus of tobacco and exported it to Great Britain and other European nations; and, more particularly, with an understanding of their marketplace orientation and their marketplace conception of the world. The marketplace difficulties encountered after 1740 by the heirs of those early settlers defined the substance of the quarrel between the American colonies and the British metropolis. And the independence and freedom the American colonials felt they needed to solve their economic problems were the same freedom and independence they desired in their personal and social affairs, and which they worshiped in the abstract. The essence of political freedom manifested itself in the colonial assemblies (and in protest demonstrations) as the lack of it materialized in the marketplace.

The continued commitment to that outlook that tied freedom for individual men to the existence of a free marketplace exerted a steadily increasing influence on American foreign policy in the years after independence had been secured. Many men who feared a strong national government because of its power to restrict or control their activities nevertheless supported the Constitution on the grounds that the new, more centralized system would enable the United States to win advantages—and prevent losses—in the international marketplace. Such men also looked to a strong government to acquire more land needed to produce the surpluses they wanted to sell on the world market.

Whether in terms of the drive to possess more land, or in their pressure to protect and expand their position in the marketplace, the Northern as well as the Southern members of the agrarian majority exerted a strong and persistent influence on American foreign policy down through the War of 1812. In the direct sense, they demanded the defeat and expulsion westward of the Indians; they agitated the seizure of Florida, the trans-Mississippi region, and all or part of Canada; and they insisted that the government act to overturn the French and British restrictions that limited or closed their foreign markets. Their indirect influence was equally important. They created the products that in turn involved the processors, merchants, financiers, and shippers in the export trade. And they generated the assertive ideological argument that justified expansion as a policy that carried freedom to other men as well as being necessary for their own freedom and material well-being. They were first the harbingers, and then the militant advocates, of America's manifest destiny to lead and reform the world.

From the outset, moreover, the agricultural majority became increasingly conscious of the vital part that its surpluses played in the prosperity and growth of the entire American economy. Not only did they supply the food and fiber for the urban population that was thereby freed for other activities, but their exports paid for much of the foreign capital that went into manufacturing, banking, mercantile operations, and other nonagricultural enterprises. Neither the Southerners who chopped the cotton and harvested the tobacco, nor the Northerners and Westerners who cropped the grains and raised the livestock, had to wait for twentieth-century economists to conclude that they were the engine of American progress. For more than a generation after the War of 1812 the Southerners carried the bulk of the international payments load, and the brunt of the battle to secure the kind of policies most appropriate to commercial, exporting agriculture. The farmers of the North and West were not inactive during that period, but most of their surplus was absorbed by the Southerners and by the increasing urban population at home, and they were preoccupied with developing a commercial agriculture west of the Appalachians.

Beginning in the 1840s, however, the Northern grain and livestock farmers again became more directly involved with foreign policy. They had begun to produce a surplus beyond the needs of the home market when the Panic of 1837 and the ensuing depression (which lowered land values as well as commodity prices) intensified that economic pressure to enlarge their overseas markets. Those difficulties also turned them toward the acquisition of virgin land at a time when the ecstatic reports about Oregon and California were reaching a crescendo. The epidemic of Oregon fever, for example, erupted first in Iowa and Missouri, from whence it spread quickly back across the Mississippi into Illinois, Michigan, Indiana, and Ohio. And some of those Northerners who wanted a chance to start over (perhaps for the second or third time), or a place to send their grown children, came to share the increasing interest of Southerners in acquiring the vast plains of Texas.

Some leaders of the Eastern metropolitan part of the political economy, such as William H. Seward, a key Whig politician of New York, read the Panic of 1837 to mean that the economy had reached the point where it needed an expanding foreign market to avoid further and even more serious depressions. And one group of urban entrepreneurs, which included flour millers and meat packers, were exporters intimately involved with (and ultimately dependent upon) the agricultural part of the economy. Their rising concern with overseas markets not only influenced metropolitan politicians on foreign policy matters, but helped increase the export consciousness of the farmers. From the time of the depression of the late 1830s and early 1840s, therefore, leaders like Seward labored to build a political alliance between Northeastern businessmen and agriculturalists by offering related benefits to both groups.

The Democrats were more immediately successful in the political arena, however, because they promised more land to the farmers of all sections of the country. The analysis underlying that strategy had first been propounded as an integrated argument by James Madison as early as 1786 - 1787, when he formulated his theory that republican government could be sustained only by "enlarging the sphere." That outlook provided the foundation upon which Madison formulated foreign policy, just as it did for Thomas Jefferson, James Monroe, and Andrew Jackson. President John Tyler and Secretary of the Navy Abel P. Upshur then applied it directly to the political situation created in the early 1840s by the expansionist demands to acquire Texas and all of the Oregon Territory. Tyler offered Texas to Southerners and Oregon to Northerners in a vain effort to control the Democratic party during the presidential campaign of 1844 and thereby remain in the White House.

Tyler failed, but the strategy was effectively used against him, and the Whigs, by James K. Polk. Along with other Democratic party expansionists like Senators Robert J. Walker of Mississippi and Stephen A. Douglas of Illinois, Polk aroused the party and the country with the imperial rallying cry of "the reoccupation of Texas and the reannexation of Oregon." The political success of their expansionist outlook and platform was due to the way it integrated several distinct themes into a coherent and dynamic whole. Most obviously, it was a straightforward promise to provide enough land, at least for the immediate future, for all Northerners and Southerners.

But it was also, particularly in the minds of men like Polk, Douglas, and some Easterners, a manifestation of the concern and determination to acquire the harbors on the Gulf and Pacific coasts that were crucial to America's overseas economic expansion. Madison himself had clearly understood that foreign markets were part of the sphere that had to be enlarged to insure the continuation of republican institutions and of prosperity, and his successors had not forgotten the lesson. The pressures for land and markets were complementary and reinforcing economic engines of expansion that were directly integrated, moreover, with the philosophical and ideological arguments that the expansion of the free marketplace was necessary for the preservation and the extension of political and social freedom. Polk was only voicing an outlook and a tradition that reached back into the eighteenth century, but he gave them classic form in his pronouncement that American expansion was justified because it involved "the expansion of free principles."

That kind of evangelical righteousness not only homogenized the economic and the philosophical forces that generate empires, but it created a powerful psychological drive that was quickly character- ized by the protagonists themselves as America's manifest destiny to lead and reform—if not rule—the world. Already justified because it was necessary and fruitful, expansion became inevitable because it was the expression of a divine logic. The concept of The City on a Hill thus became The Empire of the Globe.

III

The growing conviction that the United States possessed irresist- ible power, and was the chosen instrument of an unsullied destiny, continued to be an important ingredient in the American imperial thrust long after the War against Mexico. And, however it was adapted by other nonagricultural groups, it evolved out of the ancient faith that men who worked the land were the bearers of primary virtue. In the short run, however, that righteous confidence was muted by the internal struggle for control of the empire that was acquired by force from Mexico and through the threat of force from Great Britain, and by the shifting outlook of the Northern agrarians. Both of those factors became apparent during the War with Mexico; the first in con- nection with the drive to go beyond the boundaries of Texas and take more territory in northern Mexico, and the second during the debates over the tariff in 1845 and 1846.

As they continued to increase their production of grain, cattle, and swine, Northern farmers grew more intensely concerned with foreign markets. Those American developments coincided with the agita- tion in Great Britain to repeal the legislation that protected British agriculture against foreign competition. The Manchester Anti-Corn Law Association was organized in 1838, and the Anti-Corn Law League followed in 1839. Agricultural leaders in the Northeast, as well as in the South and West, immediately recognized the favorable implica- tions of such action for American farmers. The promise of the British market led some of them to moderate their militant demands for tak- ing all the Oregon Territory north to 54° 40′ north latitude, and prompt- ed even more to support modifications in the American tariff.

The argument that a lower tariff would promote American exports to Great Britain (and also to other countries) gained strength among Western agrarians as it became clear that the Corn Laws were going to be repealed. That turning point in British economic policy came on June 6, 1846. A short two months later, on July 30, 1846, the Walker tariff reversed the upward turn in American rates that had appeared in 1842. The coalition of Southern and Northern farmers that carried through that decision proved incapable, however, of resolving their differences over the disposition of the trans-Mississippi empire—or of agreeing on new imperial ventures.

Both groups wanted to control the western half of the continent, and the Northern agrarians became increasingly antislavery as they faced the prospect of competing against a forced-labor system. But favoring free soil did not mean agitating to free the black man. The majority of Western farmers were not abolitionists. They viewed the Negro as another rival for the bounty of the West. Their objective was to exclude both the white planter and the black man from the trans-Mississippi marketplace. That goal, and the attitude which produced it, gave Abraham Lincoln his victory over the abolitionist element in the newly rising Republican party, as well as his final triumph over Stephen Douglas. For Lincoln's policy of containing the slave labor system within its existing boundaries, without undertaking any direct action to free the black man, won him important support among Northwestern agrarians. And that strength was sufficient to check the abolitionists and simultaneously force the Easterners to promise free land to the farmers.

Douglas failed in his bid to unite and lead the country because none of his major policies spoke to either the immediate needs or the more underlying fears of the Northwestern agrarians. His argument that free labor would triumph over slave labor in the trans-Mississippi territory under the doctrine of popular sovereignty was rejected because it left too much open to too much doubt. The farmer wanted a sure thing, not the mere probability of ultimate victory after an arduous struggle. Douglas encountered similar resistance when he talked of the future rewards of expansion into areas like Cuba, or of the coming triumph of American exports in the markets of the world.

Northern farmers not only concluded that most of the immediate gains of taking Cuba (political as well as economic) would go either to Eastern businessmen or to the planters, but they had not reached the point in the commercialization of their agriculture at which export markets were regularly more important to them than the control of the free land across the Mississippi. They were businessmen, but businessmen oriented primarily to the domestic market. It is very probably true, as some modern economic historians have argued, that the Northern grain economy was committed to production for the foreign (and particularly the British) market by the end of the 1850s, but the Northern farmer did not think in those terms at that time.

For that reason, Douglas never reaped the strategic political victory he had anticipated in 1851 when he obtained the first federal land-grant subsidy for building the Illinois Central Railroad. Douglas conceived of the line not only as a way to tighten the bonds between the Northwestern farmer and his Southern customers, but as a method

of projecting Northern surpluses out into the markets of the world
as a major element in America's future economic supremacy. Douglas
might well have been elected President on that program in the 1870s
or the 1880s, but during the 1850s it was too much of an abstraction
to be effective.

There was a surge of involvement and interest in overseas markets
during the latter half of the 1850s, and particularly during the Crimean
War and the Panic of 1857. Wheat exports, for example, jumped from
8.15 million bushels in 1856 to 14.57 million bushels in 1857. But the
sporadic rise in such sales was not enough to turn the Northern farmer
outward away from his deadly confrontation with the planter. In an
ironic way, however, Douglas' loyalty to his vision of America astride
the commerce of the world carried him to the side of Lincoln and into
the camp of the Northerners who had earlier rejected him. For the secession of the South threatened the entire trans-Appalachian Northwest with the loss of egress to the open sea—and thereby its access
to the world marketplace. Faced with that prospect, Douglas supported
Lincoln and the Union.

Lincoln himself was quick to use the Douglas argument, moreover,
when the outbreak of the Civil War dramatized the changes that had
been taking place in the market patterns of the Northwestern farmers. Wheat and flour had begun to move directly eastward before the
war, but large amounts of corn and pork were still consumed in the
South. And Southerners also handled major quantities of the produce
that was exported to Europe. The eruption of hostilities soon disrupted
both of those activities, and the dislocation intensified the general
derangement caused by the war. The President feared the Northwest
might respond to the crisis by considering a settlement with the Confederacy. He countered that possibility with the argument that the great
productivity of the agrarians had created a situation in which overseas markets had become essential. Compromise with the Confederacy
was therefore impossible. The issue had to be settled unequivocally
and for all time.

I V

Southern secession hit the Northern farmer severely and dramatically. At a time when he was becoming an increasingly efficient commercial producer, he lost a traditional and still significant domestic
market and was simultaneously denied the use of the Mississippi for
the cheap shipment of his surpluses to the East Coast and to foreign
markets. The outbreak of the war also upset the economy of the Union,

created a sharp depression, and thereby further decreased the market for agricultural goods. Those painful events served to unveil the full significance of the structural changes in Northern agriculture that had been taking place during the 1850s. The grain economy had become involved in the export of a steadily rising surplus, and a similar pattern was emerging in flour and wheat.

The Northern agricultural businessmen did not recover until the combination of war orders and expanded exports to Britain (and the rest of Europe) created a boom. Then they improved their position despite the serious wartime inflation. They paid their debts, added new buildings and equipment, and bought more land. They also continued to expand their production, even though the overall rate of growth of the Northern economy decreased during the war. Compared with the Southern farmer, who turned to raising corn in order to feed himself and his army as his cotton rotted on the wharves, the Northern farmer reaped great gains from the war.

But in consolidating his new market orientation at the same time it increased his efficiency and surpluses, the war also created significant problems for the Northern farmer. As his commodities and produce went eastward for distribution to the domestic market, or transshipment to Europe, the Western farmer confronted the vital issues of transportation and control of the marketplace. He also became more concerned about the way the high American tariff rates, one of the prices he paid for the Homestead Act, which was supposed to give him cheap land, influenced the size of his foreign market. And the more agriculture became integrated and organized as a commercial system, the more the farmer was affected by the actions of his fellow agrarians and other groups in the political economy, by technological innovations, and by diseases and other natural phenomena that influenced his production.

The farm businessman very quickly focused much of his concern and agitation on the railroad system. He knew he needed reliable, fast, and cheap transportation to move his surpluses to market. For that reason, he generally urged and supported the construction of major east-west trunk lines and related feeder spurs, and directly or indirectly supplied many of the subsidies that speeded the work. Such action was a continuation of his traditional willingness to use the government for such broad economic purposes. But the agriculturalist also wanted an equitable return on his investment as a citizen, as well as reasonable treatment as an entrepreneur in the marketplace, from a transportation system that he viewed as a method of improving his competitive position. He supplied, as taxpayer, a large part of the cost of any and all internal improvements. He was not being given something for nothing by other segments of the population. The experiences of the war and postwar years, moreover, intensified the farmer's earlier awareness that the price he received for his surpluses was set on the Liverpool and London exchanges.

Such businessmen quickly and accurately recognized that the cost of transportation was one of the major overhead charges that affected their profits. It was also one of the factors of production that the farmer could reach and deal with directly. He naturally wanted low freight rates, but he also wanted rates that did not discriminate against him and rates that did not fluctuate arbitrarily and unfavorably with the time of the year and the market situation. The farmer's concern with transportation costs, which arose directly out of his routine business involvement with the foreign market, was the primary cause of his increasingly vigorous attack on the railroads.

To effect the changes he sought, the farmer assaulted the rails on the grounds that the subsidies they had taken from local and national governments defined them as quasi-public institutions, and that their arbitrary and selfish behavior posed a threat to the integrity of representative government. And he advanced the more general economic argument, taken from Adam Smith, that the railroad system, like the monetary system, was part of the structure of the marketplace itself, rather than merely another business operating in the marketplace. On that basis, the farmer maintained that the rails were subject to basic controls and regulations designed to guarantee the effective and equitable functioning of the marketplace for all entrepreneurs.

Such businessmen saw nothing radical, unreasonable, or illogical in turning to the government for aid in dealing with the transportation problem. Nor was there—despite the arguments advanced by contemporary critics and later observers in an effort to prove that the farmers were dangerous subversives, harbingers of socialism, or men incapable of accepting and adapting to the inevitable triumph of industrialism. The agriculturalist was acting wholly within the theories and traditions of marketplace capitalism when he demanded action to regulate rates and to provide competitive transportation alternatives by improving and extending the system of canals and navigable rivers.

Such immediate and fundamental concerns increasingly turned the Northern farmers away from the issues of Reconstruction after the Civil War. Whatever the individual exception, they had never as a group been actively concerned with freeing the slave and they did not provide any sustained positive support for the efforts of the Radical Republicans to extend large-scale assistance to the free black men. They were interested in blocking the resurgence of planter power in the national government, but that attitude was progressively weakened as they sought political allies against Northeastern urban leadership. For that reason, the Democratic party enjoyed a significant resurgence in the North by the end of the 1860s.

The Southern white farmer was initially preoccupied with the severe difficulties he faced as a defeated enemy in restoring production
and reentering the marketplace as an effective operator. He found
it necessary to combat many of the policies of the state governments
that came into being under national Republican leadership. He had
to struggle to maintain his position against the white business interest that took control of the cotton economy and pushed him into the
role of a sharecropper. And he had to come to terms with the freed
black man. He was thus more directly engaged in the politics of Reconstruction than his Northern counterpart. But the Southerner also steadily shifted his attention and effort to the issues that directly affected
his position as a farmer in the marketplace. The prewar alliance between Northern and Southern agricultural businessmen was revived
on the basis of a common concern to check the power of the metropolitan businessman and to obtain internal improvements that would
help all farmers.

As they became ever more involved in trying to deal effectively
with the railroads, the farmers grew more intensely conscious that
they composed a majority of the population that nevertheless regularly exercised significantly less power than a metropolitan minority composed of commercial, industrial, and financial groups centered
in the northeastern part of the country. The agricultural sector of the
American political economy accounted for the majority of the population prior to the Civil War, and it continued to do so throughout
the nineteenth century. The distribution of urban and rural population in 1870 was 9.9 million urban and 28.17 million rural; in 1900 it
was 30.2 million urban and 45.8 million rural. And the true differential between the metropolis and the country was greater than indicated
by those figures because not all of the urban centers were part of the
metropolitan sector of the political economy. Many cities, even some
as large as 100,000, were structurally and psychologically part of the
country.

The farmers confronted the additional difficulty that both major
parties emerged from the war dominated by metropolitan leaders.
That was particularly clear in connection with the Republican party,
but it was also true of the Democrats. And those farmers, Northern
as well as Southern, who identified with and supported the Democratic
party were denied substantial national representation and influence
from 1860 until after the Panic of 1873. The agricultural majority of
the country was thus effectively ruled by a metropolitan minority
long years before the American political economy became industrialized.

The accelerating commercialization of agriculture intensified the
farmer's awareness and understanding of his inferior position. The
resulting consciousness of his predicament deepened his concern to

win a greater share of economic, political, and social rewards. Whatever his more favorable view of the laws when they had been passed, he concluded well before the Panic of 1873 that the legislation voted by the wartime Union Congress had in practice balanced out in favor of nonagrarian interests and groups. His anger over that outcome was increased by the way many metropolitan spokesmen talked about the primary importance of the agricultural sector of the economy, and by the way many of their policies were predicated upon using the truth of that analysis for their own purposes. The theory about the primacy of agriculture was not simply a self-centered myth created and propagated by the farmer. Eastern financiers and other leaders spoke increasingly after 1870 of how the economy in general, as well as their particular operations, were dependent upon agriculture.

Such interpretations and arguments reinforced the agricultural businessman's traditional acceptance of and reliance upon the gospel of political economy according to Adam Smith. American farmers had been responsive as early as the end of the eighteenth century to all the main lines of argument advanced by Smith in *The Wealth of Nations.* They had taken his insistence that a free marketplace economy was essential to political and social freedom, and integrated it with the individualistic side of John Locke's philosophy. That produced an equation that causally linked the free marketplace with freedom per se. The true entrepreneur was a free producer who created plenty for all by operating freely in a free marketplace.

Smith likewise provided a solid critique of monopolies, and of the misuse of the government by special coteries of metropolitan interests. The farm businessmen were also aware that Smith offered careful and even sophisticated justification for government actions, such as those concerned with improving transportation or checking monopolies, that were designed to strengthen the structure and guarantee the freedom of the marketplace itself. And their own experience, particularly after the 1840s, steadily reinforced their understanding and acceptance of Smith's great stress on the necessity of the sustained expansion of the market as the dynamic engine of continued progress and freedom.

The farmers also extended their traditional appreciation of Smith's explanation of how the economy was inherently divided into a town and a country sector, and of his blunt judgment that the town or metropolitan sector enjoyed an inherent structural economic advantage over the country or agricultural sector. Given their internalized acceptance of the Smith-Lockean marketplace conception of the world and how it worked, the farmers' war and postwar experiences generated a steadily more intense consciousness of themselves as members of a country majority caught in an inferior, neocolonial relationship with the metropolitan minority.

The reinforcing interaction between that consciousness and the rising sense of urgency he felt as a commercial farmer to act effectively to improve his position turned the agriculturalist toward militant organization and action. Farmers had come together in various associations and clubs even before the American Revolution, but the spirit as well as the extent of such movements began to change during the 1840s. The shift became particularly significant during the Civil War, when farmers demanded government assistance against diseases that threatened their livestock, and opened a long campaign to win institutionalized recognition and influence for themselves in a federal department of government with representation in the Cabinet.

Then as the postwar boom began to dissipate at a time when they were encountering serious troubles with the railroads, the market system, and metropolitan political leaders, the agricultural businessmen began to issue tough manifestos and declarations of independence. The movement became institutionalized on a national scale with the founding the Patrons of Husbandry in 1867, and the ensuing rapid growth of the Grange and similar organizations during the next five years. Acting independently, as well as with other disgruntled businessmen like the merchants, the farmers moved to control the railroads, and to obtain other government action calculated to improve their position. By the time of the Panic of 1873 and the ensuing depression, therefore, the farmers were becoming a highly self-conscious, articulate, and increasingly militant majority of the United States.

V

The severe and baleful depression of the 1870s subjected the farmers to great adversity and suffering. Their response developed as a combination of several major alternatives. One of them, to hang on and somehow subsist and survive through individual courage and will power, and through mutual aid, was of necessity practiced by the great majority. However wrenching and painful it was, most farmers felt that course of action was more practical as well as preferable to the option of leaving the land. The travail of abandoning a personal business in which oneself and one's family had invested much psychological strength, as well as economic and physical resources, was compounded by the hardships involved in reestablishing oneself and one's family in the towns or larger urban centers that were plagued by unemployment and poverty.

The farmers revealed a similar disinterest in dealing with the depression and its consequences by making structural changes in the existing capitalist system. They did not respond to that choice as it was outlined and advocated by socialist and other radical workers and intellectuals in the cities, and they did not evolve a similar or related approach among themselves. Their commitment to marketplace capitalism as defined and developed by Adam Smith, and to the philosophical system grounding political and social freedom in such a free marketplace economy, proved impervious and resilient enough to resist the impact of the worst depression that Americans had yet experienced.

One of the major sources of that strength was the conviction that the depression could be dealt with effectively by honoring the first principles of a free marketplace economy. Many farmers consequently embraced the alternative of reforming the system so that it could and would function as they thought and believed it should. Such efforts involved the agricultural businessmen in many organizations at the local and state level, as well as in the nationwide Grange. They offered a great number of proposals, but their principal approaches can be grouped under a few main headings.

One such reform program concerned the land question. That issue was dramatized by the failure of the Homestead Act to provide a large number of people with good land at low prices, and some of the farmers concentrated on trying to revise and extend that legislation in order to accomplish the original intention. Others came to emphasize and attack what they considered the economically baneful and politically dangerous effects of the centralized ownership of vast acreages, and of speculative practices that denied anyone the use of the land.

Those approaches had the effect, directly or indirectly, of focusing more and more attention on the traditional assumption that American democracy and economic welfare were directly related to a surplus of fertile free land. Men had talked specifically about what they called the safety valve provided by the Western lands very early in the eighteenth century, and the discussion was revived during the depression of the 1870s. As a result, the famous frontier thesis began to be formulated at the grass-roots level by various agricultural spokesmen almost twenty years before it was stated by such intellectuals as Frederick Jackson Turner and Brooks Adams. Implicitly, if not overtly, that explanation of democracy and prosperity pointed toward the necessity of finding a new frontier. And that kind of reasoning, coupled with the impact of the depression, instilled the first sense of impending crisis, and even doom, that became steadily more intense and general through the 1880s into the 1890s.

All those results of the concern with land policy required time to mature, however, and in the meantime many farm businessmen were attracted to the idea of improving their competitive position in the existing marketplace. One such proposal, which appealed to South-

erners as well as Northerners, advocated the organization of cooperatives to handle merchandising, and even some producing and
marketing operations. The depression also intensified the existing concern to reform and regulate the railroads, to improve the system of
water transportation, and to organize direct trade relationships between American farmers and various European markets. The reformers also attacked the monetary system. They fought hard, and with
temporary success, to block the policy of contracting the currency
supply by withdrawing the Civil War greenbacks and resuming specie payments. They simultaneously opposed the centralization of
power over the money supply among a few large financiers. And they
opened what became a sustained and highly emotional effort to reverse the demonetization of silver that had occurred in February 1873,
shortly before the first signs of the panic and depression.

The silver mining interest was of course a principal element in the
coalition that agitated the remonetization of silver. And a significant
number of metropolitan businessmen likewise supported the reform.
But farm businessmen supplied the great strength of the movement.
They gravitated to the issue and the campaign for several reasons.
They felt that the act of demonetization provided a particularly gross
example of the dangerous and selfish way the financiers used their
vast power to control the political process as well as the marketplace,
and thereby also illustrated the corruption of metropolitan politics.
And, in truth, the farmers cut close to the bone when they made those
charges. For the men who planned and carried through the demonetization of silver did engage in collusion over a number of years to insure the success of their efforts to place the United States on the gold
standard.

The farmers advanced two principal arguments to support their
demand for remonetization. One of them concerned the domestic
marketplace. It asserted with considerable persuasiveness that the
larger money supply created by coining silver was necessary to handle
the business of a growing economy (and would therefore help generate
recovery from the depression), and that the inflationary aspects of
the move would help raise the standard of living for all Americans
—including the farmers. The other argument for remonetization
was directly related to the farmers' concern with overseas markets.
The agricultural businessmen maintained first that the purely economic
results of remonetization would expand their sales (and those of other
producers). That would occur because the nations and individuals
that sent silver bullion to America to have it coined into American
dollars would have to spend the money on agricultural products, and
on other goods and services. Even if remonetization did lower prices,
as the gold advocates asserted it would, that effect would also operate to raise exports. Finally, the farmers pointed out that remonetiza-

tion would make it possible for them to penetrate new markets in Latin America and Asian countries that based their monetary systems on silver.

In and of itself, the farmers continued, that effect of remonetization would serve to undercut the extensive power that Great Britain exercised in and over the world marketplace. That in turn would bring the metropolis and the country sectors of the world economy into a more balanced and equitable relationship; directly in connection with the English, and indirectly because weakening London was a way of weakening the New York money power that dominated the country sector of the American economy. The agrarians further maintained that remonetization would directly and significantly improve their position in the Liverpool and London commodity markets for grain and cotton. As long as silver was demonetized in the United States, they argued, British operators could and did buy the bullion cheaply in order to have it coined into Indian rupees. The profit on that operation enabled them to buy Indian wheat and cotton and undersell the American markets, or to improve Indian production and accomplish the same objective by cutting American sales in that fashion.

That multifaceted argument for the remonetization of silver on the grounds that it would enlarge the overseas market and at the same time improve the terms of trade quickly became an integral part of the farmer's case for recovering from the depression by expanding the overseas market for his surplus production. Such an export drive was a major alternative open to the agricultural businessmen, and they rapidly came to stress that solution above all others. As that happened, moreover, they increasingly related their attacks on the railroads (and their demands for improved water transportation) to the drive for foreign markets.

The antimonopoly campaign was affected in a similar, if also more complicated, manner. Some farmers stressed the argument that the big operators and trusts, by maintaining artificially high prices, prevented overseas market expansion. But others concluded that the meat processors and flour millers actually enlarged the market through their exports, and that analysis had the effect—directly or indirectly—of weakening the assault on the big operators. And, ultimately, the farmers moderated their antagonism toward established metropolitan political leaders as those men responded to the agrarian demand for larger foreign markets.

Several factors explain the consensus that developed in support of the export solution to the problems confronted by American farmers. Their deep and positive commitment to the political economy developed by Smith and Locke made them unwilling to undertake radical changes, and that attitude reinforced the inherently expansionist logic of Smith and Locke. Their economic theory and beliefs

turned them toward the overseas market. The pre-Civil War traditions of American agriculture further strengthened the appeal of that
way out of the crisis, as did the direct experiences of the war and the
postwar years.

But still another factor was crucial because it served to verify the
theory, the beliefs, the tradition, and the past experiences in an intensely
dramatic fashion. For with the fiscal year beginning July 1, 1877, rising agricultural exports rapidly improved the condition of the farmer
and at the same time played a vital role in pulling the entire American
economy out of the depression. The export of crude foodstuffs began
to increase during fiscal 1876, moving from $79 million for fiscal 1875
to $94 million. Then they jumped to $155 million for fiscal 1877, $266
million by 1880, and remained at $242 million for fiscal 1881. Over-
seas sales of manufactured foodstuffs rose from $110 million for fis-
cal 1875 to $150 million in 1877, and then spurted to $193 million for
1880 and $226 million for fiscal 1881.

The primary cause of the boom was a five-year period of miserable
weather, and widespread diseases affecting crops and animals, that
drastically reduced the output of European agriculture. The secondary cause was the ability of the American farmer, and the related
groups in the economy, to produce and deliver the food that was needed. The immediate economic results were threefold: Europe was fed, the
American economy generated increasingly strong forces producing
recovery from the depression, and the balance-of-trade position of
the United States shifted to the positive side of the ledger. It is worth
emphasizing, if only because it deeply affected the thinking of American
leaders of that time, that *the agricultural businessmen, rather than
the metropolitan industrialists, were responsible for the famous turn
of the trade balance.* As some economists later pointed out, there
were signs that the American economy had begun a slow revival from
the bottom of the depression before the boom in agricultural exports;
but the overseas market bonanza clearly played a crucial role in
strengthening and sustaining the return to prosperity. American leaders of those years, moreover, were far less impressed with the role
of nonagricultural factors in the recovery than they were with the
importance of the exports of grain and meat. The effect on all American thinking, therefore, was to extend and deepen the orientation
toward overseas markets as a crucial element in the nation's well-being.

That was particularly true of the farmers, naturally enough, but
other groups in the political economy manifested the same kind of
response. Such was clearly apparent, for example, among the producers intimately connected with the commodity crop farmers and
the stockmen. Thus the meat processors and the flour millers extended
their own efforts to penetrate and then enlarge their position in foreign markets. But the middlemen who handled the sales of the crops

and the meat, and the railroad executives (and waterway operators) who moved the foodstuffs to the ports, revealed the same increased concern with overseas markets. So did the manufacturers of agricultural implements. They not only interpreted the boom in agricultural exports as the key to increased sales of their equipment in the domestic market, but they intensified their own overseas marketing campaigns. And, finally, the Southern manufacturers of rough cotton textiles, who in many cases had a particularly close relationship with the cotton farmers, formulated their strategy of growth in terms of the export market.

The impact of the boom in agricultural exports was not limited, however, to the farmer and other businessmen whose operations tied them directly to the agricultural sector of the economy. Metropolitan leaders responded to the export bonanza by increasing their emphasis on the general importance of agriculture, by beginning to transfer the significance of the export market to their own particular situation, and by thinking more of the importance of the overseas market in the functioning of the entire economic system. In a similar fashion, key politicians of both major parties became export-oriented to a far greater degree, and on a far more permanent basis, than they had been before the depression. And some of them, like James Gillespie Blaine, reacted by making overseas economic expansion a central element in their basic program for the nation (and their own political success). Those men, along with some industrial and financial leaders, began to think less in terms of special-interest groups and more in terms of all such groups as interrelated parts of an integrated system that would come to depend more and more on exports.

Secretary of State William Seward had of course formulated his policies on that kind of analysis, and his ideas continued to be felt through men like Commodore Robert W. Shufeldt of the Navy. Shufeldt was no doubt concerned with increasing the influence and improving the condition of the Navy, and with fulfilling his personal ambitions. But his strategy for achieving those objectives was based upon strengthening the Navy as the advance agent and defender of a vastly larger strategic perimeter. Schufeldt pointed to the central importance of agricultural exports in the general economy as proof that America was becoming irrevocably involved and committed in the world marketplace, and argued that the Navy was the only military instrument capable of dealing with the new situation.

A similar though more sophisticated economic analysis was offered by civilian intellectuals. David A. Wells, who had edited the *Pennsylvania Farm Journal* in the 1850s before becoming a government economist, was one such figure. Another was Edward Atkinson, who was particularly knowledgeable about cotton textiles. They were steadily effective in promoting a growing awareness and acceptance of the

export orientation among metropolitan leaders. Directly and indirectly, therefore, the agricultural businessmen played a central part
in redefining the strategic boundaries of the United States from an
essentially defensive concept based on the continental limits to a far
more dynamic and activist conception tied to the actual and desired
position of the economy in the world marketplace. In some respects,
at any rate, that was the most subtle yet far-reaching influence the
farmers exercised on American foreign policy.

The great surge in exports also had the important effect of generating a growing certainty about the strength and power of the American
economy. That was especially noticeable among the farmers and their
spokesmen, who interpreted the boom as proof of their ability to control the markets of the world, as well as convincing evidence of their
major role in the American economy. But a number of other businessmen also read the bonanza to mean that the United States was rapidly
becoming the most powerful nation on earth. They agreed with the
agriculturalists that the nation could begin to use that strength to control more markets, and to achieve other objectives of a political and
ideological nature. That conviction was particularly significant in
determining the response of the farmers to the end of the boom and
the related decline of their economic welfare.

VI

The recovery of European agriculture was the primary cause of the
end of the bonanza export market. The cycle of bad weather came to
an end, the crop and livestock diseases ran their course or were brought
under control, and production revived. There were other factors in
the change, however, and they contributed to the continuing challenge to American farmers. One of those was the rising competition
provided by the return of Russia to the international commodity markets, and by the increasing grain production in India. Another involved
the anti-American restrictive policies devised and adopted by almost
all European nations in response to the flood of American exports.

The overseas market boom of the late 1870s created the paradoxical situation in which the American farm businessmen, who were
in a quasi-colonial position inside their own national economy, functioned as economic imperialists whose exports shook the political
economies of European nations. The vast surpluses of cheap American
food seriously disturbed the agricultural, and hence the political and
social, organization of Germany, Austria, France, and Great Britain.
*The American farmer, rather than the American manufacturer or fi-
nancier, alerted the rest of the world to the power and the dangerous
challenge of the American economy.* The specter of an Americaniza-

tion of the world, as it came to be called in the 1890s, was initially created by the sodbuster, the swineherd, the cattleman, and the cotton-chopping sharecropper.

The immediate European response of fear and anger was swiftly translated into various measures designed to prevent the American giant from overwhelming—and controlling—their economies. One countermeasure involved encouraging alternate sources of supply in Argentina, as well as in Russia and India. Another emphasized efforts to improve the productivity of European agriculture. Russia, for example, soon began to provide government assistance in storing and transporting the wheat crop. And a third consisted of various restrictions calculated to decrease or halt the importation of American agricultural products.

The policies that raised barriers against American pork and beef were carefully explained and defended on the ground that American livestock, and the related meats, were extensively diseased. The argument had some substance. The prevalence of pleuro-pneumonia among cattle, and the extent of cholera and trichinosis among swine, were significant. And there is no reason to doubt that some European officials had a sincere regard for the public health of their countries. But it is highly questionable whether American meat was more diseased than the European product, and there is no question that the habits of food preparation and use in Europe contributed extensively to the amount of sickness and death. The evidence is clear, moreover, that much of the action against American exports was generated by very powerful and effective pressure from deeply interested economic groups that had no desire to be driven out of business. That opposition remained highly effective long after the health argument had been met by a vast improvement in the condition of American livestock. The result was a rising bitterness among American agriculturalists that contributed very greatly to defining major European nations as a direct threat to the national necessities—and hence vital interests—of the United States.

The American response to the end of the boom in agricultural exports had an extensive effect on the nation's attitudes toward foreign policy. That was the case not only because the downturn involved the fundamental assumptions, analyses, and beliefs of the great majority of the people of the United States, but because those people undertook a sustained and increasingly militant campaign to solve their problems through the recovery and expansion of the overseas markets for their surpluses. Their battle for markets was not predestined to evolve into imperialism, but their ideas, beliefs, and practices did carry them to the point where they confronted a choice between embracing imperialism or changing their domestic political economy in fundamental respects. They resolved that dilemma in favor of imperial expansion because their marketplace philosophy, traditions,

and actions all combined to persuade them that such an imperial policy was the only workable solution, and that it was likewise the only
approach that would sustain and even enlarge the area of freedom.

The end of the boom initially shocked American farm businessmen
with a realization that their problems had not been solved for all time.
It likewise reminded them forcefully that Adam Smith's free marketplace economy did not function automatically. All the old problems
reappeared once the boom ended. The railroads were still powerful
and still controlled by metropolitan leaders, and the system of water
transportation was still unable to provide a satisfactory and competitive alternative. The money system remained under the control of
metropolitan gold contractionists, and the anger over that situation
was intensified by the realization that farm exports had underwritten the resumption of specie payments on a gold standard. And the
flour millers and meat processors, along with the merchants and other
middlemen, were more firmly entrenched at crucial crossroads of
the agricultural economy.

Each of those aspects of economic reality reinforced farm awareness of metropolitan power over the country. So did the political parties. The Democratic victory in the congressional elections of 1874,
which had raised hopes that a restoration of two-party politics would
bring significant benefits to the farmers, did not produce such results.
The leadership of both major parties continued to deal with the problems of the nation from the point of view of the metropolis, and on
such issues as the money question identified the interests of the American metropolis with those of Great Britain and other Western European countries.

The long-standing resentment against that attitude and its practical consequences was further intensified because the end of the boom
coincided with three developments that extended and deepened the
earlier challenge to the traditional assumptions about a surplus of
easily available land. The question, as many historians and economists
later pointed out, was not whether the continent was literally full of
people, or even whether all the nonmarginal land had been turned
to cultivation. Neither of those conditions existed. But the great majority of Americans did not approach the issue in those terms between
1876 and 1896. They viewed the problem from within the tradition
that defined a surplus of easily available and productive land a necessary condition for American prosperity and freedom. And they interpreted the situation that existed after 1880 as one that threatened
that classical foundation of American progress and liberty.

They first pointed out that while such land was not wholly occupied, it was nevertheless clear that the reservoir of cheap, good land
was being rapidly depleted. Then they argued that another significant
acreage was held by relatively few large domestic or foreign owners,
and was thus effectively withdrawn from use by American homestead-

ers. And, finally, they correctly noted that profitable cultivation of much of the remaining open land required more capital (and other assistance) than was available to the average American. That analysis produced many proposals calculated to sustain the reality of the tradition that linked American welfare to a surplus of good land. One group continued to approach the problem largely or wholly within a domestic context, and was concerned either to return some of the best land held by large American operators to the public domain, or to help Americans sustain themselves on the land that was difficult to farm. But another response was directly related to the evolution of foreign policy attitudes and proposals.

There was first of all the militant antiforeign feeling and agitation that arose among farmers of all sections against Europeans (and particularly the British) who controlled vast acreages from Texas northward to the Canadian border. That produced an anticolonialist movement of major proportions that was directed against American metropolitan leaders who were associated—indirectly as well as directly— with the foreign owners, as well as against the aliens themselves. The practical result was a movement for the nationalization of such land in order to make it available to American farmers.

The alien land issue reinforced the existing agrarian anger against the British and other Europeans over the demonetization of silver, and the restrictions raised against American agricultural exports. Those reactions were in turn generalized as well as intensified by the explicit and implicit conclusions drawn from the confrontation with the tradition that linked American well-being with a continuing surplus of land. For what happened during the late 1870s and early 1880s can only be understood as a broad grass-roots formulation and acceptance of the frontier thesis explanation of American history.

That analysis carried the farmers (and the other Americans who accepted it) into an even greater emphasis on the necessity of overseas markets. Such markets appeared as the only frontier that could sustain prosperity and freedom. The agricultural businessmen ultimately came to argue that they had to defeat the European metropolitan centers of power not only to win those markets, but also in order to realize their rightful majority rights and influence against the power of the American metropolis. The farmers who were quasi-colonials in the domestic economy thus became anticolonial imperialists in foreign affairs as a strategy of becoming equals at home.

VII

The expansionist-oriented outlook that the farm businessmen developed by the end of the export boom produced several consequences that progressively affected their actions during the decade of the 1880s. It led them to become steadily more skeptical and angry toward the majority of metropolitan leaders who responded indifferently or slowly to agricultural alternatives and pressures. That in turn extended and strengthened the development of farm leaders and organizations. Finally, the farmers concentrated ever more specifically—and militantly—on programs and policies calculated to regain the position they had enjoyed during the export boom, and to penetrate and hopefully dominate new markets in Latin America and Asia.

Cattlemen concentrated their efforts on reopening and enlarging the European market. They first demanded retaliation by the government against the British regulation that required the slaughter of all live cattle imports within ten days of arrival. In general, however, metropolitan leaders opposed that strategy. An important group of the cattle raisers then began advocating a program of inspection and control to eradicate pleuro-pneumonia. That caused conflicts with the meat processors who resisted such regulation, and led to intensified demands for antitrust legislation. Still other cattlemen turned to the remonetization of silver, or to exporting live cattle through Canada, as a way of counteracting the British refusal to remove their restrictions.

The swine feeders composed a larger group because many grain farmers began to raise hogs as a way of obtaining more profits from their corn surpluses. They tended to be more persistent about retaliation against European restrictions on pork, and continued to press for barriers against French and German exports even after they began supporting a meat inspection program. Their troubles in the hog market affected their corn problems, furthermore, and they soon agitated for government activity to enlarge the exports of that commodity.

Some of the hog producers, along with one group of cattlemen, were less militant critics of the meat processors. They argued that the big firms—Armour, Swift, and Morris—made great efforts to enlarge their exports of preserved and refrigerated meat, and expressed great skepticism that smaller companies created by antitrust action could do as well in the ruthless international competition. On balance, however, and largely because conditions did not improve in any sustained way, the drive for foreign markets during the 1880s strengthened the campaign for an antitrust law just as it continued to augment the push for federal regulation of the railroads. The battle for overseas markets had the ironic result, moreover, of improving the meat eaten by Americans.

The campaigns to reopen European markets increasingly converged with, and reinforced, the general economic nationalism manifested by the farm businessmen. The attack on foreign landowners and speculators was broadened to include British and other investors in cattle raising, meat processing, flour milling, and railroads. The arguments for the remonetization of silver steadily won more adherents in the South, as well as in the North and the West. And Southerners developed an analysis that quickly produced a proposal to store surplus commodities like tobacco, rice, and cotton in government warehouses. One of the objectives of that subtreasury plan, and the one that most historians have stressed, was to obtain short-run credit advances for the surpluses while they were held off the market. But the farmers based their argument for the program on the proposition that holding the surpluses, or controlling and manipulating the supply, would enable the American agricultural businessmen to dominate the commodity marketplace of the world—and, more specifically, to break the economic power of Great Britain. The entire approach was a product of the export orientation of the farmers.

The failure of metropolitan leaders to respond to such proposals for reopening the European markets produced several results. Farmers became increasingly angry and militant, particularly as the depression of the 1880s intensified and extended their difficulties. Some turned back toward their earlier effort to cut their losses in the existing marketplace, and to win a larger share of those rewards, by reforming the system. Their inability to win any quick or dramatically productive victories, however, reinforced the feeling that the domestic American metropolis operated as part of an international metropolis that controlled their markets and kept them in an inferior position. Such an analysis strengthened their already assertive economic nationalism and pointed them once again toward the export solution. And that extended the pressure to find and open new markets.

One element of metropolitan leadership centered in the Republican party had tried ever since the 1860s to deal with the overseas market orientation of the farm businessmen by defining the home market that would be produced by industrialization behind high tariff walls as a new and better export market. Beginning in the 1870s, and continuing with growing vigor during the 1880s, those Republican leaders sought to counter the antimetropolitan feeling among farmers by depicting men who advocated low tariffs or free trade as un-American agents of the British who wanted to dominate the American economy. Their propaganda, which ranged from wild and crude accusations of conspiracy to sophisticated and clever syllogisms, had the related objective of sustaining the Civil War image of the Democratic party as a hothouse of sedition and treason. The Republican tariff argument was thus a strategy of continuing to wave the bloody shirt to retain political power.

Three factors progressively undercut that attempt during the 1880s. One was the increasing number of metropolitan leaders who adopted and adapted the traditional export orientation of the agricultural businessmen. Various elements of the industrial part of the economy, in-

cluding relatively small hardware factories as well as giants like Standard Oil and the largest agricultural implement manufacturers, produced increasing surpluses. They had to be exported if they were to be
sold at all. The hard times of the 1880s not only dramatized that truth to
those companies, but turned other metropolitan entrepreneurs toward
the foreign markets. As a result, Republican leaders began to modify and then to change their position on the tariff.

The second factor involved the way the Democrats increasingly
emphasized the export argument in behalf of low tariffs. Southerners
had stressed that point before the Civil War, but it gained new attention as political leaders such as Representative Roger Q. Mills of Texas
began to employ it after it had been reformulated by intellectuals like
David Wells. They also added a clever argument developed by standing the Republican high tariff logic on its head. Low tariffs would not
only enlarge the market for agricultural surpluses, the Democrats
asserted, but by expanding the market for manufactured goods they
would create a big home market for the farmer. In adopting that approach, Grover Cleveland stressed the benefits to metropolitan interests, but his vigorous advocacy nevertheless attracted farm businessmen away from the Republican high tariff position.

The Democratic agitation of their new thesis on low tariffs reinforced
the general agricultural drive for new markets, which in itself was the
third element that weakened the Republicans. The convergence of
those themes was at first particularly apparent in the South, where
the traditional concern over markets for raw cotton was extended
during the 1880s by the expansion of a rough-cotton textile industry
geared to production for foreign markets. The Southern campaign
was especially vigorous because it was a manifestation of a militant
desire by a section that had been defeated in war to overthrow Northern domination, as well as the product of a close relationship between
many of the cotton producers and the textile mills.

VIII

The Southern push for new markets came to be symbolized by Senator John T. Morgan of Alabama, who waged a ceaseless struggle to
penetrate Africa, Latin America, and Asia. His battles in behalf of
an isthmian canal, and to enlarge the Navy, generated growing support among farm businessmen throughout the country, and were a
significant part of the dynamic process by which they increasingly
defined America's strategic perimeter in terms of the world marketplace. Morgan's arguments also strengthened anti-British feeling,
and contributed to the agitation for the remonetization of silver. The

Southerners also exerted an important influence on Northern metropolitan leaders. Part of that effect grew out of the challenge that the region's textile mills presented to the New England firms. The latter first responded by supporting the South's bid for the export market in rough cottons, and then gradually turned in the same direction as the economy failed to generate sustained prosperity after the depression of the 1880s. Some railroad leaders, most notably James J. Hill of the Great Northern, also came to view cotton exports to Asia as an important part of a strategy to create a continuous flow pattern of transcontinental freight traffic designed to increase profits on a regular basis.

Southern concern with overseas markets also affected Northern Republican leaders like Blaine who had not abandoned the hope of building a viable political movement in that section. Along with a few others, Blaine realized early in the 1880s that the export approach offered a promising way of holding the Western farmers while adding Southern support. Such men were aware that the meat and wheat producers of the vast trans-Appalachian region had become increasingly concerned with new markets in Latin America, and that they were beginning to talk about Asia as still another place to sell their surpluses.

The flour millers of the West, along with the meat packers, had first turned to those markets during the downturn of the late 1860s. Their interest intensified during the depression of the 1870s. Then railroad men like Hill and Stuyvesant Fish of the Illinois Central added their pressure. By the mid-1880s all elements of Western agriculture were becoming increasingly vigorous in demanding government action to open and control alternate markets. More and more farmers, for example, wanted the remonetization of silver to facilitate the direct penetration of Latin American and Asian economies, and to weaken Great Britain's position in those markets.

The farm businessmen also accepted the need for a larger Navy and for an isthmian canal. Agricultural attitudes on those issues have often been misunderstood because their critique of specific proposals has been misread as unequivocal opposition to the programs. In the case of the canal, for example, they concentrated their efforts on influencing the plans for financing the operation. They wanted it built by the government in order to avoid a repetition of the subsidies given to the railroads, to involve the government in extending the marketplace, and to insure that they would be able, through the Congress, to influence future decisions.

Their approach to enlarging the Navy (and the merchant marine) was even more subtle and complex. They were primarily determined to establish the program on the cornerstones of an advanced American technology and effective government control. They were secondarily concerned to make a sound decision about the composition of the new fleet, and at various times did disagree among themselves as well as with metropolitan leaders over the relative weight to be assigned to cruisers and battleships. Those attitudes and positions had the effect of delaying somewhat the construction of a large battleship Navy. But the Navy Department's own plan for growth called for phased development of a battle line, and the effect of the agricultural critique can easily be exaggerated. Furthermore, the policy of the farmers unquestionably contributed to the building of a better Navy, and they clearly supported its deployment and use in behalf of American economic expansion.

The agricultural pressure for markets advanced rapidly toward a climax after 1886 as continued economic difficulties interacted with the slowness and ineffectiveness of metropolitan leadership. While President Cleveland's belated emphasis on low tariffs as a way of enlarging exports added to the pressure for foreign markets, for example, his purist laissez-faire attitude prevented him from acting quickly and effectively on that proposal. That increased the impatience of the farm businessmen. Their organizations, including the Northern and Southern Alliance movements as well as the reviving Grange, persistently stressed the need to find new and larger markets.

One of the more revealing indications of the progressive integration of all the expansionist themes and policies appeared in connection with the long-standing campaign to improve the Department of Agriculture and raise it to Cabinet status. One indirect tactic employed by the agriculturalists involved attacks on the Department of State as a refuge for incompetent and aristocratic metropolitan leaders, and assaults on the appropriations for the department as a way of forcing it to use personnel to expand exports. The direct strategy called for unrelenting pressure for markets to create a Cabinet spokesman to defend and advance their interest overseas as well as at home. When that objective was finally gained in 1889, moreover, the farmers merely redirected their pressure for markets to the new official.

In a similar way, the long struggle by Western agriculturalists to win statehood for the territories became intimately involved with the rising demand for more vigorous market diplomacy. Their inability to obtain satisfaction from metropolitan leaders deepened their consciousness and resentment concerning their own inferior and quasi-colonial position as the country sector of the political economy. The farmers not only sought more home rule in their own areas, but they wanted additional votes in the Congress and the related influence in the councils of the major parties where the basic alternatives were so often formulated.

Their attitudes and activities made it apparent by 1887 - 1888, moreover, that they might well organize their own political party if existing Republican and Democratic leadership continued to be unrespon-sive and ineffective. Some metropolitan Democrats were by that time beginning to fear, with reason, that they were losing control of the party to the farmers headed by such fast-rising militants as William Jennings Bryan of Nebraska. And the more perceptive Republican leaders recognized that their party could be reduced to a metropolitan minority by the defection of angry agricultural businessmen to such a reoriented Democratic organization or to a new party.

I X

The Republicans reacted to the challenge more quickly and with great-er success than the Democrats. They did so largely because Blaine un-derstood the seriousness of the danger, and together with a few other metropolitan leaders, devised a strategy that ultimately retained the loyalty of the Western farmers. Blaine also hoped to win enough sup-port among Southern cotton interests to extend the party's power base in that region. That effort failed, but his attempt nevertheless had the effect of strengthening the general consensus on economic expansion. It was clear by the end of the first Cleveland Administra-tion in 1888 that the agrarians had two major options. They could exploit Cleveland's weaknesses and try to take control of the Demo-cratic party, or they could unite to form their own organization. The farmers are often blamed, and during those years attacked each other, for falling between those two stools. That judgment overlooks two crucial factors. First, they were at the very least as much concerned with a foreign policy solution to their problems as they were involved with domestic answers to their difficulties. Secondly, and in that con-text, Blaine was one of the few people in those years to enjoy and ex-ploit an understanding of that overseas market emphasis among the farm businessmen. Blaine's astute appeal to the farmers on that basis thus accounted for much of what has been termed their indecision or blind loyalty to party. In a real sense, Blaine defined the issue as a choice between alternate methods of market expansion and persuaded a determining group of farmers that his policy would be more effec-tive.

Benjamin Harrison shared Blaine's insight into the crisis and rap-idly committed the Republicans to an expansionist strategy in foreign affairs after he defeated Cleveland in the presidential election of 1888. He did so on the broad grounds that the entire economy required for-eign markets, and because they offered a way to hold on to a crucial bloc of agrarian votes. In that respect Harrison was acting for specific metropolitan interests that had accepted the export thesis and for the intellectuals who had generalized that analysis to the entire political economy. And in many ways he was himself an intellectual, even though he was not an academic or a New England man of letters.

Thus to conclude that Blaine and Harrison were actuated by a political motive is to miss the crucial part of the story. Since politics is defined by the acquisition and retention of power, there is no doubt at all that Harrison and Blaine were politically motivated. Once over that twig in the analytical path, it is possible to deal with the more significant obstacles of determining the outlook that guides various men in attempting to secure the power, and defines the purposes they intend and try to achieve. Blaine and Harrison did not want the power for its own sake, or to fulfill a psychotic need to control other people. They sought it in order to act upon a broad policy of overseas economic expansion that they considered necessary and desirable for the entire political economy, as well as for specific interests within it; and they concluded they could win the power by offering that program to the agricultural businessmen who had done so much since 1866 to generate both the idea itself and the pressure to act upon the idea.

Thus Harrison not only overrode his political and personal reservations to appoint Blaine as Secretary of State, but he carefully chose an expansionist to fill the newly created post of Secretary of Agriculture. Jeremiah M. Rusk of Wisconsin was an enthusiastic and untiring advocate of overseas markets for dairy farmers, livestock raisers, wheat growers, and corn producers. Harrison's other close associates, like Whitelaw Reid, shared that outlook. The widening and deepening of the agricultural unrest that occurred between the election and Harrison's inauguration only intensified their commitment to an expansionist program. The convergence of many Southern and Western farmers into the Alliance and Populist movements made it clear that the Republicans would have to act very quickly if they were to survive as anything more than a local and regional force. Harrison and Blaine were so concerned that they accepted the grave risk of splitting an already weakened party in order to save it by embracing overseas economic expansion. The showdown came early in 1890 when Blaine openly challenged the protectionists led by Representative William McKinley of Ohio for control of tariff policy.

McKinley had long been a champion of high tariffs, and regularly used the continuing industrialization of Ohio as proof of the way that protection created a home market for a diversified agriculture. He had realized from an early date, however, that foreign markets would become important when a mature industrial system had been created. In that sense, subtle but fundamental, the fight between McKinley and Blaine was over timing rather than principle. And since McKinley was intelligent, sensitive, and shrewd—as well as politically ambitious—he ultimately concluded that Blaine was correct about the crucial issue.

Blaine's strategy was a theoretical and practical work of art. Sometime during the 1870s, and perhaps a bit earlier, he had realized that the principle and practice of reciprocity offered the best of protection and free trade. He no doubt also understood, since the Grange and other farm groups had discussed and supported the policy during the mid-1870s, that reciprocity appealed to agricultural businessmen as a way of enlarging their foreign markets. And he had done much to keep the issue alive during the 1880s. Reciprocity was (and remains) a policy based on an honest marketplace exchange. The United States, as in Blaine's approach, lowers tariffs on products that it needs in return for a reduction of tariffs by another country on surplus goods that Americans want to sell. In order to open markets for Western and Southern farmers (flour, meat, and rough textiles), and for metropolitan manufacturers (oil, dry goods, and such items), Blaine confronted McKinley with a demand to revise the staunchly protectionist bill that McKinley had produced by 1890.

The ensuing battle was bitter and bloody, but Blaine won. His victory was primarily due to Western support for a strategy that promised to open new foreign markets and at the same time lower the cost of sugar. For Blaine argued powerfully that a reduction of the American tariff on sugar would not only break the barriers against flour and meat in Latin America, but that it would open the German market for American pork. And, once adopted as policy, the principle could be used to reopen and enlarge the markets of France, Great Britain, and other European nations.

Secretary of Agriculture Rusk was not idle while Blaine (and Harrison) fought McKinley. Rusk was a Union veteran who believed in direct action, and the domestic battle for reciprocity absorbed but a part of his energy. Anticipating victory there, he pressured Germany and France to arrange final surrender terms on pork, and simultaneously nagged the British to admit live cattle from the United States. In the third ring, he campaigned to expand corn exports. That effort, supported in particular by agricultural businessmen in Iowa and Minnesota, produced a major attempt to combine altruism and overseas market expansion in a private and official program of foreign aid. The strategy was to donate corn to Russia in order to relieve that nation's famine and demonstrate America's humanitarianism, to illustrate the superiority of the American free-market system, and to create a new market by changing Russian eating habits. The classic objectives of expanding markets and the area of freedom would thus be achieved.

Blaine's reciprocity program and Rusk's corn-to-Russia aid proposal established approaches that became institutionalized as central features of American foreign policy in the twentieth century. Both plans were also effective in the short run. The Harrison Administration's vigorous expansionist efforts generated a growing overseas interest in corn, reopened the German market for pork, and cleared the way for rising agricultural exports to Cuba and other Latin American economies. The widespread support for those actions made it clear, moreover, that the growing farm pressure for overseas markets was creating an increasingly deep and persuasive consensus in favor of such expansion. The movement had generated a momentum that was becoming ever more powerful.

Nothing demonstrated that more effectively than the congressional elections of 1890. On the surface, of course, it appeared that the overseas market strategy of Harrison, Blaine, and Rusk was a colossal failure. Angry farmers returned a congressional majority composed of Democrats, Populists, and dissident Republicans. But those new men were in truth at least as expansionist as the officeholders they replaced— and very probably more so. Party labels quickly proved a poor guide to foreign policy attitudes. The Populists provided the most dramatic evidence of that truth. Nebraska Senator William V. Allen bluntly told his colleagues, for example, that his supporters wanted more militant action in behalf of expansion, and promised to give them what they asked. Senators William A. Peffer of Kansas and James H. Kyle of South Dakota verified Allen's reading of the foreign policy attitudes of the dissenting farmers. And Representative Jeremiah Simpson of Kansas, crying out that "we are driven from the markets of the world," launched a campaign for overseas markets that ended several years later in a wrenching confrontation with imperialism.

Secretary of State Blaine and President Harrison were of course deeply distressed by the Republican defeat in 1890. But they had two insights into the situation that proved to be correct, and in acting on those perceptions they laid the foundation for a strategic Republican victory based on a foreign policy of overseas economic expansion. Harrison and Blaine realized that the 1890 defeat was due to three factors. Given the onrushing anger of the farmers, the Republicans lost because their expansionist program had not been put into operation quickly enough to produce tangible results, and the fight between Blaine and McKinley had divided the party and weakened the campaign effort.

They also understood, finally, that much of the Populist program (as with the proposals of other unhappy farmers) derived from agriculture's long emphasis on foreign markets. The mounting fury for the remonetization of silver (which had not been slaked by the Sherman Silver Purchase Act of 1890), the agitation for a subtreasury system of storing surplus commodities to control the market, the continuing demands for railroad regulation, and the sustained pressure for more improvements in the network of water transportation (including an isthmian canal), all evolved out of the farmers' practical and intellectual commitment to the overseas market.

On the basis of that analysis, Blaine and Harrison sustained their effort to pull the agricultural businessmen back into the Republican party by stressing just such expansion. The President's cross-country tour in 1891, for example, was a succession of speeches that explained his actions to enlarge foreign markets, and pleaded for support to sustain and extend such activities. In the narrow sense, and in the short run, the Harrison-Blaine approach appeared to fail in 1892 just as it had in 1890. The Democrats elected Grover Cleveland and maintained control of the House of Representatives. Those appearances proved to be misleading, however, because the consensus on expansion that had been so largely created by the agriculturalists proved to be more consequential in determining American foreign policy than the differences between the parties.

X

Nine events that occurred between the elections of 1892 and 1896 deepened, extended, and consolidated the expansionist outlook that the agrarian majority of the nation had evolved prior to 1892. The two that opened the sequence, the Hawaiian Revolution of January 1893, and the wracking depression of the 1890s that began with a panic in the spring of 1893, also exerted a particularly significant influence on the final integration of all the themes in that imperial *Weltanschauung*, and on the broad policy formulations that it produced.

The Hawaiian Revolution was the culmination of a century of American economic and ideological expansion into and throughout the life of the islands. The resulting power and influence excited the jealousy of other nations, and engendered persistent native resistance. The island opposition threatened to become more than merely troublesome after it won a narrow victory in the Hawaiian elections of 1890, and it was further strengthened when Queen Liliuokalani ascended the throne in January 1891. She immediately acted in ways to give meaning to her belief that Hawaiians ought to control Hawaii; and the depressing effect of the reciprocity provisions of the American tariff law of 1890, which handicapped island sugar exports to the United States, deepened her determination to implement her conviction.

Secretary of State Blaine attempted to counter the economic difficulties between 1890 and 1892 by making Hawaii a protectorate, but anti-American groups blocked the proposal. He then encouraged the pro-American interests that staged a successful coup against the Queen in January 1893 with the aid of American naval forces and a contingent of Marines. President Harrison promptly collaborated with the new rulers in an effort to annex the islands before he left of-

fice. Many farmers agreed with the President on the necessity and desirability of annexation, but enough opposed the move in the spring of
1893 to prevent action. That group favored de facto American control
of the islands to facilitate marketplace expansion across the Pacific
into Asia, but they were also concerned to honor the axiom of self-determination that was part of the free marketplace philosophy. Their confidence in the power of an American presence in the islands was the
crucial factor that allowed them to formulate a policy that seemed
to uphold ideological virtue at the same time it promised economic
success.

That same attitude provoked their great and sustained anger, however, when President Cleveland proposed to return Queen Liliuokalani
to her throne (and power). The majority of farm businessmen interpreted that recommendation as involving an even more flagrant violation of the principles and practices of freedom and self-determination than was contained in the proposal for annexation. The result
was a coalition of metropolitan and agricultural expansionists, symbolized by Republican Senator Henry Cabot Lodge of Massachusetts
and Populist Senator Allen of Nebraska, that demanded the deployment of the Navy to maintain the kind of true freedom that the pro-
American coup had ostensibly established in the islands and to insure
effective American domination of those stepping stones to the markets of Asia. Cleveland's policy also had the result of further stimulating agricultural anger against him as a particularly short-sighted and
selfish metropolitan leader.

The farmers were not merely insisting that the freedom defined by
the free marketplace political economy was true freedom. They were
also asserting that the right of self-determination had to be judged
in that light—at least in cases where the issue involved the expansion
of America's free marketplace system. That was a momentous and
far-reaching resolution of the contradiction between commitment
to the freedom of self-determination and an equally strong commitment to the necessity of expansion in order to insure one's freedom
and prosperity. It was the last step in transforming the long and urgent agricultural pressure for expanded exports into imperialism.
The farmers stopped short of embracing a policy of colonial annexation, but they revealed an implacable determination to dominate and
set limits on the Hawaiian political economy, and to define the islands
as an element in their own expansionist program.

The grave depression that began in 1893 reinforced that response
to the Hawaiian Revolution. Pervasive and continued economic difficulties heightened the farmers' already great concern for overseas
markets and increased their militance in fighting for that objective
and in battling metropolitan leaders who were slow to accept or act
on that policy. The resulting upsurge in unrest, reinforced by a sim-

ilar dissatisfaction among workers in the cities, was a major factor in completing the acceptance by metropolitan leaders of the overseas market approach that the farmers had been pushing for a generation. The other element was the direct economic pressure of the depression. Manufacturers and financial giants rapidly concluded that the industrial sector of the economy needed foreign markets at least as badly as the agriculturalists.

That ever-widening metropolitan concern for economic expansion led within five years to the general and final acceptance of the traditional agricultural outlook. That rapidly developing consensus did not prevent the eruption of serious and embittered arguments, however, over the best methods of expansion, or over which groups should formulate and execute the policy. Just such a fight, indeed, was the third important event of the period between the elections of 1892 and 1896. The issue concerned which monetary system—gold or silver— provided the best basis for economic development and expansion.

Cleveland and other determined defenders of gold monometallism launched an aggressive campaign to repeal the Sherman Silver Purchase Act of 1890 immediately after the panic of 1893. The case they advanced for gold rested largely on the necessity of maintaining the gold reserves of the Treasury in order to preserve America's international credit standing, and on the argument that gold monometallism was the standard of the world marketplace, and for that reason the United States had to operate on that basis if it wanted to expand exports.

Agrarian and other silver advocates exploded in opposition. They vigorously pressed their powerful theory that the full remonetization of silver would produce a vast expansion of American exports—industrial as well as agricultural—and asserted that result would in and of itself generate recovery and guarantee permanent prosperity. They also claimed that remonetization would accelerate and extend domestic capital formation, and thereby further strengthen the forces of economic revival at the same time it created more equity and balance in the marketplace.

The agricultural businessmen lost the battle. Treasury purchases of silver were stopped at the end of 1893. The defeat sustained the fury that the fight aroused, however, and the silverites wholly committed themselves to reversing the decision. The struggle also greatly intensified the existing economic nationalism of the farmers and focused it even more sharply against Great Britain and American metropolitan leaders who supported British policies. Similar though less highly charged conflicts shortly developed over the merits of reciprocity as against low tariffs, over the most effective kind of Navy, and over the priorities of expansion.

The men who became the major protagonists in the evolving strug-

gle actually formulated their positions long before 1896. William Jennings Bryan argued as early as 1893 that the combination of silver and
low tariffs, reinforced by the power created by the productivity of the
American farmer, would give the United States supremacy in the
world marketplace and the opportunity to spread freedom around the
globe. William McKinley took his stand on a program that combined
Blaine's argument for reciprocity with a call for an international agreement to use both gold and silver. He became so persuasive in behalf
of that expansionist strategy that the Southern and Northern delegates
to the founding convention of the National Association of Manufacturers gave him an ovation in 1895.

Long before that date, however, some Democrats had recognized
the appeal and effectiveness of Blaine's reciprocity approach, and
had begun to respond to the support that it generated. But the man
who was probably the key figure in that development, Walter Quintin
Gresham of Indiana, was a Republican who supported Cleveland
in the election of 1892 on the tariff issue. Gresham was deeply concerned
about the agricultural and urban unrest throughout the country, and
won the support of many farmers (including some Populists) because
of his sympathy with their predicament. He concluded that the depression had created a potentially revolutionary situation, and argued
that overseas economic expansion offered a way of resolving the crisis.

After he took office as Secretary of State under Cleveland in 1893,
Gresham became a central actor in the fourth and fifth events that
helped crystallize the agrarian and metropolitan consensus on market expansion. One of those episodes involved American diplomatic
and naval intervention in 1893-1894 against a Brazilian revolt whose
leaders opposed the nation's recently negotiated reciprocity treaty
with the United States. They feared it would make Brazil an American
vassal. Metropolitan business interests exerted the most direct pressure on Gresham and Cleveland to deploy the Navy against the rebellion (though the flour millers and meat packers were also active), but
that in itself revealed how rapidly the urban groups were adopting
the outlook of the farm businessmen. And the agriculturalists generally supported the militant display of force on the grounds that it
weakened the British, and because it might improve access to markets
throughout Latin America.

The farmers were more positively engaged when Gresham next
moved against the British in Nicaragua during 1894. Much of that
approval grew out of Senator Morgan's long agitation for an isthmian
canal routed through that country, and his specific proposal in 1893
to involve the United States government in constructing the waterway. Gresham's tough and shrewd diplomacy, which significantly
reduced Great Britain's influence in Nicaragua, won applause from
Populists as well as from more conservative farmers and metropoli-

tan interests. It also strengthened the existing confidence among the agriculturalists that the United States was powerful enough to achieve its marketplace objectives without having to fight any wars.

That sense of certainty exercised an increasing psychological influence on the farmers after 1894. It deepened their anger against metropolitan leaders like Cleveland who appeared cautious or timid in situations like the Nicaraguan confrontation, and it generated a momentum that carried them into making demands that ultimately provoked a war with Spain. At that point, not too surprisingly, the confidence was merely transferred to the problem of winning the war and became self-reinforcing—and therefore even more persuasive and consequential. That process was accelerated by other events during 1894 - 1895. Those incidents (the sixth and seventh in the overall pattern) involved the tariff bill finally produced by the Democrats in 1894, and the Sino-Japanese war of 1894 - 1895. Whatever the intentions and hopes of some Democrats, the Wilson-Gorham tariff of 1894 had two negative effects on overseas market expansion. By restoring sugar to the duty list, it abrogated the reciprocity treaties concluded by Blaine after 1890, and made it impossible to renegotiate such pacts. The schedule did provide free entry for a few raw materials, but even Cleveland recognized that those exceptions would not produce any significant rise in exports.

The most telling impact of the Wilson-Gorham measure came in the upper Middlewest because it destroyed the basis for the deal with Germany permitting the import of American pork products, and because it demolished the great and growing Cuban market that the flour millers and meat processors had created for those surpluses. The reaction was swift, negative, intense, and cumulative. Astute members of both parties realized, particularly after the Republicans scored a massive victory in the congressional elections of 1894, that the upper Mississippi Valley had become the pivotal region for the presidential campaign of 1896. And by that time the Wilson-Gorham tariff had served as the catalyst that touched off a revolution in Cuba that became the focus of agrarian pressure for a militant foreign policy.

Finally, the Wilson-Gorham measure also created support for the export program advocated by David Lubin of California. Lubin was a wealthy merchant who became a wealthy farmer, but he discovered in the process of that transition that the unrest and anger of agricultural businessmen were based on real rather than imagined difficulties. He proposed to meet the crisis by using government funds to pay the farmers a bounty on their exports. The California Grange was the first group to endorse his scheme, and he slowly won more backing across the nation. Lubin's greatest influence came later, however, after World War I, when the pressure for an export-debenture plan based on his idea reached a climax.

The Sino-Japanese War produced no such dramatic consequences in the development of American foreign policy. But while its effects were more indirect and subtle, they were nonetheless extensive. Most importantly, it extended the concern that various groups of agriculturalists had already manifested in the Asian (and particularly the Chinese) market, and had a similar, and probably greater, effect on the attitude of metropolitan leaders. The integration of Latin America and Asia in American thinking about overseas market expansion, a synthesis that became progressively more general during 1896 and 1897, was a quietly portentous result of the war. The conflict also moved the farmers further along in their acceptance of the need for a powerful battleship Navy.

Most political leaders recognized during 1894 that the expansionist outlook of the agriculturalists, which so explicitly combined the economic and ideological themes of the free marketplace philosophy, had become a major factor in the political situation. The continuing severity of the depression accentuated that impact, and simultaneously created more urban support for the same program. All those elements, metropolitan and agrarian, economic and political, affected Cleveland's decision in 1894 to take a militant stand against Great Britain's effort to acquire more Venezuelan territory.

The resulting crisis, the eighth event of the years 1892 - 1896, sustained the movement of the farmers toward imperialism. Once again, the crucial effects came indirectly through the reinforcement and deepening of an existing attitude. First of all, the idea of using foreign policy action to satisfy or distract the agriculturalists was publicly as well as privately recommended by a significant number of leaders. That of course enhanced the expansionist orientation, as well as sharpening its focus. The approach was so openly discussed, for that matter, that many farmers (and particularly Populists) became highly skeptical that Cleveland would translate his tough rhetoric into action. They interpreted the bombast as a desperate political maneuver.

But that in itself produced a second vital effect. The farmers concluded that even more pressure would have to be exerted before the agricultural majority would obtain its rightful influence in making policy decisions and thereby realize its objectives. And finally, the ultimate retreat by Britain again heightened agricultural confidence in America's ability to win its victories without war. In that respect, the outcome of the Venezuelan crisis significantly extended the feeling that the unilateral remonetization of silver would give the United States effective control of the world marketplace.

The final event of those momentous four years was the Cuban revolution that erupted in February 1895. In an ironic and perhaps even poetic way, moreover, the outbreak of the revolution was directly connected with a measure conceived to further such expansion. For the shock to the Cuban economy caused by the dramatic disruption of Ameri-can-Cuban trade when the Wilson-Gorham tariff law ended Blaine's reciprocity jolted the Cubans into rebellion. In an eerie preview of a pattern that would become commonplace during the twentieth cen-tury, the farm drive for export markets had established a superior-in-ferior relationship with another political economy that created all the classic problems of imperialism.

At the same time, moreover, that relationship generated the final and self-sustaining convergence of interests and ideas that produced the overt decision for imperialism. The central elements of that dy-namic process had become wholly apparent—and deeply consequen-tial—before the opening of the conventions called to nominate pres-idential candidates for the election of 1896. The economic impact of the depression, and its effect in producing a real fear of extensive so-cial unrest or even revolution, had completed the long and gradual ac-ceptance by metropolitan leaders of the traditional farm emphasis on overseas market expansion as the strategic solution to the nation's economic and social problems.

And the agricultural campaign for the extension of freedom and global enlargement of export markets reached its own crescendo in a demand for the election of a President and a Congress that would use American power to remonetize silver, to free Cuba, and to reform the world by applying the principles of the free marketplace politi-cal economy. That mighty surge of farm businessmen captured con-trol of the Democratic party and handed its presidential nomination to William Jennings Bryan.

The direct and indirect influence the agriculturalists exerted on the Republicans was less dramatic, perhaps, but it was no less extensive. Encouraged by strong pressure from Midwestern leaders as well as metropolitan spokesmen, William McKinley made the restoration of reciprocity (in general, as well as with Cuba in particular) a major element in his program to revive prosperity. He likewise promised to support Cuban freedom. And despite his formal commitment to the gold standard, he carefully and extensively presented himself as a man who would use American power in an effort to win agreement from Britain and other European nations to create an international monetary system based on silver as well as gold.

X I

To an extensive degree, indeed, the presidential campaign of 1896 was waged within the framework of analysis, policy, and national psychology that had been created after 1860 by the agricultural majority of the country. That was largely the case in connection with domestic affairs, and it was wholly true in the realm of foreign policy. In that pervasive sense, the farm businessmen emerged triumphant even though their candidate was defeated by a leader who transposed the agricultural outlook into industrial terms and gave it a metropolitan emphasis. The domestic victory of the farmers did not become fully apparent or effective until the Progressive movement flowered after the turn of the century. The result in foreign affairs, however, was clear even during the campaign, for the confrontation between McKinley and Bryan involved primarily a dispute over which methods of market expansion would most promptly and permanently restore prosperity and thereby resolve the social and political crisis.

Three factors swung the battle to McKinley. His stress on reciprocity treaties and the remonetization of silver through international agreement proved effective against Bryan's heavy-handed emphasis on the unilateral remonetization of silver to carry crucial Midwestern states. Second, McKinley used a combination of arguments for the protective tariff and for reciprocity treaties with great skill to hold labor as well as business groups in the Eastern metropolis. And, finally, the jump in wheat exports (and the associated rise in prices) that occurred late in the summer seriously weakened Bryan's argument that the depression could not be overcome without the remonetization of silver. Western farmers (and Eastern businessmen) reacted to that traditional index of economic activity just as they had since the early Civil War depression. The farm businessmen—and their role in the economy—had transformed what was originally an analysis into a pattern of response that affected the nation's politics as well as marketplace expectations and behavior. As a result, a significant number of them became sufficiently optimistic to turn away from Bryan and vote for McKinley.

Those expectations, which were shared by many metropolitan businessmen, were not promptly fulfilled. Recovery from the depression had in truth begun by the time McKinley was inaugurated in March 1897, but the gains remained diffused and uneven. The resulting disappointment first produced grumbling and impatience among the farmers and uneasiness in the metropolis, and then generated a rising pressure for action in Cuba and a growing concern to implement a program of overseas economic expansion. McKinley thus confronted a gathering storm even as he moved into the White House. Agricultural interests clamored for action to reopen the Cuban market, and metropolitan interests demanded protection for their property and investments in the island. Other spokesmen who analyzed the problem in terms of the economy as an interrelated system argued that the Cuban crisis had to be resolved so that the government and all businessmen, including farmers, could proceed with general market expansion. Metropolitan leaders particularly stressed that approach, but a significant number of agriculturalists offered the same recommendation.

Populists and other militant farmers took the lead in demanding that McKinley intervene to free the Cubans. Their action had the effect of renewing and intensifying the traditional integration of the economic and ideological themes in their expansionist thought and argument. Firm intervention to force Spain to retreat in Cuba, they cried with growing anger and impatience, would reopen the markets they needed, extend freedom for the Cubans (and thereby create an even larger market), and strike a resounding psychological blow against Great Britain and other European nations in all the markets of the world. That assault on McKinley created a political crisis involving a challenge to metropolitan authority in general, as well as to the position of the Republican party in particular.

McKinley had recognized the potentially dangerous results of such dissatisfaction even before he was inaugurated, and clearly hoped that Cleveland could terminate the Cuban crisis before he left office. Cleveland publicly warned the Spanish in December 1896 that the United States would move more forcefully if the rebellion was not handled promptly and effectively, but the problem was simply beyond the abilities or the power of the government in Madrid. Some metropolitan businessmen began at least as early as May 1897 to encourage McKinley to act more vigorously to restore peace on American terms, and the President moved to increase direct American pressure on the Spanish in June.

Neither metropolitan nor farm businessmen wanted war at that time. For one thing, they were not bloodthirsty. But a more important factor was their vast confidence that America was strong enough to free Cuba without having to go to war. And that assumption was very largely a product of the long campaign of argument and assertion by the agriculturalists that had been reinforced and seemingly proved by American victories in European markets, in controlling Hawaii, and in weakening Britain's position in Latin America. McKinley himself shared that happy belief in the efficacy of American power. That confidence was significantly challenged, however, by two developments during the latter half of 1897. One was the increasing evidence that Spain was not going to buckle under American demands—and pressure—to deal with Cuba in the way specified by McKinley. The second was the growing indication that Japan and the European powers were going to preempt and then divide the great market frontier of China. The interrelated implications of those two events were immediately recognized and discussed by farm leaders, as well as by key metropolitan decision makers.

The flour millers, meat packers, and cotton exporters (particularly the Southern textile men) promptly called for government action to protect their existing and anticipated market. Farm spokesmen talked seriously of changing the diet of the Chinese, as well as of clothing them in American cotton. In a similar way, railroad men like Hill and other industrial leaders mounted their own campaign to avoid being excluded from what came to be discussed as the next bonanza market for American surpluses.

The China crisis was the decisive factor in shifting the locus of power in formulating foreign policy from agricultural businessmen to the metropolitan leaders. Not only were urban groups more directly and intensely concerned about Asia, but the metropolis had produced an intellectually powerful and politically influential group of leaders who enjoyed direct access to McKinley. The farmers did not lack all leverage, for Secretary of Agriculture James Wilson of Iowa was a militant expansionist who enjoyed a deepening personal friendship with the President. And the growing possibility that the agricultural spokesmen in the Congress might wrench the initiative from McKinley provided them with indirect but powerful influence. In one major respect, of course, that pressure for action in Cuba was the force that finally pushed McKinley and key metropolitan businessmen into an acceptance of war.

But a war to extend classic marketplace freedoms to Cuba was neither logically nor inherently a war to accomplish that objective and at the same time project American economic power into a free Asian marketplace. Yet the second war was the war that the United States fought in 1898-1899. The agriculturalists ultimately accepted that second war, and embraced the policy evolved to harvest its rewards, but they were not directly responsible for defining the conflict in those terms. Metropolitan intellectuals, businessmen, and politicians were the principal authors of that strategy. Congressmen and Cabinet members were talking with McKinley at least as early as September 1897, for example, about controlling the Philippines as a springboard into Asia if it became necessary to go to war against Spain to end the Cuban mess. The government had developed its own military plans for such a two-front war, moreover, before Assistant Secretary of the Navy Theodore Roosevelt put his similar ideas into operation one afternoon after his superior had left the office early. Roosevelt was given a mild rebuke, but his basic orders were not revoked. They were improved. Agricultural influence was not absent even from that episode, however, for Roosevelt and other metropolitan leaders were acting upon the frontier-expansionist thesis of American prosperity and welfare.

It is highly unlikely that President McKinley was affected directly by the version of the frontier thesis developed by intellectuals like Frederick Jackson Turner and Brooks Adams. But those men did influence metropolitan leaders like Roosevelt to whom McKinley regularly exposed himself. And the President continued to discuss the problem with other men who argued the wisdom of fighting a war against Spain over Cuba, if it proved necessary, in a way that would provide a base for American economic and military power in Asia. He was also subjected to ever more insistent pressure from his political advisers to act against Spain over Cuba before the angry farmers took control of the country.

That became an increasingly real threat after January 1898 because Spain remained adamant in response to American pressure. The campaign led by key Populists became so directly challenging by March that it convinced reluctant metropolitan leaders that war was necessary to preserve the proper organization (and control) of the American political economy. At that point, if not before, McKinley opted for war. In all fundamental respects, therefore, historical as well as immediate, the war against Spain was a war of the majority of the American people.

The agriculturalists also supplied a classic moment of truth when Populist Jerry Simpson looked boldly into the implications and the consequences of the long campaign by farm businessmen to expand the free marketplace. He recognized the harsh validity of Thomas Jefferson's earlier warning that a commitment to ever expanding export markets would lead first to war and then to war again. Simpson concluded that imperial wars were more destructive of freedom than the failure to capture more export markets. He also sensed, if indeed he did not fully comprehend, that everything after the decision to go to war to extend the free marketplace to Cuba would be an ultimately unsuccessful rear-guard action to prevent those unhappy consequences.

So it proved.

The farmers fought hard to make certain that American expansion was not institutionalized in the form of traditional colonialism. For one thing, neither the Northerners nor the Southerners wanted to become involved in more problems with black men. Nor did they relish the moral and practical difficulties involved in ruling and training people who had yet to understand and accept the truths of a modern marketplace political economy. In the fundamental sense, of course, their victory against colonialism was due to their long fight in behalf of free marketplace expansion. They had created a consensus in support of an overseas economic expansion that attacked colonialism in the name of self-determination and freedom. But they also effectively opposed those Americans who flirted with orthodox colonialism between 1897 and 1900. They insured that Cuba was not annexed, and committed the United States to freeing the Philippines even as those islands were taken to provide a base for the penetration of the China market.

On all counts, therefore, the long battle of the agricultural business-

men for overseas marketplace expansion played the principal role
in the development and adoption of an imperial outlook and policy.
The occupation of the Philippines was viewed and accepted as a re-
grettably necessary—and temporary—means to the realization of
an ultimately just and progressive end. Once past that unfortunate
exception, the way lay open for the application of the classic marketplace philosophy. The Open Door Notes of 1899 and 1900, which committed the power and the prestige of the United States to the principles of self-determination and the open marketplace, were the formal
expression of an outlook and a policy that the agricultural majority
had advocated since before the Civil War.

But the policy of expanding the free marketplace led unfortunately
to wars: wars to apply the principles; and wars to defend the freedom
and the prosperity that the expansion of the principles had ostensibly produced for Americans. Finally, after long years, it became clear
that the expansion of the free marketplace had failed to bring freedom
and prosperity to all Americans, let alone to all the people of the world.
Yet at that moment the difficulty was compounded in a truly tragic
way because the view of the world that had produced the crisis was
an outlook that had been created and accepted by the majority.

There was thus no elite or other scapegoat to blame and replace.

There are only ourselves to confront and change.

If we can understand how we became an imperial metropolis in the
name of the freedom and prosperity of the country, then perhaps we
can free our minds and our wills to achieve freedom and prosperity
without being an imperial society.

ONE

The chief end of trade is Riches and Power which beget each other. Riches consist in plenty of movables, that will yield a price to foreigners, and are not likely to be consumed at home.

John Locke, 1674

All the imaginable ways of increasing Money in any Country are these two: Either dig it in Mines of our Own, or to get it from our Neighbors. . . . Riches do not consist in having more Gold and Silver, but in having more in proportion than the rest of the World, or than our Neighbors, whereby we are enabled to procure ourselves a greater Plenty of the Conveniences of Life than comes within the reach of Neighboring Kingdoms and States.

John Locke, 1691

The question is, whether small or extensive republics are more favorable to the election of proper guardians of the public weal; and it is clearly decided in favor of the latter.

James Madison, 1787

The true question . . . is the right of exporting the production of our own soil and industry to foreign markets.

Representative Felix Grundy, 1811

The expansion of our Union over a vast territory cannot operate unfavorably to the States individually. On the contrary, it is believed that the greater the expansion, within practicable limits, and it is not easy to say what are not so, the greater the advantage.

President James Monroe, 1822

The greatest improvement in the productive powers . . . seem to have been the effects of the division of labor.

This division of labor . . . is the necessary . . . consequence of a certain propensity . . . to truck, barter, and exchange one thing for another.

This division of labor must always be limited . . . by the extent of the market.

The surplus must be sent abroad. . . . It is only by means of such exportation that this surplus can acquire a value sufficient to compensate the labor and expense of producing it.

Adam Smith, *The Wealth of Nations*, 1776

The great and chief end, therefore, of Men uniting into Commonwealths, and putting themselves under Government, is the Preservation of their Property.

John Locke, 1689

He that encloses Land and has a greater plenty of the conveniences of life from ten acres, than he could have from an hundred left to Nature, may truly be said, to give ninety acres to Mankind.

John Locke, 1713

The
Tradition of Expansion
Undergoes a Mutation

THE AMERICAN farmer has never glorified the ideal or accepted the condition of self-sufficiency.[1] He has always seen himself as a creature of the marketplace, and hence as a capitalist whose wealth and welfare depended upon the profitable sale of his surplus production. He supplied himself with nonagricultural needs when and as he found that necessary, but traded for them as soon as and whenever he could. That commercial outlook, and its related behavior, were inherent in the theory and the practice of British mercantilism that guided the founding and development of the colonies, and emerged in all their glory as that system of political economy gave way to the laissez-faire marketplace capitalism of Adam Smith.

The mercantilists constantly stressed the necessity of economic expansion in generating material growth and development, as well as in creating the conditions for maximum political and social well-being. They also argued that economic liberty and success had a direct and causal part in defining freedom per se, and in realizing such freedom. The mercantilist conception of freedom, to be sure, was cast far more in terms of membership in an organic national community than the freedom defined by Smith and later political economists. It was likewise circumscribed more extensively by ideas and ideals of obligation, responsibility, and duty, and by the conviction that conscious effort and control were required to produce the general welfare. Within the limits established by those ideas and ideals, however, men were considered free to pursue their economic desires and preferences. Much of the struggle within British mercantilism developed out of the efforts to recover, preserve, or extend the liberty to advance such interests inside the boundaries of the system. By the early part of the eighteenth century, at any rate, the British mercantilist gauged his freedom to a very significant degree by the extent of his ability to enter upon various kinds of economic activity, and by the opportunities for expansion within that sphere.[2]

The drive for such economic liberty became a major dynamic force in the ultimately successful assault on the mercantilist system. And economic freedom was placed at the heart of the alternate conception of political economy developed by Smith and others after 1730. Since the campaign for economic independence and expansion, and the related liberties, was a central element in the American Revolution, it has often been assumed or asserted that the colonials were rebelling against mercantilism as well as against Great Britain's mercantilist system. Yet in truth, and whatever their wartime euphoria about the freedom to be achieved through independence, Americans generally acted within the framework of advanced mercantilist thought until after the War of 1812.[3]

The agricultural majority of the country played a major role in sustaining and maturing that American mercantilism. The farmers, individually and collectively, and large and small, generated pressure for economic expansion in the form of demands for more land to sustain and advance their commercial agriculture, and for the enlargement (and protection) of overseas markets to absorb the surpluses they produced. They also developed and agitated the pivotal mercantilist idea that such economic expansion was essential to the preservation and extension of political and social freedom.

The first great conflict in American politics, furthermore, arose out of clashing ideas about the most effective and appropriate means to realize those mercantilist axioms. That confrontation, between those who argued that the individual states could best discharge the obligation and others who insisted upon the need for a coordinated, collective effort, produced the Constitution of 1787. And it was James Madison, one of the key leaders of the Southern export-dominated agricultural economy, who formulated the most sweeping and persuasive argument for expansion in the name of present freedom, and in order to guarantee future freedom.

Madison advanced one central idea in his conversations, correspondence, and public agitation during 1786 and 1787. That theory maintained that the expansion of the area of central political authority, the creation of a national government with powers over all subdivisions, would provide the best security for republican government. "Extend the sphere," he explained, "and you make it less probable that a majority of the whole will have a common motive to invade the rights of other citizens."[4] The immediate application of that axiom required the creation of what Madison called "one great, respectable, and flourishing empire."[5] But the dynamic thrust of the principle itself was expansionist and imperial in the fundamental sense of tying republican government to an ever-expanding system. Such was the case not only in the narrow sense of assigning the primary responsibility for realizing the basic needs of the people (land and commerce, and the protection thereof) to the central government, but also in the general meaning of defining expansion as the best and most effective method for preserving republicanism in the face of an indefinitely rising population.

As Thomas Jefferson realized, Madison had blatantly reversed the traditional analysis of the causal relationship between size and freedom. British and other European mercantilists initiated that philosophical revolution (and largely carried it through), but Madison was its chief American protagonist. Along with others, including many small farmers not fully integrated into the marketplace, Jefferson was at first reluctant to accept the new equation tying freedom to empire. He feared, as did his fellow Southerner John Taylor of Caroline County, Virginia, that the expansionist means would subvert the end of freedom.

But the strength of Madison's logic, powerfully augmented by the need and desire for more land and markets, persuaded enough of the skeptical farmers to make it possible to create the Constitutional imperium. Once that decision was made, moreover, the agriculturalists took the lead in integrating the principle and practice of expansion with the axioms of natural law and freedom. In the year after the adoption of the Constitution, for example, the militant delegates to the Convention of Kentucky asserted "the natural right of the inhabitants of this country to navigate the Mississippi," and called upon the new national government to insure their right to export their surpluses by that route.[6]

Perhaps Jefferson himself revealed most clearly the enthusiasm of the convert. The acquisition of Louisiana, and the accompanying suppression of people in the territory who preferred another overlord, were justified on the grounds that they promoted "a wide spread for the blessings of freedom and equal laws." Jefferson also argued that adding Canada and Cuba would be legitimate steps in creating America's "empire for liberty."[7] But Northerners also manifested the spirit of expansion in the name of prosperity and liberty. "We have in general," explained a New York editor, "the right of doing whatever is necessary to the discharge of our duties," and carefully added that actions required for American "perfection and happiness" were included among the obligations of such duty.[8]

Other Americans, particularly those of the agricultural majority, drew upon the Physiocrats and John Locke in adapting Madison's expansionist argument to their own interests and philosophical temperaments. They were naturally receptive to, as well as flattered by, François Quesnay's judgment that agriculture was the foundation of all progress and well-being, and wholly agreed with his maxim that "an agricultural nation should facilitate an active external trade in raw produce."[9] They were equally happy with Locke's basic axiom that government existed "for the procuring, preserving, and advancing" of men's civil interests—which centered on "the possession of outward things" and the acquisition of "what they further want."[10]

What the agricultural majority wanted, it quickly became apparent, was effective action to facilitate their possession of good land and access to overseas markets. The production of surpluses of grain and livestock led rapidly during the 1780s and 1790s to a booming export trade in wheat, flour, pork, and salted beef. Vermont's export of flour to Quebec, for example, was significant enough to prompt the British to consider using that economic relationship as a way of winning the political allegiance of the population. More generally, agricultural exports accounted for about 12 percent of farm income by 1800.[11]

Small as it might seem, that figure was important in three respects. Much of the total was supplied by Southern exports of cotton and tobacco. The overseas sale of those commodities was crucial to the entire region. That concentration created a powerful political impetus for acquiring the land necessary for maintaining and expanding production, and for sustaining the area's position in the export market. Secondly, the operations of the producers of other surplus commodities were not necessarily limited by the figure of 12 percent. Some of those farmers knew that most or all of their produce went into the overseas market. Others were not as surely informed, or as deeply involved, but they were nevertheless concerned with that outlet because of their uncertainty and their hopes for better markets.

Finally, the knowledge that export markets helped make agriculture profitable exerted a direct and indirect influence on agrarian attitudes and analyses. The profitability itself attracted men into farming, and that increased the physical and political pressure for territorial expansion. And when the overseas markets were threatened, or actually closed, those crises underscored their importance. That reaction was particularly strong when such troubles coincided with domestic depressions. That kind of effect first became apparent in the 1790s, during the early phase of the Napoleonic wars, when both France and Great Britain interrupted, limited, or closed the export market for agricultural surpluses in the West Indies and European nations. Presidents George Washington and John Adams drew upon all their political skill and personal courage to avoid being pushed into wars against Great Britain and France, and those struggles over foreign policy did much to create and consolidate the first political parties in the United States.

Still more powerful pressure arose after 1806, moreover, when American farmers increasingly demanded strong action against British maritime regulations that threatened their exports, and more land to ease their general difficulties. Those campaigns for territory and markets, often waged by the same individuals and groups, constituted one of the three major factors that produced the American declaration of war against Great Britain in 1812. The other two were directly related to the way that economic expansion had been tied to domestic freedom by the mercantilists and the philosophers of natural law. As Jefferson had foreseen as early as 1785, American liberty, rights, and honor became involved through the agricultural commitment to overseas markets. In the opinion of the farm businessmen, as well as of Madison and other leaders, the exports were an essential ingredient of American development and an inherent aspect of American freedom. They held the view that free access to overseas markets was necessary in order to avoid having the American economy recolonized by the British.

The most sustained push for war against England came from commercial farmers in the West and South. The Westerners began to feel an economic pinch in 1806 and 1807, when their surpluses encountered full markets and profits consequently declined. Then the depression of 1808 dropped wholesale prices at New Orleans by as much as 20 percent. The agricultural businessmen responded with an assault against the British regulations that effectively closed Caribbean and European markets. "The dispute between us and the belligerents is not about the carrying trade," explained Senator John Pope of Kentucky in 1808, "but whether we shall be permitted to carry our surplus produce to foreign markets. . . . The necessity . . . of resisting the British orders and forcing our way into those markets where there is a demand for the article, must be evident to every one who will consider the subject."[12]

That theme was expounded and elaborated with rising urgency during the next four years as the farmers elected more and more spokesmen of their persuasion. Representative William Lowndes, a lawyer and planter from South Carolina, stated the proposition most succinctly: "The interests of agriculture and commerce are inseparable." Congressman Felix Grundy of Tennessee agreed: "The true question . . . is the right of exporting the production of our own soil and industry to foreign markets." Representative Henry Clay of Kentucky, who became the leader of the growing group of War Hawks, argued that economics and freedom were inexorably entwined. Indeed, the one seemed largely to define the other. "We are asserting our claim," he cried, "to the direct trade — the right to export our cotton, tobacco, and other domestic produce to market." The pressure became so great by the end of 1811 that the editors of the Lexington *Reporter* felt able to relax. "It appears likely that our government will at last make war, to produce a market for our Tobacco, Flour, and Cotton."

And, coupled with the related drive to obtain more land in the South and Northwest, the demands to reopen and expand the overseas market did produce the War of 1812. The formal declaration came in June, but President Madison had all but forecast the decision in his letter of January 8, 1812, to the South Carolina House of Representatives. Continued acquiescence was "forbidden," he warned, because "it would recolonize our commerce by subjecting it to a foreign Authority." And that, he explained in the idiom of the expansionist theory he had first propounded in 1786 - 1787, would damage and unsettle all the interests of the country and thereby create general unrest. Representative John Caldwell Calhoun, the brilliant young planter-lawyer from South Carolina who began to assert his leadership in the South even before he was elected to the Congress as a War Hawk in 1810, echoed and enlarged upon that analysis.

Southern agrarians "know well," Calhoun announced, that "without the market to the Continent, the deep and steady current of supply will glut that of Great Britain; they are not prepared for the colonial state to which again that Power is endeavoring to reduce us." But neither Calhoun nor other farm businessmen considered Britain the only power capable of recolonizing American agriculture. All farmers, as soon as they became involved in surplus-producing commercial agriculture, recognized their dependence upon middlemen and other traders who handled the disposal of the surplus. That was why Senator Pope and Representative Grundy carefully pointed out that they were not going to war for the carrying trade. Along with Lowndes, they understood that agriculture needed commerce, but they were deeply concerned to avoid being forced into a condition of domestic colonialism by the metropolitan powers that controlled the monetary, merchandising, and shipping elements of the marketplace.

That fear and determination increased as it became apparent that the War of 1812 accelerated the economic growth, and reinforced the political influence, of urban commercial, financial, and manufacturing interests that had begun fitfully after the first limitations of American trade in 1806. The postwar boom temporarily checked such uneasiness because the farmer shared in the prosperity. Then came the devastating panic of 1818 - 1819, and the depression of 1819 - 1820. Jefferson's blunt comment to John Adams—"the paper bubble is then burst" —caught the impact of the crash even if it oversimplified the causes of the collapse.[13] Cotton prices fell from thirty-two cents per pound in 1818 to seventeen cents in 1820. The decline continued on into 1821, when Cincinnati quotations were ten cents per bushel for corn and twenty-five cents for wheat. Whiskey was also cheap, fifteen cents a gallon, but the awareness of the basic problem returned along with the hangover.

The recovery of European agriculture after the Napoleonic wars was a major cause of the plight of the farmers. Exports climbed sharply from $52.5 million in 1815 to $93.3 million in 1818, but they dropped even more rapidly. Foreign sales remained larger than they had been prior to 1812, but that neither impressed nor helped the agricultural businessmen. The general decline in the value of exports lasted more than a decade, though some groups of farmers fared better than others. Some local wheat growers benefited from the continued flour exports by such Eastern milling centers as Baltimore, Richmond, and Rochester, and to a lesser extent from similar activities in Cincinnati. Such developments created a short-lived movement to build a regional industrial base in the Ohio Valley. Elisha Mills did establish Cincinnati as a meat-packing center after 1818, but the broad objective was not realized until much later.

Eastern grain farmers also gained some benefits from the efforts of New York exporters such as Ogden, Ferguson and Company to market wheat and flour surpluses in Europe.[14] And a few California cattlemen, particularly Thomas O. Larkin of Monterey, grew rich from the export trade in hides that was developed by Boston merchants like Bryant and Sturgis. Their operations also provided Richard Henry Dana with superb material for his career as an author, as he revealed in *Two Years Before the Mast*, but the business did not ease the unhappy condition of the great majority of American farmers.

As they would again after the crashes of 1837 and 1857, the agriculturalists had to endure severe difficulties during and following the panic and depression of 1818-1821. Maryland farmers were among the first to complain, reacting to a downturn during the late months of 1818. They announced at the end of a conference in January 1819 that prompt action was mandatory in order to remedy the "extremely defective condition of agriculture." The situation deteriorated rapidly in 1819, and by October the editors of the *American Farmer* spoke routinely and candidly of "the present gloomy state of affairs." That remained a generally accurate description of agricultural conditions for more than a decade.

James M. Garnett, president of the Agricultural Society of Fredericksburg, Virginia. warned in 1821 that "evil times have fallen upon us." His remedy was "to entreat, remonstrate, and protest" against the campaign to raise the tariff. The proper policy was to lower the rates because that would expand exports and relieve the crisis. Thomas Law of the Maryland Agricultural Society thought it obvious that "we are all impoverished"; but, while he agreed that it was vitally important to expand exports, he was appalled that a significant number of farmers were hoping for a foreign war to ease their troubles. Another farmer manifested the disenchantment with overseas markets that turned some toward the home market theory. He argued in September 1821 that the war boom was itself responsible for the difficulties — "we have been going rapidly retrograde for the last six years" — and concluded that "foreign trade has become a very hazardous lottery."

In the broader sense, the period was characterized by "wholesale foreclosures" and a serious shortage of capital. The editors of the *New England Farmer* were close enough to the truth to make their exaggeration effective: the farmer, they sighed, "passes his life continually pinched for the want of a little money."[15] As that observation suggests, the response of the agricultural businessmen to the continuing time of troubles included an insistent attack on metropolitan control of the monetary system as manifested and symbolized in the Bank of the United States. In a more general way, the attempt to cope with the problems produced a complex and contradictory set of reactions that played a major role in the demise of the American mercantilist system that James Monroe and John Quincy Adams tried to consolidate and project into the indefinite future.

That fragmentation was revealed very clearly in the sharply different conclusions that were drawn from the price decline, and from the inability of the European market to sustain agricultural prosperity. One group of farmers, centered almost exclusively in the West and North, argued that American agriculture would never prosper until it had a large home market. That turned them into supporters of Henry Clay and his American System based on a reasonable protective tariff. It also, ironically, put them in the position of giving aid and comfort to the manufacturers — a group they otherwise castigated as part of the anti-agrarian metropolis. That approach to the tariff largely dominated the thinking and action of the Committee on Agriculture established in 1820 by the House of Representatives in response to pressure from farm businessmen of all sections. The committee's report and recommendation on the tariff bill of 1824, for example, almost slavishly followed the protectionist line. The farmer, the members admitted, "looks to a market for the surplus products of his industry"; but then they pronounced the judgment that "the home market . . . is at all times to be preferred to the foreign market."[16]

Some Northerners and Westerners, however, and almost all Southerners, developed a drastically different analysis and policy. They pointed first to the example of cotton and argued that expanded production of a few primary crops offered higher rewards than controlled planting or diversification. They maintained secondly that high tariffs hurt the farm businessman in two ways. A protectionist schedule not only antagonized foreigners and thereby increased the difficulty of penetrating overseas markets, but it forced the farmer to pay higher prices for all the items he needed but could not produce for himself. It was not coincidental that the Senate, where Southerners were strongly represented, created its own Committee on Agriculture in 1825, the year after the tariff was again raised.

Neither congressional committee was noticeably creative or influential in dealing with policy matters during the 1820s. They were nevertheless important because they established the precedent of specific representation for agriculture. And the farmers steadily, if at first slowly, increased the pressure to institutionalize their role in the decision-making process in a more effective manner. In truth, of course, the agriculturalists already enjoyed leverage of that kind through the committees on public lands. And their efforts to deal with their continuing difficulties by changing land policy were somewhat more rewarding than the battle against tariff increases.

The panic of 1818 - 1819 played a catalytic role in transforming the popular agitation for a new basic land law into congressional action. The act of April 2, 1820, abolished the credit system of payment, which had rewarded the speculator more than it helped the farmer, and made it possible to buy as little as eighty acres at $1.25 per acre. That capital outlay remained too much for many farmers, however, and the manipulators and moneylenders continued to reap good harvests. The farm businessmen immediately launched new efforts to win a law that made land cheap enough to buy, and to legalize squatters' rights through the policy of preemption. The opposition to preemption was too strong to overcome during the 1820s, but the first relief act for settlers who found themselves unable to hold onto their land under the law of 1820 was passed in 1821. Ten more acts were adopted in the following decade. Another approach was offered in 1824 by Senator Thomas Hart Benton of Missouri. His strategy, which called for making the land available for less than $1.25 if it was not taken at that price during a specified period, won extensive support. It was not, however, written into law for many years.

The agricultural businessmen, and particularly the Westerners, suffered a similar defeat in their campaign to have the federal government finance and administer a broad national program of internal improvements. Once they entered the commercial marketplace, farmers became ever stronger advocates of improved transportation. They understood that lower costs in that part of their operation meant a greater chance to penetrate and hold foreign markets, and at the same time left more of the selling price in their pockets as profit. The same considerations held true within the domestic marketplace. Better transportation also offered the prospect of lower costs for the goods that the farmer purchased from the metropolis.

Jefferson advocated such improvements during his terms as President, and such American mercantilists as Albert Gallatin of Pennsylvania and John Quincy Adams developed elaborate plans for the kind of national transportation network that George Washington had envisioned as early as the 1770s. But the first major effort to transform such proposals into law and an integrated communications system, led by Calhoun in 1816 - 1817, encountered the obstacles that ultimately defeated the attempt. The key to the failure was the disagreement among agricultural businessmen. Some farmers in all sections were so involved with the practical problems of establishing themselves as commercial operators that they did not become active supporters of the campaign. Others were generally opposed because of the required increase in taxes. And another group, particularly in the flush period after the War of 1812, were satisfied with the increasing number of individual projects that the Congress approved. Such projects met their immediate needs, and they did not join the push for a national program.

The vital differences over an integrated program of improvements involved two broader issues. Many Westerners (especially prior to the panic of 1818 - 1819), and a substantial majority of Southerners, desired the improvements but feared that the more highly organized commercial and financial interests in the metropolis would reap most of the benefits. And a good many farmers, again including many who wanted such action, were seriously concerned about the constitutionality of the program. They worried that establishing the precedent of stretching the Constitution would open the way to all kinds of action by the central government against their interests, and even against their principles. Despite those powerful kinds of opposition, Calhoun managed to maneuver an internal-improvements bill through the House (86 - 84) and the Senate (20 - 15) by March 1, 1817. President Madison vetoed it as unconstitutional and on the grounds that approval could only be given on the basis of an "inadmissible latitude of construction."[17] But Madison made it clear that he supported the general objective, and urged his successor, President James Monroe, to use his influence to win support for an amendment to the Constitution that would clear the way for such legislation and action.

Monroe did precisely that, basing his argument and appeal on the same marketplace and expansionist logic that Madison advanced so powerfully in the fight for the Constitution. Such improvements would facilitate "the transportation of the whole of the rich productions of our country to market." That "would alone more than amply compensate for all the labor and expense." But there was another consideration "of still more vital importance." That was the argument that expansion provided the key to prosperity and republican government. "The expansion of our Union over a vast territory cannot operate unfavorably to the States individually. On the contrary, it is believed that the greater the expansion, within practicable limits, and it is not easy to say what are not so, the greater the advantage." The only limit, Monroe explained, involved the existence of effective transportation and communications. If that problem could be solved, then "expansion may be carried to very great extent, and with perfect safety."[18] Hence the need for a constitutional amendment to clear the way.

Westerners had grown steadily more united in support of internal improvements after 1819, but they could not win enough allies in the South and the Northeast to bend Monroe's constitutional scruples or to force a showdown on the proposed amendment. The reality of that failure reinforced their growing opposition to the existing leadership of the country; and that antagonism became ever stronger after John Quincy Adams was elected President in 1824 amid angry charges that his victory over the favorites of the South and West, William H. Crawford of Georgia and Andrew Jackson of Tennessee, was won through disgraceful bargains.

The agriculturalists bitterly assaulted Adams, and those who supported him, as men who favored the metropolis over the country, and who had created an aristocracy that threatened democracy as well as economic progress. Many Southerners shared that estimate, moreover, despite their differences with the Westerners over specific issues such as internal improvements and the tariff. The Westerners lost some of their enthusiasm for the tariff, moreover, as the rates continued to be raised and as it failed to produce a home market capable of absorbing their surpluses. Their attacks grew more general and intense as the metropolitan leaders failed to satisfy the demand for further expansion of the marketplace.

The continual restless agitation by increasingly self-conscious farmers for more land and markets, and for other measures to satisfy their particular needs, dramatized the breakdown of the mercantilist ideal—and psychology—of an organic society guided from the center by leaders with an inclusive outlook. The mercantilist habit of mind that had evolved during the Colonial era had been reinforced by the experiences of the Revolution, and had in many respects been institutionalized during the years when the Constitution had been written and put into operation. Presidents George Washington and John Adams had then sustained it through the crises over British and French interference with American trade.

Jefferson had effected a final consolidation through his recognition of the need to foster all interests of the political economy, and through the Louisiana Purchase that provided a vast reserve of resources and satisfied the agricultural majority of the country. Yet Jefferson's noble effort, through a policy of economic self-restraint and military nonintervention, to avoid being drawn into the Napoleonic wars placed too great a strain on the ideological and emotional cement that mercantilism relied upon to unite contending interest groups into an organic whole. Thus the factional conflicts that Madison had worried about in 1786-1787 began after 1806 to erode the sense of common purpose and mutual need that fed the spirit of compromise. Each interest group fought ever more vigorously to win the sanction (and power) of the national government for its essentially private programs and objectives. The War of 1812 and the related economic boom gave American mercantilism the push that extended its life into the 1820s. But the very economic development and emotional involvement that provided short-term sustenance for mercantilism also strengthened the self-consciousness, importance, and strength of each interest group.

The implications of that development became dramatically apparent in 1817 when the State of New York, impatient over the failure of the federal government to act on internal improvements, initiated construction of the Erie Canal. The inability of mercantilist leaders to resolve the very real dilemmas involved in undertaking such projects as part of a broad, integrated national program ended any possibility that mercantilism would emerge from the War of 1812 as a fully restored and viable *Weltanschauung*. Its momentum did carry it on through the 1820s, when its protagonists produced some of their best intellectual achievements. But the postwar panic and depression, coupled with the example of the Erie Canal, triggered a multifaceted revolt against the very concept of a mercantilist commonwealth, and against the men who symbolized that ideal.

The intellectual foundations of that rebellion had been solidly prepared by Adam Smith in his *Inquiry into the Nature and Causes of the Wealth of Nations*, first published in 1776. His American followers read that grand synthesis and statement of the principles of the political economy of laissez-faire capitalism as both their book of common prayer and as an operator's manual for the new system. Smith himself became America's new philosopher-king, and even the displaced mercantilist leaders were reinterpreted as early heroes according to the new gospel.

As Karl Marx was later to do with Smith himself, Smith used a very great deal of mercantilism in constructing his own system of laissez faire. Whatever the differences between them, and some were far-reaching, Smith and the mercantilists shared two important characteristics. The first was a reliance on the principle that the expansion of the marketplace was necessary for economic, political, and social well-being. The second was the axiom that economic liberty and success had a direct and causal part in both the definition of freedom per se, and in the realization of such freedom.

The drive for such economic liberty, moreover, became the dynamic element in the assault upon the mature mercantilist system. As developed by Smith, that theme was transformed into an alternate conception of reality that defined man primarily in terms of his unique and inherent "propensity to truck, barter, and exchange one thing for another" in the marketplace.[19] Smith measured man's freedom in those terms, and argued that the free marketplace system of organizing relationships between men would create prosperity and social peace without coercion. In that vital respect, Smith's creative synthesis of earlier (and concurrent) thinking supplied by the Physiocrats and John Locke marked a clear break with the mercantilist outlook. For the latter had insisted that prosperity and social well-being could be achieved only through conscious and sustained thought and action.

Because there is a persistent misunderstanding of the point, it is worth emphasizing that it was Smith, and not his critics, or the critics of the system created in his name, who defined man so very largely in economic terms. He built his system on "the propensity to truck, barter, and exchange," and upon the individual's "self-love," rather than upon any urge or propensity to realize the ideals of benevolence or freedom. "The consideration of his own profit is the sole motive which determines the owner of any capital to employ it." The ability to make such decisions in perfect freedom, moreover, realized "the simple system of natural liberty."[20] In Smith's system, therefore, and directly as well as indirectly, freedom per se was unalterably entwined with the liberty "to truck, barter, and exchange." There was no natural liberty if men were not free to act upon their own considerations of their own economic profit.

The individual's economic drive, moreover, created the division of labor that Smith credited with being a vital element in producing economic growth.[21] But he immediately pointed out that the division of labor, in turn, "must always be limited . . . by the extent of the market."[22] That point was so central to the functioning of his system that he once used the same phrase, "the surplus must be sent abroad," twice within four sentences in the same paragraph—and then again in the next paragraph.[23] And he explicitly related the principle of exporting surplus production to agriculture in discussing the growth of the United States.[24] It is apparent, therefore, that Smith did not abandon the stress on economic expansion that was so much a part of mercantilism. He instead made it *the* dynamic factor in the proper functioning and success of his own system. According to Smith's logic, therefore, market expansion was the necessary condition for the realization of individual freedom and liberty. He merely substituted a new kind of imperialism for the mercantilist variety in order to gain freedom for the individual.

There is no difficulty in understanding why American agricultural businessmen were so attracted to that crucial part of Smith's system. They read him as a man who was telling the world what they knew to be the truth. Foreign markets were essential to agricultural, and hence everyone's, prosperity. They likewise took him to their minds and hearts for his blunt judgment that "the town . . . may very properly be said to gain its whole wealth and subsistence from the country." "The cultivation and improvement of the country, which affords subsistence, must, necessarily, be prior to the increase of the town. . . . It is the surplus produce of the country only . . . that constitutes the subsistence of the town."[25]

The land, he emphasized, this time repeating the phrase in two consecutive sentences, was "by far the greatest, the most important, and the durable part of the wealth" of any extensive country.[26] There was more, much more, of the same. The "art of the farmer," Smith pointed out, requires "more skill and experience than the greater part of mechanic trades." Any man who knew his marketplace understood "how much the lower ranks of people in the country are really superior to those in the town."[27]

And then, most explosively of all, after swilling the farmer's pride almost to the point of foundering, Smith told him that he was all but trapped in an inequitable position. "The revenue of a trading and manufacturing country," Smith began quietly, and almost casually, "must, other things being equal, always be much greater than that of one without trade or manufacturing." Then the mule kick. *"What a town always is with regard to the country in its neighbourhood,* one independent state or country may frequently be with regard to other independent states or countries."[28]

The reason, Smith explained, was that "a small quantity of manufactured produce purchases a great quantity of rude produce. A trading and manufacturing country, therefore, naturally purchases with a small part of its manufactured produce a great part of the rude produce of other countries; while, on the contrary, a country without trade and manufactures is generally obliged to purchase, at the expense of a great part of its rude produce, a very small part of the manufactured produce of other countries."[29]

But since that possible relationship between two countries was based upon a structural imbalance that "always" existed between the town and the country sectors of one national economy, Smith had created a political economy that posited an internal imperialism as well as an external imperialism. The farmer had but two ways of escaping his inferior position. He could move to the metropolis. Or he could stay on the farm and work harder, cut his costs, exploit his advantage during good times, expand his markets, and attempt to manipulate the supply to his profit. It would be extremely difficult to construct a system that *through the operation of its own principles* would generate a more powerful and sustained force for overseas market expansion, and for measures designed to return higher profits from such expansion.

The farmer did not relish being told he was caught on a virtual treadmill, but he found Smith's explanation of the situation meaningful and broadly accurate. There should be no surprise, therefore, that he looked to Smith for support and guidance in agitating for market expansion, or that he did so in the name of freedom. He ripped the dying mercantilist system apart to assert and realize the superiority of his own interest at home, and to use that power to enlarge his exports. John Quincy Adams no doubt sensed in 1824 that he would never have a second chance to become President. If not, he learned it very quickly after his narrow victory. Agricultural impatience and anger thrived on his tough integrity as a mercantilist and blossomed in the warmth of his failures.

Adams had in truth pursued a vigorously expansionist policy throughout most of his public career prior to being elected President. He supported the Louisiana Purchase, backed a firm stand against British violations of American trade prior to the War of 1812, opened the way through Spanish claims for an American reach to the Pacific Coast in 1819, and applied steady pressure on the British to win more territory in the West and to break their power over markets in the Caribbean and Latin America. And he was the major protagonist in formulating the Monroe Doctrine, that militant manifesto asserting American dominance in the Western Hemisphere. It was a strong, consistent performance. But past triumphs proved insufficient in response either to the general and aggressive expansionism of the farm businessmen or to their specific demands.

Seen through agrarian eyes, Adams manifested several inexcusable weaknesses that created solid reasons for unyielding opposition. The first was simply that he was the very personification of the metropolis that had created the mercantilism that had become uncertain and inefficient as well as repressive, and of the metropolis that enjoyed an entrenched position of power that threatened to keep the farmer in an inferior condition even after that system had been demolished. Adams was talented and confident, proud and demanding, and more than a little cranky and difficult. To many agricultural disciples of Adam Smith, at any rate, he must have appeared as the Devil incarnate.

That impression was reinforced as Adams developed reservations about continuing a militantly expansionist policy, and revealed a noticeable lack of enthusiasm for either the idea or the practice of using American power to intervene actively around the world in the name of supporting or extending American-style freedom (and therefore its economic and political influence). The farmers were far more attracted to men like Henry Clay, who spoke often and boldly in behalf of such an adventurous policy. They gave Adams a cool reception as early as 1821, for example, when he forcefully opposed that kind of expansion.

"America goes not abroad in search of monsters to destroy," he warned in a Fourth of July oration. "She well knows that by once enlisting under other banners than her own, were they even the banners of foreign independence, she would involve herself, beyond the power of extrication, in all the wars of interest and intrigue, of individual avarice, envy, and ambition, which assume the colors and usurp the standard of freedom." "She might become the dictatress of the world," Adams concluded. "She would no longer be the ruler of her own spirit."[30]

The agricultural businessmen much preferred Smith's expansion of the marketplace for economic profit and liberty. They responded enthusiastically when Clay, and other Southern and Western leaders like Andrew Jackson and Thomas Hart Benton, wrapped Smith's somewhat dry and harsh logic in the more noble and comforting rhetoric that John Locke used to defend individualism and property rights in the name of man's natural freedom.[31] And they particularly liked the kind of argument advanced by Representative George Frost Strother of Virginia: "The western frontier is that portion of the world where . . . the race of man is most progressive."[32]

The first significant grumbling about Adams' foreign policy arose even as he was winning a frontier on the Pacific Coast in 1819. Some Southerners and Westerners were sure that he could have acquired Texas if he had not been indifferent or opposed to their interests. The truth was that Adams wanted Texas. But he felt the evidence favored Spain's claim, and he was unwilling to go to war. He had the same reservations against thrashing about in the Pacific northwest in order to drive the British out of the Oregon country. The farmers, and especially the Westerners, favored Senator Benton's approach. He demanded military action with the cry that "there is the East, there lies the road to India."[33]

Adams had actually begun to stress the very kind of market expansion that Smith emphasized so heavily. But the farmers were correct in judging that Adams was more interested in markets for the metropolis than for agricultural surpluses. And his failure after 1825 to regain free access to the British West Indies convinced them that he most certainly was not their man. The editors of the *Richmond Enquirer* spoke for most of them in denouncing his "clumsy and mischievous" diplomacy that had lost "the benefits of the Colonial Trade."[34]

Adam Smith and John Locke were the absentee strategists of the agricultural assault on Adams and American mercantilism. Their battlefield commander in the Southern states was John Taylor of Caroline, who exhorted the farmers to fight "for the defense of life, liberty, and property." And a remonstrance of the Virginia Agricultural Society read as though it had been copied from *The Wealth of Nations*: "National Industry is best promoted by leaving every member of society free to apply his labour and his knowledge according to his own choice, exempt from all restraints."[35] Farmers in Massachusetts cited Smith explicitly. Roger Sullivan of the Massachusetts Agricultural Society did so, for example, when he explained the "despondence" of the farmer over the "difficulty of obtaining a vent for his produce." Other agrarians in Adams' home state, such as John Lowell of the Massachusetts Society for Promoting Agriculture, questioned the value of the tariff. "The farmer is, according to the new tariff or tax, like a candle lighted at both ends. His revenue or income will be lessened while his expenses will be increased. . . . Just in proportion as the foreign article is excluded by extravagant duties in favor of the home manufacture, in the same ratio are our exports diminished, and the price of our own products reduced."[36]

As they increased the tempo of their campaign for the West Indies trade, however, the Southerners also quoted Smith. The report and petition of the United Agricultural Societies of Virginia referred to him as a man who clearly understood the need to export "surplus rude produce." "We cannot possibly sell commodities to another country," the delegates argued, "without buying to an equal amount." Hence the proper policy was to reduce the tariff. By that action "new markets would be opened, and the existing demand increased."[37]

The agrarians of the South and West needed no urging, in 1828, to send John Quincy Adams back to his ancestral home in Massachusetts. And in choosing Andrew Jackson to be their President, they picked a man ready and eager to complete the destruction of mercantilism at home, and to expand the American marketplace across the continent and the seven seas. For he was the son of a poor farmer who had left poverty behind as he became a planter by acting precisely as Adam Smith said a man should act.

TWO

The time must come when . . . our rapidly increasing numbers shall fill up our wide spread territory . . . when the great safety valve of the west will be closed. . . . When these things shall come. . . . First comes disorganization and legislative plunder, then the struggle of factions and civil war.

Thomas R. Dew of Virginia, 1836

We have just commenced exporting, yet the home market is even now completely glutted in many articles. . . . We shall be compelled to diminish our production unless a foreign market can be found.

Prairie Farmer, April 1843

Seat the United States firmly in Oregon and the commercial enterprise and the wealth of the world will centralize within our limits.

Representative Charles Jared
Ingersoll of Pennsylvania, 1845

We have surrendered our territory by negotiation in the Southwest and in the West. . . . In the Northeast, and in the North . . . and, sir, I want to see no more surrendered. . . . The right of the United States to the whole of Oregon, as far north as the Russian boundary, is as clear as the noon-day sun.

Senator James Semple
of Illinois, 1844

Oregon . . . is a mere extension of our acknowledged boundaries.

Secretary of State Abel P.
Upshur of Virginia, 1843

Texas is essential to the security of the South, the defense of the West, and highly conducive to the welfare and perpetuity of the whole Union.

Senator Robert J. Walker
of Mississippi, 1844

I regard annexation to be a vital question. If lost now, it will be forever lost; and, if that, the South will be lost.

Secretary of State John C.
Calhoun of South Carolina, 1844

Our title to the whole of the territory of Oregon is clear and unquestionable. . . . The re-occupation of Oregon and the re-annexation of Texas at the earliest practicable period are great American measures.

Democratic Party Platform, 1844

Progress, Depression, and Competitive Bidding Create a Coalition for the Expansion of the Marketplace

T HE ROWDY PURSUIT of self-interest at the White House reception following the inauguration of President Andrew Jackson typified the spirit of the free marketplace philosophy that Americans had embraced during the latter half of the 1820s. The episode might even be interpreted as providing proof, as long as the marketplace was big enough, that competition did produce a certain kind of general welfare. After the revelry, in any event, it quickly became apparent that Americans had committed themselves to that strategy of achieving prosperity and social welfare.

The agricultural businessmen had two general objectives. They wanted to reduce the inequities between the metropolis and the country within the American marketplace as it existed at any given time. They also sought to enlarge the marketplace by acquiring more and cheaper resources in the form of land, and by increasing the profitable demand for their surpluses. Farmers of all regions had generally viewed territorial expansion, and liberal land policies, as methods of improving their position within the system. And, periodically, some Northerners and Westerners had placed the same kind of emphasis on overseas markets that was a traditional part of the Southern outlook. Beginning in the mid-1830s, moreover, increasing numbers of Northerners came to stress the importance of exports in determining their relative and absolute welfare. That provided a base for an effective coalition among all agricultural businessmen against the metropolis. Such an alliance, initially based on an understanding to expand territorially in ways that would provide more land for everyone, did develop in the mid-1840s. It lasted long enough, moreover, to lower the tariff. But it soon collapsed, ripped asunder by a conflict over the division of the empire that had been won.

Thirty years before that crisis, which led on to the Civil War, the Southerners made a bold attack on the inequities of the domestic marketplace and threatened similar independent action. They launched that fight against the tariff of 1828, which raised rates to a new high. Part of the intensity of their anger was due to the decline of British prices for cotton, as the result of a financial panic, to 12 cents per pound in 1826 and on down to 8.8 cents in 1827. They faced the most unhappy prospect of paying more for their purchases while earning less for their principal surplus. That tariff-price squeeze dramatized the kind of Southern opposition to the metropolis that men like John Taylor had been preaching with increasing vigor and effectiveness since 1800.

Such views gained added strength from the support of Thomas Cooper, an English intellectual (and sometime manufacturer) who became a staunch Southerner after joining the faculty of South Carolina College in 1820. "We of the South," he cried in 1827, "hold our plantations . . . as the serfs and operatives of the North: subject to the orders, and labouring for the benefit of the masterminds of Massachusetts."[1] Cooper and Taylor were significant propagandists, but Calhoun was the political leader of the Southern fight against the metropolis. He opened the assault with *The South Carolina Exposition and Protest* of December 1828, in which he damned the tariff as "unconstitutional, unequal, and oppressive." It reduced Southerners to "the serfs of the system,—out of whose labor is raised, not only the money paid into the Treasury, but the funds out of which are drawn the rich rewards of the manufacturer and his associates in interest." "No system," he concluded, "can be more efficient to rear up a moneyed aristocracy. Its tendency is, to make the poor poorer, and the rich richer."[2] It needed no saying that the Southern agricultural businessmen were the poor becoming poorer.

Calhoun and other Southerners began preparing themselves, after 1828, to declare the high tariff system illegal—and hence null and void—if they could not win relief any other way. In the meantime, however, and as a more desirable and effective solution, they sought an alliance with the Western farm businessmen. Since the Westerners were divided over the tariff, the strongest group still attracted by the argument that the protective system would create an expanding home market, the coalition was rooted in the idea of a classic marketplace bargain between the two sections. The compromise, most openly advocated by Senators Robert Young Hayne of South Carolina and Thomas Hart Benton of Missouri, called for Southern support for the Western drive for cheap land in return for Western votes to lower the tariff.

The metropolis breathed first life into the strategy when Senator Samuel Augustus Foote of Connecticut offered a resolution on December 29, 1829, directing the Committee on Public Lands "to inquire into the expediency of limiting for a certain period the sales of public lands."[3] Senator Benton immediately denounced the maneuver. He castigated it as a metropolitan attempt to "check emigration to the West" in order to preserve its reservoir of cheap labor and thereby maintain its economic advantage over the agrarians. The idea, he charged, was to make "poor people do the work for small wages." And Senator Elias Kent Kane of Illinois accused Foote of sacrificing the "immediate and pressing interests of the new States . . . for the remote and speculative interests of some of the old."[4]

Senator Hayne then supported Benton's charge that the metropolis was attempting to limit Western prosperity and development, and that assault developed into his classic debate with Senator Daniel Webster of Massachusetts. Webster slyly slipped by the central issue of the relationship between the metropolis and the country as it had been raised in the form of land policy. He instead discussed the question of federal power versus states' rights, a strategy that produced a vigorous argument about the nullification proposals being agitated by Calhoun and other Southerners. As defined and handled by Webster, therefore, the confrontation served less to resolve the fundamental conflict than to harden opinion on both sides.

Webster undoubtedly stiffened Southern determination to forge an effective alliance with the Western farmers. Enough of them supported Benton's graduation bill to push it through the Senate in May 1830. The proposal lost in the House, but the coalition was strong enough to pass a modified preemption law on May 29, 1830. It allowed settlers who had cultivated public land in 1829 to claim as much as 160 acres at the minimum price of $1.25 per acre. And the agricultural businessmen won several more important victories in the spring of 1830. The Congress adopted the long-desired policy of pushing the Indians westward out of the way of the advancing settlers, and then authorized President Jackson to bargain with the British over access to the West Indies market.[5] And though he vetoed a measure appropriating $150,000 for a road in Kentucky, the President approved the Cumberland Road bill that promised to improve the market position of the Western farmers. That gain was followed, moreover, by the announcement on October 5, 1830, that the British had agreed to reopen the West Indian market to American exports.

Then Jackson agreed to a compromise on the tariff that satisfied enough Southerners to undercut Calhoun. The tariff bill of 1832 reduced rates to the general level of the law of 1824, and Southern congressmen voted for it by a margin of forty-five to thirty. A South Carolina convention nullified the law (as well as the old one of 1828), but no other Southern state supported the action. Calhoun stood alone against Jackson, who bluntly threatened to lead an army into the redoubt of his own vice-president. Calhoun resigned from that office on December 28, 1831, after Jackson called for further reductions in the tariff to sweeten his request for military preparations. The President won both appeals on March 2, 1832. One law authorized the use of force to uphold the revenue laws, and another provided for the gradual reduction, by 1841, of all rates in the 1828 bill that were higher than 20 percent. Those cuts were to be followed by others to lower all rates to that level by July 1, 1842. The challenge of disunion was thus effectively blunted by a combination of counterthreats and compromises.

Even more significantly, the Southern agriculturalists had been unable to consolidate an agreement with Western and Northern farmers on the best way to improve the position of agriculture in the domestic marketplace, or on the emphasis to be placed on expanding the overseas market. A good part of that failure was due to the general prosperity that the country enjoyed from the end of 1829 into 1833. Commerce and manufacturing increased their rate of growth, and that aided the food-producing farmers. Those agricultural businessmen also benefited from the developing boom in canals and railroads that improved transportation to the growing Northeastern metropolitan markets.[6] In the main, therefore, the Northern and Western farmers found it possible to dispose of much of their surpluses in the domestic marketplace, or through the existing export outlets. Southerners, on the other hand, were buying food from the West and merchandise from the North while exporting 82 percent of their cotton in 1831 (and by 1834 supplying about 75 percent of European imports), and at the same time trying to regain their position in the world tobacco market.

Given that contrast in the general position of the regions, it is particularly illuminating that the flour millers turned to the government for assistance in the export market even before the tobacco men. The millers wanted help against Spanish restrictions that threatened to cut their exports to Cuba and Latin America. Representative Henry Laurens Pinckney of South Carolina responded in June 1834 with a bill to lay higher charges on Spanish ships entering American ports.[7] The government then moved in 1835 to retaliate against the proposed Spanish policy. The threat was effective, and opened the way for a sustained rise in flour exports over the next thirty years. Those sales, which averaged $73.3 million during the period 1833-1843, rose to $198.6 million for 1843-1853, and to $512.4 million for 1853-1863. Grain farmers in the South, particularly in Virginia and Maryland, initially benefited from that boom, but the rewards increasingly went to wheat growers in New York, Pennsylvania, Ohio, Michigan, Indiana, Illinois, and Wisconsin. Michigan, for example, began to produce a surplus in 1835, and Wisconsin shipped its first load of 166 barrels via the Erie Canal in 1840.[8]

The farm businessmen also launched a campaign for general government assistance in 1835, asking specifically for a board of agriculture that would collect and publish statistics to help them cope with the fluctuations of the marketplace. That pressure was dramatically reinforced in 1836 when the tobacco farmers began demanding action against the restrictions and competition that seriously handicapped their efforts to recover European markets. The drastic decline in exports after the peak year 1790 dropped tobacco into a poor second behind cotton by 1811 ($4.45 million as compared to $7.2 million). Then, during the War of 1812, Europe turned to Cuba and other Latin American sources to meet its needs. The ensuing hard times were extended through the 1820s as England tried to stimulate production in the West Indies, as Europe raised its export duties, and as competition developed from Sumatra as well as Latin America.[9] Edmund Ruffin, editor of the *Farmer's Register*, found the crisis useful in this battle to reform agricultural practices, but his efforts did not meet the immediate need to enlarge the market. That problem became acute in the mid-1830s when the price, as well as the volume, of exports suffered a serious decline.

Maryland planters took the lead in agitating for help, and Senator Joseph Kent introduced a resolution on May 2, 1836, directing the President to place the tobacco trade "upon a more liberal footing." His attack on the monopolistic systems of France and Austria, as well as on British restrictions, won prompt support.[10] The House of Representatives quickly joined the battle, asking the President to use all possible means to relieve the tobacco farmers "from the heavy and unequal burdens" imposed by foreign governments. Neither the continued pressure applied through two major conventions held in Washington, nor a threat to retaliate, produced any major gains.[11] European governments refused to modify their systems of control, and declined to limit themselves to one source of supply.

The agricultural businessmen were more effective, however, in obtaining direct support from the government at home. That campaign, which had steadily gathered force after the Panic of 1818 - 1819, was unquestionably strengthened by the efforts of the tobacco farmers and intensified by other crop failures in 1835. In a way that was symbolic of their emergence as a pressure group of the majority, the farmers secured the creation of a special office of agriculture as a branch of the Patent Office on July 4, 1836. The victory acted as a goad rather than as a pacifier. James J. Mapes of the *Working Farmer* and Charles B. Calvert, a Maryland leader, generated "a continuous agitation" in subsequent years to expand the subdivision of the Patent Office into a separate bureau or department of the government. The editors of *The Cultivator* stated the guiding principle of the movement with refreshing candor: "Agriculture should be patronized by the Government."[12]

One man, one event, and one development played central roles in that sustained drive for direct leverage within the government. The man was Henry L. Ellsworth, who was appointed commissioner of the Patent Office in 1836. He had done extensive experimental work on a farm in Indiana, and immediately began to use his office to promote agriculture. One of his actions, for example, involved using American consuls around the world to gather information on crops and markets, and to push farm surpluses in those markets. He also won a special appropriation in 1839 to enlarge and regularize the collection of statistics. Perhaps the best indication of his interest and energy was provided by his last *Annual Report* (1844), in which he used 428 of 520 pages to discuss problems of the farmer.[13]

The long and severe economic depression touched off by the Panic of 1837 was the event that served to extend and deepen the agricultural campaign for greater influence and assistance. Cotton prices fell almost 50 percent during March at New Orleans. That shock was followed by the suspension of specie movements by New York banks on May 10, and the gradual extension of the depression among other farm businessmen. Westerners did not feel the full impact of the downturn until 1839, but then they were staggered. Farm prices dropped more than the prices of manufactured goods. And public land sales dived from 20 million acres in 1836 to 3.5 million acres in 1838.

At the same time, agricultural production continued to rise. As a result, "the matter of foreign markets for surplus agricultural produce, especially breadstuffs, assumed a new importance."[14] So also did the thrust for virgin land and an opportunity to reenter the marketplace under hopefully more fortunate (and profitable) circumstances. And, challenged by the depressing reality that past expansion had not solved all the problems of the marketplace, or provided meaningful freedom for everyone, it is not surprising that Americans began to reassert the validity of their belief that liberty and prosperity required still more expansion. Or that politicians began to offer such expansion as the program that would advance and insure their particular self-interest.

The demand for easier and cheaper ownership of land increased dramatically after the Panic of 1837. President Martin Van Buren responded promptly in his annual message of 1837, throwing his support behind Senator Benton's graduation plan and asking for a preemption law to help squatters not protected by earlier measures. The graduation bill was defeated in the House of Representatives, but preemption was extended in 1838 and again in 1840. Finally, on September

4, 1841, a permanent preemption law was passed. That legislation, enthusiastically and optimistically called the "Log Cabin bill" by Benton, was not at all generous or advanced—particularly in the context of the depression. It authorized squatters on the public domain to claim as much as 160 acres when the land went on the block, and guaranteed their right to buy it without competitive bidding at $1.25 per acre. They could follow the same procedure on land granted to canal and railroad companies if they were able and willing to pay $2.50 per acre.[15] The law was a long-sought victory for the agriculturalists, but it did not solve their difficulties or quiet their demands for more assistance.

As far as land policy was concerned, for example, Westerners in particular were beginning to respond to the campaign for free land that had gained strength among labor spokesmen in the metropolis. Thomas Skidmore of New York was one of the first to develop a line of thought that ultimately revived Madison's earlier argument for expansion to guarantee prosperity and freedom. Skidmore called for free land to preserve democracy and to insure the benefits of Smith's free marketplace, and initially proposed to divide the estates of the dead among the living as they reached legal maturity. Gradually, by the end of the 1820s, he combined Locke's emphasis on property and freedom with Smith's stress on the expanding marketplace to produce a rudimentary political economy of equality.

Skidmore's ideas were initially attacked by many reformers, but one of his early opponents, George Henry Evans, ultimately adapted and refined the argument. He produced an early version of the frontier thesis stated in terms of the Smithian political economy. That change occurred during the depression, which continued into 1843, and produced a program as well as a theory. Evans maintained that a policy of giving an inalienable homestead to any and all settlers would enable poor or unemployed wage earners to enter the marketplace as agricultural businessmen. That shift in the distribution of labor, he concluded, would improve the position of the workers who stayed in the metropolis.[16]

By the time Evans organized the National Reform Association in 1844, and began to agitate for his plan in his *Working Man's Advocate*, the reality of expansion into Oregon and Texas had created a large audience for his ideas. Those drives to the Southwest and Northwest also extended and intensified the argument that freedom and prosperity were the natural benefits of expansion. Edward Everett, a Whig writer and politician from Massachusetts, declared that expansion was "the principle of our institutions" and called for "the enlargement of the field of action" to preserve opportunity and freedom.[17] As had been the case across the turn of the nineteenth century, that kind of talk from the metropolis sounded very similar to the rhetoric of the agricultural South and West. Andrew Jackson underscored that point in 1843, when he announced that he favored "extending the area of freedom" into Texas.[18]

American penetration of that northeastern province of Mexico began in force during the depression of the early 1820s after Moses Austin secured the first colonizing charter on January 17, 1821. His son Stephen F. Austin continued the project, and Texas became part of a Mexican state generally open to immigration during 1824-1825. Americans moved in so rapidly, and established themselves (and slavery) so effectively, that Mexican authorities belatedly tried to reverse their policy in April 1830. The decision to prohibit slavery and close Texas to further colonization by Americans provoked so much opposition, however, including a separatist movement, that the area was reopened in 1833. That led only to a new boom in immigration and further tension and conflict.

The first military confrontation occurred at Anahuac on June 29-30, 1835, and fighting erupted at Gonzales on October 2. Texas declared its independence in March 1836 and adoped a constitution authorizing slavery. The victory of Sam Houston over Santa Anna at San Jacinto on April 21, 1836, roiled expansionist sentiment in the United States, and the Congress responded early in July with annexationist resolutions. President Jackson wanted to acquire Texas, but he hesitated to act because of opposition in the United States, and because of the doubt that Texas could maintain its existence as an independent nation against a Mexican counterattack. He reluctantly contented himself with diplomatic recognition.

That policy was sustained by President Martin Van Buren. He rejected a formal Texas petition for annexation in August 1837 without even submitting the question to the Congress. Texas leaders thereupon withdrew the request, and many of them turned away from the United States to concentrate on a program of expansion south along the Gulf of Mexico and westward to the Pacific. The spectacular growth of the region's agriculture, with the attendant rise in surpluses for external markets, had earlier led some Texans to advocate staying within the Mexican system on the grounds that they could ultimately exercise predominant influence in Mexican affairs. That economic power made them confident after independence had been won that they could develop their own empire.

Annexationists in the United States kept the issue alive, however, during the depression years, when the agitation for free land gathered strength, and as Americans contracted Oregon fever. That contagion became increasingly widespread after 1838, when significant numbers of pioneers began to struggle westward across the prairie and over the mountains to claim farmland in the Willamette Valley. At the outset of the 1840s, moreover, the momentum for expansion created by those factors was strengthened by several new and dynamic elements in the political economy. The most important one involved the rising surpluses of foodstuffs produced by established commercial farmers in the West. The depression drove home the necessity of finding a market at a time when no political group or coalition proved able to formulate and implement a program capable of restoring and maintaining prosperity.

One group of Westerners, following the lead offered by Senator Lewis Fields Linn of Missouri at the end of the 1830s, called for the acquisition of Oregon and the penetration of the Asian market as the best solution. Expansion into Oregon had been pushed hard by Hall Jackson Kelley of Massachusetts as early as 1828 - 1831, and he attracted support from others like Nathaniel J. Wyeth for the idea of founding a new town on the Pacific Coast. President Jackson then gave the movement a major boost (and official support) by sending an agent to inspect the region. The ensuing report generated significant interest among a number of congressmen and provided the background for Linn's activity.

Linn called upon the Congress as early as 1839 to create a territorial government for all the Oregon country, including the part settled by the British, and announced that he was prepared for war. He admitted a bit later (1841), in discussing the problem of winning the Asia market, that the English controlled the seas. But he reassured his supporters that the day would arrrive "when we might call the sea ours."[19] He then proposed, in December 1841, to begin the grand conquest by militarizing the overland route to Oregon and providing free land to all pioneers over eigheen years of age.

Missionaries, propagandists, promoters, and pioneers (sometimes one man engaged in all four operations) steadily extended the national interest in Oregon. And the Oregonians themselves dramatized the issue by adopting a provisional constitution in mid-1843. The expansionist fervor that had started in Missouri and Iowa had by that time moved eastward across the Mississippi, and in July 1843 it produced an Oregon convention in Cincinnati, Ohio. The militancy of the delegates found expression in a resolution asserting that "a surrender of *any* part of Oregon . . . was *dangerous to peace and a repudiation of Monroe's doctrine.*" Then they voted to set the boundary at 54° 40' north latitude. That served, at least in their minds, to disallow any British claims based on preemption or actual colonization (or on the Treaty of 1818, which had left the territory open to settlement by both nations).[20]

The Cincinnati expansionists were worried lest the acquisition of California be given priority in response to the pressure from two groups in the metropolis that had become seriously interested in that part of the coastline. Merchants and shippers, working through Massachusetts leader Daniel Webster, were maneuvering to claim a strip of land extending south to latitude 36°. They wanted the harbors at Monterey and San Francisco. Another group was courting the commercial farmers of the West as allies against the South. One segment of that coalition was composed of abolitionists like Henry B. Stanton and Joshua Leavitt, who realized that their religious and moral crusade against slavery was not gaining the strength required to destroy the evil institution.

Stanton shrewdly concluded as early as 1839 that the West was the key to winning national political power. The bumper wheat crop of 1842, which was harvested for falling prices, attracted considerable support for the argument that the abolitionists could win the West by promising to find and open foreign markets.[21] Westerners offered their own version of that program, however, and thereby attracted a larger number of metropolitans who were concerned to check the political power of the South. "We have but just commenced exporting," warned the editors of The Prairie Farmer in April 1843. "The home market is even now completely glutted in many articles. . . . We shall be compelled to diminish our production unless a foreign market can be found."

But Southerners had been trying for years to consolidate an alliance with the West against the Northeast, and they were not disposed to lose the battle to the metropolis. They promptly raised the ante. First they pointed to the tariff of 1842, which increased rates to an average of between 23 and 35 percent, as an example of how the metropolis pried more money out of the farmer's pocketbook even as it further restricted the chance of raising farm income by expanding exports. Next they warned from long experience about the additional tribute extracted by the metropolis through transportation costs, interest on necessary capital, speculative profits on land, and exorbitant charges for commercial services. Finally, beginning in mid-1843, President John Tyler and Secretary of State Abel P. Upshur opened a bid to keep Tyler in the White House by building a personal party composed of Western and Southern expansionists.

Tyler had become President only because William Henry Harrison (who defeated incumbent Martin Van Buren in the election of 1840) died of pneumonia a month after his inauguration in March 1841. Tyler had no significant following or power base in either the Whig or Democratic party, and relied almost wholly on a small group of fellow Virginians like Henry A. Wise and Upshur for advice on how to be nominated and elected in his own right. All three were vigorous Southern expansionists who wanted to annex Texas. That policy won Tyler some short-run encouragement from men like Senator Robert James Walker of Mississippi who also wanted Texas, but who had no intention of backing him for the Presidency.

Someone in the inner Tyler circle, probably Wise or Upshur if not the President himself, devised the strategy of offering Oregon to the North and West and promising Texas to the Southerners. Upshur made the first move, probably in response to the Oregon convention in Cincinnati. The entire American settlement in Oregon was below the Columbia River, but Upshur announced in October 1843 that he favored moving the boundary north to the 49th parallel. Two months later, in his annual message to the Congress, Tyler pushed it on to the Cincinnati line of 54° 40'. During the same months, moreover, they had been busy maneuvering to acquire Texas. Upshur finally convinced the Texans that he had the support of the necessary two-thirds of the Senate and on that basis negotiated a treaty early in 1844.

Then Upshur was killed in an explosion aboard a naval vessel on February 28, 1844. Tyler appointed Calhoun, who was convinced that he could simultaneously serve the nation and satisfy his urge to be President by uniting the South and the West with the epoxy of expansion. Given the considerable effectiveness with which that strategy was employed by other men over the succeeding few years, it is conceivable that Calhoun could have accomplished his objective if he had been more confident in the viability of the Southern society he was trying to preserve and improve. But he felt that Texas had to be acquired immediately if the South was to sustain its economy and society based on black slave labor producing a cotton crop that dominated the world market.

That analysis, so deeply rooted in the theory of the necessity to expand the marketplace, had been discussed by Southerners (and Northerners) for many years before Calhoun made it the polar star of his diplomacy in 1844. Most Americans accepted it as valid. And some, like Senator Walker, even maintained that expansion would ultimately bring an end to slavery. Other Americans continued, however, to argue about the accuracy of the analysis as applied to the South between 1840 and 1861 long after Calhoun's decision.[22] Regardless of the different conclusions that have been reached in those debates, the operative historical truth is clear and unequivocal. Calhoun and other Southerners accepted the theory of the necessity of expansion as an accurate picture of reality and acted on that view of the world. But so also did Northern and Western agricultural businessmen, and they made the same kind of argument about Oregon and foreign markets.

Given his image of the world and how it worked, Calhoun concluded that British policy toward Texas posed a mortal threat to Southern prosperity, welfare, and security. He viewed English antislavery agitation in Texas as the opening move in a vast plan to create a free trade republic that would provide a great market for British manufactures and a source of cotton that would break the South's position in the world commodity market. He also feared the British would launch an attack on slavery in the South and complete the destruction of the region's entire political economy. And there was enough evidence in support of that interpretation, a good bit of it supplied by the British themselves, to give it substance.

President Tyler mentioned those dangers when he submitted to the Senate the treaty to annex Texas, but he stressed the advantages to all sections (including markets for Western farmers). Calhoun, by contrast, boldly presented his candid analysis and added a positive defense of slavery as a necessary instrument in extending Western civilization to the Afro-Americans. He then argued that British maneuvers in Texas posed a grave danger to the entire country because they threatened to surround the United States, and concluded by raising the specter of a Southern decision to leave the Union.

The immediately negative response to Calhoun's action made it clear that he had made three major mistakes. He underestimated the anti-Southern and antislavery feeling—and fear—in the northern part of the country. As a result, he created an intense flurry of opposition among many who were neither abolitionists nor friends of the black slave. Secondly, Calhoun overestimated the active fear of the British, and the degree of general militancy, throughout the rest of the country. The majority was not ready in 1844 even to fight a war with Mexico to acquire Texas, let alone a far more severe conflict with England. Finally, Calhoun misestimated the effect of his threat of disunion. That split the Democrats despite Andrew Jackson's intervention on the side of annexation. The combined effect of those mistakes created an opposition that crushed the treaty of annexation in the Senate.

But the vote against the treaty was not a vote against expansion, as was shortly demonstrated by the nomination and election of James Knox Polk. Aided by men from the Northeast, as well as by Southerners and Westerners, Polk put the Democratic party back together again with the expansionist glue first tried by Tyler, Upshur, and Calhoun. The platform of 1844 called bluntly for "the reoccupation of Oregon and the reannexation of Texas at the earliest practicable period," and the momentum for expansion created during the convention grew ever greater during the campaign. "Whar," cried one typical Westerner, "I say whar is the individual who would give the first foot, the first outside shadow of a foot of the great Oregon? . . . Some people talk as though they were affeerd of England. . . . Hav'nt we licked her twice, and can't we lick her again?"[23]

Many Easterners joined the clamor. "Make way, I say," warned a New Jersey expansionist, "for the young American Buffalo—he has not yet got land enough . . . We will give him Oregon for his summer shade and the region of Texas as his winter pasture."[24] Henry Clay, the Whig candidate, tried to respond to such sentiment, but his awkward fence-straddling cost him votes among antislavery Northerners even as it failed to win support from Westerners committed to Polk. Coupled with the rising appeal of the low tariff argument to Westerners who had come to argue the necessity of foreign markets, the expansionist thrust carried Polk to victory in Michigan, Indiana, Illinois, and Missouri. Those states, or Pennsylvania, where local Democratic leaders like James Buchanan stressed expansion, would have given the election to Clay. In the final count, however, Polk won fifteen of the twenty-five states.

Ironically, the expansionist surge denied Polk the chance to annex Texas even though it won him a lease on the White House. Tyler claimed that victory by pushing a joint resolution through the Congress just before he left office. On the first vote, the House passed the measure 120 to 98. The Senate made a change and adopted its version by the tiny margin of two votes, 27 to 25. Almost half the "nays" in the Senate (twelve) came from the seven Northeastern states of Maine, Vermont, Connecticut, Massachusetts, Rhode Island, New Jersey, and Delaware. Even so, that section split its vote, recording four "ayes" for annexation. Far more significantly, only four of the twelve senators from north of the Ohio and west of New England voted against the resolution. Some of the Southern "nays," moreover, seem clearly to have been cast as rocks at Tyler or as gestures to ease Northern anxiety about Southern predominance in the government. And when the House considered the revised version, the vote of 132 to 76 revealed an increase in expansionist support.[25] Tyler signed the joint resolution on March 1, 1845, three days before Polk took the oath as President.

President Polk initially seemed to succeed in using the theory of expanding the marketplace as a guide to action to revive and strengthen the American political economy. But the enthusiasm for fighting Mexico in order to keep (and enlarge) Texas, and to add California, was rapidly eroded by the anger of Northerners and Westerners. Led by the Westerners, who had been promised—and expected—all of Oregon, those groups soon became determined to prevent the Southerners from moving in on all of the trans-Mississippi empire. The Western agricultural businessmen were Smithian to the core, and they defined their self-interest as hard-working, individualistic white farmers who needed land and markets. That conception of Smith's free marketplace—as a fair field with no favor—ultimately prompted them to fight to preserve and enlarge that kind of a marketplace.

THREE

Foreign powers do not seem to appreciate the true character of our government. . . . To enlarge its limits, is
to extend the dominions of peace over additional territories, and increasing millions.

President James Knox Polk,
March 4, 1845

Can there be a home market for all our produce? . . .
In very truth, when enough have been driven into manufacturing to make a home market for all our produce,
they would be numerous enough to manufacture two
or three times as much as this country could consume,
and the surplus would have to find a foreign market. . . .
Can that system be American which shackles trade
and denies to us the markets of the world? . . . No;
there is nothing about it which partakes of the freedom which we associate with the name of America.

New York Farmer, 1845

If we reduce our tariff, the party opposed to the corn
laws of England would soon prevail, and admit all our
agricultural products at all times freely. . . . The home
market is wholly inadequate. . . . Farmers must have
the foreign market, or a large surplus accompanied
by great depression in prices, must be the result.

Secretary of the Treasury
Robert James Walker,
December 3, 1845

Personal liberty is incompatible with a crowded population. . . . The spirit of enterprise that is over-spread-
ing the West and the South . . . has the love of liberty
for its means, liberty itself for its reward.

Representative Alexander Duncan
of Ohio, 1846

Oregon is the inch of ground upon which we can place
a fulcrum, giving us the lever by which to overturn
the world of British commerce. . . . We now hold in
possession the means of subsistence of the whole human
family.

Representative Andrew Kennedy
of Indiana, 1846

It is said, that if manufacturers are protected, they will
protect the farmers. God forbid that we should ever
be left to such protectors. . . . Agriculture needs protection, if any interest needs it. . . . How is agriculture
to be protected? . . . Give them but a fair field in the
markets of the world.

Representative John Francis
Collin of New York, 1846

We in the West . . . want the world's wide market.

Representative William Watson
Wick of Indiana, 1846

Illinois wants a market for her agricultural production; she wants the market of the world.

Senator Sidney Breeze of
Illinois, 1846

If breadstuffs keep up, the United States will be Fountain head of wealth instead of England.

John Murray Forbes,
October 31, 1847

We can never acknowledge the right of a State to secede and cut us off from the Ocean and the world, without our consent.

Senator Stephen Arnold
Douglas of Illinois,
1860

It is enough to say that the Valley of the Mississippi must be under one Government, cost what it may. . . . There is no alternative.

Cincinnati *Daily Gazette*, June 21, 1861

Separate our common country into two nations, and every man of this great interior region is thereby cut off from some one or more of these outlets to the sea. . . . These outlets . . . are indispensable to the well-being of the people inhabiting and to inhabit this vast interior region.

President Abraham Lincoln,
December 1, 1862

The
Belief in the Necessity of Expanding
the Marketplace and the
Coming of the
Civil War

PRESIDENT James Polk attempted from the outset to assert control of the widening expansionist movement, and to use it as an instrument for securing domestic peace and prosperity, and external advantage. And in the short run he was to some extent successful. The enthusiasm for territory and markets did produce a majority strong enough to lower the tariff and wage the war that erupted over Texas and the Mexican provinces stretching to the Pacific Coast. From the outset, however, Polk found it difficult to balance the different sets of expansionist priorities advanced by Northerners, Westerners, and Southerners. He managed to weather those cyclonic forces largely because the Mexicans accepted defeat in time to prevent the triumph of a rising movement to acquire at least the northern half of their country.

Polk might very well have attempted to ride the crest of that storm, moreover, if his representative in Mexico, Nicholas P. Trist, had not disobeyed his instructions and stayed on to negotiate a peace treaty with the increasingly worried Mexicans. But that brave act could not and did not resolve the internal American rivalry for the empire that had been acquired, or satisfy those who felt that Polk had favored the South in acting on the expansionist imperative. Those conflicts and resentments grew stronger even as Polk was leaving office, and at the end of another decade they had destroyed the ancient dream among agricultural businessmen of an alliance against the metropolis. Instead, the Western and Southern farmers were preparing to assault one another.

The election campaign of 1844 further reinforced the traditional equation between liberty and expansion, as well as the theory tying prosperity to expansion, and Polk emphasized that connection in his inaugural address. "Foreign powers do not seem to appreciate the true character of our government," he charged, also aiming his remarks at domestic critics of annexing Texas. "To enlarge its limits, is to extend the dominions of peace over additional territories, and additional millions." He added pointedly that the acquisition of Texas promised to open "new and ever-increasing markets" for the Western farmers.

The President might better have spoken to the Southern wing of his coalition (and even to himself) about the need to continue supporting the Northern and Western drive to acquire all of Oregon, for many Southerners, confident that Texas was theirs, had begun to lose interest in Oregon. Senator George McDuffie of South Carolina was only more candid than the others in expressing that lack of enthusiasm. "What is the emergency?" he demanded as early as 1843. "I have great faith," he acknowledged, "in the power of representative principle to extend the sphere of government"; but he continued that he could not understand the mad rush into a distant, empty valley. "What are we to gain?"[1] That attitude became more general after Polk won the election. At the same time, moreover, Southerners turned away from the easy land policy favored by Westerners and Northerners.

For his part, the President, concerned more to acquire California, and increasingly worried about consolidating American control of Texas, privately offered to compromise with England over Oregon as early as June 1845. He would have needed a cyclone cellar if the British had accepted. For Northerners and Westerners were demanding all of Oregon as the necessary condition of prosperity and virtue. They had created the psychological spirit of manifest expansion for freedom that John L. O'Sullivan expressed so eloquently in the July 1845 issue of the *Democratic Review*. American expansion was justified, he cried, "for the development of the great experiment of liberty and federated self-government." Representative Alexander Duncan of Ohio phrased it more succinctly and practically. "Personal liberty is incompatible with a crowded population," he explained, and added that it was also necessary to preserve the "spirit of enterprise" in the marketplace. Without expansion, monopolies would destroy "liberty itself."[2]

Many Westerners viewed Oregon as necessary in order to open Asia as a market for their increasing agricultural surpluses. That concern was understandable, though the solution was more than a bit fanciful. The export of crude and manufactured foodstuffs had jumped from $13 million in 1830 to $21 million in 1840, and by 1845 the surplus was climbing even more rapidly.[3] And between 1846 and 1850 the exports of wheat, corn, and pork accounted for about 25 percent of all American exports. Senator Sidney Breeze of Illinois, who had voted to annex Texas, bluntly termed Oregon essential "as the only vent westward for the vast surplus of the rich lands of the Mississippi basin to the shores of Asia."[4]

Representative Charles Jared Ingersoll of Pennsylvania agreed that Oregon involved more than "a mere matter of land." Given Oregon, "the commercial enterprise and the wealth of the world will centralize within our limits."[5] Some of that Eastern concern came from manufacturing and shipping interests, but Representative Hannibal Hamlin of Maine made it clear that the business groups understood the importance of agriculture. "The West," he explained, "may be the granary not only of our own country, but, give it an outlet, the granary of the world." He also included the South, for it could sell its cotton to Asians after it had been processed in the mills of New England.[6]

Westerners took the lead, moreover, in pointing out how control of Oregon was the crucial factor in overturning British commercial supremacy. It "is the inch of ground," explained Representative Andrew Kennedy of Indiana, "upon which we can place a fulcrum, giving us the lever by which to overturn the world of British commerce." Pausing to unscramble his principles of mechanics, he then noted that the lever already existed in the form of American agricultural surpluses.[7] Others were more explicit in tying that argument to the 1844 bargain within the Democratic party. Representative Orlando R. Ficklin of Illinois, for example, argued that Britain would back down rather than fight over Oregon because it "must obtain from us our cotton and provisions."[8] Easterners agreed with the analysis, though they stressed it less.[9]

Beyond winning possession of the best ports, the immediate difficulty in implementing that strategy of economic supremacy involved the lack of any effective transportation system linking the Mississippi with the coast. A rising politician of the West, Representative Stephen Arnold Douglas of Illinois, argued that, regardless of a solution to that problem, the best strategy was to organize trade along the north-south axis provided by the Mississippi. It was not at all coincidental that such a program promised to satisfy his local constituents and attract Southern support for his presidential ambitions. Thus, while Douglas was strong for taking all of Oregon (that would "destroy" British power), he opposed building a Pacific railroad until the pioneers from Chicago to Oregon had become commercial farmers with "surplus production" to export.[10]

The fervor for Oregon undoubtedly contributed to Polk's decision to take a strong position on the issue in his annual message of December 2, 1845. He coupled a claim to all of Oregon with a bold reassertion of the Monroe Doctrine. "The United States . . . can not in silence permit any European influence on the North American continent, and should any such interference be attempted will be ready to resist it at any and all hazards." Six weeks later, on January 13, 1846, he moved American troops to the Rio Grande River after Mexico refused to recognize that boundary and cede California in return for a few million dollars.

Despite those dramatic words and the portentous action, which seemed to recommit the Administration to the promises of the 1844 campaign, the President was momentarily overshadowed by his Secretary of the Treasury, the expansionist Robert James Walker of Mississippi. Walker's *Annual Report*, filed the day after Polk revived the Monroe Doctrine, provoked a long and revealing debate over the importance of lowering the tariff in order to penetrate and dominate overseas markets for agricultural surpluses. He was determined to win that campaign and made an impressive appeal to the Western farm businessmen to supply the necessary votes.

It is highly probable, moreover, that Walker was operating on an assumption held by the inner circle of the Administration that there would be war over Texas and California. That made it necessary—despite Polk's militant rhetoric—to compromise with Great Britain over Oregon to avoid the grave risks of a two-front war growing out of English aid to Mexico. And the best, if not the only, way to accomplish that delicate maneuver was through the simultaneous manipulation of the growing British sentiment for free trade in agricultural produce and the Western concern to find a market for surplus foodstuffs. The British openly discussed their role in such an operation during the debate over repealing the Corn Laws, and it seems most unlikely that American leaders overlooked that strategy. And, since Polk offered to compromise on Oregon as early as June 1845, there is good reason to doubt that he ever intended to fight for an Oregon boundary at 54° 40'.

In any event, the President and the British acted within that framework once Walker's report entered the public arena.[11] The Secretary of the Treasury came onstage bowing to his fellow Southerners. Cotton exports were "the great basis of our foreign exchange." He then concentrated on the Northerners and Westerners who produced surplus foodstuffs. "Agriculture is our chief employment . . . and if not depressed by the tariff would be most profitable." "If we reduce our tariff," he announced, incidentally revealing his awareness of the debate over the Corn Laws in England, "the party opposed to the corn laws of England would soon prevail, and admit all our agricultural products at all times freely." "The home market is wholly inadequate," he concluded, warning that the farmers "must have the foreign market, or a large surplus accompanied by a great depression in prices, must be the result."[12]

Walker prepared his argument with great care, and much of the work was invested in extensive and detailed questionnaires dispatched throughout the country. In particular, the answers to his Circular Number 2 provided considerable evidence that agricultural businessmen were turning away from high tariffs. The response of a New York farmer was perhaps atypical in long-range perception and stylish composition, but it represented a widely shared analysis. "Any tariff that lies against the trade of a nation, lies against the nation itself." "Can there be a home market for all our produce?" he continued, and answered with an eerie preview of what ultimately occurred long after he was in his grave. "In very truth when enough have been driven into manufacturing to make a home market for all our produce, they would be numerous enough to manufacture two or three times as much as this country could consume, and the surplus would have to find a foreign market." "Can that system be *American*," he asked rhetorically in a direct slap at Henry Clay, "which shackles trade and denies to us the markets of the world?" "No," he thundered, "there is nothing about it which partakes of the freedom which we associate with the name of America."[13]

Such confident militance was the product of tradition reinforced by experience and analysis. The agitation for freer trade had been accelerated, for example, by the popularization of Smith's *Wealth of Nations* by the French political economist Jean Baptiste Say. He argued that the markets of the world could absorb any and all such surpluses. And the attack on the tariff had been vigorously sustained by such Americans as John McVickor of Columbia University (and his students and plagiarizers), and William Cullen Bryant of the New York *Evening Post*. The appeal of the campaign immediately provoked renewed opposition from protectionist Easterners, even though they had to admit that the export of foodstuffs was "an important item in our commerce."[14]

The agricultural concern for the British market clearly helped Polk outflank the Westerners who continued to demand all of the Oregon Territory. By the time the Congress voted on April 23, 1846, to terminate the old agreement with Britain for the joint occupation of Oregon, the militants had lost important support in their own region as well as among Southerners and Easterners. Two days later, on April 25, they suffered a mortal blow and never regained the initiative. Mexican and American forces clashed north of the Rio Grande. Polk had decided on war before news of the skirmish reached Washington during the evening of May 9, and he promptly asked the Congress to make the formal declaration on May 11, charging that Mexico had "shed American blood upon the American soil." The vote was overwhelming: 174 to 14 in the House, and 40 to 2 in the Senate.

If judged on a short-term basis, the next three developments can be viewed as victories for Polk's expansionist strategy. First, on June 15, 1846, the Senate ratified a compromise settlement with Great Britain that fixed the Oregon boundary at 49° north latitude, several hundred miles south of the line sought by the Western militants. Second, the Western concern with export markets produced the votes to pass a bill that lowered the tariff. Agriculture had "withered," explained one spokesman, because the farmer "cannot find a good market for his surplus produce." And that analysis carried the battle.

"How is agriculture to be protected?" asked Representative John Francis Collin of New York. His answer was simple and prophetic of the outlook that would come to dominate the thinking of the farm businessmen. "Give them but a fair field in the markets of the world." Another congressman preferred to attack protection. The home market argument was "a gross absurdity. . . . If we do not find a foreign market," he concluded, the farmer would be undone.[15] Southerners often stressed the relationship between overseas economic expansion and freedom. "The expansive energies and enlarging products of our agriculturalists," explained one of them, "demand the markets of the world." And Representative John Henry Harmanson of Louisiana prophesied that Americans would carry "peace and comfort to every man's door": with surplus farm produce in one hand and a Bible in the other, Americans would soon boast that they "ruled the waves." Assuming unusual ambidextrousness, he concluded that "the fate of nations will be in their hands."[16] Westerners tended to take the reform for granted and emphasized the economics. They judged the home market argument "preposterous." America would have to construct "unbroken lines of workshops and factories before their inmates could consume the grain and other provisions raised by the farmers." Representative William Watson Wick of Indiana and Senator Breeze of Illinois wholly agreed: "We in the West . . . want the world's wide market." A mere ten counties in Illinois "could supply all the home market. We want a foreign market for our produce, which is now rotting in our granaries."[17] When it came time to vote, the West and the South cast a total of 88 votes for the lower rates of the Walker Tariff of July 30, 1846 (against 32 in opposition).

Polk's third victory came in the defeat of Mexico. That triumph not only validated the Rio Grande as the Texas border on the south, an objective that at one time mistakenly appeared to be the principal cause and purpose of the conflict, but extended the territorial empire of the United States to the California coast. Including Texas, the war added 1,193,061 square miles and gave America several excellent harbors on the Pacific. The President's successes carried a very high price tag, however, and the full extent of the cost began to become apparent even before the Mexicans surrendered.

Instead of easing the tension between Northern and Southern expansionists, the war extended and intensified their differences. The anger of those who wanted all the Oregon Territory was not appeased by the prospect or the reality of gains in the Southwest, or by the seizure of California. The final decision to compromise the Oregon Boundary was made after the declaration of war against Mexico and the protest filed during that debate by Senator Lewis Cass of Michigan pointed to the deeper divisions of the future. "We are seeking," he warned, "a doubtful good at the certainty of a great sacrifice."[18] The attacks rapidly grew more embittered. Representative Brady Preston Gentry of Tennessee charged Polk and his Southern allies with "insincerity and double-dealing." The same accusation came from Representative John Smith Chipman of Michigan. After reviewing the understanding and commitment on Oregon that had been reached prior to Polk's nomination, and then carried through the campaign of 1844, he delivered a wholesale indictment. "But lo! all at once the Administration party dropped from 54° 40' and deserted *en masse.*"[19]

That sense of the betrayal of a solemn agreement involving primary interests was a significant element in the developing division over control of the trans-Mississippi empire. It reinforced and extended the more generalized antislavery feeling in the Northwest. That movement was far broader than the abolitionist crusade, and was concerned only secondarily with freeing the black slave. The antislavery groups were determined to prevent Southerners from dominating the economic development of the Western territories, and from using that base to monopolize political power in the national government.

From an early date, moreover, such Westerners feared the consequences of any compromise over the trans-Mississippi region. Representative John Alexander McClernand of Illinois warned in January 1847 that the Northwestern farmer was already denied independent access to the Gulf of Mexico. "The vast commercial power of the Gulf" was "concentrated within the borders of slave States," and it had "been prodigiously augmented by the annexation of Texas." The danger was very real, he explained, because "extension and expansion is the condition of our political existence, and must continue to be from the adaptation of our free institutions. . . . When we cease to extend, we will cease to be, what we are now, a united and ascendant people."[20]

That ominous reading of the expansionist theory of American welfare gained substance with the approval of the Wilmot Proviso by the House of Representatives on August 8, 1846, and again on February 15, 1847. That measure, which called for the prohibition of slavery from any territory acquired from Mexico, was backed by anti-Polk Democrats, abolitionists, and antislavery Northerners. "The issue now presented," explained Representative David Wilmot of Pennsylvania, "is not whether slavery shall exist unmolested where it now is, but whether it shall be carried to new and distant regions, now free." "I ask not that slavery be abolished," he continued. "I demand that this Government preserve the integrity of *free territory* against the aggressions of slavery." Pointing out that the Louisiana Territory had gone to slavery by a count of eight states to one, he angrily concluded that "the whole of Texas has been given up to slavery. . . . An empire larger than France." "Shall we give up free territory? . . . Never, sir, never, until we ourselves are fit to be slaves."[21]

The tension created by that challenge was temporarily eased by the failure of the Senate to agree to the proviso, and by the mounting enthusiasm among various groups of Northerners and Westerners for taking all of Mexico. Some became convinced that slavery could not be imposed upon that society. Others overrode their fears about slavery with the logic of economic gain. And still others, excited by the emotional fervor of the war, wanted to punish the Mexicans.[22] But the treaty of peace negotiated by Nicholas Trist cut the ground from under the campaign, and the die-hard Oregon men were the only ones to vote against ratification.

That momentary hiatus in the conflicts between Southern and Western expansionists, and between the abolitionists and the Southern militants, might have been nurtured into a long-term compromise that might in turn have created conditions leading to the gradual and peaceful demise of slavery. One strategy for accomplishing that objective called for promptly extending the old Missouri Compromise line of 36° 30′ westward to the Pacific Coast, or to the eastern border of the California Territory. Quick, decisive agreement on the proposal might have squashed the incipient struggle for control of the trans-Mississippi empire. That approach had been discussed ever since 1820, but it was not pushed seriously until after the battle had been reopened.

The other possibility involved extending and deepening the economic and political ties between the South and the West. That might have led to the confinement and gradual decline of slavery through a mutual agreement arising out of a developing sense of common interest and purpose. There was a great deal of enthusiastic talk about constructing the economic foundations for that kind of an interregional alliance just before and during the Mexican war, and it continued for a time after the conflict ended. Much of the interest grew out of the existing trade relationships between the two regions, and the related and rising pressure for internal improvements west of the Appalachian Mountains.

Such agitation is easily understood, for that area received only $6 billion for water transportation projects between 1780 and 1860.[23] Pointing to the needs of "the vast and constantly increasing trade" of the region, Senator Breeze of Illinois submitted a typical petition on March 15, 1844, "praying for adequate appropriations for the improvement of the navigation of the Mississippi River, and the lakes."[24] And a year later a meeting of Southerners at Memphis agreed on the need for direct cooperation to secure better transportation connections. "Now is the time to meet our Western friends . . . to set the ball in motion that must bring the valley to the South."[25]

Senator Douglas of Illinois became the leading advocate of such a north-south axis, and his strategy was designed to make the Mississippi Valley the controlling center of world trade. That would "stimulate and encourage all the branches of industry," and "afford more . . . protection" to all American interests "than all the protective tariffs that the ingenuity of man ever devised."[26] He won considerable support in the Northwest, moreover, as well as among Southerners.[27] His persistent efforts to obtain major government assistance were successful in 1850, when he secured congressional approval of the first subsidy in the form of a grant of public lands to aid the construction of a north-south railroad.

By the time the Illinois Central Railroad began promoting settlement (1851) and initiating construction (1852), however, the battle was all but lost. Even the Mobile and New Orleans Railroad, which began building a line north to St. Louis in 1849, was too late. Two principal reasons explain the failure to establish a firm alliance between the West and the South. One involved the reopening of the battle for control of the trans-Mississippi West. And once again Oregon provided the spark that touched off the first cannonade. But this time it was the Southerners, rather than the Westerners, who felt betrayed by Polk. That was their reaction when he approved the antislavery territorial government in Oregon. Then Northerners revived the Wilmot Proviso and made it a major issue in the election of 1848. That combination of events rapidly destroyed the earlier Southern concern to woo the West. The region increasingly concentrated on defending and advancing a far narrower conception of its interests.

The second factor was economic, and involved the rapidly growing ties between the metropolis and the Northwestern agricultural businessmen. The network of northern canals and railroads linking the East and the Northwest created a new trading pattern that pulled the surplus-producing food farmers away from the South. At the same time, moreover, Southern transportation leaders concentrated their efforts on integrating their section on an east-west axis along the Gulf, rather than on reaching out to the Northwest. That placed Southern commercial and shipping interests under an increasing disadvantage in the struggle to control the flow of the rising surplus of the Western farmers. And that trade became steadily more vital because the South itself provided a market for proportionately less and less of the Western surplus.

The dynamic combination of increasing population, improving technology, and rising demand explains the boom in the Western production and processing of foodstuffs. Almost all the principal agricultural implements became available before 1860. The steel and chilled-iron plows and the horse rake were in general use, and seed drills, corn planters, disk harrows, and cultivators, along with mowers, reapers, and threshing machines, were put into the fields as rapidly as they could be afforded and obtained. By the mid-1850s, for that matter, the major manufacturers like John Deere, Walter A. Wood, and Cyrus McCormick were turning to the overseas market to absorb their surpluses.[28]

The increase in production was continuous and its effect was cumulative. The wheat surplus that Westerners harvested and shipped out of their region doubled in the five years between 1839 and 1844. It jumped another 300 percent by 1853. Flour traffic climbed from 800,000 barrels in 1839 to 3 million barrels in 1853. And corn shot upward by 800 percent (to 8 million bushels). Finally, pork shipments moved from 300,000 barrels in 1839 to 1.5 million barrels in 1853.[29] Those statistics, and the activity that produced them, provided the basis for the growing concern, and the increasingly expansive rhetoric, about foreign markets.

Most of those surpluses were taken by domestic consumers, but though the percentage sent abroad climbed erratically, it nevertheless rose steadily.[30] Perhaps even more significantly, the farm businessmen who produced the surplus began emphasizing the overseas market before it became a major factor in their operations. And while the precise date can be debated, it is clear that the Western farmer became structurally involved with the export market no later than the early 1850s.[31] The pattern was apparent to Senator Douglas in 1851, and he confidently anticipated the day "when we shall be able to regulate the prices of grain, provisions, and cotton" in the world marketplace. That would give the United States the power to "compel the Governments of Europe to keep the peace."[32]

Such enthusiasm was so widespread that it affected even the wool growers. The editors of the *Prairie Farmer*, for example, maintained a steady flow of reports during 1847 about the efforts of that group to find foreign markets. They were a bit slow, for three years earlier the editors of the New York *Evening Post* expressed confidence that the United States would soon "become in a few years a larger producer and exporter of wool than any other nation."[33] That particular boom never materialized, but in 1851 the farmers of California did begin exporting flour. Australia was a significant market by 1853, and shipments were being made to Mexico, Central America, Chile, the Pacific Islands, and China by the end of the decade. Those Far Western farmers and millers even penetrated the British market. It was a portentous shift in trade flows, for during the 1840s California had imported flour from both Australia and Chile.

The primary exporters of food, however, were centered along the Ohio and Mississippi rivers. Cincinnati became the meat-packing center of the nation by 1840, and was also a major contender in the production of flour.[34] But Chicago, and even Wisconsin and Minnesota, were beginning to challenge that supremacy. The wheat farmers of Wisconsin, for example, enjoyed "a period of the greatest prosperity" beginning in 1853.[35] Even before that, in 1851,a rising young economist named David A. Wells had begun to promote Milwaukee flour in the London market.[36] And flour was commercially produced at the Falls of St. Anthony, where the great St. Paul and Minneapolis mills later arose, only two years later.[37]

In some ways, however, the meat packers of Ohio and Illinois provided the clearest outline of the future. Cleveland and Chicago meat exporters seem to have been the first to try shipping via the St. Lawrence River, even though the Cincinnati processors dominated the trade.[38] The Boston and Albany Railroad experimented with refrigerated shipments as early as 1842, but that technique did not become successful until after Chicago giants like Philip Danforth Armour and Nelson Morris established themselves at the end of the 1850s. They ultimately bought many of their cattle from the high plains ranges that were first established during the late 1840s.[39] Such meat exports, especially those of pork products, led Russia to fear for its own agriculture during the 1850s, and prompted it to initiate a system of restrictions that became much tougher and more general throughout Europe in later years.

The steady shift in the flow of those Western surpluses away from moving to or through the South, to going to or through the East, was unmistakable by 1853. Almost no wheat ever went south: the highest share was 8 percent in 1849, and that dropped to 1 percent in 1853. The South handled 53 percent of Western flour in 1839, but the business declined rapidly to 31 percent by 1844, and had eased down to 28 percent by 1853. At the outset of the period of transition (1839), the South enjoyed a virtual monopoly in Western corn, taking 98 percent. The drastic loss occurred between 1844 (90 percent) and 1849, when the figure skidded to 40 percent. It slipped a bit more, to 37 percent, by 1853. The South did hold its own in pork, sliding only from 69 percent in 1839 to 58 percent in 1853.[40]

Senator Douglas recognized the shift, and realized that he needed to support the west-to-east routes as well as his project for the Mississippi Valley. Among other reasons, he could not hope to maintain and improve his position of national leadership if he lost his power base in Illinois, and his constituency was increasingly interested in shipping surpluses via the Great Lakes and the St. Lawrence. "The great and growing interest in navigation," he acknowledged, "is too important to be overlooked or disregarded."[41] Railroad leaders clearly understood the situation and pushed hard to capture all the Western trade. They often proved talented enough to combine an intra-industry analysis of their position with an appeal to the farmers. "Take Illinois" in 1850, ran one such discussion, "she produced . . . a surplus of more than 40,000,000 bushels of wheat and corn. . . . In New York this surplus would have been worth $40,000,000. In Illinois it did not net the producers more than $12,000,000. This difference is due to the charges for transportation alone. Illinois turns her vast resources to small account, for the want of more and better avenue to market."[42]

The farmers recognized and understood their needs without reading essays in the railroad trade journals. They knew they could have exported far more than they did, for example, during 1845-1847, when bad harvests throughout western Europe and in Britain created an ideal opportunity to penetrate those markets.[43] They responded by supplying capital for railroad construction in various ways, in many places even accepting railroad stock for mortgages on their farms. (The mortgages were then sold in the metropolis to raise operating funds.) That attitude and behavior were encouraged by the railroad leaders who recognized the importance of the farmers. John W. Brooks, superintendent of the Michigan Central Railroad, for example, acknowledged the interrelationship very directly as early as June 1848. The railroads, to be successful over the long run, had "to promote the welfare and prosperity" of the agricultural businessmen, "upon whose very prosperity rests the whole value of our enterprise."[44]

The developing connection with the East did not, however, end the traditional antagonisms between the metropolis and the country. For one thing, Southerners kept warning the Westerners, on the basis of their own experience, of the dangers in dealing with the Northeast.[45] That was hardly necessary. Western meat packers knew they were dependent on Eastern capital, and did not like the relationship. Very often, indeed, the metropolis was bluntly referred to as the place "where the capital which controls produce is concentrated."[46] And, despite the preemption law of 1841 (and the belated passage of a graduation bill in 1854), Eastern speculators continued to take good profits in the land market.[47]

Tension of a different kind was created by the rising productivity of the Westerners. Their power in the marketplace posed an ever more difficult challenge to farm businessmen in the East, who could not compete effectively against the better soil and vast acreages. The resulting decline did not become serious until late in the 1850s, when the rivalry between railroads for the Western surpluses produced a significant drop in freight rates.[48] At that juncture, however, other issues temporarily intervened to prevent a major confrontation. But the Easterners had begun to sense that they had no way of altering the unfavorable natural conditions, or of reversing the structural changes, that caused their troubles and suffering. That recognition of reality did not immediately move them to help the Westerners, however, and they were not enthusiastic supporters of the efforts during the 1850s to provide free land in the West.[49] Representative Thomas James Duncan

Fuller of Maine, for example, damned the proposed homestead bill of 1852 as *"unconstitutional, partial,* and *unjust."* And his colleague Representative Israel Washburn, Jr., added that he would vote against it unless Maine was given a similar subsidy.[50]

Another congressman, Timothy Jenkins of New York, spoke more bluntly about the economic factors. He placed "the stamp of condemnation" upon the bill because it would not help Eastern agriculture. Those farmers needed a profitable home market, he argued, not more surpluses from the West that would drive prices down even further.[51] When the vote came, on May 12, 1852, the East cast the great bulk of the 56 "nays." The Northwest was almost solid (34 "yeas") for the bill. And enough Easterners agreed with Representatives Charles Skelton of New Jersey and Henry Dunning Moore of Pennsylvania, to help raise the final tally to 107 "yeas." Both men argued that the settlement of the West served a double function: it was a safety valve for the discontented, and it stimulated the economy.[52] The measure was not approved by the Senate, however, and the Westerners waited another decade for the kind of a subsidy that had already been made to the Illinois Central Railroad.

Northeastern farmers were not wholly critical or negative. They supported other positive measures at the local, regional, and national levels. New Hampshire, for example, created a state commission to regulate railroads as early as 1844. Some farmers began to diversify (or otherwise change) their agriculture in order to improve their position in the growing urban markets. And another group, the dairy farmers, joined the Western campaign to penetrate foreign markets.[53] Easterners were also affected, at least to some degree, by the spirit and psychology of self-consciousness that permeated the agricultural press of the period.[54]

They likewise participated in the general movement to create agricultural clubs and societies. Whether formed on a national scale, like the American Shorthorn Association (1846) and the United States Agricultural Society (1852), or organized on a state basis, like the Indiana Horticultural Society (1841 - 1842) and the Wisconsin Agricultural Society (1851), such groups—which totaled 621 by 1849—helped ease some of the conflicts of interest. So did the effort to gain independent departmental status for agriculture within the federal government. That campaign became self-sustaining after 1849, as the problem of the surpluses evoked permanent concern. Representative Jerediah Horsford of New York, an erstwhile farmer, explained in 1852 that the proposal enjoyed his "entire approbation" because agriculture formed "the basis of our commercial and manufacturing prosperity." "I plead before this House," he cried, "the cause of farmers generally."[55] His efforts were in vain. The farm businessmen waited thirty-five years for Cabinet representation.

Easterners were also responding to the nationalistic and expansionist ideas of politicians like William H. Seward of New York. He made many direct appeals stressing the value of territorial expansion for free farmers, and the primary importance of a strong agricultural base in winning world leadership for the United States. Seward's conviction that America had a "divine purpose" to spread democracy was also satisfying, and he often combined those arguments very persuasively. "Let us cultivate and improve ourselves," he exhorted a group of Vermont farmers in 1853, "and so save and impart to the world the elements of a new and happy renovation."[56]

Seward astutely realized that America's economic expansion would ultimately involve industrial surpluses to a greater degree than farm produce, but he also understood the immediate and rising importance of agricultural exports. His argument of October 1849 for a transcontinental railroad system, for example, stressed its value in opening "new large and increasing" markets for "our surplus meat and bread." He added that such an expansion of trade would do much to weaken Britain's economic supremacy. It would shake the "pretensions" of the English by making it clear that the foundations of their dominion "were about to crumble."

The tension between Eastern and Western farmers was pushed into the background, though not permanently resolved, by the rising opposition to Southern demands to extend the slave labor system into the trans-Mississippi territory. That increasingly bitter confrontation over the Western empire was the single most important immediate cause of the Civil War. Western and Southern agricultural businessmen rapidly came to view control of that land as a necessary condition of their present and future welfare. They considered it the crucial determinant of political power (and hence freedom), as well as of economic prosperity. That estimate of the role of territorial expansion created the hothouse psychological environment that became so congenital after 1844 to the groups that decreed immediate and final solutions. The Northerners who demanded abolition—NOW!, and their Southern counterparts who insisted on secession—NOW!, unquestionably intensified the conflict. But the war came over the *extension* of slavery, *not* over the *abolition* of slavery, and that issue was defined and joined by market-minded agriculturalists rather than by moral crusaders.

The marketplace political economy of the Northern farmers did integrate political and social freedom with economic liberty in a tight causal relationship. That was, indeed, the image and explanation of the world that defined control of the trans-Mississippi West as the decisive determinant of their well-being and security. But the overwhelming majority of them applied that philosophy to themselves first and primarily, and only secondarily and incidentally—if at all—

to the black men of the country. They opposed the extension of the slave labor political economy not because they were concerned to free the slave, but because they were resolved to maintain their own freedom and improve their own welfare.

They reacted negatively, therefore, to the strategy of compromise offered after 1853 by Senator Douglas. His popular sovereignty plan, in reality a proposal to fight the issue in each territory, rapidly lost whatever initial backing it gained as the violent struggle in — and for — Kansas revealed the determined willfulness of both protagonists. Northern farm opposition to Southern projects to expand into Cuba, Mexico, or Central America further intensified the anger and militance of both sides. Whatever their differences with each other, Northeastern and Northwestern agriculturalists moved rapidly after 1854 toward an agreement on the sentiments shortly expressed by the Nebraska City *People's Press.* Paraphrasing what they called the typical Southern attitude, the editors charged that region with ruthless, single-minded selfishness: "'we care nothing about you or your rights, all we desire is to extend the area of slave Territory.'"[57]

The conflict over territory was reinforced and accentuated, moreover, by the rising Western concern with overseas markets. Much of that development was a product of the economic fluctuations of the 1850s. Even the first news of a war in Europe served to raise hopes of expanded exports. "We shall be required to supply all Europe with bread," shouted the New York *Herald* in response to the Crimean War.[58] Some observers, including Seward, saw that conflict as a preview of a future struggle between the United States and Russia for world power. That was "the great event which looms in the next twenty or twenty-five years."[59] In the meantime, however, metropolitan observers joined the farmers in welcoming the increased demand for foodstuffs.[60]

But the war did not solve the problem of the surpluses, and the late 1850s offered "no picture of booming expansion." The export of crude and processed foods jumped from $35.6 million in 1853 to peaks of $81.9 million in 1856 and $79.8 million in 1857, but then slumped to $42.6 million in 1859.[61] And despite that short boom, the rate of growth for the whole economy did not begin to rise until after 1858.[62] Yet agriculture employed almost 60 percent of all working adults and supplied more than 80 percent of the exports that "were extremely important" to the growth of the entire economy.[63] Small wonder that the Westerners increased their demands for help from the government "in *getting better prices.*"[64]

The concern with markets reached a new intensity as the Southern states began to secede after the election of Abraham Lincoln as a minority President. The "common interest of all" in the Ohio Valley "was in finding outside the valley a market for their surplus products and in receiving from the outside those things not produced within."[65] "It is enough to say," announced the Cincinnati *Daily Gazette*, "that the Valley of the Mississippi must be under one Government, cost what it may. . . . There is no alternative."[66] A bit to the north, in Michigan, Senator Zachariah Chandler was more bombastic. "We own that river," he thundered, "we bought and paid for it; and by the eternal, we are going to keep it. . . . We will make it a desert again before we let you [Southerners] steal it from us."[67]

On to the west, in Illinois, Senator Douglas was just as emphatic. *"We can never acknowledge the right of a State to secede and cut us off from the Ocean and the world, without our consent."*[68] He amplified that analysis in major speeches at Bellaire, Ohio, and Springfield, Illinois. The war, he explained, "is a war of self-defense upon our part . . . in defense of those rights of freedom of trade, commerce, transit, and intercourse from the center to the circumference of our great continent."[69] And still further west, in Iowa, "there were hard times in Cass County. . . . The rebels closed the river."[70]

Such reactions made it clear that the post-1840 shift in trade flows away from New Orleans and other Southern centers was not so complete as to make Westerners indifferent to the disruption of that market system. The flour milling industry that had developed in St. Louis on the basis of Western wheat surpluses, for example, was deeply concerned with access to the "markets of the world." The city had twenty-two mills in 1850, and by 1862 its thirty-five mills ground about 1.3 billion pounds of flour.[71] Not all of that enormous production went down the river, either to markets in the South or to be exported to foreign markets, but enough of it did to make secession a very serious economic crisis. As for the Southern market itself, even those scholars who discount it admit that it absorbed at least 20 percent of Western production.[72] That is hardly, as one such student maintains, a matter of "limited importance" even in the abstract; and it was most certainly not practically insignificant to the Westerners at the time. And much of the produce shipped to New Orleans was re-exported. For flour, the figure was 75 percent; for bacon, 40 percent; and for pork, 25 percent; and those shares involved the farmers of Ohio, Michigan, Illinois, and other Western states.[73]

Whatever the precise percentages of the trade to and through the South, moreover, the commerce was deranged by the outbreak of the Civil War. That played a major role in creating "an amount of distress that was unprecedented" in the North.[74] Business failures reached 5,935 in 1861, with losses passing $175 million. But the crisis also "greatly disturbed the market for hogs" and other agricultural products, and brought "great distress in 1861 and 1862" to Northern farmers.[75] And as commodity prices stagnated or moved downward until mid-1862, railroad freight rates jumped upward. The agricultural businessmen suffered severely.

The crisis was so deep near the end of 1862 that President Lincoln feared he would lose the support of the farmers.[76] And with good reason. The November elections produced strong Democratic contingents in Ohio, Indiana, Illinois, and Wisconsin. His response was a long, closely reasoned argument designed to prove to the Western farmers that they could neither compromise with the South nor let it go its own way in peace. The West "has no seacoast," he explained in his annual message of December 1862. "Separate our common country into two nations, as designed by the present rebellion, and every man of this great interior region is thereby cut off from some one or more of the outlets [to foreign markets]. . . . These outlets . . . are indispensable to the well-being of the people."[77] Lincoln was magnificently skilled with logic and words, but it can be doubted that those alone would have satisfied the farmers. They (and Lincoln) were saved from further immediate troubles, however, by three successive crop failures in Great Britain, and lesser troubles in France. Grain farmers, hog raisers, and cattlemen, and even cheese makers, entered a boom that lasted throughout the war.[78] That prosperity, and the demand that caused it, contributed significantly to the consolidation, extension, and improvement of Northern agriculture.

But the most important consequences appeared in other phases of agricultural development. The dramatic recovery through exports across the winter of 1862-1863 served to convince Northern farmers, and especially those in the West, of the necessity of foreign markets. It firmly shifted their emphasis from territorial acquisition to overseas market expansion, and transformed Adam Smith's theory about market expansion into an inescapable reality. That outlook guided their actions to an ever intensifying degree during the remainder of the nineteenth century.

At the same time, moreover, the export boom created a sense of vast American power that became an assumption underlying the thought of farm businessmen. Metropolitan leaders were also affected by the new sense of destiny. Other nations, boomed the *American Railroad Journal*, were now "more or less dependent" on American food surpluses. But the farmers did not need to wait for the message from the city. Food exports, cried the Commissioner of Agriculture in 1862, will enable the United States "to command the precious metals and the respect, if not the fear, of mankind."[79] The fear—and the related antagonism—came sooner than the respect. The cheese makers provoked opposition and resistance in Great Britain within two years. Not only were the American dairymen threatening to dominate the market, but they were in such a hurry to do so that they were exporting adulterated cheese. The confrontation over those issues produced the American Dairymen's Association, and also offered a preview of future efforts to block the triumph of American meat and grain exports.[80]

In an important sense, of course, the conflict over cheese was a classic example of what Smith meant when he wrote about the tension and antagonism between the metropolis and the country. For Great Britain was the metropolis, and America was the granary and slaughterhouse, of the developed and developing part of the economic world. And in many ways, moreover, the American metropolis was a part of the British metropolis. The episode also provided a portentous preview of how the American agricultural businessman, himself a domestic colonial within Smith's system, would function as an imperial expansionist in his relationship with farmers of other countries.

The wartime prosperity did postpone two major confrontations between the American metropolis and the American farmer. But the Commissioner of Agriculture's reference to commanding "the precious metals" of the world pointed toward a struggle over the monetary system, and that battle was joined within fifteen years. The other fight was foreseen far more explicitly by a shrewd observer of the political economy named Henry Varnum Poor. He warned in 1861 that the cost of transportation would "for years, if not generations to come, become the most engrossing topic of public concern."[81] He was proved a prophet in less than a decade.

FOUR

In truth, the old plantation system was re-established with the store account taking the place of the overseer's whip, the sheriff performing the duties of the ante-bellum "patter-roller," and the exploitation of men still furnishing the source of profits.

William Best Hesseltine, *The South in American History*

The only criterion by which to determine the importance and prosperity of any country is the amount and value of its exports over and above its imports.

Governor of Alabama Robert M. Patton, 1867

How many cares there are!—I think the farmers have a large share.

Judson M. Hatch to Mary Margol, 1865

We believe that this country has been run quite long enough under the direction of New England. . . . We fetch and carry, and bark, and roll over, and fight other dogs precisely as and when we are bidden by our New England master.

Chicago *Times*, November 16, 1865

Free trade with all the markets of the world is the true theory of government.

Representative Daniel W. Voorhees of Indiana, 1866

In the . . . traitorous section of Northern politics, it is consistent for Americans to advocate and plot with foreigners British Free Trade.

New York *Tribune*, April 3, 1866

It is not the question of ability to produce, but it is the question of facility and cheapness of transportation which must be solved before we can monopolize the markets of the world.

Central Committee of the River Improvement Convention, St. Louis, 1867

Politics are more than boiling.

George M. Reynolds to Luman H. Weller, 1867

Recent
Enemies Share a Similar Fate
and in Rising Anger
Confront the
Metropolis

The vast majority of Northern agricultural businessmen did not consider the Civil War a glorious crusade to free the slaves. The farmers accepted that result of the war as it occurred, and generally approved the subsequent attempt to extend civil rights to the freed black man. And a few congressmen from Western states, most notably Representatives George Washington Julian of Indiana and James Falconer Wilson of Iowa, were leading militants in the radical wing of the Republican party. But the Northern farmer never centered his attention on the black man. He was primarily involved with his own interests and problems—with the struggle over policy in the North rather than with the battle over the reconstruction of the defeated South.

As a result, the Westerners became increasingly anti-metropolitan and less concerned to continue punishing or changing Southerners. Like most people in the aftermath of a bloody civil war, they did respond to emotional references to the former enemy, and to warnings about the need to prevent the South from reestablishing what they considered its ante-bellum predominance in the national government. In a remarkably short time, however, the Northern (and particularly Western) farmers began to view their recent enemies as potential if not actual allies against the power and the policies of the metropolis.

Westerners were never fully satisfied, even during the war, with the results of their bargain with Northeastern Republicans. The postwar depression intensified their demands for more direct rewards, and at the same time aroused greater opposition to legislation that

107

favored the metropolis. The first battle erupted in 1866 over another attempt to increase the tariff. The Westerners reopened the old struggle for lower rates that they and the Southerners had waged between 1842 and 1860. Their central argument was unchanged: decrease the tariff in order to win larger export markets. The same logic, reinforced by the desire to win higher profits in the market that existed, carried the agricultural businessmen into a growing assault on the railroads, and into a militant demand to improve alternate shipping routes. Within four years, moreover, the farmers of both sections united as members of the Patrons of Husbandry, an organization dedicated to advancing the economic and other interests of agriculture.

Southern farmers were of course more directly and deeply involved with the consequences of freeing the slaves. Their prejudices (and fears) generated increasingly intense resistance to the Radical Republican effort to elevate the former slave to a more equal and truly independent position in the marketplace. But racism was by no means the only cause of Southern opposition to Northern policies. The defeated Confederates were deeply concerned to prevent the victorious metropolis from using its political and economic power to institutionalize the South as a domestic colony for the indefinite future.

Unhappily, the Southerners won their battle against the freed black man and lost their fight against political and economic vassalage. Everyone would have gained immeasurably if the results had been reversed. And it can be—and has been—argued that the victory over the former slaves did much to cause the other defeat. Unfortunately, however, the logic of that analysis is not as strong as its morality. For the metropolis might well have maintained its superior position even if the slave had become an equal in reality as well as in legal rhetoric. Certainly it did so in its relationship with Northern agriculture, and the Southerners were far poorer and weaker.

The South diversified its agriculture under the pressure of the war, producing vastly more wheat, corn, and potatoes.[1] And some Southerners argued desperately that the only hope for salvation after their defeat was in sustaining and extending that kind of multicrop production.[2] But the devastation left few options. Bad weather and crop failures in 1865 and 1867 reduced those even further. The number of horses declined 29 percent; cows, 32 percent; and swine, 35 percent. The value of agricultural implements, along with that of the land itself, fell almost 50 percent. The South after its surrender was "a land of poverty" and "one of America's colonies."[3]

Those pressures, reinforced by Northern and European demand for cotton, pushed the region back into its old reliance on that one crop. Under the new conditions, however, the merchant and the storekeeper replaced the slave-owning planter as master of the system. But the dynamics did not change, at least in the economic sense. "In truth, the old plantation system was re-established with the store account taking the place of the overseer's whip, the sheriff performing the duties of the ante-bellum 'patter-roller,' and the exploitation of men still furnishing the source of profits."[4] And the merchants "demanded that cotton, more cotton, and almost cotton alone should be grown."[5]

The crop-lien system originated in the need for credit and was consolidated by laws passed as early as 1866 that gave the landlords "a lien upon the crops of their tenants for such stock, farming utensils, and provisions, furnished such tenants, for the purpose of making their crops."[6] The Southern economy became "a vast pawn shop" involving more than 80 percent of the cotton growers, proprietors, and tenants. "Each year," reported one anguished Southerner, "the plunge into debt is deeper. . . . The struggle is woe-begone. Cares are many, smiles are few, and the comforts of life are scantier."[7] "The biggest fraud of earth," snarled a Mississippi editor, "is agriculture." "No wonder Cain killed his brother. He was a tiller of the earth. Agriculture would demoralize a saint."[8] Even a planter from the same state judged the system to be based on "extortion, genteel swindling, legitimate larceny," under which "negro and poor white men of the country made nothing."[9] But as the *Report* of the Commissioner of Agriculture made clear, the planter was no longer master—he had become "the pigeon to be plucked."[10] Cotton became "a curse" leading "to the enslavement of the South."[11]

The system did promote the revival of the production of cotton, but that only intensified the problem of an increasing surplus driving prices even lower. The high market of 1865 (90 cents per pound in New York) dropped by two-thirds in 1866, and slipped to 24.9 cents per pound in 1866. Land policies offered little or no relief because they generally operated to prevent the average farmer from breaking free of the lien system, or from diversifying his crops.[12] As a result, Southerners rapidly concentrated their efforts on three other strategies for improving their position.

One of those involved a partnership between the planters and other Southern businessmen to create a rough cotton textile manufacturing industry located in the South and controlled by Southerners. That was "a matter of prime necessity" in the minds of leaders like James Dunwoody Brownson DeBow of New Orleans and Governor Robert M. Patton of Alabama. It would enable the South to save the money that it had "heretofore paid away to the North and Europe," and thus hasten the day of financial independence. Even more important, it would raise Southern exports of cotton, which was "the only criterion by which to determine the importance and prosperity of any country." The happy result would be the end of the domestic colonialism that degraded Southerners "to a condition worse and more intolerable than that of hewers of wood and drawers of water."[13]

The realization of that grand vision took many years, much agitation, and great effort, but the activity of the late 1860s was far from insignificant. Many of the South's prewar total of 160 mills had been destroyed or otherwise closed during the conflict, and it seemed almost fantasy in 1866 to discuss controlling export markets. But Southern mills had entered the foreign business before the Civil War, and one of them, the Graniteville firm of South Carolina, reentered the national market in 1866. The West Point Manufacturing Company of the Chattahoochee River Valley of eastern Alabama provided a still more significant example. Local businessmen and planters launched the firm in 1866, and were soon selling cotton duck on the Far Western frontier. Similar reconstructions and innovations in Georgia and North Carolina restored approximately two-thirds of the South's prewar spindles to production by 1868.[14]

Northerners immediately recognized the challenge. Edward T. Atkinson, a major leader of the New England textile industry, realized that the rough textile men of the South would not be so concerned about the high tariffs favored by metropolitan companies producing finished goods that competed with British cloth. The Southerners would stand instead with the agricultural businessmen who wanted to lower the tariff in order to penetrate export markets. The proper response, Atkinson initially concluded, called for an effort to discourage the Southern industry while standing firm with other metropolitan manufacturers against a resurgence of Southern power that would lower the tariff. And, for a time, that effort was successful.

But the second Southern strategy to improve conditions called for a general effort to lower the tariff, and it promised good results through direct cooperation with Western farmers against the metropolis. The approach was predicated on a direct campaign to improve the South's position in the world commodity marketplace. Mississippi planters organized themselves for that purpose in 1865, and immediately launched a more general agitation that later created the Southern Cotton Growers Association. A complementary effort was headed by William M. Burwell of the New Orleans Chamber of Commerce, who also edited *DeBow's Review*.

Burwell concentrated on improving the Mississippi River and reestablishing the flow of export surpluses from the South, and the Northwest and West, through New Orleans. He quickly found an ally in Lewis J. Higby, a flour miller who had extracted a fortune from his wartime operations in Milwaukee and St. Louis. He arrived in New Orleans in 1868, just as Burwell and others were making their first overtures to the Illinois Central Railroad.[15] Their campaign did not immediately revive the prewar pattern of trade along the Mississippi, but it was the beginning of an effort that ultimately produced important gains for Northerners as well as Southerners.

Burwell recognized, as did other men who understood agricultural reality, that the transportation problem was derivative rather than primary. Improved transportation was necessary and desirable in order to lower costs, and thereby increase the net earnings of the farmer (and the merchant), but the vital determinant of prosperity was expanded markets. Had the markets been large and the prices high, transportation would not so quickly have become a central issue. Burwell made the point simply and directly: the rising production of Southern and Western farmers would "require a market abroad."[16] He was particularly concerned because he expected European countries to protect themselves against the economic power of American agricultural businessmen. That analysis turned him toward alternate markets in Latin America and toward new policies, such as reciprocity treaties, that were calculated to win control of those markets.[17]

The immediate political objective, of course, was to revive and strengthen the prewar efforts to build an alliance with Western farmers. And that need defined the third Southern strategy for reestablishing the region in the national political economy. Such a coalition was mandatory not only to change the tariff system, but also to win more money from the federal government for the Mississippi and the port of New Orleans, and for internal improvements throughout the South. Southerners had reason to be optimistic about the possibilities for such a partnership, moreover, because Western farmers grew increasingly restive after the end of the war.

Much of their dissatisfaction was generated by unfavorable changes in economic conditions. Despite the severe wartime inflation (a rise of 250 percent for many items), the combination of exports and war orders enabled many Northern farmers to enjoy "vigorous prosperity" through the latter part of the conflict.[18] "It has been an excellent year," reported one experienced Western observer at the end of 1864.[19] And that estimate was accepted by many others who added that "mortgages have been paid, farm buildings erected, permanent improvements accomplished, [and] farm implements and machinery obtained."[20] All seemed well: more than half the people were on the land, yet less than half the land was occupied.

Other indicators reinforced that optimistic analysis. Not only did the production of mowing machines increase by 250 percent between 1861 and 1865, but the farmers purchased some 250,000 reapers and mowers.[21] Such mechanization helped the individual agricultural businessman, and facilitated the organization of mammoth farms of as much as 11,000 acres.[22] The boom in livestock raising, coupled with the network of railroads terminating in Chicago, prompted a decision at the end of 1864 to build the huge Union Stockyards in that city. The opening on December 25, 1865, documented the demise of Cincinnati as the packing center of the nation.[23] It was also a fitting symbol of the marketplace philosophy honored by such energetic giants as Nelson Morris and Philip Armour.

Yet other developments verified the earlier warning of Representative Daniel Wolsey Voorhees of Indiana. The "high feverish flush" of wartime prosperity, he brooded in 1863, was "not the genial warmth of health." It was instead "the fierce hectic glow" of destructive "consumption."[24] The evidence in New England was particularly discouraging. Rhode Island, New Hampshire, and Massachusetts lost 10,999 farms and 424,656 acres of improved land during the war. Vermont was producing no more than "a bushel and a peck" of breadstuffs for each of its citizens—only enough to feed the state for thirty-seven days. The farmers of Maine, New Hampshire, and Connecticut supplied enough for ten days. And production in Massachusetts was so low that its people could have had bread for less than three meals on one day.[25] Western competition was becoming so powerful that it revived an old homily: "The only place that's growin' 's the cemetery."[26] The situation was serious enough for the Commissioner of Agriculture to resort to humor. "The boys are leaving the farms, and the girls are following the boys."[27] And even New York farmers, in many respects the strongest and most prosperous in the nation, began to feel the pinch. One result was a rising anger against Illinois wheat growers—as well as toward the railroads that facilitated the competition.[28]

The antagonism was not great enough, however, to block cooperation among Northern farmers in the face of a serious danger to livestock growers. A severe cattle plague struck Europe and England in 1865, and the threat to American herds provoked a common effort to secure immediate government assistance. Petitions about the "very alarming" situation poured into Washington from almost every state, and agricultural spokesmen demanded "immediate consideration" of an embargo when the Congress convened in December 1865. State Department officials added their warning that "a perfect despotism should be exercised . . . along our seaboard and borders."[29] The campaign was effective. Laws passed in December 1865 and March 1866 banned all imports of animals and hides until the danger had passed.

Westerners faced their own special and increasingly serious troubles. Pioneers in Dakota saw their fields stripped bare by grasshoppers in 1863 and 1864. An early frost struck Minnesota in 1866, ruining much of the crop and necessitating emergency relief measures. That year the grasshoppers caused heavy losses in Kansas. Westerners were also hurt by the drop in pork prices and the fall in exports. Much of that difficulty was caused by the outbreak of trichinosis in Germany during 1864 and 1865. The resulting scare, combined with production problems in the United States, created ... ...ed sustained concern until exports recovered after 1870.[30]

Other depressing factors did not produce such dramatic events, but they hurt the farmers just as seriously. Most damaging was the general drop in demand caused by the end of the war and the continued recovery of European agriculture. One farmer warned would-be homesteaders that the frontier was not a jolly place at the moment. "If a man values society, " he commented in a letter to the *Country Gentleman*, "he would not like to live here for the present."[31]Another expressed his anguish in a private note: "How many cares there are!— I think farmers have a large share."[32] Perhaps the most telling commentary came from men who were trying to sell agricultural implements. One was stoic—"some what disappointed about getting money." Another simply asked the company for help: "Please send me $75 I cannot collect enough to bear expenses." The manufacturer, not surprisingly, increased his pressure on government officials to help expand foreign markets.[33]

Many observers, both then and during later periods of economic duress, criticized the farmer for complaining about his condition, and usually added that he did not understand the economic system. In their view, the farm businessmen were either ignorant or irrational— or both. Such judgments have often been delivered, moreover, in a style and tone that implied that the farmers should have quietly accepted the setbacks as natural phenomena, and as an inevitable part of the process of industrialization in a free marketplace economy. The demand for the farmers to be passive, resigned, and noble laborers in the cause of Progress has always come from the metropolis. It is best understood as an example of sophisticated special pleading and urban provincialism. The charge that the farmers were unusually irrational has no basis in theory or fact. They exhibited typical human foibles and weaknessess—or neuroses—but nothing that set them apart as a group particularly prone to paranoia or other psychological disturbances. For that matter, as became apparent during the fight over the tariff in 1866, it was the metropolitans who first used the theory (and accusation) of conspiracy in trying to deal with agricultural opposition to their policies.

The assertion that the farmers were ignorant of the workings of the marketplace political economy is simply false. An illuminating example of their understanding was provided by the editors of the *Prairie Farmer* in connection with the postwar downturn. They explained the "general uneasiness" of the farmers in 1866 as the result of "a general stagnation" of the economy.[34] That evaluation is verified by the reports of metropolitan observers of the time, as well as by modern economists. Thorp's *Business Annals*, for example, characterized the years after the war as follows: 1865, "Boom, recession"; 1866, "Mild depression"; 1867, "depression."[35]

More than a century later, Robert A. Gordon and Abraham Abramovitz supported that crude report through their more advanced and sophisticated methods. Gordon described the fluctuations of the business cycle as moving from a peak in April 1865 to a trough in December 1867. Then came a brief recovery till June 1869, followed by a sharp decline till December 1870. The subsequent gains continued until October 1873, when a major depression struck the economy. It lasted until March 1879.[36] Abramovitz relied on an even more subtle indicator, the rate of growth of the economy. That reached a high point in the first quarter of 1864, and then declined steadily until it hit bottom exactly ten years later.[37] Given those evaluations, the term "general stagnation" does not appear ignorant or irrational. As they had been earlier, and would be again, the agricultural businessmen in 1866 were astute observers of the economic reality that provoked them to complain and agitate. The difficulties generated by the malfunctioning of the marketplace political economy acted, furthermore, to intensify other problems and antagonisms.

Some of those took an economic form, others did not; but almost all of them were related to the rising dissatisfaction with the relationship between the metropolis and the country. The Northern coalition of city and farm that had first confronted the South with a policy of containment, and then defeated the defiant Confederacy, began to unravel even as General William Tecumseh Sherman ripped through Georgia. For that matter, the strong Democratic vote in the elections of 1862 indicated that the alliance had never been put together with a cross-stitch. And the accelerating commercialization of agriculture deepened the Western farmer's awareness and understanding of his inferior position.

Whatever their view of the laws when they had been passed, and that had often been favorable, the agriculturalists rather quickly concluded that the legislation produced by the wartime Union Congress had in practice balanced out in favor of the metropolis. The only unequivocal gain for the farmers, and it could be banked only in the long future, came through the law of July 2, 1862, which opened the way to establish agricultural and mechanical colleges with capital provided by land grants. That commitment, very largely the result of a long and often lonely battle by Jonathan B. Turner of Illinois, promised intellectual and social rewards as well as marketplace profits.

Such was considerably less true of the Homestead Act of May 20, 1862. That legislation had been agitated for a generation, and was afterward uncritically acclaimed by many Americans for at least the proverbial threescore-and-ten. It offered title to a quarter-section of land to any man who would occupy it for five years and make a token payment. The law might have worked, and thereby produced important consequences for American society, if it had been passed sometime between 1785 and 1825, when the expansionist theory of American history and the logic of the safety valve were first formulated and accepted. Coming when it did, however, it was much like the civil rights legislation of the mid-twentieth century: too late, too vague, too weak, and too incidental. The best land was gone, the rules were too easily evaded, the enforcement was too feeble, and it offered little or nothing to help the farmers already operating as commercial entrepreneurs struggling to survive in the marketplace.[38]

The agriculturalists quickly recognized those weaknesses, just as they spotted the feebleness of the Department of Agriculture established in May 1862. The campaign for such action, as the House Committee of Agriculture noted, had been carried on "more or less for the last twenty years"; but it seems doubtful that it would even then have been successful if it had not been for the serious depression that hit the farmers in 1861. The committee report made it clear that a primary objective was to expand exports, and the debate followed that line of analysis.[39] Food exports keep "the balance of trade in our favor," explained Senator Joseph Albert Wright of Indiana, in a typical plea for support from the metropolis.[40]

But Wright accurately anticipated that Eastern opponents would try to sabotage the effort and produce "a mere shadow" of a department. Even President Lincoln pointed to that danger in his letter supporting the measure. He noted that agriculture was "the primary source of national prosperity," and wryly observed that "eulogistic language" produced no profits: as "the homely proverb says 'soft words butter no parsnips.'" "While law-makers have *spoken* very pleasant and truthful *words* about farming and its interests," the President continued, "they have *done* very little *for* this interest." Agriculture, "clad in homespun," was generally "elbowed aside by capital, attired in ten-dollar Yorkshire."[41]

Lincoln's support may have been crucial. Senator Lafayette Sabine Foster of Connecticut led the metropolitan attack on the legislation, protesting against "a fancy Bureau of Agriculture." The amendment he proposed would have gutted the bill. The defense was managed by Senator James Fowler Simmons, who had been a member of the Rhode Island Agricultural Society for forty years. The battle was very close, and Foster's amendment was defeated only on a tie vote. Finally after what Simmons accurately described as "a great deal of trouble," the law was passed on May 10, 1862.[42]

The metropolitan opposition angered the farm businessmen, and the experience contributed to their increasingly skeptical attitude toward their alliance with the city. So did the practical effects of much of the other wartime legislation. The revenue law of July 1, 1862, for example, did tax the high metropolitan incomes, but it also contained excise levies that hurt the farmer because they raised consumer prices. In a similar way, the farmers gained some benefits from the inflationary legal tender acts of February 25, 1863, and June 3, 1864, but those measures operated primarily to increase the concentration of financial power in the metropolis. Connecticut held more of the authorized $300 million banknotes than Kentucky, Tennessee, Michigan, Wisconsin, Minnesota, Iowa, Missouri, and Kansas. That was impressive, to be sure, but Massachusetts did even better: it controlled more than the West and the South combined.

Western agriculturalists increasingly concluded that the tariff laws filled the tills of the metropolis in a similar manner. The first bill, passed February 20, 1861, was generally moderate. It raised individual rates from 5 to 10 percent, and that resulted in an average duty of approximately 30 percent. But the subsequent legislation of 1861, 1862, and 1864 boosted existing schedules, and added levies on consumer items such as coffee, tea, and sugar. Those changes pushed the general rate to 47 percent. Farm businessmen had accepted the early laws as part of the bargain with the Northeast—as a *quid pro quo*, say, for the Homestead Act. But the later increases rapidly generated opposition after the surrender of the Confederacy. The argument that the high rates were necessary to help finance the war no longer applied, and the economic difficulties revived the concern to lower tariffs as a way of expanding exports.

Some farmers bluntly called the tariff a subsidy to the manufacturers, and the assistance given to the Union Pacific Railroad intensified such criticism. The agriculturalists were not misled by the rhetoric about free benefits. They knew from personal experience that they paid most of the taxes that financed such federal internal improvements, and also contributed much other capital for railroad construction through local and state governments. The law of July 1, 1862, for example, gave the Union Pacific 6,500 acres for every mile of track. Two years later (July 2, 1864) the subsidy was doubled. The failure to appropriate comparable sums for other internal improvements dramatized the special treatment of the railroad and aggravated the resentment. By the end of the war, as the farmer knew, the railroads, so largely financed by the citizen, were nevertheless controlled by, and for the benefit of, a small group of metropolitan capitalists.

The money to move the crops, most of which went to the transportation and commercial entrepreneurs, was likewise managed by Eastern financiers. And they used their superior political power within the Republican party to set national monetary policy. They made it clear as early as 1866 that a deflationary policy would be adopted. In their view, at any rate, the gold standard was sacred. The greenbacks would be retired, therefore, even if that decreased the operating capital available to the smaller entrepreneur. The man who had been wealthy enough to lend money to the Union in 1860 and 1861 would receive his just reward for financing freedom, and the metropolis would retain its control of the economic system.

One group of Americans launched a campaign to keep the green-backs in circulation and even increase the supply. The farmers were not prominent in that movement, and their absence has often been interpreted as meaning either that they were so prosperous as to be indifferent to the problem, or so ignorant as not to understand the issue. Both explanations are mistaken. First, the agricultural business-men concentrated their efforts on other proposals considered more important in reforming the marketplace and improving their imme-diate economic position. Second, and despite that emphasis on other measures, the farmers (including the Southerners) did exert pressure that was effective in preventing the greenbacks from being withdrawn from circulation. The Southerners hoarded specie, and the Westerners worked through the two major parties.

The farmers were further disgruntled over the failure to admit more territories as states. President Lincoln found it convenient to welcome one on the eve of two successive elections, Kansas in 1861 and West Virginia in 1863, and Nevada gained recognition in 1864 as part of the effort to insure ratification of the Thirteenth Amendment abol-ishing slavery. But no Western territories were raised to statehood to celebrate the triumph over the Confederacy, or to honor that re-gion's contribution to the victory. And the belated admission of Ne-braska in 1867 served more to intensify the agitation than to satisfy the demand for recognition.

With considerable reason, Westerners viewed territorial govern-ment as a system of quasi-colonial rule by the metropolis. The tradi-tional anger against that inferior position in the political economy was aggravated by the statistics on contributions to the war effort. Illinois, for example, had a population of 1,711,000. It supplied 259,000 enlistments to defeat the Confederacy. But Massachusetts, a center of abolitionist activity, with only slightly fewer people (1,231,000), provided merely 146,000 soldiers to free the slaves. The New Englanders did manage, however, to find enough politicians to dominate all but a few Senate committees.

All those considerations, from the tardiness and weaknesses of the Homestead Act to the distribution of committee chairmanships, con-tributed to the eruption of agricultural unrest as the economy turned downward at the end of the war. The storm had in truth been brew-ing for five years, ever since the Chicago *Times* had warned after the election of 1860 that "the Northwest will not submit to be a vassal to New England."[43] And it gathered increasing power as the Westerners began to conclude in 1862 that "New England is really now our ruler and master. . . . To her we are tributary."[44]

When the turbulence struck at the end of the war, even the first thun-derclaps were awesome. "We believe," cried the Chicago *Times*, "that this country has been run quite long enough under the direction of

New England. . . . We fetch and carry, and bark, and roll over, and fight other dogs precisely as and when we are bidden by our New England master."[45] Nor was the discontent restricted to Westerners. A New Jersey farmer warned that the American metropolis was content with its role as a junior partner in the British Empire, and therefore the agricultural businessmen had to weaken or defeat London in order to break their colonial chains at home. He called for organized political action to control the metropolis and adopt a vigorously independent foreign policy. Otherwise the farmers would "remain virtually slaves to capital and capitalists."[46]

One group of Illinois farmers, no doubt encouraged by the editors of the Chicago *Tribune* and the Chicago *Times*, held such a protest meeting in December 1865. The *Tribune* rapidly took the lead in attacking the metropolis, and in urging Westerners to demand more equitable treatment from the Congress as well as in the marketplace.[47] Iowa farmers were particularly aroused by the policies of the absentee owners of the railroads, and by the way profits on many businesses were drained eastward to the metropolis.[48] After "destroying our great highway to the markets of the world through the Mississippi," roared Henry Clay Dean of Iowa, "New England drove us into her market to be robbed by her carriers on the way. . . . The East now holds the West in her hand with a deadly grasp."[49]

The same attitude appeared in other Western states, and in territories like Dakota.[50] The feeling of farmers that they were caught in a colonial or neocolonial position was not the product of distorted perception or fantasy. The president of the New York State Agricultural Society concluded on the basis of a careful study that the agricultural businessmen were the key to the operation of the entire economy, and accurately predicted that they would provide the wealth to pay the national debt.[51] But while agriculture employed 53.1 percent of the working population in 1869, and produced 53 percent of the nation's output, the farmers received only 31.5 percent of the total income.[52] As for earning capacity in foreign markets, the exports of animal tallow and butter alone matched those of iron and steel.[53] It was not surprising, therefore, that Western leaders like Dean urged the farmers to demand the negotiation and ratification of reciprocity treaties that would encourage even greater exports of agricultural produce. That was the way to end "the robberies and oppressions of the tariff" in the domestic marketplace while expanding the overseas market.[54]

Dean was one among many. The first wave of the developing agricultural assault against the metropolis was launched in response to the effort to raise the tariff even higher. "The agricultural labor of the land," charged Representative Daniel Wolsey Voorhees of Indiana on January 9, "is driven to the counters of the most gigantic monopoly ever sanctioned by law." "Free trade with all the markets of the

world," he declared, "is the true theory of government," and demanded
that it be honored in order to expand exports.[55] That argument was
repeated endlessly during the months that followed. "Many farmers
and agricultural representatives considered the new duties so extreme
as to affect seriously the salability of their products in foreign markets."[56]

Representative John Adam Kasson of Iowa, one of the states that
led the fight, provided a revealing glimpse of how the attack on the
tariff was rapidly integrated with the battle for cheaper transportation. Everything, he explained, revolved around the necessity of larger
foreign markets. Thus it was vital to lower the rates on iron rails. "The
great burden of the West is that it costs so much to get articles to market that it leaves almost nothing as a profit."[57] A lower tariff would
reduce freight charges on the railroads and simultaneously encourage the exporters of the rails to import more agricultural surpluses.

Representative James Falconer Wilson of Iowa was willing to give
"fair and reasonable protection" to metropolitan manufacturers, but
he warned them that a farmer-be-damned policy would drive the West
"into free-trade ideas."[58] The agriculturalists of at least half the trans-
Mississippi region solidly opposed the bill, and they were supported
by their compatriots in Illinois and Indiana.[59] And the McCormick
Company, likewise interested in overseas markets for its surplus implements, added its voice to the outcry. "Agricultural implement makers *can defy the world*," asserted the leaders of the firm. "All we ask
is to be left untrammeled by onerous or special taxation."[60]

The editors of the Chicago *Tribune* delivered a blunt lecture to metropolitan policy makers. "We tell these gentlemen that they are trav-
elling to destruction as fast as they can go. They are cutting open the
goose to get all the golden eggs at once. They are legislating the Government funds into their pockets too rapidly for the permanence of the system."[61] Some Easterners saw the danger. "The practical control of
our political affairs," admitted the *Commercial and Financial Chronicle*, "is destined at no distant date to pass into the hands of the Western
people."[62] One group of Republicans proposed to meet that challenge
by controlling the vote of the South. "In a selfish point of view," one
of them explained candidly, "free suffrage to the Blacks is desirable.
Without their support . . . the long train of evils sure to follow is fearful to contemplate . . . such as a great reduction of the Tariff."[63]

Other metropolitan leaders took a broader view of the problem
and counseled compromise. They understood the risks in trying to
win the political battle with a straight power play in the South, and
recognized the grave economic consequences of damaging agriculture. "If matters are not regulated and on a fairer and juster principle,"
admonished one, "the West will be badly injured before five years."[64]
And if that happened, warned the New York Chamber of Commerce,

the farm businessmen would "soon become so restive" that they could not be controlled.

The Chamber also favored restraint on the tariff in order to avoid closing the foreign markets that were vital to agriculture.[65] That argument was also stressed by Secretary of the Treasury Hugh McCulloch. He clearly understood that his program to withdraw the greenbacks and return to a specie standard depended upon achieving a favorable balance of trade. And that could be done only by maintaining and increasing agricultural exports. The tariff "should be so framed," he explained, "as to encourage exports and enlarge our commerce with foreign nations, so that balances may be in our favor, and the interest, and in due time the principal, of our foreign debt may be paid by our surplus productions."[66]

Working with David A. Wells, who had moved on from agricultural journalism to become Commissioner of the Revenue, Secretary McCulloch tried to maneuver a mildly reformist tariff bill through the Congress. Wells had once been a strong high tariff man; but, as he privately explained in 1866, he had "changed my ideas respecting tariffs and protection very much."[67] The two men won some support from Northern textile leaders who had modified their original stand on the issue. Those manufacturers felt that lower rates might prevent Southerners from becoming effective competitors. Such help was not enough. The McCulloch-Wells effort failed.[68] The protectionists were too strong in the House of Representatives.

The high tariff forces won their victory on the strength of three factors. The crucial element was the enforced absence of Southern representatives. Those votes, added to the Western opposition, would have produced a far more moderate law. The second consideration was the strong, sustained interest-group pressure exerted by metropolitan manufacturers, and the success of one such group in striking a marketplace bargain with an important bloc of farmers. The determined, highly organized effort by the protectionists kept their ranks intact at the same time they divided the opposition.

The key man in cracking the agriculturalists was John L. Hayes, a woolen textile leader who in 1865 organized the National Association of Wool Manufacturers. His strategy was subtle and effective because he avoided going to the Congress as a manufacturing lobby that could be discounted as a private raiding party on the Treasury. Instead, Hayes maneuvered for a deal with organizations of wool growers like the Ohio Wool Growers Association that had appeared across the country from Vermont to Illinois. "Our objective," he explained to other manufacturers, "is to convince the farmers of the West who will inevitably control the legislature of this country of the absolute identity of our interests."

Hayes was not quite that persuasive during a meeting with the sheep farmers in Syracuse during December 1865, but he was effective enough to arrange a very significant *quid pro quo*. The farmers were promised support for a high tariff on raw wool in return for throwing their weight behind a rate on woolen goods that would enable the manufacturers to pay the increased domestic price and still make a profit in competition with imports.[69] On that basis, Hayes and the wool growers appealed to the Congress as a broad coalition that fairly represented the harmony of interests between the town and the country. They were influential enough to win vital votes from representatives from Ohio, Michigan, Indiana, and Illinois.[70]

Though his efforts were important, Hayes was not solely responsible for the crucial split among Westerners. His campaign benefited enormously from the extensive propaganda barrage that Henry C. Carey and others laid down against the low tariff forces. That was the third source of protectionist power. It was also the first bombardment in a long metropolitan campaign that vilified low tariff advocates as traitorous conspirators in the pay of Great Britain, as traitorous allies of the evil South, or sometimes, more generously, as merely ignorant sodbusters duped by such villains.

Carey's strategy for winning converts to protection was based less on tight economic logic than upon an emotional appeal to defeat Great Britain and win supremacy in the markets of the world. His major polemic of 1865 was a nationalistic handbook on *The Way to Outdo England Without Fighting Her*. The instructions were simple: raise the tariff and increase the money supply. That program would "gain and keep possession of foreign markets." Not, of course, for the farmer; but Carey assured the agricultural businessmen that they would be rewarded with a vast and ever-expanding home market. By concentrating on that market, moreover, the farmer would be freed from worrying about "the oppressive tax of transportation."[71]

One of Carey's associates, Treasury Department official William Elder, developed a more sophisticated argument to win the Westerners. He appealed to the widespread consciousness of being a colonial in one's own country, and to the equally general concern with export markets. The Western states, he admitted, were "Anglo-Saxon colonies." But the only way to break out of that inferior, dependent position was by adopting a policy based on the protective tariff. That would create a great home market, and also generate industrial progress in the West itself.

Elder knew, however, that the farm businessmen criticized the home market argument because, even in theory, it offered few immediate benefits. He met the issue frontally, agreeing that the farmer needed foreign markets until the country became fully industrialized. His answer was to preempt the markets of Latin America. "The time has come, the necessity is upon us, our security and prosperity demand the extension of the Monroe Doctrine to the commerce of the continent."[72] Elder's combination of candor and expansionism may well have been more effective in persuading some farmers to stay with the tariff than Carey's cruder approach.[73] It also is possible that Elder was the innovator who created the hybrid tariff policy, by mixing protection with market expansion, that James Gillespie Blaine later refined and used so effectively to keep the Western farmers in the Republican party.

For the most part, however, the metropolitan protectionists relied in 1866 on Carey's conspiracy argument. The situation was critical, he warned, because the low tariff advocates were "guided by British agents." Unless stopped, they would "make the country little more than a mere puppet in the hands of foreign traders."[74] That specter of evil men destroying the commonwealth was invoked by many high tarrif leaders. "In the . . . traitorous section of Northern politics," screamed the New York *Tribune*, "it is consistent for Americans to advocate and plot with foreigners British Free Trade."[75] "I hope," Senator Benjamin Franklin Wade of Ohio observed in horror, "we shall not be gulled by this song of free trade from across the ocean. 'Take no counsel of your enemies' is the first lesson of war."[76]

Edward B. Ward, a Detroit iron master, carried the battle directly to the Wisconsin State Agricultural Society. "The man who supports free trade," he admonished the members, "is an enemy to the country, and to the good of the Northwest."[77] And the message was dispatched everywhere in pamphlets with titles that carried the warning: *Protection Not British Free Trade*, and *The American Policy—Its Benefits to the West*. The campaign probably confused a good number of agricultural businessmen even if it did not convince them of the wisdom of protection. Those who did become true believers recited the catechism as well as Carey. "British Gold," announced the Wyandotte, Kansas, *Gazette*, "is operating to secure American legislation for British interests."[78] The more general result was a weakening of confidence among low tariff forces. "If there is any question upon which we of the West are hopelessly adrift and unsettled," concluded the Emporia *News*, "it is that of a protective tariff."[79]

The West was strong enough, however, to block a final vote in the Congress before the elections of 1866. Metropolitan Republicans were shrewd enough to avoid any serious discussion of the tariff during the campaign. They concentrated instead on refighting the Civil War, issuing dire warnings about the subversive dangers of voting Democratic, and making attacks on the character and policies of President Andrew Johnson. Johnson himself was harried, perplexed, and on the defensive about the issues of reconstruction and the changes in American society. Neither he nor other Democratic leaders rallied the farmers around the tariff issue, and the Republicans overran both the House of Representatives and the Senate.

The protectionists shortly passed the bill raising tariff rates (March 2, 1867). The farmers were neither indifferent nor resigned, but they had been defeated in the election and had lost their momentum. They were also distracted, at least for a time, by the resurgent Radical campaign to change the South in ways that would make it more nearly a modern marketplace society. And, at the same time, the farmers were briefly encouraged by the spurt in European purchases that raised prices and increased exports.[80] The impact of the boomlet that began in 1867 was enlarged beyond its true import by the intense export consciousness that existed among almost all farmers. Senator John Brooks Henderson of Missouri provided an excellent statement of that attitude in July 1866: "We want a market for our wheat; we want a market for our corn; we want a market for the thousands of agricultural productions that we have in the West for which we can get no markets in this country."[81] Local leaders sang the same song. "The first need," judged the Junction City *Weekly Union*, "is for a market for the surplus products."[82]

Cheese makers admitted they enjoyed a "large export trade that controlled the British market, and even included sales to China," but they insisted that "something must be done in opening up new markets."[83] John Deere and Cyrus McCormick were engaged in a bitter contest to win supremacy in agricultural implement markets from Europe through Latin America to Asia. And while they benefited from increased exports in 1866, the wheat farmers were worried about the "dangerous rivalry of Russia," and the harsh truth that "Liverpool prices regulate our markets."[84] Some Minneapolis leaders were so export-oriented that they were looking beyond control of the world's flour market to winning supremacy in cotton textiles. "For teas and raw silks, and the productions of that ancient, still dreaming Asiatic world we will exchange our cotton fabrics."[85] The millers themselves, however, were more intensely concerned about competition from rivals in Milwaukee and California for the existing markets.[86] They created the Minneapolis Millers' Association in 1867 in order to improve their bargaining power and capture a larger share of the exports.

Similar organizations were arising among cattlemen, as with the Colorado Stock Growers Association formed in 1867. That agricultural business, based on marketing grass and grain in what came to be called "the condensed form," was being established from Texas to Montana.[87] Portus B. Weare of Iowa provided a good example of how men carried the export orientation from one kind of farming to another. He made his first fortune by exporting prairie chickens during the Civil War, then shifted to exporting buffalo robes, next became an export broker in wheat, and finally turned to exporting live cattle. That business was not large in 1867 - 1868, but the foundations were being secured. Nelson Morris of Chicago, for example, exported some live cattle and dressed beef. And John B. Sutherland and William Davis of Detroit vied for the best patent for transporting refrigerated meat on railroads. Davis won, and his "ice houses on wheels" carried most of the slaughtered beef during the next decade.[88]

Agricultural conditions unquestionably improved during 1867 and 1868, but the extent of the gains has often been exaggerated. Statistics after the experience often blur the perception of reality. Wisconsin farmers, for example, entered a serious recession in 1867. A wheat grower from another Midwestern state tried "to save the commission" by ordering a reaper direct from the McCormick factory. And the upturn failed to solve the problems that St. Louis leaders faced in trying to recover their prewar position in the export trade.[89] The Chicago Board of Trade, moreover, was far more impressed with the underlying weaknesses in the economy than by the irregular improvement.[90] So was John W. Stokes, acting Commissioner of Agriculture. He made a direct appeal to the "rural voters" to "correct the evil" of exorbitant transportation costs, and called on the Congress to appropriate much larger sums for internal improvements.[91]

The farmers needed no prompting from Washington. They had turned away from the tariff issue and were again concentrating on the demand for more and cheaper transportation. Chicago and New York groups had tried unsuccessfully in 1863 to induce the Congress to enlarge the Erie Canal for oceangoing vessels as part of an effort to make "all nations pay tribute, and bow before the sceptre of our commerce."[92] Joined by supporters in Michigan, Wisconsin, and Minnesota, the Illinois farmers returned to the battle after 1865. All the top wheat-producing states (Illinois ranked first, Minnesota seventh, in 1869) joined the agitation within two years.[93]

The Wisconsin legislature wanted various canals, while Representative Ignatius Donnelly of Minnesota concentrated on regulating the railroads, which he considered "as important to that country as population." The Minnesota legislature, however, wanted improvements on the Mississippi River, which in its view "is now and ever will be and remain the great regulator and moderator of fare and freights" of the rails.[94] Such agitation quickly produced a major transportation convention in Dubuque, Iowa. "No general question of governmental policy," observed a Senate committee, "occupies at this time so prominent a place in the thoughts of the people." And at Dubuque the farmers and merchants discussed the best way to win control of "the markets of the world." They wanted better transportation "to control the price of breadstuffs in the very center of the world's trade."[95]

One transportation leader, John B. Garrett of the Baltimore and

Ohio Railroad, had committed himself to that general strategy as a way of surviving the bitter competition among the rails. Operating as a "virtual dictator" after taking charge of the firm in 1858, Garrett immediately moved at the end of the war to double-track his lines to the West and to acquire rights of way into St. Louis and Chicago.[96] His objective was to raise profits by giving the Western farmers "the shortest and cheapest outlet to the ocean."[97] Arguing that "exports" were the key to the prosperity of Baltimore itself, he responded favorably to the "anxiety" of Cincinnati leaders "to have the cattle business" controlled by those two cities.[98] He also acted to provide direct shipping services from Baltimore to Liverpool. The first freighter sailed September 30, 1865, and the traffic proved great enough to add four more steamers by the spring of 1869. As a result, Garrett arranged to quote the farmers a through rate from Western cities to Liverpool.[99]

Garrett next moved to deepen the Baltimore ship channel and to expand flour exports to Latin America. He won strong support from Jay Cooke of the Northern Pacific Railroad. "I have always considered Baltimore," Cooke explained, "as a natural outlet of the vast northwestern trade now being rapidly developed."[100] Garrett generated enough pressure to win a $400,000 appropriation from the Congress, and while the dredging was under way he supplied the capital to build elevators capable of holding 2 million bushels of wheat at dockside. If more railroad leaders had displayed Garrett's willingness to pursue metropolitan interests (and profits) in a way that accommodated the needs of agricultural businessmen, then much of the anger and opposition of the farmers might very well have been allayed. Such was not the case, however, particularly at the end of the 1860s, and the campaign for better and more equitable transportation grew increasingly militant and bitter.

"You cripple the great West," charged Senator Henderson.[101] The report of the central committee of the great River Improvement Convention held in St. Louis in February 1867 not only amplified that accusation, but in doing so clarified the intimate relationship between the export orientation of the farmers and their concern with transportation. If the West "can only export from the abundance of its surplus," explained the committee, "and its ability to undersell, it can monopolize the markets of the world, and . . . have a balance on the world's counter in our favor to raise our credit and pay our debts." "It . . . the question of ability to produce, but it is . . . . it is not the question of facility and cheapness of transportation," the members emphasized, "which must be solved before we can monopolize the markets of the world."

"This valley is entitled to the cheapest possible transportation," the convention declared, calling on the Congress for immediate and massive assistance.[102] Combined with the similar campaign for railroad regulation, which produced state commissions in Ohio (1867) and Massachusetts (1869), the battle for improved water navigation produced a major confrontation between the metropolis and the neocolonial agrarians. The moderate, spotty, and short-lived economic upturn did not modify the intensity of the antagonism. As many observers commented, "politics are more than boiling."[103]

More fuel was being gathered for the fire by the leaders who were organizing farmers throughout the country. A typical report told of an "enthusiastic Farmers' Club" and a "flourishing agricultural society" being formed in the same state.[104] The movement that rapidly united the agricultural resistance to the metropolis, however, and focused its energies, grew out of the efforts of Oliver Hudson Kelley of the Department of Agriculture. His tour of the South, undertaken at the instance of President Johnson, convinced him that the farmers of that section, particularly, needed sustained encouragement and help in order to improve their condition. Aided by William Saunders and a few other government officials, Kelley founded the Patrons of Husbandry on December 4, 1867.

Southern farmers responded to Kelley's initiative, and to the talented and dedicated leadership of men like David Wyatt, John T. Jones, and Putnam Israel Darden, but Westerners provided most of the early support that established the Grange as an effective organization. They also made it a national force to be reckoned with by the metropolis. For, contrary to much that has been written about the Grange, it functioned from the outset as an instrument of policy-conscious farm businessmen in all parts of the country. The minutes of a local chapter in Alabama, for example, record that the members agreed to "discuss at each meeting such subjects as would be most important to us for the advancement of our social, agricultural and financial, as well for the improvement of our literary, attainments." A few years later, reviewing the activities of his organization, Master Albert B. Smedley of the Iowa Grange made the point even more bluntly. "There can be no doubt but that this order will largely influence legislation."[105]

Although they were defeated on the tariff and transportation issues, therefore, and while some of them benefited from the short period of uneven economic improvement that began in 1867, the farmers nevertheless maintained and intensified their pressure on the metropolis. They sustained the campaign to improve their position in the marketplace as it existed, and to guarantee their long-term prosperity by enlarging the marketplace. Their general unrest, and their continued stress on exports, increasingly affected the thinking and the policies of the metropolis, moreover, even before the Grange and other organizations exerted direct influence on the legislative process.

The failure of the modest upturn of 1867 to arrest the farm agitation, for example, strengthened the concern among metropolitan interests that the greenbacks were being withdrawn from circulation too rapidly. A majority of congressmen concluded by February 4, 1868, that Secretary McCulloch's deflationary policy was dangerous enough—either on economic or on political grounds—to call a halt. They ordered him to stop the process, leaving more than $300 million of the notes in circulation. The Republicans also indicated their awareness of the agricultural ferment by equivocating on the tariff during the presidential campaign of 1868.

They were not at all hesitant, however, in reminding the farmers that both of the party's top candidates, Ulysses Simpson Grant and Schuyler Colfax, were Westerners. And regardless of the extent to which metropolitan leaders of the party understood the point (and it was probably slight), Grant had absorbed at least one of the principal ideas of his Illinois environment. Perhaps his prewar identification with the Democratic party, and in particular with Senator Douglas, explained the matter, but in any event he promptly revealed that he understood and supported the farm demand for larger overseas markets. His persistent advocacy of that policy helped them increase their influence during the next few years. Neither he nor they, however, won any major gains for agriculture.

FIVE

I am out of money and where the next corn meal is coming from I don't yet know. . . . Buffalo is very scarce now and hard to get. . . . I find it uphill business without money. I have turned pretty mean.

Mrs. L. A. Ives of Kansas,
October 1, 1872

The East wants to consolidate capital and nationalize and centralize every thing and the Union Pacific Railroad is the great lever by which to do this in the West.

Oliver P. Mason to J. Sterling
Morton, February 6, 1868

Our form of government is adapted to civilized man everywhere. . . . Great as we are, we are yet in the day of small things. . . . [Our] destiny is to grasp the commerce of all the seas and sway the sceptre of the world.

Representative Ignatius Donnelly
of Minnesota, July 1, 1868

Our diplomacy will be rescued from the subservient tone by which we have so often been humiliated. . . . And we will see [the extension] of our flag and our sovereignty over insular or continental possessions.

Representative James Gillespie
Blaine of Maine,
December 10, 1868

Too large a part of the value of [the farmers'] productions is consumed in the cost of getting them to a point where the exchanges are made. As is well known, the markets of England fix the price at which nearly all the productions of our country are sold, whether for export or consumption in our own country.

James M. Richards, President of the Chicago
Board of Trade, April 1869

The great obstacle in the way of our more rapid commercial development is the enormous cost of transportation from the West to the seaboard.

Commercial and Financial Chronicle,
November 20, 1869

Go among the farmers of the West. The hours of toil are lengthening; labor is poorly rewarded; with a ceaseless struggle to keep poverty away from their doors.

Representative Samuel Scott Marshall
of Illinois, March 29, 1870

Railways. . . . are hereby declared public highways. . . . And the General Assembly shall. . . . pass laws establishing reasonable maximum rates of charges.

Illinois Constitution of 1870

I am simply a tenant on my own farm. . . . I am not consulted as to the share of my crop which transportation companies may require to lay the surplus in a market.

Railroads are now not only national but international.

Proceedings of the Iowa State Agricultural
Society, January 1873

Cheap transportation *is vital to our prosperity.*
Proceedings of the Bloomington, Illinois
Farmers' Convention, January 1873

Let the North, especially New England, beware. The South
and West will not forever be content to pay tribute
to the North.
Lynchburg *Virginian,* April 11, 1873

Economic
Troubles Intensify Existing
Difficulties and Generate
a Rising Demand for
Larger Markets and
Cheaper Transportation

W HATEVER the gains that some farmers enjoyed during the brief revival that began in 1867, the downturn that came in 1869 inflicted increasing pain and suffering on all agricultural businessmen. They responded with rising anger, and greater determination to win the reforms—and new programs—they considered vital to their welfare. Grange membership climbed steadily in every section, and the efforts of that organization were reinforced by the activities of other farm groups. The result was a nationwide campaign for expanded markets, improved and regulated transportation, and a more equitable and effective monetary system.

The farmers won some victories. Various states passed laws, or created commissions, designed to protect the farm businessmen (and merchants) against unfair and harmful railroad practices. The Congress appropriated a bit more money for internal improvements, slowed the retirement of the greenbacks, lowered the tariff a mite, and ultimately undertook a serious investigation of the transportation problem. From a long-range point of view, however, the most important gains came in the deepened awareness and self-consciousness among the farmers, and in the inception of a new attitude among some metropolitan leaders. The latter not only recognized the seriousness of the agricultural unrest, but they began to respond to (and even adapt) the market expansionist argument that the farmers had been advocating for more than a generation. That was a portentous change, though it initially involved only a minority in the metropolis. It established the influence of the agricultural majority, and it pointed toward the ultimate acceptance of their strategy of marketplace expansion as the policy of the nation.

In the short run, however, the battles that the farmers won between 1868 and 1874 did little—if anything—to improve their position in the political economy. The metropolis retained effective control of the economic system and the policy-making process, and the economy itself continued its downward slide toward the massive depression of 1873-1879. It is important to realize, in discussing those bad years, that the farmer recognized, and generally accepted, the inherent difficulties of his particular kind of business operation. If anything, he was too understanding and enduring; certainly he complained little if at all when the marketplace rewarded him with anything close to a reasonable profit. And even during the depressions, he could distinguish between the usual woes of the world and the special pains of the marketplace, as one farmer typically did in 1869, explaining that a neighbor's problems were Freudian rather than Smithian. "He accused her of flirting with some younger men in this neighbourhood [and] he said he was drowning sorrow with whiskey."[1]

A different tone emerged when one's labor produced no purchase to hold one's own as a commercial entrepreneur—let alone leverage for improvement. Then the days were as long as weeks, and the months as years. From gathering buffalo chips at dawn to sharpening plows at midnight, the life properly provoked men to angry complaint, and women to tears and psychic terrors. Even so, the saving controls of insight and self-awareness generally held firm. As with Mrs. L. A. Ives of Kansas. "We are all well at present," she wrote a friend after three years of the agricultural depression, "and able to eat our rations of Johnny Cake for we have nothing else to eat. . . . I am out of money and where the next corn meal is coming from I don't yet know. . . . Buffalo is very scarce now and hard to get. . . . I find it uphill business without money. I have turned pretty mean."[2]

Or as with a Minnesota man who suffered hail and prairie fires in addition to low prices. "I have been trying to live on my place and with sickness and bad luck in crops have well nigh run out of everything," he finally wrote the governor in 1871. "I have been sick for months and my wife is not well from exposure and hunger and I thought that there was no other way than to ask you to help me. . . . If I can't get the money I shall lose my place after livin' from hand to mouth for three years on the frontier."[3]

Such were the personal documents—the reality—behind the growing public agitation. From the South, *DeBow's Review* reported on the "unanimous hostility to the monopolies of Eastern capital and transportation."[4] In the East, the *American Agriculturalist* said bluntly that "times *are* hard."[5] Even the Philadelphia *Press* recognized the crisis: "The farmer gets one-half of the price he received for his wheat two years ago, but he must pay nearly the same for what he buys."[6] Midwesterners made the same reports: "financial pressure," "altogether ruined many men . . . almost a panic," "hopelessly in debt," "need relief . . . something should be done," "a ceaseless struggle to keep poverty away from their doors," "ruined farmers bankrupt everybody in these small towns."[7]

"Our farmers," the manager of a Nebraska firm warned the McCormicks, "are . . . certainly in a deplorable condition."[8] And the editors of the *Prairie Farmer* summarized the general feeling with the judgment that "a crisis in our affairs is approaching and danger threatens."[9] The farm businessmen were not mollified by being told by metropolitan leaders that they were "deluded."[10] Or by the speculators who saw the crisis as a marvelous opportunity "to get good land."[11] Nor was it enough for farm wives to read learned papers proving that agricultural businessmen needed culture as much as their urban counterparts. One argued persuasively, for example, that an appreciation of color could even be important in the work routine. "A great railroad catastrophe may be the result of a locomotive engineer not having 'an eye for color.'"[12] The issue in the minds of her audience, however, was the great agricultural catastrophe caused by the failure of the railroad managers to develop an eye for the primary interest of the political economy.

Some regions, of course, fared better than others. After the best land in Iowa had been taken (by 1868), for example, the forces that ultimately produced the great Dakota boom created an early period of profitable investment. The St. Paul and Pacific Railroad and the Northern Pacific line reached the Red River; a future giant of the rails, James Jerome Hill, inaugurated steamboat service on that river; a federal land office was opened; and a stagecoach line was established. Many farmers shared the excited confidence of the Dakota Territorial Legislature: "Here is a place for a man to rebuild his fortune again; here there need be no destitute, for all that will work there is abundance."[13] But "thousands left soon after they had come," and the lasting gains were delayed at least a decade.[14]

Many in Kansas enjoyed a period of relatively good years. Crops were generally good, and livestock raising developed enough by 1870 for Armour, Plankinton Company to build a meat-packing plant in Kansas City.[15] The first big grain elevator, with a capacity of 100,000 bushels, was constructed a year later. But the prosperity was not sufficient to transform commercial agriculture into a gay adventure. The frontier was "such a desolate place," recalled one pioneer, that "the tears came in my eyes." "We never could see a neighbor's light in the evening." Nor were the profits large enough to provide many improvements. Houses were "unplastered and heated only by our cookstove."[16] And the livestock farmers were a minority because that kind of diversification required capital that most of the new settlers did not have. The majority shared the feelings of the Girard *Press*. "We are tired of this system of corn, without hogs or cattle to eat it up. Corn! Corn!! Corn!!! bah!"[17]

While it is clear that the agricultural sector of the capitalist economy revealed such variations, therefore, too much can be made of those differences. Not only were the farm businessmen faring badly as a group, and organizing to improve their situation, but some metropolitan leaders recognized the need to respond to that reality. The election of 1868 dramatized that point, for Grant's popular majority was barely more than 300,000 of a total of 5,715,000 votes. As they considered the implications of that narrow margin, Eastern spokesmen could not avoid the continuing agrarian protest.

Iowa politicians made it clear, for example, that the transportation issue had generated political forces that would not disappear after the inauguration of Grant.[18] And Representative Cadwallader Colden Washburn of Wisconsin, a staunch ally of metropolitan interests, had attacked the railroads as part of his effort to keep the farmers in line during the campaign.[19] One metropolitan observer bluntly explained the root cause of the trouble. "The East wants to consolidate capital and nationalize and centralize everything and the Union Pacific Railroad is the great lever by which to do this in the West."[20] The truth of the charge provoked an executive of the road, Grenville Mellen Dodge, to a burst of sectional anger that overrode his business loyalties. "Like all roads," he exploded, the Union Pacific was "managed a thousand miles away—the mere play thing for Wall Street, to be set up or down as a circus."[21]

Throughout the presidential campaign, moreover, the farmers stressed the export issue.[22] They maintained that pressure without interruption. The Louisville Board of Trade, for example, was only one of many groups that warned the metropolis during the winter of 1868-1869 that "cheap transportation . . . is not only a necessity to the West, but equally demanded by the best interests of the whole country."[23] And the farmers greeted President Grant with more of the same as he moved into the White House. Henry C. Wheeler of Illinois issued a bold call for an April convention to deal with "the excessive rates of transportation" that denied rural businessmen any "margin of profit." The meeting produced a strong resolution demanding that "our legal rights to transportation and markets ought to be clearly set forth and defined."[24]

The *Kansas Farmer* agreed, and urged agricultural businessmen to speak "in tones of thunder" and win their "share of government aid."[25] The message was already being heard by the more sensitive metropolitan representatives, however, as the new president of the

Chicago Board of Trade revealed on taking office. The farmer was in serious trouble, James M. Richards explained, because "too large a part of the value of his productions is consumed in the cost of getting them to a point where the exchanges are made. As is well known, the markets of England fix the price at which nearly all the productions of our country are sold, whether for export or consumption in our own country."[26]

Such truths were indeed "well known" to the agriculturalists, and the knowledge had much to do with their increasingly strong anti-British nationalism, as well as their agitation for larger markets and transportation reforms. Three metropolitan Republican leaders took the lead in responding to those emotions and demands. The prophet of the group was outgoing Secretary of State Seward, who first tried to harness the expansionism of the West to his own imperial purposes during the late 1840s and the 1850s. The others were New England politicians, Representative James Gillespie Blaine of Maine and Senator Charles Sumner of Massachusetts. A fourth key figure was incoming President Grant, who quickly revealed an understanding of the farm concern with new markets and displayed a willingness to act on that program. And, like Seward, Grant argued that various Caribbean islands were worth the effort involved in acquiring them.

Both men faced similar difficulties. The nation was preoccupied with the problems and the opportunities of the postwar era, and even men who were generally favorable to expansion divided over specific projects. Blaine offered a good illustration of that pattern, for he opposed some imperial proposals. He did reveal as early as March 1865, however, that he understood the role of commodity exports (such as wheat and cotton) in the operation of the American economy. He therefore fought measures like the short-lived export tax on cotton on the grounds that they delayed reestablishing the American "monopoly of this article in the markets of the world." That was "among the most desirable objects for the whole country that can possibly be obtained."[27] Blaine also felt that a policy favorable to the cotton interests would help the Republicans build a solid political base in the South. His commercial expansionism gave him a rapport with the farm businessmen that most other metropolitan leaders gained only much later. That market expansionism was at least as important, moreover, in generating and sustaining Blaine's anti-British posture and policies as the political strategy of attacking the British to win the votes of Irish immigrants in the Eastern cities. Blaine seriously intended, from an early date, to win economic supremacy of the world for the United States.

Sumner appealed to agricultural antagonism toward Britain for purposes that had little to do with economic expansion. Sumner was not flatly opposed to American expansion, but he was primarily concerned with other issues: freeing and helping the black man, punishing Southerners who had supported the Confederacy, establishing the Republican party as the dominant political power in the South (and hence the nation), and fostering manufacturers and other urban economic interests in the North. The crucial factor in his decision to support Seward's bid to buy Alaska in 1867 was very probably his abiding anger at Britain for aiding the Confederacy. He always considered that the American Revolution made England an interloper in the Western Hemisphere, and Britain's actions during the Civil War intensified that opposition. He was also affected, as a Massachusetts man, by the Secretary's enthusiastic argument about trade with Asia — and by the activity of his constituents in that commerce.[28] His powerful speech clearly helped produce the overwhelming Senate vote in favor of annexation (37 to 2, on April 9, 1867).[29] Neither "nay" came from an agricultural region.

Seward and the Senate expansionists did encounter resistance in the House of Representatives from congressmen of the West, as well as from men of the metropolis. Representative Jehu Baker of Illinois, for example, agreed with the editors of *The New York Times* that America had "enough territory"—"at the present time." As Baker's phrasing indicates, however, most of the Westerners hedged their opposition. The *Times* said simply that the problems of reconstruction claimed first priority.[30] But Baker displayed the kind of ideological and economic logic that ultimately carried many who fought the purchase of Alaska into open support for expansion. He admitted, even in 1867 - 1868, that he accepted the validity of the traditional arguments "governing the growth of the republic." For the moment, however, the United States possessed "a fair-sized empire" in the relatively unexploited trans-Mississippi West, and he feared that "raw, shallow, and heedless greed" would subvert necessary expansion in the future. After a period of development, he concluded, Americans could again "extend their frontiers."[31]

Many other Westerners projected the same principles to a different conclusion. Representative William Mungen of Ohio vigorously approved acquiring Alaska because it would enable the United States to "cage the British lion on the Pacific coast."[32] Perhaps the most significant Western argument for annexation was made by Representative Ignatius Donnelly of Minnesota, shortly to become a leader of the Grange and a militant advocate of the agricultural cause throughout the remainder of the century. His vigorous speech on July 1, 1868, contained the central ideological and economic themes that were even then creating a powerful force for nationalistic expansion among the farmers of the country.

Donnelly acknowledged that "the time was not ripe" for expansion because of the nation's domestic preoccupations, but immediately asserted that perfect timing was not the issue. The question had to be viewed in a "broader light." His illumination revealed that the acquisition of Alaska was "one of the necessary steps in the expansion of our institutions and nationality." "Our form of government is adapted," he explained, "to civilized man everywhere." Thus the annexation of Alaska would seal the doom of the aristocratic and autocratic British in North America and hence weaken them generally. But that was not all. "Great as we are," Donnelly promised, "we are yet in the day of small things." America's true "destiny is to grasp the commerce of all the seas and sway the sceptre of the world." That process would of course bring the nation "face to face with the four hundred millions of the Chinese empire and with the other vast populations of India and Japan." "Let us then," he cried, "while perfecting our institutions, not refuse to expand our boundaries."[33] Having offered expansion for reform, for territory, and for markets, Donnelly relinquished the floor to those who chose to stress but one of the objectives.

A good many Westerners emphasized the markets. Representative Green Berry Raum of Illinois wanted Alaska in order to speed the process of becoming "the leading commercial nation of earth" controlling "the whole of the rich trade of the East."[34] So did Representative James Augustus Johnson of California.[35] Others, like Representative Rufus Paine Spaulding of Ohio, wanted to concentrate first on establishing American predominance in the Western Hemisphere.[36] Perhaps Representatives Hiram Price and William Loughridge of Iowa best revealed the tension among (and within) the agricultural spokesmen. The latter complained bitterly of the way the metropolis made decisions committing the nation and then asked the majority to pay the cost.[37]

Price was even more critical, and stressed the need for direct and immediate help in improving the position of the farmer in the existing world marketplace. He thought it would be better to use the $7.2 million "for the purpose of removing obstructions in the Mississippi River, thus improving navigation and commerce, and enabling breadstuffs to be transported cheaply from the West to the seaboard."[38] When the vote was taken, however, on July 14, 1868, neither Price nor Loughridge said "nay." But the Westerners who did so (many of whom were from Iowa and Illinois) emphasized the points those two men had raised, rather than any basic opposition to expansion.[39]

Westerners raised more objections to Seward's later attempt to buy the Danish West Indies. The decision on that issue also came in the House, in response to a resolution offered by Cadwallader Washburn of Wisconsin. The episode revealed two important features of all congressional voting records. One was that the geographic home of the spokesman did not necessarily define his outlook. The other was that agricultural businessmen were perfectly capable of discriminating between proposals that offered them meaningful benefits and those that did not. Washburn nicely illustrated both points. He largely identified with the metropolis on economic and political issues until the flour industry turned to overseas markets to maintain its profits. And, after that, he and other spokesmen of that processing business concentrated on the markets most rewarding to them.

Neither of those conditions applied, however, in connection with acquiring the Virgin Islands. Hence Washburn moved to block the action by committing the House to the following proposition: "That, in the present financial condition of the country any further purchases of territory are inexpedient, and this House will hold itself under no obligation to vote money to pay for any such purchases unless there is greater necessity for the same than now exists."[40] The emphasis on peculiar and particular circumstances and the loopholes in that motion left the issue of expansion per se wide open for future discussion — and a different decision. Those considerations no doubt contributed to the vote — 93 to 43 in favor — as did the anger of men like Loughridge against metropolitan leaders who presumed on their power. Even so, more than half the votes against Washburn's resolution were cast by Western spokesmen, and less than half the "yeas" came from such men. [41]

The crosscurrents and eddies that characterized agricultural attitudes and actions on specific foreign policy issues between 1865 and 1868 continued to be present after the election of 1868. But the farmers, along with some metropolitan leaders, nevertheless continued to create persistent movement toward a policy emphasizing overseas market expansion. Much of the backing and filling of the immediate postwar period can be explained, for that matter, by the failure of national leaders to offer choices that spoke to the existing agricultural emphasis on such expansion. The farmers made their objectives known, but little was done to devise policies appropriate to those goals.

Blaine recognized the situation, and quickly tried to use the change in administrations to create a new feeling about foreign policy. The election of Grant, he argued on December 10, 1868, offered the country an opportunity to deal with the present and the future instead of continuing to concentrate so heavily on the past. The issues of the Civil War and Reconstruction were being handled in a satisfactory manner, he argued, and hence the time had come to step forth boldly in world affairs. "Our diplomacy will be rescued from the subservient tone" of recent years, he asserted, and the nation would proceed with "the extension of our flag and our sovereignty over insular or continental possessions."[42]

Sumner was more immediately effective, however, in focusing the new economic nationalism and the traditional anti-British sentiment among agriculturalists on the demand that London pay extensive damages for its aid to the Confederacy. His extremist speech of April 13, 1869, suggested that the bill came to $2.125 billion, and offered to settle for a deed to Canada. The agricultural support for standing firm undoubtedly strengthened the position of American negotiators in the talks that began during the summer. But there was far more than Civil War emotionalism behind the agrarian opposition to Britain. The farmers had come to focus on Liverpool's control of commodity prices as a major barrier to their market expansionism. Some of them, moreover, Easterners as well as Westerners, wanted the fertile land of Canada. And a steadily increasing number of grain producers were determined to stop the importation of Canadian wheat under the reciprocity treaty of 1854.

The issue of Canadian competition arose before Grant was inaugurated, and some Republican leaders though it would be possible to satisfy the farmers—and gain other objectives—by persuading the Canadians to improve transportation on the St. Lawrence River in return for renewing the treaty. That strategy appealed to metropolitan leaders who understood the importance of agricultural exports, who anticipated a growing Canadian market for urban products, and who recognized the need to meet the demand for cheaper transportation. "The great obstacle in the way of our more rapid commercial development is the enormous cost of transportation from the West to the seaboard," explained the *Commercial and Financial Chronicle*. "The fullest competition between the railroads and canals of both countries is the best possible means by which to obtain control of the European markets as an outlet for our surplus products."[43]

Western farm businessmen quickly counterattacked. Commissioner of Agriculture Horace Capron immediately entered a "vigorous protest" against renewing the treaty: he could not "see the justice of subjecting farmers to a direct and ruinous competition." He also revealed the intensity of antimetropolitan feeling among the farmers when he accused the pro-treaty forces of using agriculture as a pawn to win benefits for the fishing interest.[44] When that objection did not settle the matter, Capron and Western congressmen increased their pressure. Led by Representative James Abram Garfield of Ohio, they used the dispute as a platform for demanding relief from "the distress of the West, arising from a lack of cheap transportation."[45] The force of the campaign, though it was negative, was effective. The treaty was not renewed. The effort also increased the Grant Administration's concern with finding overseas markets for the farmers, and pushed it toward dealing with the transportation issue in a more direct fashion.

The President's responsiveness to the expansionism of the farm businessmen, and his understanding of the importance of agricultural exports, have been generally overlooked in the concentration on his personal weaknesses and mistakes, and on the scandals during his tenure in office. But Grant's awareness of the issue was clearly reinforced by the advice and pressure of associates like Secretary of War John H. Rawlins, who had given strong support to the expansionist programs advanced by Senator Douglas (Grant's own choice for President in 1860), and pushed the same policies in his relationship with Grant.[46] The President wasted no time in speaking to the issue, discussing the problem in his first annual message in December 1869. Rising competition from other agricultural suppliers posed a serious challenge. "Self-interest, if not self-preservation . . . teaches us also the necessity of looking to other markets for the sale of our surplus. Our neighbors south of us, and China and Japan, should receive our special attention."[47]

Agricultural businessmen agreed, but concentrated first on reducing the tariff as a way of expanding exports. The struggle was a continuation of the battle of 1866, and revolved around the same protagonists. Commissioner of the Revenue Wells, undoubtedly influenced by his study and discussions in England during 1867, advanced a strong case for reduction and reform in his *Report* for 1868.[48] His earlier opponents, Henry Carey, Representative Kelley of Pennsylvania, and Horace Greeley of the New York *Tribune*, jumped eagerly back into the pit. Kelley struck first, tying Wells to the evil Southerners who preferred "having their ships and workshops on the other side of the Atlantic" in order to keep America as Great Britain's "chief commercial dependency."[49]

Then Carey fired a salvo in the *Tribune* on May 23, 1869. Greeley moved in with heavy support on June 8, making the formal charge that Wells, and other low tariff or free trade men, were directly or indirectly paid by British money supplied by bankers like the House of Baring. "British gold" was the fountainhead of the danger. The Wells *Report* of 1868 was "bought and paid for by foreign interests." Knowingly and willfully, the metropolis "conjured up thoughts of greedy English merchants profiting at the expense of the American yeoman."[50] Such vilification continued to be a primary characteristic of the metropolitan campaign against agricultural tariff reformers for the next thirty years.

Driven on by the increasingly difficult economic conditions, the farmers nevertheless maintained their pressure for tariff reduction. Under the leadership of Horace White, the Chicago *Tribune* returned the fire of Greeley. Representative Ignatius Donnelly of Minnesota began a reexamination of his support for the high tariff and shortly reversed his position.[51] And Norman J. Colman, the increasingly influential editor of a Missouri newspaper for agricultural businessmen, opened a sustained attack on the tariff. Reared in a tradition of farm leadership in Otsego County, New York, he return d to that activity in St. Louis after trying law and politics in Kentucky and Indiana. He became an experimental farmer and served on the Missouri State Board of Agriculture before transforming the feeble *Valley Farmer* into the vigorous and exciting *Colman's Rural World*. His weekly assault on the protectionists had by 1868 - 1869 become a significant factor in the national debate over the tariff.

Such efforts not only helped counter the heavy spending of metropolitan high tariff advocates like James M. Swank of the Iron and Steel Industry, who distributed tons of propaganda throughout the West, but they also encouraged Wells and other low tariff men.[52] Wells fought back with a major analysis and evaluation of the American political economy in his 1869 *Report*, and concluded with a militant call to reduce the tariff as a means of acquiring vital overseas markets. He was deeply concerned about two characteristics he observed in the economy. One was "the tendency of affairs in the United States . . . toward an inequitable distribution of the annual surplus of production over expenditure, and to impair the power of the masses to accumulate property and better their condition." Speaking more bluntly, he restated the proposition: "the poor of the United States under the existing system tend to grow poorer."[53]

His second major worry was the propensity of American capitalism to stagnate. "There are many circumstances which seem to indicate with certainty that the present accumulation of new capital in the United States . . . is at a much slower rate than it ought to be." Stagnation was in truth even more dangerous than the term implied. For *"not to increase, . . . is to retrograde."*[54] Combined with the inherent monetary problems of the system (aggravated by such episodes as the effort of Jay Gould and James Fisk to corner the gold market in September 1869), the signs of stagnation and the grossly uneven distribution of wealth were "infusing a spirit of discontent" among many groups in the country.[55]

Wells based his program for recovery and future development upon the sustained expansion of exports. He used agriculture as the example to illustrate his analysis and to explain the need for fiscal and tariff reform. The surplus, if disposed of at all, "must find a market in foreign countries." "But the value of the surplus for exportation is much less than it would be were the currency brought to a specie standard and taxation reduced and equalized, and to this extent the American agriculturalist is placed at a disadvantage with his foreign competitor, from the very outset."[56] While he was concerned about agricultural exports, and clearly transferred that principle of marketplace dynamics to the entire economy, Wells was more interested in the future expansion of metropolitan, industrial exports. His immediate objective was effective competition with Great Britain for control of the Latin American market in manufactured goods.[57] And for those reasons he argued that the ability to export, which the farmers had already demonstrated, was *"a true test of the ability or inability prof-itably to produce for the domestic market."*[58]

That opened the way for his attack on the high tariff schedules. The existing average duty of 47 percent, he boldly concluded, was *"excessive and unnecessary, and opposed alike to the highest interests of civilization and humanity, as well as to the proper and healthy growth of all domestic commerce and industry."*[59] The reduction of the tariff would help open new markets and lower "the cost of domestic pro-duction and consumption."[60] That would make American products more competitive in the world marketplace, and the resulting rise in exports would help ease domestic discontent.

The leaders of the protectionist bloc struck back with a venomous campaign. Kelley first accused Wells of advocating and supporting "the interests of England."[61] Carey then moved to counter the low tariff sentiment among Western farmers and other Republicans (as in Minnesota) with a new pamphlet: *Review of the Farmer's Question, As Exhibited in the Recent Report of the Hon. D. A. Wells.* By that time Kelley had used his power in the House of Representatives to have the Committee on Manufactures investigate and evaluate the *Report* by Wells. The protectionists who controlled the commit-tee promptly announced that the *Report* appeared "to have been writ-ten in the interests of foreign producers and manufacturers."[62]

The strategy that had worked so well in 1866, however, was not suc-cessful in 1870. The farmers were better organized, and even more deeply oriented toward exports. And the continuing economic dif-ficulties increased the momentum created by those developments. Their anger at Britain as the overlord of the world marketplace was transferred to metropolitans whose policies and actions abetted that power, rather than to men like Wells who wanted to lower the tariff as a way of expanding exports. The tariff debate thus played an im-portant part in the process that transformed the British from a tradi-tional and general opponent into a specific and immediate enemy.

"Like rabbits," growled an Iowa Granger, "we are the prey of hawks by day, and owls and foxes by night." "We have the power; we must use it. The farmers have got the lines, why don't they drive?"[63] The Gover-nor of Iowa felt the hot wind of that anger, as did his colleagues in Min-nesota and Wisconsin. The Minnesota wheat and flour men were so concerned about new markets that they began agitating—along with the West Coast farmers—for action to open the China market. The three governors shortly journeyed to Washington to make sure that the Congress and the White House received the message.[64]

Representative William Steele Holman of Indiana responded to such pressures by offering a resolution declaring that "the policy of granting subsidies in public lands to railroads and other corporations ought to be discontinued," and directing the executive to reserve the remaining public lands "for the exclusive purpose of securing homesteads to actual settlers."[65] Others stressed the strategy of disciplining the railroads by improving and using water transportation routes.[66] All such agitation intensified as the market, despite a brief speculative flurry in June, became "depressed to an unusual extent."[67]

The protectionists confronted one particular disadvantage in 1870 that they had not faced in 1866-1867. President Grant, unlike his predecessor, responded to the agricultural campaign for markets. His concern "to revive our drooping merchant marine" was tied to that objective.[68] So was his determined bid to annex Santo Domingo. And one of the main speakers at a huge New York rally, John Fitch, emphasized the large market for Western food surpluses—and rough cotton textiles from the South—that would be created by taking the island.[69] Grant did not rely on newspaper interviews and agents, however, in advancing that cause. The island, he told the Congress, "will become a large consumer of the products of Northern farms." Deeply concerned to reverse "the balance of trade against us," he argued that annexation would have the effect of "largely increasing our exports."[70] Secretary of State Fish wholly agreed with the analysis, and added Cuba to the list of markets to be engrossed, even though he disagreed with the need to annex the islands to control their markets.[71] Fish won that tactical dispute, but not before the Westerners made it clear that they remained determinedly loyal to their traditional ideal of expanding freedom as they expanded the marketplace.

That became apparent in the long debate over recognizing the rebels who raised the flag (though not many troops) of revolution against Spanish control of Cuba. In a cameo preview of what would happen between 1895 and 1899, the agricultural businessmen confronted in 1869-1870 the vital questions of whether overseas reform and overseas market expansion necessitated and justified war. If in 1870 the Cuban rebels had been as strong, and the economic involvement of American farmers as extensive, as became the case in 1898, moreover, the result might have been the same—a crucial role for the farmers in a decision for war. Such was not the case, even though it was a Westerner, Representative John Alexander Logan of Illinois, who tried to commit the Congress to a policy of extending the rebels "the same advantages of intercourse and trade with the United States" as enjoyed by Spain. His efforts failed, but the vote was close enough (101 to 77) to indicate the seriousness of the agricultural concern with the expansion of the American marketplace political economy. For a shift of merely thirteen votes would have resulted in the House's recognizing the rebels and carrying the United States and Spain toward the confrontation that ultimately came a generation later.[72]

Given the agitation over Santo Domingo and Cuba, and the concurrent attacks on the railroads, the resolution of the dispute over the tariff was almost anticlimactic. But the agricultural businessmen did win minor reductions in the law of July 14, 1870, that affected more than one hundred items. The gains were too small even to satisfy some metropolitan reformers, however, let alone the farmers, and the issue hurt the Republicans in the fall elections. So did the campaign for cheaper transportation. One of the major rallies on that question occurred in Cincinnati during October, where spokesmen from the South and West joined forces. The two groups did reveal differences: one bloc of Southerners was primarily concerned to revive "the ocean trade of the Atlantic cities with Europe," while other Southerners and most Westerners concentrated on the railroad issue. But all agreed that "the subject of cheap and safe transportation" was "paramount" to all others, that the farmers needed new and larger markets, and that the problem was national in scope. "It is alone to Congress we can look for relief."[73]

Additional groups became involved, moreover, as farmers began to buy hogs and range cattle and fatten them on corn. Some giant operators, like those ensconced "in lonely splendor" in "great rococo mansions" on 12,000-acre estates in the Kankakee and Wabash valleys of Indiana, had been following that trail to wealth since the 1850s.[74] The average feeder never accumulated that kind of profit—or power— but he did swell the pressure for market expansion and railroad reform. It was corn, of course, that was being exported, even though the form had been changed. "For what is a hog," exclaimed one enthusiast in 1870, "but fifteen or twenty bushels of corn on four legs?"[75]

The convergence of agricultural complaints against the metropolis also manifested itself in the growth of the Grange movement in states like Iowa and Minnesota. The key organizer in Iowa was William D. Wilson, and the effort in Missouri was given an important boost when Colman began to support the Grange in his widely circulated *Rural World*. The single most significant statement of the Western attitude, however, was made by an exceptionally talented young Minnesota Republican named Cushman Kellogg Davis. His major speech of 1870, in which he discussed the rise and nature of metropolitan power in terms of "modern Feudalism," was one of those classic performances that produced an instant response and a long-term effect. Unless that power was checked, he warned, the trust—or corporation—would quickly dominate the life of the American majority just as the baron earlier ruled the European serf. The tariff and transportation problems were symptoms of the new system, and the citizen had to control the new center of power as well as deal with its specific actions. As for the leaders of his own Republican party, Davis warned them that they would go under unless they responded to the just demands of the majority.[76]

The analysis won such a generally favorable response that, as Davis later noted, it shortly made him Governor of Minnesota. The conservatives who initially dismissed the analogy with feudalism as "rank radicalism" reconsidered even before that development, for Davis had given exceptional expression to a common feeling and attitude. It was the same outlook that guided the farmers of Illinois in their battle to control the railroads for the general welfare. Their first victory in 1867, which forced railroads to load grain from independent elevators, led on to the constitutional revisions of 1870. "Railways," the new instrument of government stated simply, ". . . are hereby declared public highways. . . . And the General Assembly shall, from time to time, pass laws establishing reasonable maximum rates of charges for the transportation of passengers and freight." That explicit charge to act was extended, moreover, to provide legislation "to correct abuses and to prevent unjust discrimination and extortion in the rates of freights and passenger tariffs."[77]

Other states, other leaders, and other techniques. In Indiana, for example, a young judge named Walter Quintin Gresham shortly revealed his understanding of the same point made by Davis. The episode involved a case in which the law seemed to block any relief for the farmers of the Wabash Valley. "Well, in this instance we will have to *flex* her a little," Gresham noted wryly. "To do otherwise would fail of doing *justice*, and it may save the receiver and the court great inconvenience and trouble, for otherwise those Wabash farmers are liable to take up a part of this railroad and throw it into the Wabash River."[78]

Some metropolitan spokesmen also recognized the increasing gravity of the situation. One group, the merchants of the New York Commercial Union, did so largely because the railroads were threatening their business operations. "Our mission is to inaugurate, in its fullest sense, cheap transportation from the Mississippi to the sea."[79] That outlook soon produced effective short-run collaboration between the merchants and the farm businessmen, but it did not meet the agricultural demand for more markets. William Elder dramatized that need in a new pamphlet, *The American Farmer's Markets at Home and Abroad*, and others hoped that the increased purchases resulting from European wars would solve their problem.[80]

The Republicans nevertheless lost ground in the elections of 1870. And whatever his weaknesses, not excluding a reputedly overdeveloped taste for good whiskey, President Grant promptly offered evidence that they did not blind him to essential aspects of economic and political reality. His annual message of December 5, 1870, was filled with direct and indirect proposals for dealing with the clear and present danger of the agricultural anger and unrest. He first reiterated his argument that Santo Domingo should be annexed because of its value as a market for farm surpluses, and because that trade would help rebuild the merchant marine—which would in turn facilitate even more market expansion. Then he made a strong bid to assert leadership of the campaign for better transportation, and tried to prod metropolitan spokesmen into more effective action. "The whole nation is interested in securing cheap transportation from the agricultural states of the West to the Atlantic Seaboard." The need was great not only because the time had come to insure the farmers "a greater return for their labor," but because exports were essential to generate recovery from the "depressed" economic conditions.

Nor, finally, had Grant missed the significance of Representative Holman's resolution about saving the soil itself for homesteaders. The President came down hard on the need to protect the interests of the man who actually settled and worked the land. His sensitivity was impressive, and his concern justified. For the Montana territorial legislature, acting before the next election, passed a law prohibiting any alien from obtaining "any title, interest, or possessory or other right to any placer mine or claim."[81] Holman and the Montana legislators, in responding to specific demands concerning immediate problems, had taken some of the first—and largely unknowing—steps in the development of a general argument about the importance of the frontier in American history. And the President furthered that process by adding the prestige of his office to the proposition that free land was a crucial factor in the welfare of the country.

Grant's performance in December 1870 represented more than rhetoric and gestures. Representative Blaine, who recognized the seriousness of the problems at least two years earlier, began to concentrate on holding the Westerners in the Republican party. Other metropolitans listened more attentively to the agricultural businessmen and simultaneously maneuvered to block a new alliance between the South and the West within the resurgent Democratic party. Such increasing concern was exceedingly relevant because the farmers were in the process of deepening their self-consciousness and strengthening the power of their organizations.

The Commissioner of Agriculture forcefully reminded the metropolis, for example, that agriculture provided the basis for all economic development. Then he quoted Adam Smith on the vital role of market expansion in the health of agriculture and made it clear that wheat and flour required larger exports. One of the important elements in such improvement, he added, was the need for the "peaceful command of the seas." That was "necessary to economic independence."[82] As an illustration of what could be done, he pointed to the use of palace stock cars on the Pennsylvania Railroad, which shipped 172 head of cattle from St. Louis to New York in a mere 96 hours.[83] More than 150 times that many were exported in 1870 by men like Nelson Morris, and that trade had earlier involved three important groups in the agricultural sector of the economy.

One was composed of the processors who opened the Kansas City stockyards in 1871 to handle Western cattle. Another involved the men who were rapidly exploiting the techniques of exporting dressed beef on refrigerator cars and ships. The Easterners of the Fulton Street market in New York may have been the first to try the new method. Then came George H. Hammond of Detroit, who used the "Davis Pattern Refrigerator."[84] But the key man was Gustavus Franklin Swift of Chicago, who worked with a Boston engineer to perfect the various designs. They turned the corner in 1870-1871, and Swift thereafter devoted increasing amounts of his vast energy and shrewdness to expanding the market for chilled beef.

On the Western ranges, however, 1871 was the year of the "bad medicine." The cattlemen lost much of their capital, and by April 15 had organized to "command influence in securing cheap rates of freight."[85] One of the early leaders was John A. Campbell, first territorial governor of Wyoming, who became president of the Wyoming Stock Growers' Association. Perhaps nothing illustrated the Western integration of economics and politics quite as well as Campbell's decision to convene his stockmen's group in a joint session with the second territorial legislature.[86] The stockmen and the processors had their own particular quarrels with the railroads concerning the handling of live cattle and the servicing of the refrigerator cars, and those arguments reinforced the existing campaign to lower rates and end discrimination. That kind of agreement on railroad problems also blunted the antagonism between flour processors and grain farmers, and created an ambivalence among the farmers that remained an important feature of their attitude throughout the remainder of the nineteenth century.

The same considerations periodically divided other Western businessmen who generally supported metropolitan interests and policies. The St. Paul *Daily Press*, for example, thought it "absolute nonsense" even to consider taking land back from the railroads. That would give a man land to farm but deny him access to the market — "set before him a Barmecide feast of empty dishes."[87] But the editor of the Green Bay, Wisconsin, *Advocate* sided with the farmers. "The evil," he warned, "is a deplorable one." "I am not unfriendly to any Railroad in the State — on the contrary count myself as one of their best friends — but it is degrading to the good name of the State that they shall own, body and britches, every Legislature, one after the other."[88]

The farmers themselves recognized the value of the railroads in opening new country, and generally welcomed the efforts of men like Jay Cooke, who launched a major developmental campaign in Minnesota and Dakota after he took charge of the Northern Pacific on January

1, 1870. But their increasingly intense concern with markets overrode that consideration. The result, as John A. Millikin told the Ohio State Agricultural Society meeting in January 1872, was that all people were complaining, "to some extent, of great hardships, of unjust discriminations, and ruinous rates of charges, imposed by railroad companies." The corporations, which drew at least 60 percent of their freight from the farm economy, nevertheless followed policies that "greatly impair" the chance to turn a profit from agriculture.[89]

The legislatures of Iowa, Kansas, and Nebraska responded to the ferment and pressure with resolutions calling on Congress to act on the transportation issue. Given such aid, "cereals and other agricultural products of the Western states can at once command the provision markets of Western Europe, from which they are now excluded in consequence of the excessive cost of transportation."[90] The agitation that produced such official action was typified by the joint meeting during May 1872 of sixteen Kansas farm clubs.[91]

Tennessee farmers, operating through an Agricultural and Mechanics Association, held a similar congress in Nashville. The agricultural businessmen of Illinois, riding the momentum generated by their victories in 1870 and 1871, and called into convention by the Farmers Club of Avon, organized the Illinois State Farmers' Association in October 1872. As Commissioner of Agriculture Frederick Watts commented, in his peculiarly tortured effort to be wry, "the farmers have been brought to discover that there is work for them to do outside the precincts of the farm." Such widespread local activity, moreover, supplied much of the energy that was rapidly focused in and by the Grange movement. In some states, such as Mississippi, the Grange concentrated on local problems. But even in those cases, which included Alabama and Arkansas, the effort increased the awareness of broader issues and that affected the political dynamics of the entire country.[92] The Grange came to be viewed, moreover, as an organization defined by the activities of its more militant branches in the West. Two years after the first chapter was organized, for example, the Minnesota Grange pushed through a law defining railroads as public highways, and requiring them to observe reasonable maximum rates and fares (March 6, 1871).

The campaign in Illinois was coordinated by Stephen J. Hurlbut, Allen C. Fuller, and Jesse S. Hildrup, who had been active since the crisis of 1865 - 1866.[93] And in Iowa, which boasted more than half the nation's Grange chapters by April 1872, the key men were Dudley W. Adams and William D. Wilson. As in Illinois, the earlier farm organizations in Iowa prepared the way for Grange influence on railroad legislation. The first effort had been made in 1866, but the Senate rejected a bill approved by the House. The process was repeated twice during the next four years, and the issue created so much antagonism that both major parties supported regulation in their platforms. The Senate remained adamant, killing three more attempts in 1872, and at that point the House might well have abandoned the struggle if it had not been for the determination of the Grange. In Iowa as elsewhere, however, the agricultural need and demand for cheap transportation were so intense and widespread that the defeats served primarily to deepen the anger and strengthen the movement.[94]

Key Republican leaders recognized the danger and accurately concluded that the farm businessmen posed a greater threat to the Grant Administration than the challenge generated by party reformers like Carl Schurz and B. Gratz Brown of Missouri. Men like Blaine understood that farmers were primarily concerned with markets and transportation, with their neocolonial position in dealings with the metropolis, and with obtaining more aid from the federal government. As a party leader in Indiana told Blaine, the election battle in the West would "be hard fought and bitter," and added that they needed him "very much."[95] Grant and Fish also moved to ease the crisis. Fish made certain, for example, that the treaty settlement of the Civil War claims against Great Britain included a provision granting American commerce unrestricted use of the St. Lawrence River. On another front, the President issued a special executive order on March 31, 1871, requiring all officers of the territorial governments to obtain permission before leaving their posts. The rising absenteeism among such men, many of whom were easterners, provoked justifiable anger, Grant noted, and he expected "the gentlemen who hold those offices to stay in their respective Territories and to attend strictly to their duties."[96]

The efforts to push trade expansion, meanwhile, ranged from Washington to Latin America and on to the far reaches of the Pacific. California exporters and shippers, typified by Edward Wakeman of the Great American Land and Steamship Company, worked persistently to consolidate American influence in Samoa. That island was "of vital importance" to their plans to "control the whole commerce of the Pacific."[97] The Grant Administration responded by ordering Commodore Richard W. Meade to sail for Samoa "at the earliest possible moment." In a narrow sense, that extremely effective pressure was commercial rather than agricultural, but much of the substance of the trade was provided by the wheat and flour surpluses of the West Coast.

Westerners also scored some gains in the Congress. The appropriation for internal improvements was increased, and the tariff on manufactured goods was reduced another 10 percent. The Liberal Republicans and Democrats, by contrast, nominated one of the major leaders of the protectionist movement to oppose Grant in the election of 1872. Their candidate, Greeley of the New York *Tribune*, had a record that might at another time have served as a basis for attracting Western support. He had agitated for homestead legislation, for example, and tried in 1872 to capitalize on that earlier campaign by backing the new effort to reserve the public domain for bona-fide settlers. But Greeley was accurately viewed by the agriculturalists as primarily a metropolitan leader. His approach to the homestead issue had been far more that of the Easterner concerned about labor unrest, and in any event his high tariff views subverted his position on the land question in 1872. For at that moment, at any rate, the farmers were far more concerned with markets and transportation than with land policy. Even the question of civil service reform appeared largely as a metropolitan issue. The farm businessmen would very probably have been delighted with a spoils system that rewarded farmers rather than metropolitan machine politicians.

Given the choice that was offered, Westerners voted strongly for Grant and Republican congressmen. While they slipped a bit in the Senate (49 Republicans, 5 Liberal Republicans, and 19 Democrats), the Republicans padded their margin in the House (195 to 88 Democrats and 4 Liberal Republicans). Grant and other Republican leaders were astute enough to realize, however, that continued positive action would be required to consolidate the victory. If they failed, the Grange and other agricultural organizations might well lead the farmers into a working alliance with the Democratic party. The President immediately moved to deal with the problem by stressing the transportation issue, bluntly asking the Congress in December 1872 to facilitate "the more certain and cheaper transportation of the constantly increasing surplus of Western and Southern products to the Atlantic seaboard."[98]

The concern and pressure were effective. Minnesota Senator William Windom, who sympathized with the needs of the farmers and processors, and understood the power of the Grange at first hand, promptly introduced a resolution expressing grave concern over the transportation crisis. That led to the creation of a Select Committee on Transportation Routes to the Seaboard, which quickly became known as the Windom Committee because of the Senator's vital role in determining its approach and guiding its energetic collection of evidence. So far as the farm businessmen were concerned, and regardless of whether or not they testified before the committee, the facts were already clear. President Grant voiced at least the spirit of their attitude in his inaugural remarks on March 7, 1873, long before the Windom Committee issued its report. The need, he emphasized, was for the "construction of cheap routes of transit throughout the land, to the end that the products of all may find a market."[99]

The President, along with the metropolitan leaders to whom he directed his remarks, was promptly reminded that words were not enough. "Let the North, especially New England, beware," warned the Lynchburg *Virginian*, whose editors saw the mounting campaign for better transportation as a movement that could reunite the West and the South and restore the Democrats to power. "The South and West will not forever be content to pay tribute to the North, and the day of their enfranchisement and deliverance from a commercial thralldom which they have too long endured, draws nigh."[100] The metropolitan spokesmen who understood the situation added their weight to the movement. The "means and cost of transportation," urged the secretary of the Chicago Board of Trade, constitute "a subject worthy of the most earnest consideration, for upon its issue depends the prosperity of the whole country."[101]

The climax of agricultural agitation between the election and Grant's second inauguration came at the great convention held at Bloomington, Illinois, on January 15 and 16, 1873. It justly attracted national attention and concern, and clearly affected the thinking of politicians throughout the country. The tone was set by a dirt farmer whose pithy remarks delighted the delegates. "Mr. Bishop, of Kane," the recorder noted, "wanted present relief. He was tired of working fifteen hours a day."[102] Lawrence D. Whiting, temporary chairman of the meeting, agreed that "longer and harder hours of labor" did not help the farmer. "*Cheap transportation*," he thundered, "is vital to our prosperity." "Government must be involved in the matter," for "poverty, if not actual bankruptcy stares the farmer in the face."[103]

Many of the delegates spoke angrily of the colonial position of agricultural businessmen. "We to-day are sold, soul and body," cried one farmer named Phoenix, "in bonds to Europe, and if not there to our cities." James Shaw echoed that charge with a reference to the classic danger of "*imperium in imperio*."[104] William C. Flagg, president of the Illinois State Farmers' Association, pointed out that Adam Smith and John Stuart Mill denounced the practice of allowing natural monopolies, such as roads, canals, and railways, to be controlled by private interests. They were part of the very structure of the marketplace, and therefore had to serve all businessmen.[105] That kind of anger and analysis and discussion lead "unanimously and enthusiastically" to the adoption of three major resolutions. First, "all corporations are subject to regulation by law." Second, "cheap transportation is of vital interest to the West." And, finally, the government should provide improvements "to connect the vast interior river system with the ocean commerce."[106]

Such sentiments were not limited to Illinois. Colman of Missouri offered the same explanations and proposals. So did the Kansas State Board of Agriculture.[107] John Scott, president of the Iowa Board of Agriculture, spoke even more bluntly. "The time to trudge and the time to drudge are in the past." The "so-called market," he added, "is but the sport of bulls that toss and bears that squeeze." And Governor Cyrus Clay Carpenter caught the entire issue in one short sentence: "Railroads are now not only *national* but *international*." Hiram S.

Hyatt then cited chapter and verse from Adam Smith to document that truth.[108] Further to the west, the California State Agricultural Society offered the same arguments, and reached identical policy recommendations.[109]

Despite their serious and increasing difficulties, and their inability to win any major reforms, the farmers of all sections were in a stronger position as President Grant started his second term than they had been during the brief and uneven economic upturn of 1867 - 1869. They had analyzed the causes of their unhappy condition and produced relevant proposals to improve their position. And the increasing self-consciousness and determination created by that sustained effort contributed greatly to their ability to organize for political action. In the short run, however, they proved unable to move metropolitan leaders to act in behalf of agriculture. The men of the East who held policy-making power were far more concerned with making sure that the marketplace power of the agricultural businessmen was used in behalf of the city's conception of the national interest.

SIX

The people continue to manifest a lively determination to keep "pushing things."

Joseph H. Osborn to E. R.
Shankland, July 29, 1873

The balance of our public domain should be kept forever sacred to actual settlers.

Local centers of trade cannot meet all the necessities. . . . Hence arises the demand for cheap and speedy transportation.

Resolution, and Remarks by John
Davis, Kansas Farmers' State
Convention, April 1873

Transportation is indispensable to agricultural prosperity.

President of the California Grange,
April 1873

These men are hurt, or believe they are. They are justly anxious to mend their present condition and to prevent the depreciation of their property.

Railroad Gazette, August 16, 1873

As far as the price of crops is controlled by distant markets, all the profits and even the very existence of agriculture depend upon the rate charged for transporting its products.

William M. Grosvenor, *Atlantic
Monthly*, November 1873

What we want is a restoration of industry, a diminution of importations and an increase of export. These we are not likely to have as long as a vast volume of irredeemable currency is kept in circulation.

Secretary of the Treasury Hugh McCulloch
to Horace Greeley, June 13, 1866

[We desire to retain silver] to encourage American commerce with Mexico and with South America and Asiatic nations.

Senator Edwin Dennison Morgan of New York,
Minority Report on a Bill to
Demonetize Silver, 1868

[In connection] with the contest for final peaceful supremacy in the affairs of the world. . . . The ability of a country to maintain specie payments is due largely to the condition of its foreign trade. . . . [And] every measure which increases or improves the channels of transportation between the seaboard and the cotton and grain-growing regions of the country, or lessens the cost of freight, adds something to our capacity to compete successfully in the markets of the world.

Secretary of the Treasury George
S. Boutwell, *Annual Report*, 1872

[I] believed that [free silver] would be a very grave and serious peril to our country . . . it would place us in a position to demonetize gold and adopt silver as the sin-

gle standard to detach ourselves from the great commer-cial nations of the world and join the inferior nations.

Senator John Sherman of Ohio, Remarks
in 1893 Defending the Demonetization
of Silver in 1873

We can never have permanent prosperity until a specie basis is reached; and that can not be reached and main-tained until our exports, exclusive of gold, pay for our imports.

President Ulysses Simpson Grant,
December 1, 1873

While
the Country Concentrates on
Markets and Transportation
the Metropolis Manipulates
the Monetary
System

T HE ROLLING agrarian campaign for cheap transportation steadily increased its momentum throughout 1873. The farmers were gaining broad support for transportation improvements and reforms by the time the failure of Jay Cooke in September triggered the severe Panic of 1873 that carried the gravely weakened economy into a massive depression. That collapse of American capitalism had a paradoxical effect on the battle for railroad regulation. It helped the farm businessmen win reforms from state legislatures, but it deepened the resistance to such legislation at the national level—particularly in the Senate—and it intensified metropolitan concern with monetary policy as a crucial factor in providing relief and generating recovery.

That change of focus shortly produced an outburst of agricultural anger against the fundamental alteration in monetary policy that a small group of men carried through while most of the country, and particularly the agricultural majority, was concentrating on the transportation problem. Their action, which demonetized silver, created an issue that ultimately displaced the question of transportation in the public arena and provided a new idiom for debating the ways and means of market expansion. For that matter, the principal figures in the maneuvers that demonetized silver were concerned with that very objective. They wanted to be sure that agricultural exports would underwrite the kind of a system that the metropolis preferred—and dominated.

But the battle between the metropolis and the country had been rag-
ing since at least the 1790s, and the demonetization of silver changed
only the form—not the substance—of that struggle. Stephen Smith,
writing in 1873 to offer *Grains for the Grangers*, discussed the long
conflict in terms of America's wars for independence. The War of
1812, he explained, was "fought and won against the monopoly exercised by England on the high seas." And the Grange campaign was
being waged for "commercial freedom."[1] The agricultural strategy revealed some of the features of an enveloping guerrilla movement, as
William C. Flagg of the Illinois State Farmers' Association explained
to Senator Windom. A good many farm leaders felt it was tactically
effective, for example, not to join the Grange. "I am not a Granger,
technically speaking," Flagg commented. He, and others like him, remained free to help organize operations such as the famous Illinois
Farmers' Declaration of Independence of July 4, 1873, which the
Grange then endorsed.[2]

All agreed, of course, that the customers for the farm surpluses were
"over yonder," and that "transportation should be cheap."[3] The Minnesota Grange, ever more influenced by the dynamism of Donnelly,
moved effectively to make the railroad issue a major factor in the state
elections of 1873.[4] Iowa Grangers were even more successful. They
spoke to the issue in terms of the "production in our State which must
find a market abroad," and demanded "speedy improvement" of waterways and a government-owned, double-tracked rail line to the seaboard served by state-owned feeder spurs. Having learned that they
"could expect no quarter" from the metropolis or its spokesmen in
the West, they combined forces in 1873 with an antimonopoly party
to elect a total of 120 members to the Iowa General Assembly.[5]

Joseph Horatio Osborn of Wisconsin was a vital figure in the Western drive for markets and cheap transportation. Settling in Wisconsin
in 1844, he quickly became a successful farmer-merchant and then
a powerful agitator for the Grange. His analysis was clear and his approach was militant. Transportation improvements were "so *obviously necessary*" that he directed much of his attention and energy
to forcing the metropolis to provide transshipment facilities on the
seaboard. The failure of the government to act would be "nothing
more nor less than a *subsidy* to the railroad companies."[6] Hence he
concentrated on coordinating Midwestern Grange activity and creating a "concentrated movement" that would force the Congress to
act. He was encouraged by the gains that had been made by mid-1873,
and told a friend that he was mildly optimistic because "the people
continue to manifest a lively determination to keep 'pushing things.'"[7]

The leader of the California Grange exhorted his followers and all
other agricultural businessmen "to go into the markets of the world,

and compete with all the world with your surplus products." That strategy made cheap transportation "indispensable to agricultural prosperity."[8] A bit to the north, the Committee Resolutions of the Oregon Grange demanded improvement of the Willamette and Columbia rivers because transporting the surplus was "of almost vital importance to the farmers of Oregon."[9] As it was in Illinois and Iowa, so it was in the Far West. Other farm organizations were equally concerned with "the grain market." "Free trade and farmers' rights," cried the Oakland, California, Farmers' Club on August 23, "are what we seek."

Such constant emphasis on the market for agricultural surpluses steadily heightened the agrarian awareness of British economic power.[10] Very few of the farm businessmen even bothered, unless they were making a particular point, to note that Liverpool and London controlled the world's commodity markets. That knowledge was largely taken for granted by 1873. The significant development of that time involved the beginning of resistance to British investment in American agriculture, railroads, and government securities. Englishmen first learned of such opportunities in agriculture through the pages of the *North British Agriculturalist* and the *Mark Lane Express*. The interest was so great, and so often uncritical, that the editors of the latter journal indulged themselves in some sarcasm in the idiom of a cost-accounting balance sheet. "Everytime a cow moves her tail to switch a fly," they solemnly warned, "she exerts a force of three pounds. In the course of the summer a single cow wastes 5,000,000 pounds of energy."[11]

Such flummery did not break the spirit of the Empire, or deter the Englishman with surplus capital. Such men easily reassured themselves, as did the one who soberly concluded that "nothing, short of violence or special legislation, can prevent the Plains from continuing to be forever . . . the feeding ground of the World."[12] American farm businessmen also accepted that estimate of their future, and for precisely that reason grew ever more fretful about British penetration of the system. They were not so much worried in 1873 about money that would directly influence policy decisions as they were upset by capital that controlled marketplace operations. The reaction against specific firms like the Scottish American Investment Company, the Rathbones of Liverpool, and the Fowler Brothers, Ltd., and the more general concern about the dramatic jump in total investment between 1870 and 1874—more than 250 percent—generated the early opposition that blossomed into a massive protest movement.[13]

Another indication of similar things to come was offered by the *Nebraska State Journal*. It reported that some farmers were combining attacks on the feebleness of the Department of Agriculture with their assault on the railroads.[14] And so they were, but the campaign for a more powerful advocate in the Cabinet did not gain general support for another decade. The Chicago *Tribune* was closer to the mark. Its excellent survey of Illinois farm clubs revealed that the agricultural businessmen were beginning to integrate all the arguments they had developed since the end of the Civil War. Low tariffs would open new markets, force the railroads to lower their rates to those markets, and cut the cost of consumer goods.[15] Kansas farmers were coalescing in a similar manner. They sought "a union of heads and hands" to win "more equitable relations in the exchange of our labor." One kind of American, cried a typical speaker, "lives in the city and sells for a *living*, and the other lives in the country and produces for an *existence*."[16]

The major state convention held in Topeka on April 26-27, 1873, was one result of such growing unity and determination. The leaders were angry and impatient. Farmers ought to be taken "out behind the horse shed" for action "like the blind horse in the tread mill." Governor Charles Robinson told the group that he "would not give one fig" for the future of agriculture unless the farmers organized and won their rights. The tough rhetoric reinforced existing emotions. The resolutions began with a call to control the market so that agriculturalists would obtain "the cost of production, and a reasonable profit." Then came a demand to protect the public domain so that land would "be kept forever sacred to actual settlers." The climax was a proposal to regulate railroad rates by state and national legislative action, "and, if need be, to construct national highways at the expense of the government."[17]

Similar meetings and identical demands characterized the summer of 1873. The New York Farmers' and Producers' Convention of May defined "the duty of the hour" as controlling the cost of transportation so that "our almost limitless surplus finds foreign markets at rates to compete with the world."[18] Then came the meeting of the National Agricultural Congress, which had been organized in 1872. William J. Jackson of Tennessee demanded "a voice in affairs" for the farm businessmen. The farmer understood that he and the railroads "hinged on each other," but it was time for "equity." The South Carolina delegation insisted on action to reduce "the present extreme rates of railway and maritime transportation." And, working in conjunction with others from Minnesota, California, Vermont, Ohio, and Illinois, the Southerners produced a final report that defined cheap transportation as "a national necessity." Then, pointing to the Belgian example, they recommended "railways and trunk lines built by the State and run at fixed, uniform, and cheap rates" if all other efforts failed.[19]

That proposal, along with the identical demands of other farm groups in Iowa and Kansas, make it clear that the idea of a federal railroad line to serve as a standard of judgment enjoyed wide support long before it was projected by the Alliance and Populist movements. It is likewise apparent that the farmers were fully aware of develop-

ments in other countries that were relevant to their operations in the
United States. And it is equally unmistakable that the agricultural
businessmen formulated their demand for a national railway system
in the idiom of Adam Smith rather than within the framework provided by Karl Marx. The concept was not one of socialist nationalization, but one derived from the Smithian principle that the structural
framework of the marketplace had to be regulated or controlled by
the government in order to guarantee every capitalist an equitable
opportunity to operate in that marketplace. The farmers were simply applying Smith's argument against mercantilist joint-stock companies to the railroad corporations of their own time.

Another group of Southerners meeting in Atlanta, for example,
likewise warned that the transportation crisis was causing grave trouble. But if cheap rates were provided, then "our exports would be doubled . . . and the balance of trade would be in our favor."[20] Still another Illinois meeting gave farmer Charles Boone an opportunity to
ridicule those who said there was no need for a surplus. "The way,"
he began, "was not to produce a surplus that would need transportation. It cost so much to eat the surplus that it would be cheaper not to
produce the surplus. (Laughter.) He produced a surplus because he
was in debt. He wanted light on this point. . . . He was an overpro-
ducer because he wanted to get out of debt. But when he produced
the extra quantity, they depressed the prices and kept him in debt still.
(Laughter.)"

One delegate responded with the explanation that part of the trouble arose because Boone "had a competitor in Russia."[21] That argument was also advanced by some metropolitan leaders. Samuel B.
Ruggles of the New York Central Railroad and New York Chamber
of Commerce, for example, sounded as though he had studied with
William Seward. Russia and America were the "great competitors,"
the only *"dramatis personae* in this game." His analysis was noteworthy
because it illustrated the way that the agricultural thrust for foreign
markets was beginning to redefine the security perimeters of the United States and transform old friends into new enemies.[22] Others, like
Thomas Rimmer, a major metropolitan exporter of American grain,
viewed the problem in a narrower light. They stressed the need to match
"the extraordinary effort that the Russians are making for improving
their transportation."[23]

Most of the men who identified with the metropolis took that approach. In the West and South, of course, such leaders were ambiva-
lent. They were urban businessmen with important economic ties
to Eastern capital, and psychological commitments to city life and
to the status quo; yet they understood that much of their operation
depended on the agrarian businessman and the overseas markets for his
rising surpluses. And they admitted, at least in their intimate discus-

sions, that Eastern entrepreneurs set limits on them as well as on the farmers. One of the best illustrations of the resulting tension was provided by the flour-milling industry of Minneapolis, which began fighting for export markets—and hence low-cost transportation—as early as 1870.[24]

William Drew Washburn explained the matter to his brother at least as early as May 1869. "We have got to have other R.R. connections or we are gone up."[25] Technology rapidly complicated the problem. Hungarian millers evolved a system of using porcelain rollers to grind a finer-grade flour during the middle years of the century, but the development meant little to Americans until Red River Valley farmers began to harvest crops of hard wheat. Until that time the soft wheat of Kansas dominated the domestic scene, and also appeared to be the key to penetrating the Asian market.

Then, just after Charles A. Pillsbury entered the Minneapolis milling arena in 1869, two small Minnesota operators devised a way of grinding spring wheat. The key man in adapting and perfecting their process was George H. Christian. Washburn quickly made Christian a partner, and that combination of shrewd entrepreneurs, together with Pillsbury, rapidly transformed the flour industry. "In our first year of New Process milling," Christian once recalled, "our mills made a net profit of fifty cents per barrel; in the second, a dollar; the third year, two dollars; and in the fourth year [1874], we made four dollars and a half per barrel."[26] The short-run boom in profits did not solve the basic market problem, however, because Pillsbury and Washburn steadily expanded their production. Like their rivals in Kansas City, therefore, the Minneapolis millers added their weight to the campaign for bigger markets and better transportation.

While the Kansas City Board of Trade agreed with the farmers of the region that the Mississippi River ought to be improved, it also made a strong appeal for a good harbor at Galveston, Texas. That would facilitate the export of Missouri River Valley farm surpluses via rail connections. Such a system would make it possible to export flour to "West India and South American markets."[27] St. Louis businessmen understandably stressed the Mississippi waterway. They considered it vital to overcome "the great difficulty in the way of moving the surplus cereals of this valley to the foreign markets of the world."[28] The New Orleans group, led by Burwell and Joseph H. Oglesby, his successor as president of the chamber of commerce, argued that deepening the river and the ship channel would give the farmer another eight to ten cents per bushel. Oglesby insisted that was the best, if not the only, way to provide the farmer with "an adequate return for his labor." Burwell carried the analysis further, pointing out that the "diplomatic impediments" blocking exports were "even greater" than the physical difficulties. He demanded a concerted effort to negotiate "reciprocal trade treaties" in order to penetrate and develop alternate markets in Latin America.[29]

Most Eastern metropolitan spokemen were much slower to recognize either the economic or the political aspects of the crisis. The editors of the *Nation* spoke for that majority when they condemned a Wisconsin law establishing reasonable railroad rates as "spoliation as flagrant as any ever proposed by Karl Marx."[30] But a significant minority understood the necessity for reform, if only on purely economic grounds, and opened a counterattack within the metropolis. Charles Francis Adams of Massachusetts was the most prestigious figure in that group, and he called for direct government intervention into the marketplace (including joint ownership if necessary) to maintain competition and guarantee adequate service.

The editors of the *Railroad Gazette* flatly denied the *Nation*'s charge of communism among the agricultural businessmen. "These men are hurt, or believe they are," and "are justly anxious to mend their present condition and to prevent the depreciation of their property." Like Adams and other perceptive metropolitans, the *Gazette* recognized that the farmers were first and fundamentally men of the marketplace. "There is no question," they pointed out, "as to the importance" of the cost of transportation. "A reduction in the price of transportation would benefit them still more when prices are high."[31] The *Industrial Age* agreed, and attacked the "sleek and well-fed partisan" who did not like to have his "personal comfort interfered with by a lot of rusty farmers."[32]

William M. Grosvenor further strengthened the metropolitan reform effort with a long and candid review of the agricultural unrest in the *Atlantic Monthly*. The farmers "have got angry," he explained, because they grew weary of "complaining in vain." Then he provided a classically direct analysis of why the agrarians were so aroused about cheap freight rates. Distant markets control in a great degree the price of the whole crop, and therefore "all the profits and even the very existence of agriculture depend upon the rate charged for transporting its products." The surplus was sure to increase, he concluded, and hence America had to act or risk grave harm to a vital element in its economic prosperity.[33]

Then came the report and recommendations of the Windom Committee. The danger was great because American cereals and cotton were being challenged by Russian, Indian, and other competitors in a market that was dominated by Great Britain.[34] There were three alternatives. The nation could await the creation of a metropolitan market large enough to absorb a steadily rising surplus. It could try to reestablish the pre-Civil War pattern of selling Northern and Western food surpluses to the South, enlarging that old domestic market by having the Southerners concentrate exclusively on cotton, tobacco, and other such crops.[35] Or it could meet the crisis by overcoming Russian and Indian competition in the European market while simultaneously undertaking a program of market expansion in other areas of the world.[36]

The committee fondled the dream of recreating the ante-bellum internal trade pattern, and then came down hard for the export solution. That decision lead on to three policies. Transportation rates had to be lowered because they had not declined as rapidly as the prices paid for agricultural commodities.[37] Russia's "system of internal improvements" had to be matched or surpassed, or else that nation "will be able to drive us from the markets of the world." That would happen "unless wiser counsels shall guide our statesmanship than have hitherto prevailed."[38] And new markets had to be opened. "Every cent unnecessarily added to the cost of transportation," the committee warned in conclusion, "is to that extent a protection to the cotton planters of India and the food producers of Russia, against the farmers of the West and the cotton-planters of the South." "If we would assure our imperiled position in the markets of the world, re-instate our credit abroad, restore confidence and prosperity at home, and provide for a return to specie payment, let us develop our unequalled resources and stimulate our industries by a judicious system of internal improvements."[39]

The Windom *Report* stands as one of the key documents of late-nineteenth-century American history. It represented a deep commitment by the agricultural majority, and a significant segment of the metropolitan minority, to the proposition that American welfare depended on overseas markets. Even Senator Roscoe Conkling of New York accepted the analysis, questioning only the power of the Congress to undertake all the necessary projects. Perhaps even more significantly, the Windom *Report* formalized the process whereby the nations that blocked or challenged America's market expansion were defined as primary threats to American prosperity and freedom. And the farmer, as much a businessman as his metropolitan opponent in the domestic marketplace, had played the vital role in creating the reality that generated that conception of the world, and in developing the ideas for dealing with the specific problems.

President Grant summarized the evolving outlook very neatly in his message of December 1873: "We can never have permanent prosperity until a specie basis is reached; and that specie basis can not be reached and secured until our exports, exclusive of gold, pay for our imports."[40] A small group of shrewd and able men, well informed, determined, and crucially placed in the decision-making process, had concluded years before that the three key words in Grant's analysis—*exports*, *specie*, and *gold*—had to be reduced to one: GOLD. And during the years that the vast number of their countrymen were preoccupied with the questions of markets and transportation, they so reduced them. In their own minds, at any rate, their collusion was sanctified by the certainty that they were taking a correct and necessary step, and by the majority's commitment to the objectives of expanded exports and world economic supremacy.

The metropolitan strategy for paying for the war while avoiding an inflation that would favor debtors over creditors was always predicated upon the earning power of the debtors—the exports provided by the farmers. "What we want," explained Secretary of the Treasury McCulloch, "is a restoration of industry, a diminution of importation and an increase of export. These we are not likely to have as long as a vast volume of irredeemable currency is kept in circulation."[41] For McCulloch and others, however, the value of the exports hinged wholly on the monetary system used by Great Britain because it dominated the world commodity market. That meant gold monometallism, and hence the United States had to maintain itself on the gold standard to avoid what McCulloch called the central danger of "ruinous indebtedness to Europe."[42]

The first attempt to guarantee American integration into the gold system grew out of the efforts of two small groups of metropolitan leaders who agreed there was no other way to handle the problem. Samuel Ruggles, the New York operator who worried about Russian competition in world commodity markets, entertained the grandiose idea of unifying all the monetary (and other measurement) systems of the world as part of creating one market. He was the American delegate to the International Statistical Conferences of 1855 and 1863 that tried to accomplish that objective on the basis of the gold and the metric standards. The Latin Union monetary agreement signed by France, Belgium, Switzerland, and Italy in December 1865 increased the hopes of success despite the formal French preference for a bimetallist system including silver as well as gold. For some of the French experts favored gold monometallism, and it seemed possible that they would be able to change the policy of their government.[43]

The other group was centered in the government around Secretary McCulloch. One of his subordinates, James Pollock, Director of the Philadelphia Mint, became concerned about new discoveries of silver reported in October 1865.[44] He and others feared that any great increase in production would lower the price of silver and have the effect of removing America from the gold standard. McCulloch shortly secured a special appropriation from the Congress (in July 1866) to finance further investigations in the West. His agent verified the "vast works of the chief silver companies of Nevada."[45] By that time Ruggles had reentered the discussion (if, indeed, he had ever been out of it) along with several new protagonists. Edward Atkinson and David Wells became involved, along with Representative Samuel Hooper, a wealthy merchant from Massachusetts, Representative John Adam Kasson, a Republican politician from Iowa who pushed export expansion, and Senator John Sherman of Ohio, a major power in the orthodox wing of the Republican party. The crucial man inside the Treasury Department was Henry R. Linderman. He left his job as chief clerk of the Philadelphia Mint in 1864 to become a banker and broker, but the developing crisis prompted McCulloch to entice him back into the government as director of the Mint.

The group first moved to secure a congressional commitment to participate in the International Monetary Conference scheduled to be held during the Paris Exposition of 1867. Kasson handled the campaign in the House of Representatives, stressing the need for an agreement on universal coinage.[46] Aided by strong pressure from the New York State Chamber of Commerce, as well as the support of Kasson and Sherman, Ruggles was chosen as the chief American delegate.[47] His grand conception of the operation was the creation of a "golden chain binding in one common monetary civilization the outspread lands and waters of Europe."[48] As that rhetoric suggests, and notwithstanding his business experience and marketplace interests, Ruggles entertained a somewhat romantic vision of a universal system embracing all forms of measurement. Sherman and Kasson, who planned their European vacations to coincide with the monetary conference scheduled for June 1867, were more concerned with what they viewed as a specific threat posed by the new supplies of silver.[49] That was certainly the case, moreover, with Linderman and McCulloch, who argued that the gold standard was crucial as long as Britain refused to accept bimetallism.

That possibility appeared remote after William S. Jevons of England warned publicly in May 1867 that the increased production of silver posed a direct and serious danger. Since explicit evidence is lacking, it is possible that Ruggles missed that quasi-official alert sounded in the London *Economist* on the eve of the Paris discussions. The question is largely incidental, however, in view of his existing commitment to gold monometallism. In any event, he asked Kasson and Sherman to help swing the Paris Conference to gold. Sherman, who certainly did know the British position through his discussion with London bankers, promptly supplied Ruggles with a letter designed to reassure the delegates that the United States would support such a decision. "I feel sure that Congress will adopt any practical measure that will secure to the commercial world a uniform standard of value and exchange."[50]

The effort failed, however, and the Paris Conference adjourned without creating a new international system. That left the British astride the world commodity markets under the terms of the traditional relationships, and sent Sherman, Linderman, and McCulloch into urgent, sustained discussions. Linderman argued simply, bluntly, and convincingly that the United States had at all costs to define its monetary system in terms of British gold monometallism. That meant dropping silver. The value of gold monometallism was proved, as least to his satisfaction, by British economic supremacy, and the necessity of gold monometallism was established by the reliance of the United States on agricultural exports. His proposal was for "using silver only for subsidiary purposes."[51] Secretary McCulloch agreed, and added strong recommendations for market expansion.[52] Sherman carried his share of the load by introducing a bill on January 6, 1868, that was designed to drop the silver dollar from the American coinage system and limit the acceptance of silver as legal tender to a maximum of ten dollars. The intent was to demonetize silver.[53]

The political strategy, moreover, was based on avoiding a direct confrontation with any group—from silver miners through agricultural spokesmen to urban businessmen—who moved to open a full public debate on the proposal. That danger quickly appeared, however, in the spring of 1868. Senator Edwin Dennison Morgan of New York (a leader in the wholesale grocery trade) spotted the intention to create "a single standard, exclusively of gold," and opposed it on the grounds that such action would weaken the American drive to become the dominant economic power in the world marketplace. He wanted silver retained to expand markets in Latin America and Asia, and demanded "further popular discussion."[54] Then the Toledo Board of Trade filed a protest. That was enough for Sherman, Linderman, and McCulloch. The bill was withdrawn from further Senate consideration on June 9, 1868.[55]

The subsequent change in administrations, the abortive effort by Gould and Fisk to corner the gold market, and Western and Southern anger over metropolitan control of the money supply delayed the effort to demonetize silver for almost two years. A particularly sensitive observer might have been alerted, however, by the first report of Secretary of the Treasury George S. Boutwell in December 1869. He raised the central issue of the balance of payments, for example, and then pointed out that the problem of returning to a specie basis depended upon American exports and the nation's "financial relation to other countries." Not only was his entire argument based on exports, but he used the flour industry to illustrate the analysis.[56]

The agricultural resistance to the deflationary contraction of the greenbacks, and to metropolitan financial dominance, nevertheless indicated the wisdom of further delay. "It requires a deal of coaxing and large promises," charged Senator Timothy Otis Howe of Wisconsin in a typical outburst, "to persuade the money of New England to visit the valley of the Mississippi." "Once a year," he continued with increasing emotion, "the East talks benignly about sending money 'to the

West'—'to move our crop,' they say. . . . But, sir, do you know of any constitutional reason why the West should not have such banking facilities at home . . . as would enable her to send her own crop to market?"[57]

The gold men became increasingly concerned about silver during the winter of 1869-1870, however, and Boutwell submitted their draft law to the Congress on April 25, 1870. It was a gold monometallist bill that dropped the silver dollar and limited the legal tender use of silver to one dollar. Senator Sherman delayed action on the floor of the Senate for almost a year, until January 9-10, 1871, while debate over financial matters in the House became less central and acrimonious. Then he presented the anti-silver bill as a piece of routine monetary legislation and described it in wholly misleading terms: "It does not adopt any new principles." He did not mention the demonetization of silver. Under those conditions (which included the absence of Senator Morgan), and accepted on those terms, the bill was passed 36 to 14.

The House of Representatives was in no hurry to act, however, and the bill waited a year in committee. It finally appeared for debate on January 9, 1872, but sharp differences over the use of nickel sent it back for reconsideration. The next discussion, on April 9, produced a pointed question from Representative Clarkson Potter of New York. He did not understand the need to change existing provisions concerning silver. Representative Kelley of Pennsylvania answered with vague charges that the silver bullion interests were engaged in a conspiracy to push unwanted silver on the Treasury.[58] That was as close as anyone ever came to talking about the central fears that motivated Linderman, Boutwell, and Sherman. And they became steadily more concerned as Germany demonetized silver on December 4, 1871, and as Norway, Sweden, and the Netherlands likewise changed to gold monometallism during 1872.

But no action was taken by the House before adjournment. Senator Sherman's discussions of the crisis with Linderman were amplified by his talks with August Belmont and two representatives of the Rothschild financial empire during a long trip through the West in July 1872. The party traveled in Belmont's private railroad car and pointedly inspected the Comstock silver mine that symbolized the threat to the gold system that they valued so strongly.[59] Secretary Boutwell then reopened the campaign in his *Annual Report for 1872*. Agricultural exports were the key to America's economic health, and hence "moving the crops" was crucial. But so was a monetary system that would strengthen the United States in "the contest for final peaceful supremacy in the affairs of the world." And, recognizing the power of the agricultural businessmen who were demanding action on the railways and waterways, Boutwell concluded with an appeal to improve "the channels of transportation between the seaboard and cotton and grain-growing regions of the country."[60]

The aroused national debate over transportation clearly served to distract attention from the bill demonetizing silver when Sherman reintroduced it in the Senate in January 1872. The legislation, as well as Sherman's mode of operation, indicated that the gold men had become very careful as a result of their encounters with Morgan and Potter. The bill created a special silver dollar for trading with China and other silver-using countries, and that in itself served to create the impression that nothing fundamental was being changed—as well as speaking to the concern for increased exports. Sherman's technique was very subtle and disarming, moreover, as when he made a special point of explaining that small silver coins were being changed a bit to conform with the five-franc piece used by the Latin Union. Combined with the concern over railroads and waterways, those considerations go far to explain the Senate's routine approval of the bill on February 12, 1873. Linderman and the others could relax, at least for the moment. Silver had been demonetized.

Sherman, Boutwell, and Linderman later explained that their tiny group acted because they believed that continuing the coinage of silver "would be a very grave and serious peril to our country." "It would place us," Sherman argued, "in a position to demonetize gold and adopt silver as the single standard, to detach ourselves from the great commercial nations of the world and join the inferior nations."[61] That is very probably the most accurate short explanation of their behavior that can be written. By neglecting it, or discounting it, almost all accounts of demonetization miss the vital emphasis that the protagonists of gold placed on exports. They considered agricultural exports the key to their entire monetary system. And in overlooking that factor, the standard interpretations likewise fail to show how the general and vigorous discussion of the transportation issue—itself tied directly to the export problem—served as a screen behind which a tiny group of metropolitan leaders carried through the demonetization of silver. Finally, the oversight produces a similar failure to recognize that the subsequent campaign to remonetize silver stressed the central role of silver in expanding agricultural exports.

Important as it is, however, Sherman's account of demonetization is seriously incomplete. It says nothing about the collusion and disingenuousness of the tiny group of metropolitan leaders who carried through the action. It omits any recognition that the policy seriously favored creditors over debtors. And it ignores, in the righteous certainty of its belief in gold monometallism, the distinct probability that a silver standard "would certainly have moderated or eliminated deflationary tendencies," and "also have moderated and might have eliminated deflation in the world at large." It would, in short, "have been preferable to gold."[62] Those were the issues, moreover, along with the central matter of expanding overseas markets, that increasingly aroused the agricultural businessmen as the Panic of 1873 became the grave depression of the 1870s. Their concern with those questions, from minority metropolitan control of the farm majority to the vital importance of transportation in controlling the markets of the world, generated a massive upwelling of unrest even as the gold monometallists won their objective. The first results were a Democratic triumph in the House of Representatives and a major effort to use the power of the national government to reform and regulate the railroads, and to improve the waterways of the country.

As that campaign failed in the face of Senate opposition, and as the depression grew ever more severe, the debate turned back toward the monetary question. Then both issues were temporarily obscured by the excitement over a massive boom in food exports. Fortuitous though it was, that export bonanza exerted a major effect on American history. For, combined with the frightening impact of the depression itself, it convinced key metropolitan leaders as well as the majority of agriculturalists that overseas economic expansion provided the answer to their specific and general problems. Tradition, immediate experience, and theoretical argument were thereby transformed into the kind of assumptions and beliefs that guide individuals and move nations.

SEVEN

It is a notorious fact that the cultivation of the soil in this country is not remunerative.

Senator John Brown Gordon of Georgia, 1874

The agricultural community has unquestioned and grievous wrongs to complain of.

Cyrus McCormick, 1874

I have eat the last crust of bread and don't know where the next is coming from.

E. L. Ives of Kansas, 1875

The East has as much hold on us now as we can afford to let her have.

Nebraska State Journal, 1874

The fact soon became prominent that how to sell crops was fully as knotty a question as how to grow them. . . . The solution of this problem soon became a leading idea in the Order. . . . Transportation of farm products to market is also an outgrowth of and properly a part of the same question.

Dudley W. Adams of Iowa, Worthy Master of the National Grange, 1874

After protection unequalled for half a generation the home market has not come to us, but is as far as ever removed from the fields of agriculture.

Representative William Ralls Morrison of Illinois, 1876

The grave questions growing out of the various relations of the producing to the transportation interests of the country, are necessarily of commanding importance. . . . Our leading productions are bulky in their nature and to be made remunerative must have cheap and easy access to the markets of the world.

Governor of Minnesota J. S. Pillsbury, 1876

To a very great extent the prosperity of this country is dependent upon the quantity and price of its crops.

Railroad Gazette, 1873

In a word, we have . . . more of every kind of factory than any healthy home consumption can keep running on full time. . . . We are almost able successfully to compete in the markets of the world.

Commercial and Financial Chronicle, 1875

Those who are in favor of an exclusive gold standard use the example of England.

Cincinnati Commercial, 1876

We have it in our power now to force the remonetization of silver as coin.

Representative William Addison Phillips of Kansas, 1876

A

Massive Depression Intensifies and Extends the Movement for Overseas Market Expansion

AMERICANS had never experienced a depression as disruptive, painful, and prolonged as the collapse of the 1870s. Farm businessmen suffered particularly because their troubles had started almost five years before the Panic of September 1873. The ensuing crisis verified and deepened their existing antagonisms toward the metropolis, reinforced their commitment to the policy of market expansion, and intensified their efforts to improve and reform the transportation and monetary systems. Their rising militancy and strength, along with a similar growth of urban protest, might well have produced significant changes in the United States if a fortuitous boom in agricultural exports had not saved them and also provided the thrust that insured recovery from the terrible depression.

Even before the export bonanza, however, the cumulative power of the agricultural pressure for policies to improve the farmer's position in the overseas marketplace significantly affected the thinking of the metropolitan minority. Influential industrial entrepreneurs and leading Eastern politicians, deeply troubled by the depression and its social consequences, began to adopt, adapt, and agitate the arguments that their agrarian counterparts had been advancing for more than a decade. Even the disagreement over the monetary system began to revolve around the question of whether silver or gold would do more to enlarge the foreign market. By the eve of the election of 1876, both the embattled Republicans and resurgent Democrats had been significantly influenced by the demands for overseas economic expansion.

The failure of American capitalism that contributed so fundamentally to those developments came as part of the long decline in the rate of growth of the American economy that began during the second quarter of 1864. The two downturns in the business cycle that came in April 1865 and June 1869, and which affected agricultural businessmen so extensively, were followed by the massive contraction that began in October 1873 and lasted sixty-five months until March 1879.[1] The yearly description in Thorp's *Business Annals* became a grimly monotonous refrain—*"Depression."*[2]

The break came at the end of a period of overextension, instability, and cumulative reverses. Though they increased the market for agricultural surpluses, for example, the Austro-Prussian and Franco-Prussian wars also weakened the financial structure and forced Europeans to sell American securities. The major fires in Boston and Chicago caused huge capital losses at the same time they shook the finances of insurance companies. Then routine difficulties in marketing the farm crop in 1873 added additional pressure. The first significant failure closed the New York Warehouse and Security Company, which was deeply involved in financing the Missouri, Kansas, and Texas Railroad. Kenyon, Cox, and Company went next, and that collapse weakened the Canada Southern Railway.

Then, on September 19, 1873, as if to dramatize forever the intimate relationship between agriculture and the rest of the economy, Jay Cooke and Company closed its doors. The failure was directly related to Cooke's overextension in trying to drive the Northern Pacific deep into the Red River Valley region of Minnesota and Dakota. The ensuing panic, which began on the following "Black Friday," was brought under control by mid-October, but the economy continued to plunge downward. The wholesale price index of all commodities, for example, dropped from 81 in 1874 to 58.8 in 1879. Business failures climbed steadily from more than 5,000 in 1873 to about 9,000 in 1876 and 1877, and then topped 10,000 in 1878. And unemployment, which reached 6.7 percent in 1874, probably doubled by 1876.[3] Hundreds of thousands of men roamed the country, scrounging a meager living off the land as they searched for work. In some cases the wives and children left behind were hired at disgracefully low wages and thereby disemployed other men. As for those who still had jobs, many of them, as with the men in the Standard Oil plant near Cleveland in 1877, were paid as little as thirty cents a day. The countless strikes and outbreaks of violence provoked the use of existing state and federal troops and generated a wide movement among owners and managers to create private militias and to strengthen the government forces by building armories and providing for permanently increased enlistments.[4]

Those dramatic and disturbing events won many of the headlines in the metropolitan press, but more than half the working population was still engaged in agriculture.[5] Their difficulties can be dramatized by reviewing the steady rise in the acreage opened to the cultivation of wheat, and in the crops taken from that land. In the year of the panic, farm businessmen cultivated 29 million acres and cropped 368.3 million bushels of grain. Five years later, at the depth of the crisis, the acreage had increased to 38.5 million while production had jumped to 504.4 million bushels and when recovery finally came, in 1879, the figures were 39.8 million acres and 549.2 million bushels.[6] Gauged in production indices, food and related agricultural goods moved from 42 in 1872 to 47 in 1875, and on to 53 in 1879.[7] The cotton producers pushed their output from 3.93 million bales in 1872 to 5.76 million bales in 1879.[8] And the index of tobacco production jumped from 31 in 1872 to 42 in 1879.[9]

Such major increases, combined with the fall in prices, intensified the already great emphasis on markets and transportation. Some observers remained hopeful through 1874 that agricultural exports would save the farmer and even slow or halt the decline of the entire economy. Overseas sales of wheat and flour spurted sharply in 1873 after a drop in 1872 and repeated the gain even more dramatically in 1874. The value of all food exports also moved upward, from $169 million to $233 million (all manufactured exports totaled $97 million). But then food sales in 1875 fell back to $189 million. The great boom was three years away, even though agricultural exports continued to account for more than 75 percent of all American exports, and to contribute more than 5 percent of the gross national product.[10]

Faced with present troubles, and unaware of the coming bonanza, farm businessmen pressed hard for legislation to improve transportation, for action to expand their markets, and for a reexamination and revision of the monetary system. The Commissioner of Agriculture read the signs correctly in December 1873, warning that exports were going to receive even "more attention" because of their importance in "affording a market for our surplus products."[11] "It is a notorious fact," summarized Senator John Brown Gordon of Georgia, "that the cultivation of the soil in this country is not remunerative."[12]

"Such poverty I never saw among any people," added Frank J. Whitiek of Alabama, and that stark comment accurately summarized the plight of most Southerners.[13] Henley James, Worthy Master of the Indiana Grange, devoted his annual message to a candid review of the troubles in that state.[14] The agents of the McCormick Company reported similar distress in Illinois. George A. Wiley admitted that he had "a good many machines left on hand," for example, and similar letters undoubtedly prompted Cyrus McCormick to advise the Illinois Democratic Central Committee that "the agricultural community has unquestioned and grievous wrongs to complain of."[15]

Similar reports came from company representatives in Iowa. One of them, an established salesman, regretfully admitted that he could not order any more machines. "The work seems to drag" because he

178

could find "no reasonable prospect."[16] The depression dealt another—and crushing—blow to the cooperative enterprises of the Grange in Illinois, Wisconsin, Iowa, and Minnesota.[17] One Minnesota farmer commented that "wheat is becoming King, and through its alliance with high transportation a tyrant."[18] And a farm wife in Nebraska sadly explained the situation in that state. "Trade is dull, and some people are blue, and are almost giving away the land that has been given to them."[19]

Ben Graycroft, another McCormick representative, described conditions in Missouri by reporting on the bankruptcies of his fellow agents.[20] Even the Kansas City *Times* admitted that the men and women called "farmers—the producing classes" by the *Anti-Monopolist* "are from year to year growing poorer and poorer."[21] One of the agricultural businessmen provided a typically more direct report. "I have eat the last crust of bread," he wrote a friend, "and don't know where the next is coming from." "I expected to rough it," he added a bit later, "but *(dog my cats)* if it ain't a little more than I expected. . . . Whiskey, Hain't seen a drop in a year."[22]

The cattlemen, who were "stunned" by the panic and ensuing collapse, chose Kansas City for their mass meeting of September 1873 that led to the organization of the Live Stockmens' National Association. The first imports of live cattle into Scotland by Henry Bell no doubt encouraged the fortunate exporter, but the sale did not change the general outlook for the cattle industry. One of the men on the range recalled that the failures made him feel like he was "attending a funeral of friends daily."[23] And a bit further to the west, in Wyoming, the need for export markets soon prompted the cattlemen of that territory to organize themselves as a powerful pressure group.

West Coast farmers, acting through the Grange, likewise agitated for a *system* of marketing their surplus. Norman W. Garrelson spoke for many of the agricultural businessmen of Washington and California, as well as for his colleagues in Oregon, when he attacked the quasi-monopolistic and inefficient firms that controlled that phase of marketing.[24] Such men, as well as those in other sections, wholly agreed with David C. Cloud's judgment in *Monopolies and the People*. "Our shores are washed by oceans, which afford us highways, over which we can avail ourselves of the markets of the world. . . . Our great lakes furnish us an outlet for the surplus product of the great west."[25] The depression, accentuating conditions that were already difficult, deepened the conviction among farm businessmen that they could improve their lot if only they organized to demand—and obtain—effective action.

A large number of farmers, however, suffered additional woes caused by the assaults of nature that made it difficult for them to concentrate their energies on the problems of the marketplace. Having endured a season characterized by hot winds and baking sun, Kansans were literally swarmed under by grasshoppers. The western half of the state, where few men had capital reserves, was hit the hardest. As one farmer explained, the combination of "the grasshopper raid and the foreclosure of a mortgage" left him "utterly helpless."[26]

The citizens of the state quickly abandoned their battle to force the government to extend belligerent rights to the Cuban revolutionaries and launched a campaign for relief.[27] They were vigorously supported by neighbors in Nebraska who also endured "great distress" from the combination of the depression and grasshoppers. Conditions became so severe that the percentage of people requiring aid in various parts of the state started at 20 percent and ran as high as 90 percent.[28] President Grant responded by distributing surplus Army clothes from depots in Omaha and Leavenworth. "It was pitiable in most instances," reported one Army officer, "upon entering the poor huts to see women and children crouched shivering around their dull fires in the midst of a cloud of pulverized snow driven in upon them by the storm."[29]

The Army also acted in the Dakotas, Iowa, Colorado, and Minnesota. Governor Cushman Kellogg Davis and the Grange helped as they could in Minnesota, where twenty-eight counties were severely affected by the greedy insects.[30] But resources were limited. "We voted unanimously to give all that we had," noted the Master of the Northfield Grange, "for the relief of our suffering Brothers," and then added sadly that the treasury contained twelve dollars.[31] Davis supplied what he could through state agencies, but much of the "extreme need and suffering" went unrelieved.

Davis used the grasshopper crisis to dramatize the more general breakdown of the marketplace. "Complaints are universal," he noted, and were not limited to the plague of grasshoppers. The underlying troubles were caused by "capital — corporate and confederated — seeking its private interests through statutory means, and profaning every department of government in the effort." The railroads were the worst offenders. "The expense of moving products has become the great expense of life, and it is the only disbursement over which he who pays can exercise no control whatever. . . . The evil is a public one, affecting every citizen."[32]

And so it was, and so it did, agreed delegates to the 1874 meeting of the Vermont Grange. The railroads alarmed and antagonized them for different reasons, such as the role they played in the structural decline of New England agriculture due to the competition from Western farmers, but the Vermont Grangers nevertheless shared the general desire for lower and more equitable rates — and for larger markets.[33] The depression deepened "the listless and despondent spirit" created by the less dramatic but persistent troubles of the postwar years. One farmer in Maine estimated, on the basis of his own inquiries, that the average income of New England farmers stood at 3 percent of their investment "and $20 per month for the man's labor, after deducting farm expenses." That was sufficient to "live from the farm instead of the store," but not enough to change conditions that "weaken the courage." "The situation is not the temporary result of hard times," observed the Rutland *Herald and Globe.* "It is a permanent change in our civilization that was inevitable the moment that the railroads reached the uttermost parts of the West and solved the problem of quick and cheap transportation to the East of agricultural products."[34]

Southerners also knew the pain of special hardships, and the weakening of the will caused by constant difficulties. "Your houses are going to decay, dilapidation spreading all around," thundered William W. Land, Worthy Master of the Texas Grange, in an effort to rouse the pride of his fellow farmers.[35] Others sought relief from their "unprecedented" suffering through attacks on the "unreliability and unfaithfulness" of the freed black man.[36] But most of the Southern whites who blamed the black man also demanded governmental aid in the form of state departments of agriculture, and federal action to provide relief from the taxes of reconstruction, increased internal improvements, and market expansion.

Georgia created the first such department of agriculture in 1874, but Tennessee and North Carolina quickly followed the example.[37] The broader demand for vigorous overseas market expansion was brilliantly stated by Colonel Bushrod W. Frobel of Atlanta. "Our export trade has been so depleted," he exclaimed in December 1873, "that the balance of trade is annually against us." He called for an isthmian canal to help the West and the South grasp "the grain trade of Western Europe, and the cotton market of the world." The protection required by agricultural businessmen, he retorted to the high tariff men, "is the ability to become the active and successful competitors in the markets of the world." Cotton was a crucial export, but he argued militantly that "food controls the value of all manufactured articles . . . and, by its cheap transportation . . . the Pennsylvania miner may drop his iron on the toes of Scotland and Wales, and the western farmer crowd his flour and corn under the nose of the Russian graindealer." Cheap transportation, he concluded, was the key "to the pride and glory of the world."[38]

Similar problems confronted the Western agriculturalists who gained some benefits from a local boom that began during the depths of the depression. That growth was generated, in an ironic way, by the collapse of Jay Cooke that triggered the panic. Cooke was forced to close his doors because he had overinvested in the Northern Pacific Railroad and related efforts to develop the Red River Valley in the Dakota Territory. To meet its obligations, the company began using the land it owned to retire it debts and honor its securities. George W. Cass, president of the road, was one of the first to benefit from that policy, and he and others shortly launched a major campaign to attract immigrants to Dakota and thereby transform their losses into profits.

The determining move may have been made by John L. Grandlin, who held a Cooke note for $88,600. He combined forces (and talents) with Oliver Dalrymple to begin breaking and planting huge acreages that soon came to be known as bonanza farms. Dalrymple quickly took charge of additional large tracts secured by other investors. The Northern Pacific sold 483,141 acres (at an average price of $5.04 per acre) between September 30, 1873, and September 29, 1875, but a tiny group of twenty-three people acquired 63 percent of the total and the best land was soon gone. Within two years Dalrymple had established a corporate system of factory-style agriculture. His gangs of wage laborers, who had no stake or commitment as agricultural business-men, operated a vast array of equipment that included twenty-six plows for breaking the virgin land, forty plows for backsetting (or cross-plowing the first farrows), twenty-one seeders, sixty harrows, thirty self-binding harvesters, and five steam threshers.[39]

Such operations posed serious competitive problems for the individual farm businessmen, and extended and dramatized the kind of absentee control by metropolitan interests that had long engendered antagonism among the men who committed themselves and their families to building an agricultural society. Despite their efforts, the metropolis ran the show. In the Dakota Territory, for example, the first governor was typically appointed from an Eastern state. And, not unusually, John A. Burbank of Indiana "spent his first four years attempting to expand his personal business investments."[40] The system of factory farming also generated major economic and social consequences that deeply affected the men and women who were struggling to settle the region as agricultural businessmen. The scale and efficiency of such techniques rapidly enlarged the surplus, which in turn influenced prices and increased market difficulties. And, because it was conceived and operated solely as a technique of exploiting the land in a narrow economic sense, the corporate organization of agriculture delayed and distorted the social development of the area. For neither the owners, nor the operators, nor the wage laborers involved themselves as citizens. They literally left the country as soon as they discharged their particular responsibilities. The land was largely empty even though it returned profits to the owners. The pattern that began to develop in the Dakotas during the depression of the 1870s thus provides the clearest example of the colonial position of agriculture that produced such persistent anger among farmers throughout the country.

For that matter, even the bonanza wheat men encountered some of the difficulties inherent in the position of the smaller farm businessmen. They also had to deal with the Minneapolis Millers' Association that dominated the Northern grain market, and with the problems of a market system so largely structured by exports whose prices were set in Liverpool and London. One of the best accounts of the power of the Millers' Association was provided by George D. Rogers, an Easterner who arrived in Minneapolis in 1873 with the intention of becoming a grain broker. He was forced to transfer his wheat by shovel before he convinced the association that he would not surrender.[41] The bonanza men enjoyed more leverage than Rogers, and most certainly more than the individual farm businessman, but they could not manipulate the marketplace over any extended period. As a result, they ultimately became involved in the more general campaign to deal with the problems of transportation and exports.

Despite their emphasis on those questions, the farmers did manifest some concern with the monetary system at the outset of the depression. "We can't help believing," commented the Clinton *Age*, "that the agricultural interests of the west will be improved by an increase of the currency."[42] But a good many agricultural businessmen believed that the various proposals to end the depression by juggling the money supply were "based on a fallacy."[43] They were not, in any event, primarily responsible for the pressure that forced the government to release $26 million in greenbacks between September 20, 1873, and January 15, 1874, and prompted it a bit later to accept a figure of $382 million for total circulation. Nor were they outraged, as they would be in later years, when the Secretary of the Treasury contracted in July 1874 for a loan of $45 million through a group of financiers including the Rothschilds of London.

The farmers probably gave more attention, during 1873 and 1874, to the tariff question than to the money issue. That was the estimate of Cyrus McCormick, for example, as he groped for a strategy to maintain the good will of the farm businessmen even though he refused to cut prices as sharply as rival implement manufacturers.[44] Colman also emphasized the tariff in his editorials for the *Rural World*. The arguments were traditional. Members of the Kansas Farmers Co-Operative Association resolved that "salt and lumber shall be placed on the free list, and that there shall be made a material reduction in the duty on iron." The objectives were to lower the prices of consumer goods and weaken the claim of the railroads that high freight rates were caused by unavoidable construction costs.

California wheat producers made the same kind of argument for lowering or repealing the import duty on the jute sacks used for shipping their surpluses. The Grange and the state legislature petitioned the Congress for such action as a way of expanding exports by cutting the price. The legislature also demanded the negotiation and ratification of "a treaty of reciprocity" with Mexico in order to enlarge the foreign market. That kind of aid, along with the construction of an isthmian canal and the regulation of railroads to provide "cheap transportation," would give California farmers and other export interests a profitable competitive position in "the markets of the world."[45]

A speaker at the 1874 meeting of the Nebraska State Agricultural Society likewise stressed the connection between low schedules and enlarged exports, and called for a major campaign against metropolitan high tariff forces.[46] The protectionists became concerned about the agitation and counterattacked with a special pamphlet. The author, one of the writers employed by the American Iron and Steel Association, used the soft-sell approach. It was "safe to say that something is wrong—that a screw is loose in the body politic somewhere," he admitted, but promised that higher rates would set things right in short order.[47] The *Nebraska State Journal* countered that protectionism was one of the reasons farmers ought to revolt against their colonial position. "The East has as much hold on us now as we can afford to let her have."[48]

But the main theme of the initial agrarian reaction to the panic and depression of the 1870s involved a determined effort to better the farmer's position in the existing marketplace, and to expand his exports, by improving and regulating the transportation system. That campaign climaxed the long battle initiated in the mid-1860s and given great momentum by the agricultural downturn in 1869 and by the activities and the report of the Windom Committee. The movement was national in scope, and offered four major programs to solve the problem. That breadth and diversity provided great strength, but in all probability also generated the divisions that explain the failure to effect any major reforms or structural changes.

The general weakness was typified by the divided effort of the Grange, which by 1874 had emerged as the dominant agricultural organization.[49] Whatever its rhetoric about being primarily a fraternal, educational, and social institution, the Grange consciously and purposefully tried to function as a marketplace entrepreneur and political pressure group. Its founder proclaimed that "each Grange is of itself a Board of Trade," and the state and national bodies did their best to honor that injunction.[50] As the Ohio Grange explained, "we are bound together by . . . a common interest in the prosperity of our agricultural pursuits"—a prosperity the members defined as being tied directly "to the markets of the world."[51]

No one could have made the point any clearer than Dudley W. Adams of Iowa did in his 1874 address as Worthy Master of the National Grange. "One of the first and most proper subjects for discussion," he recalled in reviewing the early meetings, "was how to make two blades of grass grow where one grew before. During those discussions, the fact soon became prominent that how to sell crops was fully as knotty a question as how to grow them. . . . The solution of this problem soon became a leading idea in the Order. . . . Transportation of farm products to market is also an outgrowth of and properly a part of the same question." The delegates agreed, and adopted as part of the Declaration of Purposes a demand for "all facilities for transporting cheaply to the seaboard, or between home producers and consumers, all the productions of our country."[52]

One Grange approach involved the effort in such states as Illinois, Iowa, Wisconsin, and Minnesota to secure regulatory legislation. The Iowa Grange insisted that the state possessed the power, under the principles of the common law, to fix rates. "Unless there is a radical change" in the "cost of transporting this surplus to Liverpool," A. B. Smedley explained, "we shall be shut out of those markets."[53] The movement mustered enough political strength, moreover, to secure the passage of a railroad act that fixed maximum rates for four classes of freight.[54] And it appeared, after the law was upheld by the United States Circuit Court, that the control would be effective.

Even as the bill was passed, however, it became apparent that other Grangers favored different approaches. James Horatio Osborn of Wisconsin became the leader of a campaign to create a major waterway system from the Great Lakes via the Fox, Wisconsin, and Mississippi rivers to New Orleans. That route was termed "the natural outlet of this region to the European markets" in the call for a major strategy session to assemble at Keokuk, Iowa, in October 1873. As Worthy Master of the Wisconsin Grange, Osborn sought to develop "the magic touch of systematic business organization," and to that end cultivated ties with Horace K. Thurber and other leaders of the New York Cheap Transportation Association, which was composed largely of merchants. Osborn was politically shrewd enough, moreover, to maneuver an appointment in 1874 as chairman of the Wisconsin State Railroad Commission established under the Granger-influenced Potter Law.[55]

Such experience, including unsuccessful efforts to influence Representative Philetus Sawyer of Wisconsin, who held a powerful position as chairman of the House Commerce Committee, led Osborn to be skeptical of the effectiveness of state regulatory legislation. As chairman of the Keokuk meeting, therefore, he devised a strategy to hold all congressmen and senators to "STRICT, REAL, and ACTUAL responsibility."[56] The convention would organize a sustained, coordinated effort by all state Granges to focus irresistible pressure on the Congress. Osborn won the support of Missouri and most other states along the Mississippi, but the Indiana and Iowa Granges refused to commit their strength exclusively to the waterway solution. They argued cogently that the power of the railroads had to be confronted directly on the national level.

Osborn lost his bid for leadership when the National Grange declined to endorse his project for the Fox and Wisconsin rivers. Instead, Smedley moved into the key position. He was not opposed to improving the Mississippi route, but pointed out that farm businessmen would still have to control the railroads to prevent them from defeating that strategy by manipulating rates on their east-west routes. Along with Governor Carpenter of Iowa, Smedley understood that the railroad problem was "not only *national* but *international*," and concluded at an early date that state regulation would never be effective in "reaching the markets of the world as seems to be demanded in the present and must become a necessity at no distant day."[57]

His program contained five proposals for action by the federal government. First, it should improve and maintain navigation on the Mississippi and construct major port facilities at the mouth of the river. Second, it should pass regulatory legislation to maintain railroad freight rates at a level based on a reasonable profit over costs. Third, to guide the determination of those costs, and at the same time provide a truly national highway, it should (as the Indiana Grange proposed at Keokuk) construct a double-track railway from the Missouri River to the Atlantic seaboard. Fourth, as an additional lever to keep the railroads honest, it should build a ship canal around Niagara Falls and thereby provide ocean freight rates from the Great Lakes to Liverpool. Finally, the Executive Department should initiate policies designed "to restore our foreign commerce to its former condition of efficiency." Smedley dismissed the cost of such a program as a "pittance" compared with the benefits conferred on the manufacturers and other metropolitan interests by the high tariff system.[58]

In making his analysis and developing his proposals, Smedley relied extensively on the proceedings of the Windom Committee. And he wholly agreed with Senator Windom's basic premise: "Cheapen transportation between the interior and the seaboard, and our producers will command the markets of Western Europe."[59] Both men feared rising Russian competition, and they wanted to hold the advantage through a broad program of internal improvements and other aid that would match the assistance being supplied by the Tsarist government. Smedley offered almost every significant transportation proposal advocated by farm businessmen between 1870 and 1900. If his grand plan had been undertaken as national policy in 1875-1877, moreover, it would have produced significant improvements in the position and the condition of American farmers.

The one major idea that Smedley bypassed, and the fourth plan that gained support in 1873-1874, called for agricultural businessmen to market their surpluses through their own direct trade organizations. That approach won support from Chicago to Kansas City and St. Louis, and from New Orleans eastward through the South.

The project was the creature of a coalition that included the English Cooperative Union, various state Granges in the United States, and businessmen of both countries. The most important figure was Thomas Worrall, an Englishman who settled in New Orleans after the Civil War and devised the plan as a way of expanding exports while using the Mississippi River to check the railroads.

Worrall first secured British support during the winter of 1873 - 1874 and then launched his campaign in the United States through the Mississippi Valley Trading Society of London. He appealed directly to the colonial consciousness (and anger) of Western and Southern farmers, offering his plan as a way to break "their thralldom to the great cities and money power of the New England states." The argument was effective. London was attempting, fumed one Southern spokesman, "to regulate the commerce and consequently the value of money, and of labor and property, in all the other countries having commercial intercourse with her."[60] The Georgia Grange chartered its chapter of the Direct Trade Union in February 1874 as a way of ending the farmer's position as a "hewer of wood and drawer of water"; and Grangers in Alabama, Virginia, and the Carolinas soon added their support.[61]

Worrall also attracted many other Western and Southern businessmen who wanted to increase their leverage against the metropolis. Cyrus McCormick, for example, headed the Chicago chapter of the Mississippi Valley Trading Company, which gained support from Philip Armour, the Chicago Board of Trade, and some leaders of the Illinois Central Railroad. They spoke the same language about "commercial tribute" paid to the East, and entertained the same desire to expand exports. "Chicago and the northwest," explained the Chicago *Times*, "seek more direct commercial relations with Europe." Merchants and processors in Kansas City also backed the movement.[62]

The direct trade agitation undoubtedly increased the intensity and momentum of the effort to improve transportation and enlarge exports. But it also distracted its supporters from the drive to pass federal legislation. That campaign moved toward a climax between December 1873 and the opening of the Forty-third Congress on March 4, 1874. Encouraged by many Midwestern and Eastern merchants, who had their own complaints against the railroads, the agricultural businessmen steadily increased their pressure on the metropolis and the government. The Grant Administration was neither indifferent nor unsympathetic, if only because the election of 1870 had demonstrated that farm discontent could help the Democrats win control of the House of Representatives. But many members of the executive branch, including the President, were personally concerned about the crisis in agriculture. Lucius Fairchild of Wisconsin, for example, who served as American consul in Liverpool, understood the situation and added his weight to the effort. The price obtained for wheat "in our western states is controlled by the prices here," he explained to one correspondent; and pointed out that "the cheaper we can get it to the Atlantic the better we can control the market."[63]

Others, like Secretary of the Treasury William A. Richardson, approached the problem as metropolitan leaders concerned with the functioning of the political economy, and with a concern to reestablish specie payments and maintain the gold standard. "Nothing," he asserted in December 1873, "except a sound financial system, is more important to the welfare of the country than that of turning and retaining the balance of trade in favor of the United States, by a healthy stimulation of the agricultural and manufacturing industry of the country [through] the reduction in the cost of production . . . and of transportation . . . and no legislation should be neglected." And he added that the Administration had already offered "every facility" to help the tobacco growers enlarge their exports.[64]

The agriculturalists applied most of their pressure on the Congress, realizing that the professions of the Grant Administration could never be tested until metropolitan resistance had been overcome and the desired legislation enacted. The Iowa Assembly led off on February 2, 1874, with a militant complaint against the "onerous and oppressive taxation" levied by railroads and a demand for a law to stop "unjust charges or discrimination."[65] Minnesota then filed a special plea for "cheap transportation" to help Minneapolis control the grain trade of the Red River Valley, and to prevent the British—acting through Canada—from dominating the economy of that region. That danger made the issue "of national importance."

Then Missouri launched its effort to channel federal efforts into Mississippi River improvement. Representative Erastus Wells emphasized "the absolute necessity . . . for cheap and permanent methods of transporting the surplus products of the west to markets," and warned the metropolis against discounting "the urgency" of the crisis. The metropolis could delay action, he admitted, but that would produce "evil effects" reaching far beyond the immediate rewards of inaction. The best solution, he concluded, was to create competitive water routes that would force the railroads to lower rates and stop discriminating.[66]

The Missouri state legislature formalized the Wells program and added a directive to the governor to coordinate his efforts with the executives of Illinois, Iowa, Kansas, Nebraska, Minnesota, and Wisconsin. Additional pressure came from flour millers, grain dealers, and other entrepreneurs in Kansas City. Led by Robert T. Van Horn, who wanted to break metropolitan control over transportation and free Americans from the "commercial thralldom of Europe," the members of the Kansas City Board of Trade devised their own variation of the Mississippi Valley plan. They proposed a rail connection south through

Houston to Galveston, where a major port would be developed through government aid. That would give Midwesterners control of the markets of Central and South America.[67]

Wisconsin agriculturalists generally supported the Missouri emphasis on improving the Mississippi. That would "go far," the state legislature resolved on March 12, 1874, "toward solving the vexed question of transportation." But the members also favored a ship canal around Niagara Falls to improve the route "to the European markets." The vital consideration was to do something "without delay," for Westerners were tired of paying taxes and "receiving in return but a scanty part of the vast annual appropriation" for internal improvements. Lest there be any misunderstanding, the assemblymen made it clear that farmers were demanding "cheaper and more adequate means for moving the surplus."

State legislators in Illinois, who were experienced in such matters, warned that "the question of cheap transportation is agitating the people of the Northwest to an extent that has never before been equalled." "Early action" was imperative to prevent "unjust charges or discrimination," and "to provide at an early day such cheap means of transporting the surplus products of the great West as will be remunerative to the producer." And soon thereafter, one Illinois leader, Representative Stephen Augustus Hurlbut, helped bring the issue before the Congress.

He acted as a member of the Committee on Railways and Canals, submitting a long report on the wisdom of constructing a double-track freight railway from New York to Council Bluffs, Iowa, with branches terminating in St. Louis and Chicago.[68] The system was presented as the best response to the two developments that threatened to disrupt the American economy by driving the farmer from the British commodity market. First, the increased production and improved transportation systems in Russia and other East European countries posed a mortal challenge to American agriculture. "By reducing the existing unnecessary and oppressive charge for transportation," however, "the control of the foreign market will pass into the hands of the United States, and we shall be no longer dependent upon Russia and Austria to regulate the price of our crops and the value of our land."[69]

The second factor was the inability to meet the threat either by relying on the leadership of the railroad corporations or through state or federal regulation. The situation would be eased by improvements in the water transportation systems from St. Paul to the Gulf of Mexico, and from the Great Lakes to the Atlantic; but the essential remedy was a new railroad "for freight only." Built with reduced and uniform grades, and depending "for profits upon largely increased business," such a railway would enable American farm businessmen "to reach and control the foreign market by a cheap and reasonable route at a fair price."[70]

Those who backed the government railroad solution, including Grange and other groups in Missouri, Michigan, and Indiana, as well in Iowa and Illinois, offered several arguments for their plan. Those who distrusted governmental intervention in the marketplace, or accepted it skeptically, reasoned that the effort would be more successful if it involved the operation of one enterprise rather than an attempt to regulate many corporations. Others concluded that the public would be "better and more cheaply served under the governmental than under the corporate system." And others, like Representative Hurlbut, argued simply that the double-track system provided the only pragmatically effective way to deal with all the problems.[71]

If the Illinois forces had united behind Hurlbut's proposal, they might have taken the initiative from the Iowans who had been organized so effectively by Smedley and other Grange leaders. But many Illinois congressmen favored improving the Ohio and Mississippi River system, and others opposed federal action. As a result, the Congress dealt with the transportation system in terms of the regulatory bill sponsored by Representative George Washington McCrary of Iowa, chairman of the Committe on Railroads and Canals. He was particularly concerned about the ability of individual railroad corporations to manipulate classification rules, rates, and services, and deeply troubled by their awesome power when organized as pools or trusts.

Along with other Iowa spokesmen, McCrary generally supported any proposal to provide better and cheaper transportation for agricultural businessmen. But he argued cogently, as did his colleague Representative James Wilson, that the railroads would continue to carry much of the farm surplus regardless of any improvements in the waterway system. Railroad regulation was therefore essential, and the federal government had to take the responsibility. Many states would not act; some might well favor the corporations; and, even if all did act in behalf of the public, the lack of uniformity would cause confusion and ineffectiveness.[72]

Wilson offered the most compelling argument for regulation. The existing railway system was irrational, he pointed out, having been built on an ad hoc basis as part of the shift in trade routes caused by the Civil War. The broad objective was to organize and control the resulting mess by building a double-track freight line direct to the Atlantic, connecting the existing lines to improved water routes, and regulating the integrated system thereby created. That would cut costs, increase efficiency, decrease extortion and discrimination, and prevent American farmers from being "shut out of the markets of the world." Otherwise, the Russians would soon "be selling wheat in Boston."[73]

The logic of the McCrary bill persuaded a large number of spokesmen from the Midwest and other agricultural regions, winning votes in

Georgia, Alabama, Florida, the Carolinas, Arkansas, and Mississippi, as well as in Pennsylvania, New York, New Jersey, and California. Three factors account for its defeat. One was the routine political maneuvering by Democrats anxious to recover their control of the House in the coming elections. That element can be weighted too heavily, however, because many Democrats voted against the McCrary bill as representatives of the metropolis rather than as political strategists. That split between the metropolis and the country was noted at the time by many advocates of transportation legislation. Representative Richard Parks Bland, a Missouri Democrat, raised the issue because he became increasingly angry over the failure to obtain metropolitan support. "The people of the West and Northwest took up arms in the late civil war," he lashed out, "more than all else, for the purpose of forever securing to themselves free navigation of the Mississippi River and its tributaries, that their produce might find easy, cheap and ready transportation to the markets of the globe."[74] Bland was warning the leaders of his own party, as well as the Republicans, that the metropolis was taking a grave risk in persistently overriding the agricultural majority.[75]

Bland and other advocates of solving the transportation-market problem by improving the Mississippi and other river systems nevertheless voted against the McCrary bill on the grounds that water routes were cheaper, that such an alternate network was necessary to provide economic enforcement for any regulatory program, and that the railroads would never supply adequate service for the Missouri Valley and the lower Mississippi region. Some of those men added the argument that metropolitan interests would emasculate any railroad commission, and a few admitted that they wanted particular benefits for their own district or state that were not provided by the McCrary bill. Those opponents, who ranged from Wisconsin to Texas, and from Ohio and Kentucky to Oregon, withheld crucial votes during the final showdown over regulatory legislation.[76]

It would be easy to conclude that the farm businessmen defeated themselves, but the evidence does not support that facile analysis. For, in a simple political sense, a victory in the House would have been aborted by metropolitan power in the Senate. And, in the substantive realm, the proponents of the waterway system presented a powerful case for the crucial importance of creating an efficient alternative to the railroads. Futhermore, the defeat did not destroy the momentum of the movement. Indeed, the intensity of the debate, along with the seriousness of the problem and its political implications, prompted President Grant to make a special appeal for legislation to "increase the facilities of transportation from the grain-growing States of the West to the seaboard."[77] That pressure did not produce an immediate victory, but it did encourage a realignment of metropolitan

Republicans, and that ultimately led to the passage of an important measure for improving the Mississippi River.

That proposal was largely the work of James B. Eads, a perceptive engineer who gained early fame by bridging the Mississippi at St. Louis. He reasoned that jetties constructed to narrow the river would generate enough velocity to scour the sand bars that caused so many difficulties for commercial freight shipments. Eads was also persistent and persuasive, convincing businessmen from St. Louis to New Orleans, as well as agriculturalists and politicians of the region. Representative John Bullock Clark, Jr., of Missouri made a blunt appeal for support from the metropolis during the debate over the project that developed after the defeat of the McCrary bill. "Let me entreat you to do a tardy act of justice to the suffering South and West; we now come before you asking that we be paid back for all those years of toil."[78]

The congressional elections of 1874 sounded a stronger trumpet. The Democrats again won control of the House, 169 to 109, and gained ten seats in the Senate (bringing the division there to forty-five Republicans and twenty-nine Democrats). That outcome strengthened the position (as well as the concern) of Republicans like Blaine, who had warned about agricultural unrest, and Senator George Frisbie Hoar of Massachusetts, who supported the Eads plan.[79] President Grant and Secretary of the Treasury Benjamin H. Bristow responded by reasserting the vital importance of acting to expand agricultural exports.[80] More significantly, the Republican-dominated Senate approved the Eads plan for the Mississippi on February 18, 1874, before the new Democratic members could claim any of the credit. The work began in April and proceeded rapidly and effectively. Once the Democrats arrived, moreover, they awarded the Southern states a larger share of the appropriations for internal improvements. Michigan and Wisconsin had received more than the entire South had in 1872, but the 1875 bill gave that region 24 percent of the total.

Such changes prompted Republican leaders like Rutherford Birchard Hayes of Ohio, Zachariah Chandler of Michigan, and John Y. Calhoun of Illinois, who could read a political omen before many others even saw it, to begin bidding for the assistance of Blaine in 1876.[81] Their concern was warranted, for Blaine understood the temper of the agricultural businessmen and realized that the metropolis had to devise a program that would meet their needs. He recognized, for example, the importance of changing a trade expansion measure like the old reciprocity treaty with Canada that funneled most of its benefits to the metropolis. And nothing occurred between 1874 and the elections of 1876 to decrease the Republican party's need for such leaders.

"It is useless at present to discuss the depressed state of agriculture," commented the Worthy Master of one Southern Grange, "for this is painfully evident to every member of the order." Conditions continued to be "deplorable," and that sustained a mood of "general despondency."[82] "We are poor," added Kansas farmers, and endure "a great amount of suffering and destitution." The theme in Illinois was "the gradual impoverishment." Ohio agriculturalists protested the "vagrancy and want" that had become "a crying evil" in the country. Oregonians reported "a year of severe trial." And the grasshopper plague continued in such severity that the governors of Minnesota, Nebraska, Kansas, Iowa, Missouri, and the Dakota Territory agreed in 1876 to make a united demand for federal relief.[83]

The Grange had failed to effect any general or sustained improvements in the position of the farmer by 1876, and it lost members with increasing rapidity. The cooperative ventures succumbed to lack of capital, inexperienced leadership, limited potential, and the tough competition in the marketplace. They were "nothing but private enterprises," as an Illinois Granger pointed out in a candid analysis of the collapse. "It only places us upon a level with the usual competition in trade, and subjects our inexperienced agents to all the petty annoyances of adepts in the business."[84] In the broader sense, moreover, Grange leaders lost control of the early growth and failed to organize and focus their strength on one national program. And the limited effectiveness of the state railway legislation, followed by the defeat of the McCrary proposal, discouraged some farmers and turned others toward more traditional political activity.

"What we want," commented one farmer in a letter to the editor, "is practical profit . . . for in most instances a western granger's heart and pocket are synonymous."[85] Profits were elusive, however, for reasons that Charles Francis Adams, a major metropolitan leader, explained in 1875: the railroads "indeed" involved "a case of absentee ownership, with all that those words imply." And to drive home the point, Adams then compared the Western farm businessmen to the Indian population under the British East India Company.[86] For their part, the delegates to the meeting of the American Board of Transportation and Commerce emphasized that the railroads held the key to prosperity: "it is only necessary for us to supply the means of exporting our grain, bacon, tobacco, cotton, oil, and other products, at prices which will enable us to sell those products to other countries."[87]

Despite the inability to win a major victory, neither the campaign by the Grange nor other efforts collapsed like a lean-to in a prairie thunderstorm. A group of New York farm businessmen organized themselves as an Alliance during the winter of 1875-1876; the chief object, recalled the first president, "was to effect legislation in the interest of the agriculturalist."[88] Almost simultaneously, the Southern Farmers Alliance was formed by Texans to enforce the law and fight the large ranchers and land monopolists. And still another group, generally more conservative, created the Farmers National Congress during an 1875 meeting in Atlanta.

The Grange invested much of its attention and energy during 1875 and 1876 in the campaign for direct trade with Europe, and that decision contributed to later weakness. The National Executive Board approved Worrall's plan, but he then divided his effort by organizing the American Cooperative Union and opening membership to non-Grangers. That angered national Grange leaders, but many Southern Granges continued to support the plan. Their efforts had helped define railroads as public highways, and the companies as common carriers, in the new Alabama Constitution of 1875, and they were seriously upset by the Southern Railway and Steamship Association organized in 1875 by Albert Fink.[89]

Worrall made a strong effort to retain Granger support, arguing that the Mississippi Valley "finds itself in a state of commercial dependency" with a "leech at every pore." Direct trade would reward the farm businessman with independence in his own land and a handsome profit. "But if your bowels so yearn for New York and New England that you are determined to deal with them," he continued, then "submit."[90] The National Grange had no more intention of submitting to Worrall than to New York, however, and the leaders withdrew from the Mississippi Valley Trading Company to make their own arrangements for exporting to British cooperatives. That effort continued through 1876, but never produced the desired results.[91]

The persistent concern with export markets did, however, sustain the opposition to the tariff. Westerners and Southerners almost defeated (114 to 123) a House bill in March 1875 that raised rates to an average level of 43 percent, and the pressure of farm businessmen made it clear that the old reciprocity treaty with Canada would not be renewed. "At the very moment" when the nation's *true policy* and financial *necessities* impatiently demand" an expansion of exports, warned one typical group of petitioners, it was foolhardy to follow a policy "calculated to destroy our agricultural markets."

Farm businessmen were not against reciprocity per se; they demanded only that it be employed in behalf of their interests. That approach often led to short-run disagreements between different groups of farmers, just as metropolitan businessmen differed in their estimate of what would produce profits. Thus Northern and Southern agriculturalists initially split over the 1875 reciprocity treaty with Hawaii. Sugar and rice producers opposed the move even though it opened the island market to grain and meat farmers. A compromise was finally arranged, however, and agricultural operators became increasingly favorable to the reciprocity strategy as a way of penetrating and controlling markets (as happened in Hawaii).

Illinois representatives carried much of the general battle against protectionism. "In 1870," recalled Representative Horatio Chapin Burchard, "I affirmed that the high tariff had failed and would fail to give a market for our surpluses." "After protection unequalled for half a generation," William Ralls Morrison added, in a move to establish the issue for the coming election, "the home market has not come to us, but it is as far as ever removed from the fields of agriculture."[92] Such direct attacks on the weakest part of the high tariff argument prompted metropolitan protectionists to revive their charge that reduction was proposed, "not by members of Congress for the benefit of this country and its inhabitants, but by adherents of other nations for the benefit of foreigners."[93]

The rising concern about the tariff was caused by three factors that were operative throughout the country. The most important element was the growing consensus in support of the export argument that the farm businessmen had been agitating with increasing militance for more than a decade. But that was directly related to the other two: the persisting need for markets, and the way that existing exports verified the market expansion thesis and intensified the demand for more overseas sales. The great Kansas wheat crops of 1875 and 1876, for example, dramatized the necessity for markets in a region that had suffered enormously from the depression.[94] Similar surpluses troubled the flour industry in Minneapolis, but the railroads raised rates so high as to "virtually prohibit exportation from the West."[95]

The industry's leading spokesman in government, Governor James S. Pillsbury, responded with blunt talk about "the grave questions growing out of the various relations of the producing to the transportation interests of the country." His inaugural address of January 7, 1876, provided a revealing example of how, despite their differences and conflicts, the producers and processors of agricultural surpluses shared crucial assumptions and favored similar policies. "Agriculture is the primary source of wealth," he reminded the railroads and other metropolitan giants, because of "that underlying need for food." The agricultural businessmen and the milling businessmen had a common interest in "cheap and easy access to the markets of the world," and the state was a "trustee" with responsibility for insuring that both parties received their just returns.[96]

In a similar way, many farmers driven out of wheat were counting on exports to underwrite their shift to dairy operations.[97] Far to the west, fruit growers in California were beginning to manifest a similar concern with foreign markets.[98] But the most significant new development involved the rapid expansion of meat production and exports. "We cannot grow too much corn," proclaimed John Sterling Morton of Nebraska. "No matter what corn may be worth in the market . . . corn transmitted to beef, pork or mutton . . . will always pay the husbandman a handsome and satisfying profit."[99] That optimism proved unjustified, and Morton's inability to cope with the consequences cost him dearly as Secretary of Agriculture between 1893 and 1897, but in 1876 it appeared as little more than understandable overstatement.

For, exploiting the work of innovators such as Eastman, cattle kings like John Dean Gillett of Illinois and packers like Swift moved quickly to dominate the British beef market. Even Queen Victoria judged Yankee cattle "very good," and exports jumped from 1,095 hundredweight in 1874 to 144,336 in 1876.[100] Nor was that all; Midwestern swine growers benefited from an "immense enlargement of exportation," and West Coast producers were penetrating the South American and Asian markets.[101] And, as with the grain farmer and the miller, the livestock men found allies among the shoe manufacturers. They were beginning to view the export market as "of national importance."[102]

The same pattern was emerging in the South, where cotton growers were finding common purpose with the region's manufacturers of rough textiles for export. As their production returned to the highest prewar level (with the crop of 1876), the cotton men saw the textile mill campaign as one of their chief hopes for the future. Southern mills had exported to various markets before the Civil War, and the industry initiated a vigorous and effective revival.[103] Some of the firms had penetrated the Far Western market with sheetings and drills prior to the depression.[104] Such successes generated a campaign, which quickly adopted the slogan of "Bring the Cotton Mills to the Cotton Fields," to expand production. The economic objectives were integrated with the desire to restore the social cohesion of Southern society, and the urge to reassert Southern political influence in the national government. Capital was sought and obtained from cotton farmers as well as city businessmen, and the effort brought the two elements of the industry closer together. The push for overseas markets became the central theme of the joint effort.

The mill-building program was interrupted—but not terminated—by the panic. The Piedmont Manufacturing Company of South Carolina, for example, was forced to delay operations until 1875, and other projects suffered similar setbacks.[105] But the striking success of existing mills sustained the movement. "Hardly a southern mill," noted *Bradstreet's*, "failed to declare a dividend" throughout the depression, and some returns ranged as high as 16 percent.[106] Then, as the new mills began producing, the Southern owners dramatically increased their overseas sales. Exports averaged about $3 million from 1871 to 1875, then jumped more than 300 percent for the years 1876 - 1881.[107]

Northern textile men, who dominated the business as part of the general metropolitan control of industrial development, viewed Southern gains as a factor that compounded their existing difficulties. "Production must either be decreased or our own circle of consumers enlarged," they judged at the end of 1874: "We cannot accept the former alternative."[108] The analysis quickly led to action. New York merchants representing a group of Fall River manufacturers opened an effort to penetrate the British market in 1875, and Edward Atkinson, the politcally conscious leader of the Northerners, launched a major campaign to meet the emergency by expanding exports to Europe, Latin America, and Asia.[109]

Atkinson and other Northern owners were generally slower to commit themselves permanently to the overseas market, however, than the Southerners. They also lagged behind the implement firms. "Many of the leading" agricultural machinery manufacturers, Walter A. Wood, Frank D. Osborne, and Deere as well as McCormick, were "actively campaigning for foreign" markets as their production outran the capacity of the depression-ridden farmers to purchase such equipment.[110] Even more significantly, agricultural exports were affecting the general — as well as the specific — thought and policy of the railroads. Garrett of the Baltimore and Ohio gleefully predicted during 1873 and 1874 that his commitment to farm exports would save his road from the depression and transform Baltimore into "the 'Liverpool' of America."[111] Even when overseas sales declined, and his rivals launched a ruthless rate war, he relied on the export argument to defend himself against attacks from his financial backers. "Increased exports will aid our railroad interests," he maintained, "and I hope create a material improvement in business during the approaching autumn and winter."[112]

The same thesis guided others in the industry. "To a very great extent," the *Railroad Gazette* explained, "the prosperity of this country is dependent upon the quantity and price of its crops. For, with the exception of petroleum, these are the only things of which we produce a surplus. . . . When the farmers are prosperous, when they have large amounts of cotton, grain and cattle to sell, and the foreign demand is sufficient to make the prices high, then usually other business is prosperous. . . . The railroads are especially affected by the condition of agriculture, for the products of the soil form the largest part of their traffic."[113]

Related manufacturers began to apply that classical Smithian analysis to their own operations as the depression deepened. The Baldwin Locomotive Works, for example, immediately felt the pinch of the railroad decline. The firm was producing about 500 locomotives a year on the eve of the panic, but in the first quarter of 1874 the rate of production nosedived to 140 per year. Nor was it merely that exports became desirable: production would have tumbled to 46 per year without overseas orders. Other manufacturers understood the situation. "Foreign trade," announced the *Bulletin* of the American Iron and Steel Association in June 1874, "is what we most need."[114]

The industry was soon speaking openly of "overproduction," and that approach began to be generalized to the entire metropolitan sector of the economy. "In a word," concluded the *Commercial and Financial Chronicle*, "we have . . . more of every kind of factory than any healthy home consumption can keep running on full time. The present dull trade and depression in prices" point to "the markets of the world" as the way to "obtain quick relief for our languishing industries." "We shall have to compete boldly and skillfully," added the *Iron Age*.[115] But the future had already become the present. For the French and the British reported—in surprise and fear—that some American firms were even then beginning to display those characteristics in Africa as well as in Asia.[116]

Members of the Grant Administration, who had stressed exports since 1869, gave official sanction to the overproduction thesis, arguing that exports prevented the depression from becoming even more terrible and calling for the further expansion of overseas markets.[117] They also approved the admission of Colorado as a state, a move clearly designed to increase Republican votes in the coming presidential election of 1876 by pacifying some of the antimetropolitan feeling among agricultural businessmen. Colorado citizens were happy to end their neocolonial position in the political side of the political economy—"We celebrate our emancipation"—but they were far from satisfied with government policy concerning cattle and silver.[118]

The Grant Administration was not willing to go so far in support of expanding exports as to remonetize silver. Neither was the majority of other metropolitan leaders. Yet several factors combined to reopen the issue that the small group of gold advocates thought they had settled in 1873. The continuing severity of the depression and the related monetary problems prevented the question from being neglected or forgotten. The agitation for more greenbacks likewise focused attention on the currency question, as did the constant discussion of specie resumption. As a result, growing numbers of people became aware that silver had been demonetized in 1873, and the men who began to campaign for remonetization rapidly extended and focused that awareness throughout the country. From the beginning, moreover, the silverites enjoyed important sources of strength. The coalition drew support from all geographic sections of the country; its members were guided by a general theory of economic development as well as driven by specific economic interests; and it included metropolitan leaders as well as many, many agricultural businessmen.

All those elements became apparent in 1875 as the issue reentered the arena of public debate. Some of the earliest calls for action came from the Midwest. "Bring us back to the solid foundation of gold and silver," demanded the St. Louis *Republican*, warning that the failure to do so would cause serious trouble.[119] A diagnostician in Wisconsin reported ominously that "our currency patient is sick." "The fact is patent that the East is both a sponge and a lemon-squeezer, and that the West is the lemon, a large share of the juices of which is being absorbed by the sponge."[120]

As a sensitive and ambitious politician, as well as one who believed that remonetization would solve the problems of the farmer and the nation, Representative Bland of Missouri moved quickly to establish himself as the leader of the silver forces in the Mississippi and Missouri River valleys. His dedication, energy, and talent rapidly enabled him to use that regional strength as a base for national influence.

Two spokesmen of the mining industry, and of Western business interest in general, proved as passionately indefatigable as Bland. One was Senator William Morris Stewart of Nevada, a lawyer-politician who owned and operated silver mines. He knew personally, as well as generally, the results of demonetization. Nevada's economy slumped badly, and much of its population moved elsewhere, after demonetization. As a "master over judges, juries, and opponents," whose place in the Republican party was based on his close relationship with Lincoln, Stewart possessed power and influence, and he used them for silver.[121] The other Far Western leader was Henry Moore Teller, another Republican who based his career on serving as an advocate for the territories of the neocolonial West. He became one of Colorado's first (and perennial) senators, and campaigned for silver as a friend of the cattle growers, as well as an ally of the miners.

Southerners became concerned about silver because of its role in financing British cotton production in India, and as a result of their desire to penetrate the markets of silver-using countries.[122] The influence of the first argument was greatly extended when John R. Dodge, the statistician of the Department of Agriculture, carefully explained it in a public document. And, by using British wheat operations in India as his example, Dodge further reinforced the relevance of the issue for Northern and Western farm businessmen. He recounted the way an English wheat importer began his maneuvers by having £833 of silver bullion coined into 10,000 Indian rupees. Because India used silver money, that operation rewarded the Englishman with £1,000 of purchasing power. The difference, £167, paid the transportation costs on the grain to Liverpool, and "added considerably to the margin of profit."[123] It also gave the Englishman the capacity to undersell American wheat and thereby cut exports from Illinois, Kansas, or Minnesota.

The general argument about the damage of demonetization won a metropolitan hearing, moreover, from economist Henry Clay. Gold monometallism tied the United States so closely to Great Britain, he protested in 1875, that America was being recolonized. High tariffs and a nationalistic money policy were the keys to "Financial Independence."[124] Such agitation from so many sources had a prompt effect. President Grant took official notice of the mounting pressure in his annual message of December 1875, but defended gold as the only standard that would prevent Americans from laboring as "hewers of wood and drawers of water." The seriousness of the issue then prompted Blaine to present a formal statement of the case for gold.

He began with a candid admission that the United States was "suffering from prostration in business." Then he explained why the proposal to print more greenbacks, and similar plans, failed to provide a workable remedy. American prosperity depended on agricultural exports, and those, because of England's power and policy, were "inevitably and peremptorily subjected to the gold standard when sold." Hence the only satisfactory policy was specie based on gold. Blaine went on, however, to transform the routine case for gold into a nationalistic cry for world marketplace supremacy. "Give us the same basis of currency that our great competitors of the British Empire enjoy," he promised, "and we will, within the life-time of those now living, float a larger tonnage [of exports] under the American flag."[125]

Blaine provided a clear statement of the argument that gold men who favored overseas economic expansion would use throughout the remainder of the nineteenth century. He proposed to win world marketplace supremacy by overpowering Britain within the gold system. The logic was sound, and the spirit militant, but neither persuaded the silverites. Metropolitan silverites found in Francis Amasa Walker, first president of the American Economic Association and president of the Massachusetts Institute of Technology, a leader of unimpeachable credentials and brilliant intellect. The advocacy of such men prompted the Boston *Globe* and the New York *Graphic* to launch discussions of remonetization as early as March 1876. Shortly thereafter, even the editors of the *Bankers Magazine* opened their pages to metropolitan silver men. The support became so general, indeed, that the New York State Chamber of Commerce petitioned the government on May 4, 1876, to call an international conference to negotiate a bimetallist agreement remonetizing silver.[126]

The silver coalition launched its first attack in the Congress on June 3, 1876, when Bland, working with Representative Kelley of Pennsylvania, introduced a bill to remonetize silver on an unlimited basis at the ratio of 16 to 1. Senator John Percival Jones of Nevada had sounded the bugle in a soaring speech on April 24 and 25: "Beware foreign influence." "We refuse to be led up and down hill." Then, having thrown the alien agent argument back in the face of the high tariff metropolitans, Jones countered Blaine's call to expand exports through gold monometallism. World trade supremacy would come instead through the remonetization of silver.[127]

"Those who are in favor of an exclusive gold standard," agreed the Cincinnati *Commercial*, "use the example of England."[128] And it soon became clear, as the debate progressed, that the issue of silver remonetization was serving as a catalyst to crystallize many of the assumptions, attitudes, and arguments that the majority of agricultural businessmen had developed in their campaign for marketplace expansion. The crucial part of the process involved the projection of agriculture's power and primacy within the American political economy to an identical position in the world marketplace.

The farmers had concluded, as the Worthy Master of the Michigan Grange phrased it, that the United States was "a nation of exhaustless resources and power."[129] "We have it in our power now," announced Representative William Addison Phillips of Kansas (who had been a farmer), "to force the remonetization of silver as coin."[130] Metropolitan silverites echoed the theme almost to the word. "We are masters of the situation," exclaimed Kelley of Pennsylvania; and Representative Nathaniel Prentice Banks of Massachusetts, struggling to revive his sagging career by presenting himself as a Liberal Republican, compared the battle for silver to the War for Independence.[131]

The second traditional argument of agricultural businessmen that flowed into the ideology of silver was the necessity of using such power in behalf of market expansion. "The growth and extension of our commerce" was essential, reiterated Representative George Willard of Michigan, and explained once again how remonetization would enlarge exports.[132] Representative Joesph Gurney Cannon of Illinois offered one of the most succinct statements of that reasoning, pointing out that silver bullion sent to the United States to be coined into dollars would be spent to buy the surpluses of American grain, cotton, and meat—and even manufactured goods—that were at the root of the depression.[133] But Willard added another element that had long been used by farm businessmen as an additional argument for expansion: the moral necessity of enlarging the marketplace in a way that also extended freedom. "Let us not take the side of Greedy England and grasping Germany," he sermonized.[134] That theme, so implicit in the analogy with the War for Independence, supplied a self-honing philosophical cutting edge to the opposition to Great Britain and the domestic metropolitans who supported its policies.

The integration of the arguments from power, economic necessity, and moral imperative created a swelling current that carried the silverites through a predictable analysis. Those who opposed remonetization were either ignorant, self-seeking, or timid. And the weight of agricultural experience, in dealing with the financiers as well as the railroads, and the politicians as well as the land speculators, which reinforced Adam Smith's division of the political economy into the powerful metropolitan few and the weaker country majority, moved them on to the conclusion that the self-seeking —and therefore timid— metropolitan minority was responsible for the failure to remonetize silver.

"This little mischievous law repealing the legal-tender quality of silver dollars," thundered Representative Greenbury Lafayette Fort of Illinois, "was stolen through Congress, as I believe, by being hidden in the body of a long bill professing only to modify the coinage laws."[135] The reality of what had happened between 1869 and 1873 bore more than enough correspondence with that analysis to make it clear that the agriculturalists and other silverites were not evading the real world by creating paranoid fantasies. The charge was also close enough to the mark, particularly as presented by men like Fort and Bland, to provoke a disingenuous rebuttal from one of the men who had helped manage the campaign for demonetization.

Representative Kasson first tried to counter the silver assault with a vigorous presentation of the expansionist argument for gold. Given his knowledge, and his established position as a Midwestern advocate of enlarging the marketplace, he proved a strong spokesman. The gold standard was essential, he stressed, to insure "payment of the farmers of the West for their surplus products sent to Europe."[136] But he was finally stung by Bland's charge that silver had been demonetized through the maneuvers of a tiny group of men, and he responded with an elaborate and emotional denial that there had been any conspiracy.[137]

Kasson was smooth and open enough to have won acquittal on a formal charge of conspiracy, but the issue involved making fundamental public policy rather than committing a criminal act. And in that context his argument not only begged the central question, but his candor revealed more about its own limitations than about the subject. He told enough to deepen the skepticism of his opponents but not enough to allay their doubts. No one, however, not even Senator Sherman, could have met the challenge more effectively. For the only alternative to the strategy employed by Kasson was to resort to the truth: arguing simply that silver had been demonetized because gold monometallism was thought to be in the best interests of the political economy. But that would have thrown the issue back into the public arena defined simply as a question of analysis and judgment. To do that was to risk creating—in an election year—an outraged and irresistible groundswell for the free coinage of silver. The gold men recognized that danger, and confident they were acting in the best interests of the nation, chose concealment as the means necessary for preserving the virtue and the prosperity of the political economy.

John W. Foster of Ohio, a major Republican leader who later advised Benjamin Harrison (and others) on monetary policy, and served the party in many capacities related to foreign policy, summarized the situation with commendable candor. "The paralyzed condition of business and industry, the multitude of people out of employment, and the consequent dissatisfaction and desire for some change of policy" posed the most delicate and difficult crisis that metropolitan leaders had faced since the Civil War.[138] For the majority of agricultural businessmen was not simply challenging the entrenched metropolitan Republicans; it was also establishing great influence within the resurgent Democratic party. Abetted by the depression that the metropolis had been unable to prevent or control, the farmers had forced the transportation issue into the national arena, and had generated an impressive movement for overseas market expansion that had begun to attract significant metropolitan support. And the eruption of the silver agitation on the eve of a potentially explosive election had created an emotional fervor that affected the campaign for expansion, the battle for remonetization, and the struggle to break the power of the metropolis.

The resin-filled tinder had been assembled, the atmosphere was crackling hot and dry, and sparks were being struck throughout the country. Small wonder that men oscillated between violence and caution. The Republicans nominated the staidly respectable Rutherford Birchard Hayes of Ohio and prepared to use force to control the vote in the South just as they had used it against strikers in the metropolis. The Democrats selected Samuel J. Tilden, a conservative New York lawyer, and prepared to use force to prevent the black man from electing another Republican. Had it not been for the great boom in agricultural exports that developed even as the embattled rulers of the nation compromised the victory of Tilden into the inauguration of Hayes, it seems very possible that their political arrangement would have proved incapable of containing the explosive forces of social change. But the export bonanza turned the agricultural majority away from its embittered confrontation with the metropolitan minority, and at the same time turned it and a metropolitan plurality toward a policy of active overseas economic expansion. The exports that prevented domestic upheaval became the exports that required an imperial foreign policy.

EIGHT

*The vast resources of our country need an outlet, as we
have recognized so disastrously during the past five
years. Production is greater than our home demands,
and unless an outlet is found for this excess we must
still continue to feel the depressing effects.*

Secretary of State William M. Evarts,
August 1877

*The prosperity nay the very existence of our agricultural
population depend upon our export trade.*

August Belmont to John Sherman,
November 18, 1877

*The people have been "hewers of wood and drawers of
water" to Eastern capitalists and foreign bondholders
long enough. The time has come for a new order of
things.*

Sedalia, Missouri, Daily Bazoo,
June 14, 1877

*As our manufacturing capacity largely exceeds the wants
of home consumption, we shall either have to curtail
the same by shutting up a great many establishments
or we shall have to create a fresh outlet through export.*

Iron Age, July 1877

*The Farmers' Bonanza. . . . more than all other [factors]
combined, has been the means of restoring activity
to our workshops, liveliness to all kinds of business,
and prosperity to the land.*

Rural New Yorker, November 15, 1879

*We did not duly regard the first intimations of danger.
In the meantime, however, American agricultural production has assumed so extensive proportions, and
the American products have so fully established themselves in the markets of Western Europe, that the Americans have learned to know the advantages of so great
an amount of exports. . . . He that does not wish to
step back and be crushed, must keep up. Quiescence
and romance are disappearing from the world. . . .
How will the overburdened bear up in this cruel race-
track. . . . American competition . . . is the greatest
economic event of modern times.*

Alexander Peez, Austrian Official

*The land so scoffed at by the witty, so discredited by
the wise, produces the cereal that leads and controls
the exports traffic of our country.*

Philadelphia Enquirer, 1878

*Many an old clod hopper, "rude of speech," has found
out that he could talk, rise to a point of order, and venture a few remarks.*

Raleigh Farmer and Mechanic, 1878

We are now diligently hunting up other markets.

Rural New Yorker, June 1879

The bloody shirt can no longer win hegemony for the Republican party. We must find and use issues which are more applicable to the needs of the voters.
                    John Logan to John Sherman, July 19, 1879

The farmers of the Republic will control its destiny.
                              James G. Blaine, September 1878

It is to the abundance of agricultural production, as compared with our home consumption, and the largely increased and highly profitable market abroad which we have enjoyed in recent years, that we are mainly indebted for our present prosperity as a people. We must look for its continued maintenance to the same substantial resource.
                         President Rutherford B. Hayes,
                                    December 1, 1879

An
Export Bonanza Turns
America Toward
Imperialism

Both presidential candidates in the election of 1876 were affected by the intensified agitation for market expansion, and by the related campaigns for transportation reforms and the remonetization of silver. Samuel Tilden and Rutherford Hayes were alike in being intelligent observers of the political economy, as well as receptive and ambitious politicians. Hayes was less provincial, however, because he possessed a greater knowledge of the agricultural majority and was more open to its outlook and mood. He identified with the metropolis and dealt with the problems of the system from that perspective, but he did so with a broader understanding of the nature and importance of agriculture.

The difference between the two men was nicely illustrated by the scope of their proposals for expanding overseas markets. Tilden was not unaware that agriculture was vitally important in New York, nor was he ignorant of the more general troubles affecting farmers. He had been one of the Barnburners, the radical and reform wing of the Democratic party in the 1840s, and supported Polk in the election of 1844. Even his extremely lucrative law practice as counsel for railroad corporations served to acquaint him with agricultural economics and farm politics. And he served as governor of New York during the grave difficulties of the depression.

But Tilden did not move until 1878 to deal directly with the national market problem of the agricultural businessmen. Then he persuaded Representative Abram Stevens Hewitt of New York, an iron manufacturer who became a market expansionist, to introduce a bill appropriating $100,000 to open foreign markets for corn.[1] Tilden might well have done more as President, but he gave few indications that he shared the relatively broad approach manifested by Hayes. "The importance of enlarging our foreign trade," the President declared, "can not be overestimated." Export expansion was crucial "for the revival of the depressed industries of the country," and especially for the "agricultural industry, upon which the prosperity of our people so largely depends."[2]

It was not mere rhetoric. Three months before his inauguration, Hayes noted in his diary that he had decided to appoint William Maxwell Evarts as Secretary of State, and that decision was highly indicative of his outlook.[3] It also disturbed many Republicans; it was the kind of an act that provokes visceral comments on the politics of choosing a Cabinet. "For the good Lord's sake," blurted one associate, "do keep peace in the family and give every fellow a stick of candy to keep him still."[4] Some, like Blaine, disliked the choice because they feared Evarts would be too acquiescent in dealing with the South, a view derived at least in part from his able defense of President Andrew Johnson during the impeachment trial. Others reacted against Evarts' high opinion of himself—he thought he was "a clever fellow"—or against his great wealth. And at least one, Representative James Abram Garfield, discounted him because he was "so full of theory and his own cogitation that he reaches no practical conclusions."[5]

Garfield was correct about the theory and the cogitation but mistaken about the pragmatic results. Evarts had gained diplomatic experience during and just after the Civil War, and had revealed himself as a quiet but determined nationalist. He had also become familiar with the arguments and anger of agricultural businessmen concerning the importance of cheap transportation during his service as counsel for railroad corporations fighting regulatory legislation in Wisconsin. Such experiences undoubtedly helped push Evarts to the conclusion that expanded exports provided the key to prosperity and social peace. "The vast resources of our country need an outlet," he matter-of-factly told the nation. There could be no end to the depression "until some comprehensible policy be adopted to disenthrall the contracted sphere of American trade." His choice of metaphor revealed the underlying current of his thought. "It is for us to enter into the harvest field and reap it."[6]

Hayes and Evarts first had to deal with the effort to remonetize silver, however, and that problem required serious attention for more than a year. But the power of the silverites increased the Administration's concern with economic expansion and underscored the need to appease the farm businessmen. And the President and the Secretary of State, who outlined their strategy for enlarging exports even as they began to maneuver against the forces demanding free silver, increasingly concentrated on the policy they preferred. In an ironic way, however, those efforts were overlooked or discounted as the great agricultural export bonanza carried the country out of the depression.

Exports of all foods reached $216 million in 1875, and in that year all agricultural exports accounted for 78 percent of total American exports and supplied about 6 percent of the gross national product. Overseas sales of cotton textiles, dominated by the rough uncolored cloth produced in Southern mills, stood at $4,071,882. Then came the rapid expansion generated by bad weather, diseases, and war in Europe. Food sales moved to $271 million in 1877, when agricultural exports provided 6.8 percent of the gross national product. The next year food exports jumped to $352 million. In three years, considering wheat alone, American farmers opened 5 million acres and produced 135.9 million additional bushels of grain.

The figure for the next eleven quarters, through September 1881, exhilarated Americans and staggered Europeans. Food sales reached their highest point during the second quarter of 1880, when exports were moving abroad at an annual rate of $520.4 million. The yearly totals were 1879, $392 million; 1880, $488 million; and 1881, $409 million. Wheat acreage increased to 40.96 million in 1881, and production peaked at 549.7 million bushels in 1879. The share of the gross national product supplied directly by agricultural exports averaged more than 7 percent for those three years, and the farm share of all exports hit peaks of 79.8, 84.3, and 83.5 percent. Tobacco exports also increased, and raw cotton sales moved from $2.89 million in 1876 to $3.21 million in 1877, $3.25 million in 1878, and reached $4.38 million in 1880. The exports of uncolored cottons tripled between 1875 and 1878, when they topped $7 million; and they averaged more than $6 million during the next three years. All cotton textile exports climbed from $4.07 million in 1875 to $13.57 million in 1881.[7]

From the outset, but over the long run as well as for the moment, the bonanza exerted many kinds of direct and indirect influences on American foreign policy. Having long been described as crucial by agricultural businessmen, and more recently by a growing number of metropolitan leaders, the overseas market dramatically fulfilled the theory and the expectations. That consolidated the agriculturalists' commitment to the negative connotation of the export analysis as well as to its positive denotation. Once recovery had been insured through exports, it was necessary to open ever larger markets in order to prevent a major decline as well as to sustain the momentum of prosperity and extend its benefits. There was no end to the need for bigger markets. The boom had a similar effect on metropolitan leaders. It convinced many of the specific and general importance of the export market. Even those who operated solely in the domestic market, or remained skeptical of the general validity of the export argument, were forced to confront the political power wielded by farm businessmen who had been confirmed in their commitment to overseas markets (and the similar pressure exerted by metropolitans who now accepted the analysis).

Those effects of the bonanza were reinforced by its more explicit consequences abroad and at home. The impact of the massive outpouring of American agricultural exports shook the foundations of the political economies of Western Europe, and caused serious reverberations in Russia and India. The political and social consequences, which dramatized and exacerbated the economic dislocations, prompted immediate and extensive countermeasures. American pork products were restricted or prohibited by almost every Western European country, and the British closed their market for range stock imported to be fed for market. The English also moved to expand their production of cotton and wheat in India, and the Russians extended their program of internal storage and transportation improvements designed to strengthen their competitive position.

Those developments made it clear that the operation, as well as the theory and the faith, of marketplace expansion involved other peoples and powers who would have to be confronted and overcome if American expansion was to be continued. In a strange but not illogical manner, Adam Smith's analysis of marketplace capitalism and his prescription for maintaining its health were proved largely correct. The members of an agricultural majority of a political economy graced by unusual resources could be imperial expansionists in their relationship with weaker agricultural businessmen in other nations while remaining neocolonial inferiors in their relationship with their domestic metropolis. And they could do so, moreover, while their own financial and industrial overloads remained weaker than the metropolitan sector of other political economies.

The classical example of that somewhat complicated combination was provided by the United States and Britain. American agricultural exports staggered English and Scotish farmers, and disrupted the English flour industry, while rough cotton textiles exported by Southern mills simultaneously posed a serious challenge to British control of the China market. At the same time, however, the financial leadership of the United States relied on its connections with British capital, and Wall Street followed the monetary policy initiatives (and vetoes) of The City in London. Indeed, that was precisely one of the issues that prompted American agriculturalists to demand leaders who would militantly assert and use American power to achieve economic independence and win world marketplace supremacy. The farmers displayed similar antagonism toward American industrialists because of their general alliance with the financiers. Some of those manufacturing interests, such as petroleum, locomotives, and hardware, were beginning to challenge the British (and other Europeans) in foreign markets, but in any overall calculation for the 1870s and 1880s the American industrial sector remained inferior. A number of agricultural spokesmen recognized that the relationship was shifting, however, and began during the late 1870s to appeal to the industrialists to join them against the financiers.

For all such reasons, therefore, the export boom, even as it did so much to end the depression, provoked many demands for vigorous government action. Farmers agitated for countermeasures against European restrictions blocking American food exports, for policies to counteract British efforts in India (and Russia's internal improvements), for concerted probes to find and penetrate new markets, and for congressional legislation to strengthen agriculture's competitive position in all markets. Still another factor connected with the boom served to intensify those campaigns. The bonanza did not solve all the problems of all the farmers.

Even in Smith's model of capitalism, market expansion was a dynamic, not a static, phenomenon. The general welfare could not be achieved, even in theory, until all economic activity producing a surplus was integrated into one free marketplace. Furthermore, past errors and mistakes could not be overcome instantaneously. Those realities of the theory were easily observable, moreover, in the agricultural (and industrial) sector of the American political economy. Many farmers continued to suffer serious economic hardship and related social and personal difficulties. Such men and women swelled the ranks of those who agitated to sustain and extend the boom, and they added great militancy and determination to the movement. That kind of reinforcing action was partially responsible for the show of Democratic strength in the congressional elections of 1878, and for the revival of the silver issue in 1879, shortly after a compromise seemed to have eased most of that tension. And, in a similar way, the failure of the boom to provide enough for everybody also increased the concern (and the thinking) of metropolitan leaders during the political campaigns of 1880.

President Hayes and Secretary of State Evarts were sensitized to such pressure as they took office in March 1877, and they moved rapidly to deal with the crisis through market expansion. Evarts understood and acknowledged the inequities that generated so much of the unrest: capital's "excessive share of a people's industry and enterprise, in the shape of interest and rent, cannot longer be endured."[8] He likewise appreciated that agricultural exports supplied the crucial element in the functioning of the American economy.[9] Evarts had generalized and projected that analysis, moreover, as his strategy for conducting American foreign policy. President Hayes supported him without significant reservation.

"The vast resources of our country need an outlet," Evarts declared, "as we have recognized so disastrously during the past five years. Production is greater than our home demands, and unless an outlet is found for this excess we must still continue to feel the depressing effects." The significance of the analysis was underscored, moreover, by the Secretary's decision to announce it at the outset of a long interview he gave to the *Northwestern Miller*.[10] It is the duty of the government, Evarts then continued, "to protect all classes, not only the manufacturers, but the agriculturalists and miners." Hence *the* diplomatic objective was "the development of a market for American trade in American products. . . . To further extend markets for our products."

Evarts was so deeply impressed by the significance and power of agricultural exports, however, that he overestimated their strength. They "cannot be duplicated by any other country," he argued, and concluded that they "must go on increasing with the increasing consumptive power of Europe."[11] Agricultural businessmen held the same faith in the power of their surpluses, but they did not share the Secretary's optimism that the expansion of the market could be taken for granted. That difference provides a crystalline example of how serious conflicts arise between men who have reached broad agreement on a fundamental principle.

Assuming that agricultural exports would continue (almost automatically) to underwrite the functioning of the economy, Evarts assigned a higher priority to the tactical problem of expanding manufactured exports. That led him to emphasize the penetration of Latin America, and to announce that "nothing should be left undone that will tend to extend our trade" in Asia.[12] His assumption, as the British understood at the time, was that increased industrial exports, added to the agricultural export base, would "relieve the present fearful stagnation of trade."[13] Some Western spokesmen, failing to notice the stress on manufactures, welcomed the Secretary's vigorous call for overseas market expansion with unqualified praise. "Your efforts . . . to advance the commercial interests of our country," wrote one, "deserve the thanks of the whole people, especially the Mississippi Valley."[14]

There were others, however, who quickly recognized the need to spur the Secretary's concern with agriculture. If that were done, the editors of the St. Louis *Evening Dispatch* anticipated quick and final victory. "The commercial international war that England has so successfully waged with the regions of the earth is soon to culminate in her displacement as the controlling commercial power." "Commercial supremacy" would be seized by the United States. But they were careful to warn Western agricultural businessmen that they would have to "grasp the situation" and exert sustained pressure "upon the Government to aid in extending our export trade."[15]

Still another group that caught the Secretary's stress on expanding manufactured exports also understood his willingness—at least

for the present—to acquiesce in Britain's financial supremacy. Those
men quickly supplied the kind of pressure advocated by the *Evening
Dispatch*. Many chose the silver issue as the point of their attack, and
that placed Evarts and Hayes on the defensive. Such was the case even
though Evarts did not share the blanket opposition to the remonetization of silver manifested by so many metropolitan leaders. He did point
out that Great Britain was banker to the world, however, even though
he did not relish that truth, and argued that the United States did not
possess enough financial strength to create its own monetary system
including silver.[16] But, unlike other metropolitan spokesmen, Evarts
worked for remonetization through international agreement as a
sound and highly desirable objective. He did not merely mouth the
idea as a maneuver to bamboozle the silver forces. He was confident
that America's growing economic power could be used to force Britain,
Germany, and France to negotiate such a settlement.

The Secretary was thus caught in a ripping crossfire between the
advocates of free silver and the metropolitans who had no intention
of supporting his efforts to resolve the crisis. He did exert some influence, nevertheless, in the battle of 1878 that produced compromise
legislation. Representative Bland and other silverites enjoyed a strong
position after the election of 1876, for the basic Democratic strength
of 143 votes in the House of Representatives was augmented by sympathizers among the 140 Republican members. Many Missouri Republicans, for example, thought remonetization would "prove highly
beneficial" by providing "an impetus to trade."[17]

Other Westerners considered silver "the main issue" because it was
connected with other primary questions. As one editor summarized
that attitude, silver symbolized the "battle of the farmer versus the
bondholder" and the "foreign influences" of the British and Western
European metropolis. Remonetization would "go far toward restoring the debt-burdened West to something like equal footing with
the East." The people had long enough "been hewers of wood and
drawers of water to Eastern capitalists. . . . The time has come for a new
order of things." The same editor also argued that remonetization
would "strengthen the demand for our industries abroad."[18] And others
explained how Britain's refusal to agree to international bimetallism
insured gold monometallism.[19]

Iowa farmers read the silver argument in James S. Clarkson's Des
Moines *Register*, which also criticized the railroad corporations.[20]
Perhaps the *Northwestern Miller*, however, was the most influential
advocate of silver in the north central states. Its reporters and editors
pushed the issue as early as July 1877, when they explained how British operators used demonetization to undercut American exports with
Indian cotton and wheat.[21] The editors also concluded, after a long
investigation, that Senator Sherman and others had "deliberately"

killed silver in the United States.[22] The movement in the upper Mississippi region also gained the support of the increasingly influential Donnelly.[23]

In a broader sense, however, Chicago was the center of Western agitation for silver. As in Missouri and other states, Republicans like Senator David Davis and Representative Thomas Foster Tipton owed their victories in 1876 to support from agricultural businessmen who favored remonetization.[24] Many Chicago businessmen shared those views. McCormick wanted silver to help expand exports to Asia, and at one rally "not less than three judges made speeches" supporting silver.[25] Even the Chicago Board of Trade demanded strong action to secure an international agreement.[26] Similar support came from the Cincinnati Chamber of Commerce; while the Ohio state legislature, charging that demonetization had been engineered "for the benefit of bondholders of this and foreign countries," demanded free coinage.[27] Republican leaders of that state were deeply troubled by the split in their party, which pushed otherwise promising young leaders like Representative William McKinley, Jr., to "the ragged edge of free silver."[28]

Small wonder that Wendell Phillips warned that a high percentage of Westerners wanted silver, and concluded they might lash out at both major parties if it was not adopted.[29] As *Harper's Weekly* pointed out, however, "the desire for the remonetization of silver was almost universal."[30] Southern silverites, such as the editors of *Southern Planter and Farmer*, argued that silver would open new markets in Asia and terminate the "ugly" reliance on foreign capital.[31] Even the gold men admitted that "a majority of the people favor the measure," though they argued that Southerners were less excited than Westerners.[32] The strength of the popular support, combined with the effect of the depression, led such staunch goldbugs as the editors of the Augusta *Chronicle and Constitutionalist* to advise compromise. "Hunger will go through stone walls," they warned, "and men who see themselves bankrupt, not by their own fault, but by the fault of the Government and the greed of capitalists, are in great danger of listening to rash counsel."[33]

Even more significantly, the majority members of the silver commission established by the House of Representatives—who were not noted for poverty or impetuousness—also recommended remonetization. The report revolved around the crucial importance of agricultural exports in paying the foreign debts of the United States. The single gold standard controlled by Great Britain would sooner rather than later "be disastrous . . . to the entire agricultural interest." A return to silver, however, "would have a direct influence in raising the prices of our exported products." It would also help expand markets in Latin America and Asia; and that was necessary because "the west-

ern nations of Europe seem to be naturally our commercial rivals."
Such was strikingly apparent in the struggle to market industrial surpluses, which the silverites considered important to the general prosperity of the country. For all such reasons, three of the five majority
members recommended remonetization, "whatever the future policy of Europe may be."[34]

The majority report on silver, like the Windom Committee's study
of the transportation problem, created a coherent ideology from
the multiplicity of arguments that had been advanced by many individuals and groups during a long period of intellectual gestation and
dialogue. Even the minority dissenters contributed to that effect, for
they accepted the vital role of exports. Former Secretary of the Treasury
Boutwell, for example, argued that market expansion depended on
using the monetary system "accepted by other commercial nations."
"London is the financial center of the world," he reasserted, and hence
the unilateral remonetization of silver would "leave us in a less favorable condition to compete with Great Britain for commercial and
financial supremacy."[35]

Despite the opposition of such expansionist metropolitans, Bland
ran his free-silver bill through the House on November 5, 1877, by the
overwhelming vote of 163 to 34. Administration leaders knew they
might also lose in the Senate. So also did many financiers. Men like
Blaine (now a senator) were in a particularly difficult position. They
wanted the expansion but either accepted the tactical argument for gold
or feared for their political backing from metropolitan giants if they
voted for free silver—or both. The latter was Blaine's reaction, and he
applied all his talents to the difficult task of opposing unilateral remonetization while holding his wide support among Western agriculturalists. His major effort was a revealing amalgam of economic nationalism,
constitutional hair-splitting, and regretful admissions of weakness.
Great Britain, Germany, and France were the trouble-makers who
caused the crisis because of their desire to block American supremacy. But the Congress had no legitimate power to demonetize anything,
so technically the issue was not money but constitutional law. Yet
it was "difficult" to devise a way that unilateral remonetization would
be effective "as an advance movement to coerce" Great Britain and
other gold powers.[36]

The effort carried Blaine across his political tightrope, but it did
not contribute very much to a resolution of the crisis. That was handled by others like Senator William Boyd Allison of Iowa, Secretary
of State Evarts, and the metropolitan financiers who pressed for some
kind of accommodation. Allison not only knew the power of the silverites, but he welcomed the chance to outshine Blaine before the Western agriculturalists. Evarts pushed his bimetallist views inside the Cabinet. And bankers like Seligman and Belmont applied their muscle

on Secretary of the Treasury Sherman.[37] The result was a compromise authorizing the coinage of between $2 million and $4 million of silver every month (with the bullion purchased at or below the market price), and giving Evarts a warrant to call an international conference to negotiate general remonetization. That easily passed the Senate, 48 to 21, and moved through the House by an even larger margin, 196 to 71. President Hayes declined to risk broaching the sanctity of gold, even in the name of market expansion, and vetoed the law. To no avail. Enough otherwise regular Republicans, like McKinley of Ohio, spurned the metropolitan calls to duty and overrode Hayes by the same large margins.[38]

The momentum of the silverites might have produced even more favorable legislation if the export boom, and the active diplomacy of Evarts and Hayes, had not reinforced the psychological pause that came with victory and at the same time created the feeling that prosperity was on the way. The agriculturalists continued to benefit from their silver effort, however, because it strengthened an export orientation among many metropolitans and prompted them to continue agitating for market expansion. Some of those men, emphasizing the value of expansion "to turn the public thought from our unhappy internal affairs," urged Hayes to exploit the trouble with Mexico over border raids. One was particularly blunt: war would "furnish immediate employment to thousands now starving for bread."[39] The President fully shared the desire for prosperity and social peace, but he had no intention of trying to achieve them through war with Mexico. He counted instead on market expansion to revive the economy, and to prevent the decline of the Republican party into a sectional fraction.[40]

Many export expansionists shared the Administration's concern to avoid war. Senator John Tyler Morgan of Alabama, just beginning his long and vigorous career as an imperial leader, advised restraint in order to win a reciprocity treaty enlarging the Mexican market for raw cotton and rough cotton textiles, and to secure rights for a Southern railroad to the Pacific that would help open markets in Asia. Similar arguments were advanced by groups in Chicago, St. Louis, Milwaukee, and Cincinnati, and the same kind of pressure came from New York and California.[41] Mexican leaders astutely encouraged such appeals, and thereby helped Hayes and Evarts control the tension, by removing (in December 1877) all tariffs on flour and grain.

The Administration was also strengthened by increasing metropolitan pressure for market expansion. David Wells appealed directly to those leaders through the *North American Review*. "Enlarged markets in foreign countries . . . are the first national necessity of the hour; and until they are obtained . . . there are no good times ahead, and no full and profitable employment."[42] The

editors of *Iron Age* not only agreed with Wells, but reported that
his view was shared by many industrialists. "At no previous time
within the recollection of the present generation of business men
has it been so universally acknowledged that we should stimulate
our exports."[43]

Public and private action verified those statements. The National
Board of Trade, spurred on by A. C. Raymond of Detroit, resolved
in favor of export expansion. The Associated Industries of America,
headed by Henry Carey, urged the same policy. Other individuals
and firms wrote directly to Hayes and Evarts. And Howard Lockwood
launched a publication devoted exclusively to news of foreign markets and efforts to expand exports.[44] Hayes responded sympatheti-
cally to such advice and pressure, as did Evarts, and their successful
efforts to conclude a commercial treaty with Samoa (ratified by the
Senate on January 30, 1878) were guided by that outlook.[45]

Such growing metropolitan acceptance of the export argument
remained secondary in importance, however, to the pressure from
agricultural businessmen. Not only was the former derivative of
the latter, but farm surpluses began to move in anticipation of the
Russo-Turkish war. "The Turkish war is a terrible thing for Turks
and people who buy flour," Washburn wrote a friend, but he acted
quickly to exploit the opportunity.[46] Financial leaders were immediately encouraged because they keyed their analysis of the economy
to agricultural exports, and because they tied farm unrest to the
depression. "The prosperity nay the very existence of our agricultural population," August Belmont wrote Secretary of the Treasury
Sherman, "depend upon our export trade." He expected the war
to generate recovery and guarantee a return to specie payments.[47]
Perhaps the editors of the Chicago *Tribune* provided the best example of the deep roots of the marketplace outlook: they explained
the war itself as the result of Russia's need for "a more convenient
water-way to Western markets" in order to remain competitive
with American surpluses.[48]

As the *American Farmer* pointed out, however, the war was not
the only, and certainly not the most significant, cause of the boom.
The United States had become "the granary of the world," and that
power "cannot fail to make prices remunerative, and the general
business of the country to improve."[49] Other observers, such as
the editors of the Augusta, Georgia, *Chronicle and Constitutionalist*,
recognized that terrible conditions in Europe played the crucial
role in creating the market for the vast American surpluses. "The
short crop in Europe has increased American exports," they concluded, and provided a good review of the "broken and unsettled
weather" that reduced crops and facilitated disease.[50]

The French had felt the impact of American wheat exports as
early as 1872, and the European decline continued until the end

of the decade. "We are in the midst of the most extended and severe agricultural distress," judged the London *Economist* in 1879, "which has prevailed in this country for perhaps twenty years." "The same old story over again," agreed an English farmer, "low temperature, flooding downpours, no sunshine, no ripening, crops late. . . . The outlook is at present gloomy and unpredictable."[51] Many American agriculturalists expressed sympathy for the European farm businessmen, but the concern did not mitigate their own joy and confidence. The boom made many American farmers feel "very comfortable."[52] One agricultural businessman in Illinois happily recalled that the export bonanza "lifted mortgages and discharged obligations that saved thousands of farmers from bankruptcy."[53] Similar results occurred in many parts of the country, and the gains in agriculture generated an increasingly extensive recovery in transportation, industry, and finance.[54] Perhaps nothing reveals the rebirth of spirit as well as the happy candor of a young man writing his grandmother: "I spark the girls regularly."[55]

Midwestern wheat men gained additional rewards from the major export campaign launched by the Minneapolis flour industry. Part of the incitement of that effort documents the export orientation of agricultural businessmen in other sections, for Washburn and Pillsbury were concerned about the overseas sales by millers in California, Kansas, New York, and Virginia.[56] Those efforts underscored the problem: the combination of the depression and increased production turned all millers overseas. Washburn made his first sally to penetrate European markets in 1874-1875 with the idea of finding a market for the flour produced by his huge Mill B. The lack of success intensified the need. "We must make the market," commented one farm editor.[57] Many millers agreed in principle, but were reluctant to act after the first failure.

Washburn again took the initiative by dispatching William H. Dunwoody to overcome British resistance. Dunwoody lacked Washburn's exceptional enthusiasm for the project, but he was an unusually devoted and able troubleshooter, and he returned with the orders.[58] Washburn's commitment was typified by his reaction to a major mill explosion on May 2, 1878, just as he was beginning to reach for overseas sales of 100,000 barrels per year. Instead of retrenching, he moved immediately to expand production, and announced that Minnesota mills would shortly dominate the world market.[59] He no doubt meant that Washburn mills would spread-eagle the field, and they shortly did so by winning the gold, silver, and bronze medals at the Millers International Exhibition of 1880.

Wheat farmers were by no means alone in benefiting from the export boom. The "steadily increasing demand" for dried fruit from California, for example, paid significant profits in fiscal 1876-1877 and promised to become even more important.[60] Cheesemakers in Eastern farming areas, as well as those in Western states like Illinois and Wisconsin, were particularly pleased with their "increasing" sales to Great Britain and the continent, for the overseas market was crucial to their long effort to revive that specialized agricultural business.[61] And the tremendous exports of livestock provided related benefits to the corn producers, just as it gained from the similar rise in leather and shoe sales.[62]

The export of meat products almost doubled between 1872 ($55 million) and 1877 ($101 million), and reached $134 million in 1881.[63] Pork from Armour and other firms (including those on the West Coast) was eaten in every European country, and the tireless efforts of Swift opened a vast market in refrigerated beef. "All for business all of the time," as he was characterized by a close associate, Swift made more than twenty trips to England and Europe to establish the trade. "A born expansionist," he talked about the issue constantly, and more than one dinner guest finished the evening "almost drowsing in his chair from an overdose of exporting." Swift made no apologies: "I've got it on my mind."[64]

So did other processors and manufacturers closely associated with the agricultural sector of the economy. Cyrus McCormick understood that the export boom could be exploited abroad as well as at home, and launched a major effort to convince the Europeans (and others) that they could recover their competitive position by increasing their efficiency with his implements. He anticipated the "struggle," his daughter reported, "and quite naturally is eager to be in the midst of it. He feels that this may be his last great international fight, and he wants a fair field and no favor."[65] That classic statement of the central principle of the free marketplace first became a rallying cry of the American overseas push, then a demand to be won from other nations, and finally the official policy of the United States.

Railroad leaders like Stuyvesant Fish of the Illinois Central came to agitate for a foreign policy based on that axiom along with Populist leaders from Kansas, Georgia, and California. For Fish, like other railroad executives, understood the vital importance of agricultural exports to the transportation industry. Following the advice of William H. Osborne, Fish committed the Illinois Central to the export market to meet the depression crisis. Osborne cut costs and moved rapidly to extend the I.C. to New Orleans. The strategy proved valid, and traffic over the Southern division increased 300 percent by 1880. Reporting that the decision "proved to be the salvation of the property," Fish then launched a campaign to transform New Orleans into a major port.[66]

A similar outlook and policy guided the Baltimore and Ohio through its troubles.[67] President Garrett shared the view that the

Russo-Turkish war would "prove beneficial" because the rise in exports "could not fail to restore activity and profits in many classes of business."[68] The bitter struggle to control the rising export shipments, reinforced by the more personal machinations of men like Cornelius Vanderbilt, led to a rate war that forced Garrett to cut wages by 10 percent in July 1877. That touched off the violent strikes that President Hayes finally controlled with federal troops. Garrett remained committed to the export trade, however, and a year later reported happily that "the good crops of the past year have produced improved results with our railways." And he launched a sustained effort to create a European market for corn in a bid to enlarge profits even further.[69]

The continuing depression steadily increased Southern interest and involvement in textile exports. For one thing, the producers of raw cotton and unmanufactured tobacco did not reap unusual profits from the export boom. The value of tobacco exports fluctuated between $20 million in 1871 and $16 million in 1880, with highs in 1873 ($30 million) and 1877 ($29 million). Cotton fared somewhat better, but failed to enjoy any upward surge that matched food exports. But the desire of all Southerners to break free of their colonial bonds to the metropolis also did much to generate enthusiasm for the mill-building movement. "It is my dream," cried Governor of Georgia Alexander H. Stephens in 1878, to see "in every valley . . . a cotton factory to convert the raw material of the neighborhood into fabrics which shall warm the limbs of Japanese and Chinese."[70]

In more euphoric moments, some Southerners even considered bringing the black man into the movement by building mills with capital gathered from the freedman at $25 per investment.[71] Such proposals unfortunately remained good intentions. The industry generated its boom with white capital, white foremen, and white policy makers. The black man was allowed to supply capital in the form of labor (and interest paid to the storekeeper), of course, but his stock was strictly nonvoting. His benefits were marginal and limited. Such was also true for many white cotton growers, but they could identify with the enterprise more easily, and did become increasingly involved in the rising campaign for export markets. Those sales mushroomed from 12 million yards in 1873 to 111 million yards in 1877, and Southern mills shortly displaced British firms in the Shanghai-Amoy market for drills, T-cloths, and sheetings.[72] The profits were reliable and significant; typified by the Augusta Factory's ability to pay a "regular dividend of eight per cent."[73] Such success in the midst of the depression attracted increasingly fretful attention from Northern mill owners, and they intensified their own activities in the overseas market.

Southern operators, the Northerners concluded, enjoyed "a much more hopeful condition than any other portion of the country" because of their great emphasis on exports.[74] The mills along the Merrimac River from Lawrence to Manchester, and northward along the coast, responded with vigorous efforts to revive their earlier trade in rough cottons. And the mills that produced medium and fine goods assigned vastly increased attention to foreign sales. As George Atkinson advised his brother Edward, there was "a great market for cotton and woolen fabrics" in Asia. Export merchants like Horace B. Claflin of New York played a key role in the movement, which was headed by the Pepperell Company.[75]

As the German consul in St. Louis advised his government at the end of 1878, the agricultural export boom dramatized "the advantages of an expanded foreign trade" for all sectors of the economy. The involvement, he concluded, "has now become general."[76] The agricultural businessmen were exuberant and confident. They were also more insistent in demanding rewards appropriate to their crucial role in saving the political economy. "We are rapidly gaining control of this trade," reported the statistician of the Department of Agriculture, and suggested that the result might be "a social revolution."[77]

The editors of the *Rural New Yorker*, crowing about the "eminently successful" year in 1879, asserted flatly that the farmer, "more than all others combined, has been the means of restoring activity to our workshops, liveliness to all kinds of business, and prosperity to the land." Thomas P. James, Georgia's commissioner of agriculture, agreed: the activities of farm businessmen "lie at the very foundation of our prosperity." The president of Purdue University added his learned judgment: "Agriculture underlies and sustains all other interests, and is the foundation of all business enterprise and wealth." And a federal official carried the argument far enough to define cheese exports as "a matter of national importance."[78]

Such confidence and pride were not surprising, particularly when so many metropolitan leaders accepted the broad analysis and adapted it to their own operations. Young Jacob Schiff, just beginning his distinguished financial career with Kuhn, Loeb and Company in 1875, quickly came to rely on "crop conditions as the determining factor" in making his decisions.[79] That was hardly surprising: August Belmont and Secretary of the Treasury Sherman followed the same approach. And President Hayes announced his concurrence—"Agriculture is of primary importance"—and reiterated it much in the vein of the *Rural New Yorker*. There was no question of "the preponderance of the agricultural over any other interest in the United States."[80]

Other metropolitans stressed the crucial importance of agricultural exports in turning the trade balance in favor of the United States. A particularly perceptive one went on to warn, however, that strenuous efforts would be required to maintain the powerful position in world markets attained during the export boom.[81] In a similar way, the editors of the Philadelphia *Enquirer* spoke bluntly about the provincial arrogance of many metropolitans. The time had come to stop indulging oneself in "thin wit" at the expense of the farm businessman. For "the land so scoffed at by the witty, so discredited by the wise, produces the cereal that leads and controls the export traffic of our country. . . . The prosperity and welfare of a very large proportion of our people at home are intimately connected with the raising and marketing of this wheat."[82]

Both warnings were verified almost immediately. More was done to push the nation toward imperial expansion, however, than to curb the thin wit of the metropolis. The rise of serious apprehension in the midst of celebration was caused by two factors: the failure of the boom to improve the welfare of all agricultural businessmen, and the European efforts to control—even terminate—the outward economic thrust of the United States. Both developments generated prompt and sustained campaigns to improve domestic economic operations related to overseas expansion, and to use the power of the federal government to hold and enlarge foreign markets. Some of the troubles were due to the forces of nature. The continued grasshopper plague, for example, destroyed established farm businessmen as well as new investors hoping to harvest their first crop. Both were left "destitute, or almost so."[83] Other farmers hurt themselves by overexpansion and careless methods, and by ignoring warnings from their own leaders that "business principles" had to be honored with increasing care and attention.[84] But the primary causes of the continuing protests grew out of the operation of the marketplace per se, and the power of the metropolis.

The boom was based on the coincidence of tremendous American surpluses and poor supply in Europe. Prosperity was certain to be weakened as European agriculture revived. "American grain and meat," warned the *Rural New Yorker* at the outset of 1879, "can be put down in England at lower figures than those at which they can be produced at home, so that the farmer's occupation is in danger."[85] Such marketplace dynamics intensified the troubles of those who had yet to benefit from the boom. "We are growing poorer and poorer," reported such farmers, even as their colleagues paid off their mortgages and bought more land or new machinery.[86] Even the editors of the *Commercial and Financial Chronicle* realized that the depression, which they compared to "a retreating army on a terrible march," was continuing to claim human victims. "We need a more practicable statesmanship," concluded William M. Lang, Worthy Master of the Texas Grange; "one which regards the government of the State as an instrumentality for the promotion of the general welfare of the citizens."[87]

Henley James, Worthy Master of the Indiana Grange, agreed that the needs of agriculture "are almost wholly neglected." Neither the government nor the metropolis could reasonably claim credit for the boom. A sobering report came from an observer who had been "riding caboose on the noon freight" across one part of the Middle West: "the majority of farmers here are in debt." Pennsylvania and Maryland farm leaders reported their colleagues "growing poor," and "many homesteaders failed" in the Red River Valley. A later analysis of the economic pattern helps clarify the persistence of such troubles in the midst of the boom. "From 1879 to 1884 the average value per acre of wheat crop declined successively, year after year." But Adlai E. Stevenson, an Illinois candidate for election to Congress in 1878, offered much the same explanation of the "terrible condition of affairs" that had created "a cloud of almost utter despair" over parts of the state.[88]

Developments along the Red River Valley in Minnesota and Dakota produced another kind of protest. The extreme discrepancy between the profits for the few who controlled the huge wheat ranches and the gains of the ordinary farmer generated many kinds of anger and opposition. The bonanza investors "lived well. They drove the finest horses, dressed stylishly, and built pretentious winter homes in Fargo, Minneapolis, or elsewhere." And the wide publicity given the combination of "diamond shirt studs . . . kid gloves, and . . . hem-stitched hankerchief" did not contribute to a sense of community.[89] Neither did the structure of such farming, for none of the bonanza people considered the region to be their home. Their physical absence documented the reality of absentee ownership and control. Overseas investors appeared even less frequently—if at all. The resulting resentment created an anti-alien movement composed largely of conservative middle-class business and professional men who were concerned with trying to build and improve a viable society in the region. "We are so heartily disgusted with our dependent condition," one resident cried out, "with being snubbed at every turn in life, with having all our interests subjected to the whims and corrupt acts of persons in power that we feel very much as the thirteen colonies felt when they flung away their dependent condition."[90]

Those complaints and emotions were shared by many other agricultural businessmen throughout the country. Men in the Washington Territory attacked the "federal pap-suckers" who ruled them, and raged that they could only "supplicate while Congress dictates."[91] Illinois farmers mounted similar attacks on the metropolis, and others in Iowa, Virginia, and New York joined the editors of the *Northwestern Miller* in opposing foreign investors.[92] Much of the dissatisfaction continued to focus on the transportation system. Not only were the railroads' absentee owners drawing strength from foreign capital, but they controlled a vital part of the export operation and generally opposed the development of alternate routes.[93] Arguing that agricultural traffic (purchases as well as export shipments) supplied the bulk of railroad business, farm businessmen in all regions insisted that rates could be lowered even further, and warned that the concentrated economic power of the owners threatened America's ability to control world markets. "There is nothing in which our people take so much interest," noted the Denver *Weekly Times*, as "in railroads and rumors of railroads."[94]

The meat packers had their own quarrel with the rails, a coincidence of interest with farm businessmen that also manifested itself between wheat growers and flour millers. Shippers of live cattle complained not only about rates, but also about the difficulties of arranging to have the animals properly cared for en route. Armour, Swift, and other processors had to build their own refrigerator cars, and even then the railroads manipulated classification and rate schedules to obtain the same return as for live cattle cargoes.[95] Minnesota grain farmers faced the same impasse: "If the value of our exports increase, the cost of transportation augments in the same proportion, and the producer is left without profit."[96] But Washburn and other millers encountered the identical kind of discrimination, which provoked the St. Paul *Pioneer Press* to anger against the metropolitan interests that "held Minnesota in capitalistic subjection."[97] As one of the more perceptive railroad leaders later recalled, "the problem of the railroad now became the problem of the Northwest."[98] But it also became the problem of the farm businessmen (and export merchants) of the Northeast. "The rare opportunity of supplying the foreign demand for the products of our farms at *reasonable* prices must be in great measure lost," judged the *Rural New Yorker*, "unless the intervention of Congress. . . can be secured as early as possible."[99]

Such pressure prompted the *Railroad Gazette* to advise the industry to lower rates, even accept some regulation, before tough laws were forced upon it by furious farmers.[100] Instead, the owners and their allies stood fast against the two-year effort led by Representative John Henniger Reagan of Texas to pass comprehensive federal legislation. Reagan was backed by literally thousands of petitions and resolutions from all parts of the country; but the railroads developed a clever and plausible counterattack based on the vital importance of the export market.[101] Their strategy provided one of the most convincing kinds of evidence of the general acceptance of both the theory and the practice of overseas market expansion.

Reagan followed the general outlines of the earlier McCrary bill, but refined and extended that proposal to end rebates and drawbacks, prevent other forms of discrimination, prohibit pools, provide public knowledge of rates and classifications, and terminate higher charges for short-distance shipments. The opposition, led by Representatives Abram Stevens Hewitt and Clarkson Nott Potter of New York, almost took the initiative away from Reagan with their argument that the bill would "destroy this only prosperous branch of foreign trade" either by raising through-charges to the seaboard or by diverting the freight to Canadian railways and shippers.[102]

Hewitt was ready, furthermore, with a counterproposal: create a national railroad commission to rationalize the system and "develop this great foreign trade which is at length pulling us out of the quagmire into which we have been plunged."[103] The argument was effective enough to convince some Western spokesmen, such as Representative William Addison Phillips of Kansas, a former farmer, that the Reagan bill did not provide the best answer to the problem. That kind of defection raised the opposition vote, even though the bill passed the House 139 to 104, and had the effect of blocking the movement for regulation for another decade.

Many agricultural spokesmen recognized that the metropolis could use the foreign market argument less effectively against measures to improve the waterways, and also realized that a strong cross-regional coalition of Democrats and Republicans could be organized in support of internal improvements. The effectiveness of the Eads jetties had become apparent by 1878, moreover, when the Mississippi channel reached thirty feet, and that practical success added strength to the movement. So did the admission by metropolitan leaders that existing transportation facilities were inadequate.[104] The farmers and associated business interests, rallying from Virginia to Kansas, and from Texas to Wisconsin, made their first major move in 1878.[105] "We mean," announced Senator Robert Enoch Withers of Virginia, "to secure the development of our country by means of the same agencies and the same means [as the metropolis], and I for one have no constitutional scruples upon the subject."[106] Senator Windom of Minnesota agreed, demanding "a new and direct pathway to the markets of the world."[107] The alliance, mustering twenty Southern Democrats and thirteen Western and Northwestern Republicans in the Senate, and a similar majority in the House, won increased appropriations and a fairer allocation of the funds (the South was given one-third of $8.4 million).

As significant as it was, for the future as well as the moment, the victory did not cushion the shock, fear, and anger that developed as European nations began to close their markets and (a bit later) restore their own production. The dynamics of the crisis became apparent to all: given the structural weaknesses and unusual difficulties of European agriculture, the influx of American food surpluses generated continuing economic disaster, social unrest, and political upheaval. The effects, reported William H. Brewer in the Tenth Census of 1880, were known "here by the reduction of rents, there by the decrease of the value of agricultural lands, or by the . . . decrease of prices of home-grown productions . . . by distress among farmers, by emigration, by political uneasiness."[108]

Though every country was affected by 1878, Germany may have been the first to suffer. So, at any rate, it claimed: since 1874 German farmers "have been suffering from constantly declining prices" and other "evils of American competition."[109] The English, however, re-acted with "consternation" to the 1875 exports of particularly choice cattle from Illinois.[110] "A panic has almost been caused," reported the London *Agricultural Gazette* on January 29, 1877, "by the sale of the beef, which is pronounced better than home produce." Even the cheese makers avowed they were "beaten all along the line."[111]

Though some foreign observers admitted that the economic inva-sion did "save Europe from a great famine," most came to feel, at least as the crisis passed, that one way of suffering had merely been substi-tuted for another. "Agriculture has been said to be a bet with the weath-er," remarked the London *Statist*, "but the chances are no longer even."[112] Others warned that "wholesale bankruptcy of the aggre-gate agricultural interests must ensue."[113] The British also took an "ominous" view of Washburn's flour, accurately concluding that "the aggressive Yankee is contemplating a raid."[114] As one Englishman reported, "very many farmers have already been compelled to give up their farms and losses of many more have seriously crippled them. "[115]

A significant number of Englishmen began to criticize the free trade policies of their government.[116] It responded first by investigating the American success, a venture that produced some hilarious mo-ments; as when one member of Parliament attracted so many body lice that he spent much of his trip "distressingly busy . . . quietly punching himself in various parts of his body."[117] Even before the re-port was filed, however, the Privy Council moved on March 3, 1879, to end the influx of live cattle. Citing the danger from animals infected with pleuro-pneumonia, it ruled that all American imports had to be slaughtered within ten days of arrival.

That was all the encouragement needed by Germany and other na-tions. Even a socialist such as Karl Kautsky predicted ruin unless Amer-ican exports were blocked, and unless German farmers opened a market for their own surpluses.[118] German consuls in America joined leather workers in Leipzig to demand prompt and effective counter-measures. Already concerned to push German economic expansion throughout the world, and moving to adopt a neomercantilist program to facilitate that strategy and to control opposition at home, Prince Bismark seized the opportunity. Tariffs were raised on June 12, 1879, and two weeks later some American pork products were excluded. "I had the impression," he had remarked drily a bit earlier, "that under free trade we were gradually bleeding to death."[119]

The anti-American snowslide became an avalanche. "We did not duly regard the first intimations of danger," cried Alexander Peez, a member of the Austrian Reichsrath. "He that does not wish to step back and be crushed, must keep up. Quiescence and romance are disappearing from the world. . . . American competition . . . is the greatest economic event of modern times."[120] Frenchmen added that wheat exports were "one of the real causes of the influence of the American Union on the rest of the world."[121] The result was a European resistance movement against American agricultural exports that rapidly spread from Britain eastward through Italy to Greece, and westward to Spain.

The official rhetoric of the assault stressed the diseased condition of American cattle and swine. The records of the debates and private conversations, however, reveal a deep and often desperate concern to block American economic supremacy. The truth lies largely in the latter sources. American meat was not free of potentially—or immediately—deadly bacteria.[122] Invoking that standard, and submitting the reports of immaculate and expert laboratory investigations in support thereof, the Europeans justified their transgressions of Adam Smith's free marketplace in the name of human values. The criteria were of course millennial, and they were not applied to their own producers, processors, or consumers.

The British, for example, were in part reaping their own harvest, for their earlier cattle exports had helped infect American ranges. As for the continentals, especially the Germans, they preferred their pork rare—when cooked—regardless of the warnings from scientists in white smocks. The historical problem, in any event, is not to reach a mathematically exact estimate of the power of the health motive as against the forces of economic rivalry and the related concern over political and social unrest. It is rather to make it clear that, in the context of the depression and the export boom, Americans emphasized the marketplace factors. For, as in so many instances, that was the operative historical truth affecting the development of American foreign policy.

Thus metropolitan leaders like the editors of *Bradstreet's*, as well as agricultural businessmen, concluded that "most of the outcry abroad about American pork is attributable to trade jealousy."[123] Kasson had warned Evarts as early as March 4, 1878, that "all Europe is entering upon what may be styled an Era of National Selfishness," and he interpreted the outcry over health as part of that movement, intensified by the failure of various special interests to obtain the tariff legislation they demanded.[124] Kasson's view was extreme, but it increasingly gained acceptance because of the evidence.

For one thing, he cited his own interviews with European spokesmen in support of the analysis. The French ambassador in Vienna, for example, candidly warned him of coming tariff increases.[125] Other American officials reported similar exchanges. Lucius Fairchild noted that the Spanish decree against American pork referred candidly to "the insufficiency of the national production" in the country.[126] Thomas Wilson, American consul in Nantes, reported that the French packing industry acknowledged its concern with self-preservation. "The causes to which to attribute the present decadence of the pork industry are many," the Chamber of Commerce of Nantes commented in a resolution of 1879, but concluded that "we believe they are all founded on the competition with the pork made in the United States."[127]

"It was generally accepted by stock raisers and meat packers" in the United States "that the prohibition was for the purpose of preventing competition."[128] They offered two policies to restore and expand the foreign market. One was based on eradicating the diseases, thereby destroying the validity of the argument being used to justify exclusion. That approach offered the secondary benefits of involving the federal government in aid to agriculture, and cutting one kind of losses suffered by the livestock growers. The other response emphasized economic and political retaliation by the government to reopen the markets. Clearly enough, both proposals were predicated upon the necessity of continued market expansion through exports.

The editors of the *National Live Stock Journal* took the lead in the campaign for controlling the diseases. Their personal efforts began at least as early as March 1877, whey they "urged upon the Government the necessity of adopting adequate measures." Then, as the danger became clearer, they sent Judge T. C. Jones of Ohio to lobby in Washington. The campaign attracted increasing attention and support as the existing state laws proved ineffective (or were ruled unconstitutional), and as Commissioner of Agriculture William G. LeDuc of Minnesota joined the movement. The first victory, gained with the aid of metropolitan leaders like Garrett of the Baltimore and Ohio, came in 1878 when the Congress appropriated a small sum to investigate the nature and extent of pleuro-pneumonia, trichinosis, and other diseases.[129]

That proved wholly insufficient, however, and the cattlemen became increasingly concerned to obtain more government assistance as they grew ever more "alarmed at the prospect." They welcomed the renewed efforts of states like New York to control the diseases, but generally agreed that the primary and "grave responsibility" rested with the federal government. As Jones reported, however, the bill he prepared "was hurried out of sight" by the Congress.[130] The inability to obtain further action strengthened the argument of those who advocated retaliation. Such pressure reached Evarts in May 1879, and evoked more explicit concern from the Secretary than the Congress gave to the campaign for disease control.[131]

Then, on December 15, 1879, the Marine Hospital Service reported the results of its investigation into the relative prevalence of trichinosis. American pork contained no more than, if as much as, European animals.[132] That news probably tipped the balance toward retaliation, a solution that rapidly won increasingly militant support throughout the country. Yet no retaliation was undertaken. The inability to induce or force the government to act on either strategy of reopening the markets deepened the anger of agricultural businessmen toward the metropolis and intensified the attitudes and pressures that were transforming a primarily economic concern with exports into a demand for the kind of vigorous government action that produces imperial policy.

St. Louis export merchants trading in wheat and flour were exasperated over "paying tribute to the East in the shape of transportation commissions, etc."[133] New Orleans businessmen demanded "an impartial regard for the great interior interests"; only that could "emancipate" them "from the thralldom" they endured.[134] Worthy Master James M. Blanton of the Virginia Grange called for action to replace the "pseudo-statesmen and jackass politicians" who refused to deal with the problems of agriculture.[135] And from Kansas came the corollary to that complaint: "I want to see men in Congress with hay seed in their hair."[136]

The situation revived the old Grange effort to force the metropolis to recognize agriculture "as a real factor in this government by the establishment of a bureau of agriculture to be presided over by a Cabinet officer."[137] Many farmers admitted that Commissioner LeDuc was weak and ineffectual, but they argued that no man could be effective unless his power and finances were increased by congressional action.[138] The resources were so "entirely inadequate" that the existing efforts to help farm businessmen were "simply ridiculous."[139]

Such expressions of disgust and impatience over what was seen as a gross discrepancy between capacity and performance were manifestations of a sense of American power that was beginning to generate imperial attitudes, expectation, and policies. Americans "should have the market entirely in our own hands," judged the editors of the *Rural New Yorker*, concluding a discussion of the wheat and meat needs of Great Britain. Commissioner of Agriculture LeDuc spoke firmly about the world power "to which we are entitled." *Bradstreet's* warned Frenchmen and other Europeans to resign themselves to American supremacy.[140] Sharing such views, Samuel E. Adams of Minnesota, Worthy Master of the National Grange, reminded farm businessmen that the marketplace had to be kept free. He explained in 1878 that the full economic rewards would not be won until the power of the United States was used to moderate "religious intolerance" and reform the "absolute monarchies" of Europe. The marketplace had to be cleansed of the restrictive forces of "superstition, bigotry, serfdom, and despotism" in order to function with maximum effectiveness.[141]

That traditional concern with the political and social conditions required for the efficient deployment and operation of American economic power became a significant factor in the outward imperial push over the next decade, but the continued increase in production during the depression kept the immediate stress on more narrowly economic considerations. "If we could secure a monopoly of the British market, we might rest content for a few years," remarked the *Rural New Yorker* in discussing meat exports, but added that even that happy condition would not terminate the need for new markets.[142] "We, as a nation, want access to the markets of the world," summarized the president of Williams College. "On one point all sensible men agree; and that is, that one great element in securing permanent success will be our ability to compete with other nations in the markets of the world."[143] A cheese producer documented the widespread acceptance of that thesis among agricultural businessmen. "The spectre of overproduction, which has been the bugbear of the last fifteen years, has become the dread reality of 1878."[144] And, acting on that analysis, the International Dairy Fair Association organized its 1879 exhibition "to attract the attention of foreign buyers, and enlarge our markets."[145]

Other dairy groups joined the effort to revive the attack on the high tariff, a campaign also supported by the Richmond, Virginia, Chamber of Commerce.[146] "Free trade superadds to the natural control of the home market," agreed the Texas Grange, pointing out that the protective policy operated to "paralyze exportations."[147] But British restrictions on American meat exports provided the high tariff forces with a convenient example to use in reiterating their old charge about the "evil" of reduced rates and the foreign conspiracy that engineered such agitation.[148] The critics failed to muster general support and the tariff was not changed.

The agricultural businessmen and their allies did win one battle that ultimately produced significant results. That came through the creation, in June 1879, of a special congressional commission to study improvements on the Mississippi River.[149] In the narrow sense, the victory was the work of Southern and Midwestern farmers, millers, and merchants.[150] But those groups, increasingly effective in their own right, benefited from the growing national concern to sustain the expansion of foreign markets. "We are looking for export markets," cried one corn farmer in 1879, but the description applied to many groups throughout the political economy.[151]

"Many an old clod hopper, 'rude of speech,'" commented one Southerner, "has found out that he could talk, rise to a point of order, and
venture a few remarks."[152] And, whether he did so in conversation,
in letters to the editor, or during local, state, and national Grange meetings, the remarks often concerned markets—how to keep the ones
he had and how to open new ones. "We are now diligently hunting
up other markets," remarked the *Rural New Yorker*, in a summary
that applied to every region of the country.[153] Merchants, railroad
men, and processors steadily joined the search.[154] And intellectuals,
emphasizing it was "highly important" to "hold as great a control over
European markets as possible," began to demand a coherent expansionist program "divorced from partisan politics."[155]

A growing number of politicians were responding, moreover, in
a way that slowly created the official consensus for such a policy. "We
cannot hesitate," warned Representative Fernando Wood of New
York, "to enter the race for supremacy." As a onetime shipping merchant, Wood understood the meaning of overproduction: "we must
encourage and promote the adoption of such relations with other nations as will open up the markets of the world, and make the whole
universe contribute to our prosperity." "We want markets," agreed
Senator Benjamin Harvey Hill of Georgia; adding that "we think that
South America, and Central America, and the West Indies are our
proper markets."[156]

The concern for markets was strong enough, for that matter, to forge
a short-run alliance between some Southern Democrats and the Hayes
Administration. The China market for southern rough textiles suffered a temporary decline during 1878-1880, just when California
groups launched a drive to stop Chinese immigration by revising or
abrogating the Burlingame Treaty of 1868.[157] Some Southerners had
tried without success to use Chinese labor because they "thought it
would be impossible to raise cotton, cane and rice crops with free negro
labor," and that failure undoubtedly made them sympathetic to the
campaign for restriction.[158] But others feared that the abrogation or
enforced revision of the treaty would antagonize the Chinese and thereby shrink or close the market for cotton exports. "We need to continue
and increase them," cautioned one spokesman, "in China and all other
available markets."[159]

Such opposition, and similar resistance in the Northeast, was not
strong enough to prevent the Congress from passing a bill in February
1879 that established an immigration quota of fifteen Chinese per
ship. Many Midwesterners voted with their colleagues from the mountain states and the Far West. Their action was the product of antimetropolitan solidarity, and a growing concern that good agricultural
land was rapidly being occupied. But those considerations, and especially the second, were not strong enough in 1879 to keep them vot-

ing with the Westerners when it came time to override the Hayes veto. The confrontation nevertheless dramatized the need for Republican leaders to counteract the growing alienation among agricultural businessmen.

So did the failure of the 1878 international conference to remonetize silver. That fiasco served mainly, as the *Rural New Yorker* pointed out, to revive the agitation for stronger American action. Senator Allison warned Secretary of the Treasury Sherman that Joseph Medill of the Chicago *Tribune* estimated "the sentiment of the West" strongly for free silver. "I fear he is too near right," Allison added, "for a good state of public health and morals."[160] Senator John Alexander Logan of Illinois spoke more bluntly than Allison. "The bloody shirt can no longer win hegemony for the Republican party," he flatly announced to Sherman. "We must find and use issues which are more applicable to the needs of the voters."[161]

Blaine had been trying to alert other metropolitan leaders of the party to the same truth for almost a decade. The agricultural interest of the country, he reiterated in 1878, was by far the largest in the nation. That meant simply that "the farmers of the Republic will control its destiny."[162] Blaine proved an accurate prophet about American foreign policy. For the agricultural pressure for expanding the marketplace, and the growing acceptance of that outlook by metropolitan leaders, turned the United States into an imperial course between 1877 and 1897. The process was under way even as Allison, Logan, and Blaine delivered their warnings and recommendations.

President Hayes devoted much of his special message of December 17, 1878, to the vital importance of exports, and called for "every effort" to push agricultural surpluses "into new markets." He reemphasized the same theme in December 1879. Indeed, he sounded as though he was borrowing Blaine's language: "Agriculture is the leading interest and the permanent industry of our people," and hence "new and expanding markets" for its products were crucial in order to sustain prosperity.[163] Such rhetoric was far from unimportant, even as rhetoric, for it added official sanction to the language and the outlook of the agricultural businessmen from whom it was taken. But Hayes and Evarts also acted on the rhetoric, and that further strengthened the movement for a vigorous foreign policy. Their moves elicited demands for even stronger measures. In both respects, therefore, the Hayes Administration played a highly significant role in the process of redefining the American marketplace and the American security perimeter. And those changes were crucial elements in the evolution of American imperialism.

NINE

We are urged imperatively to the recreation of our commerce through the absolute necessity of procuring a market for our surplus products. . . . The Navy is, indeed, the pioneer of commerce.
Commodore Robert W. Shufeldt, 1878

Our true national policy is to determine that the day shall come when the price of our products shall not be fixed at Liverpool, when we shall consume our own and dictate the price of that which we choose to sell abroad. . . . We will reach out with shipping facilities under the patronage of Government aid, and flush the markets of the world.
Representative Moses A. McCoid
of Iowa, 1884

Good God protect us—poor European people! What shall we become?
James Camsile, 1885

[German] policy must unquestionably result (if persisted in) in disaster to the farming interests of Illinois and the Northwest.
Armour and Company to the State
Department, 1883

Having been kicked, it is time to kick back, and kick back hard, and keep on kicking until they are kicked into something like reciprocity.
Chicago *Tribune*, 1883

The American Government has miserably failed in its duty.
National Live Stock Journal, 1883

Prompt and appropriate legislation on the part of Congress . . . is imperatively demanded.
American Livestock Spokesman, 1883

The American Statesman must . . . study the resources of its rivals and thwart its antagonistic policy. In so doing no timidity should mark his actions or deference to the equanimity of his adversary control his counsel.
Representative Washington C. Whitthorne
of Tennessee, 1882

A new wave of Americanism is breaking over the whole country.
The American, 1884

We are not satisfied with the present condition or future prospects of our class. The men whose labor and success in the field saved our country from hopeless bankruptcy and restored prosperity do not receive a fair share of the profits.
State Grange of Indiana, 1882

Now, I am tired of this sort of business; and I want the American people to have as good a navy as any other government in the world.

Representative William H. Calkins
of Indiana, 1883

We want a navy. We do not want a lot of repaired old hulls and hulks.

Senator Preston B. Plumb
of Kansas, 1883

The
Redefinition of the American
Marketplace and the
American Security
Perimeter

I T IS POSSIBLE to argue that Adam Smith's theory of marketplace capitalism contains an option that points away from the kind of imperial expansion that appeared during the nineteenth century and flowered after 1900. A mature political economy, resting content with the apolitical economic advantage it enjoyed in its marketplace dealings with any undeveloped (or primarily agricultural) system, and disciplining itself to honor Smith's central axioms, might maintain its prosperity and social health without undertaking imperial activities.

As James Madison and James Monroe pointed out, however, along with other Founding Fathers, even the opportunity for one country to test itself against that challenge depends upon every other nation's willingness to make the same attempt. And, to an extensive degree, that caveat was used by the majority of Americans during the late 1880s and the 1890s to justify their own imperial expansion. They argued that their imperialism was necessary in order to create the conditions required for ending all imperialism. But that sophisticated syllogism was advanced only after the same majority had defined the free American marketplace as a free world marketplace, and asserted that American power had to be deployed and used to establish and maintain a strategic perimeter coincident with that wider American marketplace. The United States acquired its colonies, and undertook similar imperial ventures, as part of defining the American marketplace as the world marketplace, and as part of its effort to make the former free by making the latter free. Furthermore, the agricultural majority played the primary role in the entire process.

236

A few leaders like John Kasson of Iowa accepted the logic of that undertaking by the end of the 1870s and publicly advocated the necessary imperial measures. Many others joined him during the ensuing decade as they analyzed the recovery from the racking depression of the 1870s. Concluding that exports explained their welfare, agricultural and metropolitan businessmen projected that causative proposition into the indefinite future. To sustain the recovery, as well as avoid further crises, the American political economy had to acquire and maintain free and effective access to all the markets of the world.

All groups asserted, moreover, that the United States possessed the power to satisfy that primary need. The issue was to use that great strength, and the agricultural majority maintained steady and growing pressure for such action. And, from the outset, the farmers and their spokesmen argued that American power was good power because, even if it was used militantly and forcefully, it extended the free marketplace — and hence freedom itself. The conception of the American marketplace as the world marketplace not only defined the general problems of expansion, but separated the good (free marketplace) governments from the bad (closed or unfree marketplace) powers. The unfortunate existence of such unfree and unfair governments intensified the competitive rivalry inherent in marketplace capitalism, and thereby led Americans to accept the necessity of a harsh struggle for economic welfare. The battle was seen to be doubly bitter because it was necessary to create a free marketplace before Americans could achieve their final triumph in fair competition.

In the more specific sense, agricultural businessmen defined the primary enemies as those nations that blocked the expansion of their exports. Britain was particularly dangerous because it controlled so much of the world marketplace, because it prevented the remonetization of silver, because it used its Indian colony to harm American farmers, and because it unfreely restricted its own markets. Germany, Austria-Hungary, France, and others qualified for similar reasons. And smaller countries were included when they proved slow or reluctant to facilitate American economic expansion. The development of economic nationalism was thus a self-breeding process. It played a central part in defining the American marketplace as the world marketplace, and was then reinforced as the efforts to realize that concept were blocked.

Agricultural businessmen faced two other specific problems. One involved the penetration of new markets throughout the world, a difficulty that engaged Southern textile manufacturers, food processors, farm implement firms, and railroad corporations, as well as commodity and livestock farmers. Metropolitan leaders increasingly became involved in that effort for their own economic reasons, moreover, as well as because the economy relied so heavily on agricultural exports. The second complication grew out of the slowness and lack of vigor among the metropolitan leaders who held the top political offices from September 1881 through 1888, a situation that provoked farm businessmen to increasing anger and restiveness.

Finally, the projection of the American marketplace outward over the globe served to raise major questions concerning the most effective methods of accomplishing that necessary program. Agriculturalists manifested a growing demand for positive government action. They argued it was necessary because of the inherent nature of competition in the world marketplace, and in order to achieve results in connection with specific issues such as European retaliation against meat exports. But they also continued to stress the need for domestic action on the railroad and monetary issues that so vitally affected their competitive position. They increasingly agitated, however, for explicit imperial policies. Thus they called for a different and better diplomatic and consular service, provided ever stronger support for reciprocity treaties, and gave steadily greater attention to a merchant marine and an isthmian canal. And they contributed far more strength than has usually been recognized to the movement to build a modern navy.

For that matter, the relationship between the Navy and the agricultural majority supplies one of the keys to understanding the redefinition of the American marketplace as the world marketplace. Suffering from decline and derision, the Navy was an embattled institutional bureaucracy struggling to revive its fortunes, and hence its interest in overseas expansion was neither abstract nor altruistic. Naval leaders, along with the farm businessmen in the Grange and other agricultural organizations, manifested a strong sense of self-preservation, and a determination to improve their fortunes. As with the farmers, however, the Navy based its campaign for regeneration and influence on more than an egoistic assertion of self-interest.

Its top leaders offered a serious analysis of the requirements and functions of a modern navy, and they pitched their appeals to the general concern with market expansion. While they exaggerated some of their arguments, the evidence leaves no doubt of their commitment to the ideas per se. One group, typified by Rear Admiral John Rogers, stressed the elementary military weakness of the Navy. He could paint a frightful picture of defeat under the guns of Argentina, Brazil, or Chile.[1] Other officers advanced a more powerful argument predicated upon the necessity of expanding American exports. The leader of the expansionists was Commodore Robert W. Shufeldt, whose analysis contained most of the themes restated and developed a decade later by Captain Alfred Thayer Mahan. Shufeldt's widely circulated essay, *The Relation of the Navy to the Commerce of the United States* (1878), provided a neat statement of the ideas that he personally advocated in appearances before such groups as the Chicago Commercial Convention, and in intragovernmental discussions.

The central theme was unequivocal: "New markets must be found," and the Navy "is, indeed, the pioneer of commerce." Shufeldt usually sounded as though he had learned his political economy from David Wells; but, whatever the source, the student had mastered the theory of overproduction. "At least one-third of our mechanical and agricultural products are now in excess of our own wants, and we must *export* these products or deport the people who are creating them. *It is a question of starving millions.*" "*In no other way* can our commerce be reestablished. . . . In no other way can the country be relieved of its surplus products, or can additional impetus be given to its industries." Shufeldt added that America's destiny required such expansion. "No nation can be really great without an external commerce," and the exports and the Navy were "destined to carry over the world the creed upon which its institutions are founded."[2] One of Shufeldt's allies, Lieutenant James D. J. Kelley, combined the elements of economic necessity, ideological responsibility, and destined power in one classic sentence. "We are the great middle kingdom," he explained, "and an analysis of the laws underlying trade expansion proves incontrovertibly that we should rule the commerce of the world."[3]

Those were the themes that the agricultural businessmen had been agitating for almost two decades, and which led them to define the American marketplace as the world marketplace. As the editors of *Bradstreet's* pointed out, the farmers "hold their attention closely upon the pulsation of the foodstuffs markets." Or as Pat Darden, Worthy Master of the Mississippi Grange, commented, "the farmers are imbued with a money-making spirit." His colleague from Michigan agreed, and explained that "the great problem to be solved in American agriculture is how to produce crops at a profit."[4] The concern was intensified by a clear awareness that agriculture "secures us the balance of trade on which so much stress is laid," and "saved our country from hopeless bankruptcy and restored prosperity."[5]

The solution was "free and open markets in all parts of the world." "We desire," the *Breeder's Gazette* calmly announced, "to export millions of dollars' worth of livestock products." The need, therefore, as the Lecturer of the Massachusetts Grange explained, was "a national policy that will open to us all foreign countries."[6] In an effort to dramatize what the National Grange termed "the extreme importance" of exports, the *American Agriculturalist* translated one portion of them into the transportation equivalents. The grain exported from New York City from January 1 through July 8, 1880, if hauled in forty-bushel wagons pulled by two horses, would require a line 15,151 miles long composed of 3.2 million horses and 1.6 million drivers. Then, to make the point even sharper, the editors noted that the grain would fill a string of boxcars stretching 1,455 miles.[7]

All agreed that it "will be very essential to have the foreign markets all open."[8] Leading spokesmen from every agricultural region developed that theme in the form of an argument from necessity. Representative Samuel Wheeler Moulton of Illinois, who had earlier farmed in Kentucky and Mississippi, called the foreign market the "great desideratum." "No country in the world has a greater interest in finding foreign markets." And he quoted a friend across the Mississippi River to cinch his argument: "Every important industry we have in Iowa, agricultural or manufacturing, is as utterly dependent on a foreign market as it could possibly be with absolute free trade."[9]

Representative Washington Curran Witthorne of Tennessee warned the metropolis that it was time for foreign policy "to become responsive to those demands and necessities." A political economy either expanded or died: "there is 'no pause'—unless followed by death and decay." "It is the law alike of population and trade that such a tide must move forward."[10] The consensus among agricultural businessmen on such expansion was nicely illustrated when Kasson, serving as a Republican congressmam from Iowa after a tour of diplomatic duty, congratulated Whitthorne on his analysis. "My mind has long been full," he accurately noted, "of this subject of extending the commerce and navigation of the United States."[11]

The bright-tobacco farmers likewise became increasingly concerned about larger foreign markets after 1879, when the price decline turned them abroad.[12] And though he stressed the needs of the cotton farmers and textile mill owners, Senator Morgan of Alabama spoke for all Southern agriculturalists in making his demands for expansion. The depression had been caused, he explained, by the inability of American farmers "to reach the wealth of other countries to relieve the financial poverty of our own." "Our home market is not equal to the demands. . . . We must enlarge the field of our traffic. . . . Extend the area of our trade throughout the known world, barbarous as well as civilized."[13]

The pressure of necessity, so clearly revealed by the general use of imperatives like *must*, was relieved by a sense of confidence in the power of the United States. "The dream of political independence without the fact of commercial independence," emphasized Representatives Moses Ayer McCoid of Iowa and Henry Safford Neal of Ohio, "is soon and easily dispelled." "Our true national policy is to determine that the day shall come when the price of our products shall not be fixed at Liverpool, when we shall . . . dictate the price of that which we choose to sell abroad. . . . We will reach out with shipping facilities under the patronage of Government aid, and flush the markets of the world."[14] Kasson added that Americans held the "natural domination of the Pacific and of the coasts bordering upon it."[15]

Representative Samuel Jackson Randall assured the agricultural businessmen of the Northeast that the only danger was a failure of will. "To stand still is to let others pass us in the race."[16] House colleagues from Wisconsin and Texas agreed with that estimate. Burr W. Jones of Madison, Wisconsin, urged the nation to "commence in earnest the contest for equality in the markets of the world," and Thomas Peck Ochiltree warned laggards that "the day has come when no party dogmas will be allowed to stand in the way of . . . protection for a foreign trade."[17] Or as Charles B. Chess of Kansas commented in an open letter, "the wary German will soon be forced to tax the air about the cans to suppress the importation of American canned beef."[18]

Such confidence and determination upset many Europeans. "Whatever premises you start with," concluded the *London Statist*, "whatever deductions you make, in arguing the merits of a particular trade, the inevitable question comes, sooner or later, 'But what will America do?' America is the hobgoblin in the happy dream of traders in the present day."[19] Another spokesman put it even more starkly. "Good God protect us—poor European people! What shall we become?"[20] Americans viewed the issue differently, asserting that their expansion would liberate and improve the world.

Representative Charles Edward Hooker of Mississippi provided a typical expression of that faith in announcing his belief "in the power of our country to extend its civilization, its laws, its morals, its high sense of duty everywhere." America's "contribution to the material welfare of the people" of the world, agreed the National Grange, is "incomparably greater than any other country has offered."[21] That attitude was so general, indeed, that it provoked Representative Benjamin Butterworth of Ohio, himself a market expansionist, to warn of the inherent dangers. "Doubtless it is our mission on earth," he commented in 1882, "to make free and to civilize and Christianize the world. But I hope we will not commit suicide in the attempt. I hope it may not be written on the tomb of this Republic, 'Here rests a brave and generous people who lost their own liberties in attempting to give freedom to all the world.'"[22]

Most agriculturalists felt that the proper policies, if only the metropolis would adopt them, would produce the freedom and the markets without catastrophe for anyone. As that failed to happen, however, the farm businessmen and their spokesmen became increasingly militant. The *Western Rural and American Stockman* commented in 1884, for example, that a major war was justified only if "necessary to protect some important interest," but immediately noted that control of an isthmian canal qualified as such an interest. "European powers should be taught to keep their hands off this continent. They do not belong here." Weaker powers could expect the worst: "There is no particular objection to giving the Guatemalian a drubbing."[23] And reformer Henry Demarest Lloyd typified the final confluence of necessity, confidence, and morality. "If nobody can lick us we need not be afraid to play the just and generous big brother among the nations."

He wanted Chicago to be "the greatest seaport in the world. . . . With foreign consent and cooperation—or without."[24]

Edward Atkinson and James Jerome Hill never became that pontifical or provocative, at least in public; but they provided excellent examples of how the export performance of agriculture—and the ideas so long agitated by the farm businessmen—affected metropolitan leaders. Atkinson told members of the American Agricultural Association, and other farmers, that he was much concerned with "the export of our surplus." The "chief duty" of American leaders was to "remove obstructions," he added, because "this nation has a function in the world that is yet almost a vision." That ideal, which he summarized as the principle of "equal opportunity to all," was directly related to the truth that "this country never needed the world for a market so much as it does now."[25]

Hill was more ebullient. "In his midnight talks to his friends he raved about the trade of the Orient as Napoleon raved of India to Narbonne. . . . 'I will reverse the immemorial course of trade eastward over the seas and turn it from Suez to Seattle. . . . Our white bread is like the lotus; no nation that once eats it will change to poorer diet. I will make wheat flour as cheap as rice for the millions of the Orient, and our farmers will profit by a new demand.'"[26] Hill verified the substance, if not the exact rhetoric, of such reports in his own published writings.[27] From the beginning, he explained, "we knew it was necessary to look to Asia for part of our traffic."[28] Without agricultural exports, cotton from Alabama (and rough cotton textiles from Georgia), as well as wheat from the Dakota Territory (and flour from Minnesota), the Northern Pacific could never fulfill Hill's dream of dominating transcontinental transportation. By the end of the 1880s he spoke almost constantly of the need to control world commerce, and candidly admitted that meant overseas expansion. The old lesson of territorial expansion was no longer relevant: "We have to unlearn such ideas."[29]

Hill was unique only in the grandeur of his expansionist vision, his talent, and his determination. Garrett of the Baltimore and Ohio followed the same strategy; George W. Perkins of the Chicago, Burlington, and Quincy fully understood the central importance of agricultural exports; and Fish, who counted very heavily on crop reports delivered every four days in making decisions for the Illinois Central, rivaled Hill in his energy, ability, and grasp of the significance of overseas markets.[30] Other industries tied to the agricultural part of the economy likewise stressed exports. Farm implement manufacturers boosted their foreign sales from $611,152 in 1864 to more than $3 million in 1883 and 1884.[31] And Washburn alone was exporting about 30 percent of the production of his three major mills.

The development of the expansionist outlook among those entrepreneurs who inhabited the zone of transition between the pure agricultural and metropolitan sectors, such as Washburn, Swift, and Armour, is further illuminated by the career of David Lubin. His early business in Sacramento, California, was a wholly mercantile activity based on commerce in finished products. His success enabled him, early in the 1880s, to fulfill a promise to his mother by visiting Palestine. In addition to whatever religious experience he may have undergone, Lubin returned convinced that the small farmer was the essential element in a democratic social and political order.

Lubin acted on his analysis during 1884-1885 by shifting much of his capital and his abilities to the production of wheat and fruit, and by becoming a Granger. He immediately verified the rhetoric of the farm movement by losing money on his first crops. The existing market was too small, given transportation costs, to return a profit. Beginning with his militant participation in the Fruit Growers Convention of September 1885, Lubin launched his own crusade to regulate the railroads and expand the marketplace. And, by the end of the decade, his campaign for an export bounty on agricultural surpluses had become a significant force affecting foreign policy.[32]

Metropolitan spokesmen applied similar pressure. David Wells hammered away at the necessity of expansion, warning in 1882 that otherwise "we are certain to be smothered in our own grease." He may have intended that remark as a pun, for lard was an important item in agricultural exports, and Wells constantly stressed "the national dependence upon those foreign markets for continued prosperity."[33] Another commentator, Richard H. Edmonds, agreed with the analysis but concluded on a more confident note. "What the past has been all may now know; and if we are to judge the future by the light of the past, then the United States must ever hold a commanding position in the grain markets of the world."[34]

Louis P. Brockett, a regular ghost writer for the Republicans, emphasized the importance of the commitment to a free marketplace. *"The* empire" was America's "moral power over the nations of the earth." Editors of *The American* agreed, asserting that the expansion of the United States was "in the interest of mankind everywhere." "Our industrial independence is the basis of our political independence," and therefore "we shall not abandon our markets to be a fattening place for Manchester or London." Such imperial freedom would not bring war, however, for "the nation that wants to fight the United States . . . we doubt it is to be found."[35] Another writer who also served in the diplomatic corps, M. M. Ballou, discussed the interrelationship between expanding freedom and exports by explaining how it would be necessary to reform Cuba in order to make it a profitable market. The businessman could thus discharge his moral obligation while meeting his marketplace responsibilities.[36]

Other metropolitans emphasized the economic responsibilities.

Chauncey M. Depew took it for granted that everyone understood that agricultural exports were "the main cause of our extraordinary prosperity for the last few years." Leonard Hazeltine, a New York commission merchant, explained to any doubters that "prosperity, starting from the farmer, goes down into every branch of trade and commerce."[37] The New York *Commercial Bulletin*, the *Commercial and Financial Chronicle*, and *Bradstreet's* repeated the message throughout the entire era.[38]

Others who urged the vital importance of following the lead of agricultural businessmen were willing to accept any imperial consequences. "Isolation will not be possible for us very long," the New York *Tribune* pointed out in 1883: "Inevitably there will arise somewhere, before many years, a necessity for interposition by the United States." "American enterprise should surely seek foreign markets," warned the *Commercial and Financial Chronicle;* "not merely with the purpose of disposing of an occasional surplus . . . but for the permanent supply of great populations which are to be clothed, fed and transported from place to place." Trade "with the outer world," amplified the New York City Chamber of Commerce for the benefit of the Senate, "is as important to us as it ever was to England. . . . Our sole resource is to open new markets to our people."[39]

Such expansion was becoming "a public duty." Woodrow Wilson, then a young political scientist with political aspirations, wholly agreed with the business community about the need for a "vigorous and consistent line" on the "extension" of the market.[40] The process of redefining the American marketplace as the world marketplace was hurried along by the arguments of liberal Republican politicians like Carl Schurz.[41] He termed those who dragged their feet on market expansion "the curiosities"; and for himself he asserted that "the greater" such expansion "the more promising will be the development of our industries." Schurz was troubled by the experience of "periodical stagnation," and sounded like Adam Smith in explaining that "the more limited the market is, the more easily will it be glutted." Hence he called for "a larger field of operation" and did so confidently — America was "the one great Power with an absolutely free hand in foreign affairs."[42] Though he was a New York manufacturer and a Democrat, Representative Abram Hewitt could agree with Schurz on the analysis and the prescription. "Our prosperity will continue only so long as there is an adequate market for our products. . . . The situation, if not alarming, is very serious."[43]

Even the financiers moved slowly along toward a general statement of the export thesis. They had always recognized, as Alexander Mitchell, president of the American Bankers Association explained, the importance of farm surpluses in turning the balance of trade, and in controlling the outflow of gold (which was the key to specie resumption).[44]

The inability of manufacturers to match the volume or value of agricultural exports undoubtedly contributed heavily to the reluctance of most bankers to support active measures for market expansion prior to the mid-1880s. So did their own dependence on Britain. And, finally, the financiers were more orthodox marketplace capitalists, far more content to rely on private power with minimum governmental activity. By the end of the decade, however, more and more money men agreed that "the fullness of time" had created the need for the manufacturer to "complete such arrangements as are needed to extend his trade."[45]

The attitude of the financiers clearly restrained (even blocked) many metropolitan politicians who were more sympathetic to vigorous expansion during the early years of the decade. That in turn intensified the anger of agricultural businessmen toward the metropolis. Some key metropolitan politicians, such as Frederick Theodore Frelinghuysen of New Jersey, who served as Secretary of State under President Chester Arthur, personified the kind of metropolitan expansionism that further antagonized the farmers because it emphasized industrial exports. Even so, Frelinghuysen's acceptance of the proposition that the American marketplace was the world marketplace dramatized the broad consensus that developed after 1877 among major national leaders.

The dynamic force that moved those men was candidly described in 1884 by a diverse group of spokesmen after discussions with individuals and organizations throughout the country. "The people everywhere . . . appear to have become absorbed by a realization that the internal development of this country has reached a point where an external commerce is necessary for its prosperity . . . and that the markets must somewhere be found for the disposition of the surplus."[46] It is very helpful, in understanding how that process affected thinking about policy, to eavesdrop on politicians discussing the problem of being successful in politics.

"When you take the nine Republican States that begin with Ohio and end with Kansas," Blaine wrote Garfield just before they took charge of foreign policy in 1881, "you have the very heart of the Republican party."[47] That region, as both men very well knew, was one of the two centers of sustained and militant agitation by agricultural businessmen for overseas market expansion. They concluded that such expansion offered the best preventive therapy to keep the heart beating. Not only do their actions verify that conclusion, but so also do accounts by widely different protagonists of that time. The British Minister to the United States, for example, concluded very quickly that Republican strategy was based on "propounding the policy of sole supremacy over South America,—a policy which certainly is likely to be popular among the constituencies."[48]

Somewhat later, in 1891, Edwin Hurd Conger, a farm businessman from Iowa who became an influential Republican politician (and diplomat), revealed a good bit more of the story in trying to persuade Wisconsin farmers that the Republicans would win more markets than the Democrats. Conger recalled that he had been deeply worried that the bitter intraparty fight between conservative Senator Roscoe Conkling of New York and President Garfield and Secretary of State Blaine would destroy the party. But Garfield reassured him: "Mr. Conger, do not be alarmed. We shall develop a policy during my administration which will make the Republican party more popular with the people of this country than it has been since the day of its birth." The program was based on a wide network of reciprocity treaties opening new markets for American agricultural and industrial surpluses, and Conger recalled the evening in 1881 when Blaine explained to him—and others, including Representative McKinley of Ohio—"how it would provide an additional market for American cereals, American beef, and pork, and American farm machinery."[49]

Conger may not have remembered the exact language, but there is no reason to question the substance of his story. It is valuable, moreover, beyond offering an excellent illustration of the extent to which, by 1880-1881, the conception of the American marketplace as the world marketplace had been accepted by one group of major Republican leaders. For it also provides a central episode around which to discuss an important problem of analysis and interpretation. The question involves the reasons for the *apparent* slowness in translating that expansionist consensus into a coherent imperial policy—and an empire.

The answer is composed of several factors, the first of which is a more balanced sense of time. Viewed from the middle of the twentieth century by men who sometimes seem obsessed by a hyperconsciousness of rapid change, a decade or two can seem almost a lifetime. Hence it is perhaps natural to view American leaders of the last part of the nineteenth century as awkward and inefficient—or simply not guided by an imperial outlook. Ironically, a good many of the agricultural businessmen who were so deeply concerned about overseas economic expansion came to feel the same way. Their impatience as protagonists is more comprehensible, however, than the lack of perspective manifested by so many later observers.

Even if one dates American imperialism by the taking of the Philippines and the enunciation of the Open Door Notes (1898-1901), the period under discussion is only twenty years. For half that period, 1880-1890, the United States was engaged in a series of wars to contain and defeat the Indians of the trans-Missouri West. Yet, even granting the effect of that distraction, American leaders can hardly be termed indifferent or inefficient expansionists. They moved firmly and irrevocably into Samoa in 1878, helped Europeans control Morocco in 1880, opened Korea by themselves in 1882, maneuvered for open access to a free marketplace in the Congo in 1883 - 1884, claimed rights to Pearl Harbor in 1887, finished the job in Hawaii in 1893, intervened in Venezuela and Brazil between 1893 and 1896, established effective control of Cuba and the Philippines by 1899, and dispatched more than 5,000 troops to China in 1900 as part of claiming fair shares throughout that vast nation. Surely that performance qualifies for passing marks as an imperial achievement over twenty years.

Considered more rigorously, the twenty years become ten, for there can be no question about the imperial nature of American policy during the 1890s. The central problem, therefore, is to understand the hiatus of the 1880s. Here a second factor enters in the form of a disagreement among metropolitan leaders about the readiness of the American economy to enter the imperial struggle for supremacy. It was an argument about timing and can be clarified by examining the views of Representative McKinley. For he was present during Blaine's briefing in 1881 and then, nine years later, again confronted Blaine in a major fight over tariff policy.

McKinley based his career on Ohio, which was developing manufactures during the late 1870s and the 1880s. He responded by mastering the theory, practice, and politics of the protective tariff. He became an outstanding advocate by presenting the case for high rates in terms of high wages for the worker, a large home market for the agricultural businessman, great profits for the metropolitan industrialists, and economic independence from Great Britain for everyone. But McKinley was also an intelligent and shrewd politician, a close observer of what was happpening throughout the political economy, and he enjoyed considerable ability to recognize and adjust to emerging changes, pressures, and ideas. And it is clear that he did not allow his rivalry with Blaine to deafen him to a truth just because Blaine uttered it first.

McKinley began in 1882, shortly after the 1880 - 1881 confrontation with Garfield and Blaine, to offer asides about expanding the overseas market as part of his argument for protection. Those remarks make it clear that the crucial difference between McKinley and Blaine concerned *when*—not *whether*—to undertake a major expansionist program. The main thrust of McKinley's analysis pointed to the need for America to become stronger, and after 1881 he increasingly defended protection as the best way to build the power required to defeat Great Britain for control of the world marketplace.[50] McKinley might very well have moved more rapidly in the direction of imperial expansion if Blaine had continued on as Secretary of State at the beginning of the 1880s. For he would have been responding to Blaine, who understood more clearly than any other Republican leader that the politics of the period after 1876 was shaped and energized by the expansionist outlook and policy that the agricultural businessmen developed and agitated so persistently and vigorously. He was also in an excellent position to urge the metropolis to act on that knowledge.

Representative George Washington Glad, a Greenback Democrat from Maine who grasped that reality better than many of his more illustrious colleagues in either party, made the point very simply. "Now, gentlemen," he announced at the outset of 1883, "we need this commerce. The West needs it; the South needs it. There is no use to talk in this enlightened age about any class or section of the country that can do without ocean commerce. It is essential for the life of all sections."[51] Or, to consider the issue from another angle, Senators Aaron Augustus Sargent of California and Hannibal Hamlin of Maine did not force President Hayes and Secretary of State Evarts to act contrary to their true beliefs in sending Shufeldt to open Korea "with a view to the encouragement and extension of American commerce."[52] The expansionist outlook had become the basis of thought about American foreign policy. The pragmatic question involved who was prepared to act on that consensus most effectively, and in a way that would meet the demands of the agricultural majority.

Blaine and Garfield were ready. Blaine made that perfectly clear in appointing his old expansionist friend, Robert Roberts Hitt of Illinois, as First Assistant Secretary of State. Garfield revealed his intentions in his inaugural address: "The interests of agriculture," which has "done much to secure" the nation's prosperity, and which "furnishes much the largest part of all our exports," "deserve more attention from the Government than they have received."[53] That approach, as Blaine explained, "had for its ends some great objects—objects which I know the President considered of very great consequence to the American Union and to the future of this country."[54] But their projected imperial collaboration for the expansion of the American marketplace was aborted by the assassination of Garfield on July 2, 1881, as he walked with Blaine to a railroad station in Washington.

That murder was the third (and decisive) factor that delayed the development of an imperial policy. Blaine's vigor and verve—and the political attractiveness they generated—were too much for incoming President Chester Alan Arthur, a lawyer-politician from New York, and the Secretary of State was forced to resign. The change did not involve a dramatic shift from expansion to anti-expansion. Arthur and his choice as Secretary of State, Frederick Frelinghuysen, favored market expansion. But they were far more staid, unimaginative, and cautious, and approached expansion in terms of their more narrow metropolitan outlook. That difference in orientation was the fourth factor that slowed the expansionist thrust. The metropolitan part of the economy was not as vigorously united on expansion as the agricultural majority, and Arthur was not the kind to create more enthusiasm through his own leadership.

The President did state his concern with "successful competition in distant fields of enterprise," and added his support to the campaign for a better Navy. [55] As for Frelinghuysen, he could enunciate the theory and necessity of expansion as well as any leader of the late nineteenth century—and mean every word of the lecture. "A nation of 56 million inhabitants can never cease to be an important factor in public affairs, and when that nation is wealthy even out of proportion to its vast population; when it pushes its enormous natural products into every country, underselling the local markets . . . it cannot expect to hold aloof . . . and cannot consider itself isolated either politically or commercially."

Alvin Adee, the highly influential State Department bureaucrat who served well into the twentieth century, once recalled that Frelinghuysen "used to talk to me by the hour about all this." Adee also provided, in a typical display of his perception and thoroughness, a major insight into the reasons that Frelinghuysen and Arthur were less vigorous than Blaine. Both approached the problem of expansion as though they were preparing a legal brief, reasoning methodically and formally from the assumption of necessity to a list of prerequisites and structural requirements. They were great systematizers; so excellent, indeed, that they were inclined to reason present possibilities out of existence on the grounds of unpreparedness. The key to Frelinghuysen's orientation to the future was his estimate that "stability of government" and "a sound system of banking" were vital to sustained expansion.

That was a fifth reason for the interruption in vigorous action on the majority's demand for expansion. Frelinghuysen considered the existence of an integrated financial structure, headed by "a parent Intercontinental bank in New York," as "the most important" element —"whereby the whole system could be harmoniously controlled." And the bankers were not ready, in the early 1880s, to push the creation of such a system. The Secretary of State thought such an imperial extension of the American economy would "come in the end," but felt it "was impossible so long as revolution and financial irresponsibility continued to sap the energies and credit of the Spanish American States." [56]

President Arthur made a similar analysis. He wanted "a series of reciprocal commercial treaties with the countries of America," "the establishment of the consular service . . . on a salaried footing," "measures to favor . . . a steam carrying marine," and a "uniform currency basis for the countries of America." He mentioned the importance of Europe, Asia, and Africa, but stressed transforming the Western Hemisphere into an American marketplace. [57] The ever-increasing pressure from agricultural businessmen, reinforced by the economic downturn that began in 1882, gradually forced Arthur and Frelinghuysen to increase the tempo and intensity of their expansionist efforts. Unlike Blaine (and a few others), however, who recognized the situation and initiated action, Arthur and Frelinghuysen moved largely in response to urgings from high party members. Secretary of the Treasury William Windom, who had been appointed by Garfield, continued his efforts to enlarge the marketplace. "Fail to give our farmers and manufacturers the open markets of the world," he warned in December 1882, "and there will be a giant glut at home, prices will go down, and prosperity will diminish."[58] Arthur heard the same message from his own choice to head the Treasury, Hugh McCulloch. He devoted most of his 1884 report to the issue of exports because the subject was "of so great importance." Not only had the export boom ended for agriculture, but increasing numbers of manufacturers needed "a market for their surplus." Market expansion was thus "the question which now comes to the front." "Unless we can share in the trade which is monopolized by European nations, the depression now so severely felt will continue, and may become more disastrous."[59]

But McCulloch revealed the attitude of the Arthur Administration in his remark that the issue "now comes to the front." The agricultural businessmen—and Blaine—had been saying that in 1879 and 1880. Arthur did finally manifest a sense of urgency in 1885: "One of the gravest problems which appeals to the wisdom of the Congress is the achievement of the most effective means for increasing our foreign trade and thus relieving the depression under which our industries are now languishing."[60] But such intensity came much too late to moderate, let alone overcome, the dissatisfaction and antagonism generated by the earlier failure to win any victories for agriculture.

The farm businessmen quickly discovered, moreover, that President Grover Cleveland was even more phlegmatic than Arthur and, in important respects, even more narrowly oriented to the metropolitan sector of the political economy. And the new Secretary of State, Thomas Francis Bayard of Delaware, was more galling to the agriculturalists than Frelinghuysen. Like their predecessors, Cleveland and Bayard were marketplace expansionists, but their orthodox laissez-faire approach reinforced their metropolitan provincialism. Their willingness to allow expansion to happen when it happened was the sixth and last factor accounting for the failure to carry through immediately on the militant expansionism of the agricultural businessmen. The farmers finally affected Bayard in 1886, and he reluctantly admitted that "the demand for new markets for American products has become almost imperative."[61] His use of the qualifier next to an absolute term perfectly reveals his outlook—and explains the embittered attitude of the agricultural majority toward such metropolitan leaders.

From the point of view of the agricultural businessmen, the strong metropolitan orientation of Arthur and Frelinghuysen, and Cleveland and Bayard, posed one of the major problems within the expansionist outlook. In response, the farmers progressively defined the American government, as well as those of European nations, as an onerous opponent. Indeed, many came to consider it simply bad—hostile, wrongheaded, one-sided, inequitable, and tainted. That judgment and feeling gained great impetus at the outset of the 1880s from the clearly revealed differences between Blaine and Frelinghuysen.

Many later evaluations of Blaine sound very similar to the one offered in 1880 by Sir Edward Thornton, British Minister to the United States. "Blaine is a noisy mischievous demagogue and most unscrupulous; he hesitates at no falsehood."[62] Hence it is illuminating to note the shift in opinion of those who dealt with him as a rival. Thornton still considered him "ambitious, impetuous, and somewhat imperious" a year later, but had come to recognize that he was "undoubtedly an able man and may modify his views."[63] After their first encounters, Thornton admitted that Blaine was "a good man of business"; and Sackville-West soon added that "he is not a man to be set aside so easily."[64]

As for policy, the *Pall Mall Gazette* accurately noted that Blaine favored actions "which would tend to increase the export trade of the United States at the expense of that of Great Britain."[65] But Blaine did not limit his concerns—or ambitions—to Britain. He inherited the problem of German restrictions on all American pork products except ham and bacon, and the difficulty created by similar restrictions on flour exports.[66] The analyses Blaine received from abroad reinforced his own feeling that the conflict was commercial rather than hygienic, and underscored his awareness of the seriousness of the confrontation.[67]

Just before Blaine took office, moreover, on February 18, 1881, the French moved against pork exports. That action was turned into a panic when English papers promptly printed a wild report by George Crump, British Vice-Consul in Philadelphia, on the horrible deaths supposedly suffered by those who had eaten American pork. The swine breeders and meat processors, already angry and worried, became incensed. There was sufficient public evidence to convince them that all three countries were engaged in deadly commercial warfare. Even the Bordeaux Chamber of Commerce criticized the French decree as being based on inexact information, and because it hurt the French consumer and "caused great interests to suffer to the extent of millions." And a French paper spoke angrily against the "system of warfare," adding that the "Academy of Medicine has stated that the danger is enormously exaggerated."[68]

The impact of those reports was intensified when it became known that Consul Crump "refused to make answer" to "many questions" asked him by the New York Produce Exchange; but "did reluctantly admit . . . that when he wrote his report he was aware that the mortality among hogs in 1880 was not greater than in 1879." *Bradstreet's* spoke of the "strong feeling . . . justly aroused." Blaine called it "widespread alarm." The British Minister agreed with both, explaining that "when an American's pocket is touched, he is not likely to keep his temper."[69]

All were correct. The Cincinnati Chamber of Commerce, the Indianapolis Board of Trade, and the Merchant's Exchange of St. Louis assured Blaine "that the hogs of the State of Ohio and of the whole West have been. . . singularly free from disease of all kinds."[70] Specific packers reported their exports "seriously interrupted"—"our *losses* are likely to be *severe*"—and demanded action. One processor in Chicago "now employing 500 pairs of hands would have 2,000 constantly at work but for the trichinae scare."[71] Every section clamored for retaliation. *"The necessity for immediate action is most urgent,"* a group of Virginia livestock men had warned the Congress in 1880, and the failure to prevent further restrictions provoked great rancor.[72]

Big operators like Armour, who had long since defined their marketplace as the world marketplace, did not wait for the government to act. They counterattacked through their corporate consular service. "We have for some time," Armour told Blaine, "been engaged in some effective work, we think, in bringing about the repeal, or at least the modification of the prohibitive decree."[73] Even such giants needed assistance, however, and the smaller businessmen who lacked the resources to establish their own foreign service had no choice but to turn to the government. And though the editors of the *Prairie Farmer* thought it was natural for the French to fight back against the American farm businessmen who were "so depressing their interests," they accepted the inevitability of the conflict and demanded the government wage it with no quarter given or asked.[74]

Blaine had been worried about the danger at least as early as 1879, and he moved quickly to counter the "sudden and disastrous" danger.[75] He followed his first vigorous protest, which was "especially satisfactory" to many agricultural businessmen, with a government inspection.[76] When that indicated that American meat was no more diseased than any other, he blasted the French for a "mistaken and wrongful" action that triggered a general assault on American interests. The livestock industry was "one of the greatest and most wholesome branches of the export trade of this country," and he was honoring his "duty and grave responsibility to watch over the interests of its producers and exporters." American agriculturalists were "rightfully entitled to a prompt and effectual modification of the attitude" of the French Government.[77]

Then, perhaps taking an idea offered by Kasson, and surely encouraged by Armour's report that his men advised "strong pressure," Blaine prepared to win concessions during the scheduled negotiations for a new commercial treaty with France. He no doubt felt that the additional pressure from California wine growers would strengthen his hand, and so told his agent to warn France "discreetly" that the Congress would pass "at least defensive if not retaliatory legislation."[78] And the House responded on April 10, 1882, by directing its concern and support to measures as "will encourage and protect our export trade."[79]

The counteroffensive initiated by the agricultural businessmen, and then organized and focused by Blaine, was temporarily effective. The French shortly suspended their prohibition, and many farmers (and metropolitans concerned with export expansion) anticipated that the victory would lead to the reopening of all European markets. The assassination of Garfield denied Blaine the chance to exploit the French retreat either diplomatically or at home, however, and President Arthur and Secretary Frelinghuysen claimed credit for the success.[80] They needed whatever support that assertion attracted, for the agricultural businessmen did not transfer their confidence in Blaine to his successors.

Senator Morgan of Alabama spoke for many Southerners concerned with market expansion when he expressed his "deep regret" that Blaine was being forced out of the Cabinet.[81] The two men had collaborated very closely in planning the great Atlanta International Cotton Exposition of 1881, a major effort in the campaign to conquer the cotton and cotton textile markets of the world. They agreed that goal was a "vast subject," as the special State Department handbook described the objective, but were confident that the "world offers a field large enough for . . . all the manufactures we can produce." "If Mr. Blaine did nothing else as Secretary of State," the editors of the Atlanta *Constitution* commented, "than to explain the chances and circumstances connected with the export of our cotton goods, he would deserve the thanks of the country."[82]

Morgan and other Southerners viewed cotton exports, and especially the rough fabrics from a regional textile industry, as the lever with which to emancipate themselves as an economic and political colony of the metropolis. The mills were "the weapons peace gave us," explained the Atlanta *Constitution*, adding that "the conflict between New England and the South as the true seat of cotton manufacture has just fairly begun. . . . The south can win—and win it will." Within that framework, as one Baltimore enthusiast explained, the Exposition was "the celebration of the marriage of cotton growing to cotton manufactures."[83] Even Edward Atkinson realized that there was no longer any chance to keep the South as a raw material farm for the New England mills, and *Bradstreet's* warned any doubters that the world market was the only way to handle the new competition.[84] Blaine and Morgan not only agreed on that point, but Blaine saw collaboration with Southerners like Morgan as one way to begin rebuilding the Republican party in that region.

Blaine also viewed the Exposition as part of his push to establish American predominance in the Western Hemisphere. He sought that objective for itself, and in order to provide the United States with an impregnable base for its global expansion. Perhaps nothing reveals the integrated sweep of Blaine's outlook more clearly than his view of Hawaii: the United States, he explained, "regards the Hawaiian group as essentially a part of the American system of the states, and the key to the North Pacific trade."[85] "The interests, commercial and political, of the United States, on this continent, transcend in extent and importance those of any other power, and where those immense interests are deeply involved this government must preserve a position where its influence will be most independent and efficient."[86]

Blaine wholly agreed, therefore, with the Hayes-Evarts decision that "the policy of this country is a canal under American control."[87] Pressure from East Coast shippers of West Coast grain surpluses, as well as from Midwesterners and Southerners, contributed significantly to the increasingly vigorous measures that Hayes took to control the maneuvers of Ferdinand de Lesseps to build a canal. Representative Jay Abel Hubbell of Michigan, for example, argued that the canal was the key to the exports that would underwrite prosperity. "Give us a ship canal and we shall find the solution of the Chinese problem. . . . We can have an almost unlimited commerce with that country if we now embrace our opportunities."[88]

The House of Representatives, worried lest foreign capital extend the pattern established by British control of the Suez Canal, established a committee to review the entire problem. Its members called for "the speedy acquisition" of naval bases to guard all possible routes; and, a bit later, recommended that the Clayton-Bulwer Treaty "should now be finally and formally abrogated."[89] Garfield (and probably Blaine) added personal pressure which undoubtedly reinforced Hayes in standing firm behind his definition of the canal as "virtually a part of the coast line of the United States."[90] That conception of the canal explains why Blaine moved so vigorously to block European influence in Colombia: maneuvers of that kind were "an uncalled-for intrusion" in a region where American interests ranked "before those of any other power."[91] The "fixed purpose" of the United States was to control *any* canal.[92]

Blaine based his strategy on the proposition that rivalries among Latin American nations had to be prevented or controlled by the United States. Otherwise, Great Britain or other European powers would use the troubles to subvert American dominance. There was no conflict between intervention to maintain peace and intervention for economic expansion. "To attain the second object," Blaine explained, "the first must be accomplished."[93] The troubles in Colombia, the conflict between Mexico and Nicaragua, and the war between Chile and Peru threatened to open the way for the British, and the Secretary's interventions were designed to block London and thereby advance American interests.

Blaine was also concerned with personal and more general political objectives at home. He had committed his career to the forging of a powerful alliance between metropolitan Republicans and Western agriculturalists, with additional support to be won as it proved possible from Southern cotton interests. And he concluded that Arthur and Frelinghuysen might very well foreclose the future of the party by failing to give the West and the South the kind of foreign policy they demanded.[94] Blaine's concern to prevent that outcome clearly guided his attempt, in November 1881, to commit his successor to a Pan-American peace conference. He undoubtedly considered himself vindicated by subsequent events. For, despite much support for the conference by petitioners from Vermont through Nebraska to California, and from Texas to Iowa, Arthur and Frelinghuysen quietly withdrew the invitations in August 1882.

That negative action had been anticipated much earlier, and provoked considerable criticism and agitation even before the formal cancellation. Much of the interest in the conference was directly related to the rising demand to open new markets by negotiating reciprocity treaties. That approach, argued *Bradstreet's*, was "much more effective" than any other "in attaching those countries to the United States." "It should be a matter of concern," the editors added, in view of the clear need to export the great agricultural surpluses, that the government failed "to foster trade, to find new markets."[95] The pressure in Congress, which involved representatives from Louisiana, West Virginia, Florida, and Illinois, finally moved Kasson to defend Frelinghuysen as a wholly reliable expansionist not to be compared unfavorably to Blaine.[96] The Secretary himself was disturbed enough to explain the cancellation to Senator Windom, long a leader in the push for markets, who had also left the Cabinet. "Such a Congress at this time would probably be of little benefit . . . and might be very injurious," Frelinghuysen argued, pointing out that the United States could easily be outvoted on crucial issues.[97] He held firm despite continuing pressure from Illinois, Ohio, Missouri, and other agricultural states.

When it became clear that the decision would not be changed, farm businessmen shifted their attention to an attack on Frelinghuysen for refusing to continue Blaine's tough line against European restrictions on American meat exports. The Secretary had quickly dropped all talk of retaliation and made it clear that he preferred to try to reopen the markets through negotiations based on eradicating the dis-

eases in the United States.[98] The majority favoring retaliation drew
strength from the mounting evidence that the restrictions were part
of a broad European counterattack against the economic power manifested by American agricultural businessmen. One consul reported
that the "determined attack" included "petty exactions" as well as
major obstacles. Another recounted candid admissions by various
officials that the measures were a response to the "stupefying" power
of American farmers.[99] Such views reached the farmer through his
own papers like the *Breeder's Gazette*, as well as in stories reprinted
from major dailies like the New York *Herald*.[100] Their deepening animosity was reinforced by support from metropolitan shippers who
demanded action through such organizations as the Chamber of Commerce of the State of New York.[101]

Then the Germans excluded all American pork. Armour and other
livestock spokesmen immediately increased their pressure. Unless
reversed, the policy would "unquestionably" cause "disaster to the
farming interests of Illinois and the Northwest." "Any wise retaliatory
measure" would be satisfactory so long as it was instituted "promptly"
and brought "speedy repeal" of the offending regulation.[102] The New
York *Herald's* cry for "avenging the American hog" was supported by
general "excitement" and "very vigorous efforts" to pass retaliatory
legislation.[103] The German measure likewise strengthened the conviction that the nations that opposed the expansion of the free American
marketplace were dominated by "selfish landlordism" and undemocratic aristocracies.[104]

Frelinghuysen incensed many agricultural businessmen when he
rebuked Aaron Sargent, the American Minister in Germany, for even
mentioning the possibility of retaliation. Sargent had been a strong
expansionist during his service in the Congress, and he wholly agreed
with the movement for retaliation. He thought it the "only argument
which would be effective."[105] The *Rural New Yorker* typified the anger
toward Arthur and Frelinghuysen for submitting "to such foolishness
as is practiced against the United States." "Stockmen ought to begin
a row at once." The *National Live Stock Journal* agreed, charging that
the government "has miserably failed in its duty." And the *Breeder's
Gazette* demanded a policy that would "bristle with retaliation at every
point."[106]

President Arthur, worried by the criticism, considered stronger action. But Frelinghuysen argued for continuing the moderate approach
on the grounds that the French retreat (on November 27, 1883) would
tip the battle against all restrictions. The German prohibition remained,
however, and the President's uneasiness prompted him to create a commission to study the question of diseased meat. But then he retreated,
tossing the issue to the Congress: "Is it not advisable to provide some
measure of equitable retaliation in our relations with governments
which discriminate against our own?"[107]

Josiah Bushnell Grinnell, one of the most articulate and justly prestigious agricultural spokesmen, tried to reestablish some confidence in the Arthur Administration through an open letter to the *Western Rural*. The act itself documented the intensity and seriousness of the opposition, and Grinnell did not present a convincing case for the farmers to moderate their anger. He agreed that the expansion of exports was a matter of "grave concern," and reported that the government was trying to help. He added that the President had personally given "good proof of his interest," and called for inspection laws to reopen all foreign markets.[108]

Grinnell surely winced as the French reaffirmed their prohibition even before his letter was printed. Then it became known that Frelinghuysen had dissuaded Arthur from acting on his inclination to take a firmer stand. That confirmed the farm businessmen's estimate of the Administration as a creature of the metropolis and produced a concerted effort to make policy in the Congress. "Having been kicked," the Chicago *Tribune* roared, "it is time to kick back and keep on kicking until they are kicked into something like reciprocity."[109] The President had lost whatever chance he had to provide positive leadership and thereby maintain the confidence of Western farm businessmen. The initiative passed to the Congress, but it also shifted to the groups that favored inspection rather than retaliation. That meant a sounder long-range program, but the strategy did not produce any immediate victories.

The forces favoring inspection had been active since 1880; but they did not begin to gather strength until 1882 (after Blaine left office), when Emory Storrs, a Chicago broker representing packers like Morris, failed to persuade the Privy Council to modify or remove the British ten-day slaughter order. Deeply disappointed that Blaine was no longer Secretary of State, and "very much depressed" by their losses, the swine breeders reluctantly endorsed inspection on condition that it would be implemented by "radical measures."[110] The serious battle for an inspection system opened in April 1883 when the Wyoming Stock Growers Association decided on a campaign to force the Congress to take action.

As revealed during the major meeting in Chicago on November 15 - 16, 1883, however, the inspection forces were deeply divided among themselves. Some, including railroad men who feared a bad precedent was being established, resisted federal action. Others, as with many packers, fought the kind of tough legislation that was needed. And still another group (mustering Armour, as well as many farmers) hoped the battle for inspection could be used to force Arthur to overrule Frelinghuysen and retaliate. The leaders of the Wyoming Stock Growers Association, who masterminded the complicated maneuvers, credited Senators Plumb and Wilson with the work (and influence) that produced a workable—and hopefully effective—law. That was probably an accurate estimate, though they had important help from metropolitan Republicans like Senators Henry Bowen Anthony of Rhode Island and Warner Miller of New York who also understood the crisis. The final bill, passed May 29, 1884, created a Bureau of Animal Industry "in order to promote the exportation of live stock from the United States."[111]

The legislation did ultimately improve the quality of American meat products, thus rewarding domestic consumers with a windfall from the storm over exports. But it did not ease the demands for more immediate action by the government, and the failure of the Arthur Administration to produce *any* improvement saddled the Republican party with a burden that not even Blaine could carry to victory in the election of 1884. The tone of the agricultural anger was nicely illustrated by the protests from the Topeka, Kansas, Board of Trade. Europeans "have maligned the American hog," they resolved, and called for retaliation in the form of prohibiting the import of "all articles of luxury" from the offending countries. The concerted effort to "punch up Congress" involved a special delegation from Illinois; petitions and resolutions from packers in Chicago, Milwaukee, St. Joseph, St. Louis, and Boston; formal demands from the state governments of Ohio, Indiana, and Kansas; congressional efforts by politicians from Rhode Island to California and from Texas to Iowa; and embittered editorials in almost every agricultural newspaper or journal.[112]

Horace White understandably warned Carl Schurz that he foresaw "a foreign policy looming up in the distance at variance with national traditions and involving enormous expenditures and no end of jobbery."[113] Farm spokesmen were complimenting congressional supporters for their "savageness," attacking Frelinghuysen for being "too respectable" and following a "fifty year old diplomacy," and demanding "a strong diplomacy" to protect the "vast interests" of agriculture. "Blockade with a vengeance," roared one editor who, though he did not "desire the government unnecessarily to embroil us in a war," nevertheless demanded "our rights protected at all hazards."[114] The same editor, Milton George of the *Western Rural*, whose feel for the attitudes of agricultural businessmen in the upper Ohio, Mississippi, and Missouri valleys enabled him to gain wide support for the Northern Farmers Alliance, also provided a central insight into what was happening throughout the country.

For, after encouraging militancy, he cautioned prudence because he sensed that "the average American is much puffed up with his nation's power."[115] The editors of the *Rural New Yorker* also understood the phenomenon: an economic nationalism was defining various other nations as enemies on the basis of their response to American overseas economic expansion. The angry threats and demands were "not meaningless," they pointed out, because the underlying outlook was "undoubtedly shared by a majority." The editors thought the wild talk "about using the iron-hand" was "buncome," but admitted that the "denunciation of 'princes, potentates, principalities and power'" was all of a piece with the equally tough rhetoric about market expansion.[116] And so it was, for the agricultural businessmen were carrying the logic of Adam Smith and John Locke to its inherent conclusions. Freedom at home depended on freedom abroad; and the world markets required for prosperity at home defined the American marketplace as the world marketplace and thereby delineated the security perimeter of the political economy.

Secretary of State Frelinghuysen tried to channel the militancy into support for his more placid strategy of market expansion.[117] He assured Western and Southern congressmen that he shared their concern, but insisted that such objectives as more trade with Latin America could "be best accomplished by negotiation, with the several states, of Reciprocity Treaties which shall cover the different needs."[118] That offered the strongest possibility "to gain the control of those markets for the products of our fields and factories."[119] Such talks did not satisfy the farm businessmen. The time had arrived, declared Representative Witthorne of Tennessee, particularly concerned to expand tobacco exports, for the government to "become responsive to these demands and necessities." "No timidity should mark [its] action or deference to the equanimity of [its] adversary control his counsel." "This struggle cannot be postponed."[120]

"We are not satisfied with the present condition or future prospects of our class," added the Indiana Grange. "The men whose labor and success in the field saved our country from hopeless bankruptcy and restored prosperity do not receive a fair share of the profits."[121] That kind of intense self-consciousness and sense of community among the members of the agricultural majority created a powerful and aggressive economic nationalism. The men of the land, as the Texas Grange pointed out, were united by "class interests based upon occupation, trades, employment and professions." They were becoming contemptuous of leaders who allowed even "the weak and effeminate government of Spain . . . to prescribe conditions . . . prejudicial to American productions."[122] The attitude was widespread, as indicated by the testimony of Erastus D. Goodwin, a Connecticut farmer. He wanted tough measures to drive Great Britain "from the markets of the world," and an end to "discrimination in favor of our manufacturing interests."[123]

"A new wave of Americanism," summarized one editor, "is breaking over the whole country."[124] One of the most striking aspects of that nationalistic drive for markets involved the way it led Southerners to reassert their eighteenth-century tradition of demanding government aid. Senator Morgan provided much of the leadership in that movement, but others like Senator Joseph Emerson Brown of Georgia, Representative Ezekiel John Ellis of Louisiana, and Representative Thomas Peck Ochiltree of Texas documented the wide extent of that attitude. "The state takes the lead," declared Ochiltree, in the drive for "a market for our surplus products." "We have passed that era in our history when the Federal power was restrained. . . . The day has come when no party dogmas will be allowed to stand in the way of development and protection for a foreign trade."[125]

Ochiltree's remarks offer a partial explanation for the failure of the agricultural majority to gain its objectives immediately. He was reading a process as an achievement, not an uncommon propensity, and hence foreshortened time. The agricultural businessmen did win their strategic battle for the acceptance of the market expansionist outlook in a remarkably short period, although the struggles over the kind of expansion, and for control of the process, are apt to obscure that truth. William E. Curtis of the Chicago *Inter-Ocean* provided a very neat description of the major dilemma over control. Until the neocolonial agriculturalists captured control of the American government from the metropolis, they faced the necessity of working with their domestic overlords in order to defeat Great Britain—yet the metropolis was tied to the global enemy.[126]

Once that situation is understood, much that appears contradictory in the behavior of the farm businessmen becomes comprehensible. They are often presented, for example, as opposing the improvement of the diplomatic and consular services. But they actually played a large role in the demand for expansion and increased efficiency. The National Grange, for example, called upon the Secretary of State in 1881 to extend the publication of consular reports. Their primary objective, however, was to reform both branches of the department so they functioned to meet the needs of agriculturalists seeking world markets.

In their minds, at any rate, that was "but simple justice."[127] Their votes against measures for merely sustaining or enlarging the existing services were part of a broad effort to force the changes they deemed necessary. Senator Plumb of Kansas, who labored diligently throughout the 1880s to educate metropolitan Republicans on the necessity of satisfying the agricultural businessmen, explained the situation very clearly in 1884. He strongly supported the consular service, but insisted that it be reorganized to meet the need for world markets. His attacks were designed to create a government agency organized to deal effectively with the substantive issues confronting the nation.[128]

A growing number of metropolitan leaders recognized the validity of Plumb's warning, and that served to increase the pressure on Arthur and Frelinghuysen. One of the major figures in that process was Senator George Frisbie Hoar of Massachusetts. "The American people," he bluntly told other metropolitans in 1884, "are entitled to have their great business interests dealt with by statesmen who are not constantly flinching and cringing." No one could mistake the targets of his attack: "We are groping still blindly after new policies which shall increase our exports."[129] Bankers continued to discount such cries of urgency, but they were persistently countered by other metropolitan leaders who complained that "the avenues of commerce all over the world have been seized by rival nations," and who warned that agricultural exports were "the most important factor in maintaining the commercial prosperity of the United States."[130]

Such agitation belatedly affected President Arthur and Secretary of State Frelinghuysen, and moved them to somewhat more vigorous action. They stoutly defended the existing reciprocal trade treaty with Hawaii against metropolitan high tariff critics, and made a major effort to win approval for a similar treaty with Mexico. They won that long fight (on March 11, 1884) by the narrow vote of 41 to 20 in the Senate, but the struggle revealed that agricultural businessmen remained very skeptical of Frelinghuysen's concern for their interests. They were more interested in the Cuban market for its potential to absorb meat products, flour, other foodstuffs, and rough cotton textiles.[131]

The Administration did make one energetic effort to aid agriculture, but it affected Southerners rather than Northern or Western farmers. For that matter, given Frelinghuysen's outlook, he may have viewed the Congo more as a market for Northern textile manufacturers than for the Southerners who applied almost all of the pressure to penetrate that region. But President Arthur understood Blaine's domestic political strategy in supporting the Atlanta Cotton Exposition, and he may have been making his own move to strengthen the Republicans in the South.[132] In any event, the bizarre episode leaves no doubt about the convergence in expansionist thought of the concern to export "civilization, order, and security" along with cotton textiles, "canned fruit, milk, and beef."[133]

The classic, formal statement manifesting the final integration of those two themes in the free marketplace outlook did not come until the promulgation of the Open Door Notes by the Administration of President William McKinley at the end of the century. But the efforts of Senator Morgan and his expansionist allies were guided by the same spirit—and almost produced the language—of that later document. Morgan's imperial conception even included freedom for the Southern black man—after he had been exported to Africa. The Senator thought the freedmen would strengthen the American power base in the Congo, but his primary concern was to evade a racial confrontation in America.

The motives of Henry Shelton Sanford, Morgan's principal ally in the Congo operation, were somewhat less complicated. He wanted influence, fame, and money. The son of a wealthy New England manufacturer, he served in various diplomatic posts prior to the Civil War and then, after that conflict, invested much of his capital in Southern agriculture. A very shrewd entrepreneur, he cultivated friendships with Presidents Grant and Arthur, Senators Morgan and Chandler, and various leaders in New York business and politics. He entered the Congo maneuvers after Henry Morton Stanley, the Welshman who thought he was an American, discovered Livingston in Africa and almost simultaneously recognized the possibilities for American exports.

Stanley projected a fantasy market. He first calculated that "just one Sunday dress" for the Congolese would require 320,000,000 yards of good American cotton sheeting. "I found," he recalled, "that two Sunday dresses and four every-day dresses would in one year amount to 3,840,000,000 yards. . . . I would have to provide for night dresses also, and these would consume 160,000,000 yards. Then the grave clothes came into mind, and . . . I really feared for a time that the millions would get beyond measurable calculation. However . . . 16,000,000 yards will be required." By that time, of course, Stanley was indulging himself in marketplace play, but it was a most revealing kind of amusement.

It was Sanford, however, rather than Stanley, who devised the basic political strategy. The United States would recognize King Leopold's International Association of the Congo, itself a front organization designed to give Belgium a foothold against the British and the French in Africa, in return for free commercial access to the Belgian colony. The result, Sanford explained, would provide the market "for relief from the overproduction which now threatens us in some of our manufactures."[134] Morgan's sustained efforts won Senate approval for official action to assist such "furtherance of our commerce."[135] Arthur then recognized Leopold's agency and later dispatched two naval vessels to support the American official sent to explore what Frelinghuysen described as "the prospective rich trade" that "should be opened to all nations on equal terms."[136]

The Congo trade remained prospective, but the pressure for markets continued to plague Arthur and Frelinghuysen. And the great difficulty of satisfying the expansionist demands of the agricultural majority was nowhere more apparent than in the struggle to control a canal route, acquire an American merchant marine, and build a modern navy. For while the farm businessmen wanted the exports, they were determined to expand freedom at home as well as abroad in the process of extending American power in the world marketplace. Their imperial thrust was in that very important respect directed as much against the domestic American metropolis as against Great Britain, Germany, and France.

Senator Morgan quickly established his position as the most persistent advocate of a canal who also stressed its rewards to the agricultural sector of the political economy. "There can not be anything done for the southern people of equal advantage," he explained in one version of his standard speech, "to the building of the Nicaragua Canal, so as to give us access to the eastern Asiatic countries. . . . We shall harvest that wealth of the Indies."[137] But he had capable assistance from other Southerners from Virginia to Texas and, as he acknowledged, additional help from Northern and Western farm groups. Oregon agriculturalists, along with their counterparts in California and Washington, demanded "immediate and favorable action" on the issue. They argued the canal would enable them to defeat Russian and Indian wheat growers, and agreed with the cotton men that it would give Americans an insuperable advantage in "this great Chinese market."[138] The Leavenworth, Kansas, Board of Trade favored the project because it would help overcome the transportation advantage held by Kansas City.[139] And the National Grange included the canal as part of the transportation system that it termed "the public highways."[140] Many metropolitan interests also agitated for a canal. "If our natural prosperity is to continue," summarized one such spokesman, "we much reach foreign markets with our manufactures."[141]

But Frelinghuysen's maneuver to secure a canal route through Nicaragua smacked too much of traditional British colonialism. The convention he signed on December 1, 1884, created a protectorate that upset enough expansionists—metropolitan as well as agrarian—to prevent ratification in the Senate. But the treaty did muster a majority of the votes, and that show of strength dramatized the basic commitment to imperial expansion that had emerged from the consensus on the necessity of enlarging exports on a sustained basis. The split among the expansionists between those who favored annexation and those who preferred to establish American predominance in less formal (and demanding) ways accounted for much of the delay in consolidating the new American security perimeter. Until the tension was resolved, the insistence on expanding freedom had the effect of slowing the expansion of the marketplace.

Similar conflicts delayed the push for a merchant marine and a navy. Metropolitan shipbuilders and merchants provided the early pressure to acquire a commercial fleet, but Blaine quickly generalized the issue in terms of the entire economy.[142] He first stressed the danger of "becoming tributary to Great Britain," and his concern to expand textile exports to South America and Asia.[143] Within a year (by 1879) he added the arguments that a merchant marine would help market "all the countless products of the fertile West," and likewise do much to solve the monetary problem by ending the gold drain to England.[144]

Agitation for American shipping by farm businessmen had clearly influenced Blaine. The *Northwestern Miller*, for example, steadily demanded a national marine throughout 1877 and 1878; and spokesmen from Nebraska and Michigan added their voices to the campaign.[145] Additional metropolitan interests joined the battle as a result of the agricultural export bonanza of the late 1870s, concluding that the trade raised the "most serious" issue of "whether we are to continue to give away the freights."[146] Others emphasized the argument that the agricultural businessmen would continue to fill the holds of a great fleet.[147] All such advocates agreed with the New York *Tribune* that "the avenues of commerce all over the world have been seized by rival nations."[148]

The disagreement arose over how to meet the challenge. Oregon Grangers favored buying the ships, and Dakota spokesmen pointed out that "the increased value of the wheat crop alone would be many times greater than the amount necessary to start these steamship lines."[149] Others, including Blaine, insisted that "Americans should build ships for their own purposes," a view backed by those who considered the merchant marine a school to train "great merchants and famous captains who will find and develop new markets for American production."[150] Yet those economic nationalists, who were largely responsible for the failure to start buying a fleet, were opposed by other expansionists who feared that federal appropriations would line the pockets of a few metropolitan corporations.

Such men shared John Wanamaker's concern to find "an open door to new markets," but they fought hard to block his proposal to subsidize the shippers in the same way the railroads had been aided. They wanted a national program. Senator Plumb effectively summarized their position. "I want that which ministers to the commerce and the prosperity of the entire country," he insisted on March 3, 1883. "I want something which gives us an outlet at the mouth of the Mississippi for the flour, the wheat, the pork, and the beef. . . . If we cannot have a policy which shall minister to the foreign commerce of this country, which shall give it a chance to be enlarged . . . then I do not want any shipping bill at all."[151]

Similar divisions slowed the effort to construct a modern navy. President Hayes raised the issue in December 1880 when he described a building program as an "unquestionable service to the expansion of our commerce."[152] No one could have stated the connection between market expansion and a new strategic security perimeter any more clearly. One of the central questions about how best to expand was immediately posed by a metropolitan expansionist: "Our war vessels should take the form of swift cruisers rather than of the huge monsters owned by Europe."[153] That view, so often attributed solely to agricultural spokesmen considered opponents of a navy, was in truth held by the Navy's own leaders.

Officers like Shufeldt and Kelley recognized that a new fleet would have to be built over a period of time. They also understood two crucial factors that many impatient expansionists overlooked. First, battleships are extremely vulnerable in combat unless they are supported by destroyers and cruisers. Second, a first-rate navy is based on sound and extensive technology and sophisticated industrial production. While naval officers (and their civilian allies) often used the enlarged rhetoric of battleships to convert others to their long-range objectives, therefore, their serious thoughts were not so very different from those of the agricultural spokesmen who fought the propensity to take a short cut to the final goal.

Some farmers used the same argument for buying naval vessels that they employed in the debates over a merchant marine. Blaine's counterfire was devastating: the United States "cannot make a navy by graduating cadets at Annapolis." But the return salvo was equally effective: "The Senator may as well understand that the men of the West and of the South and of the great producing regions, insist that they have paid tribute to New England long enough, and if they can buy ships anywhere else cheaper, they insist that they have a right to do so. . . . Kentucky wants nothing except fair play and a free contest."[154] The exchange was a stand-off. Blaine's economic nationalism was shared by the agricultural businessmen, and in their view that meant an American Navy to expand the American marketplace throughout the world.

Hence they responded positively to President Arthur's call for a navy "to protect . . . the highways of commerce, the varied interests of our foreign trade." And they wholly approved his blunt assertion that "we must be prepared to enforce any policy which we think wise to adopt."[155] Their complaint against Arthur was that he refused to act on his own rhetoric. As Representative Hilary Abner Herbert of Alabama explained the issue, farm businessmen wanted true independence because they "must export," and they could not have "freer trade and fairer play in the markets of the world" without a navy. Or as Representative William Henry Calkins of Indiana commented, "I hope to see in my lifetime the American Navy standing . . . at the head of all the navies of the world."[156]

The broad agricultural support for a modern navy was revealed in many forms. No farm groups petitioned the Forty-eighth Congress, for example, against beginning a construction program. The opposition memorials from farm states originated in small pacifist or religious groups, and in no way represented the views of the majority of the farmers.[157] Such centers of the agricultural economy as St. Paul and Cincinnati, moreover, spoke vigorously of "the absolute necessity for a prompt and large increase in the naval forces of the United States" to further "our commercial interests abroad."[158] And Senator Vest of Missouri, a staunch spokesman for the farmers in their battles against the railroads and other corporate powers, argued simply that "commercial supremacy and naval power are inseparable."[159]

Senator John Franklin Miller of California provided an excellent example of how freedom and economics were being integrated in marketplace expansionism. "If this nation intends to take its place, as it should take its place, among the great nations of the earth and contend . . . for the commerce of the western hemisphere, it is time that she should be prepared to meet either the encroachments or attacks of those powers which have become jealous of this great nation . . . whose example of free government and free institutions is spreading the contagion of free thought and the freedom of individual action among all the peoples of the globe . . . and engendering and exciting the hatred and malice and unfriendliness of imperialists and monarchists throughout the world. . . . The time has come now . . . when new markets are necessary to be found in order to keep our factories running. Here lies to the south of us our India, and if we have the nerve, and the foresight, and the sagacity to utilize it by proper methods we shall have new markets for our products and for our manufacturers."[160]

One of the most telling commentaries on agricultural support for a navy came from Representative James Burns Belford of Colorado. He could not resist the provocation to tease the farm spokesmen about being landlocked sailors. "I have been edified and electrified," he once joshed, "by the learned discourses of Rear Admiral Calkins, from Indiana, and of Commodore Anderson, from Kansas, the western part of whose State does not contain water enough to freshen a salt mackerel."[161] His colleague from Illinois, Representative Benjamin Franklin Marsh, made the point more directly. Restoration of American sea power was favored "by the people of the sparsely settled districts of the West" because they needed overseas markets.[162]

But Blaine's opponent in the early confrontation over how to acquire the new navy, Senator James Burnie Beck of Kentucky, spoke an equally important truth because he understood and shared the antimetropolitan feeling of the agriculturalists. And that was a powerful force because it was reinforced by firm technological fact as well as by an experienced, hardened skepticism about the judgment of metropolitan leaders. Beck stated the issue very neatly in response to urgent pleas to proceed immediately on the basis of existing European construction techniques: "Let us wait and see whether they are such ships as we ought to duplicate or not."[163] Even Representative Ezekiel John Ellis of Louisiana, who wanted a navy "heart and hand" in order "to obtain commercial supremacy," admitted the strength of that argument.[164]

The agricultural resistance to rapid and uncritical action was based on two objections. "We want a navy," explained Senator Plumb. "We do not want a lot of repaired old hulls and hulks." Despite his general support for a building program, Senator Vest agreed that American technology did not inspire confidence.[165] That view gained major support, moreover, because the Navy itself admitted that "great deliberation" was required—many issues remained an "open question." The entire subject, concluded the Report of the Naval Advisory Board of October 25, 1883, "should be carefully studied and decided upon."[166]

Shufeldt further agreed that "the first thing we ought to do" was to "make a Navy with reference to the protection of our people and our commerce abroad. . . . Then afterwards I would like, perhaps, in the not very distant future, to build larger ships."[167] The agricultural businessmen appear still less negative and obstructionist in the light of Secretary of the Navy William Eaton Chandler's blunt talk about the difficulty and uncertainty in meeting the technological requirements. "Never in this country has any steel been manufactured in large quantities subjected to such rigid tests."[168]

No mills had ever rolled such plates. No shipyard gangs had ever fabricated such ships. No armorers had ever forged such rifles. And once those problems began to be explored, the inquiry raised the fundamental issue of whether the fleet should be built through subsidies to private interests, or through public shipyards.[169] Representative Whitthorne summarized the view of many agriculturalists in one sentence: "We need speed; we need guns, and we need armour," so "make your experiment first."[170] Representatives Richard William Guenther of Wisconsin and John Frederick Dezendorf of Virginia added that the construction of the Navy should not create another metropolitan monopoly; hence the government should provide its own shipyards and other necessary plants.[171]

Many metropolitan expansionists, including President Arthur, understood and accepted the need to proceed carefully in order "to secure judicious designs and honest and economical construction."[172] The failure to begin building a battleship fleet second to none was not due to any lack of expansionist ardor, but rather to a realistic and sophisticated concern to design and fabricate the relevant kind of ships in the best and most responsible manner. And, despite its internal differences, the expansionist movement did appropriate more than $30 million for the Navy during 1883 - 1884. The definition of the American marketplace as the world marketplace had led the Navy to relocate the security perimeter of the country, moving it outward from the continental limits to the furthest reaches of the seven seas. And the agricultural businessmen, who had played the key role in expanding the marketplace and the conception of it, provided astute support for the resulting needs of the Navy.

Despite the differences over methods and tactics, and the confrontations over who should determine policy, the transformation of the drive for exports into a sophisticated imperialism designed to expand freedom as well as markets became self-sustaining during the years of Garfield and Arthur. A strong majority of Americans accepted the necessity of market expansion. The sense of necessity thus produced actions that created the conditions that defined foreign affairs as a struggle for economic supremacy against unfree foreigners. And that battle required the use of American power against foreign governments and peoples. The farm businessmen who produced the surpluses that changed the lives of Europeans thus began to demand that the American government change the lives of still other peoples in order to open new markets for their continuing surpluses.

Those pressures for expansion were intensified, furthermore, by two domestic experiences that came to a climax as the economy wobbled into another recession that became another depression. The great continental fund of wealth-producing farm land seemed to be gone—taken, occupied, filled up—and the acceptance of that apparent truth led to the demand for a new frontier in overseas markets. The intellectual and emotional impact of the confrontation with the seeming end of the frontier was greatly heightened, moreover, by the evidence that vast acreages of the land had been seized by foreign capitalists and American metropolitan operators closely associated with foreign capitalists. Those reinforcing experiences not only strengthened the already powerful spirit of expansionist economic nationalism, but intensified the feeling among the neocolonial American agriculturalists that they would have to defeat their domestic imperial overlords before they could embark upon their own imperial expansion of the free marketplace.

TEN

America . . . has its rapidly growing "colonies" in the far west.

Comment of an Englishman, 1881

What right or title has a foreign cattle company to public land which has been settled on by a citizen of the United States under the homestead law?

J. D. Sargent to the Public Land Commissioner, 1883

Upon their fences they have posted at intervals notices as follows: "The son of a bitch who opens the fence had better look out for his scalp."

George W. Fairfield to the Surveyor General, November 1883

We are rapidly utilizing the whole of our continental territory. We must turn our eyes abroad, or they will soon look inward upon discontent.

Representative John Adam Kasson of Iowa, September 1881

Poverty is the mother of many things in this world.

B. A. Arnold of Colorado to the Public Land Commissioner, 1883

We frequently take occasion to refer to the fact that in this country of ours "Westward the star of Empire takes its way.". . . The development of the West . . . is the development of the nation.

Western Rural, January 5, 1884

We are now on the threshold, in my judgment, of a development outward, of a contest for the foreign commerce of the world.

Senator Preston B. Plumb of Kansas, May 1884

American soil is for Americans, and should be exclusively owned and controlled by American citizens and those intending to become such.

Joint Resolution of the State Legislature of New Hampshire, August 1885

We have practically reached the limit of our public domain.

Henry George, April 1886

Everywhere there is unrest and discontent.

Representative William Joel Stone of Missouri, 1886

Are we the servile and supple tool of foreign capitalists, or are we going to preserve this country for our own people?

Representative James Burns Belford of Colorado, 1884

The
Closing of the Continental Frontier,
Like the Closing of the European Markets, Turns
America Toward
Imperialism

G IVEN THEIR strong traditional commitment to the marketplace conception of reality, and the experience they could so easily interpret as confirming that conception of the world, American agriculturalists moved from a continental to an overseas imperial outlook with relatively little intellectual difficulty or emotional shock. The one bothersome rut in the road to empire was the experience and sense of a special freedom-as-liberty created and enjoyed, especially after 1819 - 1820, by controlling a relatively unpopulated continent. The achievements of the earlier age of mercantilism, grounded in a different sense of freedom-as-community, were distorted when not forgotten.[1] It was not at all by accident that the agricultural businessmen of the 1880s and 1890s invoked the names of Andrew Jackson and Patrick Henry instead of James Madison and John Quincy Adams.

The identification of oneself within the marketplace tradition of freedom-as-liberty created a powerful obligation to expand freedom while extending the marketplace. That responsibility could be met by opposing the actions of the less free European nations that blocked farm exports; and by carrying the principles and practices of the free marketplace to the peoples of the less fortunate societies in Africa, Latin America, and Asia that American farm businessmen viewed as new and necessary markets. Opposition to the one and penetration of the other clearly qualified as enlarging the area of freedom.

But the transition from continental to overseas imperial expansion was eased—and speeded—by the closing out of the frontier of easy opportunity that had underwritten the freedom-as-liberty. The syllogism that facilitated the change was somewhat complicated, but not so difficult as to lose any of its persuasiveness. One: the vast surplus of cheap (often free) and easily farmed land had provided a means of avoiding the confined, undemocratic, aristocratic, and monarchical existence of Europe. Two: that land also produced a spiraling surplus that proved the necessity of expanding the marketplace. Three: the unfree European governments closed their markets to thwart the spread of freedom by curtailing it at its source. Four: the unfree American metropolis passively supported, or actively collaborated with, those efforts of the unfree European nations. Five: the expansion of the marketplace would restore freedom at home and extend it abroad.

The developments that greased the slide toward imperialism involved the deepening conviction that the kind of land that underwrote freedom-as-liberty was coming to an end, and a similar certainty that the termination of that classic free land-free marketplace equation had been speeded by American metropolitans allied with foreigners who were closing or otherwise controlling the overseas markets. The results were an embittered campaign against the metropolis and its alien allies that magnified the existing determination to win supremacy in the world marketplace, and a quickened confidence that expanding exports would enlarge the freedom of the customer as well as the liberty of the producer.

Those imperial forces drew their strength from roots that reached deep into the soil of the 1840s, when the concern for the amount of free land first became a matter of sustained national concern. The additional fears evoked by the debates after the Civil War about the abuses of the preemption laws and the weaknesses of the Homestead Act were intensified by the depression of the 1870s and the related increase in foreclosures and tenancy, the rise of the cattle industry, the rapid success of the bonanza farms, and the swelling consciousness among farm businessmen of their neocolonial position in the political economy.[2]

The bonanza farms incited widespread opposition because they removed vast acreages of virgin land from the market, they were controlled by wealthy metropolitan individuals or powerful metropolitan syndicates (with alien connections), they exerted great leverage in and on the marketplace, and they contributed little if anything to the building of a viable social order.[3] Those features provided a substantial basis for extensive criticism and militant antagonism. The metropolis was neither receptive nor sympathetic to such criticisms during the latter part of the 1870s because the huge farms were presented as exciting examples of triumphant American enterprise and as illustrations of the romance of the Great West.

Thus the owner was often pictured as a man who lived "in town in his own house or stops at the best hotels, smokes the best cigars, is full of good stories, and takes life in an easy, jolly way." And the operation itself was described with an exaggerated flair that charmed the urbanite. "I've seen a man on one of our big farms start out in the spring and plow a straight furrow until fall. Then he turned around and harvested back." Or with statistical data that staggered the imagination, as with the calculation that a single day's harvest would fill seventy-five boxcars.[4]

The ordinary farm businessman also read such accounts, however, and knew that men like Representative John Wilbur Dwight of New York (as well as metropolitan entrepreneurs who did not hold public office) owned such farms. They likewise understood the kind of truths that an anonymous writer finally began to tell the metropolis at the end of the 1870s. He had gone West with eyes wide in wonder to return with lids narrowed by the dangers. He noted the "conspicuous absence of women and children," or "anything that could be called a home." They are "simply business ventures," he concluded, "skinning the lands without any compensating benefits." They had "not one redeeming feature," and would very probably cause a revolt among the farm businessmen.[5] The author was observant and perceptive, and his evaluation was strengthened (and his forecast verified) by concurrent developments in other parts of the West and in the South.

As was so often the case in the evolution of the expansionist and imperial consciousness, an immediately favorable development spawned a troublesome consequence that reinforced the existing momentum for expansion. That was particularly true in connection with the export boom of the late 1870s, for its ramifications greatly augmented the formulation of the frontier thesis and the surge of anti-alien feeling among the agriculturalists. The boom speeded the occupation of the remaining farm land and attracted foreign investment to the West and Southwest. Many of those business operations, domestic and foreign, evoked a surging antagonism among farm businessmen.

The beginnings of the movement can be illustrated by reviewing the career of one foreigner who became a minor hero to some American agriculturalists because he accepted the logic of their central arguments against the metropolis. The man was Moreton Frewen, a member of the British aristocracy who came to the United States in 1878 after sustaining heavy gambling losses and after breaking off an affair. Frewen possessed a sense of humor about both of his propensities, and once remarked that he had decided it was wise to "push on west" because the Philadelphia females "were very agreeable to behold." Some were "big and blonde and often beautiful," and the brunettes were "not less perfect."[6]

He and his brother pushed on with a flair. They crossed the Big Horn Range in Wyoming in December 1878 and (with brother Dick doing much of the early work) purchased land on the Powder River and founded the 76 Ranch. The next summer they acquired 2,000 cattle from Oregon and launched a second operation on Crazy Woman's Creek. Within three years they owned nearly 15,000 head, and when Moreton bought his brother's share in 1882 and incorporated at $1.5 million, he was a major figure in the high-range livestock business.[7]

Frewen manifested many of the characteristics and attitudes that antagonized nonranching farm businessmen, and in those respects typified the kind of operation that generated the drive to nationalize the land for use by Americans. But he also worked with Thomas Sturgis of the Wyoming Stock Growers Association against the beef packers and the railroads, became a major advocate of remonetizing silver, and tried very hard to reopen the British market for feeder cattle.[8] Those activities won him a significant measure of acceptance and support—and some influence. His very uniqueness dramatizes the overriding negative reaction to foreign capitalists and underscores the more general conflict between the ranchers and the cereal farmers. At the same time, his operations also illustrate the very important antimetropolitan feeling among large and wealthy ranchers that did so much to prevent the coalition of expansionists agricultural businessmen from destroying itself in internal conflicts.[9]

Frewen is thus very helpful in isolating the various themes that came together to create the anti-alien movement, and the experiences that led to the grass-roots formulation of the frontier thesis. Two of those elements, the great flow of foreign (and largely British) capital into American agriculture, and the nature of the operations of the American and alien ranchers, reinforced each other from the outset. The most illustrative counterpoint to Frewen is provided by William Scully, the son of an Irish landed family who came to America in 1851 and rapidly acquired vast acreages across the Midwest in Illinois, Kansas, and Nebraska. He established a no-nonsense system of tenant farming that harvested a fortune—for himself. Scully prescribed the crops, and specified that the tenants pay all the taxes and finance all improvements above the ground. He controlled well over 100,000 acres in merely two fiefs of his kingdom—two counties in Kansas and two in Nebraska.[10] Scully was not unique, for other investors held huge tracts in Florida and other states.[11]

Scully did become a primary target, however, for the nonranchers who attacked alien capital; and, because of his quasi-feudal operations, became a symbol of the entire issue. But the primary assault was directed against aliens in the cattle industry. Not only did most British capital enter that phase of agricultural business, but such was known from the beginning—along with British elation over the profits. Despite their reputation for verbal reserve, the Englishmen sent more words than pound notes, and most of them were circulated in agricultural newspapers. The Earl of Dunsmore, for example, explained that he was buying into ranching in Montana to recover financial losses in London.[12] And Lord Airlie concluded, on the basis of his operations in Colorado, that "with a capital of something less than $20,000, a man ought to be able to make a very good start of a farm of 640 acres." Having vented that casual arrogance, he added as an aside that he "would not advise anyone to go to Texas."[13]

Another outspoken Englishman candidly described America as an aspiring empire "which has its rapidly growing 'colonies' in the far west."[14] One of the major figures to incite the American colonials was James S. Brisbin, who provided an enthusiastic report of how an occasionally resident landlord could enjoy personal freedom and improve his health while "reaping a rich reward." "A herd ought to yield an annual increase of at least 25 per cent," and the resulting "miracle of the nineteenth century" ought to yield a net profit of $36,500 in five years. To cinch his case, he reported on an American syndicate headed by Judge David W. Sherwood of Connecticut that had been organized "to realize the largest possible profits."[15]

The individual who talked most bluntly about the practice that provoked much of the early antagonism was W. Bailie Grohman. "You or I," he gleefully told his fellow Britishers, "can to-day make ourselves entirely at home, disporting ourselves as virtual owners of the land, without paying one penny for it. . . . There's no trouble about title, deeds, surveyors, and lawyers."[16] Mrs. L. L. Snowden of Colorado offered a typical American judgment of the process. "A poor man does not get justice. . . . The justice of the peace" in her county was "an Englishman . . . [who] has not declared his intention of becoming a citizen."[17] Another warned that the people were becoming "aroused in righteous indignation" by "fraud after fraud" practiced by two large English cattle companies.[18]

The arbitrary occupation of the land by foreigners was only one of the offenses.[19] American operators, individual and corporate, followed the same practice, and both groups progressively enclosed vast tracts to exclude settlers and block access to water.[20] An investigation of the situation in 1881 and 1882 left no doubt that "many ranchers or herders had settled on the public lands without claim or pretense, or title or possessory right, and have inclosed large tracts of the same with fences."[21] Beyond issuing verbal blasts against the practices, however, the Arthur Administration did little to stop the activities. The violations continued unhindered, and by the end of 1882 the Matador Cattle Company operating in Texas proudly claimed more than 1.5 million acres.[22] Given that success, it is somewhat surprising that thirty-one additional firms enclosed only 3 million more acres.

Many metropolitan spokesmen worried only that "large amounts of European capital are still required," an attitude that extended and hardened the anger of the farmers.[23] "What right or title has a foreign

cattle company," asked one embittered man who had been ordered
to remove his home from his land, "to public land which has been
settled on by a citizen of the United States under the homestead law?"
Kansas farmers wrote fiery petitions against "syndicates and individuals" alike, and a Nebraska man was outraged by the arrogance of
the giants. "Upon their fences they have posted at intervals notices
as follows: 'The son of a bitch who opens the fence had better look out
for his scalp.'"[24]

"Men are inclosing areas equal to small kingdoms," cried the editors of the Wyoming *Sentinel*, *"and, contrary to law, hiring men to
pre-empt."* Sturgis of the Wyoming Stock Growers Association realized the danger and concluded that fencing was not "the wisest method"
of using the public lands. A confrontation between agricultural businessmen on that issue was "likely to be disastrous." The Cheyenne
Leader, judging in January 1883 that "public opinion is now at a fever
heat," agreed that "the fences that have been built upon the public lands
must go."[25] Secretary of the Interior Teller bluntly warned President
Arthur that the situation was alarming and presented an overpowering case for vigorous countermeasures. The "frequent frauds" had
produced "numerous complaints," he explained, and pleaded with
the Congress to act. Another report concluded that "the pre-emption
laws are now the hope of the land-grabber and are the land-swindler's
darlings."[26]

But the President failed to counter the rising clamor, and the anger
against foreign capitalists and illegal fencing converged in a powerful movement against alien landholders.[27] The *National Live Stock
Journal* and the *Breeder's Gazette* admitted that the British were using
"our own territories" as colonies in order to compete with American
cattlemen, and the editors soon abandoned the argument that American
farmers could win the battle simply by raising better cattle.[28] The steady
rise in alien holdings likewise produced an increasing number of careful analyses by individual businessmen. William Godwin Moody
warned that the "lands of our country are rapidly going into the hands
of a few," and concluded from his own research trip through the West
that the combination of foreign and metropolitan acquisitions posed
a serious danger to the free marketplace. The frontier process was
unhappily coming to an end. Moody saw no alternative but to accept
the inevitability of corporate farming and control it by regulatory
legislation.[29]

Such fatalism was rare among farm businessmen. While they agreed
most emphatically that the giants had to be restrained, they vigorously
reasserted the axioms of the free marketplace and on that basis moved
to reclaim the land taken illegally by American and foreign capitalists—and to find a new frontier. Their maturing consciousness thus
integrated the concerns about preemption, tenancy, alien appropria-

tion, and bonanza holdings into the frontier thesis. That process was abetted by the Census Report of 1880, which was studied very carefully by agricultural leaders like John J. Woodman of Michigan, the Worthy Master of the National Grange. His report in 1884 was a major effort to evaluate the structural position of agriculture.

Woodman attacked alien ownership of land, for example, as part of the general pattern whereby the metropolis was extending its power over farm businessmen. Another ominous indicator was the continuing rise of tenancy.[30] The traditional free marketplace system, he warned, was "in danger of being disrupted and over-thrown." Farmers had to act promptly. Working within that framework, the Grange committee on agriculture stressed the need for foreign markets, attacked foreign nations that discriminated against American exports, and demanded "immediate attention by the government" to "the plain requirement that our foreign service be planned and conducted with the purpose of supporting and protecting commerce."[31]

The assault on alien landholders and the campaign for foreign markets became so interwoven with the concern about the end of the continental frontier that it soon became difficult—if not misleading—to separate the various strands of expansionist thought. It is nevertheless useful to review how the frontier thesis became a conscious part of the general expansionist outlook. Henry George was probably the first man to reinject the issues into general debate after the Civil War, doing so through his 1871 discussion of *Our Land and Land Policy*. But then a House of Representatives report of 1874, *Geographic and Geological Surveys West of the Mississippi*, suggested rather clearly, if peripherally, that the kind of land suitable for traditional farming was not inexhaustible.

The question was dealt with far more directly in 1877 - 1878 by John Wesley Powell, director of a federal survey of the Rocky Mountain region. His *Report on the Lands of the Arid Region of the United States* (1878) left no doubt that such land was being rapidly occupied. The first response, however, was a vigorous debate about what kind of land policy was appropriate to the drier regions that remained open. Many felt that the proposal to distribute such territory in larger grants would create a situation akin to feudalism headed by an "aristocratic and wealthy few, each owning lands sufficient for a European principality." George helped turn the discussion back toward the question of what to do now that the frontier was ending when he published *Progress and Poverty* (1879). His single-tax remedy (and various proposals for modifying land policy) were neither illogical nor unappealing, but they did not mesh easily and naturally with the expansionist spirit of the era.

Given the marketplace-expansionist conception of reality, the end of one frontier implied the need for a new frontier. One of the earliest explicit statements of that logic came from Kasson of Iowa. "We are rapidly utilizing the whole of our continental territory," he announced in September 1881; adding, in his characteristically assertive manner, a strong recommendation as to the proper policy. "We must turn our eyes abroad, or they will soon look inward upon discontent."[32] Perhaps the mosts revealing aspect of the process of formulating and accepting the frontier thesis involved the way that the increasing worry about the land that might be reclaimed from illegal owners led all groups to conceptualize ever more consciously about the importance of surplus land in the succesful operation of the free marketplace.

The popular statement of the issue was typified by a proposition offered by Secretary of the Interior Teller in 1883: "Public lands, suitable for agriculture, should be disposed of only to the actual settler under the homestead laws."[33] In a fascinating manner, the concern with that issue led many men, even though they did not immediately accept Kasson's judgment about the policy required to sustain the vital dynamic of the frontier process, to accept the frontier thesis itself. The result was another debate about the tactics and the timing of expansion, rather than a confrontation over the issue of whether or not there was an alternate way of underwriting freedom and prosperity.

Thus the early 1883 discussion of the merchant marine not only revealed how all facets of the expansionist consciousness were coming together in one inclusive outlook, but also provided examples of how the frontier thesis was becoming a major idiom of thought. "The time may come," admitted Representative Joseph Gurney Cannon of Illinois, "when we have fully developed this continent, when we will have to look elsewhere for a market." He disagreed with those who argued that the hour had arrived, but he accepted the axiom that the frontier would have to be shifted from the continent to the world. He simply held that one could not accelerate the inevitable: "You had as well try to fill a sieve by pouring water into it."[34] A metropolitan spokesman argued that interpretation even more explicitly. "Our country," asserted Representative William Wallace Grout of Vermont, "is the certain future center" of the world marketplace. But the process could not be forced. "Wait till this empire in the West is developed."[35]

The other reading of the situation, however, rapidly gained majority acceptance. As a Southerner phrased it in February 1883, the export trade "is a safety valve upon the market."[36] "We frequently take occasion to refer to the fact," the editors of the *Western Rural* pointed out, "that in this country of ours 'Westward the star of Empire takes its way.'" "The development of the West . . . is the development of the nation," and overseas markets had become essential to the West.[37] "We have been busy with ourselves," admitted Representative Miller of California, who then argued forcefully that "the time has now come . . . when new markets are necessary."[38] Repeated warnings that the continental frontier would "become exhausted" in "a very few years" accelerated the projection of the frontier overseas.[39] "We are now on the threshold, in my judgment," commented Senator Plumb in advocating a merchant marine, "of a development outward, of a contest for the foreign commerce of the world."[40] Exports, agreed metropolitan expansionists like the editors of *Bradstreet's*, are "an escape valve for the overproduction of this country."[41]

One of the most significant developments was the report of the commissioners appointed by the House of Representatives to explore new markets in Latin America. They used the term "earth ocean" to define the great continental land mass from the Mississippi to the Pacific and then, pointing out that government aid had been crucial for the development of that frontier, called for similar action to exploit the frontier of the sea. "The people everywhere," they concluded, "appear to have become absorbed by a realization that the internal development of this country has reached a point where an external commerce is necessary for its prosperity . . . markets must somewhere be found."[42]

The continuing discussion and agitation prompted politicians from the metropolis, as well as from agricultural regions, to push the issue as a major theme in the election of 1884. Agricultural impatience and dissatisfaction with Arthur and Frelinghuysen had helped the Democrats win a powerful majority in the House of Representatives in 1882 (they jumped from 135 to 197, while the Republicans dropped from 147 to 118), and the spokesmen of both parties began a serious attempt to consolidate the antiforeign and expansionist sentiment behind their leadership. The publicity became self-breeding as the discussion of known evidence sparked the revelation of new information.

All the troubles of the agricultural businessmen seemed to be personified, for example, by the operations of the Marquis de Mores in the Dakota Territory. As a French aristocrat who entered the military elite through his education at St. Cyr and Saumur, and then acquired additional capital by marrying the daughter of a Wall Street financier, he symbolized the power of the metropolis as effectively as a monument on the prairie. The marquis formed a corporation "affiliated with the Mellon brothers" to combine all livestock operations from breeding to packing.[43] He and other European gentry established the general image of an investment process that actually drew most of its capital from many "ordinary businessmen."[44]

Even the more favorable and humorous stories about the giants were characterized by a derogatory tone. Thus the Earl of Aylesford, who held 37,000 acres in Texas, while a "hale fellow well met with all the cowboys," was a desperate drinker who left "bottles lying around as thick as fleas on a goat."[45] The standard picture was a bleak landscape of hard men—"one of the worst I have ever met"—using "three car-loads of post and wire" to run enclosures with perimeters of more than fifty miles that denied bona-fide farmers access to water and land.[46] The reports about acquisitions totaling 500,000 acres in Iowa and Minnesota, added to those about similar developments in other Western and Southern states, produced wide acceptance of a comparison between American farmers and Irish serfs.[47]

Eastern farmers fully supported their Western and Southern colleagues against what the *Rural New Yorker* called "plutocratic immigration," and "arrogant encroachments," even though some of them doubted that the entire country was being slipped into the vest pockets of foreigners.[48] For that matter, Representative William McAdoo, a Democrat from New Jersey, presented the first bill (December 11, 1883) designed "to prevent aliens other than *bona fide* settlers from owning lands in the Territories of the United States." That is not as surprising as it may appear, for many of the original colonies and early state governments approved such legislation, and that tradition reinforced the efforts of metropolitans to win the support of the agricultural majorities in their parties.

The first major debate, which developed around two of the five resolutions introduced in 1884, was led by a team of metropolitan and agricultural spokesmen in each party. The career of one of them, Senator Charles Henry Van Wyck, a Republican from Nebraska, provided an example of the process that was turning continental expansionists into overseas market expansionists. He had used his law practice in New York as a base for election to the House of Representatives in 1858, 1860, and 1862. Then, after service in the Civil War, he settled on the Nebraska frontier as a farmer and won election as a Senator. He was not only a leader in the movement against foreign corporations, but a spokesman for the increasingly angry opposition to metropolitan rule of the territories.

The bitterness against that colonial position in their own society, along with the constant opposition to the railroads, was repeatedly injected into the discussion of alien landholdings. The situation as of December 1883 concerning the home states of the men appointed by the federal government to serve as governors and secretaries of state in the territories clarifies the intensity of such opposition:[49]

TERRITORY	RESIDENCE WHEN APPOINTED	
	Governor	*Secretary*
Arizona	Nevada	California
Dakota	New Hampshire	Ohio
Idaho	Iowa	Idaho
Montana	New York	Michigan
New Mexico	Ohio	Wisconsin
Utah	Kentucky	Pennsylvania
Washington	New Jersey	Colorado
Wyoming	Iowa	Pennsylvania

The Democrats moved first, and substituted a resolution introduced on January 21, 1884, by William Steele Holman of Indiana for the earlier one offered by McAdoo. In addition to McAdoo, the metropolitan Democrats manifested their support for the agriculturalists through Representative Charles Brown Lore of Delaware. The Republicans countered with a bill proposed by Lewis Edwin Payson of Illinois, which won strong backing from metropolitans like Newton Wright Nutting of New York. It soon became apparent that the primary struggle concerned which party could be the most militant, rather than whether firm action should be taken.

Holman rather successfully integrated the railroad issue and the frontier thesis with the alien landholding question. He first demanded that all land granted to railroads be returned to the public domain if the terms of the subsidies were not fulfilled. Then he proposed a declaration that "it is in the highest public interest that . . . all of the public lands adapted to agriculture . . . be reserved for the benefit of actual and bona fide settlers." "The safety of our institutions," he explained, "rests on the ownership of the lands by the people." That would not only insure the continuance of the frontier process, but would end the threat from "great capitalists of Europe." Supported by metropolitan as well as Southern Democrats, and of necessity by many Republicans, Holman's resolution passed by the resounding margin of 251 to 17.[50]

Payson led the Republican counterattack which took the form of a bill "to prevent unlawful occupancy of the public lands." He stressed the danger from domestic corporations along with the threat from abroad on the grounds that the activity, as James Wilson of Iowa termed it, was "entirely un-American" regardless of the nationality involved. The debate over the Payson measure produced an even greater number of statements of the frontier thesis. It won bipartisan metropolitan support, for example, from Republican William Kelley of Pennsylvania and Democrat McAdoo of New Jersey. Both were deeply concerned to sustain the frontier process in order to avoid grave social troubles.

Others like Representative James B. Belford of Colorado stressed the need to establish American independence at home and abroad. "Are we the servile and supple tools of foreign capitalists," he thundered, "or are we going to preserve this country for our own people?" He also warned the Democrats to vote for the Payson bill or be forever damned as men "in the interest of corporations and monopolists, English capitalists, and everything of that sort." The Democrats were no such fools as that and, striking their own blows against "the minions of some lisping lord and the satraps of some capering count," insured passage of the Republican measure.[51]

Such bipartisan nationalism and antiforeignism was greatly intensified by the presidential campaign of 1884. Not unexpectedly, Blaine's strategy was effectively summarized in his slogan of "America for Americans," a promise to create an overseas "commerce which leaves no sea unexplored, and a navy which takes no law from superior force." The land, Blaine cried, "should be disposed of only to actual settlers and to those who are citizens of the Republic, or willing to become so."[52] The Democrats dealt with that issue by listing alien landholdings in their campaign handbook and by promising prompt action. In some respects, moreover, they spoke more explicitly to the market expansionism of the agricultural businessmen. They promised faster improvement of the Navy and the Merchant Marine, and assured the farmers that they would reverse the Republican policies that had lost "the control of the markets of the world" to the British.

But many agriculturalists were skeptical of Grover Cleveland's commitment to their interests and needs. His meteoric rise to the national arena was predicated wholly on satisfying metropolitan leaders who were not noted for their concern for farmers. "The nomination of Cleveland," summarized a resolution of the New York Farmers Alliance, "raises the issue of whether the sovereignty of the people shall be overshadowed by the corporations which they created. He must be defeated if we would maintain our liberties."[53] That attitude almost carried New York state for Blaine despite the blunder by one of his supporters that alienated Irish and other Catholic voters in New York City.

Blaine later concluded that the episode cost him the election, and historians generally accepted his analysis, noting that a mere 600 votes would have put him in the White House. That analysis is mathematically correct and strikingly dramatic, but it is nevertheless more useful to evaluate the election from another perspective. In the broadest sense, Blaine lost because he could not recover the initiative that he and President Garfield had established in 1880-1881, but which had been lost by Arthur and Frelinghuysen. That was apparent in Connecticut and Indiana, which voted for Cleveland after helping elect Garfield. Those electoral votes would have tipped the 1884 election to Blaine just as effectively as a victory in New York.

Blaine was likewise hurt by the refusal of metropolitan Republicans to act on his strategy of recognizing the importance of the agricultural West by admitting more territories as states. His appeal in the West was underscored by triumphs in California and Nevada, which had voted Democratic in 1880. And, though defeated himself, Blaine helped the Republicans gain twenty-two seats in the House and two in the Senate. Blaine's overwhelming agricultural support (he carried every Western state north of the Mason Dixon line except Indiana) was more significant in the evolution of American foreign policy, moreover, than Cleveland's victory in the electoral college. For his popularity was based on a willingness to respond to the farm demand for expanding the free marketplace. That pressure ultimately returned Blaine to the post of Secretary of State as part of the Republican acceptance of his outlook and strategy.

In the meantime, Cleveland immediately faced aggravated demands for action on the alien land issue. Representative William Calvin Oates of Alabama introduced the Democratic bill "to prohibit aliens and foreigners from acquiring a title to or owning lands within the United States" even before Cleveland was inaugurated. Senator Plumb did the same for the Republicans.[54] Then, on February 25, 1885, the Congress acted against unlawful fencing. Clearly enough, a majority agreed with the evaluation offered by Norman C. McFarland, the outgoing Commissioner of the General Land Office. "The time is near at hand when there will be no public land to invite settlements or afford citizens of the country an opportunity to secure cheap homes."[55] Or, as a Minnesota Alliance meeting declared shortly after Cleveland's first speech as President, agricultural businessmen wanted "a free and open market," and keeping American land for American farmers was an essential part of that program.[56]

Cleveland did not seize the opportunity to assert his personal leadership by immediately using the law against fencing public lands. Instead, he handed the problem to William A. J. Sparks of Illinois, his choice as General Land Commissioner. Sparks did move quickly, issuing a special order on April 3, 1885, that suspended final action on acquiring full title to public lands in parts of Nebraska, Kansas, and Minnesota, and in all of Colorado, Wyoming, Utah, Dakota, Montana, and Washington. His justification was "the great looseness and irregularity" that allowed "wealthy speculators and powerful syndicates" to acquire great acreages. Given the approaching end of the frontier, drastic measures were necessary: "hundreds of millions of acres . . . should be wrested from illegal control."[57]

Though the order was clearly intended to deal with the issues raised by the agricultural businessmen, it provoked an embittered outcry by thousands of settlers who were denied their land patents. The intensity of the reaction, which put the Cleveland Administration on the defensive throughout much of the West, cannot be fully understood except in the context of another presidential action that also affected the cattlemen. He issued two orders (April 17 and July 23, 1885) terminating the grazing of cattle on Indian reservations, and followed those (on August 7) with a belated directive that all illegal fencing of public lands "be immediately removed."[58] Cleveland had tried to handle the fencing crisis through local politicians. When they "payed no attention," however, he acted despite heavy opposition pressure from the ranchers.[59]

Sparks and the President thus managed to define themselves as the major enemy of two groups that had earlier focused considerable anger on each other. The antagonism between the settlers and the ranchers did not evaporate, but the Cleveland Administration became a lightning rod that attracted much of the embittered emotional voltage. The cattlemen were outraged because they were being forced to move their animals from land they considered open, and because they were being forced to shift the cattle to overgrazed areas just before the onset of winter. They promptly devised strategies and programs of opposition.

Some wanted to fight openly with all the political muscle they could develop. They were bitter and sarcastic. "Thou shalt have no other Gods than William Andrew Jackson Sparks," mocked the editors of the Cheyenne *Daily Sun*, "and none shalt thou worship. Thou shalt not raise cattle upon the land, neither sheep or asses nor any living thing, but only corn the same as the State of Illinois."[60] Others counseled "great care and judgment," concluding the most effective maneuver was to "keep away from Congress" and "remain quiet." That might prevent more restrictions and facilitate delays and ineffective enforcement.[61] As one such operator remarked: "We are not as yet hurrying any, although it may subject us to a little inconvenience." He was more concerned to evade additional rules "should they get ugly."[62]

The crop farmers did not ignore the continued violations by the cattlemen, but they did concentrate their attention on foreign ranchers and on Commissioner Sparks. As one farmer complained to Senator Charles Frederick Manderson of Nebraska, the order suspending land patents "caused a wonderful amount of suffering this winter." The outcry over the practical problems, which involved the possible loss of the land as well as the inability to borrow money, was reinforced by the resentment of many who concluded that Sparks operated "upon the assumption that a very large proportion of settlers on the public domain were dishonest."[63]

"Protest and wail, prolonged and intensified as the months passed," forced Sparks to modify the order on December 3, 1884, and ultimately drove him from office. But as one of many harried Democrats complained, the original order continued "working political mischief" for the remainder of Cleveland's term in office.[64] "Sparks is a thousand times more particular about a homesteader's exact compliance with each infinitesimal iota of the law," complained a Kansas editor, "than he is with a railroad grant or the stock ranch of an English syndicate. Yet that is the general style of this great business administration." Another dismissed him as "a red tape dude," the "biggest old nuisance that ever a pioneer community had to depend upon for titles to well earned lands."[65]

Even the Administration's efforts to defend itself contributed to the convergence of the concern about the end of the frontier, the antimetropolitan anger of the agricultural neocolonials, and the demand for effective laws against alien landowners. Thus Secretary of the Interior Lucius Quintus Cincinnatus Lamar's attempt to reassure the farm businessmen served largely to give official sanction (and circulation) to the long-developing equation between free land and economic and political freedom. If the unoccupied public domain is "exhausted or permitted to pass into the hands of the few," he agreed at the end of 1885, "the power of the Government to lawfully enforce the principle of the equality of her citizens will be greatly impaired."[66]

The crisis produced three broad responses. One stressed domestic reform. The chief advocate of that approach was Henry George. "We have now practically reached the limit of our public domain," he bluntly answered Lamar in 1886, and went on to sound yet another call for the adoption of his single-tax program.[67] George attracted significant (and dedicated) support for his program, but he was trying to modify a commitment to the marketplace outlook that was too deep and too intense to be shaken. The vast majority of agricultural businessmen who were affected by his blunt talk about the end of the frontier formulated their response in terms of the new frontier of overseas market expansion.

A second proposal was offered by metropolitan leaders like Edward Atkinson and a few agricultural spokesmen.[68] They stressed the importance of intensive and diversified agriculture. The argument was based on sound premises; for, as later developments proved, the land could be farmed far more productively. But the argument was weak in two crucial respects. First, farming of that kind required capital, chemistry, and technology that were not available to the average agricultural businessman during the last quarter of the nineteenth century. Second, more surpluses required even larger markets, and hence the argument served to reinforce the existing pressure for overseas economic expansion.

The third approach included a plan to acquire capital in the form of land and a larger share of the profits, as well as an argument pointing to such market expansion. The majority of the farmers settled on an integration of the demands to force aliens off the land and to balance the relationship between the metropolis and the country. Those proposals reinforced the antagonism toward European countries that blocked exports, as did the rapidly growing fear that the surplus of free land was almost exhausted—however much might be recovered from aliens and giant American syndicates. And the failure of the metropolis to act vigorously and effectively on any of those options further intensified the expansionist attitudes.

The reaction against what one Westerner called "Commissioner Sparks' 'Cranky doctrines' regarding our Territory," greatly speeded the convergence of all such agricultural criticisms.[69] The more perceptive metropolitans recognized that the farmers had sound arguments. "There seems to be no reason," charged *Bradstreet's* in discussing Montana, "why the national government should go as far east as New York to find a governor." Such was "the worst kind of policy."[70] And, for their part, the Westerners could analyze the problem with considerable sophistication. "We come more directly in contact with the central power at Washington than is ever the case with the inhabitants of a state. . . . In the great questions that affect us, to Congress we must appeal. At the same time we are not granted a single vote and hardly a single voice in the national legislature."[71]

The pressure was increased as some metropolitans followed agriculturalists in comparing the holdings of foreign capitalists to British control of Ireland. America was threatened, thundered the *Rural New Yorker*, with "the worst features of the cruel landlordism that has for centuries cursed shackled Ireland." The "evil" of alien land ownership "has become so flagrant and its results so intolerable that prompt Congressional legislation . . . is urgently demanded."[72] New York leaders like William Dodsworth, editor of the *Daily Commercial Bulletin*, joined other newspapers and magazines in warning of the danger in the rising antimetropolitan feeling among the farmers. One writer claimed that twenty-nine foreign owners held an area in the United States that was larger than Ireland, and even the Secretary of the Treasury decried "the dependent relationships" typical of Europe.[73]

Robert P. Boise, Worthy Master of the Oregon Grange, typified many farm businessmen in tying the alien land issue to the questions of silver and metropolitan predominance.[74] Another significant development involved the way that the end of the frontier was viewed as increasing the danger of unrest—or even revolution. Richard James Oglesby, who became Governor of Illinois after serving as chairman of the Senate Committee on Public Lands, put the issue bluntly in February 1886 as part of an attack on Scully's holdings in that state. "Uncle Sam has no more farms to give away. This I say generally. . . . The land within the humid region"— "the 100th meridian separates the arid from the humid"—"has been taken up." The result "will inevitably produce land-hunger." "The alien landlords will have to go. They are a luxury we cannot afford. . . . It is alike our interest and our duty . . . to prevent the creation of agrarian monopoly . . . as that which now threatens revolution in Great Britain." "The landowner," he concluded, "is not a revolutionist."[75] "There is no greater safeguard against public disorder, tumults, and riots," agreed Representative Payson, in a major statement of congressional judgment, "than a generally distributed ownership of lands and homes."[76]

Payson's rival in pushing legislation against alien land ownership, Representative Oates of Alabama, tied the entire movement directly to foreign affairs, explicitly defining the legislation he introduced during

1886 - 1887 "as a part of the foreign policy of this country."[77] Representative McAdoo promptly added, as petitions with nearly 150,000 signatures began to arrive, that the frontier was "the safety-valve of republican institutions. It is the outlet for popular discontent."[78] Similar fears were expressed by Senator Plumb, a leader in the effort to repeal all preemption laws as another move to aid the farmer. He admitted, moreover, that such action was at best a stopgap. It could not forestall the consequences "which will inevitably result from the fact that there are no more public lands subject to settlement."[79]

The House and the Senate acted first—though independently—to repeal preemption.[80] They could not agree on the same legislation, however, and the final law was not passed until 1891. In the meantime the Senate approved its version of alien land legislation on June 1, 1886. It was not a strong bill. It did not touch existing acquisitions, drew the line at "more than 20 percent of the stock" in corporate enterprises, and ordered canal, rail, and turnpike corporations to return or sell all land not used for those purposes after ten years. As Plumb admitted, the slap on the wrist would come only in the future.[81]

The debate in the House was far more energetic, and the bill itself a bit tougher. "Everywhere there is unrest and discontent," worried Representative William Joel Stone of Missouri, who admitted "the gravest apprehension." "It takes no prophetic eye to see the day when we must meet the dangers of an overcrowded population." Payson demanded the limit on foreign share holding be cut to 10 percent, and argued that no alien acquisitions should be inherited. "Much anxiety" just had been created, for "it may happen that the nation which failed to conquer us with its arms may yet prevail with its treasure." A clearer expression of bipartisan nationalism could hardly be imagined.

A significant group of worried spokesmen from the South and West fretted that the bill would open the way for a general assault on property rights, and that was equally revealing of the agricultural businessman's commitment to marketplace capitalism. Those men tried to recommit the bill for further refinement, but most of them accepted defeat (127 to 85) and joined the overwhelming majority that passed the measure (210 to 6, with 106 not voting).[82] The dispute between the House and Senate was finally resolved by a conference committee in favor of the milder Senate version. "It is not of as wide scope as I should like to have it," Senator Plumb acknowledged, "but it is a beginning in the right direction."[83]

Some disagreed. The mining interests wanted an exemption and tried to wring a tear (and enough votes) with the claim that "foreign capital has assisted the poor mine owners at times."[84] Their effort failed because the majority demanded more stringent legislation. Some states, such as Montana and Indiana, had passed laws in 1885, and others followed the congressional action with tougher laws. The most embittered onslaughts occurred in Illinois and Kansas, largely in reaction to the operations of Scully.[85] But Iowa, Wisconsin, Nebraska, Minnesota, Mississippi, Washington—and even Connecticut—acted in a similar vein.[86]

Other farm businessmen concentrated on sustaining the pressure for stronger national legislation. The Farmers Alliance of Falls County, Texas, demanded an end to the policy that was making "serfs of American freemen," and pointed out that the land question was merely another facet of the monetary policy that kept the farmers under the thumb of the metropolis. Massachusetts and Maine agreed that "America was created for America and not for English capitalists." The Denver *Republican* asserted that alien ownership was "contrary to the spirit of independence." And the resurgent Grange revived its earlier call for a Cabinet post for agriculture as a means of solving all such problems.[87]

The Iowa legislature spoke for the overwhelming majority of agricultural businessmen when it reminded the Congress that the first duty of government was "to adopt such policies as will best promote the growth of National power and insure prosperity to the Nation and its citizens."[88] An Illinois legislator had said the same thing in 1885: the duty of the government was to pursue a policy designed to "best promote the growth of national power and insure prosperity to the nation." It should change policies that increase the "wealth of citizens of other nations."[89] Or, as one Kansas farmer wrote to the Chicago *Tribune*, "the farmer at the end, toils chiefly for the various organized representatives of capital that crouch and wait and gamble for his surplus earnings."[90]

The anger toward the alien landowners, the concern over the end of the frontier, and the demands for government action converged in a rising tide for overseas market expansion. The Secretary of the Interior recognized that truth in his Report for 1887 by giving first consideration to the closing of the frontier. It was a doubly prophetic change, for in other years top priority had been given to the battle to wrest the continent from the alien Indians.[91] As that war was closed out, the struggle for overseas markets began in earnest. No one made that clearer than railroad and agricultural magnate James Jerome Hill, the confident and energetic sometime tutor of President Cleveland. Power, he explained, came to "those who controlled the commerce" of the world. In the past, America had been a continental world unto itself. But that frontier was gone. "We have to unlearn such ideas."[92]

But Cleveland proved unwilling—or unable—to unlearn his laissez-faire economics and to broaden the limits of his outlook. He was a narrow metropolitan spokesman who favored overseas economic expansion for industrial interests, and he ultimately proved willing to facilitate such market expansion by providing free raw materials for the factories. But he offered no direct response to the angry agricultural majority proposing only to improve its position by helping the manufacturers. The strategy had a certain logic to it, but Cleveland could not translate the theory into reality fast enough to stabilize the economy or win reelection.

ELEVEN

A foreign market becomes more and more necessary.
                                    Bradstreet's, August 1883

Nearly 90 percent of our exports are farm products. Should we not be benefitted by a national policy that will open to us all foreign countries that need our products?
                                    William H. Earle, Massachusetts
                                    State Grange, 1883

The political pot has begun to boil.
                                    Western Rural, 1884

This majority is, and always has been, without representation in Cabinet positions.
                                    Kansas State Board of Agriculture,
                                    February 1886

We need a market for a greater or less surplus all the time.
                                    Breeder's Gazette, 1887

What is to become of this surplus? . . . What are we to do? If the foreign market is closed against us our agriculture is prostrated at a blow.
                                    Representative Roger Q. Mills
                                    of Texas, 1884

Doubtless there was overproduction. . . . Our home market is not equal to the demand. . . . We have outgrown the home market and must seek markets abroad if we would continue to prosper.
                                    Senator John Tyler Morgan
                                    of Alabama, 1882

The real and most immediate "silver danger" is that which impends over the American farmer, and grows out of the competition of the wheat of India.
                                    Western Rural, 1885

The great question is, Shall this Government issue a declaration of financial independence?
                                    Senator Thomas Mead Bowen
                                    of Colorado, 1886

The price of the farmers' crop is totally at the mercy of these railroad managers. . . . There is no steadiness, no system.
                                    Joseph Medill of The Chicago Tribune, 1883

Just as soon as the owner of property puts his property to a public use he puts it under the direction of the public.
                                    Western Rural, 1886

The men who stand between the farmers and the foreign markets hold seats in the Congress of the United States.
                                    Breeder's Gazette, 1886

Persistent
Economic Troubles and Unresponsive Metropolitan
Leadership Arouse the
Farmers and Consolidate
the Consensus on
Overseas Economic Expansion

THE FLUCTUATIONS of the economy during the 1880s hurt many farm businessmen, heightened their self-consciousness, and intensified their demands for recognition and effective assistance. Vast numbers of agriculturalists joined new local, regional, and national organizations, and the Grange enjoyed a slow but influential revival. All such groups accepted the market expansionist outlook. Large numbers of metropolitan spokesmen also adopted that analysis, and the theory was formalized as an overproduction thesis that explained the persistent recessions and depressions that damaged all elements of the political economy.

That explanation of the recurrent troubles generated a sense of impending doom that amplified the implications of the frontier thesis and added to the urgency of finding overseas markets. Those intellectual and psychological pressures, coupled with the rise of organizations capable of serving as instruments for action, produced a surge of agricultural protest that steadily reinforced the fears of metropolitan leaders and impelled them onward toward empire. Farmers reinvigorated their campaign for better transportation, renewed their demands for the remonetization of silver, rekindled the battle for Cabinet representation, reasserted their claim to full representation in the Congress, and sustained their efforts to reopen European markets and find new outlets for their surpluses.

The agricultural businessmen won some victories, as with the passage of the Interstate Commerce Act of 1887, but the Cleveland

Administration proved reluctant to meet agricultural needs. That failure generated the forces that astute Republican leaders like Benjamin Harrison and Blaine parlayed into a short-run victory in 1888, and a long-range triumph predicated upon imperial expansion. Blaine had formulated that strategy before Garfield was assassinated, and the depression and recession of the 1880s, and his narrow defeat in 1884, strengthened his commitment to that solution to the problems of the party and the nation.

The rate of growth of the economy turned downward at the beginning of 1881, but the export bonanza camouflaged that crucial indicator until after the business cycle peaked in 1882.[1] The shift "became pronounced early in 1883," however, and by the end of that year many farmers were "just barely making a living."[2] The crisis month was August, when the editors of the *Commercial and Financial Chronicle* winced at the "sudden and striking cessation of industrial activity," and *Bradstreet's* cried out that a foreign market "becomes more and more necessary." Unemployment climbed toward 8 percent by May 1885, when the *Western Rural* stated bluntly that the nation was in a "business depression."[3]

The subsequent upturn carried into March 1887, but then another reversal occurred. That lasted through April 1888. The yearly summaries in *Thorp's Business Annals* provide a good sense of the erratic movement that caused so much pain and difficulty: 1883—Recession; 1884—Depression; 1885—Revival; 1886—Revival; 1887—Prosperity; and 1888—Short Recession.[4] The fluctuations severely affected even those states that were developing more balanced economies (such as Ohio and Wisconsin), and caused grave troubles in states like Nebraska, Kansas, Georgia, and Mississippi that remained primarily agricultural.[5] Chicago cash prices for Number 2 wheat dropped from a range of between $0.95 5/8 to $1.43 1/4 in 1881 to a spread of $0.69 1/2 to $0.96 in 1884, and continued generally low throughout the following years.[6] Wheat and corn earned fair prices at the same time, moreover, only in 1883 - 1884. Wheat farmers in Kansas, for example, suffered hardship in 1885, 1887, and 1888, while corn growers felt a similar pinch in 1887.[7]

Yet wheat acreage and production continued to move upward. The area under cultivation increased from 40.7 million acres in 1882 to 46.5 million in 1888, and the crops from 553.7 million bushels in 1882 to 618.4 million in 1889.[8] Export prices fell steadily from an index number of 109.4 in the second quarter of 1882 to a low of 77.4 in the last quarter of 1886, and recovered only to 85.8 by the end of 1888.[9] Mortgage rates fell so little as to offer no meaningful help to the agricultural businessman.[10] The significance of such statistics was neatly summarized by the editors of the *Western Rural*: "Things with us are very much at loose ends."[11]

Farmers were aware of such quantitative data to a far greater extent than many observers have recognized (both then and later), and they followed the discussions about what it meant and often contributed directly to the dialogue.[12] "You underrate the reading tendency of the farming community," one knowledgeable editor warned an official in the Cleveland Administration. "Many years' experience with the correspondence of a very wide area has shown me, that although no literary ability or elegance of diction prevails, there is, underlying the illiteracy, a sturdy and honest desire, by reading and study, to improve."[13]

Many metropolitans grievously underestimated the agriculturalists. "One could hardly imagine," remarked one such Eastern provincial in commenting on an excellent diplomat from the country, "that so intelligent and courtly a Gentleman, of fine presence and manner, could come from 'out West.'"[14] Another equally capable individual, Representative Erastus Johnson Turner of Kansas, provided one of many effective replies to that attitude. "There seems to be a very serious apprehension on the part of some of our Eastern friends. . . . They seem to think that all that is necessary is to go out there and break up the sod, plant crops, and immediately you are insured a bountiful return. This is absolutely not true."[15] As the editors of the *Rural New Yorker* commented, ignorance and inferiority did not account for the anger of the farm businessmen.[16]

"Pioneering is hard enough under the most favorable circumstances," Senator Plumb warned his metropolitan colleagues. "There is always disappointment. The burden falls first and hardest upon the wife."[17] "My washings are so hard to do," agreed one such woman, "it tires me completely out for a day or so."[18] "We are beginning our eleventh year in Kansas," commented another farmer, "with great hopes (thank God for hope), for each year we have grown poorer since we came here."[19] "If you have any seeds," came a plaintive cry from Rabbit Dawson in Nebraska, "plas send me some as i am a poor man and lost my crop with the hail last august and cant aford to buy."[20] "Even after a decade on a western farm," concludes one authority, "families spent only $500 or $600 annually for both living and operating expenses."[21]

The agricultural businessmen knew perfectly well that their relative income was far below the metropolitan level.[22] They were angry, as the Arkansas State Horticultural Society told the Congress, because their interest was "less fostered and less encouraged," and because they received the "fewest direct benefits from the taxes paid in." Eastern farmers agreed wholeheartedly: "legislators have ignored our interests." Small wonder that the farmers held such views, for *Bradstreet's* casually acknowledged that "much more consideration is shown the agricultural interest in Europe than has been the case with us."[23]

What Nebraskans called the "universal business depression" hit Southerners with particular force. "Cotton farmers have but little money," one contemporary survey noted, and tied that harsh truth to the general "demoralization." The region's loss in comparative standing intensified the bitterness toward the metropolis. "'Northern brains and capital' as the phrase goes," ran the denunciation of one agricultural leader. "They want to civilize us from without." And Texans lashed out at policies so long and deeply "oppressive to our people."[24] But it was equally important that Delaware farmers joined the battle against a government that appeared indifferent to developments that might "reduce the farmers of America to a serfdom far worse than the tenant system imposes upon Ireland." And that leaders of Cleveland, Ohio, shared the anger because their city "has long labored under the disadvantage of being considered a 'way station' on the road to the metropolis."[25]

Westerners were not only outraged by "bonanza nabobs" from America and Europe, but thoroughly weary of metropolitans who "lorded it over us" in national affairs and even controlled many county governments.[26] "We believe the great mission of our government," summarized a Nebraska farmer, "is to see that all classes have an equal chance in the great race."[27] Such action could begin, added those in the territories, by extending full citizenship to the colonials west of the Missouri River. That demand was echoed by agricultural businessmen in all regions, moveover, in their cries for Cabinet influence. "This majority is, and always has been," cried the Kansas State Board of Agriculture, "without representation in Cabinet positions." Texans agreed, adding that farmers were "unequally depressed and unjustly oppressed;" and the Burlington County, New Jersey, Board of Agriculture insisted upon leverage "commensurate with the importance of Agriculture."[28]

Such serious, continuing difficulties and the related self-consciousness produced a multiplicity of organizations designed to improve the farmer's position in the political economy. Such activity began first among the agricultural businessmen in the upper Midwest, the plains states, and the ranching regions in Colorado, Wyoming, and Montana. Cattlemen founded the National Cattle Growers Association in December 1883 behind leaders like Sturgis of the Wyoming Stock Growers Association, John Clay of Chicago, and George W. Simpson of the Bay State Cattle Company of Boston.[29] An equally important development involved the revival of the Northern Farmers Alliance. It had been started by Milton George in October 1880 in connection with a rally on the railroad question, and had grown rapidly for a two-year period before losing its momentum. But as one of the chapters reported early in February 1884, the depression and the mounting dissatisfaction with the metropolitan leaders of both parties sparked an upsurge of interest and action. Other evidence prompted George to report an "unusual disposition among the farmers throughout the entire West to organize into a concert of action."[30]

"The political pot has begun to boil," he whooped; and, aided by David A. Wood, a key man on his staff, George moved to capture the dissidents for his organization.[31] He did just that, and by the end of 1885 the Alliance claimed over 232,000 individual memberships. Most of the members at that date were Northern farmers, but the rise of the Southern Alliance rapidly swelled the total to somewhere between 2 million and 3 million.[32] In Virginia, for example, a Farmer's Assembly organized by Robert Beverly laid the foundation for the first Alliance chapter created in 1887. The major Southern push, however, came from Texas, Louisiana, and Arkansas. The Texas Alliance and the Louisiana Farmers Union merged at the end of 1888 with the Agricultural Wheel that had been founded in February 1882 (and claimed 500,000 members on the eve of the consolidation).

The driving leadership of William Walker Tedford established Wheel chapters throughout the Southern Mississippi Valley, and did much to generate the dynamism of the Southern Alliance (known formally as the National Farmers Alliance and Co-Operative Union of America). The choice of the name Wheel offers a valuable insight into the character of all the farm movements. It was taken from the writings of the Physiocrats: "Agriculture is the great wheel or power that controls the entire machinery of the world's industries. . . . Who could live without the farmers?" Tedford gave way after the merger to such men as C. W. Macune of Texas, Leonidas LaFayette Polk of Virginia (who founded the *Progressive Farmer* in 1886), and Thomas Edward Watson of Georgia.

Many other organizations played an important part, however, in stimulating and sustaining the drive to improve the position of the agricultural businessmen. Such local clubs never became generally known, but they were major factors in the enhanced self-consciousness, clear arguments, and determination that became so apparent throughout the decade. The 1884 agenda of one such group in Ohio typified the approach. The members began with a discussion of debt in January, moved on in March to a review of how to invest any profits they made, examined agricultural literature in June, and explored the theories of competition and overproduction in October.[33] The results of such study were often communicated to metropolitan leaders known to be concerned with agriculture. An Iowa farmer advised *Bradstreet's* in April 1884, for example, that he had netted all of $1.68 per head in raising 100 pigs to 300-pound hogs.[34]

Former Grange members provided much of the strength of the Northern and Southern Alliances, but a renewal of the Grange in the Northeast extended the base of the burgeoning protest movement.[35] The

Farmers Mutual Benefit Association, led by John P. Stelle, was particularly strong in Illinois and Indiana, but also mustered some members as far east as West Virginia and on west into Kansas.[36] Additional power was created through the Farmers Congress, the American Farmers Union, and the Orange Growers Protective Union, organized by Californians in 1885 to deal with the transportation difficulties involved in marketing fruit surpluses.

And the Colored Farmers National Alliance and Cooperative Union, founded in 1886, claimed 1 million members by 1891. The black farmers and field hands did not exercise much direct influence on national policy. They probably did exert two kinds of indirect pressure, however, because of the general threat they posed to the emerging post-Reconstruction pattern of white control throughout the South. In a narrow sense, they provided an added spur to the imperial expansionism of men like Senator Morgan. More significantly, they were a constant reminder that the new Southern political economy had to be managed effectively in order to contain actual and potential dissidents. That served to reinforce the market expansionism of Alliance members, as well as that of Southern manufacturers.

From the outset, however, the Southern Alliance revealed the same deep commitment to the marketplace philosophy that characterized its Northern counterparts. "Let the Alliance be a business organization for business purposes," intoned Macune, and his injunction was honored because its assumptions were generally shared.[37] Uriel S. Hall, a major figure in the Missouri Alliance, was not at all unique in offering "closely developed arguments full of allusions to John Stuart Mill and other economists."[38] The "growing restlessness" of American farmers was not due to a break with classical theory, but rather to a determination to see it honored in practice as well as in campaign speeches.[39]

The issue, as another Alliance leader explained, concerned practicing the principles.[40] Even the field hands, described by one of them as the incipient proletariat of the system, proudly asserted they were "not ready to rebel against that system." Indeed, nothing dramatizes the loyalty to capitalism quite as well as the behavior of men who were "in the field at work by six o'clock in the morning and came in as the sun went down." "I have," added another, "worked, day after day, sixteen long hours each day, and for pay so small I am ashamed to write it down."[41] Yet they continued to honor "private ownership," asking only that the "laws shall be so adjusted that they will give the landless classes an absolute and unquestionable right to an abode upon the soil of our own country." As that field worker knew, the farm protests movement included many supposed landowners who sought only to own their land. "Business men," as Milton George accurately termed them.[42] Not "muttering malcontents," added the St. Paul *Pioneer Press*, but men of the marketplace faced with "probable ruin."[43]

"All we demand," explained William Peffer of Kansas, "is a just measure of the profits realized over labor in connection with capital."[44] "There is no good reason," added the editors of *The American Nonconformist*, why Western farmers "have to be so poor." The objective, agreed George, is "an equal opportunity to enjoy the pursuit of happiness and prosperity."[45] The issue, George and Macune explained, involved the abuses of the system that "endanger the structure itself, and tend toward ultimate dissolution and loss of all control"—"to prevent riots." "The producers of this country form the great conservative and conserving element whose power must stand between the nation and the foes which now threaten its well-being."[46]

Such avowals of orthodoxy were unnecessary to anyone familiar with the agricultural majority; but for metropolitans and others who thought largely in stereotypes, the assurances were documented beyond cavil during the long discussion of the depression and recession of the 1880s, and in the related and persistent emphasis upon market expansion as the key to prosperity, justice, and freedom—and social stability. For as Representative Milo White of Minnesota explained, the concern with exports was steadily heightened by the growing fear that "the tendency of the times" was "toward the increase of millionaires and tramps."[47]

Some Northeastern farmers turned to diversification in order to control the "ready market" of the cities, but the region did not become indifferent to the importance of exports.[48] Samuel L. Boardman, onetime secretary of the Maine Board of Agriculture, held that the farmer should continue to harvest the crops "which the foreign markets require." And the Massachusetts Grange insisted that Northwestern agriculturalists, whatever their own sales to the urban centers, should support all efforts to secure a national policy "that will open to us all foreign countries that need our products."[49] That was a hardheaded business policy designed to protect their local interest, but it also bespoke an honest camaraderie. Both elements reinforced the drive for market expansion.

The concern of the Northern Alliance to create a State Department and a Department of Agriculture that would "collect correct information on all domestic and foreign agricultural production" was but one of many indicators of the rising pressure for action in behalf of that policy.[50] The interest in Latin America, for example, was anything but fantasy. Provision exports to Brazil jumped 400 percent between 1885 and 1891, and similar gains were made in trade with Nicaragua, Guatemala, and Mexico.[51] Cargo manifests documented the reality of the overseas trade. Of the shipments to the West Indies and Latin America from 1884 to 1889, for example, 26 percent was supplied directly by the states of California, Georgia, Illinois, Iowa, Kansas, Louisiana, Maryland, Michigan, Minnesota, Missouri, North Carolina, Ohio, Oregon, South Carolina, Virginia, and Wisconsin. Their participation was undoubtedly much higher, for many of their products were transshipped through Philadelphia, New York, and Boston.[52] More generally, the Secretary of Agriculture reported that the share of crops exported in fiscal 1887 ran as follows: cotton, 69.1 percent; tobacco, 52.5 percent; wheat, 27.9 percent; cheese, 20.2 percent; and meat, 8.4 percent.[53]

The livestock interests understandably wanted to increase their exports, and their intense campaign to reopen European markets and penetrate other areas was directly tied to that need. "We want a market for a greater or less surplus all the time," explained the *Breeder's Gazette*.[54] Having despaired of moving metropolitan leaders to retaliate against European restrictions, and having become increasingly concerned to control animal diseases, the breeders and stock feeders shifted their efforts to secure effective health measures.[55] The same concern to raise exports prompted similar campaigns against adulteration in meats, lard, and cheese.[56] And still another industry tied to the cattle growers, the leather and leather goods trades, joined the push for export markets "to dispose of a surplus."[57]

Rising competition from Russia and India aggravated the problem and further hardened the existing animosity toward England.[58] "Great Britain is hedging us round about," warned the Massachusetts Grange, demanding a solution to the problem of "overproduction."[59] Minnesota Alliance leaders agreed, complaining that American farmers were "deprived of all commercial rights in disposing of the products." The nation faced being displaced "in the market of the world," worried National Grange leaders, and vigorously reasserted the farmer's right "to equal opportunity in the pursuit of happiness."[60] Most agricultural businessmen came to accept the overproduction thesis during the mid-1880s, and they spoke candidly about taking advantage of another European war. "We will do the best we can," one commented, "to feed the people at the best price we can get."[61]

One of the best indicators of the degree to which the traditional market expansionism of the farmers had been formalized in the overproduction thesis was provided by the increasing exaggeration and shrillness of those who opposed the theory. "Don't be afraid of overproducing," asserted one such spokesman, "we cannot glut the markets." "The fraud of overproduction," cried another, will carry Americans in "a backwards rush toward barbarism."[62] But Senator Allison, never one to risk creeping out on a limb, properly concluded that the overproduction thesis provided good political ammunition against Cleveland and the Democrats who "sleep in the presence of this depression."[63]

Such agitation affected politicians of the grain and livestock regions on a wholly nonpartisan basis. "I feel I cannot attach too much importance," wrote a Nebraska leader, "to have Nebraska go to London next year." The state needed "one more *grand boom*."[64] Democrats from agricultural areas were in some ways more impatient and fretful about Cleveland's inaction than the Republicans. "No country in the world has a greater interest in finding foreign markets for our immense production," exclaimed Representative Samuel Wheeler Moulton of Illinois, greatly disturbed that nothing was being done to change the policies that "shut and destroy foreign markets." Agreed, vowed his Democratic colleague William Ralls Morrison: "What we want is a market."[65] He also wanted presidential leadership that would prevent a debacle in the next election.

Along with Morgan of Alabama and Bland of Missouri, Representative Roger Quarles Mills of Texas became one of the perpetual-motion market expansionists of the Democratic party. He was an overproductionist who asked one question over and over: "What is to become of this surplus? Year by year it grows greater. . . . Our crops are now far beyond the requirements of our home consumption. . . . What are we to do?" His answer never varied: "We must either have the foreign market or none."[66] But Republicans like Senator Plumb were equal to the challenge, and boldly asserted that "instead of being controlled by, we should be able to control foreign markets."[67] Plumb was concerned for Kansas millers, as well as wheat farmers, and he had able support on that issue from his colleagues in Minnesota and New York.

Minneapolis millers exported one-third (or more) of their production from 1880 through 1892, and they tried hard to attain—and then hold—the 40.3 percent reached in 1887.[68] Washburn described the strategy with his usual bluntness: "Run both mills 'red hot' and for all there is in them, and have a wide-awake, aggressive organization and 'carry the war into Africa.'"[69] The most elegant testimony to such expansionism came in the poems written by William Crowell Edgar of the *Northwestern Miller.* Thus to Pillsbury for Christmas, 1885:

> *I hope that Beloochistan and Siam*
> *Of Pillsbury's Best will grow as*
> *fond as I am,*
> *And distant Madagascar folk request*
> *That missionaries bring them*
> *"Pillsbury's Best."*

And to Samuel H. Seamans, on the same holiday, Edgar wrote:[70]

> *An Empire may be the New Year find,*
> *Well built to suit your master mind,*
> *And from this Empire every hour*
> *May you export a car of flour.*

California and Oregon millers published no poems, but they worked just as hard to capture markets in Asia.[71]

The McCormick Company felt the spur of similar competition from Walter A. Wood, John Deere, and A. R. Farquhar as the domestic market for implements became more nearly saturated. Wood enjoyed "a large and rapidly increasing export business" reaching around the world, and he and Farquhar pushed hard to obtain government aid in opening more markets. The McCormick firm counted more on its own efforts, and those produced "a marked improvement" during the mid-1880s. The pressure from other firms ("many requests") did evoke a direct response from the government, however, and the Midwestern firm undoubtedly benefited from the official efforts to win "that share in the world's trade to which the superiority of their manufacturers entitles them."[72]

Southern cotton interests likewise intensified their pressure for a more vigorous diplomacy. The depression was "about the darkest period the cotton goods trade ever experienced in this country," and some operators wanted to organize a pool in order to limit production and share the domestic market.[73] But the great majority accepted overproduction as a fact of life and turned instead to foreign markets in Latin America and Asia. Led by such men as John F. Hanson and David A. Tompkins (who also played a key role in the cottonseed oil export business), the Southerners organized another cotton exposition to generate "a tidal wave" of exports. "We must have more customers," Hanson explained, to absorb "the excessive production of our mills."[74]

Texans as different as Macune of the Southern Alliance and Senator Samuel Bell Maxey agreed that exports provided the answer. Macune wanted to "force the world to pay a just and fair price," and Maxey stressed the need for "an outlet for our surplus" textiles.[75] Senator Brown of Georgia offered an insight into the similarity of the policy advocated by otherwise contrasting and antagonistic individuals. "The nerve that runs the American's pocket," he candidly remarked, "is one of the most sensitive in his organization."[76] When that was "tingled," as Brown termed the action, men like Senator Morgan and Representative Hilary Abner Herbert of Alabama joined forces to demand "a bold line of policy"—particularly in Asia—to obtain the necessary markets.[77]

Northern textile spokesmen added their weight to the demand. The reason, as Senator William Pierce Frye of Maine explained, was "one of pure business." The export market, added another observer, "is where they make their money."[78] A similar convergence of interests tied Southern tobacco farmers to manufacturers and Northern commission merchants. All of them wanted the Cleveland Administration to "secure a fairer and less restricted commerce for our surplus tobacco." Otherwise, "the despondent frame of mind" would continue to generate political unrest.[79] The warning was not exaggerated, for the "disappointed, dissatisfied, and dejected" tobacco men shortly began to join the Alliance movement.[80]

The growing metropolitan agreement on the necessity of foreign markets became apparent during a September 1884 meeting of merchants, shippers, manufacturers, and commission agents. Great Britain influenced their thinking in the same way it affected agricultural businessmen. South America, explained one, "represents twenty American Indias, whose unsupplied and inviting trade fields we will find most profitable." Many emphasized the great market for provisions of all kinds, cotton textiles—"we want to supply the cotton shirts and pants"—and agricultural implements. And all applauded former President Grant's strong plea for government action to create a fleet of merchant ships. "I would subsidize," he roared, "and subsidize them big."[81]

Some conservative financiers acknowledged that agricultural exports were beginning to make it possible for them to expand.[82] They savored the prospect of being "able to buy up steadily and largely . . . America's securities held abroad," for that opened the way to become "absentee creditors."[83] Such men did not immediately become vigorous expansionists, but their shifting emphasis did strengthen the metropolitan concern with overseas activity.[84] The editors of *Bradstreet's* (and other journals) contributed significantly to that process by printing persuasive essays on the necessity of opening more markets for the entire economy.[85] "The end to be kept steadily in view," they emphasized, "is to create new markets for American products." Farm businessmen had performed a vital service by clearing "the path for wider and freer commercial expansion," and the time had come to transform that trail into a highway of American supremacy.[86]

The first annual report of Carroll D. Wright, Commissioner of Labor, was both a sign of the times and an influence upon them. Overproduction was a permanent feature of the economy, he announced in 1886, and then explained how, beginning with European restrictions, the decline in agricultural exports had adversely affected the railroads and every other part of the economy. The problem was complicated and intensified by the great efficiency of modern machinery and the disappearance of the continental frontier, but the solution was simple and unequivocal—markets had to be opened. Wright's report might well be viewed as the symbol of the consolidation of a metropolitan majority in favor of market expansion. And a striking example of the changes that were taking place was provided by Carl Schurz, who became president of an organization formed to help expand the marketplace by publishing the *United States Export Almanac*. He and his associates, who included Wells and Atkinson, offered the State Department 20,000 free copies of the first issue to aid the cause, and as a gesture of appreciation for the approval of the operation by Secretary of State Thomas Francis Bayard.[87]

The Cleveland Administration was not even that responsive to the demands for Cabinet representation for agriculture, however, until well after the congressional elections of 1886, when the Republicans cut the Democratic margin in the House from forty to seventeen votes. By then it was too late, for Western and Southern Democrats were attacking the Democrat in the White House almost as bitterly as the Republicans.[88] Cleveland finally signed the law in February 1889, but by that time the Republicans had parlayed the anger of farm businessmen into a general political victory. The Administration handled the campaign for admitting Western territories as states in the same fashion. By the end of 1887, after repeated failures to win some victory, the Westerners were enraged. They became furious as nothing was done during the election year. "The present Administration has appointed nearly every officer from non-residents," thundered one colonial. "The people have been tyrannized over and robbed and plundered by them to a degree that is almost beyond mention."[89] Even then the Democratic leaders dragged their feet, but the Republicans finally pushed through a bill admitting North and South Dakota, Montana, and Washington less than two weeks before Cleveland left office.[90]

Cleveland's failure to provide effective leadership during the troubled years of the mid-1880s is explained by two interrelated and reinforcing characteristics. His conception of marketplace capitalism was narrowly orthodox, a limited contractual outlook that distorted even the principle of laissez faire that he (and others) mistakenly thought to be all of Smith's political economy. And Cleveland was unimaginatively dedicated to the metropolis that he largely defined as the confined and constricted world of corporate enterprise. That combination led him to describe his governorship of New York as "a business engagement between the people of the State and myself." Carried on into the Presidency, his outlook created a situation, as one Alliance leader aptly described it, in which the Democratic party became "like the man who was so tall he never knew when his feet were cold."[91] Even conservative farm leaders predicted that "a crisis and a catastrophe can not long be deferred."[92]

The distrust and apprehension were greatly increased by Cleveland's early and unsuccessful attempt to manipulate the silver issue to his political advantage within the limits of his narrow outlook. Though far from content with the outcome, the silverites had acquiesced at the end of the 1870s in the compromise that produced the Bland-Allison law. The issue was revived, significantly, by broad-gauged metropolitan spokesmen who became concerned about the way British entrepreneurs used demonetization to undercut American farmers with Indian wheat.[93] But Cleveland viewed the problem solely in terms of his fear about the outward flow of gold caused by the depression.

That outlook led him into an elaborate maneuver to manipulate the new concern for silver to consolidate gold monometallism.

The key figure in the deception was Manton Marble, editor of the New York *World* and a prominent member of the metropolitan wing of the Democratic party. The strategy was to use the known British opposition to international bimetallism to end the threat from the silverites.[94] Secretary of State Bayard agreed to provide the money for Marble to go to Europe "and 'mouse' about for fresh information, if any there be, on the silver question." Secretary of the Treasury David Manning thought it all a good joke, and asked Marble to play the role of "a silver tramp." Marble promptly opened discussions with Lord Iddesleigh to insure failure. The British spokesman honestly replied that it "would be only a waste of time" to bother Lord Salisbury.[95]

One can only sympathize with the agricultural businessmen and other silverites who tried to fathom the diversion as it occurred. They were forced to read between the lines of the public press in an attempt to extrapolate the truth, and they understandably made mistakes, attributing the collusion to the wrong individuals. Had they known the full story of what was happening, the protest movement would have erupted in full fury much sooner than it did. "We are taking advantage of every legal opportunity," Manning reassured Marble, "to maintain the gold standard." And, as in the past, the goldbugs relied on the farm businessmen to save the day. "Our great crops, just coming in to a fairly needy market, can keep us swimming for some time to come."[96]

The British routinely rejected bimetallism; and, having won the rigged case, Cleveland used the verdict as a plea for killing silver. "I recommend," he intoned in December 1885, "the suspension of the compulsory coinage of silver dollars." He then acted on his own suggestion by drastically cutting the purchases of bullion. To appease the die-hards, Secretary of the Treasury Manning proposed a tariff change to provide free raw materials for metropolitan businessmen, arguing that would help the farmers by increasing domestic demand as the manufacturers expanded their exports.[97] But the Administration overplayed its hand. Another lawyer, shrewder if not more powerful, recognized the mistake even as the maneuver was being planned. Benjamin Harrison concluded as early as March 1885 that Cleveland was creating "a wide and bitter break in his party." "If we are left half a chance, we can beat them in 1886."[98]

Harrison was a shade optimistic. The victory did not come until 1888. But his analysis was correct because Cleveland opened the way for the Republicans to assume the leadership of the mighty movement of expansive economic nationalism that the agricultural majority had been generating for two decades. Cleveland's assault on silver not only indelibly defined the metropolitan Democrats as friends of

Great Britain and Germany—already considered the most dangerous and hated rivals—but the intense agrarian reaction to his performance dramatized the opportunity for those Republicans who were
less perceptive than Harrison and Blaine. The upsurge of opposition
likewise convinced those who were reluctant to make such an accommodation that the compromise was nevertheless the price of political survival.

The crucial development was the consolidation of the image of American goldbugs as the willing accomplices of British control of the world
marketplace. The analysis exerted such a continuing and pervasive
influence, and contributed so much to honing a hardened but negative economic nationalism to a positive and assertive imperial edge,
that it should be seen in all its clarity as it was formulated in the mid-
1880s by agricultural leaders. The *Western Rural* provided a classic
statement of the argument in answering Cleveland's rhetoric about
the danger of silver. "The real and most immediate 'silver danger,'"
the editors countered, "is that which impends over the American farmer, and grows out of the competition of the wheat of India, now looming up in the near future."

"Stop the coinage of the silver dollar," they continued, "and the
price of silver immediately and rapidly falls, and with it the rupee of
India." That meant, in 1885, that the British operator gained a 15 percent premium on his Indian wheat. "Having driven the farmer into
such a position . . . and made him dependent upon a foreign market
for 84,000,000 bushels of wheat, at or below cost, let the gold standard men beware that they do not finally deprive him wholly of this
foreign market by Indian competition." "We should have long since
made New York the monetary center of the world, where European
kings and others would have come, crowns and hats in hand, to borrow. We should have made this country the very center and circumference of the financial and industrial power and of the civilization
of the earth."[99]

Even if the analysis had been wholly paranoid fantasy, it would
remain the operative historical truth in understanding the imperial
outlook of American farm businessmen. It was actually based very
largely on evidence supplied and verified by the British. *Bradstreet's*
explained the system as clearly as the *Western Rural*. "A low exchange
gives the exporter a larger number of rupees in exchange for the sterling price of his merchandise, and he is therefore able to sell more cheaply in the consuming market." The members of the Indian Silver Association considered the situation so harmful to their nation that they implored the British to terminate the double standard that underwrote the
manipulations.[100]

American silverites could also cite the candid admissions of British
officials to document their case. The Royal Commission on Gold and

Silver concluded that there was "no doubt" about the validity of the analysis. "There is no question at all," remarked H. Wollaston Blake, Director of the Bank of England. "I have always said there was a bounty," added William Fowler.[101] "I do not say that England would lose her natural advantage if she parted with the gold standard," summarized Bertram Currie, another London financial leader, "but if she did she would be in a very great danger of losing her supremacy."[102]

And that, of course, was precisely the objective of the American agricultural majority. They wanted world economic supremacy and hence sought an "independent policy" calculated to defeat the "British nabobs." "The West and the South," warned one Republican, "sustain the Silver coinage . . . in defiance of Banks, and Capitalists, and the domination of England and Germany in regard to silver." "The great question is," cried Senator Thomas Mead Bowen of Colorado, "shall this Government issue a declaration of financial independence? A declaration not only against Europe, but against the organized enemies at home. . . . England rules the financial markets of America."[103]

The Cleveland Administration continued to supply fuel to men like Bowen, Bland, and Frewen who built the bonfires of the campaign in the mid-1880s. Secretary of State Bayard casually dismissed the threat of Indian competition as "distant and little to be feared." Secretary of the Treasury Manning called the argument about silver "illusory."[104] "It is not strange," Bland remarked, "that the intelligent people in the wheat-growing and cotton-raising States are opposed to this war on silver." Nor is it surprising that Cleveland became known to many as "a most pliant tool" of "Lombard Street, London, and Wall Street." "Give us relief" through the "free coinage of silver," cried the Indiana Grange in 1886, and the demand was echoed across the entire nation.[105]

The interlocking nature of the developments of the mid-1880s is nicely illustrated by the way the heated debate about silver strengthened the revived campaign for transportation improvements. Those who denied the significance of silver usually explained the competitive strength of India in terms of the railroads and shipping lines provided by the British for Indian commodity producers, an argument that had the unintended result of giving the agricultural businessmen an opportunity to thrash the metropolis with its own flail. Other factors were more important, however, in generating the drive that finally produced the Interstate Commerce Act of 1887. The persistent efforts of Representative Reagan kept the issue alive through the first part of the decade, and the related investigations and debate extended the agitation and made it clear that some action would have to be taken.[106]

A more indirect but nevertheless powerful force was generated when the West and South overrode President Arthur's veto of the River and Harbor Bill of 1882. The vote was important in demonstrating the power that the agricultural coalition could muster, and the legislation included an appropriation for a major study by a Mississippi River Commission. Its inquiry and report contributed greatly to the acceptance of the idea that the transportation system was a public highway that had to be dealt with on an integrated national basis to insure the general welfare. As Senator Harrison explained, the need was for "a people's highway," and that was "obviously not a sectional but a national work." Indeed, "a national duty."[107]

"Rules should apply to it," added others, "because it holds the life and property of the nation in its hands," and because it was the key "to the elevation of our material interests from a condition of semi-vassalage to foreign nations to one of financial independence."[108] "The roads are public necessities. . . . In no sense of the word a private business enterprise"—"a great public highway."[109] The farm businessmen were wholly correct in arguing that Adam Smith sanctioned such regulation. "Competition is the life of trade," commented one farmer from West Virginia, and pointed out that controls were needed to preserve a free and open marketplace. "It is the duty of the State," summarized the Worthy Master of the Oregon Grange, "to provide highways for the people."[110]

Those views were reinforced by the continued inability of state governments to provide effective regulation of the railroads, by the narrow conservatism of the courts in undercutting or overruling even those efforts, and by the arrogance and abuses of most railroads. Many agricultural businessmen (including processors) recognized the interdependence of the farmer and the rails, and were "not unmindful that reductions in rates had been going on."[111] They countered very forcefully, however, that the rates continued to be manipulated in a wholly arbitrary manner, and that discrimination was standard procedure. "There is no steadiness, no system . . . and the whole country is kept in a tremor of expectancy as to whether prices are going up or down from this unregulated cause."[112] The farmers also pointed out that the decline in rates did not prevent the corporation from making high returns on watered stock, and added that the existing drop in freight rates did not solve the problem of meeting the competition of subsidized producers.[113] Even as the depression was dramatizing all such complaints, moreover, *The New York Times* bluntly concluded that "most great railway kings are selfish, dishonest, corrupters of the courts and juggling manipulators of the stock markets." The *Western Rural* preferred its own idiom: "Writing letters to railroad managers is as effective as fighting battles with blank cartridges."[114]

The vehemence and widespread strength of the movement increasingly worried leaders in both parties. Reagan's bill passed the House for a second time on January 8, 1885, by the strong majority of 161 to 75. Then, less than a month later, Senator Shelby Moore Cullom, a Republican from Illinois, pushed a first draft of his bill to establish a national regulatory commission through the upper house. He and many other Republicans were seriously concerned that the party would lose its crucial agricultural support and wither into a metropolitan faction.[115] That fear increased as Cullom's investigating committee took the full blast of the depression-blown anger of the farm business-men. He admitted to one reformer that the sense of urgency triumphed over the admitted weaknesses of his proposed legislation: the impor-tant thing was "to get some bill passed."[116]

That was finally accomplished in February 1887 despite the oppo-sition of those railroad men (and others) who fought it simply be-cause they wanted to maintain their freedom of action, and the crit-icism of others (including merchants and farm businessmen) who feared it would hurt rather than help overseas economic expansion by ending the practice of offering through (and even special) rates for export shipments. While the law did produce some improvements, such as shifting goods to lower freight classifications, and enabling some agricultural businessmen to win local victories, it did not solve the transportation problem.[117]

Senator Van Wyck of Nebraska had warned in 1886 that the long agitation culminating in the Cullom investigation and the sustained congressional debate would produce a law incapable of fulfilling the expectations that had been generated. The country would "expect some radical and effective legislation," and none would be forthcoming. He was proved correct. "There is a screw loose," concluded Southern Alliance leader Polk. "The wheels have dropped out of balance. The railroads have never been so prosperous, and yet agriculture lan-guishes."[118] Grangers and stockmen shared that view, and the dissatis-faction fed a constantly growing demand for tougher regulation or outright government ownership of a double-tracked line across the country.[119]

The mounting unrest gradually prompted the Cleveland Administra-tion to begin using foreign policy to ease the threat to orthodox metro-politan conservatives. That strategy was suggested by some Democrats at least as early as February and March 1885, as it became clear that the farm businessmen were going to cause trouble during Cleveland's term in office. "A little saltpetre is good for the nostrils now and then," advised one spokesman, "and we haven't had a smell of it in twenty years." Another was more sophisticated and discreet. "I hope," he wrote Marble, "that you have said a good word for commercial trea-ties, upon which the destiny of the country and party now vibrates. In truth there is no principle, no party, no country that is not based on colonies or trade."[120]

Some evidence suggests that the Administration took office with that strategy partially formed in its mind. Cleveland's top patronage man, for example, was Postmaster General Donald McDonald Dickinson, a known expansionist. Secretary of State Bayard remarked soon after the inauguration that "it seems to me that the time is very opportune for our effort to penetrate China and Japan with American railroads, [and] rolling stock."[121] And other leading Democrats began immediately to discuss Cuba as though it would be the first target of opportunity. Many people assumed that the proposed reciprocal trade treaty with Spain would secure "almost complete commercial monopoly. . . . Annexing Cuba in the most desirable way."[122] Cleveland may also have been affected by the support from established American planters (like George K. Thorndike), the New York Produce Exchange, and the New York Chamber of Commerce—some of whom saw a chance to move into the Philippines at the same time.[123]

In any event, the President discussed the issue with his own group. One sure indicator was the memo prepared by an anonymous adviser from Westchester County, New York. Marked *STRICTLY CONFIDENTIAL*, with the additional warning *SHOULD BE CAREFULLY KEPT FROM PUBLICATION*, it argued that annexation was part of "the tradition and policy of the Democratic party," and defined Cuba as "the most important territory which should be added to the US." The writer stressed the economic advantages, and in conclusion offered to organize a syndicate to buy the island.[124] Representative Abram Hewitt of New York added his support, and in doing so indicated that he expected—"as is probable"—some action. And Smith M. Weed made it clear that Cleveland had considered the issue. "I believe, with you," Smith noted in April 1885, "that that mission [to Spain] is, and will be during your administration, of more importance than any other Foreign Mission."[125] Then, at the end of the year, as many Democratic congressmen and advisers were growing concerned that Cleveland was alienating 80 percent of the party, Bayard offered the hope that "the death of the King of Spain [would] lead to important results as to Cuba."[126]

But Cuba was not that easy to pluck—or squeeze—and the Administration did not carry through. The increasing opposition to Cleveland's policies (and lack thereof)—Representative Morrison of Illinois called it a "slap in the face"—finally induced the President to send a special message to the Congress on August 2, 1886, in which he reassured the farm businessmen that he sympathized with their plight and appreciated their "hard, steady, and often unremunerative toil."[127] The words were empty, the tone condescending, and the effect negative. The results of the off-year elections made it perfectly clear that words were insufficient, and Cleveland assumed a more aggressive *posture* in foreign affairs.

But the President was simply too narrowly metropolitan to comprehend, let alone respond to, the agricultural conception of overseas market expansion. His approach was based on a loosely held version of the trickle-down theory of helping agriculture by aiding the metropolis. Later manifestations of the early interest in Cuba, for example, were cast within that framework.[128] He did support the naval building program, and set a close watch on British maneuvers to extend their control over the mouth of the Orinoco River in Venezuela.[129] But agricultural businessmen already supported an enlargement of the Navy and the Merchant Marine; and, for that matter, the significant jump in appropriations (in 1888) came long after Cleveland began to emphasize foreign policy gestures as a way of coping with the farm protest movement.[130]

The same considerations held true in connection with the increasing vigor of the push into Latin America. The pressure that sustained the Blaine strategy of marketplace expansion into that region came from Southern and Western farm spokesmen, and from metropolitan leaders who had accepted the economic and political necessity of such maneuvers. The enabling legislation to hold a Pan-American conference was kept before the House and the Senate, for example, by men from Missouri, Ohio, Illinois, Colorado, and Maine; and Democrats like Wells repeatedly urged Cleveland to act in order to strengthen the party.[131] But the President did not even use foreign policy with any verve or imagination.

The resolution that authorized another Pan-American conference was handled by Representatives James Bennett McCreary of Kentucky, Charles Edward Hooker of Mississippi, and Bland of Missouri—with a bipartisan assist from William Walter Phelps of New Jersey. McCreary's proposal, as Phelps gleefully noted, was almost a carbon copy of Blaine's earlier project. "I am not advocating anything but sound Democratic doctrine," McAdoo shot back: "We want no unnecessary foreign complications; but . . . we have always maintained, coupled with our declaration of non-intervention, the strongly maintained right to preserve this continent. . . . The Americas belong to the Americas."

Hooker emphasized the need to expand economically into and around the Gulf of Mexico—"the American Mediterranean." Adam Smith, he reminded those who had forgotten, stressed that "every market must be availed of; and that which is ours by the natural laws of trade must no longer be yielded to foreign nations, if we would prevent the calamity of having an overplus of production." But expansion in the name of the natural laws of trade would make the region "blossom like the rose." Bland emphasized the necessity of remonetizing silver in order to create such a free and prosperous community, and clearly hoped to gain new recruits for his movement by backing the conference.[132]

Cleveland and Bayard bowed to the will of the expansionists after the bill was passed on May 10, 1888, but displayed no enthusiasm or vigor. They reacted in the same fashion, but with even less effect, to the increasingly angry demands of the livestock industry to reopen European markets. The meat growers made it clear from the outset that they expected Cleveland to follow through on the creation of the Bureau of Animal Industry by taking "vigorous action." Representative Benjamin Le Fevre, an Ohio Democrat, tried to prod his colleagues and the Administration into some meaningful policy initiatives, but he evoked no coherent or effective reply.[133]

Cleveland even failed to respond to a pointed warning—"our people are impatient"—offered in November 1885 by his own Commissioner of Agriculture, Norman J. Coleman. Coleman knew the temper of the agricultural community better than any other member of the Administration, and worked hard to meet its needs, but he was never able to exercise significant influence on the President. Cleveland blandly announced that "there are no questions of difficulty pending with any foreign government," thus discounting the European restrictions on meat exports, and declined to wet an oar to help the economy catch what he admitted was "that irresistible tide of commercial expansion." He was sorry about the restrictions on meat exports, but offered nothing beyond "strong hopes" that they would be removed.[134]

That did not satisfy the livestock men. The cattle raisers were particularly weary of counting on hope after the collapse of Frewen's grandiose plan to evade the British slaughter order by exporting live cattle through Canada.[135] But the swine breeders contributed their full share, throughout the spring and summer of 1886, to the swelling disgust and bitterness against the strict legalism and diplomatic reserve of Cleveland and Bayard. Their "sensitiveness on the constitutional question [of inspection], and the wise statesmanship in their objections," snarled the *National Live Stock Journal*, "are things calculated to excite wonder in the minds of ordinary mortals."[136]

"The men who stand between the farmers and this foreign market," added the *Breeder's Gazette*, "hold seats in the Congress of the United States." The *Western Rural* caught the tone of the agricultural confidence in American power, particularly when it was used for the purposes of freemen. "If this Government would always be prompt in demanding justice it would have no difficulty that would be likely to lead to war. We are a powerful nation and war with us means serious loss of life and money." Even the *Rural New Yorker* became disgusted with the inaction. "Nothing is likely to be done unless we retaliate."[137]

Republicans quickly caught the mood of the livestock men and moved to adopt a more aggressive policy as early as January 18, 1886, when Representative Ransom Williams Dunham of Illinois (a grain and provision merchant who had served as president of the Chicago Board of Trade) introduced retaliatory legislation. Representative Phelps of New Jersey, a friend of Blaine who had served as Minister to Austria in 1881, and Senator George Franklin Edmunds of Vermont quickly took charge of the campaign, however, and managed it well enough to upset Bayard considerably.[138] The Secretary of State quickly let it be known that he was concerned with "unjust hardships inflicted on American commerce," but not so concerned as to employ retaliation. That was "wholly unprecedented," and he would have nothing to do with the Edmunds bill. That reaction did not surprise the livestock men, for they had discovered long before that Bayard was "fertile in expedients" of delay, evasion, and inaction.[139] The Administration remained unmoved, moreover, despite its losses in the election of 1886, the terrible weather on the Western ranges from the summer of 1886 through the winter of 1887-1888, and the sustained demand from the cattlemen.

The "big die-up," as it quickly became known to the ranchers, began with extremely dry and hot weather through May, June, and July 1886.[140] Then came a winter of terror, with snow that buried houses and winds that toppled trains off the tracks. "The weather since I wrote you on the 15th [January]," reported one man a week later, "has been snow and wind. . . . If the present weather keeps on . . . and should we have a cold snap . . . we will lose a good many cattle." Three weeks later he had concluded that "God Almighty intends to close out the range business altogether. On the 30th January it turned a little colder and snow began to fall and kept it up until Monday when that night it went to 6 below zero and Tuesday 22 below and Wednesday night 30 the coldest this winter. . . . What the loss will be I do not pretend to say . . . there is nothing we can do to save the cattle."[141]

It is highly doubtful whether President Cleveland (or any other metropolitan leader of his outlook) enjoyed the slightest understanding of the emotional shock to the men who were forced to stand by immobilized as their animals died horribly on the ranges. He could not muster very much understanding for the Texas farmers who had been grievously scarred by the drought. He vetoed a bill to give them some seeds. There "seems to be no doubt," he commented, that seeds would help; but he could "find no warrant for such an appropriation in the Constitution." He did offer a bit of salt, however, with the remark that the bill "is in no manner properly related to the public service or benefit."[142]

He remained true to his orthodoxy when a Democrat from Iowa warned him that the people "are terribly in earnest and feel deeply." Finally, after repeated demands to retaliate "blow for blow," and a sustained petition drive (including two from the Chicago Board of Trade), Cleveland boldly suggested getting tough by prohibiting pork imports from Germany and France. The irrelevance of the proposal was surpassed only by the disgust of the livestock men. They had been unable to muster all their potential strength because of a division between those who emphasized the need to attack the big Chicago meat packers and another group that concentrated on the drive for markets. The irony, of course, was that the antimonopolists (centered in St. Louis) were equally concerned to enlarge the market. They merely adopted different tactics to accomplish the common objective. They won a short-run victory when the Senate agreed to investigate the problem in May 1888; but by the time the committee headed by Senator Vest reported, many of them had shifted their attention back to demands for retaliation against the European enemies. [143]

The livestock men exerted considerable influence on the evolution of American foreign policy. They contributed greatly to the intensification of economic nationalism, and focused it sharply and aggressively against Great Britain, Germany, and France. In the process, furthermore, they reinforced the existing attitude that America's expansion was justified and good because it served to enlarge the free marketplace at the expense of aristocratic and tyrannical governments. "As we have often said," noted the *Western Rural*, "England and Germany are a great deal more interested in preventing competition than they are in preventing the introduction of disease."[144] And, finally, the stockmen deepened the feeling that America possessed the power to accomplish its objectives without war if only metropolitan leaders would serve the national rather than their special interest.

The Cleveland Administration did develop its particular kind of metropolitan concern with market expansion across the Pacific with the agricultural protest movement, and especially the anger at Germany and Britain, firmly in mind. That was particularly true in connection with the renewed struggle for control of Samoa.[145] But the President's greatest contribution to the approaching triumph of the expansionist imperial outlook so long developed and advocated by the agricultural businessmen came through his belated but vigorous campaign for a lower tariff. The reason for that influence was simple and powerful: however unintentionally, his dramatic tariff message of December 6, 1887, crystallized the entire discussion of the tariff in terms of export markets.

Cleveland's strident call for lower rates also divided his own minority metropolitan wing of the Democratic party, for whose benefit the policy was primarily intended, and that in turn created a crucial opening for expansionist Republicans like Blaine and Harrison. Thus the cliche that the tariff was a "purely business question" offers an important insight into the evolution of American foreign policy. The President's conversion to low rates occurred quite slowly, and took place almost entirely within the framework of a concern for industrial exports. Democrats like Representatives Bland, Frank Hunt Hurd

of Ohio, and Mills of Texas had been agitating the issue for years, and
the President's own Secretary of the Treasury had advanced the argument as a major feature of his annual reports. Those men saw the policy as a classic way to implement Adam Smith's axiom concerning
the freedom of an expanding marketplace. "The farmers need no protection," explained a Southern Democrat in 1883: "All we want is an
open field and fair play. We want an opportunity to reach the markets of the world."[146]

The campaign waged by those men increasingly disturbed Republican protectionists, and they countered with an extensive and steadily
more extremist campaign to maintain the true faith among Western
agriculturalists. Swank sounded the bugle in February 1883. "The
time has fully come," he shrilled, "to throw off all lethargy, to dispense
with all modesty . . . to exercise all energies in a united and determined
effort" against the damnable foes who were a motley crowd of foreign
agents "in direct receipt of English money"—"trimmers and cow-
ards."[147] The reinforcements quickly swung into line: the Metropolitan
Industrial League, the Association for the Protection of American Industries, the Eastern Pig Iron Association, and finally (January 1885) the
American Protective Tariff League.

The battle indeed involved "considerable expense and trouble,"
as one subordinate complained, but it was most certainly not carried
out, as Swank once claimed, "very quietly."[148] There were millions
of words, many of them in the titles of the pamphlets, and most of them
were wild. *Proof of British Influence in American Tariff Legislation*
was packaged with the more sarcastic *Has the British Lion Worn Out
His Paws?;* while the less emotional reader was seduced with an appeal to his concern for justice, *Producers and Consumers. Some Plain
Facts Which Show How Protection Benefits All the People of Our
Country.* An appeal was also made to those with an open mind: *Which
Is Best for Farmers, Protection or Free Trade?* And staff officers like
McKinley offered still more subtle arguments to prove that world
markets could not be conquered until "the British policy" was defeated
at home.[149]

The low tariff forces nevertheless gained ground by creating confusion and winning converts throughout the West. That was probably a factor in convincing Cleveland to support his Secretary of the
Treasury's low tariff efforts. But the crucial factor was the sense of
crisis that Bayard tersely expressed in November 1887. "The situation
is most serious—and the make-shift remedies are exhausted."[150] The
President made his decision during a tense conference with Mills,
Manning, Senator William Freeman Vilas, and Representative John
Griffin Carlisle.[151] But, wholly in character, Cleveland defined the low
tariff in narrowly metropolitan terms.

One could not end all tariffs, he explained, because they provided funds needed by the government, and because an income tax on metropolitan wealth was unthinkable. Hence the solution, as Manning (and probably Marble) had long explained, was to remove the tariff from raw materials. Given such assistance, the metropolitan industrialists could lower their prices and penetrate foreign markets. And that would in turn create the domestic demand to absorb all the agricultural surpluses that did not find overseas markets as other nations responded to the American action by lowering their tariffs (and removing other restrictions).[152]

As it happened, of course, men like Mills had to develop and explain that classic imperial inversion of the protectionist logic about the home market. Cleveland's outlook was so narrowly orthodox and metropolitan that he fretted almost exclusively about the inability of his Eastern supporters to understand the subsidy he was handing them. He would have done far better to worry about how best to exploit the beautiful argument that Mills offered him to destroy the Republican power base among agricultural businessmen in the West.[153] His choice was not based on ignorance. Cleveland had been advised, perhaps as much as three years before his famous low tariff message, of a compromise policy that would solve the central dilemma. That strategy was based on using the bait of no tariff on sugar to win concessions opening new markets for all agriculturalists. The suggestion was originally made by one metropolitan Republican to another metropolitan Republican, and it bitterly divided the metropolitan wing of that party just as effectively as Cleveland's proposal divided the metropolitan wing of the Democratic party.[154]

But the difference proved as sharp as Occam's razor. The Republicans had leaders who understood the problem, who recognized the opportunity, and who proved sensitive enough to realize that political power arises from the fountainhead of the majority. In particular, the Republicans had Blaine and Harrison. But it was not so much that those men surpassed Cleveland as it was that the agricultural businessmen had committed themselves to reaching freedom and prosperity by traveling the high road of overseas market expansion. That meant that Americans would travel the imperial highway to liberty and welfare. Nothing is inevitable until men close off their options, but that is what happened during the four years after Cleveland was defeated in his bid for reelection.

TWELVE

The problem of our statesmen today is to maintain the Western farmer in comfort, in honor, and in wealth by a business in which he is forced to underbid the naked Oriental.

Senator George F. Hoar of
Massachusetts, 1887

We do not mean to be contented with our market.
Benjamin Harrison, Campaign Speech, 1888

The average farmer of to-day is in poor circumstances and receives a very small return for his labor and money invested.

State Grange of Massachusetts, 1889

The South has been the tail of the dog of industrial empire.

William H. Ballou, 1889

I am an exporter, I want the world.
Charles L. Lovering, Massachusetts
Textile Executive, 1890

The Great West has thus far acted as a safety valve; but it is nearly closed, and it is very evident that something must happen ere long.

Fred Grundy, 1890

The farmers have the call in this Congress.
The Chicago *Tribune*, 1890

There will be no tariff legislation this session unless a silver bill is passed.

Senator William Morris Stewart
of Nevada, 1890

If the Alliance can hold full one-half of our Republican voters in such states as Kansas and Nebraska our future is not cheerful.

President Harrison, 1890

We have a surplus production in these great valleys for which we must seek foreign markets. . . . It has been a source of constant thought and zealous effort on the part of the administration . . . to secure larger foreign markets for our farm products.

President Harrison, 1891

The American producer, whether on the farm or in the shop, can knock the hind sights off the producer anywhere else on the face of the earth.

Populist Representative
Thomas Edward Watson of Georgia, 1892

I am a free trader—absolute. . . . It so happens that we have a very large agricultural surplus. . . . We have no market here. The farmers must of necessity seek a foreign market. . . . Why, Mr. Chairman, we are driven from the markets of the whole world. . . . We believe that the money question is a part of the great question of trade, or so mixed up with it that you can not separate them.

Populist Representative Jeremiah
Simpson of Kansas, 1892

Metropolitan Republicans Commit Themselves to Market Expansion to Hold the Western Farm Businessmen and Sustain the System

M ETROPOLITAN leaders faced a complex set of difficulties as the economy wobbled through the depression and recession of the 1880s, and as the hardening anger and antagonism of the farm businessmen threatened their control of the political economy. The central question was whether any segment of the metropolis could maintain enough strength among agriculturalists to prevent them from taking control of one party, or from creating a new political organization that would dominate the future. Had the farm businessmen in the Democratic party committed themselves to an all-out bid to control their party after the election of 1886, and had they succeeded by 1892, they might very well have emerged as the established leaders of the country. The effort almost succeeded, after all, even though it was not initiated until 1890.

Even that handicap might not have proved insurmountable, moreover, had it not been for one group of astute and determined Republican leaders who agreed with the policy of overseas market expansion and who used it to revive and maintain the position of their party—and the power of the metropolis. Without Harrison and Blaine, and other equally energetic Republicans like Jeremiah M. Rusk and Whitelaw Reid of New York, the agriculturalists might very well have led the nation as it embarked upon their program of economic expansion. For it was their program, and their long-term dedication to it, that determined the outcome.

Blaine, Harrison, and the others merely understood and accepted what had been wrought by the agricultural majority, and then adopted

319

and adapted it for the entire political economy. Their commitment to that political and economic strategy emerged clearly during the presidential campaign of 1888, and they affirmed the decision despite the wrenching struggle it produced within the Republican party, and despite its short-run failure to satisfy the agriculturalists. Their analysis and faith were justified, however, within six years. For they had taken the initiative in defining and acting on the alternatives *within* the expansionist outlook developed by the majority. That placed all other groups, and particularly the more militantly reformist wing of the farm protest movement, at a disadvantage they never overcame.

The Blaine-Harrison wing of the party faced a similar danger after President Cleveland's tariff message of December 1887, and they might not have recovered the initiative if the expansionist version of the low tariff argument had been accepted as the doctrine of the Democratic party. Even Blaine was undecided about how to counter the challenge. His first response, most probably determined by a concern to protect his position with metropolitan high tariff leaders, stressed the home market.[1] He very badly wanted to be President, and that early reaction appears as an effort to insure his renomination.

He quickly dropped that tactic in the face of the widespread ferment within the party and throughout the agricultural South and West. For in addition to the strong support for Harrison as the next nominee, there was considerable interest in such men as Walter Quintin Gresham and Rusk. Gresham won approval for his understanding of the importance of the transportation issue and for his opposition to railroad abuses, for his independence of metropolitan interests, and for his refusal to damn the silverites out of hand. He was pushed very hard by Teller of Colorado and other party leaders in Nebraska.[2] Rusk, a close friend of Garfield who had been offered a diplomatic post by Blaine in 1881, made his career as a two-term governor of Wisconsin who fully comprehended the vital role of market expansion in the well-being of the agricultural businessmen.[3]

Rusk threw his support to Harrison, an unusually intelligent and shrewd lawyer-politician who knew the problems and the temper of the farmers through his service in the Congress (and especially his work on the Mississippi River Commission), and through his relationship with his son, Russell Harrison, a rancher and newspaperman who served as secretary of the Montana Stock Growers Association for more than a decade. As a political operator, Harrison could be hard and yet respect the pragmatic limits of ruthlessness; he knew when to draw back from those actions, as one Westerner described them, that "might be sliding the steel a little too deep."[4]

Combined with his personal reserve and his involvement in his private life, Harrison's abilities and toughness provoked some contemporaries (like the ambitious young aristocratic crusader Theodore

Roosevelt) to angry opposition. But those characteristics also enabled him to perform very effectively as a campaigner when he chose to engage his talents and energy in that phase of politics. That was demonstrated as early as the Republican convention, where it became apparent that Harrison was the choice of a coalition of metropolitans and Westerners who favored market expansion. One such man was Senator George Frisbie Hoar of Massachusetts. He began shortly after the Republican gains in 1886 to emphasize the need for policies designed to help "western farmers to send their grain to Europe." "The problem of our statesmen today is to maintain the Western farmer in comfort, in honor, and in wealth by a business in which he is forced to underbid the naked Oriental." Such was also necessary to maintain the "balance of trade" that underpinned the entire economy.[5] Another supporter was Senator Plumb of Kansas who, along with Kasson of Iowa, had pushed such market expansion for a decade. Perhaps the most illuminating indicator of what was happening within the hierarchy of the party came when Senator Sherman turned to overseas economic expansion as a way of solving the silver and agricultural problem.[6]

The selection of Levi P. Morton of New York as vice-presidential candidate provided another sure indicator of the outlook of those who backed Harrison. Morton had long been involved in international trade and finance (as well as the purebred livestock business), and — like Rusk — had been on the diplomatic list prepared by President Garfield and Secretary of State Blaine. While Morton was a gold man, his argument hinged on the advantage that gold offered in winning markets for "cotton, wheat, corn, flour," and in making New York "the clearing house for the commercial exchanges of the world."[7] That spirit was also apparent in the platform. For, while it reasserted the value of a high tariff, it also stressed the need for "prompt action" in strengthening the Navy and building a merchant marine as part of opening "new and direct markets for our produce." That theme was reiterated — "extension into better markets" — as part of the tough attack on Cleveland's foreign policy for "its inefficiency and its cowardice." McKinley even charged that the Democrats served "the interests of Europe."[8]

Harrison quickly made it clear that he would emphasize market expansion rather than the high tariff. He was no doubt influenced by the steady reports of trouble in the West. Alliance men from Nebraska, complaining that agriculture was "greatly depressed," asserted that the condition could "be controlled by legislation" and demanded action on money, transportation, and markets. One of Rusk's friends in Wisconsin cautioned that "the Grangers can be heard at the outside door." And Senator Plumb and Medill of the Chicago *Tribune* explicitly warned that the tariff would "be especially obnoxious in the west . . . and is going to hurt us materially . . . if it is not in some way qual-

ified."⁹ Harrison was also guided by the views of Reid and Blaine who
understood the problem and pushed market expansion as the answer.

It is apparent, however, that Harrison had been thinking within
that framework for most of the decade. Stanton J. Peelle of Indiana,
for example, one of his earliest supporters for the nomination, spoke
directly in that idiom to Kasson just before the campaign was launched.
"We must recognize the outward march of our industrial enterprises
and as a progressive people, we must recognize changed conditions."¹⁰
Harrison left no doubt about the matter once he opened his front-porch
campaign. "We do not intend to be contented with our market," he
declared. "We should seek to promote closer and more friendly commercial relations with the Central and South American States."¹¹ That
theme, so reminiscent of Blaine, was the central message of his speeches
to the hundreds of delegations that visited him in Indianapolis. Defining himself as a student of markets rather than a scholastic theo-
rist, Harrison repeatedly called for market expansion furthered by
a merchant marine and protected by a navy. The chief rival and enemy
was the British Empire (and its domestic friends). Harrison's stay-at-
home campaign was extremely effective. "We could safely close these
headquarters," reported one Easterner, "and he would elect himself."¹²
That was an exaggeration born of elation, but the delegations that
were excited by their trip and aroused by the candidate did prove effective when they returned home.¹³

But Blaine was also sought by many local leaders in the West and
responded with some of the most effective speaking of his career.¹⁴
Once defeated for the nomination, indeed, Blaine relaxed and thoroughly enjoyed the battle against Cleveland and Bayard. "Your election," he enthused to Harrison, "will seal our industrial independence
as the Declaration of '76 . . . saved our political independence." That
was the spirit of his own effort. "I have now just left him after his lunch,"
recounted Mrs. Blaine on one occasion, "roast lamb, cabbage, stewed
rhubarb and cream, whisky and water . . . and crackers and cheese,
reading aloud Ingall's screed in the *North American Review* on Cleveland." For his own part, Blaine fired away at Cleveland for not retal-
iating to open markets for American livestock men, and happily honored his earlier injunction to expose Bayard as "a humbug and a
poud."¹⁵

The Democrats never mounted an effective counterattack against
such vigorous nationalism and expansionism. Cleveland tried to use
foreign policy to rally support, but his efforts were as feeble as they
had been during his four years in office. The famous episode of "Murch-
ison's letter," in which a California Republican named George A. Os-
goodby hoodwinked the British Minister into avowing his preference
for Cleveland, has often been used to explain the outcome of the election. The ploy supposedly turned enough New York Irishmen back to

the Republicans to determine the electoral count. The logic is weak, for Harrison's popular margin in the state was 7 million votes. It is more probable that Cleveland squeaked through to victory in New York in 1884 because he was then Governor; then lost by a sizable margin in 1888 because many people had become disaffected. Cleveland's margin over Harrison in popular votes (less than 100,000 of more than 11 million) was due to the population differential between the Democratic South and the Republican West.

Harrison promptly carried through on the expansionist nationalism of his campaign in choosing key Cabinet members. The major decision involved making Blaine Secretary of State. Despite serious personal reservations, and a fearful estimate of Blaine's ambition, Harrison finally selected his rival. He did so because of the great direct and indirect political pressure, and because he recognized that they shared the same expansionist outlook. That was also an important element, along with their Western strength, in selecting Rusk as Secretary of Agriculture and Senator Windom of Minnesota as Secretary of the Treasury. The same stress on expansion was apparent in the choice of Benjamin F. Tracy, a New York lawyer and judge who was also a highly respected gentleman horse-breeder, as Secretary of the Navy. And John W. Noble, the new Secretary of the Interior, firmly believed that the end of the continental frontier meant that the United States had to open a new frontier by building "a greater commerce" in the world marketplace.[16]

The Administration moved immediately to translate its expansionist rhetoric into a vigorous foreign policy. Because the President and other major leaders were so continually concerned about the agricultural protest movement that was steadily increasing in size and militancy, their diplomacy cannot be fully understood unless it is reviewed within that context. The broad setting was determined by the economy. The rate of growth turned downward in the fall of 1889 and did not reverse itself until the spring of 1892. The business cycle followed a similar course between July 1890 and May 1891, and the unemployment rate in 1890 - 1891 fluctuated between 4 and 5.4 percent.

Those patterns reinforced the existing self-consciousness that was expressed so directly by an Illinios farmer: "For the past ten or twelve years the conviction has been gradually forcing itself upon us that something was wrong in our affairs. . . . We have been steadily going behind." "It looks like," added an agriculturalist on the West Coast, "disunion and poverty is reduced to a science among farmers."[17] And the Massachusetts Grange concluded that "the average farmer of today is in poor circumstances and receives a very small return for his labor and money invested."[18] Many Western farmers were additionally hurt by drought in 1889, and again in 1890. "It is going to be a bad thing for this country if these dry seasons continue," a South Dakotan warned, "for many people are getting discouraged and they have good reason to be as things are going."[19] "Cheyenne is yet poor," reported a leading rancher, "and business in all lines is very dull."[20] All such circumstances intensified the antimetropolitan feeling of the farm businessmen. The West was "an underdeveloped country," complained a Western Granger; and one politician cautioned another that "the country is pretty sensitive . . . thinking the great cities are getting an undue share of the patronage."[21]

Southern agriculturalists manifested the same anger and emotion. "The South has been the tail of the dog of industrial empire," one man complained, echoing the members of a Danville, Virginia, Alliance chapter who organized to escape "the insufferable thralldom of a worse than Egyptian bondage."[22] A Georgia farmer protested bitterly about the sharecropping system, concluding that at most a man had "generally half of every Saturday to work his own little plot." And one of the "best known and most intelligent planters in Alabama" reported that he turned a profit of $972.64 on seventy acres.[23] Suffering a slump of their own, Southern textile men agreed on the "absolute necessity" of opening new markets. "If legislation be necessary, by all means let us have legislation. But give us a foreign market."[24]

More and more Northern mills made the same demand. Charles L. Lovering, treasurer of the Massachusetts Mills of Lowell, described the situation with fabled Yankee directness: "I am an exporter. I want the world." Such men turned increasingly to the China market as a way to meet Southern competition, which had gained an additional comparative advantage because of increased labor costs in the North caused by reform legislation.[25] Northern flour millers faced less trouble on that count from the Southern processors, but both groups hammered away at Harrison and Blaine for quick market expansion. The Southerners argued that the Brazilian market was "very important," but admitted they would be satisfied with "any market."[26]

Despite their differences, the livestock men and the meat processors also united in demanding prompt and effective action to reopen their markets. The Omaha and Chicago Boards of Trade, the Kansas City Commercial Exchange, and the Boston Chamber of Commerce all told Blaine privately and publicly that they needed "a foreign market."[27] Overseas market expansion offered "a way of escape for the harassed cattle-feeder," argued the editors of *Breeder's Gazette*, and cried out for "some Moses . . . to open the doors of European ports to the unrestricted entrance of our cattle." "With a fair field and no favors, the magnitude to which our livestock exports would obtain would revive, enlarge, and enrich the industry to an extent little imagined."[28]

The anger over the British role in the market troubles of the stockmen was reinforced by continuing English investment in land, and in flour milling, brewing, and mining.[29] One result was a renewed demand for stronger legislation against alien landowners. Kansans discussed the issue in terms of "land gods." Macune's *National Economist*, the official publication of the Southern Alliance, termed the foreign activity "a deadly monster." Whatever the labels, most agreed with Macune that the process was Britain's "modern plan of conquest."[30] Still another issue directly related to British economic power, the remonetization of silver, was agitated ever more strongly and bitterly.

Senator Stewart of Nevada advised Harrison even before the inauguration that he planned to push the issue as forcefully as possible. It was "more important" than any other question because "a sufficient supply of money" would revive business.[31] "It will not do to assume that the country is prosperous while the farmers and producing classes are becoming more involved in debt."[32] Many Westerners came to share Stewart's "great hopes" that the Harrison Administration would "refrain from all negotiations and connections with the bond holders of Europe and assert the financial independence of the United States."[33]

Stewart again explained the issue very carefully to Harrison in April 1889. "A financial crash" was highly probable unless the proper policy was promptly adopted. All the worry about British power was unwarranted. "The United States, without the cooperation of any other nation, can raise the price of silver to par with gold at the ratio of 16 to 1." That would help everyone, "and particularly our farmers" who suffer from Indian competition. If that was not done, the result would be "stagnation and despair." "There is no reason why the United States should allow England to longer dictate our financial policy. Financial independence is almost as essential to the prosperity of this country as political independence."[34]

Even the Indiana Grange agreed with Stewart, and the President's political advisers warned him that he "must go faster" because the Southern and Western farm businessmen were organizing a revolt.[35] That became dramatically apparent in June 1889 when Senator Plumb's free-coinage amendment passed by a wide margin. And, while not as shocking, the demands for other assistance in the marketplace nevertheless underscored the widespread concern for economic expansion. The National Grange called for a consular system improved to help "the disposal of our surplus agricultural products," for example, and Westerners renewed the call for action on an isthmian canal. That would "do more toward cheapening freight," asserted the editor of the *Pacific Rural Press*, "than two Interstate Commissions."[36]

Others continued to press the attack on the railroads, however, and intensified the demand for an American merchant marine.[37] The Pacific Coast Commercial Conference, which involved agricultural interests and flour millers, asked for the same kind of government aid favored by the Farmers National Congress. And the Inter-State Deep-Harbor Movement, composed of delegates from eighteen states west of the Mississippi, called for subsidies sufficient to create a Gulf port that could end the "enormous loss in transportation expense." The editors of the Springfield, Illinois, *Republican* did not exaggerate: "Our farmers and stockmen are ready to honor the man who will solve this question of transportation so that cheap, safe, and rapid steamship communications may be had with the nations of Central and South America."[38]

Whatever the emphasis, whatever the specific proposal, the farm businessmen were manifesting a new urgency, stridency, and militancy. "The promotion of agriculture," announced the National Grange, had become the nation's highest priority. America should "become a more powerful nation," and "take the advance of all the nations of the earth." "We demand of Congress that every just facility shall be granted for the purpose." The objective, because it was the necessity, was a policy "that will give this nation the commercial supremacy that belongs to it."[39] Southern Alliance leaders accepted the analysis and developed the argument for the necessity of market expansion from a quotation from Adam Smith.[40] The livestock men and the meat processors stated the issue just as bluntly: "Wonder what Uncle Sam would do if it was not for the farmers of the West, anyhow?"[41]

The farm businessmen also increased their stress on the power of the United States and vigorously asserted their confidence that freedom went hand in hand with America's market expansion. "We desire free, open and fair competition," asserted the Worthy Master of the New York Grange. True enough, agreed the editors of the *Pacific Rural Press*, who moved left with the times and became an Alliance paper. But they thought it wise to be candid and admit that open trade was "aggressive." The British Empire was not built "on the lust of conquest or a desire to teach school," they pointed out, but on the necessity "to secure a better market." Hence the question of colonialism, "annexation," had to be decided strictly on the criteria of whether or not it was "to our advantage." Thus anything that threatened "to interfere with the liberty, happiness and prosperity of any people on this hemisphere" had to be opposed for all sound and just reasons.[42]

The argument among agricultural businessmen was not over *whether* to expand but over *how* to expand. A West Coast farmer stated the approach of one group simply and directly—force would not be needed. "The word of this 70,000,000 nation will be very apt to carry respect wherever it makes itself heard."[43] But others insisted on the need for "an intelligent and aggressive effort." "The markets of these countries *ought to be opened* . . . for the surplus produced in this country"—"at once." Such a policy was deemed politically wise, moreover, as well as economically necessary. It would "greatly strengthen the hold of the present administration upon our people."[44]

Harrison and Blaine had reached that conclusion even before they took office, and moved rapidly to make the word of the 70 million heard through a larger navy and other amplifiers. The confrontation with German and British naval units in Samoa had triggered the tightly packed charge of agrarian animosity toward those nations and produced an outburst of militant expansionism in January 1889, and the Congress had promptly voted a special appropriation of $100,000 to strengthen the American position in Pago Pago. Blaine sent three vigorous expansionists, headed by Kasson, to the subsequent discussions in Berlin, and they consolidated the claim. That won wide approval, and there was no great opposition to participating in the joint protectorate over the islands.

Blaine supplemented that move across the Pacific with two other thrusts. He encouraged Horace Allen's enthusiastic labors to expand American commercial, industrial, and financial operations in Korea. And Vice President Morton provided economic help for Allen through his own firm, a move that dramatized the growing metropolitan involvement in such expansion.[45] The Secretary of State also acted on his view that Hawaii was part of "the American system." He was in the process of deciding that the annexation of the islands was necessary (if he had not already done so), and picked John L. Stevens, a close expansionist friend from Maine, to watch over American interests.

They very probably began to discuss intervention shortly after the anti-American movement won a narrow victory in the February 1890 elections. For that matter, such conversations may have been opened when it became clear that free entry for sugar into the United States might be used as a bargaining lever to open markets in Europe and Latin America. It was apparent that any change in the laws on sugar imports would affect the tight economic relationship between the United States and Hawaii. In any event, Blaine tried to win Hawaiian approval for a protectorate. The proposed agreement included a proviso granting the United States the right to land military forces at its own discretion. The rejection of that approach only intensified the concern to maintain control.

The Harrison-Blaine strategy of using sugar to expand markets for American surpluses developed through the convergence of four factors, all of which involved the agricultural businessmen. One was the long agitation for reciprocity treaties that had engaged farmers as well as manufacturers, and which Blaine and Garfield had sought to focus on Latin America. The second was the ultimately successful campaign, in which the agriculturalists played a major role, for the Pan-American conference that Arthur and Frelinghuysen had canceled. The third was the acceptance of the agriculturalists' expansionist outlook by the majority of the metropolis. And the fourth was the surging protest movement that underscored the need for quick and effective action to open new markets.

Blaine and Harrison viewed the Pan-American conference as a major opportunity to implement the expansionist outlook and thereby resolve many economic and political problems.[46] The vigorous interest and enthusiasm manifested by farmers and processors, as well as the continued warnings from political advisers, reinforced that approach.[47] Cattlemen considered the conference of "vital importance." The Mississippi Valley Wheat Growers Association, which was also concerned about pork exports, thought it a first step to "control the markets of the world." The Omaha Board of Trade and the Chicago Produce Exchange "cordially endorsed" the meeting, and other Westerners added their approval. Flour millers and cotton textile men, "deeply interested," discussed "our commercial occupation of such markets" as a "necessary, temperate and substantial maintenance of our Monroe Doctrine." And one particularly excited individual offered his "mite to help on the conquest commercially of South America."[48]

Harrison tapped another source of support when the conference opened in October 1889 by asking the Congress to expand the Merchant Marine through mail subsidy legislation. That further sharpened the focus on market expansion and reinforced the interest in the conference. Agricultural businessmen responded enthusiastically. Groups from Ohio to Kansas, and from Wisconsin to Louisiana, favored action that would break British power over a market that "rightly belongs to the American producers." "There is no time to be lost," the Pacific Coast Commercial Conference warned. "American interests are spreading." Those men, wanting to be "wholly independent of England," demanded "equal terms in the open market." Cincinnati spokesmen, concerned for America's "rightful supremacy," were pointing for the trade of "China, Japan, India." And the *National Economist* added its plea for a subsidy. "The supreme need of the farming class is a foreign market."[49]

Blaine neatly outlined his approach to the conference by listing his priorities in ascending order. "A great gain" would be the increase in "common confidence." "A greater gain" would be "to draw the people of all American nations into closer acquaintance." "The greatest gain" would be the proper regulation of "commercial relations."[50] His original strategy called for establishing American predominance through a customs union, but the conference rejected that plan in favor of reciprocity treaties. Blaine and other American leaders promptly seized upon that proposal and made it into the grand strategy of the Harrison Administration for solving the problems of the political economy through overseas market expansion.

The necessity of effective action became urgent during the winter of 1889-1890 because the farm businessmen began to seize the initiative. The normally conservative members of the National Farmers Congress shifted to blunt attacks "on the self-respect" of the government for failing to act "with a strong hand" against rivals who were "appropriating" trade and "thereby threatening great danger to our interests." The National Grange, weary of the "gloomy" lot of the farmer, resolved for free silver and demanded "new markets, new exchanges, and increased opportunities" for exports.[51] And the founding of the Trans-Mississippi Commercial Congress indicated that stockmen, flour millers, and other agricultural businessmen were overriding their differences to present a solid front against the metropolis.

But the most portentous development involved the simultaneous December meetings in St. Louis of the Southern Alliance, the Northern Alliance, the Farmers Mutual Benefit Association, and the Colored Farmers National Alliance. William Alfred Peffer, an influential newspaper editor and a long-time Republican leader of farm businessmen in Kansas, provided the nation with an excellent summary of what was happening that same month. "There is a feeling of unrest among the farmers of this country," he announced bluntly, "and they are forming local, county, state, and national associations . . . in a common effort to improve their condition." The policies of the metropolis, arbitrary, inequitable, and unjust, had produced a determined movement "to remedy these wrongs, to obtain their just proportion of the profits arising from their labor, and to restore themselves to their normal place among their fellow men." It was "the greatest revolution ever peacefully inaugurated."[52]

The joint conference that evolved in St. Louis documented that analysis with demands for the remonetization of silver, for the improvement and control of transportation, for an end to alien landownership, and for "a better system of handling and disposing of what we produce."[53] The latter proposal offers a vital insight into the outlook of the agricultural reformers, for it was a plan to establish facilities for storing commodity crops and thereby controlling the world marketplace and its prices. Though they offered it first for cotton, the advocates soon included wheat and other crops. The program became known as the subtreasury plan because of its similarity to earlier projects for the monetary system, and because the farmer would be able to obtain loans to 80 percent of the "local current value" of the crops in storage.

The classic marketplace strategy underlying the subtreasury proposal evolved from American and European traditions and experiences. The Russian efforts to reestablish their position in the world market were widely known and reported, for example, and the American farm businessmen acknowledged that debt, as well as one to a suggestion first offered during the French Revolution.[54] The objective was made perfectly clear by Harry Kinney of South Carolina when he presented the idea in *Frank Leslie's Illustrated Newspaper* on November 30, 1889. "The practical result of the plan would be to prevent the Liverpool Cotton Exchange from dictating the price of our product." Farm businessmen were of course attracted by the tactical benefit of obtaining an immediate return on their annual investment, but control of the marketplace was essential to win that gain.

As Harry Tracy explained in detailing the project to Alliance members, the aim was to replace British control with American control. "Nothing is plainer than the following: *If domestic price is governed by foreign quotation, then effective measures should be inaugurated for preserving the same ration between the supply and demand for money that prevails in the foreign market.*"[55] The marketplace would be dominated by controlling and manipulating the major source of supply. It would defeat "the great money power of England and Germany," and the United States would "soon become the banker of the world, and . . . draw interest from all the nations of the world."[56] No metropolitan expansionist ever devised a more imperial project for controlling the world marketplace.

The vigorous agitation of the subtreasury proposal, which served to strengthen the movement for silver as well as the general spirit of assertive nationalism, was a major facet of the booming militancy of the agriculturalists.[57] "Motions and countermotions were as thick as falling leaves," the *Country Gentleman* reported of one Ohio farm convention, and the description applied to the entire movement. Yet several themes became predominant. Underlying all of them was the feeling best expressed by the *Rural New Yorker*. "The farmer, East as well as West, has become aware that there is a screw loose somewhere in his trade relations." "The great West has thus far acted as a safety valve; but it is nearly closed, and it is very evident that something must happen ere long."[58]

Farmers from Delaware to California, and from Florida to Minnesota, were bone weary and raw-nerve angry about having "the rural geese plucked so early and often." Convinced they were growing relatively—if not indeed absolutely—"poorer day by day," they were through waiting for beneficence from the metropolis. "Brother farmers, we have been the tail end of God's creation long enough."[59] The recommended solutions included everything from "100 good farmers upon the floor of Congress" (and "trade a few senators for some solid old farmers") to government control of communications to insure a free and open marketplace.

But all the proposals involved the overproduction thesis and the related demand for overseas market expansion. The farmers of Minnehaha County in Minnesota stated that basic article of faith as well as any farm group. "The prosperity of the nation depends upon the prosperity of the agricultural people, and, further, the prosperity of the farmers depends upon their ability to sell their surplus to foreign nation. . . . Therefore we demand that your honorable bodies remove as many as possible of the barriers of commerce."[60] "This feeling of the desirability of extending our border," admitted the editors of *Country Gentleman*, referring to economic frontiers, "intensified by the accelerating and bewildering rapidity with which that extension has gone on, grows stronger and stronger."[61]

The principal opponent was defined as the American metropolis allied with its counterpart in Britain. It was time for a new Declaration of Independence against "the dictation of British lords" and "Wall Street bullionists."[62] "We feed the nation, we clothe it, and furnish about nine-tenths of the value of all articles exported from our ports," cried one letter writer. "And in return are allowed the privilege of sending millionaires to Congress to expend our money." The farmer, added an editor, created a wealthy metropolis that in return gives "the masses a stone instead of bread."[63] The attack on railroads and other "such combinations as destroy legitimate competition" was so embittered because those corporations supplied some of the "indispensable necessities of our business and welfare."[64] Preaching the gospel according to Adam Smith, as it so often did, the *National Economist* explained that the railroads were simply "taking from the country and giving to the city." That, explained Alliance president Polk, was why the farmers demanded "the most rigid, honest, and just . . . control and supervision of the means of public communication and transportation"—or, failing that, "government ownership."[65]

Such was "not communism," but simply a desperate effort to preserve "individual enterprise" from a crisis that was "a menace to our national life."[66] The editors of the militant *Farmers Advocate*, who carried on a running battle with Peffer's *Kansas Farmer*, made the point as explicit as humanly possible. "Every wise alliance man will be ready to assure the business man of the town and villages that our movement is not hostile to his interest," they announced in 1890. "It is well to have it understood from the first, that ours is not a class movement, but rather a reform movement."[67]

That was an accurate assessment of the vast majority of agricultural businessmen. It held true at the end of the century as well as when it was made, and remained valid through the first two-thirds of the twentieth century. The point is central to any understanding of the development of the farm protest movement between 1889 and 1900. A small group of agriculturalists did develop an understanding and acceptance of some kind of socialist alternative to marketplace capitalism. Yet most of those men failed to carry their evolution of that concept beyond the point of shifting the proposal for nationalizing the communications, transportation, and monetary systems from the idiom of Smithian capitalism to the idiom of nonrevolutionary socialism. That was not as great a change as many metropolitan leaders initially feared, nor as great a change as many agriculturalists thought.

At the outset, however, the intensity and determination of the reformers gave them tremendous impact and momentum. Despite Blaine's sensitivity, Secretary of Agriculture Rusk probably played the crucial role in alerting the Administration to the *urgency* of the crisis. President Harrison (and others) indicated such was the case, and the record supports that analysis.[68] While Harrison, Secretary of the Treasury Windom, and Secretary of the Navy Benjamin J. Tracy all stressed market expansion in their annual messages of December 1889, for example, none sounded the crisis alarm. And Blaine was still primarily involved in the Pan-American conference. But Rusk knew the agricultural situation at first hand, and his friend James Harvey Sanders, editor of the *Breeder's Gazette*, warned him from the outset about the "blasts" he was receiving "from all over the country." Rusk went immediately to the Cabinet with the unhappy news.[69] He also alerted Whitelaw Reid, Minister to France.[70]

Between speeches to various farm groups, Rusk asked Blaine to take "especial pains" to use the consular service to help the farmers find markets.[71] He likewise pleaded "strongly" for congressional help, an effort that had an important part in forcing the meat inspection bill introduced by Senator Edmunds to the floor for consideration on February 11, 1890.[72] That was not enough to satisfy the livestock men, however, for they had watched many a piece of proposed legislation wither and die in the heat of metropolitan opposition, or freeze to death in the winter of its indifference. Sanders privately warned Rusk that even Blaine was being attacked for treating agriculture in a "cavalier manner." Then, the next day, he publicly criticized the Administration for a lack of action that was "little short of suicidal." The issue was one of *"will"*—not power or possibility.[73]

Rusk shortly told Blaine that it was "extremely important that we should increase our exports of live animals and meat products."[74] Blaine responded with an order for action that used Rusk's analysis—and much of his language.[75] The discussions with Rusk (and probably Reid) crystallized Blaine's strategy for using reciprocity to solve the nation's economic problem—and the political crisis facing the Republican party. Rusk spoke publicly of his pressure on Blaine, Reid came home from Paris, and Senators Plumb and Allison jammed the meat inspection bill through the Senate.[76]

Then Blaine made an emotional personal plea to the McKinley wing of the party to write the reciprocity strategy into the tariff bill before the House sent the measure to the Senate.[77] The effort failed. The subsequent talks among Secretaries Rusk and Blaine, Senators Plumb and Allison, and Minister Reid and President Harrison were unfortunately unrecorded. But the essence of the story can be reconstructed. The force exerted by the agricultural businessmen, and the Democratic attempt led by Senator Voorhees of Indiana and Representative Mills of Texas to take leadership of the movement, forced the Harrison group to use increasingly powerful pressure on the reluctant Republican metropolitans. "The farmers," the Chicago *Tribune* remarked with characteristic bluntness, "have the call in this Congress."[78]

A significant number of farm groups, including some Grange and Alliance chapters, favored the export bounty plan advocated by Lubin.[79] Others stressed reciprocity treaties, "a policy of spirited retaliation," or a combination of the two approaches. But, whatever the proposal, the theme was to "do everything possible."[80] As Senator Voorhees and other Democrats perceived, there was "a deep, strong current of discontent, anxiety, and alarm . . . and that current is growing swifter, stronger, and more threatening every hour. The spirit of unrest, irritation, and reproach is abroad amongst the tillers of the soil to an extent never before known in American history." Then he turned to the attack. "Where is that home market? . . . The farmer is hunting for it. . . . Home market! What lies have been told in its name!"[81]

Republicans had been fearfully anticipating that assault for two months, their letterboxes overflowing with "ominous warnings."[82] "Times are very hard," they were informed, and the farmers "read and think for themselves." The combination, many agriculturalists promised, would produce results that would "astonish" the Republicans if drastic action was not taken immediately.[83] Senator Plumb understood that mortal danger and frightened Reid with his knowledge. "What we want is trade," Plumb cried in January 1889, and when it was not forthcoming he told Reid that the "west and northwest . . . were in open revolt." Already aware that Harrison was "less cheerful" than a bit earlier, Reid reported that the President "confirmed Plumb's discouraging statements about the condition of the west."[84]

The only possibility of holding the agricultural businessmen, and thereby maintaining metropolitan control of the political economy, was in defeating the metropolitans who were either too narrow or too uncomprehending to accept the policies that were necessary. The President and others knew that the effort would produce what one Western Republican accurately called a "political explosion" within the party, but they proceeded with the assault.[85] Aided by such old friends and expansionist allies as Representative Hitt of Illinois, Blaine attacked McKinley on April 10, 1890. The Secretary told him bluntly that the tariff bill was "injudicious from beginning to end," and that it would "protect the Republican party into speedy retirement."[86] Reid and Rusk joined the battle with public and private salvos.[87] Clearly on the defensive, McKinley parried for time. Complaining that "we have been beaten in every instance" that reciprocity was attempted, he asserted that the drawback provision in his tariff bill did enable exporters "to go out and capture the markets of the world."[88]

McKinley was understandably uncertain about how the metropolitan powers of the party would divide on the issue, and he was hedging until that crucial information could be obtained. Mills immediately moved in to destroy a divided opponent by stressing overseas market expansion. That was "the real question," and the farmers now understood that the Democrats would "open the way to the foreign market." "I want you to pass your bill," he taunted McKinley, "and go with it out West." "You will hear a storm that will be worse than a Nebraska cyclone blowing around your heads."[89] And that was precisely what the Harrison group feared when the House passed McKinley's bill on May 21 without a reciprocity clause.

They recovered some ground, however, when the Congress finally passed the Sherman Anti-Trust Law six weeks later. The crucial factor was not the bill itself, or even the generally favorable response among agriculturalists. The vital point was the indication that the metropolitan conservatives were willing to compromise. For while it carried Sherman's name (he had first introduced it in 1888), the legislation was largely written by corporation lawyers and other metropolitan leaders in prolonged collaboration with the Senate Finance Committee. Its value as a deterrent to the concentration and consolidation of metropolitan economic power was highly questionable from the outset. But it was significant in the more general context because it represented a metropolitan willingness to enact the fundamental axiom of the political economy of the agricultural majority into federal law. As a measure "to protect trade and commerce against unlawful restraints and monopolies," the legislation gave official sanction to the traditional demand of the farm businessmen for "a fair field and no favor."

Harrison and his allies faced more difficulty in persuading their metropolitan associates to accept a new silver law. Yet that was essential. Led by Senator Stewart and Teller, the silverites knew the swelling demand for remonetization gave them the power to create chaos if the gold men refused to compromise. "The excitement of the West is not temporary," Stewart noted simply. "The people will have relief or know the reason why." He was therefore adamant. "There will be no tariff legislation this session unless a silver bill is passed."[90] Stewart's position was further strengthened by the continuing agitation for stronger alien land legislation. The failure of the Congress to toughen the law of 1887 led many states to pass their own legislation, and the movement was increasingly tied to the silver issues.[91] Representative Edward Payson Allen of Michigan explained the argument very neatly when presenting a Grange petition. The early remonetization of silver "would have fenced out foreign capital and given our own people the benefit of the interest and dividends."[92]

The expansionist nationalism of the silver campaign was assertively displayed during the National Silver Convention of November 1889 in St. Louis. Gold was variously described as the lever of British supremacy and the cause of American stagnation. "We ought to have this trade," shouted Bland, and called for the election of politicians with the "courage of men—statesmen—not the timidity of mice." "The United States can play a lone hand," agreed Edward D. Stark of Ohio, "and ask no odds of any nation on the globe. . . . Some of us here will see this country assume the commercial and monetary hegemony of the world."[93] That imperial outlook was rapidly becoming the primary theme of the silver campaign. The domestic benefits of remonetization were not discounted or ignored, but the movement was arguing that no such gains could be harvested until the Wall Street-London axis was defeated.

That analysis reinforced the already powerful thrust for markets. "Rally to the FLAG of American freemen," came the rebel yell from Arkansas. "Go to work at once, before the British conspirators . . . force you into cruel serfdom." "Let us abandon English and Germans as our financial school-masters," another told Allison. "New York will become the exchange capital for the world," summarized Bland, as he paraphrased John Quincy Adams' old cry to cease being a cockboat in the wake of the British man-of-war. Stop being "simply tail to the London kite."[94]

Harrison and Blaine agreed with that sentiment, and also understood the theoretical argument for using silver to increase the money supply and ease the troubles of the economy. And, confronted with Stewart's ultimatum, they mustered enough metropolitan support to pass the Sherman Silver Purchase Act of July 14, 1890, which required the government to buy 4.5 million ounces of silver each month and pay for it with Treasury notes redeemable in silver as well as gold. Many businessmen, moreover, were "urgent" and "most anxious" to win some kind of international agreement on bimetallism. "Everything in reason will be done," Harrison promised, "and I hope an easier money market will be the result both for business and political considerations."[95] The resulting conference held in Belgium during 1892 did not remonetize silver, but it did serve to document the Administration's deep concern to use silver in expanding trade "with China, Japan, and Central and South America, and at the same time with the nations of Europe."[96] That objective was sought more immediately in a resumption of the fight with McKinley over adding a reciprocity clause to the tariff bill.

McKinley may well have been impressed (and softened) by the metropolitan action on the antitrust and silver issues even before the Harrison-Blaine group and the farmers mounted an offensive to persuade him that it was time to move on market expansion. He undoubtedly learned from men like Allison and Sherman that many "an old wheelhouse" was ready to leave the party unless "the rotten McKinley bill"—

that "hellish legislation"—was changed.[97] But Harrison and Blaine, along with Rusk, Reid, Foster, and Hitt, delivered the message personally and forcefully.[98] Reid became so concerned, indeed, that he pushed his sarcasm to the edge of insult. "Please consider these points," he wrote McKinley, "to see whether the gain to our farmers from the exclusion of Canadian pork is going to warrant shutting the French market against American pork packers."[99]

The metropolitans who influenced McKinley came under similar siege. As close observers of such infighting, the editors of *Bradstreet's* concluded that Blaine's conversion of Senator Edmunds was the move that opened the way to victory. Blaine not only unleashed his own anger, as when he smashed his hat during a discussion with senators, but used the agricultural and metropolitan forces that were available.[100] "What a market," cried one agricultural editor in appreciation of his efforts; a Mississippi River boatman agreed that the Secretary had "proved himself a statesman"; and a Southern leader ruefully admitted that Blaine "never staggered at or struck upon anything so timely."[101] Senator Cushman Kellogg Davis of Minnesota explained the agricultural support in one pithy sentence: "It is the conviction of the American people that we should seek other opportunities than the home market."[102]

Blaine's awareness of the need for metropolitan support prompted him to balance his appeal to the West with assurances to the manufacturers. His own vigorous efforts were reinforced by those of Senators Hale, Frye, and Aldrich, and Representative Hewitt.[103] The uneasiness manifested by many bankers and other financial leaders also contributed to the Secretary's success, as did strong backing from meat and flour processors and cotton textile men (processors and manufacturers who were especially interested in the Cuban and Brazilian markets).[104]

The final version of the tariff bill (which took effect in October 1890) contained a reciprocity section delegating power to the President to use carrot-and-stick diplomacy to expand American markets. He could authorize free entry for the sugar from those countries that granted American exports similar privileges. That meant the Republicans could offer the farmer cheap sugar and export markets in countering Cleveland's promise of free raw materials and markets to metropolitan manufacturers. It represented a classic capitalist effort to resolve internal political and economic problems through overseas market expansion, and the Harrison Administration tried very hard to use it to open European markets for meat products before the congressional elections in November.

That maneuver had been mentioned by Reid as early as June 1890, and Rusk may have pushed the strategy a bit earlier.[105] Reid seems to have carried the fight, however, explaining bluntly that "the stake is so big, . . . besides the political advantage for the administration

just now."[106] His efforts, reinforced by the interest of farm businessmen in using reciprocity as a weapon of retaliation, won active aid
from Blaine.[107] Rusk supplied additional persuasion, and the battle
was carried directly to McKinley in the last stages of the fight over
the tariff.[108] The argument may have helped win the battle for reciprocity per se, but that victory came too late to help the Harrison-
Blaine group in the elections of 1890.

Nothing could have saved the Republicans in November 1890. The
party was divided, the Harrison Administration had not delivered
enough tangible rewards to satisfy the silverites or other market expansionists, and the agricultural protest movement had reached a
crescendo. The disgruntled Republican farmers who joined the Democrats or the new Populist parties were the primary factor in the defeat.
The first People's party was organized by Texans in June, and others
were created in Nebraska, Colorado, South Dakota, North Dakota,
and Minnesota in time for the election. One Republican noted early
that "the Alliance is making considerable progress," adding a resigned
but revealing comment about the defectors: "It is the old gang and
I can expect nothing from them."[109]

The Republicans did the best they could by papering over the Blaine-
McKinley fight, and by stressing the future benefits of the reciprocity legislation.[110] Others accurately realized that "the benefits from
the reciprocal trade" strategy would not appear soon enough to help.[111]
They argued that the combination of a very dry summer in much of
the West and high mortgages was simply too much to overcome.[112]
And some felt that the Harrison-Blaine effort to help the black man
and rebuild Republican strength in the South through a strong election control bill would hurt the party with Western farmers.

One observer reported that Blaine himself argued that the party
should change its strategy and cultivate the Southern Alliance.[113] And
it seems very unlikely that Western farmers waxed enthusiastic about
risking their coalition with Southern white agriculturalists in order
to pass a law that they were inclined to resent as a further extension
of metropolitan power and authority. Though strongly backed by
Harrison and Blaine, the election control bill had barely squeaked
through the House in July 1890 (by six votes), and it had been shelved
in the Senate.[114] Whatever its role in the election, the measure was
killed by the Democratic victory and the momentum of the farm
protest movement. For while they increased their margin in the
Senate (from 2 to 8), the Republicans were swamped in the House
(235 to 88).

"Our election disaster," Harrison wryly commented, "is too large
a topic for a Sunday evening letter. . . . If the Alliance can pull one-
half of our Republican voters in such states as Kansas and Nebraska,
our future is not cheerful." Rusk bluntly called it a "political blizzard"—
"a disaster." And another, admitting the party was "very badly beaten,"

feared that "one more such . . . may prove a very great defeat"—the end of the party.[115] His point was clear, for in the crucial states of Indiana, Illinois, Iowa, Kansas, Nebraska, and Minnesota, the Republicans suffered an exact reversal. They had elected forty-four representatives from those states in 1888, but in 1890 the Democrats and Populists carried that many districts—and the Republicans in 1890 claimed three less (fifteen) than the Democrats had in 1888.

"We must pass some legislation which will be distinctly in the interest of the farmers in the central and western States," ran one of many similar warnings from party leaders. "You have no idea of the strength of this feeling."[116] Though he was undoubtedly surprised by the extent of the defeat, Harrison did have a clear sense of the situation. And, despite estimates from some advisers that Blaine's attack on McKinley had lost many votes, the President immediately and unequivocally reasserted his commitment to the strategy of overseas market expansion and to reciprocity treaties and related measures as the proper tactics.

Representative government, he noted pointedly, "makes it imperative that we shall save our working people from the agitations and distresses which scant work and wages that have no margin for comfort always beget." That lesson had been driven home to "a very unusual degree by agitation and organization among farmers looking to an increase in the profits of their business." Overseas markets, "so directly helpful to the farmer," would therefore be "further and very largely increased." "From the time of my induction into office," he reminded the nation, "the duty of using every power and influence given by law . . . for the development of larger markets for our products, especially our farm products, has been kept constantly in mind." "No effort has been or will be spared to promote that end," he continued, and pointedly reminded France that good relations with the United States depended upon "substantial progress" in reopening the market for American meat surpluses. Cuba was of "peculiar importance" because of "the extent and development of our trade." And the nation was called upon with "added urgency" to improve all transportation routes and services, and to create an inter-American bank to facilitate market expansion in the Western Hemisphere.[117]

The agricultural uprising persuaded more metropolitan leaders to accept Harrison's analysis and program.[118] Leonidas Polk of the Southern Alliance was essentially correct in discerning a strong movement toward imperialism within the metropolis. The irony was that the members of the Ocala meeting to which he made that analysis resolved in favor of measures that increased the expansionist momentum. That was the effect of the demands for free silver, the subtreasury storage system, and transportation reforms, just as it was of the call for further action against alien landownership.[119] The overriding concern of the agricultural businessmen, as the Minnesota Alliance pointed out, was "free and open markets." "The most important question," Governor Boies of Iowa added, "is how to extend the markets." For on that basis, as Populist Tom Watson explained, the farmers were confident that "the American producer, whether on the farm or in the shop, can knock the hind sights off the producer anywhere else on the face of the earth (Applause)."[120]

Harrison's response to the election (and the Ocala Convention) was a remarkable cross-country tour organized and executed as a campaign for overseas market expansion. He took his Postmaster General for political chores and Rusk as the hard-sell spokesman for exports. The lecture tour, which began in earnest at Jonesboro, Tennessee, on April 14, 1891, and concluded a month later in Omaha, Nebraska, was a continental variation on one theme: "the necessity of larger markets."[121]

April 14, Jonesboro, Tennessee: "We have the power, if we will, to put our flag again on the sea and to share in the world's commerce."

April 16, Anniston, Alabama: "I am sure you will unite with me in those efforts we ought to make . . . to reach out to other markets and enter into competition with the world for them (Cheers)."

April 17, Memphis, Tennessee: "[There is] a great trade in South America that we shall soon possess."

April 18, Galveston, Texas: "We are great enough and rich enough to reach forward to grander conceptions than have entered the minds of some of our statesmen in the past. If you are content, I am not. . . . (Great and prolonged cheering)."

April 21, Del Rio, Texas: "I want to say, from the time of my introduction into office until this hour, I have had before me constantly the need of the American farmer for a larger market for his products (Cries of 'Good, good,' and cheers)."

May 8, Seattle, Washington: "I am thoroughly discontented with the present condition of things. We may differ as to methods but I believe that the great patriotic heart of our people is stirred, and that they are bent upon recovering that share of the world's commerce which we once happily enjoyed."

May 13, Omaha, Nebraska: "We have a surplus production in these great valleys for which we must seek foreign markets. . . . It has been a source of constant thought and zealous effort on the part of the administration at Washington to secure larger foreign markets for our farm products."

The thought and the effort continued unabated for the duration of Harrison's Administration. It was "the era of the battle for a market," the President remarked a few months later, and he was determined that the United States would emerge victorious.[122] One of his most important gains came in winning increased support from within the metropolis. That steady shift to expansion was caused by several factors. McKinley, for example, shrewdly recognized the response Harrison had evoked on his continental tour and prepared to emphasize exports.[123] Others, like Senator William Eaton Chandler, called more bluntly for a foreign policy that would "have the . . . effect of diverting attention from stagnant political discussions."[124]

Charles S. Smith, president of the New York Chamber of Commerce, argued that a serious panic had been averted by the exports supplied by the farm and the cotton textile industry. Another said flatly that market expansion provided the only program capable of keeping "our factories running and our people employed in time of a reduced home demand, and to lessen costs through increased production." And Jacob Schiff warned that it would be very dangerous, because of the need to finance agricultural exports, to repeal the silver purchase act. "We are antagonizing old and settled channels of trade," added *Iron Age*, asking for a powerful navy, "and are undoubtedly cultivating antagonisms which may bear bitter fruits someday."[125] Andrew Carnegie, who was one of the first to recognize the necessity of an export market to maintain production during slack times, bluntly told the British that the epoch of their supremacy was drawing to a close. The Harrison-Blaine reciprocity strategy insured that outcome, and Carnegie offered the old empire a junior partnership in the new imperium.[126] He pointed brazenly to Cuba as the example that best proved his point, and many other metropolitans came to share his enthusiasm for that market.

Harrison and Blaine moved very rapidly to penetrate the Cuban and Brazilian markets once the reciprocity legislation was passed, and their success evoked great interest and considerable economic involvement.[127] The "magic wand of reciprocity," cried the Boston *Journal*, has defeated "British intrigue"; and Senator Hale warned the Democrats that they dared not repeal reciprocity.[128] Stuyvesant Fish of the Illinois Central was particularly pleased with the prospects — and the reality — of increased freight shipments south to New Orleans. His only complaint about the reciprocity treaties was that "they do not go far enough."[129]

Hill of the Great Northern was busy, meanwhile, pushing his grandiose plan to embrace the markets of Asia with exports of cotton to Japan, Southern cotton textiles to China, and Western meat, flour, and grain to the entire region. The first agent he sent to scout the prospects arrived in Japan in August 1892, and the resulting seventy-two-page report filed in May 1893 was widely distributed in St. Paul. It rapidly attracted interest and support throughout the country, and made it clear that Hill originated the idea that Edward H. Harriman tried to act on after 1900. Their famous struggle for control of the en-

tire network of Northwestern railroads (and a connecting link to the
East Coast) grew out of Hill's vision of an American world marketplace.

A significant testament to the strength of such metropolitan expansionism came from George Douglas Perkins, president of the Chicago,
Burlington and Quincy Railroad. Perkins was an articulate Smithian
who opposed government intervention in the marketplace. "The 'hig-
gling of the markets,' as Adam Smith puts it, will bring about very
much better results as to prices than the arbitrary exercise of the powers of government." But Perkins almost totally failed to comprehend
the marketplace outlook of the farm businessmen who supplied him
with freight. "If the lunatics like Peffer, Bellamy & Company could
have their way we should simply lapse into barbarism." He was shrewd
enough to realize, however, that the broad support for such action
made it "not wise" to "make any show of resistance."[130]

The developments that upset Perkins served as a spur to Harrison,
Rusk, and other Administration leaders. "The wires are hot," summarized the *Rural New Yorker*, "with accounts of distress and discontent among the farmers." The Kansas City *Times* understood one cause
of the trouble and expressed it bluntly. The metropolitan "East has
a tendency to intolerance and arrogance of which it is but partly conscious. Its attitude toward the West is exactly the attitude of Western
Europe towards this country."[131] Underneath that factor was the bedrock economic difficulty so clearly described by Benjamin H. Clover
in a letter to the editors of the *National Economist*. "At the age of 52
years, after a long life of toil, economy and self-denial, I find myself
and family virtually paupers. . . . What once seemed a neat little
fortune and a house of refuge for our declining years . . . has been
rendered valueless."[132]

"The land in the West," cried another in 1892, "is all gone." "The
West has served as a great safety valve to the nation. But . . . there is
no more West to go to. What in God's name is to become of us?"[133]
That analysis had become so common that Representative Walter
Gresham of Texas made it the theme of a major speech to Southern
and Western farmers a year earlier. "Where shall we go? We must
go abroad. . . . We must open up our harbors, build up our navy and
merchant marine . . . and go upon the high seas. When we do this the
prediction of Napoleon . . . will be fulfilled . . . when he said 'I have
now put into the power of the United States to humble Great Britain
on the high seas.'"[134] The frontier thesis was widely agitated by C.
Wood Davis, a Western commercial leader and member of the National
Board of Trade who wrote widely on the basic causes of the agricultural crisis. The manufacturer would have to join the farmer, he explained, in the "search for distant markets" and stand shoulder to

shoulder in the "sharp competition with Europe for the trade of other countries." "Our rulers must in the absence of the safety-valve heretofore existing in the public domain find means of opening distant markets."[135] Davis also discussed the analysis with politicians like Senator Plumb, who passed it on to Rusk.[136]

Although Democratic spokesmen continued to press for a low tariff as the best method of expanding the marketplace, the Administration's reciprocity program began to generate increasing support.[137] Populists and other market expansionists like the Chicago Board of Trade made a more effective point by complaining that reciprocity had neither reopened nor enlarged the vast European markets.[138] But Rusk and others labored very hard, and with growing effectiveness, to counter that criticism. The Secretary thought "the duty of the hour" was to inaugurate a long-range program of market expansion that would meet the legitimate needs of the farm businessmen, and even viewed foreign markets as "one of my hobbies."[139]

Rusk also extended government aid to Charles J. Murphy, who had been struggling since 1887 to create a European market for surplus corn. Weary of being "treated like a long-haired crank with a flying machine or the recipe of the elixir of life," Murphy finally persuaded the New York Produce Exchange to subsidize his performances in which he cooked and served corn dishes at fairs and exhibitions. He was happy to extend the fruits of American freedom, moreover, and argued that his efforts rendered "a philanthropic service worthy of our best endeavors," as well as providing "a sane, practical, and speedy benefit to the farming interests."[140]

Secretary Rusk approved that integrated approach, and also shared Murphy's desire to penetrate the markets of "China, Japan, and British India."[141] Their outlook led directly to a major effort to encourage freedom in Russia while opening a new market there by providing aid for the victims of the famine that became serious in 1891. The Russian relief movement was initiated, however, by Benjamin F. Tillinghast, an editor of the Davenport, Iowa, *Democrat* who had long been concerned with market expansion for farm businessmen.[142] The plan provided a classic preview of how Americans would combine philanthropy, market expansion, and ideological assertiveness during the 1890s and the twentieth century.

At the outset, for example, Tillinghast met resistance from those who opposed giving aid to governments that did not qualify as free by American standards. That attitude was reinforced, in all probability, by the slap at Tsarist persecution of Jews by President Harrison and others. But Tillinghast and Governor Boies overcame such resistance with help from Rusk and the flour millers of Minnesota, who had begun to collect food at the beginning of December.[143] Harrison joined the effort with the suggestion that the government supply free ocean transportation as a mixed-economy supplement to the aid given by Hill and other railroad men.[144]

The Democrats blocked that proposal in the House, but they could not stop Rusk from sending Murphy to Russia to exploit the opportunity.[145] And the effort in Iowa and Minnesota, together with the work of other groups throughout the country, did deliver a significant amount of food to the Russians. The humanitarian impulse was of course a major factor in the enterprise. But so, also, was the concern with a marketplace benefit. "Uncle Sam," summarized the Washington *Star*, "will later on reap an advantage by securing through the introduction of this cereal a new market for his most important crop." Secretary Rusk, according to the report, remarked that the action was like "throwing bread upon the waters with a string tied to it."[146]

Even if garbled or invented, the comment was typical of Rusk's blunt, single-minded concern with market expansion. Other Administration leaders periodically complained that his penchant for the hard line would undo all the long labors to reopen the German and French markets for American meat products.[147] That objective was achieved, however, by using the reciprocity power and the meat inspection system created in 1890-1891, and the French offered their first serious compromise on December 4. Harrison candidly admitted that he was "very anxious to get a market" because he knew he was working against time—as well as vigorous and effective opponents.[148]

That urgency, intensified by the May 1891 convention in Cincinnati that brought Populists and other reformers together to discuss a third-party movement, very probably contributed a good bit to Harrison's angry militancy in handling the crisis with Chile, and to Blaine's maneuvers to acquire Hawaii.[149] The President first became involved in the Chilean revolution that erupted in January 1891 when he detained, as a precautionary measure, a rebel ship loaded with war supplies. Then in May the crew broke free and raced southward from California. Harrison ordered hot pursuit and the Navy finally captured the ship in Chile. The tension increased throughout the summer and erupted on October 16, 1891, in a saloon brawl between American sailors and Chilean hecklers. The President, who was then exploring the possibility of acquiring a naval base in Peru in order to strengthen the American position in the Pacific, was clearly ready to go to war.[150]

The general outburst of nationalistic assertiveness, reinforced by similar support from Republican businessmen, prompted the President to overrule Blaine's argument for a more subtle application of power.[151] Harrison's ultimatum (originally formulated on December 9, 1891) was sent on January 21, 1892, and he waited only four days before advising the Congress that it was free to declare war. By then, however, Chile had apologized, and some foes of the Administration promptly attacked Harrison for unwarranted militancy. The more lasting result was nationalistic satisfaction and an increase in the existing feeling that America was powerful enough to secure its objectives without war.

During the height of the Chilean crisis, moreover, Harrison was also seeking a way to consolidate American power in Hawaii. The native resistance to the existing informal American predominance in the islands was increased by the tariff act of 1890 which ended Hawaii's special position in the American sugar market. Queen Liliuokalani had made it clear when she took power in January 1891 that she intended to reassert islander control, and she steadily increased her authority and support. But the tariff change also upset American sugar kings, who became ever more convinced that a coup offered the only way to deal with both problems.

Blaine alerted Harrison on August 9, 1891, that "Hawaii may come up at any unexpected hour." "I hope," he added, "we shall be prepared to decide it in the affirmative." The President was not sure how to handle the situation despite his fear that American power was "in jeopardy." He was determined, however, to meet the "very apparent and very pressing" "necessity of maintaining and increasing our hold and influence."[152] By the spring of 1892, the Administration was preparing the way for annexation without much concern for secrecy. "More or less talk," *Bradstreet's* reported, "has been had lately about a project for the annexation of Hawaii," adding that the Chairman of the House Committee on Foreign Affairs "has been sounding leading members."[153]

The ultimate confrontation over that issue made it clear that the Blaine-Harrison wing of the party had been correct in their estimate that market expansion offered the best strategy for checking the agricultural unrest and maintaining metropolitan control of the country. For the determination to maintain American authority in Hawaii not only moved formerly reluctant metropolitan leaders like McKinley further along toward imperialism, but it brought the Populists into a foreign policy coalition with Republicans like Henry Cabot Lodge. That outcome had been foreshadowed in the long campaigns for overseas markets and silver, and the convergence began to become apparent through the winter of 1891-1892, as even the *National Economist* admitted that reciprocity had won a major victory for American farmers.[154]

The Populists and other agricultural businessmen continued to stress the importance of silver and the subtreasury program for enlarging and controlling foreign markets, but the Harrison Administration eased its way through those issues with a combination of finesse, hard facts, and good fortune.[155] An increasing number of metropolitan leaders, for example, politicians like Henry Cabot Lodge as well as businessmen, were manifesting a more receptive attitude toward some accommodation on silver. That somewhat blunted the impact of the angry cry that "Lombard Street and Wall Street were twin brothers," at least for the moment, particularly as Harrison was able to avoid turning to Wall Street for funds to maintain the Treasury gold reserve.[156]

The President encountered less trouble from the subtreasury proposal because the agriculturalists were divided over its merits, and because its advocates failed to develop a specific plan that was persuasive enough to dramatize the issue and win general support.[157] The split became apparent in the inability to agree on one carefully drafted bill to place before the Congress. The weaknesses were so serious that the legislation was tabled, and the proponents never generated enough popular indignation to revive the proposal.[158] The market expansion of the farm businessmen was more effectively mustered during the 1890-1892 debates on trade and the Navy.

Harrison's determination to strengthen the fleet was always tied to economic expansion, and Secretary of the Navy Tracy summarized the approach in 1889 in stating that the Navy involved "a practical business question of insuring our property and our trade."[159] Metropolitan support for naval construction was extended by the writings of Captain Alfred Thayer Mahan, who had accurately sensed as early as 1889-1890 that the end of the continental frontier would produce a significant "change in the thoughts and policy of Americans as to their relations with the world outside." He viewed Blaine's triumph in the bitter battle for reciprocity as a turning point in the process of moving outward "to seek the welfare of the country."[160] Mahan's direct influence, which reinforced that of other imperialist intellectuals like Brooks Adams, touched rising metropolitan politicians like Theodore Roosevelt and Lodge, as well as established leaders like Tracy (who counseled regularly with Mahan).

But Mahan also affected spokesmen of the agricultural protest movement like Senator James Henderson Kyle of South Dakota, a civil engineer who shifted to the Congregational ministry before entering politics. The tie between Mahan and Kyle was highly indicative of the way that many metropolitan leaders were coming to emphasize the kind of reformist expansionism that the agricultural businessmen had stressed for a generation. For Mahan's talk about the opportunity and duty to extend Western and Christian values through the expansion of American economic power was very similar to the argument of the farmers that expanding the free marketplace extended the area of freedom.

That spirit was apparent in Kyle's arguments for the unilateral remonetization of silver, which typified the way that markets and freedom were wholly integrated by the Populists. "Here is the syllogism," explained Kyle:[161]

1.   Our prices for cotton and wheat are regulated by the European market. . . .

2.   East India and the United States are competitors for that market. . . .

3.   Considering quality . . . the market is ours. . . .

4.   If Asiatic bills of exchange, however, fall below par, the East Indian has the advantage of us. . . .

5.   Demonetization . . . has furnished cheap silver bullion and hence lowered Asiatic exchange. . . .

6.   Free coinage of silver would bring it to a par with gold, and also raise Asiatic exchange to par. . . .

7.   Therefore, free coinage . . . restores to our farmers the European market. . . .

"Now comes the time," added a Western Alliance leader, in an idiom that became increasingly popular after 1890, "for a declaration of Independence." Time for America to "again establish an independent business, to be run independently of monarchical money."[162] Or as Nelson A. Dunning of the Alliance explained, "instead of being led by the older nations of Europe," the United States should "lead the South American States and Mexico up to the plane of civilization, financially and socially, that we occupy."[163] Given the triumph of the reformers, added a utopian novelist, America would be so strong that it "could snap her finger in the face of all nations without fear."[164]

Such market expansionism was beautifully formulated by Populist leader Polk: "The broad world is our market." The editors of the *National Economist*, who regularly read *Bradstreet's* and State Department Consular Reports to strengthen their arguments, constantly stressed that theme.[165] Populist Representative John Davis of Kansas made the point simply and forcefully: "We do not want a new policy. But to return to the old policy—the policy which was practiced from 1812 to 1860."[166] The accuracy of that analysis explains why the Populists quickly confronted themselves with the question of the Navy's role in marketplace expansion.

The farm criticism concerning the issues of technology and the enforcement of contracts was not only designed to produce a better navy, but did in most cases help produce a stronger fleet.[167] The vigorous agricultural support for trade expansion, including an isthmian canal and a merchant marine, was matched by a disinclination to protest naval appropriations.[168] Many Western spokesmen, like Senator Jonathan Prentiss Dolliver of Iowa and Representative Clinton Babbit of Wisconsin, joined Southerners like Senator Morgan and Representative Hilary Herbert, and metropolitans like Lodge, in providing active support for what the *Rural New Yorker* and the *North Pacific Rural Spirit* called the "good work" of Secretary Tracy and President Harrison.[169] When some conservatives like Herbert misunderstood the nature of agricultural criticism, moreover, Populists like Tom Watson promptly advised them they were "mistaken."[170]

The primary issue at the end of the Harrison Administration was whether or not the new Navy met sufficiently the needs of the political economy. One group of agriculturalists argued that it did: America was powerful enough to make any nation "slow to provoke or bring on a war," because they knew it "would end in disaster to themselves."[171] Representative William Jennings Bryan of Nebraska offered a clear statement of the views of that minority. "I believe in a sufficient navy," he explained, adding that "we have this now, either in existence or in construction. We do not need more."[172]

The momentum toward a larger navy that was inherent in market expansion was nicely revealed, however, in the assumptions and reasoning of Populist Representative Jeremiah Simpson of Kansas. In many respects, Simpson saw deeper than any other major leader of the agricultural protest movement into the dilemma of free marketplace expansion. As he moved ever closer to a final confrontation with the fateful choice between accepting the marketplace as it operated or embarking upon an imperial policy to make it operate as it should, Simpson progressively isolated himself from the imperial consensus that was uniting the metropolis and the country.

That process was particularly revealing because at the outset he offered a classic statement of the position of the more militant agricultural reformers. Like most Western Populists, Simpson was a Republican who left the party when in his view it "became the champion of special interests."[173] Unlike any of them, however, he had served as a brave and resourceful merchant seaman before settling in Indiana and then Kansas to provide his wife and daughter a more stable family life. His farming experience including raising cattle—and being wiped out during the terrible years at the end of the 1880s. He came to the Congress, in the estimate of the editors of the *Rural New Yorker*, as "a remarkable man with a strong personality and a good heart and head." And he quickly established himself there, as elsewhere, as "one of the best rough and tumble debaters" of the era.[174]

"Why, Mr. Chairman," he roared to the House in April 1892, "we are driven from the markets of the whole world." That defined the crisis, for "it so happens that we have a very large agricultural surplus. . . . The farmers must of necessity seek a foreign market." His solution was pure Adam Smith. "I am a free trader—absolute. . . . If left to take care of themselves men will trade with other men who will give them good bargains. . . . I want to trade where I can get rich instead of getting poor." He emphasized the need for market expansion by quoting the Governor of Illinois on the end of the frontier: "'We have some very serious problems to face. Our country is filled up. There is no west to go to. We are full, and we will have to acquire Canada, British America, and Mexico, or overflow.'"

Simpson was not calling for territorial conquest, but for "an enlightened policy or system which would open up friendly relations with foreign countries, which would give us a market for our surplus, [and] we would say to the Canadian people 'Come in under the American flag; join us under a common government, and let us be one people.'" Commercial expansion would lead to economic and political union. Free trade was the proper and effective policy, Simpson reiterated, and pointed to Great Britain's economic supremacy as proof of the logic and as the example to emulate. He accepted the need for a merchant marine, stressed the need for an equitable transportation system, and explained the agricultural emphasis on the money issue with typical clarity. "We believe that the money question is a part of the great question of trade, or so mixed up with it that you can not separate them."

At the outset, Simpson avowed so much confidence in a pure Smithian marketplace that he discounted the importance of force. "I do not believe we need a navy at all. If we attend to our own business, dealing fairly and justly with other nations, I do not believe we need any navy to defend us."[175] Some of that rhetoric was purposeful exaggeration to dramatize his central point, and much of the assurance was grounded in the assumption of overweening American power that was so deeply held by all agriculturalists. But he was also convinced that the existing Navy was large enough, and that an open field with no favor would produce the general welfare of the world under American leadership.

The example provided by Simpson made it clear that the Blaine-Harrison bet on the market expansionism of the agricultural majority was based on an astute reading of its outlook, and the program of reciprocity treaties proved effective in checking the strength of the low tariff Democrats and Populists before those groups developed an overpowering momentum. Thus Blaine and Harrison, with strong help from men like Plumb, Rusk, Reid, and an assist from McKinley, not only devised the strategy that preserved metropolitan (and Republican) control of the political economy, but the strategy itself committed the United States to a program of imperial expansion on a global scale. For that matter, it might well have enabled the Republicans to consolidate their advantage in the election of 1892 if Harrison and Blaine had been able to campaign as they had in 1888.

THIRTEEN

What a peculiar man you have to deal with in the President.
> E. B. Wall to Senator William F. Vilas, 1893

The most insidious and destructive foe to the farmer is the "professional" farmer who, as a "promoter" of granges and alliances, for political purposes, Farms the Farmer.
> Secretary of Agriculture J. Sterling Morton, 1893

You fail utterly in your appreciation of the calamitous circumstances confronting the American farmers today. . . . Your interests are chiefly those of a banker and corporation lawyer.
> Representative Joseph Sibley to Secretary Morton, 1894

I can say with emphasis that the most business-like occupation I ever engaged in, is farming.
> W. H. Warren of Georgia, 1894

The most striking fact about the whole thing is that the number of our people to-day wholly dependent on foreign markets is larger than the number of those employed in the protected industries.
> Populist Tom Watson, 1894

I believe, gentlemen, that the time has come for the United States as a great nation to take its place as one of the great commercial nations of the earth.
> Populist Jerry Simpson, 1894

The gold bugs . . . have "cornered" not only the silver, but the government.
> North Pacific Rural Spirit, 1893

A silver standard . . . would make us the trading center of all the silver-using countries of the world, and these countries contain far more than one-half of the world's population.
> Representative William Jennings Bryan, 1893

I take my pen in hand to let you know that we are starving to death.
> Mrs. Susan Orcutt to the Governor of Kansas, 1894

I am not a pessimist, but I think I see danger in the existing conditions in this country.
> Secretary of State Walter Q. Gresham, 1894

There will be no war as long as the money power controls the politics of this country. . . . When the pops get in, there will be a war if John Bull does not attend strictly to his own affairs.
> Southern Mercury, 1895

I would extend the Monroe Doctrine to . . . the assistance of every people seeking to establish the Republic.
> Henry Demarest Lloyd, 1895

Metropolitan
Democrats Lose Control of
Their Party to the
Agricultural Businessmen

G ROVER CLEVELAND secured the Democratic nomination for the Presidency in 1892 as the spokesman of the metropolitan wing of that party, and reentered the White House in 1893 without enlarging his outlook on the political economy. His primary concern with overseas markets was to enlarge metropolitan exports, a course he felt would provide a sufficient domestic market for agricultural surpluses. He did manifest a heightened awareness of the possibility of relieving his increasing political difficulties by appealing to the assertive, anti-European nationalism that had been generated by the farmers. But Cleveland was wholly unprepared to carry through on that approach in any way that would satisfy either the emotional or the economic demands of the agricultural movement. He thus lost control of the party to the silver-market expansionist wing led by the Populists and William Jennings Bryan.

Cleveland's traditional narrow metropolitan attitude created serious troubles for him even before the grave depression of the 1890s compounded his problems—and those of the nation. Western skepticism and opposition were immediately deepened by his appointment of J. Sterling Morton, Jr., as Secretary of Agriculture, and by his vacillation toward the Hawaiian revolution. The depression, an economic crisis at least as severe as the disaster of the 1870s, and psychologically and politically more disruptive because it occurred at the end of a generation of instability and suffering, severely increased those difficulties.

The President immediately revealed the narrowness of his outlook (and temperament) by responding to the depression with a willful campaign to repeal the Sherman Silver Purchase Act. That effort outraged the silverites, antagonized a significant number of metropolitans who favored other approaches to the silver issue, and fractured the Democratic party. None of his subsequent efforts to appease the agricultural businessmen reestablished the confidence and trust that are essential to effective leadership. Cleveland was discarded because he failed as a metropolitan leader of the expansionist movement, and because he never seriously tried to rally Americans in opposition to an imperial policy.

Such weaknesses were apparent during the campaign of 1892. He had no great desire or concern to continue in politics after 1888, and metropolitan Democrats undoubtedly used his self-consciousness about his "disinclination to enter again upon any kind of work" in persuading him to serve as a bulwark against a takeover by the agriculturalists.[1] They also appealed to his righteous concern to "eliminate" dangerous and "unworthy" men, and to prevent "the dangerous and reckless experiment of free, unlimited, and independent silver coinage."[2] Perhaps the most illuminating example of the attitude of the men around Cleveland is provided by Thomas Francis Bayard, who returned to duty in 1893 as the American Ambassador to Great Britain. If Cleveland had not been nominated, he commented, "our ship of state would have pounded herself to pieces in treacherous sands of false finance."[3] Such emotion (and purple rhetoric) from Bayard signaled a visceral involvement.

Similar intensity powered the Populists, who viewed Cleveland as a flunky of "the aristocracy of the East." "The Northern Democrats," thundered Tom Watson, "have ruled the South with a rod of iron for twenty years."[4] The first thing Cleveland had done after election in 1884, he added, "was to truckle to Wall Street."[5] The Republicans were no better, for the two parties "are but one," and between them there was "comparatively little difference."[6] Lincoln himself "could not get the Republican nomination to the State Legislature from the Springfield district," scoffed another, and that was why the good Republicans like Gresham were so uneasy and restless.[7]

A number of Republicans who had joined the Populists, and other reformers, tried to have the third party nominate Gresham. He was not that restless. Others wanted "a 'whoopin' ol' canvas" for Simpson, but that proved impossible because of his Canadian birth. The Omaha convention turned instead to a more traditional protest leader, James Baird Weaver of Iowa, who since the 1870s had served as a sometimes elected Greenback politician. He campaigned on a platform that one sympathetic student of Populism calls "the basic document" of the movement.[8] After invoking "the blessing of Almighty God," the delegates presented their version of the watershed analysis of American history that had become increasingly common after the mid-1880s depression. Due to the malfunctioning of the free marketplace, caused in part by willful abuses and in part by the results of unfair and ruthless competition, the political economy was polarizing into "two great classes—tramps and millionaires."

The demonetization of silver was both a cause and a symbol of that derangement of the natural order which threatened "terrible social convulsions, the destruction of civilization, or the establishment of an absolute despotism." The avowed objective, therefore, "identical with the purposes of the National Constitution," was to muster the majority for the eradication of the evils and the correction of the malfunctions. The answer was the restoration of a truly free marketplace economy, which in itself would contribute greatly to making men "intelligent, virtuous, and temperate." The economy rested on the production of vast agricultural surpluses, and hence all primary reforms involved "wise and reasonable legislation" to facilitate the profitable exchange of those surpluses for other necessary and desirable products.[9]

The first necessity was the free and unlimited coinage of silver. A graduated income tax was also required to help prevent the dysfunctional concentration of economic power. Government ownership of the railroads was needed because, as a structural part of the marketplace itself, the transportation system should be operated in the interest of all businessmen. The delegates then called for the end to alien ownership of land, and for other measures to distribute what remained of the continental frontier to the producing agricultural entrepreneurs. And, finally, they demanded various reforms to reestablish and guarantee the freedom of the political side of the political economy.

The Populist platform was indeed a basic document setting forth the crystallized consensus of the agricultural majority as it had developed over a period of three decades. Populists exulted over the "new Declaration of Independence." The nationalism of the movement produced much enthusiastic redundancy. "Its principles are American; its leaders are Americans; its platforms are American." And in keeping with their awareness that overseas markets were "thoroughly agitating" the farm businessmen, many Populists stressed "free commerce with all nations" as part of their effort to act "for our own interest and our own improvement."[10]

Some of their campaign rhetoric was exaggerated. And much of the language used by their opponents was provocative: "a slap in the face to the people of the Eastern states," "mad scheme of the howlers and cranks," "comic and grotesque," "monstrous travesty," "impudent and half-crazed," "a tale told by an idiot," "the witches' cauldron was a plaything to it."[11] But the more astute leaders within both major parties recognized the hard realism of the Populist analysis and acknowledged the need for an effective response. Representative Mills of Texas, for example, saw the possibility of pulling the Republicans who moved into the Populist ranks on through the party into the Democratic fold. He wooed them by promising that his low tariff strategy would do more than the reciprocity of the Republicans to enlarge the overseas market.[12]

That argument was weakened because Bayard reasserted the proper metropolitan conception of Democratic "duty." The primary objective was to change the tariff so that "our manufacturers will find their way open to expanded markets in which they may profitably compete."[13] McKinley sought to exploit the gap between Mills and Bayard with his recognition of the need for foreign markets.[14] He also related the end of the continental frontier of "unbounded fertile soil" to the reciprocity treaties that "fostered agriculture . . . directly." He was not ready to try unilateral remonetization of silver, but he did support bimetallism and attacked Cleveland frontally as a man "dishonoring one of our precious metals."[15]

Other Republicans also warned that the country could not afford another dose of the "humiliating diplomacy of Grover Cleveland and Mr. Bayard."[16] The party platform promised that reciprocity would "give us control of the trade of the world," the "extension of our foreign commerce," and the "achievement of the manifest destiny of the Republic in its broadest sense." Harrison sustained that theme in his letter of acceptance on September 2, 1892. Overseas market expansion under reciprocity had launched "the commercial crusade of the United States," a campaign that would bring victory "in the battle of the markets." Underscoring the importance of exports to Cuba, he urged the farmers to support those who had opened such "new, large, and increasing markets."[17]

Western Democrats grew worried by September, reporting that the Republicans were "working like nailers" and providing a battle "such as we never had before."[18] But Harrison went home to comfort his dying wife and did not repeat either his front-porch campaign of 1888 or his 1891 cross-country tour for market expansion. Blaine, a spent and ailing imperial giant, appeared almost not at all. And Plumb, a major force west of the Mississippi, had died. As a result, the Western Populist parties, so largely composed of unhappy and angry Republicans, elected Cleveland.

But a significant number of Western Democrats, including important conservatives, were upset and worried by Cleveland's narrow metropolitan outlook, and uneasy about his personality and temperament. "What a peculiar man you have to deal with in the President," remarked one of them in the course of a long discussion about the feel-

ing among Westerners that metropolitan Democrats wanted "to elect
Mr. Cleveland without the aid of any States west of Indiana." The
evidence on that point was so clear that all agreed that the experience
"should be a lesson to us in the West."[19] The skepticism of an Iowan
of lesser rank was perhaps even more indicative of that apprehension.
He wrote Richard Olney, the corporation lawyer Cleveland selected
as Attorney General, that the President failed to "comprehend, even
in a moderate degree, the threatening and portentous condition of
the country." That estimate had created, even among agricultural
conservatives, "a feeling of dread."[20]

Harrison candidly expressed a similar fear in his last annual message of December 1892, warning of the dangerous consequences if
the Democrats destroyed the reciprocity system. He also emphasized
the increase in exports to Cuba, arguing that gain was typical of the
harvest to be gathered. The first imperial fruits of reciprocity, however, ripened in Hawaii. Under steady pressure from the determined
Queen Liliuokalani, and threatened economically by the free-sugar
proviso of the 1890 tariff, American leaders in the islands engineered
a coup with the cordial assistance of Blaine's appointee, Minister John
L. Stevens.

Stevens called in the Marines to cow the Queen on January 16, 1893,
recognized the new white government the next day (on his own initiative), and on February 1 proclaimed a protectorate. Blaine, out of
office since June 4, 1892, died just before the culmination of his efforts.
Harrison submitted the treaty of annexation to the Senate with the
blunt judgment that the restoration of the Queen would be "undesira-
ble, if not impossible." Possession of the islands by any other power
would endanger American "safety" and the "peace of the world."

Agriculturalists generally favored annexation or a strong protectorate. The *National Economist* presented the revolution in a favorable light; while the *Indiana Farmer*, pointing out that "the business
of the Islands has been mainly in the hands of the people from the United
States for some years past," assumed that annexation would be approved.[21] The editors of the *Pacific Rural Press* acknowledged the
dangers of annexation, but then argued that "Hawaii is the key to the
whole commerce of the Pacific Ocean." "It can scarcely be doubted,"
the editors concluded, that the episode would "form a precedent for
the accession of Cuba," and would "mark the entrance of America
into a wide field as a world power."[22]

That was a shrewd assessment of the expansionist outlook of the
time and a prophetic estimate of where it would carry the nation. Metropolitan support for annexation, which included the New York *Tribune*
and the New York *Independent*, manifested the same convergence
of ideology and economics that characterized agricultural thought.
"It is our duty," explained the *Commercial Advertiser*, "to assist in

the elevation of all peoples, and when in any given case the fulfillment of these obligations is accompanied by so many manifest advantages to us, our course seems to be plainly indicated."[23]

Cleveland antagonized all such expansionists on March 9, 1893, by abruptly withdrawing the treaty of annexation from the Senate. The President was not against colonies per se, but followed two primary guidelines: whether the specific operation was in the national interest as seen from his particular metropolitan point of view, and whether annexation was the best method. "I do not say that I should think annexation in all circumstances and at any time unwise," he wrote Schurz, "but I am sure we ought to stop and look and think."

Schurz spoke for a majority of market expansionists when he replied that, *in general*, colonialism was unwise and unnecessary. "All the advantages we might gain by it can be secured without irrevocably abandoning the safe, time-honored tradition of our government."[24] But many viewed Hawaii as the exception that proved the rule. While Cleveland was entirely sincere in his desire to evaluate the situation, it is clear that he was even more concerned to end the threat of silver. And he did not want that struggle complicated by a simultaneous battle over Hawaii. As with his action in raising the low tariff issue in December 1887, however, Cleveland's maneuver on Hawaii served to increase and sharpen the interest in foreign policy. It had the effect of dramatizing the tactical question of how to expand.

In a wholly unintended way, moreover, his selection of J. Sterling Morton as Secretary of Agriculture intensified the concern with foreign policy and further antagonized the farm businessmen. As Morton once remarked in a moment of insight about himself, he was "an out-and-outer" who considered "*all*" legislation "which invades the economic domain" as "pernicious and the forerunner of evils greater than it alleges itself able to cure." "The relation of Supply to Demand is the sole regulator of value, whether the commodity be soap, salt, or silver."[25] Morton had been connected with agriculture throughout his life, and viewed himself as a man who helped Nebraska by helping the farm businessmen. Agriculture, moreover, was "the basis and foundation upon which the superstructure of all the commerce of the world is reared."[26]

His efforts to bring the railroads into Nebraska helped him win a lucrative position as counsel for the Chicago, Burlington, and Quincy line. True to his pure laissez-faire view, he fought the railroads over their abuses while defending them against legislative restrictions. He displayed the same determination to save the system when he became Secretary of Agriculture, and acted with characteristic self-righteous zeal. "There are very few out of this job-lot of statesmen," he remarked arrogantly in 1887, "who understand economic principles and fewer still who will adhere to them against the threats of voters."[27]

When particularly upset, which was the case a good deal of the time, Morton revealed a contempt for the "multitude of most egregious unmitigated apes" and a fatalism similar to that manifested by Brooks Adams. "I wish I lived in another planet," Morton once blurted to Perkins. "This one is evidently going wrong."[28] He dedicated himself, however, to saving what he could as Secretary of Agriculture. He realized he faced a difficult and trying ordeal, but entered upon the crusade with the "systematic and untiring" efforts of a man who believed himself an isolated and unappreciated savior. The primary difficulties were the backlog of "vicious legislation" and "the common enemy, the Populists and Republicans."[29]

Morton first wielded the patronage sword against Western Democrats and bureaucrats who favored the tariff. That provoked an angry outburst.[30] Next he stopped the traditional distribution of seeds, a practice that had become a symbol with little meaning. And then he acted in a manner that created the impression he was terminating the effort to push corn into European markets, a misunderstanding that provoked still more antagonism.[31] Within his framework, however, Morton was seriously concerned to expand exports and to that end acted on existing congressional legislation to create the Section of Foreign Markets on March 30, 1894. And he appointed agents "to investigate the demands of foreign markets," and dispatched what he called "propagandists in the same missionary work."[32]

But Morton did not comprehend Adam Smith's clear authorization for government action to maintain a free and open marketplace, and he simultaneously launched a campaign to end the system of meat inspection created under Harrison and Rusk. The expense, he argued, was not justified by the results; and, in any event, foreigners ought to be satisfied with the far less rigorously inspected meat eaten by the American consumer. To complete his clean sweep, he attacked the reciprocity system as "a massive humbug."[33] Those moves incited a storm of protest from farmers, processors, and exporters. Morton was bitterly attacked for failing to realize that the "work of opening the markets" was "a function of the government."[34]

The reaction stung Morton deeply and contributed to his violent outburst against farm businessmen who allowed themselves to be deceived and misled "by pretended friends" and "sinister advisors." "The most insidious and destructive foe to the farmer," he sermonized, "is the 'professional' farmer who, as a 'promoter' of Granges and Alliances, for political purposes, *Farms the Farmer*." The proper policy for farmers was to "keep in the furrow" during the day and read Adam Smith's *The Wealth of Nations* at night. That epic, he explained, "is to political economy as the New Testament is to the Christian religion."[35]

That was like telling the disciples that they ought to attend a seminar with Jesus Christ, and neither Morton nor Cleveland ever recovered from the ensuing outrage. The Grange, which Morton considered "a sort of huge 'bunco' establishment," erupted in rage against the "premeditated slanders" of a man "no way qualified" for the job. "The imperative duty of the President is immediately to take steps to secure a Secretary of Agriculture who shall be in accord with that interest."[36] Alliance leaders asserted he was too narrow to grasp "the dignity of his position," and demanded a replacement who had the proper appreciation of those whose exports "creates the balance of trade in our favor with the nations of the world."[37]

"You fail utterly," warned Representative Joseph Crocker Sibley of Pennsylvania, "in your appreciation of the calamitous circumstances confronting the American farmers to-day." "Your interests are chiefly those of a banker and corporation lawyer." The analysis was further strengthened by Morton's response. He whined that he had been "misunderstood and misrepresented," asserted contradictorily that any "real farmer" would agree with what he had said, and arrogantly told a national leader of the Alliance that "nothing can be more complimentary than your condemnation. . . . Be kind enough, therefore, to continue your assaults."[38] The farmers obliged, typing the Secretary as "Grover's Fool," and recalling Secretary Rusk with a fondness increased by their realization that they had lost a special friend. Rusk was a "great man," acknowledged militant reformers like the editors of the *National Economist*, and others praised him with equal generosity. The antagonism toward Morton was increased even further by his snarling attacks on silver, which accentuated his unwillingness to embark upon a vigorous program to reopen old markets and secure new outlets.[39]

The storm over Morton soon became part of the hurricane of the depression. The first warning signs appeared in 1892: investments in the railroads slowed and construction activity declined. Then the collapse of the National Cordage Company and the Philadelphia and Reading Railroad early in 1893 prepared men like Nebraska banker Charles G. Dawes for the worst. When it came, on May 5, 1893, the panic prompted him to remark that "it is at last upon us." The subsequent depression, which in its primary phase covered two cyclic fluctuations lasting well into 1898, was capped by another downturn that did not end until December 1900.[40] Unemployment mushroomed, almost quadrupled, by the end of 1893, reached 18.4 percent in 1894, remained above 12 percent through 1898, and was still twice the 1892 figure (3.0 percent) in 1899 (6.5 percent). Real earnings for the entire economy, which declined 18 percent between 1892 and 1894, averaged 15 percent lower until 1898. Gross farm income dropped at least that much, and may have gone even lower during much of the period.[41]

Southern agriculturalists were hit particularly hard because their condition was "bad" before the panic. By the end of the summer, the reports had become wrenchingly familiar—"debt, poverty, and despair."[42] But similar conditions existed throughout the country, and "despair" was reported in Minnesota as well as Mississippi. "Times are hard," sighed the *American Swineherd*, and descriptions of the "stagnation" were filed from New York, Ohio, Indiana, Nebraska, and Colorado. A state investigation in Washington revealed "pitiable" and harrowing conditions, and a Nebraskan warned Morton that "much real suffering was the lot of many."[43] "Never in my life of forty-five years of responsible activity have I seen a time," John Sietz wrote from Ohio, "when in spite of the hardest labor, strictest temperance, plainest frugality, and closest economy, the 'average farmer' has grown so poorer."[44]

The metropolis was not spared. August was a very bad month: "never before has there been such a sudden and striking cessation of industrial activity. . . . Commerce and enterprise were arrested in an extraordinary degree." By the end of the year, when 491 banks and 15,000 businesses had failed, "the want and misery were everywhere." "The business year 1893 promises to go into history," concluded *Bradstreet's*, "with heavier net losses in financial, commercial and industrial circles throughout the United States than in the more severe panic periods of the past eighty years."[45]

Conditions rapidly became even graver. "The panic of last year is nothing," concluded James Hill in 1894, "compared with the reign of terror that exists in the large centers. Business is at a standstill, and the people are becoming thoroughly aroused." That estimate does much to explain the increased tempo with which metropolitan leaders completed their conversion to the agricultural doctrine of overseas market expansion. A Southern commercial entrepreneur who shifted to agriculture offered eloquent testimony on the appeal of that overview, and on how the daily experience of the farmers reinforced that image of the world. "I can say with emphasis that the most business-like occupation I ever engaged in, is farming."[46]

"The most striking fact about the whole thing," commented Populist Tom Watson, "is that the number of our people today wholly dependent on foreign markets is larger than the number of those employed in the protected industries." And to underscore the point he reprinted his own earlier call to "knock the hind sights off" any rival, and the long explanations of the central importance of foreign markets offered by Populists Simpson and Peffer.[47] Simpson reiterated his expansionist outlook after the onset of the depression. "I believe we can safely tear down the custom-houses and challenge the world for competition in its markets. I believe, gentlemen, that the time has come for the United States as a great nation to take its place as one of the great commercial nations of the earth."[48]

The depression swelled the agricultural chorus for market expansion into a mighty roar. Western, Southern, and Northeastern farmers of all political persuasions joined in demanding a canal, a merchant marine, a strong navy, and any other measure that would help "relieve the glut."[49] Fish of the Illinois Central understandably thought the vital importance of exports was "too obvious to need comment," and concentrated on working with fellow rail magnates like Hill, and Senators Morgan and Cullom, to capture the Asian trade that he called "the new West."[50] It is not at all inconceivable that Fish took that striking metaphor from the reports of Professor Frederick Jackson Turner's paper on the frontier thesis that circulated through the Chicago and New York newspapers in 1893.

"Our frontier is almost gone, Professor Turner tells us," *The New York Times* reported, for example, and added that "we are getting land hungry again." Turner eloquently expressed an idea that had permeated American thinking from the beginning of the eighteenth century. The frontier-expansionist conception and explanation of American reality was an idiomatic (and romantic) statement of Adam Smith's marketplace-expansionist model of the world. Not only had it been developed and stated by many agricultural spokesmen during the years after the Civil War, but the metropolitan aristocrat Brooks Adams formulated it in 1893 - 1894 in a form that was even more grandiose than the version offered by Turner. The two men exerted a significant influence, moreover, on such young imperial expansionists as Theodore Roosevelt and Senator Lodge.[51]

Specific economic needs prompted other metropolitan leaders to intensify their demands for overseas markets. "All of us were for more trade ," Oscar Straus reminded a Board of Trade and Transportation banquet in 1893, "a trade that would reach the four quarters of the globe, carried in American ships under the Stars and Stripes." Some entrepreneurs concentrated on Asia, while others like Bethlehem Iron and Steel also sent agents into Latin America.[52] Their rhetoric rested on bedrock statistics. Agricultural exports continued to supply more than 5 percent of the gross national product from 1894 through 1900; but processed items accounted for a greater share of food exports in all but two years after 1888, and that indicated the steady industrialization of the economy.

That became ever more apparent after 1887 in the decline of the agricultural share of all exports. With the exception of 1892, those dropped steadily from 76.4 percent in 1887 to 61.6 percent in 1900. The big jump in exports of finished manufactures came between 1894 ($135 million) and 1896 ($181 million); while the increase in semimanufactured exports occurred in two large spurts (from $76 million in 1896 to $98 million in 1897, and from $117 million in 1899 to $153 million in 1900). The same kind of industrial gains appeared in the rise of the share of manufactured exports in the gross national product. That edged upward from 2.5 percent in 1896 to 3.1 percent in 1900.

It was not surprising, therefore, that metropolitan spokesmen began to generalize about the necessity of expansion. "The industrial demand of the day," noted Hawthorne Hill in the *Engineering Magazine*, "is for markets abroad. The whole people are awakening to it."[53] And still others, like Carnegie and Albert Shaw, editor of the *Review of Reviews*, offered a metropolitan version of the agricultural marriage of reform and prosperity. "We belong to a race that must lead and rule in the affairs of men," Carnegie asserted; while Shaw explained how "a colossal trade" in Latin America and Asia would "promote the material and moral development" of those peoples.[54]

The bankers also edged closer to the imperial threshold. There would be no quick recovery from this depression, unfortunately, because there would be no "big exports" of agricultural surpluses as had been the case in 1878. "The decline in wheat and silver has therefore been more talked of in Wall Street than the stock market, outside of the 'Industrials'; for upon the future of wheat raising in this country, for export, the Trunk lines, as well as the Granger roads, are largely dependent for their Eastbound traffic."[55] Many financiers concluded that it was vital to obtain an agreement for international bimetallism and their strength prompted Morgan to approach the British for just such a compromise. Their cold refusal turned the balance back toward the goldbugs.

And Cleveland took his advice and reassurance from the goldbugs. "Nothing is more vital," he warned the nation in his inaugural address, than "a sound and stable currency." His first major response to the depression, therefore, came on June 30, 1893, when he called the Congress into special session for the purpose of repealing the Sherman Silver Purchase Act.[56] The embittered confrontation actually began much earlier, at the end of April, when the government made it clear that it would fight for gold by borrowing funds from a metropolitan syndicate with European connections. Virginia Democratic leaders immediately denounced that move as "an Unholy Alliance" with "the Bonded Money Sharks" of Wall Street.[57]

Such anger was understandable, for August Belmont and Jacob Schiff (who had become frightened) manifested great concern lest agricultural exports earn enough gold from Europe to ease the crisis and spoil the chance to repeal the silver legislation. The country, they feared, might conclude "that matters were on the mend," and hence "the greatest promptitude" in repeal was vital.[58] The main themes in the ensuing struggle were clarified long before the Congress assembled on August 7, 1893. Many Southerners, for example, stressed that demonetization in 1873 was "the greatest cause" of their continuing troubles, and demanded free coinage or effective agreements with silver-using countries in order to win "absolute control of the trade of all such countries."[59] After blaming Germany, Great Britain, and France for "the degradation of silver," the Texas Alliance announced that "the time has come for America to assert her right of commercial supremacy."[60]

Populist Governor Davis H. Waite of Colorado agreed, and promised during a big Denver rally in July to "seek to open up new markets" by coining a Colorado coin to facilitate trade with "Mexico and the South American republics." He also spoke angrily and militantly against metropolitan power allied with foreign countries. "If it is true that . . . we are only a province of European monarchies," he thundered, "then we need another revolution. . . . For it is better, infinitely better that blood should flow to the horses' bridles than our national liberties should be destroyed."[61]

Metropolitan goldbugs promptly edited Waite's "If" out of his remarks, otherwise distorted his speech, and tried to kill the silver movement by presenting "Bloody Bridles Waite" as a typically subversive silverite. Western agriculturalists were neither fooled nor intimidated. "The goldbugs," shot back the *North Pacific Rural Spirit*, "have 'cornered' not only the silver, but the government." And even the more conservative *American Agriculturalist* revealed a new militancy. "The East has treated the West somewhat as England has treated the United States."[62] Metropolitan silverites joined the resistance to Cleveland. Senator Hoar, for example, who was a vigorous bimetallist, concluded that repeal might very well hurt exports more than the purchase of the bullion. Brooks Adams fought the gold forces with tracts against the financiers (*The Gold Standard*) aand helped Senator Lodge prepare his attacks. Speaker of the House Thomas Reed agreed with Lodge that silver would help control Asian markets. And, after the silverites greeted the convening Congress with a huge Chicago rally, Republican leaders like Harrison and Reid came out against repeal. That was "no remedy," and would instead produce "greater stringency, more failures, more mill stoppages and more reduction of wages."[63]

The disagreement among metropolitans also ripped the Democratic party. But the President would not listen to those who counseled compromise. That prompted one Cabinet member to fear the worst. "If the Democratic party divides on this question, the split will be as disastrous as the one that occurred in Charleston in 1860."[64] The party did divide, and the results were nearly as disastrous. The depression and all the nation's other troubles, Cleveland advised the Congress, were "principally chargeable to Congressional legislation touching the purchase and coinage of silver by the General Government." The issue was wisdom and morality against stupidity and avarice. "This matter rises above the plane of party politics." The Virginia Alliance delivered the answer of all militants: "The money power of the world is now turned against us . . . and there sits in the presidential chair, armed with the veto power, the most pronounced and determined opponent of silver money, inviting and awaiting the dictation of Europe."[65]

Representatives Bryan of Nebraska and Bland of Missouri led the counterattack by Western Democrats. Bland charged that Cleveland had "lost the spirit of 1776," while Bryan stressed the power of the United States to force Britain to accept silver, a victory that would lead to world economic supremacy. "A silver standard, too, would make us the trading center of all the silver-using countries of the world, and these countries contain far more than one-half of the world's population. What an impetus would be given to our Western and Southern seaports." "Why not reverse the [goldbug] proposition and say that Europe must resume the use of silver in order to trade with us? But why adopt either gold or silver alone? Why not adopt both and trade with both gold-using and silver-using countries?" As for Great Britain, "suppose we try bringing her to terms by action. . . . Let me appeal to your patriotism. . . . Are we an English colony or an independent people?"[66]

Why not, indeed, echoed Populists like Davis and Simpson. "Why should we trim our sails," snarled old sailor Simpson, "to fit the breeze of any country?" "Our position in the world," cried Davis, "justifies higher ambitions than mere existence. . . . To reach our most cherished and reasonable destiny as a commercial and civilized people we must have a sound, stable, pure, and plentiful currency." "It will thus be seen," he added somewhat unnecessarily, "that this silver fight is comprehensive."[67] Such passion proved unavailing, however, against the President's righteous will and his ruthless control of patronage. Those finally forced the repeal bill through the House on August 28. "It is time to begin sounding the notes of national independence," cried the *Indiana Farmer*, and called upon the agricultural businessmen to override "the whims and influence" of alien powers.[68]

Many implored the Senate to save silver.[69] Senator Stewart had come very close to understanding the collusion that had demonetized silver between 1868 and 1874, and opened the attack by recalling Senator Morgan's warning of those years that "the most mature deliberation" was essential in such major decisions. Then he emphasized the importance of "the trade of China, Japan, India, and other Oriental countries." And to cinch the argument, Stewart and others quoted Sir Richard W. Fowler's admission that American demonetization of silver could only mean "the complete ruin of the agricultural export interests of the United States."[70]

Senators Allen and Peffer attacked the arrogance of the metropolis, challenged its leaders to "tote fair," and argued that silver would boost exports and thereby relieve a situation "full of peril." "Nothing but food satisfies hunger."[71] "My theory," explained Senator Teller of Colorado, "is that the United States is big enough and rich enough to control the whole currency question throughout the world." "To the south of us," added Populist Senator Kyle, "are possibilities of empires" that would "lift the burdens from the backs of our farmers and laboring men." And, equally important, it would facilitate a return to "old fashioned Jeffersonian Democracy." The problem was to defeat "the money lenders of the East."[72]

Neither the argument nor the anger was stilled by Cleveland's victory on October 30, 1893, when the Senate killed silver by a vote of 48 to 37. Some began to organize for "the elections of 1894 and 1896."[73] Metropolitans like Brooks Adams, and Boston businessmen, and even Perkins of the C. B. & Q., organized themselves to win some kind of bimetallism.[74] Others joined that effort or turned to reciprocity treaties as a way to facilitate market expansion.[75] Populists emphasized the neocolonialism of the South and West, and redoubled their efforts to assert American power through remonetization. A California Alliance chapter attacked Cleveland as "unpatriotic and Un-American." The *Southern Mercury* resorted to searing satire: "Americans should willingly make any sacrifice to please these 'beastly' English" in order to satisfy Cleveland and other "English money lords." Taubeneck concentrated on the "deep and wide gulf between the interests of the East and those of the South and West." The key to "commercial independence from the East is first to become financially independent. That is . . . dictate the financial policy of our government to [our] interests as the East has done." Silver was vital because it would "place the farmers of the South and Northwest upon equal footing in the market of the world."[76]

The nearly universal antagonism did influence the Cleveland Administration. Yet the reaction was complicated and complex, and must be differentiated very carefully. Secretary of the Treasury John Carlisle's *Annual Report* of December 1893 provides a good outline of most of the approaches that the government considered. He first repeated the traditional defense of gold as the key to penetrating and controlling markets. Next he asked the Congress for authority to meet the gold needs of the government through public bond issues. Then he reiterated the argument that free raw materials would enable the manufacturers to dominate the world market. The bond proposal was designed to avoid going to American and European bankers, and at the same time engage the assertive nationalism of the agricultural majority in support of metropolitan dominance. That would hold the monetary line while tariff changes opened new markets and relieved the economic crisis.

Cleveland's move toward a more assertive foreign policy thus continued to be guided by his fundamental commitment to the metropolis, and his heightened concern to use industrial expansion to control the farm uprising. Those were the primary considerations behind his striking pronouncement in December 1893: "The world should be open to our national ingenuity and enterprise." The editors of the *Indiana Farmer* wholly approved the sentiment but, as with other agriculturalists, recognized that Cleveland was not using it in their context—or with their needs primarily in mind. It was, after all, "the only allusion made to the farmer's interest."[77] The President had indeed concentrated on the importance of removing the tariff on raw materials to facilitate the overseas exports of manufacturers.

One final complexity needs to be clarified. Cleveland's Secretary of State, Walter Gresham, did possess a more inclusive and integrated conception of market expansion as the answer to the problems of the political economy. His appointment was a reward for leaving the Republicans during the election of 1892, a decision taken on the grounds that the more broad-gauged metropolitan leaders of that party were unable to break free of the special interest.[78] The irony, of course, was that he agreed to become the agent of a man far narrower than Republicans like Harrison and McKinley. For in truth Gresham analyzed the crisis very much as those men, and accepted overseas market expansion as the method of relieving the pressures within the political economy.

He had made that clear in his early dealings with Morton about enlarging European markets for meat exports, and he did so again during the height of the battle over silver. Carl Schurz made a strong appeal (appropriately entitled "Manifest Destiny") for "enlarging our commercial advantages" in the October 1893 issue of *Harper's*, and Gresham promptly told him it was "the best article of the kind that I have seen."[79] Schurz wanted America "powerful and respected," and argued only about "how this end can be most surely" won. He warned against colonialism of any kind, even the British "administrative" colonialism in India, insisting that the United States could obtain all the economic objectives "without taking those countries into our national household . . . without assuming any responsibilities for them."

Such was precisely the idea behind the Harrison-Blaine reciprocity program, and its effectiveness was one of the causes of a rebellion in Brazil that prompted Gresham to intervene in the new imperial style. The rebels wanted to abrogate the reciprocity treaty negotiated by Blaine in 1890-1891 because they feared it was harmful to the Brazilian political economy. And they gained significant strength in December 1893 when Admiral Saldanha da Gama came over to their side.

Metropolitan leaders in the United States like Oscar Straus, W. A. Crossman and Brothers, and William Rockefeller, president of Standard Oil, quickly asked for assistance in maintaining their strong trade position.[80]

Gresham had already expressed his own fears that the rebels might succeed, and promptly ordered the Navy to prevent any "substantial interference with our vessels."[81] By that time, moreover, the Secretary had already seen to the removal of a rear admiral who had been unenthusiastic about the interventionist policy. But the replacement also proved a reluctant imperialist. Gresham maneuvered still another change of command, and the third choice was properly militant. When the rebels moved to stop a merchantman from unloading, he wasted no shots across the bow. One round was fired dead on target to italicize the verbal message that followed: "I will sink you."

The single-shot intervention was effective, and the rebellion shortly collapsed. Taking no chances, Gresham nevertheless kept five naval vessels on the scene despite the danger from yellow fever. In retrospect, of course, the operation was a small affair. But in and of itself it served to dramatize the great relative power of the United States in dealing with weaker nations. It reinforced the existing confidence in American strength. It was symbolic of the imperial action that was becoming increasingly frequent, and it demonstrated the Cleveland Administration's prompt and energetic response to pressure from metropolitan businessmen. It also provides a very useful reminder that America's imperial foreign policy was evolved and put into operation by civilian leaders who did not hesitate to overrule military men who disagreed.

Cleveland's position on Hawaii, however, lost whatever support among the agriculturalists that the Brazilian affair may have gained him, and in addition generated strong opposition. The President's investigation of the coup established the fact of American intervention, and he tried late in 1893 to arrange a transfer of power back to the Queen. Agriculturalists marched in the front rank of the angry rebellion against that proposal, which also aroused many metropolitan spokesmen. Senator Hoar, for example, was told to "Give the Old Pumpkin Head Hell," and to "Come down on him like a hawk." And a leader of the Home Market Society reported that "a good many Democrats say that the attitude of Cleveland is indefensible."[82]

Farm businessmen saw the proposed "reinstatement of monarchy" as a flagrant violation of the principle of the free marketplace. Some Populists criticized Harrison's initial intervention, but insisted on maintaining the controls necessary to "trade products to our advantage whenever possible." The most significant development was the evolution of an informal coalition between metropolitan and Western Republicans, Populists like Davis, Simpson, Peffer, and Kyle, and dissident Democrats. Republican expansionists like Hitt of Illinois led the effort to censure Cleveland's proposal to restore the Queen, and though it was defeated, he won the votes of many Western Populists. "It seems ridiculous," Kyle charged, "to suppose that the United States Government ever contemplated the use of force for the purpose of restoring a monarchy." He and Peffer, along with other farm spokesmen, wanted to recognize the new government in the islands and establish a protectorate.[83]

The interpenetration of economics and political morality was very strikingly displayed in the debates, and even those who refused to condemn Cleveland revealed the same desire to extend freedom along with markets.[84] Another portentous omen was the agreement between Senators Teller and Lodge on the desirability of annexing Cuba as well as Hawaii.[85] Yet the most significant indicator of the winter of 1893 - 1894 may have been the special and limited nature of the Populist outrage about the scandal in providing armor plate for the Navy. Carnegie's plants not only failed to produce quality steel, but the weaknesses were masked and not reported. Such episodes verified, of course, the earlier insistence of the agriculturalists on proceeding carefully in building a new navy. Watson's *People's Party Paper* noted that vindication, but concentrated on a bitter indictment of Carnegie, and on an impassioned attack on Cleveland for his failure to punish the offenders. But Watson did not assault the idea of a big navy, or the necessity of such a force.[86] Once again the issue involved honest and effective means rather than the nature of the ends.

Such was likewise the case with the swirling struggle to revise the tariff. That battle was affected by the fight over Hawaii, as well as by the steaming disaffection among agricultural Democrats over the repeal of the silver purchase law, and the continuing collapse of the economy. Senator Mills of Texas took the lead in trying to hold the farm businessmen with his argument that a low tariff would "throw wide the gateways and permit them to enter every market."[87] Despite his efforts, the party's leaders met serious resistance from the outset.

Their heated attacks on the reciprocity strategy, and on the Bureau of American Republics created during the Harrison Administration, led important metropolitan and agricultural groups to fear the worst. Fish of the Illinois Central became worried early in 1892, for that matter, that the Democrats would destroy the basis of his firm's heavy export traffic in "bread-stuffs, beef, and hog products."[88] A spokesman for the Cleveland Administration tried to reassure other skeptics like Carnegie that the proposed change to a low tariff schedule would be "thoroughly judicious, progressive, and excellent," but he was not successful.[89] Carnegie insisted that the reciprocity strategy was essential because it provided great assistance in the "contest with foreign manufacturers."

Similar fears about reciprocity prompted a large number of farm implement manufacturers to exert very heavy pressure on Representative Wilson who managed the bill in the House. Charles W. Marsh, editor of the *Farm Implement News*, headed the campaign that involved almost every major firm except McCormick. The McCormicks were in no sense unconcerned with finding markets for surplus production, and were for that matter ready to merge with Deering as early as 1890 in order to command a greater share of all markets. But they played a lone hand: "We as you know are not given to . . . working on nobody else's wood pile but our own." Others, however, agreed with Deering that the repeal of reciprocity would cause "very serious results."[90]

Representative James Albertus Tawney of Minnesota led a vigorous attack to prevent Wilson from dropping the reciprocity section of the tariff of 1890 on the grounds that it was crucial to the welfare of Western agricultural businessmen and processors. He stressed the way reciprocity had expanded the market for flour, meat, and other provisions in Brazil and Cuba, and charged that the movement for repeal was another example of Cleveland's damaging pro-British policy.[91] The wool growers were also antagonized. Some of them understood the value of reciprocity and fought side by side with Carnegie on that issue. Most of them, however, were appalled by the prospective reduction of the rates on wool.[92]

The early and sustained outcry prompted the Grange and others to predict major defections among the farmers. Watson's *People's Party Paper* called for the defeat of the bill and flatly predicted that, if it did pass, the Democrats would be a minority party for an indefinite future.[93] Although the reasons for that outcome were more complicated than he allowed, the prophecy was largely correct: the bill did indeed contribute heavily to the Democratic demise. For, even in the form it passed the House of Representatives on February 1, 1894, the legislation contained four provisions that gravely weakened the Cleveland Administration.

First, it clearly sidetracked reciprocity as a major weapon in market expansion. That was because Wilson opposed the approach and refused to extend the crucial proviso for delegating power to negotiate such treaties to the President, and because the duties on refined sugar subverted the arrangement that opened the German market to American meat exports. Second, those same sugar rates denied the farmer any effective lever against domestic refiners. Third, the wool growers went unprotected. And fourth, the very modest income tax proviso (needed for revenue as well as to soothe the more militant reformers) antagonized crucial metropolitan interests. The bill was an invitation to mayhem by the Senate, and the Senate obliged.

Two of the more extreme expansionist counterattacks were made by Senator Lodge and Moreton Frewen. Frewen was no longer ranching in Wyoming, but he remained an active silverite. His scheme called for raising the duty on diamonds. That would exert enough pressure on Cecil Rhodes to force the British mining king to persuade Rothschild to agree to international bimetallism. It would also have rewarded Frewen with a larger than tidy fortune through speculation: "I alone shall know how the cat may be made to jump." "More than thirty senators expressed serious interest in the maneuver, including metropolitan spokesmen like Lodge, Chandler, and Quay, as well as Southerners and Westerners, but it was never tried.[94]

Frewen's grandiose idea may well have been the suggestion that led Lodge to make his attempt, on May 4, 1894, to use the tariff "to force England into some action" on silver. "By closing to a certain extent our markets to her products and those of her colonies," he explained, Great Britain could be defeated. Senator Stewart welcomed such "financial war to obtain financial liberty, freedom, and independence." Lodge and other Republicans were of course aware that the move might aid them with the agriculturalists, but there is no warrant for dismissing it as an empty political gesture. Lodge and his metropolitan allies were seriously trying to win international bimetallism, and many of them saw London as America's main rival for world economic supremacy. In any event, the amendment mustered twenty votes in defeat.[95]

The efforts to save reciprocity also failed, even though important metropolitan groups supported the wheat and flour interest and the livestock growers and meat processors. They understood that the provisions in the Wilson bill pertaining to sugar would lose the German and Cuban markets, as well as block additional expansion. Packers and exporters in Chicago, Cincinnati, Toledo, and other centers repeatedly warned of those consequences, as did metropolitan leaders like Senator Hoar, the editors of *The Nation*, and Senator Redfield Proctor of Vermont.[96] Proctor was particularly incensed about the subversion of American economic control of Cuba, and denounced the Wilson bill as a measure to "Perpetuate the Territorial Jurisdiction and the Financial and Commercial Power of Great Britain in America."[97]

The Cleveland Administration was warned privately, moreover, of the grave danger in not retaining reciprocity. And, finally, on July 16, 1894, Germany formally advised Gresham that the legislation would work "an injury to the German sugar trade" that would not go unchallenged.[98] That underscored the other attacks on the bill from the Philadelphia Board of Trade and the flour industry. Senator William D. Washburn stressed the loss of "new markets," damned the damage to existing gains in Cuba and elsewhere, and effectively quoted Representative Henry Gray Turner of Georgia (and other Democrats) to dramatize the willfulness of the Administration: "The proposition," vowed Turner, "is to repeal the reciprocity clauses by express and explicit provisions."[99]

The Administration overrode Washburn.[100] It then dismissed the warnings from Senator Kyle about leaving wool on the free list, ignored Senator Richard Franklin Pettigrew's harsh accusation that the legislation "robs the farmer," and discounted the other signs that farm businessmen were ready to transfer their loyalty back to the Republicans.[101] Cleveland continued to emphasize free raw materials for manufacturers and allowed the bill to become law without his signature.[102] That maneuver failed either to mollify the Democrats who had been outraged by his narrow and willful approach to the bill, or to appease the Western agriculturalists. Thus the Wilson Tariff Law contributed significantly to what Watson called the "all-round catastrophe" for the Democrats in the election of 1894, in which they lost control of the Congress. Republicans and Populists both scored gains, but the Republican resurgence was far more impressive. Even the militant *Southern Mercury* was pleased by the Republican victory, though of course it expected little if any improvement.[103]

That was neither irrational nor narrowly partisan, for the economic crisis was extremely severe. "I take my pen in hand," one farm wife explained to the Governor of Kansas, "to let you know that we are starving to death. . . . My husband went away to find work and came home last night and told me that we would have to starve. He has been in 10 counties and did not get no work. . . . I haven't had nothing to eat today and it is 3 o'clock."[104] Such conditions hurt the Democrats not only because they were in power, but because Cleveland failed to provide relief — or hope for the future. Watson's harsh judgment — they "dodge and shuffle and straddle" — was accepted by thousands of agriculturalists throughout the country. The party, warned one member, is "ragged and broken up."[105]

The Republicans, on the other hand, were attracting positive support for their push for market expansion. As one agricultural editor noted, "the Western mind is essentially imperial in its tendencies and reaches out to grasp new possessions for the country and the race," and the Republicans spoke to that outlook through their positions on reciprocity and silver. Cattlemen and implement dealers, as well as meat processors and wheat farmers, responded to the cry of "free and fair access to the markets of the world."[106]

Metropolitan Republicans helped by maneuvering adroitly to attract moderate silverites. Clarkson of Iowa emphasized the importance of that strategy long before the silver law was repealed. "A million of honest men do not rise up in revolt unless they have some actual grievance," he told the National Republican League in May 1893, and called upon the party to respond to the farmers on the monetary issue. "If the Farmers' Alliance shall help to bring this about, it will not have existed in vain."[107] Aided by the receptiveness of Clarkson and others, the Alliance did contribute a very great deal to the Republican recovery. Harrison swung the Indiana convention to support high tariff measures designed to force England to accept bimetallism, and he and others produced similar Republican declarations in Ohio, Kansas, Minnesota, Iowa, Illinois, Michigan, South Dakota, Nebraska, Missouri, North Carolina, Tennessee, Georgia, Montana, Idaho, Nevada, Wyoming, Colorado, California—and even Vermont.[108]

Senator Lodge was one metropolitan who gave Westerners serious reason to believe that the party favored bimetallism. Charles Francis Adams was another: he had abandoned gold monometallism and confidently predicted that "the game is now absolutely in the hands of the United States."[109] Senator James Donald Cameron of Pennsylvania spoke candidly about the grave mistake the party had made in demonetizing silver in 1873, "and, what was worse, doing it with a foreign air of conspiracy," and urged Western Republicans to maintain their pressure for free silver.[110] And Representative Thomas Brackett Reed, powerful metropolitan politician from Maine, based his campaign for the party's presidential nomination on a silver alliance with the Western agriculturalists. "Cheap silver," he argued, "is an effective stimulus to Asiatic exports." "We have got to consider silver and the tariff not as two issues but as one."[111]

For that matter, it was a former Republican, Secretary of State Gresham, who provided the Cleveland Administration with its broadest view of the crisis through his recognition of the general "danger in the present condition of society."[112] "What is transpiring in Pennsylvania, Ohio, Indiana, Illinois, and in regions west of there, may fairly be viewed as symptoms of revolution." "The honest men (and a large majority of them are honest) firmly believe that they are oppressed." The trouble was overproduction: "our mills and factories can supply the demand by running seven or eight months out of twelve."[113] The solution was overseas economic expansion.

Gresham came under great pressure to provide strong support for a Nicaraguan canal. Senator Morgan's long effort was coming to a climax, and he demanded satisfaction. "There can not be anything done for the Southern people of equal advantage . . . so as to give us access to the eastern Asiatic countries for our cotton." Aided by Westerners, he moved the Congress toward a showdown on the issue, and a House Committee urged direct action to claim "the rich commercial territory to the Western Pacific."[114] Full of "gloomy forebodings" about the domestic situation, Gresham seized upon the British intervention against Nicaragua's effort to reassert its control over the Mosquito Indian reservation. He adroitly maneuvered the British out of their position in the area and strengthened American influence. It was a very effective bit of diplomacy, but it did little or nothing to satisfy

Morgan or Westerners like Peffer and Cullom. Having given "more than ordinary attention" to the question, Peffer proposed buying land for a canal from Nicaragua with silver bullion. The objective was trade expansion and related world reform, for "commerce is the most active, the most efficient, and the most powerful civilizing agency known or recognized among men."[115]

Illinois Central president Fish was so concerned about the canal issue that he arranged "a long talk" with Gresham. He reported the Secretary "spoke most encouragingly" and promised to do all he could "to stimulate the enterprise."[116] But nothing was done to translate the rhetoric into effective action. The expansionist coalition had become strong enough to prevent special interests from weakening the momentum for overseas markets, as when Morgan and others blocked an effort by sugar growers to abrogate the old reciprocity treaty with Hawaii, but it was not yet powerful enough to force Cleveland to act positively.

The "lethargy or indifference" of the government on the canal issue, a matter of "transcendent importance," provoked the Seattle Chamber of Commerce to complain bitterly about the delay in developing "the imperial domain" of the West. "Suppose in the future," suggested Representative William Baker, a stockman from Kansas, "we do less for Massachusetts and more for . . . Indiana, Illinois, Iowa, Nebraska, Louisiana, Mississippi, Alabama, Georgia, North Carolina, Kansas, Kentucky, and Florida." "Whenever we ask for anything you do not agree with us about," added Senator Peffer, "you call us unreasonable." "The time is here when we must speak plainly about these things. . . . The medicine must be taken."[117]

The Master of the Virginia State Grange became so disenthralled with Cleveland that he appealed to McKinley. And the Secretary of the Chicago Board of Trade agreed that the farmer could hardly be blamed for insisting that "the plate [be] passed round to his table once in awhile."[118] Other Western businessmen joined their expansionist allies in the South (and in the metropolis) to organize the National Association of Manufacturers. That organization blossomed quickly from a seed planted by the editors of *Dixie*, a Southern trade journal. They proposed a meeting to discuss the penetration of the Mexican and South American markets, but the response produced a national meeting concerned with expansion throughout the world.[119]

The founding session of the National Association of Manufacturers convened in Cincinnati on January 22, 1895, and the keynote address was delivered by the Governor of Ohio—William McKinley. His commitment to reciprocity and overseas market expansion was forceful and unequivocal. "We want our own markets for our own manufacturers and agricultural products; we want a foreign market for our surplus product. . . . We want a reciprocity which will give us foreign markets for our surplus products."[120] Other speakers explained the depression in terms of the decline in agricultural exports, stressed the need for government aid in market expansion, and attacked Great Britain as the principal rival to be defeated and replaced.

That assault on England, so much a part of the agricultural outlook since the 1870s, signaled another step along the way to the creation of a full consensus between the metropolis and the country. The farmers may have temporarily slowed that process, however, by the intensity of their reaction against the Cleveland Administration's February 1895 contract for another gold loan from the Belmont-Rothschild syndicate. "It takes three times the corn" to pay taxes as before "John Bull, Cleveland, John Sherman, and Rothschild and Co. took charge of the financial policy of this country," the *Southern Mercury* had screamed after the first such loan, and the editors reacted even more extremely in 1895. Senator Stewart told Cleveland he was the captive of an "alien gold trust"; and then, in a second biting, sarcastic letter, he congratulated the President on his feeble foreign policy, his "union of interest" with Britain, and his success in persuading England "to manage and control our domestic affairs."[121]

The mushrooming silver agitation provided William Hope Harvey with a long-sought opportunity to exploit his considerable talents. After ten years as a wandering frontier entrepreneur, Harvey earned his first real success as a mine superintendent in the Colorado silver boom. He invested those profits in Utah real estate, but the depression destroyed him before the Mormons could make him rich. He returned to Chicago and struck a mother lode as an advocate of silver and market expansion. Harvey was not an original thinker, much less a primary force in the silver movement, but he was a shrewd operator able to spot and ride the ninth wave of a popular movement.

Harvey offered nothing new except a dynamic and remarkable ability to crystallize all the arguments of the silverites in provocative and persuasive prose. One of his major tracts, for example, *The Great Debate Between Hon. G. Horr and William Harvey*, was a clever put-on in which he appeared as a spokesman for the farm silverites against an imaginary financial expert. That format was a classic appeal to the country against the metropolis, and his major theme was merely a lucid restatement of the twenty-year-old argument that remonetization would give America control of the world marketplace. "If the silver using nations of the world could bring their silver to the United States and exchange it for the products and wares which they needed and get a fair exchange, they would not part with their metal anywhere else for less. We could take all the silver they have in any one year, and then go to work and raise and make the same things over again and ask them to come again. . . . If we had the principal trade of India, China, Japan, and South America, which we would have . . . our virtual monopoly of the trade of those countries that now supply Europe with many articles would put these articles under the control of our traders and we would fix the price to Europe."[122]

Harvey's propaganda was powerful and effective during the next three years, and particularly in its influence in casting the argument about market expansion as a choice between silver and reciprocity, but he was not responsible for the imperial market expansionism of the agricultural majority. He merely expressed and reinforced that outlook. That was already being done with great effectiveness, furthermore, by Populists like Senators Allen, Kyle, and Peffer, by Representative Simpson, and by others who wrote letters to the editor. That became unmistakably clear during the early 1895 debates over Hawaii, the Far East, and the Navy.

Senator Kyle dramatized the convergence of the metropolis and the country on overseas market expansion by standing shoulder to shoulder with Senator Lodge to attack Cleveland's Hawaiian policy. The islands should be annexed because they were vital to the Asian trade, and American naval units should be constantly on station to block foreign interference. Allen joined them in the charge against the Administration after explaining his political economy with an explicit reference to Adam Smith.[123] Agreeing with Kyle that the islands were vital to the new security perimeter of the United States, Senator Teller explained the imperial conception of the national interest. "If it is necessary that we have those islands either to preserve peace at home or abroad, or to maintain our commerce or encourage our commerce, then we have the right to secure them."[124]

Metropolitan leaders like the editors of the *Commercial and Financial Chronicle* shared that concern to control Hawaii, a desire that was heightened by the war between China and Japan. Cleveland was far more responsive to pressure from those interests, and pointedly announced that the Asian conflict "deserves our gravest consideration by reason of its disturbance of our growing commercial interest."[125] The President's interest in exports to Asia was strengthened by his friendship with Hill of the Great Northern, who not only impressed Cleveland but used the relationship to push the importance of Asian trade.[126]

Such developments created a crisis for the more militant reformers within the agricultural protest movement. Nothing dramatized that confrontation, or the ultimate resolution in favor of expansion, as effectively as Simpson's struggle with the question of whether or not to support additions to the Navy. His study of the Sino-Japanese war reinforced his estimate that the fast cruisers were more effective than battleships, and his judgment that America possessed enough ships "to protect our interests both at home and abroad." The vital policy change, he reiterated, involved a switch to free trade.

Then Representative Eugene Francis Loud of California quietly asked Simpson how he planned to emulate Great Britain's free-trade successes without also building an American version of the Royal Navy. The Populist replied simply that the continental frontier provided employment for a "vast population," and hence there was no need for "taking to the sea." The big Navy "may become necessary in the future, when the territory of this country becomes more densely settled," but not until then. But the question hung in Simpson's mind, perhaps caught on the peg of his earlier argument about the end of the continental frontier necessitating a drive for overseas markets.

He shortly took the floor again in order to revise his initial rebuttal. In a moving speech, Simpson admitted his *non sequitur*. "It is my opinion that, if we should adopt the policy by means of which Great Britain today controls the great ocean-going trade of the world, we may . . . regain our lost ground. If such conditions should arise there may be some excuse for an increase in our Navy."[127] But, as Simpson realized, the crucial factor was not free trade but the commitment to overseas markets as the solution for domestic troubles. Five days later, therefore, referring to the recent American intervention in Brazil, as well as to the Sino-Japanese war, he announced his support for building more cruisers.[128]

Senators Allen, Peffer, and Kyle reached similar conclusions and voted for both naval appropriation bills. No agricultural groups attacked their action. "The best way in the world to preserve peace," explained Peffer, "is to be ready for war." Watson's *People's Party Paper* revealed a similar concern with export expansion by rejoicing over Japan's defeat of China. Watson agreed with State Department spokesmen (and other metropolitan leaders) who felt that Japan's victory created "America's Opportunity to Penetrate China." It would open "large opportunities" for enlarging the export of raw cotton and rough textiles. Not surprisingly, Watson shortly thereafter denied that the Populist party was even so much as tinged with socialist ideas.[129]

Pleased by the outcome of the war, the State Department promptly claimed a full share of the benefits. "This country will expect equal and liberal trading advantages." And, after pressure from metropolitan interests, the American representative in China was directed to employ "all your efforts" in line with the policy of "keeping foreign markets open" in order to "secure expanded privileges of intercourse, trade, and residence in which our citizens may share."[130] As hopeful as Watson and other expansionists were, however, there were no immediate orders from Asia large enough to ease the agricultural pressure on the Cleveland Administration.

That opposition rose another notch when the President failed to display any marked vigor in responding to the further British interven-

tion in Nicaragua at the end of April 1895. Cleveland was denounced
by the Assembly of his own state of New York, as well as by the Connecticut State Senate. Even earlier, in March, Gresham and other advisers who anticipated the British move warned that the country was
demanding a "positive. if not aggressive" foreign policy. One such
counselor argued openly for "a war to straighten things out."[131]

Such advice hit the President at a time when the continuing depression, the overwhelming defeat in the elections of 1894, the intensified
outrage of the silverites, and the renewed debate and criticism about
Hawaii had shaken his confidence and strength. "I have been dread-
fully forlorn these many months," he admitted on February 12, 1895,
"and sorely perplexed and tired."[132] He was also under bipartisan
pressure in the Congress to take a stronger position against the British attempt to seize a large area, including a region that would give
it control of the Orinoco River, from Venezuela. Representatives Leonidas Felix Livingston of Georgia and Hitt of Illinois won unanimous support for a resolution that stressed the importance "of our trade and
other relations with those people."[133] The Senate promptly added
its endorsement. The French were also active. Their pressure on Santo
Domingo in March was followed in May by similar maneuvers against
Brazil.

Cleveland was fully aware, moreover, that the public attacks on
him were strengthened by the developing alliance between metropolitan and Western Republicans who favored expansion.[134] Stung by
the "vehement criticism" across the country, and urged by Cabinet
members like Olney and Whitney "to beat the tomtom in the Venezuelan matter," the President defined the issue as "the most distinct of home
questions" and finally displayed some vigor in using foreign policy
to control the ever increasing domestic unrest.[135] The decision was
not merely political, and most certainly not hypocritical, because
Cleveland was a strong nationalist, seriously (albeit cautiously) concerned about the overseas market expansion within his metropolitan
outlook.

But he was using foreign policy in the sense that he was acting on
a narrow metropolitan view that did not integrate the agricultural
sector of the political economy into its analysis, and which defined
benefits to the farmers as a consequence of gains for the metropolis.
Standing up to Britain over Venezuela was a political equivalent of
his strategy of free trade in raw materials. Neither represented the kind
of inclusive outlook manifested in the Harrison-Blaine-Rusk approach
to reciprocity. The emphasis on manufacturers was revealed in several episodes during May. The first occurred when Don Dickinson,
a major Democratic politician in Michigan, issued a militant call for
market expansion after a conference with Cleveland. The President's re-

sponse, given the preliminary discussion, indicated that he was emerging from his earlier depression. "In due time it will be found that the Administration has not been asleep."[136]

Then, when Gresham died on May 28, Cleveland replaced him as Secretary of State with Olney, who had already become active in pushing a strong policy for domestic as well as overseas objectives. His experience and analysis were far more narrowly industrial than Gresham's, however, a consideration that increases the significance of a series of articles published anonymously in the Baltimore *Sun* on May 26, 27, and 28, 1895. They were actually written by Frederick Emory, an important bureaucrat in the State Department, and they emphasized the value of foreign markets for industrial surpluses. "The time has come when our manufacturers must help to swell the volume of our export trade." "It has been the task of Mr. Cleveland's foreign policy," he then explained, "to prepare the way for them, to insure a hospitable reception for them."

All such indicators prompted Watson and other Populists to conclude that Cleveland was using foreign policy to weaken the agricultural movement. As with Simpson's dilemma over the Navy, however, Watson and the others were caught in the coils of their own expansionism. Thus, Watson did not attack the opposition to Great Britain, but instead manifested deep contempt for the President's methods and purposes.[137] In a similar way, agricultural businessmen were concerned with other issues of expansionist activity as much as—and in some cases more than—they were involved over Venezuela. That was particularly true in the summer of 1895.

Many expansionists, attracted by the jump in exports to Cuba after the reciprocity treaty of 1891, increasingly focused their attention on that island. Western spokesmen like Teller and metropolitan leaders like Proctor differed over the wisdom of annexation, but they agreed early in 1894 that nothing should be allowed to weaken or disrupt America's economic control of Cuba. And Teller, though he was not a Populist, was an eloquent advocate of the free marketplace expansionism that the agricultural majority had developed to a high pitch. "The Monroe Doctrine," he explained, "merely declares that we will not tolerate any interference in affairs in this hemisphere by European powers. . . . We have a right to intervene."

That right, he candidly asserted, was based on economic and ideological criteria: in cases where "commerce is destroyed and lives are wasted," America had the power and the right to "say to those people, 'Now you have gone far enough. You have disturbed the commercial world. You are destroying your civilization, and it is time for you to come to a halt.'" Peacefully if possible, "but if that cannot be done, does anybody deny the right of this Government, in the interest of humanity, in the interest of the business of the world and the race, to say, 'You must put an end to this condition, or we shall compel you to do so'?"[138]

That kind of highly integrated and ideologically supercharged free marketplace expansionism could not in the end be mollified by the gestures—however sincere—of those who entertain a more limited conception of such expansion. Hence Cleveland's unwillingness to save reciprocity with Cuba provoked immediate and rising antagonism among Westerners and Southerners. Perceptive observers like Senator Wilkinson Call of Florida realized as early as December 1894 that the termination of reciprocity would very probably serve as the catalyst touching off another revolutionary outbreak in Cuba, and he began to agitate to purchase the independence of the island from Spain. Minnesota citizens, acutely aware of the market for meat, flour, and other provisions, shortly petitioned the government to buy the island outright.[139]

Then, when the revolution did erupt on February 24, 1895, other Midwesterners raised a general cry to drive Spain from the Caribbean. The *National Stockman*, for example, first compared the revolt to the American Revolution, and then added a marketplace note. "Aside from this the commercial interests of this country would probably be advanced by Cuban independence." And by September the impatience with the lack of forthright action by Cleveland prompted the Chicago *Tribune* to ask, in its characteristic assertive manner, "Why do we wait any longer?"[140] The agitation over Cuba thus compounded Cleveland's dilemma and reinforced his propensity to resolve it by taking a strong stand against the British advance in Venezuela.

The Administration did that on July 20, when the President and Olney bluntly asserted American predominance in the Western Hemisphere. But the note was not published and hence had little effect on the mounting clamor for tough diplomacy. For that matter, the information that did reach the public served mainly to fuel the agitation.[141] Impressed by the analysis offered by Peter Brooks, a large American operator in Cuba, Olney concluded that the idea of buying the island offered a workable solution to the new complication. "Spain cannot possibly succeed" in crushing the revolution, the Secretary decided, and stressed the need for a clear policy. Cleveland understood the logic of that argument, but was not ready to act.[142]

Instead, he moved to deal with all such issues through a vigorous reassertion of the Monroe Doctrine against the British pressure on Venezuela, an action he viewed as challenging American interests. That strategy emerged clearly in his annual message of December 2, 1895, written before the English reply to the tough note of July had been received. The President began by discounting German restrictions on American food exports, promulgated in response to the end of reciprocity, as only "somewhat injurious." The Cuban revolution admittedly damaged "commercial exchanges" and aroused "sentimental sympathy" and "adventurous support among our people," but the primary problem was "enforcing neutrality laws." He next attacked the silverites as "a serious menace to our prosperity and an insidious temptation of our people to wander from the allegiance they owe to public and private integrity."

Cleveland then turned that kind of righteous moralism on the British. Declaring that the Monroe Doctrine "is essential to the integrity of our free institutions and the tranquil maintenance of our distinctive form of government," he concluded that "we may properly insist upon this doctrine without regard to 'the state of things' or any changed conditions here or elsewhere."[143] While the tone was assertive, the remarks were unfocused and indeterminate simply because the President did not know whether the British were going to give him a victory of some kind or provide the occasion for even stronger rhetoric.

The latter was the case. Lord Salisbury curtly refused to acknowledge that the Doctrine enjoyed any standing in international law, and slyly offered to discuss the concrete issue of Venezuela if the United States would state its economic, political, or strategic interests in a straightforward manner. The British answer was powerful enough to infuriate both Cleveland and Olney, and they vented their anger publicly on December 17 in a presidential message heard round the world. The crucial sentence provided an answer to Salisbury's request for specifics. American predominance in the Western Hemisphere was "important to our peace and safety as a nation and is essential to the integrity of our free institutions and the tranquil maintenance of our distinctive form of government."

That was the vital part of the performance simply because it formalized the extension of the American marketplace and security perimeter that had been initiated during the depression of the 1870s and sustained by Blaine and Harrison. The assertion that domestic American welfare depended upon hemispheric predominance was a classic projection of the frontier outlook, a well-nigh definitive application of the marketplace conception of the world, and an emotionally intense manifestation of the militant nationalism generated by the agricultural majority. As Cleveland remarked to an intimate, the message "caught the national spirit perfectly."[144]

A Cabinet member's diary entry was equally revealing. Former Representative Wilson, who had become Postmaster General in April 1895 after the infamous tariff bill had become law, offered his succinct commentary on January 3, 1896. The crisis and the President's handling of it "has dwarfed or relegated to the background all other and lesser foreign questions on which the Republicans were getting ready to attack the Administration for its weak and 'un-American' foreign policy, and to that extent has done us good politically."[145] The message did serve, as one observer wrote Secretary of Agriculture Morton, "like an electric spark kindling the fires of patriotism," but the blaze quickly subsided for want of fuel.[146]

It was Cleveland's unwillingness to move on down the imperial highway, rather than any overwhelming opposition from the metropolitan business community, that allowed the Venezuelan crisis to wane as rapidly as it had waxed.[147] The President had no intention of following through with a vigorous program to expand overseas markets. That was precisely what angered the agricultural businessmen, moderates as well as Populists, and they immediately stepped up their efforts to take control of the Democratic party in order to put such a policy into operation.

"The only war that Mr. Cleveland can engender," commented the St. Louis *Grocer*, "is a war led by the bankers of Wall Street against the commercial and agricultural interests of this country. In that war Mr. Cleveland has the position of Commander-in-Chief." "Pity the extremity of a discredited Administration," agreed the *American Grocer* of New York, "which drives it into a startling bit of jingoism with a view of galvanizing it into new life."[148] The *People's Party Paper* had offered that analysis as early as June, when it attacked Cleveland's resort to "warlike complications" as an effort to maintain "the perpetual bondage" of the West and the South. "The war scare is a fake," Watson snorted in December.[149] "There will be no war," agreed the *Southern Mercury*. But "when the pops get in," the editors promised, "there will be a war if John Bull does not attend strictly to his own affairs." The *Pacific Rural Press* argued that there would be no war on different grounds. "War with us would mean the breaking up of the British Empire"—"she will not fight."[150]

William T. Stead, expansionist editor of the *Review of Reviews*, admitted to Chicago reformer Henry Demarest Lloyd that Cleveland had engineered a clever maneuver against the protest movement. Lloyd himself was ready for war, comparing the British action to the "firing on Fort Sumter, or Bunker Hill." "I would extend the Monroe Doctrine to the defense of every Republic as far as Andora and San Marino, and to the assistance of every people seeking to establish the Republic." That was the only way, the necessary way, "to fulfill our mission to defend and *extend* liberty." "But it is too much to hope for," he concluded sadly.[151]

All of it, in the nineteenth century, yes; but much of it, no. Agricultural leaders like Senator Allen and William Jennings Bryan were even then moving to recapture the initiative on Hawaii and silver, and to force intervention in Cuba. Others were agitating for the restoration of the reciprocity strategy of market expansion, and for other measures to relieve the continuing depression. "There are some who think that the only business man is the man who lives in some great city," cried Bryan in November 1895, "and who is engaged in commercial pursuits. But I would impress upon your minds that every producer of wealth is a business man."

Bryan had no need to convince the agriculturalists, as he surely knew, for they had been trying to educate the metropolis to that truth for a generation. He was instead trying to impress himself on the agricultural businessmen as the man who could penetrate and control the markets they needed, and extend the freedom they treasured, by winning the presidency and remonetizing silver. "I say, let us restore silver and then let England adopt bimetallism because the United States has it."[152] Cleveland never had a chance against Bryan and it required all of William McKinley's sophisticated expansionism, hard will, and political shrewdness to keep the Nebraska expansionist from entering the White House.

FOURTEEN

I do believe that the sober, candid, thinking, patriotic people of this country fully realize the necessity of promptly taking steps . . . to extend the interests of our commerce.

Populist William Allen, 1895

It would not be good policy, just now, for Spain to pick any quarrel . . . with the United States.

Farm, Field and Fireside, 1896

The only thing that can remove this threat of danger to business stability is the settlement of the question and the restoration of peace to the island and this can only be brought about by firm and decisive action on the part of the United States.

Senator Henry Cabot Lodge, 1896

If Cuba were free she would pass under American trade influences.

People's Party Paper, 1896

The only trouble is it is better not always to say the truth. It is better not always to speak of money and property and property interests. . . . Let it be placed upon some higher ground.

Senator John Sherman, 1896

The poverty in this state is something more than you can conceive.

John H. Tibbles to Senator Allen, 1896

Foreign markets are essential to the prosperity of the American farmer.

State Grange of New York, 1896

Give us protection and reciprocity treaties with such countries as we can trade advantageously with.

Wisconsin Farmer, 1896

We demand the establishment of an economic and financial system which shall make us masters of our own affairs, and independent of European control.

Populist Party Program, 1896

Let us restore silver and then let England adopt bimetallism because the United States has it. . . . There are some who think that the only business man is the man who lives in some great city.

William Jennings Bryan, 1895

The East is not the battleground.

Postmaster General Wilson, 1896

I think the advance in price has come to stay. This ought to make McKinley votes, put the farmer in better humor and upset the theory that Bryan and his followers have been advancing.

William H. Dunwoody, October 1896

It is a business man's state.

Iowa State Register, November 6, 1896

The
Climactic Debate over Silver
or Reciprocity As the Best
Method of Expanding
the American
Marketplace

T HE ELECTION of 1896 was such a deeply emotional struggle because it involved a confrontation between a divided metropolis and a divided country over the highly charged issues of how best to extend the freedom of the marketplace and at the same time expand the marketplace. The basic choice was explicit. William Jennings Bryan insisted that the unilateral remonetization of silver was the only way to attain both objectives. William McKinley argued that reciprocity and international bimetallism provided the only sure route to such freedom with prosperity. The coalition headed by Bryan added that control of the markets of the world needed to be supplemented by classical Smithian reforms at home. While not dismissing the need for some changes of that kind, McKinley stoutly maintained that the expansion of the marketplace would generate welfare for all members of the system.

The election dialogue was carried on in a context defined by three factors. One was the continuing depression. The second was the common desire to expand the free marketplace. The third was the Cuban revolution. Within that framework, a majority of the agricultural businessmen were initially inclined to support the Populists and other reformers in a bid to take command of the Democratic party and refashion it as the instrument of their solution to the ills of the political economy. Yet a strong minority of the farm businessmen leaned toward the answer to those problems recently developed by the Republican leaders who stressed bimetallism and reciprocity. McKinley and his allies transformed that minority into a slender majority in the crucial states of the upper Mississippi and Missouri valleys, and they came to power as the Cuban and Far Eastern situations presented serious challenges to the rhetoric of all expansionists.

The failure to offer bold and effective leadership in a similar crisis lost Cleveland and his coterie of metropolitan Democrats their only chance, feeble though it was, to maintain control of the country. The President made no move to apply his vigorous reassertion of the Monroe Doctrine to the Cuban revolution, or to implement it through a program of market expansion. Militant agriculturalists who had been advocating such action for more than a decade promptly seized the initiative. Populist Senator Allen of Nebraska returned to Washington in December 1895 convinced that "the sober, candid, thinking, patriotic people of this country fully realize the necessity of promptly taking steps . . . to extend the interests of our commerce." "The people of this country have become dissatisfied with the foreign policy that has been pursued," and "a firmer policy should be adopted."[1]

Allen then introduced a three-part resolution designed to change the policy. The government "should promptly recognize the revolutionists of Cuba, who are now honestly struggling to secure their independence, . . . as composing an independent nation." Furthermore, "all islands in close proximity to the mainland of the United States . . . should, as speedily as possible, by Treaties of purchase, be annexed . . . as essential to our safety in times of war and the convenience and necessity of our commerce in times of peace." And, finally, while the government "should not needlessly or hastily embroil itself with any foreign power, and should only resort to extreme measures in cases of actual necessity," it should nevertheless be "firmer and more prompt . . . in maintaining the rights of American citizens abroad."[2]

The Senator next reactivated Blaine's plan for a Pan-American union "for the purpose of promoting the general, industrial and commercial welfare" of the nations of the Hemisphere, and to secure them "from European or other foreign encroachment." He integrated silver into his foreign policy by specifying that the union have a common silver coin of "full legal tender" in all countries.[3] "We must be," he added, "the exclusive judges of when the [Monroe] doctrine is to be applied."[4] The performance promptly earned Allen the first of many letters of "sincere congratulations" for his "Americanism," and the note cast a revealing light on the outcome of the presidential election. "If you were as sound on finance as you are on true Americanism, I would be ready to worship at your shrine."[5]

But Allen and other silverites were convinced that a sham toughness in foreign policy was being used to block them on silver, as well as to avoid effective market expansion, and they remained adamant about combining the two questions because they considered them inexorably entwined. Silver, as they had been arguing since the 1870s, would expand the marketplace in and of itself, and at the same time weaken the aristocratic power of Britain, Germany, France—and now Spain.[6] The power of that analysis was clearly revealed in the support it received from agricultural businessmen who were not Populists. *Farm, Field and Fireside*, for example, viewed Spain as a mere puppet of the British, and hence saw action against Spain as a blow against England. Its editors warned the British, furthermore, that America "will have a hand in the 'Eastern Question' whether England likes it or not."[7]

The *National Stockman* agreed, supporting the Cubans because they were "struggling for the same rights for which our revolutionary forefathers fought."[8] The *Western Rural* shared the view that action in the Middle East might be required, but emphasized the need to send naval units to Cuba to protect American trade and lives.[9] And the *Rural New Yorker*, asserting that "the rebellion is fully justified," expressed its views in an editorial poem:[10]

> *Off yonder in the ocean blue*
> *Fair Cuba strives in freedom's battle,*
> *She has a right to look to you*
> *For manly words—not idle prattle.*

The petitions, resolutions, and letters that flowed into the Congress provided persuasive evidence that such editors knew their readers. The Topeka Philosophical Society demanded support for the Cubans "from the standpoint of patriotism, political economy, and material commercial interests." Citizens in Spokane, Washington, agreed, as did Alliance members in North Carolina who wanted "no backing down." Iowans though Cuba ought to be dealt with "as a warning to powers which have thought to question . . . the Monroe Doctrine." The attitude that a move against Spain would weaken all "monarchical tendencies" was widespread, appearing in Grange petitions, private letters, and resolutions from state legislatures.[11]

Such broad support encouraged other leaders to offer rival resolutions, and the Senate finally approved Morgan's move to force Cleveland to recognize the Cuban rebels as belligerents. Cuba was "so closely" tied to "the political and commercial welfare of our people," and so "universally regarded as part of the continental system of America," Morgan argued, that prompt action was necessary. The war was "doing serious harm to the rights and interests of our people on the island, and to our lawful commerce," and it was time to establish "the security of life and property . . . permanent peace and a government that is satisfactory to the people of Cuba."[12] The vote on February 28, 1896, was overwhelming—64 to 5.[13]

The resolution greatly disturbed Cleveland and other metropolitan spokesmen who intensely disliked the rebels, who fretted that intervention of any kind would delay or prevent economic recovery, and who felt more generally that American expansion would develop without such risky militancy.[14] Senator Lodge understood such resistance and worked persuasively to overcome it, arguing that Spain would back down rather than fight—and adding that business would not suffer seriously even if war did erupt.[15] "The only thing that can remove this threat of danger to business stability is the settlement of the question and the restoration of peace to the island and this can only be brought about by firm and decisive action on the part of the United States."[16]

Some businessmen closely tied to agriculture shared the fear that strong action would do more damage than good, but they were overbalanced by the farmers who agreed with Lodge.[17] *Farm, Field and Fireside* expressed the majority's confidence in American power, and its desire to expand trade relations with a free Cuba.[18] Populist editors wholly accepted that view, and even reprinted articles from *Farm, Field and Fireside.*[19] It soon became apparent, moreover, that a significant number of metropolitan spokesmen shared that confidence and desire.

When it reached the House, the Morgan resolution on Cuba was ignored in favor of a measure submitted by Blaine's old expansionist ally, Representative Hitt of Illinois. Referring to "the numerous petitions" demanding action, Hitt called upon the Cleveland Administration to recognize that "a state of public war exists in Cuba." The "only permanent solution" would be "establishment of a government by the choice of the people of Cuba," and their efforts deserved formal (and consequential) recognition. Furthermore, in view of "the very close relations" between Cuba and the United States "in consequence of its proximity and the extent of the commerce between the two peoples . . . the United States should be prepared to protect the legitimate interests of Americans by intervention, if necessary."[20]

Hitt used no evasions in presenting the resolution. "Wherever American interests are imperiled we land marines if necessary; and if it is necessary for the protection of a vast property in the midst of extreme confusion and disorder, we can land a sufficient force for protection."[21] The co-leader of the House action was Representative Robert Adams, Jr., of Pennsylvania, a graduate of the Wharton School of Economy and Finance, who also laid great stress on American investment and business on the island, and on trade with it.[22] His arguments served to highlight the metropolitan support for strong action that was developing among Andrew Carnegie, labor leader Samuel Gompers, and such spokesmen as the *Journal of Commerce*, the *Commercial Advertiser*, and the *Financial Record.*[23]

Hitt's resolution passed the House on March 2, 1896, by the vast margin of 262 to 17—but its gross emphasis on economic considerations upset enough senators to force a compromise. Senator Sherman, aging rapidly but still an astute judge of political sentiment, candidly discussed the need to rephrase the call for action "upon some higher ground." The Hitt analysis was "in substance . . . true," but "it is better not always to say the truth. It is better not always to speak of money and property and property interests." He understood, he added, the analogy with the American Revolution.[24]

Sherman's estimate of the substance of American interests in Cuba should be kept in mind, for he shortly became Secretary of State; but it is also essential to realize that he underestimated the degree to which the Populists and other agriculturalists had integrated the political and economic freedoms of the marketplace. They were not at all reluctant to admit their concern with exports to Cuba, but they properly insisted that they viewed the expansion of the marketplace as essential to liberty as well as to profit. That was why they demanded a presidential campaign stressing that vital interrelationship, and why they chose silver as the instrument and the symbol of their expansion.

The agricultural businessmen were contemptuous of the Cleveland policy of providing a breathing space so that Spain could reassert its control in Cuba. The United States, Olney told the Spanish Minister after protracted Cabinet discussions, wanted "to cooperate with Spain in the immediate pacification of the island." The object was a solution "which will prevent all thought of intervention by rendering it unnecessary." The President was making an "official expression" of his "anxiety," and of "his earnest desire for the prompt and permanent pacification of that island." The Cleveland Administration feared that protracted conflict would force Spain to abandon Cuba "to the heterogeneous combination of elements and races now in arms against her." That outcome induced "the gravest apprehension," and prompted the President to offer his good services to help arrange a settlement that would leave "Spain her rights of sovereignty, . . . yet secure to the people of the island all such rights and powers of local self-government as they can reasonably ask."[25]

Olney's note makes it clear that the advocates of American intervention were largly correct in their analysis of Administration policy, but it also reveals that they overlooked or discounted one important consideration. For in its concern to terminate the revolution before it further damaged American interests and disrupted American politics, the Administration did take the first step toward full-scale intervention. The uninvited offer to help end the uprising, coupled with the specifications for a settlement, bespoke an American intention to set limits on Spanish action. Olney made that clear when the Spanish refused the offer of good offices. "The situation here and in Cuba," the Secretary bluntly replied, "must be bettered."[26]

That was precisely what the Populists and other agriculturalists intended to do by winning the election of 1896 for domestic reform and the expansion of the free marketplace to Cuba and elsewhere through the remonetization of silver. They counted on the continuing depression to help them defeat those who exhibited, as some metropolitan spokesmen admitted, the "superciliousness" and "arrogance" of men who "posed as the 'holier than thous' end of civilization."[27] "The poverty in this state," one constituent wrote Senator Allen, "is something more than you can conceive." And others reported on the "extreme and unusual drouth" that increased the "many hardships and privations."[28]

The accounts from other states were no better. New York Grangers defined 1895 as a year "long to be remembered by the farmers of our land," a time when "a large class of the honest toilers of the land are gradually nearing the gulf of financial ruin." Pennsylvanians warned that the depression "threatens to drive us to the wall." Illinois reported "a state of great depression," and offered a clear idea of why the farmers were so incensed: "We ought to be prosperous, but we are not." And conditions in Kansas were so bad that many were "in the slough of despondency."[29] Agricultural spokesmen, militant and moderate alike, also knew how deeply the farm businessmen were committed to the theory and the reality of the export market. "There is good reason," as the *National Stockman* remarked, "for devoting more attention to our foreign trade." Agricultural exports carry not only the farmer, but the balance of trade for the entire economy. "Any person who opposes" efforts "intended to further our commerce with Japan and the east," remarked *Farm, Field and Fireside* in praising Senator Morgan, "is simply turning his hands backwards on the dial of history." "Foreign markets," summarized the New York Grange, "are essential to the prosperity of the American farmer."[30]

Reform leaders like Senator Benjamin Ryan Tillman of South Carolina, along with others like Allen and Peffer, combined reform and expansion in their efforts to control the corporations and thereby produce a better navy.[31] Tillman wanted such a fleet "to have the nations of the earth consider us as being one of the powers"—so that "any country in Christendom" would "think once, twice, and thrice before it goes to war with this country."[32] The "boasted 'home market,' for which the protectionists clamor," he added, "can no longer purchase the products of our home factories."[33] Such persistent concern with overseas markets belatedly prompted Edward Atkinson to study a phenomenon of such "very potent influence." His first estimate of the number of agricultural businessmen directly tied to the export demand revealed how little he understood the relationship. He placed it at about 2 million. Then, under criticism, he recognized how narrow his study had been and drastically revised the total upward to about 10 million for part of Northern agriculture.[34] A significant number of the farmers who had known that for a generation began in 1895 - 1896 to support Lubin's proposal for an export bounty on agricultural exports as a way of earning a profit on their operations.

The New York Grange, for example, changed its mind and joined fellow members in California, Oregon, Washington, Pennsylvania, Ohio, and Wisconsin in approving the approach.[35] A major bounty rally in Worcester, Massachusetts, produced additional backing from groups in San Francisco, Seattle, and Bath, Maine, from various Atlantic coast shipbuilders, and from the National Farmers Congress. Representative Elisha Edward Meredith of Virginia ultimately introduced a bill to create such a system, but it never came to the floor for discussion and decision.[36] Tillman was one of the few militant reformers to support the bounty plan, and that does much to explain why it failed to become a major issue in the nineteenth century.[37]

The bulk of Populist and Democratic leaders concentrated almost exclusively on silver, giving secondary attention to improving and controlling the transportation system. "The truth is," as Secretary of Agriculture Morton unhappily admitted in March 1896, "that the silver fallacy has been growing in public estimation for the last six months. . . . The propaganda of the 16-to-1 crowd have penetrated every back county in Texas and all the other states with their fallacies and wind. It looks now as though they might carry the National Convention at Chicago."[38] Morton was proved correct on both substantive points, but Senator Stewart offered a far more useful analysis of why silver became such a powerful element in the campaign. "The Populist party is a band of reformers, and they desire victory in order that they may accomplish reforms, and by co-operation with other reformers in establishing an independent policy for the United States, they will have a reasonable chance to secure all the reforms they desire. But with Rothschild's millions in control of the Administration, no reform whatever is possible."[39]

Other farm businessmen of less pronounced reformist ideas accepted the basic premise: remonetization would enable America to displace Britain and expand a truly free marketplace around the globe. "Our monetary system," asserted Elwood Furnas, president of the Iowa Alliance, "should be governed by the Monroe Doctrine as well as our territory."[40] The editors and letter writers of the whole range of agricultural publications gave eloquent and angry witness to their understanding and acceptance of the argument. They took particular pleasure from Lord Balfour's candid opinion that unilateral remonetization would "force Bimetallism on the world whether England likes it or not."[41]

Some Southern textile men joined the movement hoping that free silver would expand their exports to Latin America and Asia.[42] Senator Marion Butler of North Carolina, a leading Populist, spoke for agriculturalists of the region in calling the silver issue "by all odds the most momentous to our future liberty and prosperity." The reformers, he declared, were patriots ready to "fight to the bitter death the infamous British gold conspiracy."[43] Butler may have been influenced by Brooks Adams, for he shared his concern about "the decay of civilization." And, like Adams, Butler wanted silver to expand the American marketplace and "to rid this country of foreign debt and foreign dictation."[44]

By the spring of 1896 such agriculturalists had reached the point of committing themselves to the silver analysis and program. The process through which that had occurred was surely understandable, and the analysis itself could be defended with considerable force as a marketplace approach to a marketplace problem. They might very well have won the election, moreover, if they had supplemented silver with other expansionist proposals to attract the farm businessmen who were not wholly persuaded by the silver argument. That, rather than any other weakness, was the primary failing of the silver movement. For the conservative metropolitans who were so deeply frightened and antagonized by silver would not have voted for Bryan in any event; and the chance for agricultural businessmen to attract a solid labor vote was minimal at best. Silver had become so central, so wholly the cause and the answer, however, that it blinded Bryan (and his associates) to the full meaning of what was happening in the Western Republican parties. And Bryan was the key figure, for he had been aiming for the Democratic nomination since 1894, and the more militant reformers had no choice but to accept him once he fulfilled that ambition.

The indicator that Bryan—and Populist leaders—missed became apparent during the Republican state convention in Idaho, though it had appeared as early as 1894 in other states. First, the delegates condemned Cleveland as vehemently as any Democrat. Second, they heaped high praise on Senator Fred Thomas Dubois for his "fearless position taken in behalf of the free coinage of silver, protection to American industry and reciprocity, one and inseparable."[45] The second resolution was crucial, for it revealed the possibility of developing a package approach that could counter the appeal of free silver among Western farmers. Seeing only the big silver sky, the Democrats and Populists missed that small cloud far down on the horizon.

But it was not a cloud to William McKinley, who had been working just as hard as Bryan for a presidential nomination. It was instead almost precisely the package of protection, reciprocity, and some kind of commitment to silver that he and other astute Republican leaders were preparing to offer the workers and capitalists in the cities and the farm businessmen in the crucial states of the upper Midwest. One sign of that evolution came in a letter of November 9, 1894, from William J. Fowler of the *American Cultivator* to Senator Cushman Kellogg Davis of Minnesota. Fowler viewed the resurgence of Republican power in the elections of 1894 as offering the party a second chance to embrace the Harrison-Blaine reciprocity strategy, add a strong stand for bimetallism, and capitalize on the opportunity to rule the country "during the next quarter of a century."[46] Davis understood the argument and agreed that the strategy could be very effective in exploiting the agricultural reaction against the Wilson tariff.[47]

Davis was undoubtedly a major participant, along with others like Pillsbury, in the policy discussions that began in May 1895 and culminated six months later in the decision to launch a major drive for reciprocity, and for retaliation to open the European markets for American surpluses. The *Northwestern Miller* opened the campaign with a long feature article on December 27, 1895, and it attracted so much favorable attention that it went into production as a pamphlet within two weeks.[48] The effort rapidly became integrated with the support for the revolution in Cuba, and dramatized how the agricultural concern to expand the free marketplace was focused on that specific foreign policy question.[49]

The response of the editors of *Farm, Field and Fireside* was just as significant, perhaps more so, for they were strong silver advocates who joined the campaign for reciprocity. Their long article at the end of January praised Blaine and again tied the issue to Cuba. The problem was to find "a statesman large enough" to put reciprocity and silver together and thereby realize Blaine's old cry of "America for Americans."[50] The *Western Rural* immediately echoed that slogan, and made the same connection with Cuba. "'America for Americans' is now the phrase, not only with reference to the Monroe Doctrine, but with a view to reciprocal trade. . . . If independent Cuba, with a warm side towards the United States, could be thrown into the scale, it would make a vast increase in our commerce."[51]

The livestock growers and the packers immediately joined the battle. Samuel W. Allerton led the processors in a public campaign focused on Representative Joseph Gurney Cannon of Illinois. "Restore reciprocity, open the markets of the world for our cattle, hog products, and canned goods. . . . The foreign exchange is made south and west of the Alleghenies. Restore reciprocity." "An old farmer," writing to the *Country Gentleman*, agreed that the answer to the depression was "to take possession of the world's markets."[52] Wool growers added their weight, complaining that the Wilson tariff "very seriously compromised" "our international business relations." The *Pioneer Press* prophesied accurately that many farm businessmen in the West "will be more interested in getting a higher tariff on wool than in securing the free coinage of silver."[53]

The editors of the *Rural New Yorker* were unusually perceptive and well-informed agricultural leaders, and they did not miss the significance of what was happening among the Northern farmers. Their light touch was typical of the way they often made a central point. "It must be," they noted on April 4, 1896, "that the Cuban question and the chance that McKinley will secure the Republican nomination have made our readers forget our great book offer."[54] Always a bit more heavy-handed, the *Northwestern Miller* intoned three weeks later that reciprocity "will rise to worry several of the politicians."[55] It did just that to Bryan and the Populists. The reason was that it intrigued such key Republican leaders as Whitelaw Reid, Senator Stephen Benton Elkins of West Virginia, Representative Nelson Dingley, Jr., of Maine, and Speaker of the House Thomas Brackett Reed. Flour king Pillsbury returned from his conversations with Reed "greatly encouraged," while Elkins and Reid concluded that "the reaction to the Wilson Bill" was one of the basic explanations for McKinley's strength.[56]

McKinley had established his credentials with the industrial market expansionists by committing himself to the protection-reciprocity strategy at the founding convention of the National Association of Manufacturers. The N. A. M. proved an effective pressure group, and immediately launched a drive for reciprocity and a campaign to capture Latin American markets. The National Board of Trade shortly added its strong endorsement of reciprocity, and *Bradstreet's* reported as early as January 18, 1896, that such pressure was being felt by many members of the House.[57] The intensity of the Democratic and Populist commitment to silver is perhaps best revealed by the way it blinded them to what was happening in the South—and in the House of Representatives.

McKinley's strategy for winning the Republican nomination relied heavily at the outset on obtaining the endorsement of Southern state conventions, and he campaigned vigorously for those delegates. And his combination of protection and reciprocity evoked a positive response from the Southern mill owners who were increasingly interested in those policies. Even those who remained Democrats made it clear that they agreed with David A. Tompkins that reciprocity treaties were essential in expanding their exports. The Southern Textile Manufacturers Association, organized in May 1896, not only stressed reciprocity in its Declaration of Principles, but voted to cooperate with the N.A.M. and the New England Cotton Manufacturers' Association in a joint effort to enact that policy.[58] Southern leaders like Senator Morgan responded by supporting the old Blaine strategy.

But not Bryan. He also missed or discounted the testimony before the House Ways and Means Committee during the winter and spring. Those hearings were explicitly focused on "Reciprocity and Commercial Treaties," and undoubtedly grew out of the Republican concern to exploit the agricultural reaction against the Wilson tariff.[59] Flour millers attended in force, constantly pressing in with their demands for foreign markets "to avert ruin." They provided a classic example of what the committee described as "Private Enterprise Searching For New Markets." But meat packers, provision handlers, and livestock raisers added their voices for reciprocity in general—and with Cuba in particular.

Industrialists and other metropolitan businessmen appeared to support the same policy. The National Board of Trade was followed by the Cleveland Chamber of Commerce and a strong presentation from the Assembly of the State of New York. The latter posited the "inevitable destiny" of the United States, and continued with a list of urgent demands that included "the acquisition of Cuba by the United States, preferably by purchase." Then, after the Farmers Headquarters in Clarinda, Iowa, interposed its resolution declaring "most emphatically for reciprocity," the Pittsburgh Chamber of Commerce added its judgment that new markets were "an imperative necessity."

The Philadelphia Board of Trade and the Boston Chamber of Commerce then prepared the way for John W. Gates, president of the huge Illinois Steel Corporation. "We got into Brazil in good shape," he reported, and then stepped aside while his top manager stressed the importance of the Cuban market. Like Carnegie, they were "willing to sell [their] surplus at a loss in order to keep the works running," but they preferred to operate at a profit with the aid of reciprocity treaties. They were supported by a report from the N.A.M. that emphasized the lessons of Brazil and asked with "particular emphasis" that they be applied to Cuba.

McKinley unquestionably digested that vital document, though he probably missed a similar study undertaken by the Wisconsin State Bureau of Labor.[60] It polled a sample of farmers by questionnaire and supplemented that information through informal interviews to discover how the agricultural businessmen of the state explained their depressed condition. Admitting they sometimes followed "old ruts," the farmers accepted their share of the blame. But they also attacked the Wilson tariff as "very injurious." Their positive proposals mentioned silver and transportation, but concentrated on two other policies: protection on such items as wool, and reciprocity treaties. All their answers were predicated upon the need for foreign markets, and a few integrated protection, reciprocity, and silver as explicitly as the Idaho Republicans.[61]

The Minnesota millers were so determined about the issue that Pillsbury agreed to be a delegate to the Republican convention "mainly because he desired to be in a position to urge the necessity of a reciprocity clause in the party platform." Understandably, the Northwestern Miller gave him credit for "the conspicuous place" of reciprocity in the campaign.[62] The judgment was overgenerous. It tells more about the pressure that McKinley had already responded to by the time of the convention than about why he responded. The answer to that question is simply that McKinley embraced reciprocity as a result of his encounter with Blaine in 1889-1890, and because his subsequent analysis of the political economy led him to stress overseas economic expansion.

McKinley was an unusually sensitive and shrewd politician, and he indicated as early as January 1896 that he was not going to campaign on "extreme protection." Pillsbury's efforts reinforced McKinley's decision to emphasize reciprocity, but they did not force it upon him. Pillsbury was a strong man, but not powerful enough to break McKinley's "irresistible will."[63] That became apparent in the way McKinley outmaneuvered the metropolitans who thought they had captured him in a net of gold during the St. Louis convention.

McKinley was a bimetallist with clear sympathies for silver. That "strong leaning," as observant members of Cleveland's Cabinet called it, won him the support of men like Francis A. Newlands, John G. Garrison, and Myron A. McCord, as well as the confidence of many agricultural businessmen who were not hard-line silverites.[64] The Western Rural, for example, spotted the way McKinley men were approving silver in various state conventions, and became increasingly concerned lest McKinley's record and rhetoric on silver keep the Western farmers in the Republican fold.[65] And metropolitan leaders like Senators Lodge and Hoar were deeply concerned to present a solid front on bimetallism.[66] Finally, those views were shared by Marcus Hanna, the tough, brilliant political manager who had committed himself to McKinley in 1888.

The ensuing and bitter intraparty fight arose because the Eastern Republicans who controlled the state machines that McKinley had to defeat to win the nomination also understood his silver sympathies. An official of the National Union Bank laid it on the line in mid-May, less than a month before the convention. "There is a very ugly, hostile feeling growing up here among financial and business men against McKinley because of his silence on money subjects. The leading foreign banking houses give out that the large gold exports are occasioned by distrust of their correspondents abroad as to his soundness. . . . Urge him to make a plain statement against free silver."[67]

The convention fight forced McKinley to give ground. But he did not surrender. He reluctantly accepted an explicit pledge to gold, but in return obtained a commitment to bimetallism and an explicit attack on the Democrats who "pawned American credit to alien syndicates."[68] That was not enough for the hard-line silverites led by Senator Teller, and they stalked out of the convention in a display of righteous nationalistic expansionism. The United States, they declared, "can not much longer exist free and independent" unless it employs silver to enlarge agricultural (and other) exports.[69] "Stripped of everything else," as Teller later explained, "the simple question is, Are we in favor of having a system of our own?" Crying "Yes!" and adding that "it is cowardly to say that we must ask the permission of Great Britain," Teller missed McKinley's fundamental agreement on the primary issue of "having a system of our own."[70]

The Republican platform left no doubts, made no equivocations, on that issue. The Democratic repeal of reciprocity was termed "a National calamity," and the policy would be restored "to secure enlarged markets for the products of our farms, forests, and factories. . . . Reciprocity builds up foreign trade and finds an outlet for our surplus." Foreign policy "should be at all times firm, vigorous, and dignified." That meant Hawaii "should be controlled by the United States"; a canal "built, owned and operated by the United States"; the "continued enlargement of the navy"; the "purchase of the Danish West Indies"; and a commitment that "everywhere, American citizens and American property must be absolutely protected at all hazards and at any cost." As for Cuba, Spain had "lost control," and the "Government of the United States should actively use its influence and good offices to restore peace and give independence to the island."

Bryan answered that silver would do all that—and more. He had been developing his argument since the late 1880s, when he sided with Bland on silver and with Mills against Cleveland over the proper use of a low tariff. His formulation of a definitive statement was complete in all essential respects by January 1894, when he tied the entire political economy to agricultural exports that carried the balance of trade. "I am not," he avowed, "in favor of the reciprocity which you have had last year, but I am in favor of commercial freedom."[71] And the key to that was unilateral remonetization of silver.

The degree to which he had integrated all facets of his concern to expand the free marketplace around silver was revealed during a routine appearance at a university debate competition. While waiting for the decision of the judges on the winner of a competition over the Venezuelan boundary issue, Bryan filled the time with a speech on

"The Monroe Doctrine Applied to the Silver Question." That meant remonetization "without waiting for the aid or consent of any other country."[72] Even men like Bland, who held that silver would "double the foreign market for our goods, and give us such a period of prosperity as we have never known before," could not match Bryan's single-minded dedication.[73]

Senator John Warwick Daniel of Virginia did offer, however, a superb performance as temporary chairman of the Democratic convention after the goldbugs had been driven from the scene. He was joyful beyond measure that the party had finally found an issue that enabled it to throw off the onerous label of un-American that the protectionists had pinned on it a generation earlier. The protectionist goldbugs were the true alien sympathizers whose policies assisted Great Britain in asserting and maintaining its "commercial supremacy over the world." The United States, he continued, possessed "a natural base of fixed empire," and the time was long since past "to declare the financial independence of the United States." Brethren of the East," he thundered in warning, "there is no North, South, East or West in this uprising of the people for American emancipation from the conspiracy of European kings, led by Great Britain, which seeks to . . . make American manufacturers, merchants, farmers, and mechanics hewers of wood and drawers of water."[74]

Then Bryan did it even more effectively in a speech closing out the discussion on the platform. He first vented the spirit of the farm businessmen's sure knowledge of their underlying primacy in the political economy. "Burn down your cities and leave our farms, and your cities will spring up again as if by magic; but destroy our farms and the grass will grow in the streets of every city in the country." He then compressed Daniel's long list of occupations into a perfect charge against the metropolis: it made "the definition of a business man too limited in its application." Farmers were as truly businessmen as lawyers, bankers, or industrial magnates. Bryan had used that phrase—and the idea behind it—so long that it reverberated in the agricultural press as effectively as it did in the convention hall.[75]

The demand for the government to help businessmen, Bryan pointed out, involved no break with sound American traditions. "We today are inventing no new principles . . . we are simply applying to new conditions those principles which must forever live if the people still retain their love for our form of government." Indeed, Bryan thundered, "it is the issue of 1776 over again." Then he launched his fervent nationalistic attack on gold monometallism as a British policy that would subvert American freedom and prosperity—nay, that had already done so. "Let England have bimetallism because the United States has it." It is often forgotten that his militant assertion of anti-metropolitan, anti-British sentiment provided the context for his famous conclusion. "We will answer their demand for a gold standard by saying to them: 'You shall not press down upon the brow of labor this crown of thorns. You shall not crucify mankind upon a cross of gold!'"

Bryan settled the platform debate and the nomination fight with one speech. "The money question is paramount to all others." "Gold monometallism is a British policy, and its adoption had brought other nations into financial servitude to London. It is not only un-American but anti-American." That bold attack dominated the platform. "Trafficking with banking syndicates" was condemned, and Blaine's reciprocity strategy was blamed for the loss by farm businessmen "of access to their national markets." While implicitly recognizing the weaknesses of the Wilson tariff, the question of revision was left moot. And nothing more than "sympathy" was offered to the Cubans.

But Bryan and silver were enough for Teller and other displaced Republicans and independents. They met in St. Louis on July 22 as the National Silver party. First they reviewed all the arguments that the agricultural businessmen and others had developed for silver. Second, they promised that remonetization would expand the marketplace and restore prosperity. Finally, they agreed to support Bryan. "A vote for Bryan," cried Teller, "is a vote for industrial and financial independence of the American people from foreign domination and control."[76]

Most Populists undoubtedly agreed with that proposition. But a significant number thought other measures were also needed for full liberation, and more than a few even had doubts as to whether silver was the most promising of several instruments for producing domestic equity and international market supremacy. The dissatisfaction of those reformers (who were divided among themselves) was increased by their reluctance to accept the consequences of their own strategic mistake in scheduling their convention after the Democrats had acted. Going with Bryan meant going behind Bryan. But they enjoyed very little freedom of action because they had not created the kind of broad support, or effective state organizations, that provided the strength to survive certain defeat if they nominated a third ticket.

The choice was between a coalition with the Democrats that offered some immediate influence (and a chance for more) and a gallant gesture of determined and militant reformism. The majority of the delegates clearly favored the first alternative, and the angry rhetoric of the minority has to be discounted as an indicator of its actual strength. For even those who advocated more extensive changes operated within the political economy of the capitalistic marketplace. That had been apparent between 1887 and 1896, and it was again demonstrated after the election.

Senator Allen's keynote address stressed that very point, and he argued that silver offered the best way to preserve and improve the marketplace system. The defeat of the British would leave the American metropolis weakened and isolated and open the way for reform. That analysis became the preamble of the platform. "The influence of European money changers has been more potent in shaping legislation than the voice of the American people. . . . We demand the establishment of an economic and financial system which shall make us masters of our own affairs, and independent of European control." The remonetization of silver was thus the means of insuring "the welfare and prosperity of this and future generations."

The Populists went on to reassert the importance of better and more equitable transportation as a part of the structure of the marketplace. In good Smithian fashion, they called for government ownership "to the end that all may be accorded the same treatment." They likewise reiterated the argument for some form of a subtreasury system that would likewise help farm businessmen attain marketplace supremacy. And, in a forecast of later pressure, they demanded the government "should recognize that Cuba is, and of right ought to be, a free and independent state."[77] The nomination of Tom Watson as the candidate for vice-president was a revealing assertion of party identity, for he had pushed market expansion throughout his career.

Neither the Populists nor Bryan ever paused to consider the possibility that they could lose decisive votes from their own power base. "The contest upon which the common people of this country have entered," Bryan promptly announced, "involves not national union but popular liberty and the maintenance of the rights of the people as against their taskmasters of the East."[78] That was perfectly true at one very important level of analysis, and wholly accurate as an estimate of the neocolonial resentment and determination to gain more equity in the management and the rewards of the political economy. Indeed, those aspects of the developing social consciousness of the farm businessmen had created a vigorous movement of assertive, nationalistic expansionism. And, in that fundamental sense, Bryan's emphasis on freedom was a wholly consistent corollary of his stress on silver.

Yet it nevertheless blinded him to the pragmatic political effectiveness of Blaine's sophisticated appeal to the neocolonial agriculturalists. A program that delivered farm businessmen a greater share of the marketplace (while promising them even more), and flattered them without hypocrisy in the process, filed the cutting edge of colonial antagonism into the kind of rounded, softened resentment that was an accepted part of marketplace competition. Blaine's strategy for holding farm businessmen in a coalition with metropolitan businessmen spoke to a kind of shrewd realism about freedom that protected the agriculturalists against confusing rhetoric with reality.

Instead of concentrating first on rallying his hard-core supporters, Bryan opened his campaign on August 12 in Madison Square Garden. Even metropolitan Democrats who passionately opposed Bryan were dumbfounded. "The East is not the battleground," Postmaster Wilson noted in his diary.[79] The speech was not poor, though Bryan, lacking a sounding board of farmers, did not perform with his usual dynamism. The trouble was simply the irrelevance of the message in that milieu. While workers were angry with old-line metropolitan leadership, for example, McKinley had a deserved reputation as a man who dealt fairly with labor. In the context of the depression, moreover, the logic of protection spoke more directly to the wage earner than the silver argument. And, as revealed by the difficulties of building a solid coalition between labor and agriculture in the industrializing sections of the Middle West, workers shared in varying degrees the anti-farmer attitudes of their employers.

One astute Republican from the West, Clarkson of Iowa, understood why Bryan faced such a difficult problem in the metropolis. "I think you realize in some degree," he wrote a friend in Utah, "although you could not fully unless you were here to learn of the distrust and prejudice among Eastern capitalists against Western people." "Eastern people," he continued, "are provincial. They do not realize, as I often tell them, that the whole prosperity of the country, the very salvation of finance and banking and honor, all depend on the Western people."[80] Bryan of course agreed with that estimate, but he failed to exploit its implications.

McKinley dealt with the challenge far more astutely by opening his campaign sitting on his front porch in Ohio while Bryan entered the lion's den. Only then did he issue his letter of acceptance. It was a masterpiece based upon leaving the door open for bimetallism, stressing reciprocity as the way "to afford new markets for our surplus agricultural and manufactured products," and subtly countering Bryan's disdain for unity by appealing for union "to increase our power and influence abroad."[81] The insinuating effectiveness of the combination had been revealed two months earlier, when the pro-silver, pro-Bryan editors of *Farm, Field and Fireside* displayed a wrenching ambivalence induced by the appearance of Blaine's ghost, the militant call for action on Cuba, and the uneasiness that McKinley's record gave substance to his bimetallism.[82] At almost the same moment, West Coast silver spokesmen verified that fear: "McKinley is not owned by Wall Street."[83]

McKinley's acceptance letter was a typically sober and serious document, but it was also marked by a tone of relaxed confidence that contrasted strikingly with the anxiety manifested by many other politicians and observers. "Considerable excitement" was one of the milder descriptions of the situation offered by observers in the Middle West and the trans-Missouri region.[84] Metropolitan Democrats were perhaps even more concerned. Postmaster General Wilson reported as late as August and September that New York businessmen were "not at all confident that Bryan may be defeated."[85]

Given his political shrewdness, as well as his temperament, McKinley's display of confidence can partially be explained as a move to establish a positive mood among Republican fieldworkers. But his estimate that the peak danger was past, expressed more than a month before his letter of acceptance, was much more than a psychological gambit.[86] It was based on three solid considerations: first, confidence in the correctness of the strategy that concentrated on winning the upper Middle West; second, a sense of assurance that he had devised an appeal that would hold crucial agricultural votes in those states; and third, full trust in the effectiveness of Hanna and other key fieldworkers like Charles G. Dawes.

It is highly probable, moreover, that McKinley caught the upward turn of the wheat market before many other observers. The *Country Gentleman* first noted "a tendency to advance" on July 23, and a week later reinforced that estimate with reports of "a better feeling."[87] The opportunity created by unfavorable crops in Europe and a short harvest in America did not produce a general feeling of confidence, however, for another month. Then a very keen Minnesota flour miller committed himself to a forecast of "higher prices."[88]

Protagonists and commentators began explaining the outcome of the election in terms of the advance in wheat even before the voters went to the polls, and historians later sustained the analysis. To avoid having it considered in too narrow a context, as a kind of wheat-up-Democrats-down thesis, the episode needs to be reviewed within a broader framework. The rise in wheat came at the end of a long process in which the metropolis itself had come to accept the export analysis developed and agitated by agricultural businessmen. It occurred, moreover, to men suffering the third year of a depression who thought about such indicators in the context of agricultural exports having ended the massive depression of the 1870s. And it happened in the midst of a campaign being waged at the climax of a six-year argument about how best to expand exports. The two contenders were stressing that very issue.

Thus the nation was not merely predisposed to view the jump in wheat prices as a central development, but it would have required a drastic reversal of deeply entrenched assumptions and beliefs for it to have done otherwise. "Anything which has a bearing upon our foreign trade," noted the *Prairie Farmer*, "has a particular interest at this time."[89] As the turn in the market began to appear well founded, Western Republican leaders talked bluntly to metropolitan financiers. "The best way to elect Bryan is to hold on to the money" needed to move the crops, and by flour millers and other processors to meet their requirements.[90]

As the gains continued, undercutting the silver argument that wheat could not rise unless the price of silver jumped, one Bryan journal charged the improvement in the market was all a maneuver by Hanna to defeat the Democratic-Populist coalition.[91] And surely the money that went west to market the crops was as important as the funds that Hanna collected for his intensive campaign throughout the upper Mississippi and Missouri valleys. For it helped mightily to give substance to the rhetorical campaign against silver and in behalf of reciprocity. Hanna felt confident enough about Iowa, for example, to refuse a request for additional funds.[92]

The Germans also supplied an assist by announcing new restrictions on American meat exports.[93] That reinforced McKinley's persistent and heavy emphasis on reciprocity.[94] The president of the National Livestock Exchange even carried his battle for votes for reciprocity into Texas. "Reciprocity would open for our surplus the foreign gates of commerce . . . and the resultant beneficial effect would soon be felt in every channel of commerce."[95] Through all such developments, Hanna's dedicated labor—"he is working incessantly and vigorously"—delivered the message to marginal and undecided voters.[96]

The growing impact of the export boomlette manifested itself in economic analyses, letters to the editor, editorial judgments, and political reports from the battleground. It "certainly helped many farmers," ran a typical comment from the West in a long symposium in the *Rural New Yorker*.[97] The *Pacific Rural Press* judged it the most remarkable short-run expansion in the history of California wheat business.[98] And the editors of *Manufacturers Record* compared it favorably—and hopefully—with the boom at the end of the 1870s: "This enormous increase in foreign exports completely changed all business conditions," and might well "mark the beginning of a general revival."[99]

A member of a survey crew working in Illinois, "asking everybody about politics," reported as early as September 24 that he had been "unable to find a single Bryan man among the farmers. They all say the Democratic farmers will vote for McKinley."[100] Minnesota observers felt confident a month later: the exports won McKinley votes by upsetting "the theory that Bryan and his followers have been advancing," and by putting "the farmer in better humor."[101] Bryan clearly felt the same way, for he belatedly rushed to Minnesota in a last effort to win the vital Middle West. Leaning very heavily on the importance of agricultural exports, he tried too late to persuade the farm businessmen that silver would make America "the mistress of the world's commerce."[102]

He failed there as elsewhere in the region. He ran third in Minnesota behind a Silver-Republican candidate for governor (who won that office)—far in the rear of McKinley. Perhaps the most perceptive summary of McKinley's success among farm businessmen came in a terse comment from the editors of the *Iowa State Register:* "It is a business man's state."[103] Bryan had not matched his insight into the truth that the agriculturalists were as truly businessmen as their metropolitan counterparts with a program that convinced them he would improve business. McKinley not only succeeded in that struggle, but he promptly called the Congress into special session to implement his strategy of market expansion for all businessmen.

FIFTEEN

Now don't you fellows fool yourselves by thinking that we will be able to give McKinley instructions.

Marcus Hanna, 1896

[We] have a concern with [Cuba] which is by no means of a wholly sentimental or philanthropic character . . . Beside this large pecuniary interest. . . . It can not be reasonably assumed that the hitherto expectant attitude of the United States will be indefinitely maintained.

President Grover Cleveland,
December 1896

United States battle ships should be sent without delay to Cuban waters.

Populist Senator Allen,
February 1897

Especial attention should be given to the reenactment and extension of the reciprocity principle . . . [to open] new and advantageous markets for our surplus agricultural and manufactured products.

President William McKinley,
March 1897

Why should we not act? . . . There is no nation . . . upon the face of the earth with which we have such immediate, such direct, such important commercial and other relations. . . . Why should we not act? . . . We have lost the advantages of the Cuban market.

Senator John Thurston of
Nebraska, May 1897

Cuba would be worth more to our commerce than Alaska.

Farm, Field and Fireside,
June 1897

New markets . . . [constitute] the paramount need of the agricultural interests at this time. . . . Japan and China offer the most tempting fields for the increase of our wheat exportation.

Prairie Farmer, July 1897

The extraordinary, because direct and not merely theoretical or sentimental, interest of the United States in the Cuban situation cannot be ignored. . . . The chronic condition of trouble . . . injuriously affects the normal functions of business, and tends to delay the condition of prosperity to which this country is entitled.

Secretary of State John Sherman
to Spain, July 1897

I am not lying awake at night over the condition of Cuba. . . . I am more concerned about the condition and prosperity of our own people.

Populist Jerry Simpson, January 1898

What we all want is Chinese trade.

Commodore George Dewey,
January 1898

[We] respectfully and earnestly urge . . . the prompt and energetic defense of existing treaty rights of our citizens in China, and . . . the preservation and protection of their important commercial interest in that Empire.

New York State Chamber of Commerce
to President McKinley, February 1898

War is not only coming. . . . The real, the insidious first entrance upon war has already been made.

Representative James R. Mann
of Illinois, March 8, 1898

The Boston men . . . said for business one shock and then an end was better than a succession of spasms.

Senator Lodge to President McKinley,
March 21, 1898

We as Populists ought to be candid. Since 1896 all the leading Populists in National, State and county conventions have declared in some way favorable towards freeing Cuba. . . . All this talk about imperialism is but the old howl of the Federalists when they arrayed themselves against Mr. Jefferson for securing to this Nation the Louisiana purchase. . . . Stand firm for [a policy] which will put us in touch with five hundred millions of Asiatic consumers.

J. S. Woods, Letter to the Editor,
Southern Mercury, July 21, 1898

Onward
to War for the Free American
Marketplace

McKinley moved to honor his commitments to reciprocity and bimetallism as soon as he won the election. The decision to intervene in Cuba, with force if necessary, was made less than a year after his inauguration as President. The strategy adopted, should force be used, called for a two-front war to seize and hold an American base in the Philippines. The acceptance of war as an instrument of policy involved a process similar to the dynamics of a man starting down a sand dune to the sea. Once the objective is defined, and the movement started, the steps become longer and longer and the speed increases. There is a crucial instant when the mass of the man becomes great enough to compact the sand, and on the next step it suddenly exerts a force of its own. The man either stops in a jarring halt or becomes almost airborne.

Historians cannot film the process of going to war as a physicist can record the flight of a man down a sand dune. Hence they cannot perfectly isolate the pivotal instant. But they can with confidence say that the decision occurred within a certain period. And with the McKinley Administration that moment came long before the President wrote his special war message of April 1898 to the Congress. The primary force producing the war against Spain was the marketplace-expansionist outlook generated by the agricultural majority of the country during the generation after the firing on Fort Sumter. That social consciousness involved an image of the world as a free capitalist marketplace in which personal and social freedoms were causally integrated with economic liberty and welfare, in which ideas and experience were merged as beliefs, and which promised ideal results from necessary actions.

The agricultural businessmen played a smaller, but by no means insignificant, part in the crucial definition of the war as an instrument of American expansion in Asia. But it was the metropolitans, rather than the agriculturalists, who explicitly formulated the war against Spain over Cuba as a war for the free marketplace in the Far East. The acceptance of that conception marked the shift in policy-making initiative away from the farm businessmen to metropolitan leaders. It was a decision of principle implemented with plans to fight a two-front war, and to hold some portion of Spain's Pacific empire as a springboard to the Asian marketplace.

The integration of Cuba and China was the product of five developments. The traditional interest in the China market was heightened by the rising exports (particularly of Southern rough cotton textiles) of the late 1880s and 1890s, the Hawaiian coup and the agitation over annexation, and the Sino-Japanese war. Next came the climax of the silver movement, which had always pointed to China as one of the markets to be won by remonetization. Then the outbreak of the Cuban revolution provided a major focus for agricultural agitation to save and enlarge that market, and to force the metropolis to act more vigorously and more generally to enlarge the free marketplace. That pressure steadily pushed the government to demand more of Spain, and into its own discussions of forceful intervention. Those talks led to contingency planning by the Navy. The first actionable result was a June 1, 1896, report by Lieutenant William Wirt Kimball: "War with Spain, 1896, General Considerations of the War, the Results Desired, and the Consequent Kind of Operations To Be Undertaken."[1] The "strategic importance of Manila" defined that Pacific port as part of a war over Cuba. The connection became determinative by the end of October 1896, when the Administration committed itself to preparing a full war plan by January 1, 1897.[2]

Private and official concern with the Asian market was an integral part of that conception of a war with Spain. Hill of the Great Northern was beginning to ship Southern cotton (and textiles), as well as flour, to the Far East; and his operations were paralleled by various other entrepreneurs headed by the American-China Development Company, John J. McCook of the law firm of Alexander and Green, and James H. Wilson.[3] The latter two, aided by such members of the Cleveland Administration as Secretary of War Daniel S. Lamont, transformed the visit of the high Chinese official Li Hung Chang into a state occasion, and succeeded in having Secretary of State Olney instruct the American Minister to China to use his "personal and official influence" to obtain contracts for American firms. The editors of the *Rural New*

Yorker added that Li's visit should be exploited to expand agricultural exports.[4]

The farm businessmen were more influential in connection with Cuba.[5] Their agitation and demands forced Cleveland to increase his pressure on Spain, and provoked him to serious thought about setting a deadline for obtaining satisfaction from Madrid. In a draft version of his annual message of December 1896, for example, Cleveland warned the Spanish that American patience had "its necessary limitations." The United States would sooner rather than later "be compelled to protect its own interests and those of its citizens, which are coincident with those of humanity and civilization." He indicated that a grace period of a month would be granted, after which the consequences "would be almost inevitable."[6]

Delivered as written, those words would have produced war in January 1897, the date toward which the Navy had pointed in making its plans. But they were not spoken. The armed forces were not ready, and Cleveland, whatever his own fears and preferences, was not a man to leave a war on the doorstep for an incoming Administration. In the message that he did deliver, however, the President warned that America's patience would not "be indefinitely maintained." The demand for satisfaction rested on a concern "by no means of a wholly sentimental or philanthropic character." The "large pecuniary stake" of the United States played an important part in the rising clamor for action. Spain would have to pacify the island quickly or face the prospect of more forceful intervention.[7]

Agreed, cried the chorus of militant agriculturalists, demanding that "something should be done." Led by Senators Allen and Morgan, the expansionists greeted McKinley with a call for sending battleships to Cuban waters "without delay."[8] McKinley resisted such pressure because he preferred to free Cuba without war and because he knew that powerful metropolitan interests opposed that solution to the problem. Those men wanted peace for recovery from the depression followed by the undramatic conquest of the markets of the world. War would "seriously damage all of our commercial and financial interests."[9]

The agricultural militants, warned some metropolitans, were trying "to disturb confidence and so do something for silver." The same men attacked metropolitan war hawks as selfish or short-sighted agitators who wanted "the balance of their countrymen to save them from loss." If for no other reason, war should be avoided because it would hurt the farm exports that maintained the system by pulling it out of depressions.[10] There were two other metropolitan attitudes that deserve attention because they pointed toward the consensus that finally developed.

One was the view, manifested in the *Wall Street Journal* and the *Com-*

mercial and Financial Chronicle for a short period after Cleveland's message, that a war would not cause much disruption in the economy. Indeed, it might even "stimulate rather than depress business," and would further serve to unite the divided country.[11] That estimate gradually attracted more support during 1897, and was finally adopted by many who originally opposed intervention of any kind. The other opinion involved a wider appreciation of the agricultural majority and its problems.

Philip Armour, for example, felt that "better times, and better prices for grain and stock," would convert more dissident farm businessmen "than any missionaries we might send to talk to them."[12] Stuyvesant Fish, who shared Armour's strong sense of being part of the agricultural economy, expressed an enlarged understanding of the monetary difficulties faced by the farmers.[13] And William E. Dodge told the New York Chamber of Commerce, after a trip through the West, that he had been ignorant and mistaken. "I came back very deeply impressed with the conviction that I had not been entirely informed, and those living in the East were not entirely informed, as to the condition of things in very large portions of our country."[14]

McKinley had been very deeply impressed with the agricultural majority much earlier, of course, and intended to continue his efforts to further its interests as he aided the metropolis. He was also his own man. "There are idiots," John Hay remarked, "who think Mark Hanna will run him!"[15] Some of the men who were mistaken on that point, such as John W. Gates of the Illinois Steel Corporation, enjoyed considerable power themselves and were inclined to think they could work their will by calling Hanna on the telephone. It is true that the President listened to powerful metropolitan leaders, and avoided antagonizing them whenever that was possible. But he also displayed great skill in maneuvering them into positions where they had little choice but to do what he had decided to do, and he possessed a will that no metropolitan giant could break.

Gates learned that lesson sooner than many. He was trying to secure a high appointment for a close friend who had opposed McKinley's nomination, and in the discussion with Hanna mentioned the large ore purchases of his firm. He then suggested that Hanna's company could count on a large share of such business if he used his influence on the President. Hanna put it aside with a shrug. "Well, I am not paying much attention to the ore situation." When Gates persisted, Hanna was blunt: "You do not quite understand my position. . . . I cannot tell who will secure the prize." McKinley made such decisions.[16]

"After you have talked with him," Hanna told another group of Republican leaders, "you will find that he knows more about politics than all of us." "Don't fool yourselves by thinking we will be able to give McKinley instructions."[17] A similar failure to understand the

situation misled some farm leaders, for example, to view the appointment of John Sherman as Secretary of State as a sign of presidential
weakness and as proof of metropolitan control of the Administration. "We can expect no . . . aggressive foreign policy," they complained.[18] That judgment was correct in the sense that neither Sherman
nor McKinley was ready to declare war on the day of inauguration, but
it was profoundly mistaken in that it missed McKinley's unreserved
commitments to end the Cuban crisis and to push overseas economic
expansion.

McKinley appointed Sherman for several reasons. It was of course
a shrewd political maneuver, not least because it was a gesture of respect and honor to an aging major leader of the party with strong ties
to the metropolis. It was also a way to remove Sherman from the scene
of the action in the Senate while replacing him with Hanna, who promised to provide excellent intelligence, liaison, and organization. But
McKinley also knew that Sherman shared the view that foreign policy—explicitly in connection with Cuba, as well as generally—"must
be controlled by commercial interest."[19] Finally, the President was
aware that Sherman's weakened condition would make it easier to
control foreign policy from the White House.

The President revealed his concern with market expansion in making other appointments. Frank A. Vanderlip, Assistant Secretary of
the Treasury, for example, was an avid metropolitan expansionist.
Cornelius N. Bliss, who became Secretary of the Interior, was a se-
nior partner in Bliss, Fabyan and Company, one of the leading exporters of cotton to China. And James Wilson of Iowa, the new Secretary
of Agriculture, was another Rusk—one of many indicators of how
much McKinley had learned from Harrison and Blaine. Wilson was
a farm businessman who moved into politics during the first great
campaign to improve and regulate the railroads after the Civil War,
became known as "a Granger Congressman" during the 1870s and
1880s, and then served as a professor and director of the agricultural
experiment station at Iowa State College.

"Tama Jim" was a militant, indefatigable market expansionist who
accepted the overproduction analysis of the capitalist marketplace.
"We first produced wheat in abundance, and sent it abroad. Then came
pork, and now we have beef, and next it will be butter."[20] He favored
an isthmian canal, steamship and naval building programs, agricultural attachés for all embassies and legations, the annexation of Hawaii,
and viewed China as a major market for all American surpluses. McKinley responded quickly and positively to Wilson, and the Secretary of
Agriculture soon became one of the President's close personal friends
and important policy advisers. He was a powerful influence for a vigorous expansionist policy.

McKinley's strategy was predicated upon fostering and accelerating the recovery of the economy—and then sustaining it—through bimetallism, reciprocity, and an enlarged merchant marine. Bimetallism "will have early and earnest attention." "Especial attention should be given to the re-enactment and extension of the reciprocity principle of the law of 1890." "The end in view ought always to be the opening up of new markets for the products of our country. . . . Let us move out to new fields steadily and increase the sale for our products in foreign markets. It should be our settled purpose to open trade wherever we can."[21]

Those repeated references to overseas market expansion in McKinley's inaugural address documented the triumph of the agricultural majority in the long battle to determine the substance and tone of American foreign policy. Thereafter, as had been increasingly the case since the 1880s, the differences involved the techniques of expansion and the degree of emphasis on intervention to expand freedom as well as markets. Those disagreements were often heated, and sometimes raised important issues. But no significant effort was made to reopen the question of whether or not the nation should predicate its welfare on the inherent necessity of market expansion, or to reexamine the question of whether or not reforming others in the image of America's conception of freedom was logically and morally a necessary part of reform at home.

McKinley hoped that recovery from the depression would moderate if not forestall bitter debate over the tactical questions. He agreed with agricultural and metropolitan spokesmen who stressed the role of farm exports in achieving that immediate economic objective.[22] And he received reassuring reports from the railroads verifying that analysis. Frank Thompson of the Pennsylvania system wrote him directly of the 10 percent increase that led him to expect "decided improvement." And Fish of the Illinois Central was full of confidence that the "excellent crops" would, as usual, produce "business for the mills, for the railroads, and for every line of trade."[23]

Against that background, the President acted quickly to secure an agreement on bimetallism. "I am exceedingly anxious that we should carry out the pledge of our platform to promote international bimetallism, and everything I can do in that direction will be done." The congressional maneuvers were completed even before McKinley was inaugurated, and his appointees, a bipartisan group composed of Senator Edward Oliver Wolcott of Colorado, Democrat Adlai E. Stevenson of Illinois, and Charles J. Paine, sailed for France on May 8 to open negotiations for a conference with all European powers.[24]

Reciprocity was dealt with even more energetically. The President called the new Congress into special session and the Senate began work on the day of the inaugural. As had been the case with Harrison, Blaine, and Rusk, the campaign for reciprocity was paralleled by an effort to lower or remove barriers against American meat exports. Wilson told Sherman to "press it vigorously until American exporters receive just and fair treatment." The Secretary of State acted immediately. Both efforts won support from agricultural businessmen and their spokesmen.[25]

Typifying the consensus on market expansion, the congressional debate was not so much about reciprocity as it was a discussion of the problem within the framework of reciprocity. There was broad agreement, for example, that America was wholly committed to what Senator Nelson Wilmarth Aldrich of Rhode Island called "the bitter contest which is going on among the leading nations of the world for industrial supremacy." Individuals and groups that had formerly been opposed or indifferent to reciprocity, such as Democratic Senators Morgan of Alabama and George Gray of Delaware, and the McCormick Company, now supported the strategy.[26]

A small Populist contingent belatedly followed the lead of Tillman and joined the Grange and other groups in backing the Lubin export bounty plan. Their participation created an eddy of debate that briefly attracted some attention, largely because Senators Frank Green Cannon of Utah and Butler of North Carolina tried to prove that the expansionism of the agricultural businessmen was better than that of metropolitan entrepreneurs because it did not lead to colonialism. Their logic was so tortured, and the issue itself so secondary, however, that even the other Populists largely ignored the performance. When the vote came, Lubin's plan mustered a puny ten votes.[27]

Reciprocity did much better, being favored by a House proposal and an even more extensive Senate proviso. Both were included in the final bill passed on July 7, 1897, and the Senate version granted McKinley wide powers to negotiate such treaties during a two-year period. The House, however, insisted on the right to review all agreements before they went into operation. That restriction was not as important in explaining McKinley's failure to produce dramatic and profitable results, however, as the rising clamor for action against Spain and the increasing concern to penetrate the China market.

McKinley moved slowly and carefully—"very deliberately," as Senator Lodge noted—on Cuba during the first two months after he took office.[28] His typical very-close-to-the-buttoned-vest approach misled many people, including Lodge and other metropolitan expansionists, as well as the agriculturalists. For a time, the farm businessmen were themselves busy praising Secretary Wilson's vigorous effort to reopen old markets and penetrate new ones, agitating various expansionist measures such as a bill to add agricultural attachés to foreign legations, and adding their optimistic prognostications about the Asian market.[29] Increasingly, however, they focused their attention and pressure on Cuba.

Senator Allen pushed his campaign to recognize the rebels so heatedly that the Washington *Post* warned that "a spark might drop in at any time and precipitate action."[30] There were two sparks. One was Senator Morgan, who took over the battle with his resolution of April 1 to recognize "a condition of public war" in Cuba and extend "all the rights of belligerents" to the revolutionaries. The other was the increased ferocity and destructiveness of the rebels and the Spanish. That created intense emotion about the mistreatment of Americans and a heightened concern over the destruction of American economic interests.[31]

Morgan argued powerfully that the only way to reverse the sharp and severe drop in exports to Cuba was to create an independent Cuba tied to the United States. Populists like Allen vigorously supported that analysis, but so did Republicans like Senator John Meelen Thurston of Nebraska and Senator Francis Emory Warren of Wyoming, Democrats like Representative John Sharp Williams of Mississippi, and Populist-Democrats like Curtis Harvey Castle of California. "Why should we not act?" Thurston argued. "We have with her, or had with her, a great and an advantageous trade relation. . . . Why should we not act? I will put it upon no other grounds than purely commercial grounds, if you please. . . . We have lost the advantage of the Cuban market."[32]

Metropolitan expansionists like Lodge agreed with Thurston that the case for intervention could be made solely on economic grounds, and often presented that argument with great vigor. Many of that group shared the agricultural concern to spread freedom, moreover, although they often defined it more narrowly. Those men were opposed in the spring of 1897, however, by a stronger contingent of metropolitans who wanted peace in order to proceed with recovery at home and to pursue less dramatic economic expansion.[33] They tried to blunt the influence of the hard-liners with petitions of their own. More than 300 of them from New Orleans and Charleston, as well as Boston, New York, and Philadelphia, for example, signaled their support of McKinley in May. It was a curious kind of support, however, that pointed toward their ultimate willingness to intervene. They wanted peace to end the great economic losses and to quiet the unrest generated by the war in Cuba, but they asked the President to use his power and authority to secure that result.[34]

Most agriculturalists demanded far more direct intervention. Their resolution calling on McKinley to recognize the rebels as belligerents passed the Senate 41 to 14 on May 20, 1897; a demonstration of power that moved one group of peaceful expansionists to escalate their own efforts with a proposal to buy Cuba. McKinley would probably have gone along with that plan if it had ever become actionable (he kept it alive for months), but he was far too realistic to place much hope in that approach. The evidence is strong, indeed, that the President anticipated the ultimate necessity for intervention and war even as he came into office.

Assistant Secretary of State William R. Day, who was less militant than Secretary Sherman, felt that the President "probably" considered intervention from the outset. Another insider supported that estimate on the basis of his conversation with McKinley during the search for the right man to send as Minister to Spain. He quoted the President as saying that "if nothing could be done with Spain, he desired to show that he had spared no effort to avert trouble."[35] Other indicators reinforce that analysis. Senator Eugene Hale of Maine told the Senate during the debate over belligerency for the rebels that the President was in full control of the situation; and the editors of *Farm, Field and Fireside* quickly spotted the important liaison between McKinley and Representative Hitt of Illinois, who had been a militant expansionist ever since his service with Blaine. And Senator Francis Emory Warren of Wyoming, who discussed the issue with McKinley in June, told a friend that the President was ready to act.[36]

Actually, of course, the President had already acted, and it was only Warren's intense concern to be "selling them goods or provisions or anything else we manufacture or grow" that blurred his normally good political eyesight. McKinley sent William James Calhoun to investigate conditions in Cuba, supported an appropriation of $50,000 to aid Americans on the island, negotiated a new treaty of annexation with the American-dominated government of Hawaii, and appointed a special commission to report on the construction of a canal in Nicaragua. Most agriculturalists supported those moves, though the militants of course wanted more direct action.[37]

Some observers were dismayed, however, by what they took to be the assumption of many war hawks that the Spanish could be bluffed into surrendering Cuba.[38] Others, like Populist Jerry Simpson, did not speak to that point because they shared the traditional confidence in the efficacy of American power. But Simpson did display the contradictions of a man under increasing difficulties in trying to resolve the tension generated by the outlook of expansion for prosperity and reform. Thus, on the one hand, he vigorously defended the "absolute necessity" of an appropriation to build a naval coaling station at Pearl Harbor. Those who wanted to spend the money at home were mistaken. "It is plain that we should follow the line of action that Great Britain has so wisely followed in establishing naval stations throughout the world." But, on the other hand, he opposed the relief appropriation for Americans in Cuba on the grounds that charity began at home.[39]

While Simpson wrestled with the dilemma of expansion and reform, McKinley increased the pressure on Spain. The dreary and distressing reports from Calhoun, and the encouragement for stronger action from Secretary of Agriculture Wilson and others, were no doubt factors in the appointment of Stewart L. Woodford as Minister to Spain.[40] He was known to be sympathetic toward the Cubans, and some metropolitan businessmen thought him "too close to the war hawks." That fear was probably reinforced by the approval manifested by the militant agriculturalists who thought that "some important results are likely to come," and by the Army's refusal to allow Tasker H. Bliss, Woodford's military aid, to take his family to Madrid. The high command considered the risk of war far too high for such amenities.[41]

The editors of *Farm, Field and Fireside* either had a good source of official information or the Administration was very closely attuned to the outlook of the agriculturalists. Probably both. They advised the President on July 3, in any event, that Woodford's instructions "should ask the virtual independence of Cuba, for the sake of the lives and safety of our own citizens, for the sake of commerce, for the sake of humanity." The heart of the Administration's dispatch dated July 15, 1897, stressed that "the extraordinary, because direct and not merely theoretical or sentimental, interest of the United States in the Cuban situation cannot be ignored, and if forced the issue must be met honestly and fearlessly, in conformity with our national life and character."[42]

"Not only are our citizens largely concerned in the ownership of property and in the industrial and commercial ventures which have been set on foot in Cuba through our enterprising initiative and sustained by their capital, but the chronic condition of trouble and violent derangement in that island constantly causes disturbance in the social and political condition of our own people. It keeps up a continuous irritation within our own borders, injuriously affects the normal functions of business, and tends to delay the condition of prosperity to which this country is entitled. . . . Assuredly Spain can not expect the Government to sit idle, letting vast interests suffer, our political elements disturbed, and the country perpetually embroiled, while no progress is being made in the settlement of the Cuban problem. . . . You will not disguise the gravity of the situation, nor conceal the President's conviction that, should his present effort be fruitless, his duty to his countrymen will necessitate an early decision as to the course of action which the time and the transcendent emergency may demand."

Perhaps no official document of the era provides as clear a statement of the expansionist outlook that had been generated and shaped by the agricultural majority. Spain was held responsible for a prosperity to which the United States was "entitled." Misrule in Cuba, rather than the failure of the domestic political economy, was the actionable cause of America's difficulties. Equally important, the message established McKinley's deep concern with the increasingly aggressive demands for direct intervention by the militants headed by the agriculturalists and their spokesmen. That agitation was a product of the same conception of America's needs and objectives. The definition of the United States in terms of an expanding free marketplace and the frontier process had created a "transcendent emergency" that could only be resolved by a foreign power acting within that framework—or by war.

There was a short interlude of deceptive calm on the Cuban front while Woodford familiarized himself with the situation in Spain. The principal subject of discussion was Japan's resistance to the annexation of Hawaii. Even Lodge reported that "everything is quiet here."[43] The editors of *The Nation* and *Railroad World* were more perceptive. "The most critical of all the Cuban struggles," reported the former, "are going on in the various inland towns and cities of the United States, where our Senators and Representatives are in the thick of the fray." A bellicose speech by Senator Cushman Davis in St. Louis was typical of the action by such militants that "McKinley has most to dread. They will force his hand infallibly." Such men, agreed the railroad spokesmen, have transformed the Cuban issue into "a standing menace."[44]

In at least one respect, *The Nation* was wholly correct. The agricultural militants did force McKinley's hand insofar as the timing of his ultimate military intervention. And, in doing that, they closed the door on the last chance to free Cuba without war. The farm businessmen were also the leaders (and the chorus) that generated the outlook and the attitude—and the trade—that made Cuba so much more central in American thinking during the mid-1890s than it had been during the previous years. In those fundamental respects, therefore, the agricultural majority could not evade a major share of the responsibility for the war against Spain.

But the farmers were not primarily responsible for the Administration's decision to fight the war, if it proved necessary, with a two-front global strategy. Nor did they make the decision to intervene. Those choices were made, in that order, during the last months of 1897 and the first days of 1898. For that matter, the President's July 1897 instructions to Woodford very probably represented a firm decision to force the issue with a full understanding that the result would very likely be war. One man who spent a week with McKinley and his close advisers at the end of August reported that everyone expected Spain to reject the offer of good offices and the deadline for settlement on American terms. The group then examined the effect of war on domestic economic conditions, concluded it would be relatively minor, and turned to the problem of exploiting the victory for overseas economic expansion. On that, he reported, "there is as yet no well considered plan."[45]

Public commentators also anticipated war; and Woodford himself was so pessimistic that he advised the President directly of his "serious apprehension."[46] Such was the context in which McKinley began discussing the importance of the Philippines with Assistant Secretary of the Navy Theodore Roosevelt and others. Roosevelt, a vigorous war hawk, personally submitted a formal memorandum advising the President to "take and retain the Philippines," and other high politicians soon supported that advice.[47] The Administration had already indicated its strong interest in the China market, and in August demanded (and received) the right for American merchants to reside in Hangchow province. Metropolitan and agricultural pressure for that market, and concern about European powers preempting it, continued to increase through August into October. James Hill asked the farmers to support his grand design to control the Far Eastern market, for example, and demanded more vigorous action from "our public men."[48]

The tension over Cuba eased a bit when on October 20, 1897, a new and ostensibly liberal government came to power in Spain. However, the importance of the change was not as great as some expected or claimed, if only because American officials had become so disenchanted with both the Spanish and the rebels that it would have taken dramatic new developments to alter their outlook. Secretary of Agriculture Wilson admitted that all would be well if the new government followed American specifications, but he did not expect that to happen. New York merchants hoped for more, petitioning the Spanish government for "improved trade relations," and Secretary of State Sherman allowed himself some optimism. But he coupled his promise of "benevolent expectancy" with a blunt and ominous warning that "peace in Cuba is necessary to the welfare of the people of the United States."[49]

That remark not only expressed the general feeling of the Administration, but revealed the impact of the clamor for intervention. Farm spokesmen discounted the new Spanish government and called for prompt action "when affairs are ripe." The mood was aptly expressed by a Southerner: "We have much to gain and little to lose by a war with Spain." The Administration could hardly discount the talk, for the Democrats had gained in the off-year elections, and the failure of the effort to negotiate an agreement for international bimetallism was sure to provoke more anger among the agriculturalists.[50]

McKinley had already made it clear that he was preparing for any eventuality. After long conversations with and about Fitzhugh Lee, he changed his mind about removing the extremely militant interventionist that Cleveland had appointed consul general in Havana. Instead, the President sent Lee back to Cuba. Next he instructed Woodford to preserve "full freedom of action."[51] And then he detached the battleship *Maine* from the North Atlantic squadron, and allowed the remainder of that unit to proceed with its scheduled war maneuvers in the Gulf of Mexico. Woodford commented laconically that Spain had no choice but to comply with American demands; otherwise "her last attempted defense against our immediate and effective intervention will be gone."[52]

Then the Germans, already under fire from Secretary Wilson and other farm businessmen for their "markedly unfriendly" harassment of American meat exports, seized the port of Kiaochow in China's Shantung province on November 18, 1897, and raised the specter of a wholesale assault to partition that divided and enfeebled nation.[53] American leaders were seriously disturbed; but, partially because of the time factor, partially because there was no immediate countermaneuver the Administration could undertake, and partially because action in Asia hinged on intervention in Cuba, President McKinley stressed Cuba rather than the Far East in his annual message of December 6, 1897.

McKinley left no doubt that he had committed himself to intervention of some kind. The most obvious sign was his blunt warning that the United States would act after one last grace period—"a reasonable chance"—for Spain. The record would make it clear that any decision "to intervene with force" would "be without fault on our own part." But there was another indicator, less direct but perhaps even more decisive. He threw down the gauntlet to the Populists and other agricultural militants by flatly asserting that he would not recognize the rebels. That was "premature," "indefensible," and "unwise."[54] When it came, intervention would be defined by the President. McKinley was ready, despite his deep preference for achieving American objectives without war, to go to war in order to secure peace.

Administration action was in line with the President's rhetoric. It moved the *Maine* to Key West, reinforced the Pacific fleet, and denied Woodford's request to come home to deal with personal matters.[55] Three portents appeared immediately. The metropolitan resistance to forceful intervention began to crumble, the militants reasserted the importance of expanding marketplace freedoms to Cuba, and the two theaters of action—Asia and Cuba—began to be linked by metropolitans and agriculturalists.[56] Senator Allen led the counterattack on McKinley, demanding "speedy and effectual Congressional recognition of the political independence of Cuba," and presenting the classic argument of the agricultural businessmen as reformers with great power and emotion.[57] He and the other militants were essentially correct in charging that metropolitan conservatives, and especially financiers, exerted a strong force against prompt intervention and recognition of the Cuban revolutionaries. Such men had become marketplace expansionists, but they were expansionists who preferred in the Cuban situation to achieve the objectives without war, and expansionists who placed greater stress on the freedom of Americans to penetrate the market than upon the freedom of the Cubans to govern their own marketplace. The Kansas City Board of Trade discovered the difference firsthand when it tried and failed to persuade the Philadelphia Board of Trade to join it in a petition demanding the recognition of Cuban independence.[58]

Agriculturalists argued that American expansion into Hawaii and Cuba was neither subjugation nor conquest. It was "an act of humanity" that would bring the "practical peace" so badly needed in the world. America was "the source of light and hope to mankind." "We are now a great nation, with commerce to be opened up and extended as much on the Pacific as the Atlantic," and it was a "plain duty" to annex Hawaii and remove Spain from Cuba. That would place the United States in "a condition to command a peace."[59]

The propensity to link Cuba, Hawaii, and the rising concern over America's position in the China market became very pronounced during the January debate in the Senate over annexing Hawaii. Senator Davis of Minnesota, "very busy" with the drive to pass that measure, reported that "the intervention of European powers in the affairs of China and Korea is having a beneficial effect upon the prospects of the treaty."[60] Senator Hoar became so disturbed about the integration of all the crises that he asked President McKinley if the Administration was planning to claim a share of China. Assured that was not the case, Hoar approved the annexation of Hawaii.[61]

The Administration wanted to avoid the partition of China because that "would tend to destroy our markets."[62] The Committee on American Interests in China, which later became the American Asiatic Association, was organized on January 6, 1898, to insure that the government acted effectively in behalf of that policy. It represented a convergence of Southern and Northern cotton textile manufacturers, as well as a coalition of metropolitan exporters, manufacturers, and financial leaders. The group's first action was to petition the New York Chamber of Commerce on January 13, asking it to take "immediate action" to notify the State Department of the deep concern over events in Asia that "may ultimately prove highly detrimental to the trade privileges now enjoyed."

The Chamber responded by going straight to McKinley with a strong request for an "energetic defense" of American rights, and similar action for the "preservation and protection" of "important commercial interests." One of the prime movers in that effort, which rapidly established close liaison with the government, reported that McKinley was very receptive and sympathetic. "With President McKinley and his Cabinet associates, with frequent personal calls and correspondence, we keep in good accord. . . . Our suggestions and resolutions . . . have been received with warm appreciation."[63]

Metropolitan political leaders like Senator Lodge were equally concerned to deploy American power: "the ports of China must be open to all nations." So were silverites like Senators Teller of Colorado, Stewart and Jones of Nevada, Cannon and Joseph Lafayette Rawlins of Utah, Warren of Wyoming, Kyle of South Dakota, George Turner of Washington, and Morgan and Edmund Winston Pettus of Alabama.[64] Such pressure prompted McKinley to shuffle his diplomatic appointments in order to send "an older and more experienced man," Edwin H. Conger, to the China cockpit.[65]

Much of the simultaneous agitation for action on the Cuban front came in response to the Administration's own moves. The President's Christmas Eve appeal for support for a Red Cross relief drive, for example, was followed by a directive extending all Navy enlistments about to expire, and an order sending the *Maine* to Havana. The decision on the *Maine* had the effect of pushing Cuba ahead of Hawaii and China in the Senate debates on expansion. "There may be an explosion in Cuba," Senator Lodge commented to a close friend, "which would settle a great many things. We have got a battleship in the harbor of Havana, and our fleet, which overmatches anything the Spaniards have, is massed at the Dry Tortugas. This action on the part of the administration has had a very cooling effect on Spain."[66]

Lodge's eerie premonition about an explosion in Havana was less significant than his remark about the effect of the visit on the Spanish. For it is highly probable that the *Maine* was sent to notify Madrid that the decision to intervene had been made, and hence the time for peaceful surrender was very short. That was certainly the message and the tone of Representative Hitt's vigorous defense of the President, offered on January 19, 1898, in an effort to control the surging agitation of the silverites, Populists, and other agricultural militants.

The angry impatience of those who wanted immediate intervention manifested itself in every mail delivery. The legislature of Mississippi gave notice in a joint resolution of its belief that it was "the duty of the United States Government to at once intervene, peacefully if it can, but forcibly if it must."[67] Some of the most revealing reports, however, came from the men who were trying to collect money for the Red Cross relief project. Governor Holcomb of Nebraska assured the national director that he would "heartily cooperate," but then warned him not to expect a large remittance. "I feel . . . that I represent the unanimous sentiment of Nebraska people in expressing the opinion that would our national government extend to the struggling Cuban patriots the recognition to which they are entitled and which humanity demands, these contributions for the starving would be unnecessary."

The Governor of Washington reported the same attitude throughout his state. Governor Andrew E. Lee of South Dakota was blunt to the point of disrespect. "To my mind it is little less than criminal on the part of our government to . . . pass the contribution box for food to preserve the lives of Cubans for slaughter by Spanish bayonets. The efforts of Cuban relief should be to softening the hearts of Spanish bond holders who are dictating the policy of the McKinley administration." The Governor of Illinois, John R. Tanner, was less brusque, but his message was the same: such measures were only "palliative." He told the people of the state that the "proper course" was to use "all the influence and power of the Government to put an end to the civil war in Cuba, . . . insisting that the freedom and independence of the Cuban people shall be respected."[68]

The Red Cross was a quasi-governmental operation, and the Administration quickly learned of those sentiments.[69] McKinley also knew that agricultural exporters wanted "prompt and efficient measures" to halt the "great and increasing loss of trade" with Cuba; and, significantly, that the demand of the Wilcox Lard and Refining Company was now supported by bankers and manufacturers.[70] That was particularly important information because the situation in Cuba was deteriorating very rapidly. Consul General Lee, for example, was alerted to "maintain frequent communications with the United States squadron in Key West."[71] And Representative Hitt held "repeated consultations" with McKinley just before he defended the President on the floor of the Congress.

Advising the critics to give closer attention to McKinley's annual message of December 1897, Hitt flatly asserted that the President was pushing vigorously to drive Spain out of Cuba, and clearly implied that force would be used if it proved necessary.[72] The *Western Rural* joined *The Nation*, Washington newspapers, and attentive congressmen in taking the speech as a clear sign that intervention was only a matter of time.[73] Spanish leaders did not need to read the Hitt speech. Woodford made it clear in his mid-January talks that the President was ready to act. Spain almost immediately (February 1) revealed its refusal to surrender without a fight, and began to strengthen and deploy its naval forces.[74]

John J. McCook and his expansionist associates, who were interested in the China market at least as much as in Cuban possibilities, then provided a push calculated to increase the momentum for war. Their connections with Cuban revolutionaries turned a political profit in the theft from the mails of a letter written by the Spanish Minister to the United States. Other letters had very probably been obtained but never used. But this one was an impatient and indiscreet note written in a moment of emotional stress by an understandably frustrated and angry man who was watching his beloved country again being forced to the wall by a nation that had been slashing away at the Spanish empire for two centuries. McCook handed the letter to Secretary of State Day for the President on February 9, having made sure it would be published in the New York *Journal* on the same day. It was an effective maneuver, for the letter angered many heretofore reluctant expansionists and added more evidence that Spain would not surrender without a fight.

Less than a week later, Senator Lodge's foreboding about an explosion in Havana proved tragically correct. The *Maine* erupted in fire and death twenty minutes after taps on February 15, shook with secondary blasts, and settled to the bottom. No one has ever provided a wholly convincing explanation of whether the cause was faulty design, carelessness by an officer or an enlisted man, or external malice and skill; and, if the latter, whether it was Spanish war hawks, revolutionary war hawks, or conservative Spanish-Cuban annexationists. There is no question, however, that 266 men lost their lives; or that, on balance, the act moved Spain closer to ultimate defeat.

The sinking did give McKinley a bit of added leverage in his effort to free Cuba from Spanish rule without armed intervention. The President's strategic political problem at home, which he faced every day after December 4, 1897, was to withstand the constantly increasing pressure from the silverites, other agriculturalists, and metropolitans like McCook and Roosevelt, while he maneuvered on three other fronts. He needed to complete preparations for war, edge the metropolitan conservatives into accepting military intervention, and hold the door open for a last-minute capitulation by Spain. Given that situation, the end of the *Maine* helped him by shocking the Spanish and the metropolitan conservatives, and by dramatizing the cost of war and thereby inducing some second thoughts (however short-lived) among some of the militants.

The President needed any help he could find, for the pressure for war was approaching the point of congressional revolt. Silverites and other expansionists roared for intervention as "the beginning of a sound business policy" that would demonstrate America's "settled determination to be supreme in the affairs of our half of the world." The markets might be obtained through the operation of "natural laws," but that kind of "progress is slow" and America could not afford to wait in China—or any other region of the world. Even the Populist *Southern Mercury* supported the expansion of Asian markets for Southern textile mills.[75]

The *Maine* tragedy did prompt some spokesmen to caution against war. But they argued from the premise of superior strength—"we have the power to compel peace"—that the agriculturalists had developed as early as the 1870s. The editors of the *Western Rural* and Carl Schurz agreed that Spain would surrender if America remained patient. And the editors of *Farm, Stock, and Home,* arguing simply that "Spain is weak," concluded that "the whole business has been badly managed."[76] A more accurate judgment would have been that McKinley's need to prepare for war began to subvert his efforts to gain more time.

That happened sooner, in all probability, than he originally anticipated. Representative George Brinton McClelland, reading McKinley's
annual message of December 1897 and other events as sure indicators
that war was coming, warned early in January that the Army was "absolutely unprepared for war." The common assumption that American
power was "invulnerable" was "unfortunately" mistaken.[77] The Navy,
of course, presented far less of a problem. But Assistant Secretary
Roosevelt was worried, despite his 1897 discussions with McKinley,
that all preparations had not been made to move into Asia when the war
began. Hence on February 25 he seized what was left of the day after
Secretary John D. Long went home slightly indisposed and used it to
send all kinds of orders, including one to Commodore George Dewey to
"start offensive operations in Philippine Islands" as soon as hostilities erupted. Roosevelt's fears were groundless. McKinley had discussed that strategy with others, including Senator Orville Hitchcock
Platt, and had quietly settled on just that course. Thus, while his su-
periors substituted better orders for many of Roosevelt's efforts, they
did not bother to revise the two-front war directive to Dewey.[78]

The Army was another matter, and McKinley shared McClelland's
view that it was far from ready. An appropriation for additional fire-
power was discussed and passed in February, and National Guard units
reported receiving their quota assignments at the same time.[79] But
those measures were insufficient, and his knowledge of such weakness pushed McKinley into an extremely difficult dilemma. He had
to be ready to go to war in April because of the demands and limits
of the climate in Cuba, yet if he asked Congress for the necessary funds
he would undercut his own attempt to gain time against the war
hawks.[80]

As usual, McKinley maneuvered very adroitly. He first warned
Spain, on March 1 and 3, that the top of the hourglass was almost empty.
Then, on March 7, he called key representatives and senators into urgent conference at the White House. That was the day after Germany
took a ninety-nine-year leasehold on the vital section of the Shantung
province, an action everyone knew would prompt a Russian coun-
termove. The President told the congressmen that "war was inevitable" and asked for money.[81] The Congress met the request for $50 mil-
lion, as the President knew it would, by a vote of 311 to 0 on March 8, the
day the Russians occupied Port Arthur and Talienwan in Manchuria.
McKinley then used the congressional uproar for immediate action
to swing the last reluctant metropolitans into line for war. He of course
hoped the Spanish would capitulate, but he knew there was no turning back—or any other direction—if they did not surrender.

McKinley was unquestionably prepared to go to war, and to fight
the war with a two-front strategy, whenever he judged the agricultural militants on the verge of splitting and taking control of the Republican party, and thereby displacing the metropolis (and the party) as

the dominant force in the political economy.[82] He was not, therefore, running an elaborate bluff, and most certainly not scrambling desperately to maintain his control. It was one of the most striking displays of presidential nerve and finesse in the nation's history.

The President counted on the agricultural war hawks, led by the Populists and the Silverites, to push the die-hard metropolitan conservatives over the line. That would save him, whatever the Spanish did, from having to split the head of the party to avoid severing the head from the body. The militants wasted no time in performing as anticipated. "I am the jingo of jingoes," cried Senator Allen joyfully, as he saw the long campaign approaching victory. With the help of Southern allies like Senators Butler, Call, and Morgan, the United States was going to meet its responsibilities as Cuba's "elder brother" and displace Great Britain as the monarch of the marketplace.[83]

Allen's claim to a place in the vanguard of the agricultural spokesmen who forced the issues cannot be denied, but he had much assistance. Even Simpson, who avowed a primary concern for the condition of American society, bowed to the emergency and voted for three new battleships. And the editors of Populist and silver papers constantly agitated the issues, arguing that war would extend freedom and exports, and concluding that, if it brought the remonetization of silver, it "would not be an unmitigated evil."[84]

But the Populists were in truth but the whitecaps on the ground swells of agricultural expansionism. The more conservative farm businessmen had been agitating overseas markets for more than a generation before the Populists appeared. Indeed, the vast majority of Populists were erstwhile Democrats and Republicans who had been part of that expansionist movement. Editor E. S. Jones of the *Prairie Farmer* candidly acknowledged the economic stake involved in the crisis. "Stripped of all questions of sentimentalism," the issue was trade. Trade "of especial importance to farmers of this country. With normal conditions prevailing, Cuba has been a large consumer of our agricultural products, and should be a much larger consumer of them than heretofore, with the establishment of peace and sound government." Those conditions would create a "large and permanent demand."[85] The political spokesmen of the moderate and even conservative agricultural businessmen argued just as powerfully for intervention.

Such a combination of fury and reason enlisted in behalf of freedom and trade had the expected effect on the metropolis. The "head of a leading stock Exchange house" was reported on March 9 as concerned lest the "internal dissension" over Cuba delay and weaken "the extension of commerce with the rest of the world." Stuyvesant Fish of the Illinois Central verified the same shift of opinion. And on March 15 Cleveland Dodge told Secretary of War Russell A. Alger that the businessmen were deeply concerned about the continuing discord. "They are willing to go to any extreme to avoid it." Alger's reply provided a good insight into Administration thinking on the issue. He emphasized the economic disruption, and made it clear that he was ready to "meet this question and settle it forever now."[86]

Such evidence makes it clear that the financial and industrial laggards were moving toward war *before* Senator Redfield Proctor delivered his famous speech of March 17, which has so often been credited with turning the tide in the metropolis.[87] Just as Proctor had been an expansionist toward Cuba for many years, so metropolitan attitudes had never been wholly pacific. The legislature of the State of New York, for example, appealed to McKinley on January 31 to secure peace "by whatever means necessity may require."[88] A large delegation of New Yorkers then discussed the problem with the President early in February, stressing the need to settle the issue before May or June in order to plant and harvest the sugar crop. The continuing uncertainty, steadily increased and made more threatening by the agricultural campaign for war with silver, would have completed the metropolitan conversion to war even if Senator Proctor had never spoken.

The President's messages to the metropolis were far more important than Proctor's words. Personal emissaries, associates acting as campaigners, and political appointees serving as errand boys usually accomplish more than speeches in such circumstances. McKinley used all those approaches after the White House conference on appropriations—and had no doubt done so before.[89] Once the metropolitan tide began to flood, moreover, it crashed upon the White House with almost as much force as the agricultural surf. The same militant cry came from New York, Boston, and Philadelphia: "With force if we must."[90]

A sizable group of Republican leaders began during the last week of March to demand an immediate declaration of war. They feared the Populist and Democratic agriculturalists would exploit the consensus for war to their immediate and long-range advantage.[91] McKinley held them off with a firm assertion of his will cloaked in the folds of the constitutional division of powers (and a telegram campaign for peace very probably organized by Hanna) until he completed his preparations and offered Spain one last chance to surrender without war.[92] He gave the Congress its head on April 11, but acted as Commander in Chief even before the representatives and senators could settle their differences and pass a war resolution. As a result, the declaration of war voted on April 25 had to be dated April 21 to cover the naval action initiated by the United States on April 22, 1898.

The editors of the *Southern Mercury*, failing to distinguish between McKinley and Cleveland, "never believed that there would be any war." When it came, therefore, they largely explained it as a diversion engineered by the metropolis.[93] But one Texas Populist could not accept either the faulty analysis or the evasion of responsibility. His sharp rebuke was far closer to the truth about the immediate and historical role of the agricultural businessmen. "We as Populists ought to be candid," J. S. Woods admonished the editors. "Since 1896 all the leading Populists in National, State, and county conventions have declared in some way favorable towards freeing Cuba."

"All this talk about imperialism," he continued, "is but the old howl of the Federalists when they arrayed themselves against Mr. Jefferson for securing to this Nation the Louisiana purchase and the opening of the mouth of the Mississippi river for the benefit of trade and commerce. . . . Let the southern and especially Texas Populists stand firm for a policy which will put us in touch with five hundred millions of Asiatic consumers, where the people of Texas, the South, and the West, can sell all of their surplus products, cotton goods, wheat, flour, iron and beef; then we will be free from the power of Lombard Street and England will no longer be able to dictate and control the prices of productive labor in the South. Give us an exchange market in Cuba, Porto Rico, the Philippines, Caroline Islands, and in China and Japan. . . . Let no Populist be led astray by the scare-crow of words manufactured by such men as Cleveland. . . . Free commerce is what we want. . . . The capture of these islands . . . means universal free trade for this nation and an expansion of our National thought, commerce and trade, and it further means death to the cruel and dishonest methods of gain heretofore imposed upon us in the South and West by the bondholders of Europe and New England."[94]

Other agriculturalists in the West and Northwest echoed his analysis. "The war is upon us," commented the editor of the *Western Rural*, and then went to the point. "It is of our own making and was inspired by the principles of humanity . . . the spirit of liberty and progress." Once the war for a free marketplace in Cuba had come, the editors of the *Rural New Yorker* turned to Asia and explained why nations were edging toward war in China. "Once make them believe that they should have two suits of clothes, and you create a clothing trade. . . . American manufacturers are, or ought to be, able to hold their own in foreign trade. American farmers may expect a constantly increasing foreign demand for food and, indirectly, the opening up and civilizing of Africa and China will increase this demand."[95]

The agricultural majority had played the primary causal role in generating the ideas, emotions, and policy that produced the war against Spain, and struggled persistently to define the war as one to extend the freedoms of a marketplace society as well as to expand exports. The farm businessmen subsequently supported the policy developed by the metropolis from their outlook and ideas. And for that reason the war for the free marketplace led on to a marketplace empire.

CONCLUSION

*One thing at a time is a good rule, but this does not pre-
vent looking ahead. . . . China and Japan will soon
require some attention. . . . Our commerce with Cuba
. . . will be too important to ignore, but it can never be
more than a bagatelle as compared with what is likely
to develop with the Orient.*

Western Rural, April 1898

*Our ability to produce so greatly exceeds our capacity
to consume that wider markets are necessary. . . . We
can expand our commerce without . . . conquest in
the Far East.*

Southern Mercury, June 1898

*I must not be understood . . . as opposing the acquisi-
tion of proper harbors in all these islands. . . . Let us
fortify all those places if necessary, and secure all the
facilities proper, and then let us quit. . . . I would erect
and sustain an independent republican form of government in all Spain's possessions.*

Populist Senator Allen, July 1898

We must keep the Philippines.

Chauncey F. Black, Chairman of the
National Association of Democratic
Clubs, September 1898

*[The Peace Treaty] will vastly extend the influence of
the United States in checking oppression, repressing
the unjust aggressiveness of the European Monarchies
and widening the sphere of liberty in the world . . .
[and] will open to American commerce a vast field
for expansion and will furnish a great and expanding
stimulus to our manufacturing and natural production.*

Joint Resolution of the Legislature of
South Dakota, February 1899

*The policy of the "open door" with the Philippines . . .
will enable us to use our moral advantage in securing
the same "open door" with all parts of the Chinese Empire.*

Wallace's Farmer, January 1899

*Unless a vigorous policy is pursued . . . these markets . . .
in the territory already occupied or threatened by Russia
. . . will be eventually closed to our trade, as has recently been the case by the French in Madagascar.*

Southern and Northern Cotton Textile Manufacturers to Secretary of State John Hay,
January 1899

*There is but one thing that will regulate and make farm-
ing profitable, and make it profitable for every crop
raised and for every section of the country. I can sum
the whole thing up in two words—oriental markets.
Give us the oriental markets.*

John C. Hanley of the National
Farmers Alliance, August 1899

We feel that the great power of this Government and very large sums of money have been expended to widen the market for our manufacturing industries. . . . We believe there should be no discrimination and that the same energies and efforts ought to be put forward by the Government for advancing the markets of agriculture in all foreign countries.

Aaron Jones, Worthy Master of the
National Grange, March 1899

The permanency of the present prosperity, therefore, lies very largely in our ability to continue this condition of things and become not merely a bread and meat exporting nation, but an exporter of manufactured products as well.

Wallace's Farmer, May 1900

Through
the Open Door to Empire

T HE WAR to drive Spain from Cuba opened the door for the establishment of an American marketplace throughout the world. However they differed over the means—among themselves, and with their metropolitan counterparts—the farm businessmen had never been thinking simply or only about Cuba. Cuba was but the temporary focus and symbol of their general, inclusive drive for overseas economic expansion. The decision for war raised three primary questions. The first concerned how much of what kind of freedom was to be carried through the door thus opened to empire. That issue continued to be debated well into the twentieth century, but the discussion never transcended the marketplace outlook of the agricultural majority. The second question involved the extent of the empire, and it produced practically no serious disagreement. For, almost from the outset, the farm businessmen had defined the American marketplace as a global marketplace, and the metropolis accepted that conception.

The third issue concerned the problem of structuring and exploiting the global marketplace empire while honoring the broad commitment to a free marketplace. By definition, as well as pragmatically, that was the most difficult problem confronted by all American leaders. They devised a broad strategic answer predicated on holding the Philippines as a base for deploying the power of the United States to establish and uphold the classic marketplace principle of a fair field with no favor—an open door for all entrepreneurs. Though that strategy was formulated as a policy by the metropolitan minority that had reasserted and consolidated its control of the political economy, it was a manifestation of the outlook developed and shaped by the agricultural majority. Not surprisingly, the farm businessmen agreed in principle and in practice; insisting only that the Filipinos be educated and trained to full membership as free members of the marketplace system. That caveat was accepted by metropolitan leaders because it was an agricultural version of the position they had taken during the dispute over recognizing the Cuban revolutionaries.

That earlier confrontation came to a climax after President McKinley made it clear in his annual message of December 1897 that he opposed such action. He bluntly asserted that the rebels had failed to create a functioning, responsible government, and candidly insisted that American interests and objectives required the creation of a certain kind of government in Cuba. The President reiterated those arguments in his war message of April 11, 1898, clarifying his reasoning in the process. The current war dramatized a long series of uprisings that repeatedly "subjected the United States to great effort and expense . . . caused enormous losses to American trade and commerce, caused irritation, annoyance and disturbance among our citizens, and . . . shocked the sensibilities and offended the humane sympathies of our people." Hence the issue was going to be dealt with in a manner that promised to end such losses and distractions, and to establish a functioning marketplace society.

That policy was based on the performance—and lack of it—by the revolutionaries, as well as upon McKinley's own assumptions and preferences. One of those was undoubtedly the sense of Anglo-Saxon superiority manifested by most Americans. At that time the attitude as manifested toward Cubans was not racism. The essence of racism is a belief in the *inherent and permanent inferiority* of another ethnically defined group of people. McKinley's Anglo-Saxon—more accurately, American—sense of superiority was based on the conviction that the United States was more advanced and civilized than other societies. He did not say, nor did most other Americans say, that the Cubans and the Filipinos were inherently and permanently inferior. The President and the majority of Americans said only that those peoples were not yet able to sustain their development toward civilization without further education and guidance. They did not foreclose the possibility of continued progress.

Such an attitude of superiority is of course a manifestation of the worst kind of arrogant, self-centered superciliousness. And it can—and does—devolve into racism under several conditions. Sustained inability by the outside group to realize the a priori criteria of civilization often produces the conclusion that the failure is explained by inherent inferiority. A second force transforming a sense of superiority into racism is a flat rejection by the foreigner of the values and criteria of civilization as defined by the more powerful society. Both those causes have been operative in the development of American attitudes toward other peoples, along with the power of traditional beliefs about the inherent inferiority of some peoples. Racism has existed among Americans, and still exists among Americans.

The point here is that the charge (or assumption) of racism does not help clarify McKinley's refusal to recognize the rebels, or his unwillingness to hand the island over to them as soon as the Spanish were defeated. For that matter, the dispatches of the Administration make it clear that the President and others feared that such action would very probably lead to a racist bloodbath *within* that island. It is also likely that McKinley worried lest a hands-off policy expose the island to the power of American entrepreneurs who, if not all racists, were clearly interested in establishing their private control over the island.[1] McKinley wanted to use American power in ways that would transform colonial Cuba into a society that could take its place in America's free marketplace system. He was in that central respect a thoroughly modern American metropolitan.

The irony was that the leaders of the agricultural majority sought precisely the same objective. They accepted—even anticipated—the need for extensive American investment and other forms of assistance and leadership in reaching that goal. Their intense opposition to McKinley was based on three other considerations. One was the depth of their commitment to the principle of the free political side of the marketplace outlook, and the related emotion that had been generated during the long battle to force the metropolis to accept their outlook and meet their needs. They were unusually familiar with the limits and restrictions on political and economic freedom in the territories under metropolitan rule of the marketplace.

The second element explaining their anger was a belief in the ability of any man to function successfully in the free marketplace once he gained the opportunity. That faith was the product of their conception of human nature and it had been deeply reinforced by a century of frontier expansion across the continent. In their view, the average man operating as a farm businessman had built America into the strongest nation in the world. They extended the Cubans the ultimate respect of assuming they could, given the proper circumstances, perform in the same fashion.

The third factor, which supplied the spark to ignite their supercombustible combination of idealism and rational calculation, was a mistaken judgment of McKinley. They erroneously viewed him, in those first days of the battle over the declaration of war, as a mere instrument of a metropolitan coalition determined to subvert the expansion of the free American marketplace into traditional British colonialism. There were such men in the metropolis, but they did not constitute even a strong plurality, and they most certainly did not manipulate McKinley. Believing otherwise, the militant agriculturalists defined the issue in terms of immediate recognition of the rebels and unequivocal independence for the Cubans.

As Senator Warren aptly observed, their reaction to the President's war message was "red hot sure enough."[2] Allen, Butler, and others, convinced that McKinley was preparing to hand the island over to "a greedy syndicate of bondholders," waged a ten-day struggle that forced the President to employ all his will, finesse, persuasion, and power.[3] The militants were in the end defeated by the weakness in their own case. Men initially moved by their idealism concluded, no doubt many of them under the tutelage of the Administration, that there were two flaws in the Allen-Butler argument.[4]

One was the lack of convincing proof that the rebels were capable of controlling and structuring the island as a free marketplace political economy. That being the objective, even for the militants, their inability to establish a high degree of probability for that outcome led to major defections among their early allies. John W. Springer, president of the National Live Stock Association, made the point in opposing both the annexationists and the militants. To the former, he said bluntly that Cuba "is not our territory, never was, and we don't want it." He was equally direct to the latter. "The people are not capable of self-government and are ignorant and church bound in the worst degree. I approve McKinley's course."[5]

In an ironic way, the annexationists also weakened the Allen group. For the clear proof of their existence subverted the argument of the militants that it was possible to turn the island over to the Cubans. Men who wanted a free marketplace for American expansion, and who accepted the need for American initiative and capital, came to see the danger in exposing a devastated economy and a weakened, misruled, and divided people to the overwhelming power of the giant operators. Some government control was required to prevent the free marketplace from being monopolized by the syndicates.

As a result, the militants failed to force McKinley to recognize rebel leadership. They did win, however, after a wild three-day debate, a formal disavowal of "any disposition or intention" to annex the island. Most agricultural businessmen were satisfied with freeing Cuba from Spanish control and promising self-government. And in truth that action did extend the political freedom of the marketplace to Cuba. No significant number — if any — of the militants stood ready to allow Cuba to use its freedom to move out of the American marketplace. Significantly, even Senator Allen carefully qualified his demands for recognizing Cuban independence with the word *political*. They wanted and expected Cuba to become even more fully integrated into the American marketplace than it had been between 1890 and 1895. So did the great majority of farm businessmen.

They also displayed an increasingly strong desire to control Hawaii as a vital base in the battle for the Asian market. Allen also led the militants in that fight, which clearly revealed the limits of their concern to expand freedom. For when freedom was used against the free American marketplace conception of reality, then freedom became unfreedom and intervention was justified as preserving and extending freedom. There was no hypocrisy involved, merely a different estimate of whether freedom would be misused and thereby weaken freedom.

The primary limitations on freedom came not from evil or ignorant men, but rather from defining freedom in terms of the marketplace. Honest, intelligent, and well-meaning men could and did disagree over their estimate of reality—or the probabilities—within that framework. But to define freedom as including action removing a vital element from the American marketplace required a different conception of freedom. Had the militants thought the Cuban rebels were ready to sign a reciprocity treaty with Great Britain (or another European power) rather than with the United States, there would most assuredly have been no great fight to recognize them as the legitimate government of Cuba. The same estimate governed their policy toward Hawaii.

The McKinley Administration's decision to intervene forcefully in Cuba prompted it on March 16 to change its strategy for the annexation of Hawaii. The leaders switched from treaty ratification by the Senate to acquisition by joint resolution, a procedure requiring significantly fewer votes and opening the way for the expansionist majority in the House of Representatives to exert direct pressure on the Senate. The congressional debate and the more general discussion made it apparent that the agriculturalists viewed Asia as part of the American marketplace. Senator Teller expressed the attitude with his usual bluntness. "Mr. President, we want those islands. We want them because they are the stepping way across the sea. . . . Necessary to our safety, they are necessary to our commerce."[6]

Petitioners from Kansas and Nebraska made the same argument. The islands were deemed important for defense, and "essential to our maintaining control of the commerce of the Pacific." "Without commerce, especially of meats, grains, cotton and manufactures, we cannot attain the highest degree of prosperity," reasoned the Nebraskans, "and our growing commerce on the Northern Pacific would be immensely benefitted by a control over Hawaii."[7] While they supported it, the farm businessmen correctly understood that the push across the Pacific was primarily the work of the metropolis. The editors of the *Western Rural*, commenting on McKinley's dispatch of troops to hold the Philippines immediately upon word of Dewey's naval victory, *assumed* the islands would be held after the war. The cotton textile journal, *Manufacturers Record*, expressed its agreement by quoting the Chicago *Times-Herald*: "It is safe to say that the United States will not fail to use them for the expansion of our market in the Orient." The Populist *Southern Mercury*, looking forward to the "role reserved for us in the Orient," added only that America must also be sure to expand freedom. And Secretary of Agriculture Wilson, long a vigorous expansionist, beamed over the "new world" that had been opened by the victory.[8]

Some agriculturalists saw the Asian market as a way to break free of British control of the marketplace.[9] James J. Hill computed the potentialities of the new opportunity in the same way that others 'had once calculated about Africa. "If those Chinamen would only take 1 bushel [a year], that would only give them about three-quarters of a pound of flour a week, but it would take 400,000,000 bushels of wheat to supply them. . . . Now that is a market that is capable of expansion. That market may be expanded."[10] Stuyvesant Fish of the Illinois Central and the implement manufacturers agreed, but so did the National Grange. It asked the Department of Agriculture to push "our corn products in China," and warned the State Department to act "vigorously" to prevent the "disintegration" of China.[11] And the General Business Agent of the National Farmers Alliance and Industrial Union, who also spoke for the National Grain Growers Association, revealed that those organizations were working closely with Hill to control the Asian market.[12]

"The people out there," a Midwestern newspaperman told the metropolis, "have taken hold of the new question, namely, the adoption of a foreign policy by this country, with an eagerness that shows them willing to drop free silver and fight along some other line."[13] He was mistaken about one point. "The people out there" had taken hold of the issue thirty years earlier. The same was true of Southerners. "We want a market for our raw cotton other than English markets," explained one producer, advancing the same argument used by Western farm businessmen. "I am an expansionist, an 'imperialist,' if you will," acknowledged a Texan. "Somewhere in the Orient will be another cotton market rivaling Liverpool, with spindles and consumers galore. So be it."[14] Southern textile manufacturers agreed with such producers, but in doing so revealed how they had come to think of themselves as part of the metropolis. They talked now about *the* industry, rather than about the *Southern* industry. The "we" they used meant all manufacturers.[15]

For that reason, Southern cotton millers very probably exerted more direct influence on American foreign policy after the declaration of war against Spain than any other group in what for a generation had been a majority coalition of businessmen who viewed themselves as members of the agricultural part of the political economy. The flour millers were also active, and were concerned with Cuba as well as Asia, as were the meat packers, provisioners, and implement manufacturers. But, having accepted the outlook of the agriculturalists, metropolitan leaders increasingly made policy within an industrial framework.

McKinley and other Administration spokesmen dealt with the crucial China problem within that context. They were far more concerned with clocks, kerosene, and steel than with corn, lard, or salted beef. McKinley addressed the National Association of Manufacturers, not the National Grange. He used force in China for more markets for iron rails and locomotives, not against Germany for pork. And most certainly not against Great Britain to reopen the market for live cattle, for London had become an ally in the fight for an open marketplace in Asia. Secretary of Agriculture Wilson acknowledged the shift in an interview with the editors of *Wallace's Farmer*, one of the most influential of the new agricultural papers. The "question of expansion— new and larger markets," he told them, "is a profitable subject." But the profits would increasingly come from the home market created by export orders for the metropolis.[16]

Wilson had sensed the shift (perhaps unconsciously) as early as May 5, 1898, when he discussed the reasons for his militant expansionism in a typically candid letter to Frank McCoy. He was delighted with Dewey's victory at Manila. The "wonderful enlargement of American influence" meant that "in the future we shall control the Pacific Ocean." Then he defined the nature of the conquest. "We *manufacture* faster than customers at home can consume, and we need an outlet for American enterprise."[17] Wilson was also one of the first to understand the interlocking nature of the difficulties involved in structuring the Asian (and world) marketplace to insure American supremacy, and that perception undoubtedly strengthened his established influence with the President.

The problem was to consolidate American power in Asia, use it to create an open marketplace while at the same time honoring the commitment to a free marketplace, and accomplish both objectives without constant war. Wilson pinpointed the essential factors involved in a workable solution long before the Spanish sued for peace. "We shall have to take the Pacific Islands," he first noted, "not only Hawaii and the Philippines, but the Caroline or the Ladrone Islands." That could only be done, of course, within the framework of an obligation to "teach these poor people to govern themselves." But, given that power base, the United States could then insist upon the principles of an open marketplace. "We are not omnipotent, and can't thrash all Europe at once, but these countries really needed something to bring them to a realizing sense that they are not omnipotent either."[18]

McKinley did not make a firm decision on the Philippines until the end of the summer, and the public debate continued for still another six months. One of the men who had worked with Rusk in the campaign to expand corn exports to Europe provided one of the best commentaries on that irresolution and heated argument among expansionists. "There has been more or less confusion in the public mind regarding what the policy of expansion involves," explained Francis B. Thurber, president of the United States Export Association. He then proceeded to illustrate that confusion even as he described it.

The policy of expansion "has been mixed up with the idea of imperialism, whatever that may mean, but, as I interpret it, imperialism means absorbing vast foreign territories into our Union with all the rights of citizenship to their populations." Thurber did not consider that either required or desirable; but "the expansion of our markets" was "absolutely necessary in view of our increasing productive capacity. . . . We must have a place to dump our surplus, which otherwise will constantly depress prices and compel the shutting down of our mills . . . and changing our profits into losses. I do not believe in imperialism . . . but I do believe in a policy of expansion which will give us the control of some markets which will be a steppingstone to others in a wider zone of influence which such control would enable us to exercise."[19]

The policy Thurber defined as imperialism was of course a version of colonialism in which citizens of the colony became limited citizens of the metropolis. Americans understandably thought within that framework for two reasons. First, it was their understanding of the British imperial system. They disliked it for that reason. Second, it was the process Americans had evolved and institutionalized at a very early date for handling their continental expansion under the plan of territorial government. The resistance to using it in overseas market expansion can be comprehended more fully in the context of the long battle by American agriculturalists against such limited citizenship, as well as in the light of their concern to avoid another racial problem when such territories were admitted to statehood, the fear of economic competition from such new possessions, and the realization that the Pacific Islands were minor markets.

Some Western farm businessmen, such as the editors of the *Western Rural*, initially viewed those islands as meaningful outlets for surpluses. So did some Southern cotton growers and textile men.[20] But that analysis was never accepted by the majority, and the issue was quickly defined in terms of the relevance of the islands to the China (and the world) market. The editors of the *Western Rural* made the shift within two weeks. "We need these points of departure in every ocean and as outposts for the protection of our commerce. The commerce of America must be extended. It has but just begun with China and the Orient."[21]

The central issue soon became one of deciding how much to take, and how to structure American control. The editors of the *Southern Mercury* spoke for a tiny group that argued (at least in the beginning) there was no need to take anything. The China market was necessary because "our ability to produce so greatly exceeds our capacity to consume." But "we can expand our commerce without . . . conquest in the Far East. We may gain our share of the world's trade without annexing an acre of land overseas." The very great majority of agricultural businessmen accepted the necessity, however, of taking some portion of the Philippines. Many hoped at the outset to limit the size of the acquisition, but acquiesced—with varying degrees of enthusiasm—in McKinley's decision that it was impolitic and impractical to attempt such a piecemeal approach.[22]

The willingness to compromise on acquiring one major colony grew out of the recognition that market expansion in Asia required a secure base of operations, and the argument that the action could be redeemed by training the Filipinos for self-government and independence. "Our duty," concluded the *Western Rural*, "requires us to stand for liberty everywhere. If any of our citizens or our trade and commerce even are to be injured by an unjust, cruel and despotic rule, . . . we will take a hand in the correction of the evil. It is national altruism. It is better than the Monroe Doctrine and is adapted to the 20th century. The Monroe Doctrine and the clam-like policy were our swaddling clothes." "Henceforth it should be our mission to help extend Anglo-Saxon liberty, education and commerce, and open the way for Christianity to every part of the globe."[23]

Other agricultural spokesmen echoed that recommendation. Massachusetts Grange leaders accepted it, as did the editors of other farm publications. The Philippines were necessary to insure the extension of the American marketplace; and that was necessary not only for American welfare, but because such expansion would extend freedom throughout the world. The proposition would be proved by discharging the duty to "fit them for the highest degree of liberty and self-government."[24] The farm businessmen reached that position, moreover, at least as soon as their metropolitan counterparts. Acting under the impetus of the National Civic Federation, an organization formed as a permanent symposium of key industrial, financial, and labor spokesmen, metropolitan leaders formally compromised their policy differences during an August 1898 meeting at Saratoga Springs.[25]

Their consensus was most effectively stated by Carl Schurz, who had always accepted the necessity of market expansion while opposing traditional colonialism. Exports, he had long argued, "will save us from the suffocation so much dreaded." "I fully agree," he reiterated at Saratoga: "We cannot have too many." But the United States could obtain the required bases and ports "without burdening itself with any political responsibilities in the regions concerned." Hence the proper policy was to occupy the outposts "until they are thoroughly pacified"; and then, having obtained the required economic and military footholds, withdraw. That would extend freedom by "exerting civilizing influences upon the population of the conquered territories," and "gain commercial opportunities of so great a value that they will more than compensate for the cost of the war." The agriculturalists found no difficulty in supporting a position they had developed in their own discussions. [26]

McKinley reportedly told a delegation from the Saratoga conference that it had "pointed the way to the nation, because it has brought a unanimous agreement between the expansionists and the anti-expansionists." [27] The President had in truth seen a good way down that path as early as May 11, when he and the Cabinet decided to hold a coaling station in the Philippines. But the Administration was undecided about how much more to acquire, and the Saratoga meeting may well have encouraged McKinley to resolve the dilemma by demanding the entire archipelago. [28] The unequivocal decision on that point was not announced by the President until October 25, 1898, though his propensity to move in that direction was clear by mid-September.

The farm businessmen of the upper Middle West may well have played a significant—if indirect—part in his final decision. For the President used an invitation to open the Omaha Exposition as a means to test—and mold—public opinion much as President Harrison had done in 1890 during his cross-country tour. Like Harrison, McKinley took along a militantly expansionist Secretary of Agriculture. Wilson used the opportunity, as had Rusk, to press hard for bold action. Unlike Harrison, however, who had taken an unequivocally expansionist line from the outset, McKinley began somewhat cautiously.

The President soon concluded, however, that he could speak his predilections more candidly. And on the return trip he evoked enthusiastic responses when he declared that "what we want is new markets, and as trade follows the flag, it looks very much as if we were going to have new markets." [29] The reaction of the Midwesterners verified the concurrent estimate of a West Virginia politician. "I have never yet met a man from the masses of people who does not believe that we should, with a masterful hand, hold firmly by the great markets which American blood and iron have obtained for our commercial flag." [30]

Whatever its precise influence, the popular support for expansion certainly encouraged the President (along with Secretary Wilson's urgings) to go all the way in the Philippines. And, as so often proved to be the case, his estimate of the general outlook proved accurate. The peace treaty with Spain, which transferred the Philippines (and other Pacific islands) to the United States, was ratified by the Senate within two months. The vote was close, but several factors need to be considered in evaluating the significance of the narrow margin. *Most obviously, the two-thirds rule in the Senate always means that even the smallest possible victory (in this case, 57 to 27) represents a two-to-one majority.*

There is considerable evidence, moreover, that a significant number of Democrats who voted against the treaty in order to keep the issue alive for the 1900 presidential election campaign would have voted for it if their support had been needed for ratification. Despite opposition among sugar and tobacco planters, for example, the South manifested strong support for establishing American power in Asia. "It is a cold question of business," explained one textile manufacturer, and many shared that attitude.[31] Chauncey F. Black, former governor of Pennsylvania and chairman of the National Association of Democratic Clubs, was a vigorous expansionist who used his position to win support for the view that "we must keep the Philippines." His efforts prompted others to observe that "there is a very strong undercurrent in the party in favor of expansion." Hence it is very questionable whether Bryan's last-minute campaign in behalf of the treaty played a major part in the vote for ratification.[32]

It is possible that a division on annexation per se would have gone the other way. Certainly some senators would have voted "Nay" if the issue had been separated from the other provisions of the treaty. But presented in that form, the question would have been decided by a simple majority, and on balance it seems doubtful that the decision would have been reversed. Everyone agreed on the need for "proper harbors," as Senator Allen called them, and there was a broad consensus in favor of some kind of protectorate. Allen himself wanted to "erect and sustain an independent republican form of government," and that kind of imperial reformism was at the core of Bryan's outlook and proposals.[33] Finally, it is important not to analyze attitudes as they existed on February 6, 1899, in terms of the later reaction against the war to repress the Filipino revolt. That long, brutal, and ugly war against the forces led by Emilo Aguinaldo generated some militant opposition and extensive disenchantment with the policy of formal colonialism. But there was no broad demand to withdraw, and most certainly no widespread movement to abandon the struggle for overseas markets. Indeed, there was an increase in the support for a still bigger navy and a large merchant marine.

Agricultural businessmen strongly approved the Open Door policy promulgated later in 1899 even though, in the narrow sense of policy making, it was very largely formulated by metropolitan leaders. The reason for that support is apparent. The policy represented the essence of the outlook, attitudes, and specific proposals that the farm businessmen had been promoting for more than a generation. It was their policy in the deepest sense of being a manifestation of the social consciousness they had developed and molded. Many farm leaders understood what was happening, and even named the policy before Secretary of State John Hay drafted the dispatches. Perhaps the editor of *Wallace's Farmer* was the most perceptive and knowledgeable of that group.

"The policy of the 'open door,' the policy followed by England," he explained on January 13, 1899, "with the Philippines, whose trade after all amounts to little comparatively, will enable us to use our moral advantage in securing the same 'open door' with all parts of the Chinese Empire, whether under Russian, German, or English influence. That trade will be valuable from the beginning. . . . We need this Oriental trade." It is very likely that editor Henry Wallace, through his friendship with Secretary of Agriculture Wilson, was privy to the discussions at the highest level of the McKinley Administration. But other editors, like those of the *Farmers Review*, had been talking about "open ports" throughout 1898; and the flour millers and Southern textile leaders translated their concern for an open marketplace into sustained direct pressure.[34]

Other farm businessmen joined that campaign when it became apparent that European powers and Japan were not honoring either the letter or the spirit of Hay's first Open Door Note. He had asked on September 6, 1899, for "perfect equality of treatment for commerce" in the Chinese marketplace, including the spheres of influence claimed by other nations. As the situation deteriorated, agricultural spokesmen became increasingly concerned and militant. Midwesterners wanted "a bold and determined stand."[35] Senator John Lowndes McLaurin of South Carolina spoke forcefully for the textile manufacturers who were already dealing directly with the Secretary of State. "The 'open door' policy is what we need and want." And Hill of the Great Northern, acquiring control of the Chicago, Burlington, and Quincy to further his grand strategy of expansion into Asia, carried his case for a strong policy directly to the White House.[36]

Such pressure reinforced the Administration's own deepening concern over the "critical posture of affairs" created by extensive unrest in China that was turned against foreigners by the Boxers and the Empress Dowager, and by the Russian maneuvers to exploit the upheaval to extend its control. The United States moved first on July 3, 1900, with a stronger Open Door Note promising "uttermost accountability" for any and all who visited "wrong" upon American citizens. Hay likewise reasserted the intention to guard and protect "all legitimate American interests," and added a broad commitment to "bring about permanent safety and peace to China, preserve Chinese territorial and administrative entity, protect all rights guaranteed to friendly powers by treaty and international law, and safeguard for the world the principle of equal and impartial trade with all parts of the Chinese Empire." McKinley then sent troops, more than 5,000, to help restore order—and keep the marketplace free and open for Americans.

The *Prairie Farmer* responded with a lead editorial urging Iowa and Nebraska farmers to choose expansionist senators in the coming election. They were needed because "the most lasting and greatest benefit" for agricultural businessmen "must come from a well-defined and aggressive national policy which will open the best-paying markets of the world to western farm products."[37] Bryan seriously misjudged the depth and extent of such marketplace expansionism, and for that reason was forced to revise his initial strategy of emphasizing imperialism in his second campaign against McKinley. He offered no strategic alternative to McKinley's policy, and the country had little desire to reopen the tactical debate over the Philippines.

The intensity of agricultural involvement in foreign policy declined sharply after 1900 as the Boxer Rebellion was suppressed, as American forces gradually isolated and defeated the Filipino insurgents, and as the home market absorbed a greater proportion of a stabilized production. The combination of domestic demand and reliable foreign purchases in cotton and tobacco underwrote a period of prosperity for most farm businessmen. The farmers turned back to the foreign market, however, as World War I orders first eased a serious domestic recession and then created a wild export boom.

The agricultural businessmen never again looked inward to the extent that they did between 1900 and 1914, for a second era of technological improvements and methodological advances created new surpluses that the domestic market could not absorb at high prices. They first revived the export bounty plan agitated by David Lubin in the 1890s, and then advocated a combination of Blaine's reciprocity strategy and a modified version of the Populist subtreasury plan for controlling the market by manipulating the supply. None of those approaches proved satisfactory, and the farm businessmen did not find a rewarding marketplace until the government again became a major customer during World War II, and the subsequent wars, interventions, and aid programs of the Cold War era.

Over the years that became a century the farmers were unhappily proved correct in their analysis of the 1860s—under a capitalist marketplace political economy their welfare depended upon overseas market expansion. As it had in the nineteenth century, that outlook led in the twentieth century to wars and other interventions to expand and defend the American free marketplace that agricultural businessmen had first defined as the world marketplace. The American colonials who had used expansion to gain a more equitable and profitable relationship with the metropolis became in the process an integral part of an imperial American metropolis.

After the imperial decade of the 1890s the future could have been different only if more agricultural businessmen had followed the lead of those once Republican farmers who came to understand after 1898 that a different world required a different conception of the world, a different conception of freedom and a different conception of how to realize that freedom through a different political economy. Those farmers, concentrated mainly in the Middlewestern states of Wisconsin, Minnesota, Iowa, Nebraska, and Kansas, with comrades scattered through other Northern states, began the arduous task of evolving such a new social consciousness behind the leadership of Eugene Debs.

They were warm, intelligent, and courageous men and women. The metropolis occasionally indulged them with a smile as hicks with a heart—but only until, with their comrades in the cities, they built the nucleus of an American socialist movement. Then the smiles became grimaces and the clever phrase was replaced with an ugly label—subversives. And from its point of view, the metropolis was perceptive and accurate.

For Republicans who become socialists do pose a fundamental challenge to those whose social consciousness remains locked within the framework created by Adam Smith. Just as socialists whose social consciousness remains locked within that framework, or the one created by Smith's greatest student, Karl Marx, similarly pose a fundamental challenge to socialism.

A changing reality creates the need for a new social consciousness, and even impels men and women toward that new image of the world. But the new vision does not come automatically. It emerges slowly and painfully from the moral and intellectual imagination of specific men and women. If it does not come, as it did not come between 1860 and 1900, then the old social consciousness is forced to be sufficient unto the need. Forced because there is no alternative, and forced because that is the only way to make it function. Force and the provocation of force are fundamentally alike in being the product of the failure of moral and intellectual imagination.

The Republican farmers who became socialists after 1898 did not suffer from that failure. Their example is conceivably useful for today's Republicans.

And Democrats.

And Socialists.

All of us.

POSTLUDE

Again and again in history, ideas have cast off their swaddling clothes and struck out against the social systems that bore them.

Max Horkheimer, 1946

From
Empire to Community

Historians are often asked for the meaning of their reconstruction and analysis of the past. More often than not, the questioner inserts such adjectives as "real" or "deeper" before the word "meaning." They are usually next asked what to do about the meaning. That is often the question that was intended in the first place.

But it is not a question that the historian *qua* historian can answer. The citizen as historian has one primary responsibility: to do his best to reconstruct what happened and to explain how and why it occurred. To do that well, one must first imagine, and then cultivate, a conscious, controlled, and creative schizophrenia.

That wrenching discipline can be made easier, or in practice evaded entirely, through two devices. One can turn the truism that all things are relative into an excuse for indulging everyman's propensity to be an advocate of his own truth, and his desire to perform that service in an accomplished and influential manner. One can also distort the truism that we can get closer to the truth than our own opinions into a justification for cosmic indifference.

The schizophrenic discipline of the historian is a harrowing way to stay sane. And of course very few men or women manage to master it. Certainly not I. But the effort must be made if the citizen as historian is to offer anything of value as a historian—to himself, to other historians, or to other citizens. To the extent that my disciplined schizophrenia has been creative, my study of the past offers three primary meanings.

449

First. The agricultural majority of the country developed, through the interaction of existing ideas and continuing experience, a marketplace image or conception of the world and how it worked—and of how it could be manipulated to attain their objectives. That marketplace outlook defined primary values, such as freedom and equal opportunity, as being necessary and worthy per se, and as being necessary to the proper functioning of the marketplace. The integration of the concern with freedom and the concern with economic profit and welfare led to a central conviction that it was necessary to expand the marketplace, and to expand it as a free marketplace, if freedom, profit, and welfare were to be realized. That proposition, transformed from an analysis into a belief through the processes of internalization and reinforcement, provided the dynamic causal force for a steady movement by the majority toward an imperial foreign policy.

Second. The metropolitan minority of the nation gradually accepted the expansionist aspects of the agricultural conception of the world. Its members did so because they were themselves businessmen who shared the fundamental premises of that outlook, because the farm majority was a vigorous and persistent tutor, and because their experience verified and reinforced the lesson they were being taught. They adopted the imperial outlook during the same years that they consolidated their control—still as a minority—of the political economy. The result of those interacting processes was a war against Spain and the formulation of a grand strategy for such imperial expansion of the free American marketplace.

Third. The agricultural expansionists who tried to maintain an operating balance between the expansion of freedom and the expansion of the marketplace were unsuccessful. So, ultimately, were the metropolitans who recognized that problem and made the same effort. They failed for two reasons. The metropolitan leadership that consolidated its control of the system entertained a narrower conception of freedom than the one held by the reformers on the farm or in the city; and it also offered a different analysis of how the freedom of the free marketplace developed and matured. That was the secondary cause of the failure.

The primary cause was simply that the overwhelming majority of farm businessmen shared the more conservative views of the dominant metropolitans. Indeed, they had generated and shaped that outlook. And, for that matter, many of the reformers soon acquiesced or assented. The result was an overpowering imperial consensus that defined freedom in terms of what existed in America; or, in its most liberal form, in terms of what Americans sought for themselves.

Those meanings that I offer as a historian do not, however, tell me what to do as a citizen. Nor can they tell any other citizen what to do as a citizen. He can, of course, if he so chooses, undertake the tortured schizophrenia of the citizen as historian, conduct his own study and evaluation of the materials I have used, and then engage me in dialogue as a historian about the validity and nuances of our historical investigations.

But the meanings of my history do raise questions for me as a citizen, and for other citizens as citizens. Like every other citizen, I must deal with those questions as a thinking and feeling man. I do not have to be a historian to confront those issues. Neither does any other citizen. It will help all of us to read other historians—along with philosophers, political theorists, economists, and others—but we do so to become citizens who think more incisively about the questions.

The first question is whether or not the *inherent character* of the marketplace conception of reality sets limits on the nature of freedom. My answer to that question is Yes. Freedom as the liberty to compete in the marketplace—to "truck, barter, and exchange," as Adam Smith called it—is a limited and limiting conception of freedom.

The second question is whether or not the *operation* of the marketplace system limits the realization of freedom even within the limits established by its conception of freedom. My answer to that question is Yes. Action on the belief in the marketplace outlook generates the kind of domestic and international imperialism so perceptively foreseen—and candidly discussed—by Adam Smith himself.

We can as citizens deal with the question of what to do, therefore, only after we cope with the issues raised by the meaning of the history. The problem of what to do, furthermore, is defined by one's conclusions about those issues.

Thus a citizen answering No, or Partially, to the questions just posed faces a problem that is different than my problem. If he answers No, he can proceed with his business-as-usual. If he answers Partially, then he must undertake an analysis that leads to policy and action calculated to modify the mistakes and make it possible for him to answer No at some future date. Depending upon the degree of his Partially, his reforms will be minor or major. In either case, it is possible that the agricultural majority of the nineteenth century offers him some warnings and some insights.

Anyone like myself who answers Yes to those questions faces a severe and demanding task. As Populist Jones of Texas said to his colleagues in 1898, let us radicals in the 1960s be candid. To begin with, it is wise to recognize that we may not be able to provide wholly satisfactory resolutions of all the problems that explode out of that Yes answer. A measure of humility and self-skepticism is as essential to radicals as to any others. Probably more so. We do not have all the answers now, and it is profoundly unradical to assume that we will devise them in our own time.

Radicals confront many extremely difficult questions. The central one concerns a different conception of freedom. It is very easy, in dealing with that problem, to change the language of the marketplace conception of freedom yet retain most of its limiting substance. "Doing *one's* own thing," after all, is not so very different from doing what Adam Smith advised. Stopping there might produce a more relaxed marketplace society, but in essentials it would remain a marketplace society.

"Doing *our* own thing" exposes one to similar dangers unless *our* is defined very carefully, and unless our decisions about the things are made and acted upon through very carefully defined processes.

The definition must be inclusive, for otherwise we posit ourselves as an elite dispensing our brand of freedom to the rest of society in some kind of an enforced mass feeding.

Yet it must not be inclusive in a literal, operational sense. No meaningful conception of freedom can survive in a mass democracy, for we have learned the painful way that mass democracy becomes very little democracy.

Hence it is essential for radicals to devise workable plans and procedures for decentralization that will enable all of us to realize a richer and more creative conception of freedom. We need models of autonomous yet interacting regional political economies that will function as communities. And we need political movements to create the support required to put those plans into operation.

If we do not meet those requirements, then there will very probably be corporate cells controlled by a board of directors. And the odds are high that such a system could—and would—be made to work.

A second important problem concerns the same issue that plagued the nineteenth-century agricultural majority. Those men and women embraced imperialism in the name of freedom, as well as in the practice of expanding the marketplace. Heresy though it may be, it seems very likely that radicals must accept the truth that there is a broad area in which every people is an island unto themselves. Imperialism in the name of community—at home or abroad—is a vastly more horrible travesty than imperialism in the name of the free marketplace.

The constant battle to distinguish between fraternal assistance and aid insisted upon in order to produce the same kind of community as ours is a struggle that radicals have lost about as often as liberals or conservatives. Doing our thing in our way must not be allowed to become doing your thing in our way.

To confront that issue is to confront the question of whether or not there is a time to accept short-run defeat rather than to win a minor battle by becoming more like the enemy. I think there are such times. I do not think they come often. But I do think they come most often in the beginning and at the end of a social movement, when the sense of urgency is most intense.

And because just now we are just beginning, I suggest that we be very careful about winning when it requires us to become more like what we find so unacceptable. For those kinds of victories can very easily change us into small businessmen promoting a marginal product.

BIBLIOGRAPHY
AND NOTES

THIS STUDY is based on a wide range of sources that provided the most direct and extended access to the experience, thought, and action of the agricultural majority of the country; and to the interaction concerning foreign affairs between that majority and the leadership of the metropolitan minority. Some of the materials are well known to scholars. Many other items are not generally known or used. A full listing of the materials that I consulted would require excessive space, if only because many of the items proved of marginal value in connection with this subject.

Hence this bibliography is sharply restricted to the primary materials that offered the most continuing assistance. Some manuscript sources and newspapers are not listed despite the citations to them in the footnotes because I used them only in dealing with specific events. In a few of those cases, the first suggestion came from a friend or an interested colleague, and I limited my exploration of those collections to developing the lead. Most of the isolated references to newspapers not listed below refer to clippings contained in archival or manuscript collections, or to items mentioned by the correspondents (which I verified).

Research in primary materials for a study of this kind could in theory be continued until one had read everything. I stopped after six years when the investigation of new materials began to produce redundancies on all central points and themes.

I am of course indebted to other scholars in several fields. Save for a few exceptions, however, such as Paul Wallace Gates and Fred Albert Shannon, I turned to their work only after I had gone extensively into the primary sources. I have indicated in the footnotes where I found their contributions directly relevant and helpful. I have followed the same practice in dealing with the vast number of published primary sources, particularly government documents, that I consulted.

Record Groups of the National Archives of the United States

16 Department of Agriculture
17 Bureau of Animal Industry
38 Office of the Chief of Naval Operations
40 Department of Commerce
43 Records of United States Participation in International Conferences, Commissions, and Expositions

46 Records of the Senate
56 Department of the Treasury
59 Department of State
80 General Records of the Department of the Navy
104 Bureau of the Mint
128 Records of the Joint Committees of the Congress
166 Office of Foreign Agricultural Relations
233 Records of the House of Representatives

*Materials from the Manuscript Collections of the
Following Men and Women, and Organizations*

Brooks Adams, Charles Francis Adams, Henry Cullen Adams, Benton Aldrich, James Franklin Aldrich, Russell A. Alger, William Vincent Allen, William Boyd Allison, American National Cattlemens Association, Rasmus B. Anderson, Christopher Columbus Andrews, Chester Arthur, Sarah G. Baird, Wharton Baker, Thomas Bayard, Albert Beveridge, Frederic de Billier, George N. Black, James G. Blaine, Charles R. Boardman, Edward S. Bragg, Joseph G. Cannon, Henry Castle, William E. Chandler, Samuel M. Chapman, Chicago, Burlington, and Quincy Railroad, James S. Clarkson, Grover Cleveland, Solomon Gilman Comstock, Henry Allen Cooper, Jacob Calvin Cooper, Shelby M. Cullom, Albert Baird Cummins, Dane County, Wisconsin, Agricultural Society, Cushman Kellogg Davis, J. C. Bancroft Davis, James William Dawes, Leonard W. Dibble, Grenville M. Dodge, William E. Doggett, Jonathan P. Dolliver, John S. Donald, Ignatius Donnelly, Duke University Records of the Patrons of Husbandry and the Farmers Alliance, Clarence J. Dunder, William H. Dunwoody, William Crowell Edgar, Stephen B. Elkins, Isaac L. Ellwood, William L. Ellwood, John J. Esch, Rudolph Evans, William Evarts, Lucius Fairchild, Hamilton Fish, Stuyvesant Fish, Joseph Foraker, Henry D. Fox, Everett W. Frazar, Moreton Frewen, S. Adelbert Gardiner, Augustine V. Gardner, James Garfield, Joseph B. Gill, John G. Gregory, Walter Gresham, William G. Haan, Eugene Hale, William D. Hale, Murat Halstead, Benjamin Harrison, Eugene G. Hay, John Hay, Fred G. Hesse, Lewis J. Higby, George F. Hoar, Halbert L. Hoard, Silas A. Holcomb, George W. Holdrege, T. C. Hord, Illinois Central Railroad, Illinois State Grange, Joseph R. Jones, John A. Kasson, Elisha W. Keyes, Samuel J. Korkwood, Charles L. Kurtz, John F. Lacey, William G. LeDuc, John Lind, Henry D. Lloyd, Henry Cabot Lodge, Jonathan P. Lord, Frank O. Lowden, The McCormick Collections, Hugh McCulloch, William McKinley, John R. Maltby, Manton Marble, Charles Mason, R. W. Meade, Lewis T. Michener, Mississippi Valley Trading Company, Ltd., John B. Moore, J. Sterling Morton, Albinus Nance, Nebraska Farmers Alliance, Nebraska Railroad Commission, Knute Nelson, Josiah A. Noonan, North Star Grange, St. Paul, Minnesota, Richard J. Oglesby, Joseph H. Osborn, Thomas B. Page, Charles G. Pearson, George D. Perkins, Arthur Pickford Family, Otis A. Pray, Pomona Grange No. 12, Hennepin County, Minnesota, Whitelaw Reid, Minnesota Grange, Richfield, Minnesota, Thomas C. Richmond, Theodore Roosevelt, Rosendale Agricultural Club, Rosendale, Wisconsin, Jeremiah M. Rusk, William E. Russell, Henry S. Sanford, George R. Schaefer, Robert Schilling, John Sherman, Henry H. Sibley, William H. Smith, John C. Spooner, William McK. Springer, Oscar Straus, Henry C. Taylor, James W. Taylor, Joseph N. Teale, Hubert E. Teschemacher, John B. Thomas, Russell Thorp, Ruben G. Thwaites, Daniel A. Tompkins, William Toole, Benjamin F. Tracy, Charles R. Van Hise, Francis J. Walker, William F. Vilas, Francis E. Warren, Cadwallader C. Washburn, Elihu B. Washburn, Luman H. Weller, David Wells, William Whitney, Cyrus Woodman, John R. Young

*Reports of the Boards, Commissioners, Departments, and
Institutes of Agriculture of the Following States*

Alabama, California, Colorado, Connecticut, Florida, Georgia, Illinois, Indiana, Iowa, Kansas, Kentucky, Louisiana, Maine, Massachusetts, Michigan, Minnesota, Missouri, Nebraska, New York, North Carolina, North Dakota, Ohio, Pennsylvania, Texas, Virginia, Wisconsin

Proceedings of the Following Organizations

Agricultural and Mechanics Society of South Carolina, American Agricultural Association, American Bar Association, American Cotton Manufacturers Association, Chicago Board of Trade, Colored Farmers National Alliance, Farmers and Laborers Union of America, Farmers National Alliance, Iowa Farmers Alliance, Illinois Farmers Institute, International Deep Waterways Association, Michigan State Farmers Institutes, National Cattle Growers Association, National Association of Stock Breeders, National Farmers Alliance and Industrial Union, National Farmers Congress, National Silver Conventions, New York Farmers, Ohio Farmers Alliance, National Patrons of Husbandry, State Patrons of Husbandry (of Alabama, Arkansas, California, Colorado, Delaware, Illinois, Indiana, Iowa, Kansas, Maine, Maryland, Massachusetts, Michigan, Minnesota, Mississippi, Missouri, Nebraska, New Hampshire, New Jersey, New York, North Carolina, Ohio, Oregon, Pennsylvania, South Carolina, Tennessee, Texas, Virginia, Washington and Wisconsin), Pennsylvania Farmers Alliance, Railway Conventions at Saratoga, New York, Southern Commercial Convention, Trans-Mississippi Commercial Congress, Virginia Alliance, Western States Commercial Congress, Wisconsin Farmers Alliance, Wyoming Stock Growers Association

Newspapers and Other Periodicals

Advance Guard, Albany (Oregon) *Democrat, Alliance Advocate, Alliance-Independent, The American, American Agriculturalist, The American Breeder, The American Cultivator, The American Economist, The American Farmer, American Miller, American Non-Conformist, American Railroad Journal, American Stock Journal, American Swineherd, American Thresherman, American Wool and Cotton Reporter, Anti-Monopolist, Boot and Shoe Recorder, Boston Journal of Commerce, Bradstreet's, Breeders Gazette, Bulletin of the National Association of Wool Manufacturers, Butcher's Advocate, California Farmer, Charleston News and Courier, Chicago Dairy Produce, Chicago Inter-Ocean, Chicago Produce, Chicago Tribune, Chronicle and Constitutionalist, Cincinnati Populist, Cincinnati Price-Current, Colman's Rural World and Valley Farmer, Colorado Price-Current and Live Stock Journal* (becomes *Daily Denver Stockman*), *The Cotton World, The Country Gentleman, The Cultivator and Country Gentleman, The Cultivator, Daily Commercial Bulletin, The Dairy World, The Dakota Farmer, The Davenport* (Iowa) *Democrat, DeBow's Review, Dixie Manufacturer, The Drover's Journal, Dry Goods Economist, Dun's Review, The Elgin Dairy Report, Farm and Factory, Farm, Field and Stockman* (becomes *Farm, Field and Fireside*). *Farm Implement News, Farm Journal, Farm Machinery, Farm, Stock and Home, Farmer's Advance, Farmer's Call, The Farmers Alliance, Farmer's Register, Farmers Review, The Grange News, Great West, Hoard's Dairyman, The Homestead, Hunt's Merchant Magazine, Iowa Farmer and Breeder, Iowa Homestead, Implement Age, Indiana Farmer, Industrial Age, Journal of Agriculture, Kansas Farmer, Frank Leslie's Illustrated Newspaper, Lima* (Ohio) *Sentinel, Live Stock Report Issued Weekly by Clay, Robinson and Company, London Economist, London Live-Stock Journal, London Times, Louisiana Planter, Manufacturers Record, Mark Lane Express, Massachusetts Ploughman, Merchant's Association Review* (of San Francisco), *Michigan Farmer, The* (London) *Miller, Milling and Grain News, The Million, Milwaukee Advance, The Union Signal, Minnesota Farm Journal, Moline Daily Republican, Montana Farming and Stock Journal, The National Advocate, National Corporation Reporter, National Economist, National Farm and Fireside, National Live Stock Journal, National Provisioner, National Stockman and Farmer, National Watchman, Nebraska Farmer, New England Farmer, New York Herald, New York Produce Exchange Reporter, New York Produce Review, The New York Times, Normanden, North British Agriculturalist, Northwest Pacific Farmer, North Pacific Rural Spirit, Northwestern Farmer, Northwestern Live Stock Journal, Northwestern Miller, Ohio Farmer, Ohio Populist, Ohio Practical Farmer, Ohio Swine Journal, Omaha Bee, Omaha World-Herald, Orange Judd Farmer, Pacific Rural Press, People, People's Call, People's Paper, People's Party Paper, Plough Boy, POP, The Populist, Practical Farmer, The Prairie Farmer, The Progressive Farmer, Review of the Trade of India, Rural Life, Rural New Yorker, The Silver Knight-Watchman, The South, South*

Omaha Daily Stockman, Southern Agriculturalist, Southern Cultivator and Dixie Farmer, The Southern Mercury, Southern Planter and Farmer, Southwestern Miller, The State Record, Sugar Beet, St. Paul Daily News, Star, Textile Manufacturer, Textile Record, Textile World, Topeka Advocate, Trade and Export Journal, Traffic, Vox Populi, Wall Street Journal, Wallace's Farmer, The Western Advance, The Western Farmer, Western Ploughman, Western Rural and American Stockman, Western Swineherd, Western Stockman and Cultivator, Willamette Farmer, Wisconsin Farmer and Northwestern Cultivator, Wisconsin Signal, World Trade

Unpublished Manuscripts of a Historical Nature

R. D. Bittinger, "History of the Patrons of Husbandry in Kansas, 1872-1882" (MA Thesis, University of Kansas, 1960); E. C. Brook, "The Struggle for the Adoption of the Interstate Commerce Commission, 1872-1887" (PhD Thesis, University of Chicago, 1925); H. J. Brown, "The National Association of Wool Manufacturers, 1864-1897" (PhD Thesis, Cornell University, 1949); P. F. Buckner, "Silver Mining Interests in Silver Politics, 1876-1896" (MA Thesis, Columbia University, 1954); O. L. Burnette, "The Senate Foreign Relations Committee and the Diplomacy of Garfield, Arthur, and Cleveland" (PhD Thesis, University of Virginia, 1952); C. E. Chapman, "History of Deere and Company, 1837-1911" (MA Thesis, University of Iowa, 1949); Chen-Han Chen, "The Location of the Cotton Manufacturing Industry in the United States, 1880-1910" (PhD Thesis, Harvard University, 1939); C. B. Cowing, "Speculation on the American Exchanges. The Principal Ideas Affecting the Evolution of Trading, 1892-1936" (PhD Thesis, University of Wisconsin, 1955); W. E. Derby, "A History of the Port of Milwaukee, 1835-1910" (PhD Thesis, University of Wisconsin, 1963); R. B. Duncan, "Papers Relating to American Agricultural Exports, 1830-1850" (PhD Thesis, Cornell University, 1938); P. L. Erickson, "Destitution and Relief in Nebraska, 1874-1875" (MA Thesis, University of Nebraska, 1937); J. S. Ferguson, "Agrarianism in Mississippi, 1871-1900. A Study in Non-Conformity" (PhD Thesis, University of North Carolina, 1952); H. L. Flanagan, "The Cotton States and International Exposition, 1895" (MA Thesis, University of Georgia, 1950); L. W. Fuller, "The Populist Regime in Colorado" (PhD Thesis, University of Wisconsin, 1933); H. A. Hoard, "A Historical Survey of *Hoard's Dairyman*" (MA Thesis, University of Wisconsin, 1923); G. E. Hunsberger, "The Development of Tariff Policy in the Republican Party" (PhD Thesis, University of Virginia, 1934); R. L. Hunt, "A History of the Farmers Union in Texas" (PhD Thesis, University of Wisconsin, 1934); V. O. Johns, "Development of Flour Milling Industry in Kansas" (MA Thesis, University of Kansas, 1923); F. C. Kuester, "The Farmers Alliance in Nebraska" (MA Thesis, University of Nebraska, 1927); D. M. Leach, "The Tariff and the Western Farmer, 1860-1890" (PhD Thesis, University of Oklahoma, 1964); E. M. Mack, "Life and Letters of William Morris Stewart, 1827-1909. A History of His Influence on State and National Legislation" (PhD Thesis, University of California at Berkeley, 1930); N. R. Mahnken, "The Congressmen of the Grain Belt States and Tariff Legislation, 1865-1890" (PhD Thesis, University of Nebraska, 1941); C. L. Marquette, "The Business Activities of C. C. Washburn" (PhD Thesis, University of Wisconsin, 1940); R. C. Miller, "The Populist Party in Kansas" (PhD Thesis, University of Chicago, 1928); G. H. Miller, "The Granger Laws. A Study of the Origins of State Railway Control in the Upper Mississippi Valley" (PhD Thesis, University of Michigan, 1951); S. N. Murray, "A History of Agriculture in the Valley of the Red River of the North, 1812-1920" (PhD Thesis, University of Wisconsin, 1963); N. L. O'Connor, "The Influence of Populist Legislators upon American Foreign Policy, 1892-1898" (MA Thesis, University of Oregon, 1958); R. M. Packard, "The French Pork Prohibition in American Diplomacy, 1881-1891" (PhD Thesis, Harvard University, 1954); A. C. Radke, "John Tyler Morgan, an Expansionist Senator, 1877-1907" (PhD Thesis, University of Washington, 1953); W. B. Ranney, "American Newspaper Opinions of European Alliances and Alignments, 1871-1894" (PhD Thesis, Johns Hopkins University, 1935); L. J. Scheidler, "Silver and Politics, 1893-1896" (PhD Thesis, University of Indiana, 1936); H. B. Schonberger, "The Foreign Business of the McCormick Harvesting Machine Company" (MA Thesis, University of Wisconsin, 1964); E. A. Scott, "The Grange Movement in Oregon, 1873-1900" (MA Thesis, University of Oregon, 1923); M. Y. Scott, "The Life and Political Career of William Vincent Allen"

(MA Thesis, University of Nebraska, 1927); M. Small, "Robert Schilling and the Origins of Populism in Wisconsin" (Mss. in Wisconsin State Historical Society); F. L. Smith, "The Populist Movement and Its Influence in North Carolina" (PhD Thesis, University of Chicago, 1929); R. A. Smith, "A. J. Rose, Agrarian Crusader of Texas" (PhD Thesis, University of Texas, 1938); O. C. Stine, "Economic History of Wheat in the United States" (PhD Thesis, University of Wisconsin, 1921); T. Stirton, "Free Trade and the Wheat Surplus of the Old Northwest, 1839-1846" (MA Thesis, University of Chicago, 1952); J. F. Tucker, "British Agriculture Under Protection and Free Trade, 1815-1895" (PhD Thesis, University of Pennsylvania, 1957); J. W. Whitaker, "The Rise and Development of Beef Cattle Feeding in Illinois and Iowa, 1840-1900" (PhD Thesis, University of Wisconsin, 1965); E. A. White, "The Republican Party in National Politics, 1888-1891" (PhD Thesis, University of Wisconsin, 1941); E. T. White, "The Farmer of the Western North Central States and the Tariff, 1887-1893" (MA Thesis, University of Maryland, 1947); G. G. Williamson, "Cotton Manufacturing in South Carolina, 1865-1892" (PhD Thesis, Johns Hopkins University, 1954); J. B. Workman, "Governor William Larrabee of Iowa and Railroad Reform" (MA Thesis, Iowa State Teachers College, 1935)

NOTES

Chapter One

1. W. B. Hesseltine, "Four American Traditions," *Journal of Southern History* (February 1961), 3-32; P. W. Gates, *The Farmer's Age: Agriculture, 1815-1860* (New York, 1960), 413; R. C. Loehr, "Self-Sufficiency on the Farm," *Agricultural History* (April 1952), 37-41; C. P. Nettles, *The Roots of American Civilization* (New York, 1938); and A. M. Simons, *The American Farmer* (Chicago, 1902). Also see M. M. Cleworth, "Twenty Years of Brown County Agricultural History, 1880-1899," *South Dakota Historical Collections*, 17 (1934), 175-176; and A. Bogue, *From Prairie to Corn Belt* (Chicago, 1963), M. B. Bogue, *Patterns from the Sod. Land Use and Tenure in the Grand Prairie, 1850-1900* (Springfield, 1959).

2. Here see W. A. Williams, *The Contours of American History* (Quadrangle Paperback edition, 1966), and the materials cited therein. For a clear statement of such mercantilist thought, see J. Steuart, *An Inquiry into the Principles of Political Economy* (London, 2 volumes, 1767).

3. W. A. Williams, "The Age of Mercantilism: An Interpretation of the American Political Economy, 1763 to 1828," *William and Mary Quarterly* (October 1958), 419-437.

4. J. Madison, "The Federalist No. 10," published originally in the New York *Packet*, November 23, 1787. But also consult his long letter to T. Jefferson, October 24, 1787.

5. J. Madison, "The Federalist No. 14," published originally in the New York *Packet*, November 30, 1787.

6. *Address of the Convention of Kentucky, to the United States in Congress Assembled* (St. Louis, 1884).

7. J. D. Richardson (ed.), *A Compilation of the Messages and Papers of the Presidents, 1789-1897* (Washington, 1896-1899), 1:358, hereafter cited as Richardson, *Messages*; H. A. Washington (ed.), *The Writings of Thomas Jefferson* (Washington, 9 volumes, 1854), 5:444.

8. New York *Evening Post*, January 10, 1803.

9. F. Quesnay, Note to Maxim IX in "The General Maxims for the Economic Government of An Agricultural Kingdom." A stimulating essay on the Physiocrats is R. L. Meek, *The Economics of Physiocracy* (London, 1962).

10. *The Works of John Locke* (London, 12th edition, 9 volumes, 1824), 10:10, 42. Also consult S. S. Wolin, *Politics and Vision. Continuity and Innovation in Western Political*

Thought (Boston, 1960), esp. Ch. 9; and C. B. MacPherson, *The Political Theory of Possessive Individualism: Hobbes to Locke* (Oxford, 1962).

11.   R. E. Lipsey, *Price and Quantity Trends in the Foreign Trade of the United States* (Princeton, 1963), 51.

12.   For ease of reference, these and subsequent quotations may be found in G. R. Taylor, "Agrarian Discontent in the Mississippi Valley Preceding the War of 1812," *Journal of Political Economy* (August 1931), 471-505; and M. K. Latimer, "South Carolina—A Protagonist of the War of 1812," *American Historical Review* (Spring 1956), 921-929. The debates as reproduced in the *Annals of Congress*, Volumes 22-25, are filled with the analysis.

13.   T. Jefferson to J. Adams, November 7, 1819: in *The Writings of Thomas Jefferson*, edited by P. L. Ford (New York, 1895), 12:144-145.

14.   B. H. Wall, "Ebenezer Pittigrew's Efforts to Control the Marketing of His Crop," *Agricultural History* (October 1953), 123-131. Also see G. R. Taylor, *The Transportation Revolution, 1815-1860* (New York, 1957), esp. 190-198; and Gates, *The Farmer's Age*.

15.   Gates, *The Farmer's Age;* and consult *American Farmer*, April 23, October 1, 1819; July 6, 13, September 7, 1821.

16.   *Report of the Committee on Agriculture Upon the Subject of Increasing Duties, March 19, 1824*. House of Representatives, 18th Cong., 1st Ses. (Washington, 1824).

17.   Richardson, *Messages*, 1:584-585. The conflict over internal improvements is nicely reviewed by G. Dangerfield, *The Awakening of American Nationalism: 1815-1828* (New York, 1964). A fuller discussion is provided by Taylor, *Transportation Revolution*, which contains an excellent bibliography.

18.   Richardson, *Messages*, 2:144-183.

19.   A. Smith, *An Inquiry into the Nature and Causes of the Wealth of Nations* (New York, Modern Library edition, 1937), 13. This difference between Smith and the mercantilists is noted by W. C. Mitchell, *Types of Economic Theory*, ed. with an introduction by J. Dorfman (New York, 1967), 55-60.

20.   Smith, *Wealth of Nations*, 14-15, 355, 651.

21.   *Ibid.*, 3, 13.

22.   *Ibid.*, 17. The background of Smith's imperial outlook is discussed by E. A. Benians, "Adam Smith's Project of an Empire," *Cambridge Historical Journal* (1925), 249-283.

23.   *Ibid.*, 353, 645.

24.   *Ibid.*, 540, 541-542, 545.

25.   *Ibid.*, 356-357.

26.   *Ibid.*, 241.

27.   *Ibid.*, 127.

28.   *Ibid.*, 641.

29.   *Ibid.*, 642.

30.   J. Q. Adams, *An Address Delivered at the Request of a Commission of the Citizens of Washington . . . on the Fourth of July, 1821* (Washington, 1821).

31.   The classic reviews of this development are A. K. Weinberg, *Manifest Destiny. A Study of Nationalist Expansionism in American History* (Baltimore, 1935); and H. N. Smith, *Virgin Land. The American West As Symbol and Myth* (Cambridge, 1950). On Smith and freedom, see J. W. Hurst, *Law and the Condition of Freedom in the Nineteenth-Century United States* (Madison, 1956). Justice John A. Campbell's remarks, "Freedom, free action, free enterprise—free competition," are in B. Twiss, *Lawyers and the Constitution* (Princeton, 1942), 137.

32.   *Annals of Congress*, 33:838.

33.   Smith, *Virgin Land*, 25 (but see all Ch. 2).

34.   F. L. Benns, *The American Struggle for the British West India Carrying Trade, 1815-1830* (Bloomington, 1923), 160; and in general for the political manifestations of the push by farm businessmen for the Indies market.

35.   J. Taylor, letter to the editor, *American Farmer*, July 20, 1821; *ibid.*, January 14, 1820, 332-333.

36.   Sullivan and Lowell, reports as printed in *American Farmer*, May 25, 1821, February 8, 1822.

37.   *American Farmer*, January 4, 1822, 321-324.

Chapter Two

1. T. Cooper, "Dr. Cooper on the Tariff . . . July 2, 1827," as quoted in J. Dorfman, *The Economic Mind in American Civilization, 1606-1865* (New York, 1946), 2:535-536.

2. *The Works of John C. Calhoun*, ed. by R. K. Cralle (New York, 6 volumes, 1851-1856), 6:1-59.

3. *Register of the Debates in Congress*, 6:1:3.

4. *Ibid.*, 6:1:4, 22, 14.

5. *Ibid.*, 6:2:1138.

6. A. M. Johnson and B. E. Supple, *Boston Capitalists and Western Railroads. A Study in the Nineteenth Century Railroad Investment Process* (Cambridge, 1967), 2-21, 24, 29; Taylor, *Transportation Revolution*, 237; G. R. Taylor, "American Economic Growth Before 1840," in R. L. Andreano (ed.), *New Views on American Economic Development* (Cambridge, 1965), 59, 66, 70-71; M. Abramovitz, "Long Swings in American Economic Growth," in Andreano, *New Views*, 403, and 424-425 for the reprint of the yearly description of conditions from Thorp's *Business Annals*.

7. *Register of Debates in Congress*, 10:4:4522-23, 4795-4796.

8. A. L. Kohlmeier, *The Old Northwest as the Keystone of the Arch of American Federal Union. A Study in Commerce and Politics* (Bloomington, 1938), 31-32, 51.

9. C. E. Gage, "Historical Factors Affecting American Tobacco Types," *Agricultural History* (1937), 43-57; J. C. Robert, *The Tobacco Kingdom* (Durham, 1938).

10. *Register of Debates in Congress*, 12:2:1381.

11. *Report of the Select Committee of the House of Representatives on Tobacco, February 18, 1837. Report No. 239.* 24th Cong., 2nd Ses. (Washington, 1837); *Message from the President Upon the Subject of the Tobacco Trade, October 3, 1837. House Executive Document No. 41.* 25th Cong., 1st Ses. (Washington, 1837); then see *Congressional Globe*, 7:61, 225; 8:168, 183, 253, for the continuing efforts to enlarge the market.

12. E. D. Ross, "The United States Department of Agriculture During the Commissionership: A Study in Politics, Administration, and Technology, 1862-1889," *Agricultural History* (1946), 131; *The Cultivator*, September 1837.

13. C. C. Taylor, *The Farmer's Movement, 1620-1920* (New York, 1953), 71, argues that "until about 1860, farmers' organizations were for the most part concerned with technical problems of production rather than with problems of markets and prices." My research strongly suggests, to the contrary, that the farmers were directly and pointedly involved with markets and prices.

14. T. P. Martin, "Cotton and Wheat in Anglo-American Trade and Politics, 1846-1852," *Journal of Southern History* (1935), 299. Also see here, as elsewhere, the work of Douglass North on American economic growth.

15. R. M. Robbins, "Preemption—A Frontier Triumph," *Mississippi Valley Historical Review* (1931), 331-349; and F. T. Carlton, "An American Utopia," *Quarterly Journal of Economics* (1910), 428-433, review the long battle. R. G. Wellington, *Political and Sectional Influence of the Public Lands, 1828-1842* (n. p., 1914), is a very useful study.

16. See *The Radical* (January 1842); *The Free Enquirer* (December 10, 24, 1831); and the files of *Working Man's Advocate*. A brief summary appears in J. Dorfman, *Economic Mind*, 2:641-645, 684-686. More extended treatment can be found in J. R. Commons, et al., *A Documentary History of American Industrial Society* (Cleveland, 11 volumes, 1910-1911), 7:299-307, 8:32 ff.

17. E. Everett, *Orations and Speeches on Various Occasions* (Boston, 4 volumes, 1878-1879), 1:33, 260.

18. A. Jackson to A. V. Brown, as quoted in J. Parton, *Life of Andrew Jackson* (New York, 1860), 3:658. Also see Washington *Globe*, February 12, 1843, and Albany *Argus*, March 29, 1944. Another item is reprinted in *Niles National Register*, June 8, 1844.

19. *Congressional Globe*, 10:279 (and also 396).

20. Linn's activities can be followed in *Senate Document No. 470*, and *House Report No. 101*, of the 25th Cong., 2nd Ses., as well as in the *Congressional Globe*. The Cincinnati resolution can be found in R. W. Van Alstyne, *American Diplomacy in Action* (Stanford, 1947), 568.

21. A good review of this development is offered by T. Stirton, "Free Trade and the Wheat Surplus of the Old Northwest, 1839-1846," MA Thesis, University of Chicago, 1952.

22.   The discussion about the role of expansionism in Southern development is endless: much material is in Weinberg, *Manifest Destiny;* a recent symposium is in *The Journal of Economic History* (December 1956); after which proceed to the work of E. C. Barker and G. Genovese.

23.   *Niles National Register,* April 20, 1844.

24.   *Young Hickory Banner,* October 15, 1845.

25.   The votes are recorded in the House and Senate *Journals,* January 25, February 27 and 28, 1845.

Chapter Three

1.   *Congressional Globe,* 12:198-199 (hereafter cited as *CG*).

2.   *Ibid.,* 14:A:178-179.

3.   United States Department of Commerce, *Historical Statistics of the United States* (1960 edition), 545.

4.   *CG,* 15:445. Also see St. Louis *Missouri Reporter,* June 24, 1845; and *Hunt's Merchant Magazine,* 16 (1847), 36-37.

5.   *CG,* 16:A:241.

6.   *Ibid.,* 15:187-188.

7.   *Ibid.,* 15:A:212. See also the analysis by J. D. Cummins of Ohio at 15:336.

8.   *Ibid.,* 15:328.

9.   See New York *Herald,* September 28, December 12, 1847. And consider J. M. Forbes to P. S. Forbes, October 31, 1847: "if breadstuffs keep up the United States will be the Fountain head of wealth instead of England"; as quoted in Johnson and Supple, *Boston Capitalists,* 80.

10.   R. W. Johannsen (ed.), *Letters of Stephen A. Douglas* (Urbana, 1961), 140, 127-131; *CG,* 15:258-260.

11.   See here London *Times,* January 3, 1846; A. L. Kohlmeier, *The Old Northwest as the Keystone of the Arch of American Federal Union. A Study in Commerce and Politics* (Bloomington, 1938), Ch. 5; *CG,* 15:159, 261, 313, and A:179, 343, 459, 753.

12.   *Report of the Secretary of the Treasury, December 3, 1845,* 6, 13.

13.   *Ibid.,* 478-487. The unusually useful replies to Circular No. 2 begin on 431.

14.   Rep. C. Hudson of New York, *CG,* 15:A:459-461. See also 15:459-460, 995.

15.   *Ibid.,* 15:A:760; 15:1008, 1021-1022.

16.   *Ibid.,* 15:A:733, 745, 748.

17.   *Ibid.,* 15:A:1057, 1040-1043; 15:1105, 1124. This market expansionism is also documented in E. E. Lampard, *The Rise of the Dairy Industry in Wisconsin. A Study in Agricultural Change, 1820-1920* (Madison, 1963), 61; C. W. Wright, *Wool-Growing and the Tariff. A Study in the Economic History of the United States* (Boston, 1910), 53-54; and B. H. Hibbard, *Marketing Agricultural Products* (New York, 1922), 137.

18.   *CG,* 16:A:26-31.

19.   *Ibid.,* 16:A:59-60; 16:A:323. And see the study by John Hope Franklin.

20.   *Ibid.,* 16:A:102-103.

21.   *Ibid.,* 16:A:315.

22.   Weinberg, *Manifest Destiny,* 160-180; J. D. P. Fuller, *The Movement for the Acquisition of All Mexico, 1846-1848* (Baltimore, 1936). Also see S. A. Douglas to Polk, August 25, 1845; Douglas to S. Treat, February 19, 1848; and Douglas, "Autobiographical Notes" [1859], in *Douglas Letters,* 119-120, 157, 472-473.

23.   E. L. Ross, "A History of Rivers and Harbors Appropriations Bills, 1866-1930," PhD Thesis, Ohio State University, 1938.

24.   *CG,* 13:396.

25.   Records of the Memphis Convention of 1845, from notes loaned by W. B. Hesseltine.

26.   S. A. Douglas, *An American Commercial Union and Alliance* (Washington, 1889), 36.

27.   See, for example, *Western Journal,* 1 (1848), 173; and *Niles National Register,* July 31, August 7, 1847.

28.   W. T. Hutchinson, *Cyrus Hall McCormick* (New York, 2 volumes, 1930, 1935), 2:405, 427; and J. P. Lord to C. S. Lord, December 23, 1855: *Jonathan P. Lord Papers;*

as well as the standard accounts of agricultural technology beginning with L. Rogin, *The Introduction of Farm Machinery in its Relation to the Productivity of Labor in the Agriculture of the United States During the Nineteenth Century* (Berkeley, 1931).

29. The statistical data used in this study have been selected for each specific instance after a thorough consideration of the alternate data, and after discussions of the problem with Eric Lampard and Mort Rothstein. R. A. Billington, *Westward Expansion* (New York, 1949), 401, provides a useful table.

30. Taylor, *Transportation Revolution*, 185, 194.

31. Compare, for example, Martin, "Cotton and Wheat," 293-319, and M. Rothstein, "America in the International Rivalry for the British Wheat Market, 1860-1914," *Missisippi Valley Historical Review* (December 1960), 401-419.

32. As quoted in Martin, "Staff of Life," 2.

33. Wright, *Wool-Growing*, 153-154. Such glowing expectations can be found, however, in most agricultural journals of the period.

34. Lippincott, *Manufacturing in the Ohio River Valley*, esp. 114-117, 175-185.

35. J. G. Thompson, *The Rise and Decline of the Wheat Growing Industry in Wisconsin* (Madison, 1909), 40.

36. Odle, "American Grain Trade," 248-249.

37. *Report of the Federal Trade Commission on the Grain Trade* (Washington, 7 volumes, 1920-1926), 1:75.

38. *Hunt's Merchant Magazine*, 437-440.

39. A. E. Sheldon, *Land Systems and Land Policies in Nebraska* (Lincoln, 1936), 174; P. W. Gates, "Cattle Kings in the Prairies," *Mississippi Valley Historical Review* (December 1948), 381; and on pork exports see S. Robinson, *Facts for Farmers, Also for the Family Circle* (New York, 2 volumes, 1867), 1:57.

40. The basic analysis of this redeployment of trade was made by L. B. Schmidt, "The Internal Grain Trade of the United States, 1850-1860," *Iowa Journal of History and Politics* (January 1920-January 1922), but also see *Eighth Census, 1860, Agriculture*, clvii. It has then been discussed by Billington, *Westward Expansion*, 401, 801-802, and Taylor, *Transportation Revolution*, 161-164. It was then rediscovered by A. Fishlow, "Ante-bellum Inter-regional Trade Reconsidered," *American Economic Review. Papers and Proceedings* (May 1964), 352-364; and R. Battalio and J. Dagel, "Structure of Ante-Bellum Southern Agriculture: South Carolina, A Case Study," mimeographed, 1968; all of whom seem largely unaware of the earlier work. They have not added much beyond details. On balance they exaggerate Southern losses.

41. Douglas to Woodsworth, March 5, 1850; Douglas, "To the Citizens of Chicago, October 1850"; Douglas to Breeze, January 5, 1851; and Douglas to Matteson, January 2, 1854: all in *Douglas Letters*, 188, 197, 201, 273.

42. *American Railroad Journal*, August 7, 1852, 506.

43. Martin, "Cotton and Wheat," 299-306.

44. F. Merk, *Economic History of Wisconsin During the Civil War Decade* (Madison, 1916), 241-243; R. E. Riegel, "Trans-Mississippi Railroads During the Fifties," *Mississippi Valley Historical Review* (September 1923), 156-157; and Taylor, *Transportation Revolution*, 97-98. The quotation from Brooks can be found in the Michigan Central Railroad, *Annual Report, 1848*, 23.

45. B. B. Kendrick, "The Colonial Status of the South," *Journal of Southern History* (February 1942), 15, offers a succinct characterization of the region's experience.

46. See, for example, *Norris' Chicago Business Directory* (1846), 18-20; and Clemen, *The American Livestock and Meat Industry* (New York, 1923), 137-138.

47. R. P. Swierenga, "Land Speculator 'Profits' Reconsidered: Central Iowa as a Test Case," *Journal of Economic History* (March 1966), 1-28.

48. F. Merk, "Eastern Antecedents of the Grangers," *Agricultural History* (January 1949), 7.

49. Shannon, *Farmer's Last Frontier*, 52; F. A. Shannon, "The Homestead Act and the Labor Surplus," *American Historical Review* (July 1936), 642-643, 645-646; St. G. L. Sioussat, "Andrew Johnson and the Early Phases of the Homestead Bill," *Mississippi Valley Historical Review* (1918), 253-287.

50. *CG*, 21:A:386, 289-292.

51. *Ibid.*, 21:428-430, and see 729-737.

52. *Ibid.*, 381, 477. The House vote is at 21:2:1351.

53. Lampard, *Dairy*, 62. Also see *The Democratic Review* (June 1852), 492, for stress on foreign markets.

54. A. L. Demaree, *The American Agricultural Press, 1819-1860* (New York, 1941), 94.

55. *CG*, 21:A:746-748; and see 491, 892-894.

56. G. E. Baker (ed.), *The Works of William Henry Seward* (New York, 1884), 176-190.

57. Nebraska City *People's Press*, September 20, 1860. And consult E. H. Berwanger, *The Frontier Against Slavery. Western Anti-Negro Prejudice and the Slavery Extension Controversy* (Urbana, 1967).

58. New York *Herald*, September 16, October 2, 1853.

59. *Ibid.*, September 21, 1853. Also see the Chicago *Tribune* editorial on "America's Great Foe," October 26, 1853; and the Sacramento *Daily Union*, October 7, 1854.

60. Richmond *Daily Dispatch*, January 13, February 13, 1854; *The Wisconsin Farmer and Northwestern Cultivator*, April 1854, 73; Chicago *Tribune*, January 18, March 25, 1854; and *The Cultivator*, January 1855, 27-28.

61. D. C. North, *The Economic Growth of the United States, 1790-1860* (Englewood Cliffs, 1961), 213, 284. Other figures can be found in the Treasury *Report for 1866*, 348; J. Nimmo, *The Proposed American Inter-Ocean Canal in Its Commercial Aspects, Report for the Treasury Department, August 7, 1880* (Washington, 1880), Appendix 19; and Gates, *Agriculture and the Civil War*, 417.

62. Here see Abramovitz, "Long Swings," 403; and R. A. Gordon, *Business Fluctuations* (New York, 1952), 216.

63. J. G. Williamson, *American Growth and the Balance of Payments, 1820-1913. A Study of the Long Swing* (Chapel Hill, 1964), 4; F. H. Hitchcock, *Agricultural Exports of the United States, 1851-1902* (Washington, 1903), 7-8; P. K. Whelpton, "Occupational Groups in the United States, 1820-1920," *Journal of the American Statistical Association* (September 1926), 342, 339; North, *Economic Growth*, 135; and Harris (ed.), *American Economic Growth*, 76.

64. *Prairie Farmer*, November 4, 1858; and the reports in that paper (and in the Chicago *Tribune*) on the farmers' convention at Centralia, Illinois, September 1858. Gates, *Agriculture in the Civil War*, 218-219; and also see Massachusetts Board of Agriculture, *Eighth Annual Report, 1860* (Boston, 1861), 10 ff.

65. C. R. Fish, "The Decision of the Ohio Valley," *Annual Report of the American Historical Association* (Washington, 1912), 155-164.

66. Cincinnati *Daily Gazette*, June 21, 1861.

67. Detroit *Post and Tribune, Zachariah Chandler: An Outline Sketch of His Life and Public Services* (Detroit, 1880), 186.

68. Douglas to Lanphier, December 25, 1860; Douglas to Belmont, December 25, 1860: *Douglas Letters*, 504, 505.

69. These speeches are quoted at length in Fish, "Decision," 161 ff.; and in A. Johnson, *Stephen A. Douglas: A Study in American Politics* (New York, 1908), 481.

70. Atlantic, Iowa, *News-Telegraph*, January 3, 1968; one of a series reviewing the early history of the area from various primary sources.

71. W. W. Belcher, *The Economic Rivalry Between St. Louis and Chicago, 1850-1880* (New York, 1947), 28-29; H. Steen, *Flour Milling in America* (Minneapolis, 1963), 40-41.

72. Fishlow, "Ante-bellum Trade," 353. Also see Taylor, *Transportation Revolution*, 161-164.

73. Gates, *Farmer's Era*, 221.

74. W. G. Moody, testimony before Senate Committee on Education and Labor, *Relations Between Labor and Capital* (Washington, 5 volumes, 1885), 85.

75. E. Z. Russell, et al., "Hog Production and Marketing," *Yearbook of the United States Department of Agriculture, 1922*, 189; Gates, *Agriculture in the Civil War*, 4-5; H. C. Hubbart, *The Older Middle West, 1840-1880* (New York, 1936), 154-160; F. L. Klement, "Middlewestern Copperheadism and the Genesis of the Granger Movement," *Mississippi Valley Historical Review* (1952), 683-686; Thompson, *Wheat in Wisconsin*, 57.

76. See Klement, *Copperheads*, 3-11; and Hubbart, *Older Middle West*, 191.

77. A. B. Lapsley, *The Writings of Abraham Lincoln* (New York, 8 volumes, 1905-1906), 6:194-198. Richardson, *Messages*, 6:134-135.

78. Gates, *Agriculture in the Civil War*, 210-214, 223-224, 245, 375; E. D. Fite, "The Agricultural Development of the West During the Civil War," *Quarterly Journal of Economics* (1906), 264-265; Russell, "Hogs," 190; Cochrane, *Railroad Leaders*, 26; Hubbart, *Older Middle West*, 219-220; L. L. Tucker, *Cincinnati During the Civil War* (Columbus, 1962), 21-22.

79. *American Railroad Journal*, October 5, 12, 1861; *Report of the Commissioner of Agriculture for 1862*.

80. Gates, *Agriculture in the Civil War*, 210-214, provides a convenient review of this early battle; but for extended treatment see Lampard, *Dairy*.

81. *American Railroad Journal*, October 5, 12, 1861.

Chapter Four

1. Gates, *Agriculture in the Civil War*, 104.

2. W. A. Cocke, "Breadstuffs and Cotton," *DeBow's Review* (April-May 1867), 363-364.

3. Gates, *Agriculture in the Civil War*, 379, 373; D. F. Dowd, "A Comparative Analysis of Economic Development in the American West and South," *Journal of Economic History* (1956), 560. Also see Shannon, *Farmer's Last Frontier*; R. A. Easterlin, "Interregional Differences . . . ," in *Trends in the American Economy in the Nineteenth Century* (Princeton, 1964), 85-86.

4. Hesseltine, *The South in American History*, 544.

5. Shannon, *Farmer's Last Frontier*, 92.

6. Law of December 15, 1866: Legislature of Georgia, *Acts of 1866*, 141. G. L. Anderson, "The South and Problems of Post-Civil War Finance," *Journal of Southern History* (1943), 184-185.

7. C. V. Woodward, *Origins of the New South, 1877-1913* (Baton Rouge, 1951), 129, 131 (quoting C. H. Otken, *Ills of the South*, 21-22).

8. *Hind's County Gazette*, August 16, 1871.

9. Woodward, *New South*, 183. Also see J. S. Ferguson, "The Grange and Farmer Education in Mississippi," *Journal of Southern History* (1942), 497-512; M. B. Hammond, "The Southern Farmer and the Cotton Question," *Political Science Quarterly* (1897), 450-475; Hammond, *The Cotton Industry: An Essay in American Economic History* (New York, 1897).

10. C. W. Howard, "Condition of Agriculture in the Cotton States," in *Report of the Commissioner of Agriculture for 1874*, 236.

11. *The South*, as quoted by G. R. Woolfolk, *The Cotton Regency* (New York, 1958), 111.

12. P. W. Gates, "Federal Land Policy in the South, 1866-1888," *Journal of Southern History* (1940), 303; S. V. Connor, "Early Land Speculation in West Texas," *Southwestern Social Science Quarterly* (1962), 362.

13. J. D. B. DeBow, "The South Should and Must Manufacture for Herself," *DeBow's Review* (February 1867), 173, 176; Governor Patton of Alabama, "The New Era of Southern Manufacturers," *DeBow's Review* (January 1867), 59-60. Also see Anon., "Progress in Southern Manufactures," *DeBow's Review* (June 1867), 567-570.

14. See here the following items: M. C. Copeland, *The Cotton Manufacturing Industry of the United States* (Cambridge, 1923); V. C. Clark, *History of Manufacturers in the United States* (New York, 1949), 2:108; H. Young, *From the Cotton Field to the Cotton Mill. A Study of the Industrial Transition in North Carolina* (New York, 1906), 60-61; and U. S. Department of Commerce, *Bulletin No. 128* (March 1914), 16.

15. Burwell's operations can be followed in *DeBow's Review* (July 1867, June 1869). The activities of Higby are revealed in *Lewis H. Higby Papers*. Also see J. Douglas to W. Osborne, November 9, 1868: in Cochrane, *Railroad Leaders*, 316. The broad question of Southern rails is dealt with by J. F. Stover, *The Railroads of the South, 1865-1900* (Chapel Hill, 1957); and by D. M. Potter, "The Historical Development of Eastern-Southern Freight Rate Relationships," *Law and Contemporary Problems* (Summer 1947), 416-448.

16. *DeBow's Review* (July-October 1868).

17. See his testimony before the Windom Committee, *Report of the Select Commit-

tee on Transportation Routes to the Seaboard with Appendix and Evidence. Senate Report No. 307. 43rd Cong., 1st Ses. (Washington, 2 volumes, 1874), 2:853-855.

18.   Fite, "Agricultural Development of the West," 278.

19.   C. E. Margol to Weller, January 1, 1865: *Luman Hamlir Weller Papers.*

20.   *Report of the Commissioner of Agriculture for 1866,* 5.

21.   Gates, *Agriculture in the Civil War,* 233; Rogin, *Agricultural Machinery,* 36.

22.   P. W. Gates, "Cattle Kings in the Prairies," *Mississippi Valley Historical Review* (1948), 383.

23.   H. C. Hill, "The Development of Chicago As a Center of the Meat Packing Industry," *Mississippi Valley Historical Review* (1923), 253, 258, 262.

24.   *CG,* 34:4:A:78.

25.   Gates, *Agriculture in the Civil War,* 374; E. S. Carr, *The Patrons of Husbandry on the Pacific Coast* (San Francisco, 1875), 56-57.

26.   R. L. Hart, "The Regeneration of Rural New England," *The Outlook* (1900), 506.

27.   *Report of the Commissioner of Agriculture for 1870,* 255. Also see Z. A. Gilbert, "Changes in Our Farming," *Maine State Board of Agriculture Report for 1872;* and H. F. Wilson, *The Hill Country of Northern New England* (New York, 1936), 56-57, 97-98.

28.   L. Benson, *Merchants, Farmers and Railroads* (Cambridge, 1955), 80-81.

29.   *CG,* 36:1:19-20, 37-38; Dudley to Seward, February 2, 1866, and Anderson to Seward, February 13, 1866: *National Archives of the United States,* Record Group 59 (hereafter cited *NA,* followed by record group number). Also see letter of the Commissioner of Agriculture of April 17, 1866: *NA* 16.

30.   See, for example, *Country Gentleman,* April 5, 12, 26, and May 31, 1866.

31.   Letter from "HMS," *Country Gentleman,* May 18, 1865.

32.   Hatch to Margol, May 3, 1865: *Weller Mss.*

33.   Wellman to McCormick Co., January 12, 1866, and Hays to McCormick Co., April 20, 1866: *The McCormick Manuscript Collection.* Also see Hutchinson, *McCormick,* 2:431-432.

34.   *Prairie Farmer,* March 31, 1866.

35.   As reprinted in Abramovitz, in *New Views,* 424-425.

36.   Gordon, *Business Fluctuations,* 216.

37.   Abramovitz, *New Views,* 403. Other relevant studies include F. D. Graham, "International Trade Under Depreciated Paper, the United States, 1862-1879," *Quarterly Journal of Economics* (1922), 220-273; Special Consular Report, *Wages of Farm Labor in the United States,* 256-267; S. Lebergott, "Wage Trends, 1800-1900," in *Trends in the 19th Century,* 449-499; S. Lebergott, *Manpower in Economic Growth: The American Record Since 1800* (New York, 1964); C. D. Long, *Wages and Earnings in the United States, 1860-1890* (Princeton, 1960); and J. D. Bowman and R. H. Koehn, "Agricultural Terms of Trade in Four Midwestern States, 1870-1890," mimeographed, 1967.

38.   The literature on the Homestead Act is enormous. The earliest and most consequential criticism developed during the late 1860s and the 1870s, and is dealt with below. The historical critique was launched by P. W. Gates, "The Homestead Law in an Incongruous Land System," *American Historical Review* (1936), 652-681; and F. A. Shannon, "The Homestead Act and the Labor Surplus," *ibid.,* 637-651.

39.   *CG,* 32:1:855-856.

40.   *Ibid.,* 32:1:1690-1692.

41.   Department of Agriculture, Bill No. 269.

42.   *CG,* 32:2:1756; 32:3:2014-2017. Also see Ross, "The Department of Agriculture During the Commissionership," 133-134, 142.

43.   *Chicago Times,* December 10, 1860.

44.   *Milwaukee See-Bote,* October 1, 1862.

45.   *Chicago Times,* November 16, 1865.

46.   Letter to the editor, *The Cultivator and Country Centleman,* April 5, 1866.

47.   H. L. Dante, "Western Attitudes and Reconstruction Politics in Illinois, 1865-1872," *Journal of the Illinois State Historical Society* (1956), 156-158.

48.   J. B. Workman, "Governor William Larrabee of Iowa and Railroad Reform," MA Thesis, Iowa State Teachers College, 1955, 19.

49.   H. C. Dean, *Crimes of the Civil War, and the Curse of the Funding System* (Baltimore, 1869), 358; but see all of Ch. 8, "The Sectional Character of the Funding System."

50. See, for example, H. R. Lamar, *Dakota Territory, 1861-1889. A Study of Frontier Politics* (New Haven, 1956), 99, 145; Klement, "Copperheadism and the Grange," 680-684; J. E. Boyle, *The Financial History of Kansas* (Madison, 1908), 33; and E. B. Robinson, *History of North Dakota* (Lincoln, 1966), 123.

51. J. S. Gould, as reported in *Report of the Commissioner of Agriculture for 1867*.

52. E. C. Budd, "Factor Shares, 1850-1910," in *Trends in the 19th Century*, 397; R. E. Gallman, "Commodity Output, 1839-1899," ibid., 26. But also see Dowd, "A Comparative Analysis . . . West and South"; Lampard, *Diary*, 88-89, 119, 128; R. E. Lipsey, *Price and Quantity Trends in the Foreign Trade of the United States* (Princeton, 1963), 45; and D. Winch, *Classical Political Economy and Colonies* (Cambridge, 1965), 96-99, 134.

53. *Report of the Secretary of the Treasury for 1866*, 310-312.

54. Dean, *Crimes*, 364, 358-359.

55. *CG*, 36:1:154.

56. C. L. Miller, *The States of the Old Northwest and the Tariff, 1865-1888* (Emporia, 1929), 22.

57. *CG*, 36:4:3688.

58. *Ibid.*, 36:4:3497, 3515.

59. *Ibid.*, 36:4:3725; Wells, *Diary*, 2:542; H. K. Beale, "The Tariff and Reconstruction," *American Historical Review* (1930), 276-294, and materials cited therein.

60. McCormick Co. to Smith, February 2, 1866: *McCormick Mss.*

61. Chicago *Tribune*, June 22, 1866; and see June 26, 28, 1866.

62. *Commercial and Financial Chronicle*, July 7, 1866.

63. Brewer to Sumner, July 7, 1865: as quoted in Beale, "Tariff," 279.

64. Ray to Trumbull, February 2, 1866: *ibid.*, 281.

65. Action of 1867.

66. *Report of the Secretary of the Treasury for 1868*, xvi.

67. Wells to Atkinson, July 17, 1866: *Edward Atkinson Papers*.

68. See Atkinson to Senator Henry Wilson, July 7, 1866: *ibid.*

69. Here, in addition to the *Reports* of the National Association of Wool Growers, and the state documents such as the *Eighteenth Annual Report of the Ohio State Board of Agriculture, 1863*, see the study by Brown.

70. Beale, "Tariff," provides a useful analysis of the vote.

71. H. C. Carey, *The Way to Outdo England Without Fighting Her* (Philadelphia, 1865), 39-40, 46, 95.

72. W. Elder, *How the Western States Can Become the Imperial Power in the Union* (Philadelphia, 1865), 18-24.

73. See, for example, the discussion in *The Cultivator and Country Gentleman*, August 30, 1866, on how long it would take to create the home market.

74. H. C. Carey, *An Open Letter to Mr. Colfax, February 10, 1865* (New York, 1865), 1, 7, 13, 16. This is one of the many pamphlets that Carey prepared. They were broadcast through the West and can be found in most collections.

75. New York *Tribune*, April 3, 1866.

76. *CG*, 32:4:3756; and 32:4:3689.

77. E. B. Ward, *The Farmer and the Manufacturer* (Detroit, 1868).

78. Wyandotte, Kansas, *Gazette*, January 26, and March 2, 1867.

79. Emporia *News*, February 22, 1867.

80. *Commercial and Financial Chronicle*, August 10, October 12, 1867; *Country Gentleman*, January 25, 1866; T. Veblen, "The Price of Wheat Since 1867," *Journal of Political Economy* (1892), 68-70.

81. *CG*, 36:4:3753.

82. Junction City *Weekly News*, March 9, 1867. Also see Anon., "The Grain Crops and Food Prices," *DeBow's Review* (November 1867), 457; *Report of the Commissioner of Agriculture for 1871*, 296 (speaking about 1867).

83. *Country Gentleman*, February 8, 1866; X. A. Willard, in *Report of the Commissioner of Agriculture for 1866*, 358, 373, 378; Gates, *Agriculture in the Civil War*, 207.

84. *Report of the Commissioner of Agriculture, 1871*, 296; *Country Gentleman*, November 8, 1866; and H. Davis, "California Breadstuffs," *Journal of Political Economy* (September 1894), 528-529.

85. *Minneapolis Tribune,* January 7, 1868.

86. Steen, *Flour Milling,* 172-173.

87. *Report of the Senate Select Committee on Interstate Commerce. With Appendix.* Senate Report No. 46. 49th Cong., 1st Ses. (Washington, 1886), 1:27.

88. N. Morris to Nimmo, April 20, 1885: in *Treasury Department Report on Cattle,* 198; C. H. Taylor, *History of the Board of Trade of the City of Chicago. In Three Volumes* (Chicago, 1917), 1:369-370.

89. A. B. Irwin to C. McCormick, July 1, 1867: *McCormick Mss.;* S. Waterhouse, "St. Louis—The Commercial Center of North America," *DeBow's Review* (October 1867), 315-317.

90. Taylor, *Chicago Board of Trade,* 347.

91. *CG,* 39:5:A:50-54; *Report of the Commissioner of Agriculture for 1867,* viii, ix.

92. *Proceedings of the National Ship Canal Convention, Chicago, June 2-3, 1863* (Chicago, 1863); Gates, *Agriculture in the Civil War,* 349-355; *Transactions of the Illinois State Agricultural Society* (Springfield, 1861-1864), 5:82.

93. See L. B. Schmidt, "The Westward Movement of the Wheat Growing Industry in the United States," *Iowa Journal of History and Politics* (1920), 396-413.

94. *Senate Miscellaneous Document No. 22.* 39th Cong., 1st Ses. (Washington, 1865); *Senate Select Committee on Interstate Commerce,* App., 98; *CG,* 36:4:3464; *Senate Miscellaneous Document No. 54.* 39th Cong., 1st Ses. (Washington, 1866), Minnesota Legislature action of January 25, 1866.

95. *Senate Select Committee on Interstate Commerce,* 1:2-3; *Country Gentleman,* January 25, 1866; *Proceedings of the Mississippi River Improvement Convention, February 14-15, 1866* (Dubuque, 1866); and Milwaukee *Sentinel,* February 13, 16, 1866.

96. *Bradstreet's,* September 10, 1887.

97. *Railroad Gazette,* June 25, 1870.

98. Garrett, *Address to the Board* (Baltimore, 1865); B. F. Grove to Garrett, May 24, 1866: *Baltimore and Ohio Railroad Archives,* courtesy of Howard Schonberger.

99. Garrett to H. Allan, December 27, 1870: *ibid.*

100. Cooke to Garrett, February 8, 1872: *ibid.* The B. and O. campaign for flour exports is documented in *Hearings Before the Special Assembly Committee on Railroads of the New York State Assembly, 1879* (Albany, 1879), 3:2999. Hereafter cited as *Hepburn Report.*

101. *CG,* 39:1:253.

102. Anon., "Improvement of the Mississippi River," *DeBow's Review* (November 1867), 467-468, 593; *Proceedings of the River Improvement Convention Held in St. Louis, February 12 and 13, 1867* (St. Louis, 1867). Also see Missouri *Republican,* October 4, 1865; and Waterhouse, "St. Louis," 315-317.

103. G. M. Reynolds to L. H. Weller, August 4, 1867, and V. M. Mixer to Weller, "Confidential," August 26, 1867: *Weller Mss.*

104. *Country Gentleman,* August 8, 1867.

105. R. Partin, "Black's Bend Grange, 1873-1877: A Case Study of a Subordinate Grange of the Deep South," *Agricultural History* (1957), 53, 57; State Grange of Iowa, remarks of Smedley, *Journal of Proceedings for 1873.*

Chapter Five

1. C. Philips to L. H. Weller, January 31, 1869: *Weller Mss.*

2. L. A. Ives to Weller, October 1, 1872: *Weller Mss.*

3. Quoted by G. C. Fite, *Farmers Frontier, 1865-1900* (New York, 1966), 56.

4. *DeBow's Review* (July 1869).

5. *American Agriculturalist* (December 1869).

6. Philadelphia *Press,* July 30, 1869.

7. In sequence from: Chicago *Tribune,* September 1, 1869; J. Edgar to C. McCormick, November 25, 1869: *McCormick Mss.;* J. Edgar to C. McCormick, December 17, 1869: *ibid.; Country Gentleman,* March 3, 1870; Rep. Marshall of Illinois, March 29, 1870, in *CG,* 42:7:235; and O. H. Loomis to C. McCormick, November 5, 1870: *McCormick Mss.*

8. Nye, Colson and Co. to McCormick, January 2, 1872: *McCormick Mss.*

9. *Prairie Farmer,* March 26, 1870.

10. *Nation,* April 8, 1869, 269-270.

11. See, for example, J. P. Lord to C. S. Lord, November 13, 1871: *Lord Mss.;* and *Report of the Commissioner of Agriculture for 1869.*

12. L. J. Williams, "What Is Good for an Artist, and What an Artist is Good For," *Transactions of the Kansas Board of Agriculture, 1872,* 411-417.

13. *Council Journal of the Eighth Session of the Legislative Assembly of the Territory of Dakota* (Yankton, 1869), 203.

14. Robinson, *Dakota,* 123-127, 135.

15. Boyle, *Financial History of Kansas,* 49.

16. A. E. Bingham, "Sixteen Years on a Kansas Farm, 1870-1886," *Collections of the Kansas State Historical Society* (Topeka, 1923), 15:501-524, 506, 511.

17. Girard *Press,* September 26, 1872.

18. W. L. Weller to L. H. Weller, March 8, 11, 1868: *Weller Mss.*

19. *CG,* 39:5:A:294.

20. O. P. Mason to J. S. Morton, February 6, 1868: *J. Sterling Morton Papers.*

21. C. Dodge to W. T. Sherman, November 6, 1869: *John Sherman Papers.*

22. See, as illustrative: *Country Gentleman,* January 23, 1868; Lampard, *Dairy,* 121-122; R. L. Jones, "Ohio Agriculture in History," *Ohio History* (1956), 229-258; and *Ohio Agriculture During the Civil War* (Columbus, 1962).

23. *Remarks of Thomas M. Monroe, of Dubuque, Iowa, Before the National Board of Trade, December 1868* (Richmond, 1869); and see *Cheap Transportation a Public Necessity* (Dubuque, 1869), for reports on similar meetings in New Orleans and Keokuk.

24. The best accounts of this convention in Bloomington can be found in the *Prairie Farmer* and the Chicago *Tribune* during March and April 1869. There is a useful review in Commons, *Documentary History,* 10:42-44.

25. *Kansas Farmer,* April 15, 1869; and see *Country Gentleman,* April 22, 1869.

26. *Country Gentleman,* April 22, 1869.

27. G. Hamilton [Mary A. Dodge], *Biography of James G. Blaine* (Norwich, 1895), 196-197.

28. E. L. Pierce, *Memoirs and Letters of Charles Sumner* (Boston, 1894), 3:42; Sumner to F. Lieber, October 8, 1866, and J. Sherman to Sumner, September 6, 1867: *Charles Sumner Papers.*

29. U. S. Senate, *Journal of Executive Proceedings,* 40th Cong., 1st Ses., 675-676. The two dissenting votes were cast by Fessenden of Maine and Morrill of Vermont. Fessenden first tried to kill the treaty by moving to postpone consideration until after the date scheduled for adjournment. Of the twelve who voted "yea," four were from Western states (Michigan, Missouri, Wisconsin, Nebraska).

30. *The New York Times,* July 16, 1867.

31. *CG,* 39:1:606-609.

32. *Ibid.,* 39:4:3659.

33. *Ibid.,* 3660.

34. *Ibid.,* 3813.

35. *Ibid.,* 3625-3628.

36. *Ibid.,* 3810.

37. *Ibid.,* 3620-3625.

38. *Ibid.,* 3807.

39. The vote is recorded in the House *Journal,* 40th Cong. 2nd Ses., 1067. Westerners accounted for 21 of the 43 "nay" votes. The decision was 113 to 43.

40. *CG,* 40:1:792.

41. *Ibid.*

42. *Ibid.,* 40:1:58.

43. See *Commercial and Financial Chronicle,* November 20, 1869; and J. W. Taylor to H. McCulloch, November 13, 1868: *James W. Taylor Papers.*

44. *Report of the Commissioner of Agriculture for 1868,* 3.

45. *Ibid., 1869,* 7; Memorandum filed by Western congressmen with Secretary of State Fish, December 21, 1869: *NA* 59; and J. A. Garfield to Fish, January 28, 1870: *Hamilton Fish Papers.*

46. Much of this section is based on discussions with William Best Hesseltine, who reviews Grant's expansionism in his biography; and on research flowing from those talks.

47. Richardson, *Messages,* 9:3991.

48. For the effects of the trip to England, see London *Times,* September 2, 1867, and

The New York Times, September 4, 1867. Then read the *Report of the Special Commissioner of the Revenue, 1868*. House Executive Document No. 81. 40th Cong., 2nd Ses. (Washington, 1868).

49. *CG*, 40:1:454.

50. New York *Tribune*, June 8, 28, 1869; D. M. Leach, "The Tariff and the Western Farmer: 1860-1890," PhD Thesis, University of Oklahoma, 1964, 293; and see H. R. Ferleger, *David A. Wells and the American Revenue System, 1865-1870* (Ann Arbor, 1942), 299-303.

51. M. Ridge, *Ignatius Donnelly. The Portrait of a Politician* (Chicago, 1962), 126.

52. See the revealing account of the protectionist propaganda in the New York *Herald*, September 27, 1891.

53. Wells, *Revenue Report, 1869*, xl-xli.

54. *Ibid.*, xxvi, x.

55. *Ibid.*, xxxi, xxxiv.

56. *Ibid.*, xlvii, xlix.

57. *Ibid.*, lxi.

58. *Ibid.*, xxxviii.

59. *Ibid.*, lxxii.

60. *Ibid.*, lxxiv.

61. *CG*, 42:1:370-375.

62. *Examination of Statements in the Report of the Special Commissioner of Revenue by the Committee on Manufactures*. House Report No. 72. 41st Cong., 2nd Ses. (Washington, 1870), 65.

63. C. C. Taylor, *The Farmers' Movement, 1620-1920* (New York, 1953), 128-129.

64. *Country Gentleman*, October 7, 1869, May 12, 1870; *Report of the Commissioner of Agriculture for 1869*, 586; *Annual Message of Governor Horace Austin* [of Minnesota] for the Year 1869 (St. Paul, 1870); and R. N. Current, *Pine Logs and Politics. A Life of Philetus Sawyer, 1816-1900* (Madison, 1950), 65.

65. *CG*, 41:2:2095.

66. *DeBow's Review* (March 1870); *Country Gentleman*, June 3, 1869.

67. Taylor, *Chicago Board of Trade*, 416.

68. Richardson, *Messages*, 9:4007-4008.

69. New York *Tribune*, April 6, May 13, 1870.

70. Richardson, *Messages*, 9:4016.

71. *Ibid.*, 4031.

72. The fight over recognizing the Cuban rebels can be followed in *CG*, 41:1:59, 276, 711-712; 42:5:4436-4439, 4447-4479, 4483, and 4507.

73. Baltimore *Gazette*, October 7, 1870; *Report on the Cincinnati Convention of 1870* (Cincinnati, 1870), 7, 8, 108, 11, 50-51. On the relevance of this mounting campaign for improved water transportation, see R. W. Fogel, *Railroads and American Economic Growth. Essays in Econometric History* (Baltimore, 1964), 23-24.

74. P. W. Gates, "Hoosier Cattle Kings," *Indiana Magazine of History* (1948), 1-24.

75. J. S. Wright, *Chicago: Past, Present, Future* (Chicago, 1870), 213.

76. This account is drawn from a commentary by Davis on a copy of "Modern Feudalism" in *Cushman Kellogg Davis Papers*.

77. Illinois Constitution of 1870: Article II, Sections 2 and 5.

78. M. Gresham, *The Life of Walter Quintin Gresham, 1832-1895* (Chicago, 1919), 1:370-376.

79. New York *Herald*, July 8, 1870; *The New York Times*, October 16, 1870.

80. W. Elder, *The American Farmer's Markets at Home and Abroad* (Philadelphia, 1870).

81. Richardson, *Messages*, 9:4053-4054, 4058, 4060, 4065; the law was again passed in 1874.

82. *Report of the Commissioner of Agriculture for 1871*, 449-451, 453-454, 458.

83. *Ibid.*, 230.

84. Taylor, *Chicago Board of Trade*, 369; O. E. Anderson, *Refrigeration in America. A History of a New Technology and Its Impact* (Princeton, 1953), 49; *Annual Report of the New York Produce Exchange, 1879* (New York, 1880), 505.

85. M. Frink, *Cow Country Cavalcade. Eighty Years of the Wyoming Stock Growers Association* (Denver, 1954), 39-40.

86. *Wyoming Stock Growers Association Collection*; also see W. T. Jackson, "The

Wyoming Stock Growers Association: Political Power in Wyoming Territory, 1873-1890," *Mississippi Valley Historical Review* (1947), 571-594.

87. St. Paul *Daily Press*, January 7, 1872.

88. C. D. Robinson to J. A. Noonan, January 30, 1872: *Josiah A. Noonan Papers*.

89. *Ohio State Board of Agriculture Report for 1872*, 12-13, 15-16.

90. *House Miscellaneous Document No. 124.* 42nd Cong., 2nd Ses. (Washington, 1872). For Kansas and Nebraska see *Senate Miscellaneous Document No. 51.* 42nd Cong., 2nd Ses. (Washington, 1872).

91. Fort Scott *Monitor*, June 14, 1872.

92. See, for example, the *Daily Arkansas Gazette*, December 28, 1872; G. D. Davis, "The Granger Movement in Arkansas," *Arkansas Historical Quarterly* (1945), 340-352; J. S. Ferguson, "Agrarianism in Mississippi, 1871-1900. A Study in Non-Conformity," PhD Thesis, University of North Carolina, 1952, 66, 506; Partin, "Black's Bend Grange," 53, 57.

93. See *Prairie Farmer*, November 4, December 2, 16, 23, 1865, and March 3, 1866; then consult G. H. Miller, "The Granger Laws. A Study of the Origins of State Railway Control in the Upper Mississippi Valley," PhD Thesis, University of Michigan, 1951.

94. On the farm emphasis on cheap transportation, rather than on discrimination between shippers, see Miller, "Granger Laws," 207, 312.

95. O. P. Norton to Blaine, July 27, 1872: Hamilton, *Blaine*, 302. Also see the comment by Harper and Brothers, August 14, 1872, *ibid.*, 305.

96. Richardson, *Messages*, 9:4095-4096.

97. Wakeman to Meade, January 13, 1872: *R. W. Meade Papers*, a collection that contains much material on the economic forces involved in the push for Samoa. Grant's concern with Latin America is apparent in C. Butterfield to Evarts, August 13, 1877, and to Hayes, November 27, 1877: *NA* 59.

98. Richardson, *Messages*, 9:4149-4150.

99. *Ibid.*, 4176.

100. Lynchburg *Virginian*, April 11, 1873.

101. Taylor, *Chicago Board of Trade*, 473.

102. There are several useful records of the Bloomington meeting. The best two are *Windom Report on Routes to the Seaboard*, and *Transactions of the Department of Agriculture of Illinois, 1872.* This comes from the former, 657.

103. *Illinois Transactions for 1872*, 227-228, 229.

104. *Ibid.*, 233, 281.

105. *Ibid.*, 253-254.

106. *Ibid.*, 294-295.

107. G. F. Lemmer, *Norman J. Colman and Colman's Rural World. A Study in Agricultural Leadership* (Columbia, 1953), 72; Secretary of the Kansas State Board of Agriculture, "To the Farmers of Kansas, February 27, 1873," copy in Morton Mss.

108. *Iowa State Agricultural Society Report for 1872*, 97, 107, 208, 221-222.

109. *California State Agricultural Society Report for 1872*, remarks of President C. F. Reed. Also see *Pacific Rural Press*, November 16, 1872.

Chapter Six

1. S. Smith, *Grains for the Grangers* (Chicago, 1873), 35.

2. *Windom Report on Routes to the Seaboard*, 2:646.

3. *Ibid.*, 649.

4. See, for example, I. Donnelly, Diary, entry of January 30, 1873: *Ignatius Donnelly Papers*; Donnelly, *Facts for the Grangers* (St. Paul, 1873); and Miller, "Granger Laws," Ch. 6.

5. Iowa State Grange. *Journal of Proceedings for 1873*; "The Anti-Monopoly Party in Iowa," *Iowa Journal of History* (1954), 289-325; and Miller, "Granger Laws."

6. J. H. Osborn to W. R. Taylor, March 22, 1873: *Joseph Horatio Osborn Papers*.

7. Osborn to E. R. Shankland, March 26, 1873; Osborn to E. R. Shankland, July 29, 1873: *Osborn Mss.*

8. E. S. Carr, *The Patrons of Husbandry on the Pacific Coast* (San Francisco, 1875), 94-95.

9. Oregon State Grange, *Journal of Proceedings for 1873.*

10. See, for example, the good account in Carr, *Patrons on the Pacific,* 100-102.

11. *Mark Lane Express,* as quoted in Brayer, "When Dukes Went West," *The Westerners Brand Book. Denver Posse, 1948* (Denver, 1949), 59.

12. C. W. Dilke, *Greater Britain. A Record of Travel in English-Speaking Countries During 1866 and 1867* (London, 1872), 90.

13. J. J. Madden, "British Investment in the United States, 1860-1880," mimeographed paper, 1957, 43; *Hepburn Report,* Volume III; and A. W. Currie, "British Attitudes Toward Investment in North American Railroads," *Business History Review* (1940), 208.

14. *Nebraska State Journal,* March 9, 1872.

15. Chicago *Tribune,* March 17, 24, 29, 1873.

16. H. Bronson, *Farmers' Union and Tax Reform* (Lawrence, 1873), 3, 4.

17. This account of the Topeka Convention is taken from the *Kansas State Board of Agriculture Transactions for 1872.* But also consult the Topeka press.

18. This convention can be followed in Commons, *Documentary History,* 10:68; and in J. Periam, *The Groundswell. A History of the Origins, Aims, and Progress of the Farmers' Movement* (Cincinnati, 1874), 320.

19. The best account is in *Indiana State Board of Agriculture Report for 1873;* but also see *Prairie Farmer,* April 5, July 12, and August 10, 1873.

20. *House Miscellaneous Document No. 106.* 43rd Cong., 1st Ses. (Washington, 1873).

21. *Windom Report on Routes to the Sea,* 2:658.

22. *Ibid.,* 333.

23. *Ibid.,* 176.

24. Red Wing *Argus,* April 14, 1870.

25. W. D. Washburn to C. C. Washburn, May 10, 1869: *Cadwallader Colden Washburn Papers.*

26. W. C. Edgar, *The Medal of Gold. A Story of Industrial Achievement* (Minneapolis, 1925), 41; J. Gray, *Business Without Boundaries. The Story of General Mills* (Minneapolis, 1954), 15, 29; and Steen, *Flour Milling,* 63, 284-285. The Christian report was only slightly exaggerated.

27. *Windom Report on Routes to the Seaboard,* 2:639-644.

28. *Ibid.,* 689.

29. *Ibid.,* 893, 895; 853-855.

30. *The Nation,* July 17, 1873.

31. *Railroad Gazette,* August 16, 1873.

32. *Industrial Age,* August 20, 1873.

33. W. M. Grosvenor, "Railroads and the Farms," *Atlantic Monthly* (1873), 591-610.

34. *Windom Report on Routes to the Seaboard,* 1:176-177, 38, 45, 129, 251-252.

35. *Ibid.,* 44-45.

36. *Ibid.,* 34, 43.

37. *Ibid.,* 14-23, 71-78.

38. *Ibid.,* 251-252.

39. *Ibid.,* 252.

40. Richardson, *Messages,* 9:4198.

41. McCulloch to H. Greeley, June 13, 1866: *Hugh McCulloch Papers; Secretary of the Treasury Annual Report for 1865; ibid., 1866,* esp. 9-10. The background of the silver and gold coinage in the United States can be followed in N. Carrothers, *Fractional Money* (New York, 1930), 76-79, 90-92, 105.

42. *Secretary of the Treasury Annual Report for 1867,* xxix.

43. This part of the story can be followed in H. B. Russell, *International Monetary Conferences: Their Purposes, Character, and Results* (New York, 1898); and H. P. Willis, *A History of the Latin Monetary Union* (Chicago, 1901). Also see D. G. B. Thompson, *Ruggles of New York: A Life of Samuel B. Ruggles* (New York, 1946).

44. J. L. Ringwald to Pollock, October 17, 1865: *NA* 104.

45. *House Executive Document No. 29.* 39th Cong., 2nd Ses.

46. See, for example, *CG,* 36:3:2653-2654.

47. Beckwith to Seward, June 29, July 17, 1866: *NA* 59; National Board of Trade, *Proceedings for 1870* (New York, 1871), 228.

48. Ruggles to Seward, July 18, 1867: *NA* 59.

49. Here see Hooper to Sherman, April 9, 1867; J. Cooke to Sherman, April 15, 1867; and J. Yates to Sherman, May 3, 1867: *Sherman Mss.*

50. Ruggles to Sherman, May 17, 1867; Sherman to Ruggles, May 18, 1867: *Sherman Mss.*

51. *Annual Report of the Director of the Mint* (Philadelphia, 1867), 8-10. The discussion can be followed in Knox to Linderman, August 1867: *NA* 104; Linderman to McCulloch, November 23, 1867: *NA* 104; Sherman to McCulloch, December 23, 1867: *NA* 56; Sherman to McCulloch, December 23, 1867: *NA* 104; McCulloch to Linderman, December 26, 1867, January 2, 1868: *NA* 104.

52. *Secretary of the Treasury Annual Report of 1867*, xx, xlii-xliii.

53. The most pertinent recent studies of this campaign have been provided by P. M. O'Leary, "The Scene of the Crime of 1873 Revisited: A Note," *Journal of Political Economy* (1960), 388-392; J. A. Dindahl, "Economic Factors in Specie Resumption: The United States, 1865-1879," *Journal of Political Economy* (1961), 30-48; and W. T. K. Nugent, *The Money Question During Reconstruction* (New York, 1967), which contains an excellent bibliography. My own research was undertaken independently of theirs, but I have benefited from their analyses.

54. *Report of the Senate Committee on Finance, Senate Report No. 117.* 40th Cong., 2nd Ses. (Washington, 1868), 8-14.

55. *CG*, 39:3:2959.

56. *Secretary of the Treasury Annual Report for 1869*, x, xii, xiv. Then see Pollock to Boutwell, March 7, 1870, and Pollock to Knox, March 10, 1870: *NA* 104.

57. *CG*, 41:1:704; and see *ibid.*, 733-734, for the remarks of Senator Morton of Indiana.

58. *Ibid.*, 42:3:2316.

59. San Francisco *Daily Evening Bulletin*, September 3, 1872.

60. *Secretary of the Treasury Annual Report for 1872*, ix-xi, xix-xx, xxiii.

61. Sherman, remarks in *Congressional Record*, 25:3:1061. For Boutwell, see G. S. Boutwell, *Reminiscences of Sixty Years in Public Affairs* (New York, 1902), 2:151-152.

62. M. Friedman, A. J. Schwartz, *A Monetary History of the United States, 1867-1960* (Princeton, 1963), 134.

Chapter Seven

1. Abramovitz, *New Views*, 403; Gordon, *Business Fluctuations*, 216.

2. Abramovitz, *ibid.*, 424-425.

3. S. Lebergott, *Manpower in Economic Growth*, 178-179, 187.

4. Here see the seminal work of Herbert Gutman; and such studies as R. V. Bruce, *1877: Year of Violence* (Indianapolis, 1960).

5. A. S. Tostlebe, *Capital in Agriculture. Its Formation and Financing Since 1870* (Princeton, 1957), 46, gives the figures of 53.0 percent for 1870 and 49.4 percent for 1880.

6. H. Working, "Wheat Acreage and Production in the United States Since 1866. A Revision of Official Estimates," *Wheat Studies* (June 1926), 260-261, 237, 245.

7. E. Frickey, *Production in the United States, 1860-1914* (Cambridge, 1947), 35-43.

8. R. E. Lipsey, *Price and Quantity Trends in the Foreign Trade of the United States. A Study by the N. B. E. R.* (Princeton, 1963).

9. The statistics can be reviewed in F. A. Hitchcock, *Agricultural Exports of the United States, 1851-1902. U. S. D. A., Division of Foreign Markets. Bulletin No. 34* (Washington, 1903); *Historical Statistics of the United States*; and in I. Mintz, *Trade Balances During Business Cycles: United States and Britain Since 1880* (New York, 1959); and *Cyclical Fluctuations in the Exports of the United States Since 1879* (New York, 1967).

10. The comments in Taylor, *Chicago Board of Trade*, 495, and in *Report of the Commissioner of Agriculture for 1877*, 187, are also helpful. O. V. Wells, "The Depression of 1873-1879," *Agricultural History* (1937), 237-249, reviews the crisis in the context of increasing exports.

11. *Report of the Commissioner of Agriculture for 1873*, 11.

12. *Congressional Record*, 2:6:12 (hereafter cited as *CR*).

13. F. J. Whitiek to Sibley, May 8, 1876: *Henry H. Sibley Papers.*

14. Indiana State Grange, *Journal of Proceedings for 1874.*

15. G. A. Wiley to McCormick, June 24, 1874; J. S. Buck to McCormick, May 21, 1874; and McCormick to Illinois Democratic State Central Committee, July 29, 1874: *McCormick Mss.*

16. H. R. Grattan to McCormick, June 5, 1874: *ibid.*

17. G. Cerny, "Cooperation in the Midwest in the Granger Era, 1869-1875," *Agricultural History* (1963), 204-205.

18. *Statistics of the State of Minnesota for 1873*, 188.

19. Letter to the editor, *Prairie Farmer*, October 17, 1874.

20. B. Graycroft to McCormick, June 13, 1874: *McCormick Mss.*

21. *Anti-Monopolist*, August 6, 1874; Kansas City *Times*, January 21, 1873.

22. E. L. Ives to Weller, June 4, 1875, and E. L. Ives to Weller, later in 1875: *Weller Mss.*

23. L. Atherton, *The Cattle Kings* (Bloomington, 1961), 157; New York *Evening Post*, September 24, 1873; Taylor, *Chicago Board of Trade*, 493; J. G. McCoy, *Historic Sketches of the Cattle Trade of the West and Southwest* (Glendale, 1940), 309-312.

24. Oregon State Grange, *Journal of Proceedings for 1873.*

25. D. C. Cloud, *Monopolies and the People* (Chicago, 1873).

26. A. H. Lackerp to I. N. VanHoesen, December 14, 1874: *McCormick Mss.*; and see Boyle, *Financial History of Kansas*, 49.

27. Remonstrance from the Legislature of Kansas . . . to Recognize the Rights of Cubans, January 27, 1874: *NA 46, S-43-A-H9.2.*

28. P. L. Erickson, "Destitution and Relief in Nebraska, 1874-1875," MA Thesis, University of Nebraska, 1937, 81.

29. Fite, *Farmers Frontier*, 69.

30. There are excellent accounts of the Minnesota aspects of the crisis in the *Sibley Mss.* See, for example, the "Confidential Circular by State Grange Representatives." Also see *Executive Documents of the State of Minnesota for 1873, 1874,* and *1875;* and the annual messages of Governor Davis. It is important to remember this background when, in later years, Davis became chairman of the Senate Foreign Relations Committee.

31. A. W. Riddle to Sibley, July 6, 1874: *Sibley Mss.*

32. Governor C. K. Davis, "Inaugural Address of January 9, 1874": *Executive Documents of the State of Minnesota for the Year 1873,* 3-11.

33. Vermont State Grange, *Journal of Proceedings for 1874.*

34. H. G. O. Smith, quoted in *Report of the Commissioner of Agriculture for 1874,* 189-190. The entire article, "Does Farming in New England Pay?" is very illuminating. Also see Rutland *Herald and Globe*, August 28, 1879; and *Sixth Report Upon Vermont Agriculture,* 1879-1880.

35. Texas State Grange, *Journal of Proceedings, 1874.*

36. See, for example, the remarks of J. W. White, Worthy Master of the Virginia State Grange, *Journal of Proceedings for 1873.*

37. See, for example, the petitions from the Grange of Hamilton County, Florida, December 26, 1873; the Belmont Grange, Sumter County, Alabama, May 1, 1874; and the Goldwater Grange, Tate County, Mississippi, April 11, 1874: *NA 46, S43A-H8.3.*

38. B. W. Frobel, remarks of December 1873, in *Windom Report on Routes to the Seaboard*, 2:745-751.

39. There are many accounts of the bonanza farms in the Dakota territory, but a good introduction is provided by H. E. Briggs, "The Great Dakota Boom, 1879-1886," *North Dakota Historical Quarterly* (1930), 78-108; and H. M. Drache, *The Day of the Bonanza. A History of Bonanza Farming in the Red River Valley of the North* (Fargo, 1964).

40. W. T. Jackson, "Dakota Politics During the Burbank Administration, 1869-1873," *North Dakota History* (1945), 118. R. R. Dykstra, "Town-Country Conflict: A Hidden Dimension in American Social History," *Agricultural History* (1964), 195-204, provides an excellent discussion of how colonial consciousness develops in such situations. Also illuminating is M. Bronfenbrenner, "The High Cost of Economic Development," *Land Economics* (1953), 93-104, 209-218.

41. See his account in Federal Trade Commission, *Grain Trade*, 2:141.

42. The Clinton, Iowa, *Age*, April 17, 1874. Also see the Kansas *Daily Commonwealth*, November 9, 1873.

43. J. E. Follett to Osborn, November 30, 1894: *Osborn Mss.*

44. See Hutchinson, *McCormick*, 2:96-97, 334-337, 594-595; and the materials in the *McCormick Mss.*

45. Resolution of 1873, in E. G. Cutler (ed.), *History of the State of Kansas* (New York, 1873), 396-397. Also consult Petition of the California State Grange, January 22, 1874: *NA* 46, S43A-H8.3/86; Resolution of the California Legislature, February 2, 1874: *ibid.*; and Concurrent Resolution of the California Legislature, February 26, 1874: *ibid.*, S43A-H9.2.

46. *Prairie Farmer*, October 10, 1874.

47. *The Case Plainly Stated. The Rebellion of the Farmers of the Northwest* (n.p., 1874), 5-8.

48. *Nebraska State Journal*, August 21, 1874.

49. Estimates of Grange membership vary to an extensive degree. The most recent attempt to solve the problem is a careful study by R. L. Tontz, "Memberships of General Farm Organizations, United States, 1874-1960," *Agricultural History* (1964), 143-156. He places Grange strength in 1875 at 451,605 *family* memberships, and allots them sectionally as follows: Midwest, 206,134; South, 138,448; West, 15,206; and Northeast, 40,308.

50. O. H. Kelley, quoted in National Grange, *Proceedings of the Session of 1874*.

51. Ohio State Grange, *Journal of Proceedings for 1874*. Also see the 1874 proceedings of other state units, such as Arkansas.

52. National Grange, *Proceedings of the Session of 1874*; and such Grange publications as D. W. Aiken, *Political Tracts for Granges, No. 1* (n.p., 1874).

53. Iowa State Grange, *Journal of Proceedings for 1874*.

54. *Journal of the Iowa Senate for 1874* (Des Moines, 1875), 65.

55. Osborn to L. Allen, December 18, 1873; H. K. Thurber to Osborn, May 16, 1874; and, for a sample of support in Wisconsin, M. K. Young to Osborn, July 29, 1874: all in *Osborn Mss.* A copy of the Call is also in Osborn's correspondence; but also see *Chicago Times*, January 28, 1874.

56. Osborn to E. R. Shankland, December 29, 1873: *Osborn Mss.*

57. *Report of the Iowa State Agricultural Society for 1872*; Iowa State Grange, *Proceedings for 1874, 1875*.

58. *Ibid.*; Smedley's report is in National Grange, *Proceedings of the Session of 1874*. Also see his testimony before the Windom Committee.

59. *St. Paul Weekly Press*, April 10, 1873.

60. Memorial from Duff Green, Dalton, Georgia, December 16, 1874: *NA* 46, S43A-H8.3/88. Also see *Branch Family Papers*, No. 2718; *New Orleans Price Current*, April 1, 1874; *New Orleans Times*, June 18, 1874; and *Galveston Daily Mercury*, June 5, 1874.

61. *What to Do with Products. Practical Tracts for Grangers No. 1* (Washington, 1874); Alabama State Grange, *Proceedings for 1874, and 1875*.

62. See the folders on the Mississippi Valley Trading Company in the *McCormick Mss.*; A. P. Perkins to Worrall, August 1, 1874: *Mississippi Valley Trading Company Collection*; *Chicago Times*, October 15, 1874; and *Kansas City Journal of Commerce*, July 1874.

63. L. Fairchild to G. W. Hazelton, April 13, 1874: *Lucius Fairchild Papers*.

64. *Secretary of the Treasury Annual Report for 1873*, xi-xii, xxiv, 60.

65. This document and the subsequent items can be found in the document series published by the respective states; in *NA* 46, and 233; and many are reprinted in the *House Miscellaneous Document No. 164.* 43rd Cong., 1st Ses. (Washington, 1874).

66. *Cheap Transportation of the Products of the West. Speech of Representative Erastus Wells of Missouri in Congress, January 31, 1874* (Washington, 1874).

67. *Daily Journal of Commerce*, October 23, 1874; C. N. Glaab, *Kansas City and the Railroads. Community Policy in the Growth of a Regional Metropolis* (Madison, 1962), 188 ff.

68. *Double-Track Freight Railway from Tidewater on the Atlantic to Council Bluffs on the Missouri. House Report No. 479.* 43rd Cong., 1st Ses. (Washington, 1894).

69. *Ibid.*, 3.

70. *Ibid.*, 3-5.

71. As representative indicators, see the petitions from Missouri Granges introduced by Rep. Bland, *CR*, 2:5:4594, 4976; remarks by Rep. Willard of Michigan, *ibid.*, 2:3:2233; memorial by G. G. Hubbard, February 23, 1874 (Washington, 1874); and speeches of Rep. Hurlbut, *CR*, 2:2:1966-1967.

72.   *CR,* 2:1:783, 1941, 1946; and *Commerce by Railroad Among the Several States. House Report No. 28.* 43rd Cong., 1st Ses. (Washington, 1874).

73.   *CR,* 2:3:2044 - 2050, 2208, 2419, 2427 - 2428.

74.   *Ibid.,* 2:3:2249 - 2250; also see the comment of Rep. Willard at 2:3:2234.

75.   H. G. Roach, "Sectionalism in Congress, 1870 - 1890," *American Political Science Review* (1925), 504 - 507, has an excellent analysis of the division between the metropolis and the country.

76.   See, as illustrative of the pro-water route forces, the arguments presented in *CR,* 2:2:1129; 2:3:1296, 2148, 2156, 2243 - 2244, 2249 - 2250, 2623; 2:4:4529 - 4533; and 2:A:196.

77.   Grant, Special Message of June 18, 1874: Richardson, *Messages,* 9:4220.

78.   *CR,* 2:5:4529.

79.   See Hamilton, *Blaine,* 311; J. G. Blaine, *Political Discussions: Legislative, Diplomatic, and Popular, 1856 - 1886* (Norwich, 1887), 122; and Hubbart, *Older Middle West,* 255, for a convenient review of the election in the Middlewest.

80.   Richardson, *Messages,* 9:4239; *Annual Report of the Secretary of the Treasury for 1874,* xxiv - xxxi.

81.   Hayes to Blaine, June 16, 1875; Chandler to Blaine, August 15, 1875; Calhoun and W. E. Gapen to Blaine, August 21, 1875: all in Hamilton, *Blaine,* 373, 375, 376.

82.   North Carolina State Grange, *Journal of Proceedings for 1875* and *1876.*

83.   State Granges of Kansas, Illinois, Iowa, Ohio, and Oregon, *Journal of Proceedings for 1875;* also see the relevant materials in the *C. K. Davis Mss.*

84.   Report by S. J. Frew, Illinois State Grange, *Journal of Proceedings for 1875.*

85.   *Spirit of Kansas,* July 6, 1876.

86.   C. F. Adams, "The Granger Movement," *North American Review* (April 1875).

87.   *Railroad Gazette,* December 25, 1875.

88.   Letter to the editor from F. P. Root, in *Country Gentleman,* December 25, 1890.

89.   State Granges of Mississippi, Tennessee, and North Carolina, *Journal of Proceedings for 1875.*

90.   T. Worrall, *Direct Trade Between Great Britain and the Mississippi Valley* (Manchester, 1875), 1, 8. The story can be followed in *Rural Carolinian,* September 1876; Wisconsin State Grange, *Bulletin* (July 1875); *The Granger,* February 1876; National Grange, *Proceedings of the Sessions of 1875* and *1876;* J. W. A. Wright, *Europe and the Grange* (n.p., 1876); and in the *Osborn Mss.* and the *Mississippi Valley Trading Company Mss.* Also see the forthcoming work by Howard Schonberger.

91.   Resolution of Ontario County, New York, Agricultural Society, February 2, 1875: *NA* 46, S43A - H9.1. Also see, in the same file, the Michigan petition signed by 400 citizens.

92.   *CR,* 4:4:3328, 3316.

93.   The organized campaign of petitions charging such foreign influences are in *NA* 46, S44A - H7.1.

94.   G. L. Anderson, "From Cattle to Wheat: The Impact of Agricultural Developments on Banking in Early Wichita," *Agricultural History* (1959), 10 - 12.

95.   E. B. Washburn to C. C. Washburn, August 5, 1875: *Washburn Mss.* Also see G. G. Tunnel, "The Diversion of the Flour and Grain Traffic from the Great Lakes to the Railroads," *Journal of Political Economy* (1897), 343.

96.   *Minnesota State Executive Documents for 1875,* 1:20 - 25.

97.   Lampard, *Dairy,* 295.

98.   W. W. Cumberland, *Cooperative Marketing. Its Advantages as Exemplified in the California Fruit Growers Exchange* (Princeton, 1917), 16.

99.   Morton to Nebraska Board of Agriculture, January 1876: *Morton Mss.*

100.   Gates, "Cattle Kings," 391 - 395; J. T. Critchell and J. Raymond, *A History of the Frozen Meat Trade* (London, 1912), 191, 387, 424.

101.   *Report of the Commissioner of Agriculture for 1876,* 237, 241.

102.   Keene Bros. of Lynn, Massachusetts, to Rep. W. R. Morrison, July 31, 1876: *NA* 233, HR44-A - F38.6.

103.   The best studies of the early Southern mills are P. J. Hearden, "Cotton Mills of the New South and American Foreign Relations, 1865 - 1901," MA Thesis, University of Wisconsin, 1966; R. W. Griffin, "Reconstruction of the North Carolina Textile Industry, 1865 - 1885," *North Carolina Historical Review* (1964); J. Blicksilver, *Cotton Manufacturing in the Southeast: An Historical Analysis* (Atlanta, 1959); and G. G. Williamson,

Jr., "Cotton Manufacturing in South Carolina, 1865-1892," PhD Thesis, Johns Hopkins University, 1954.

104. *Hepburn Report*, 3:2896.

105. *Manufacturers Record*, May 31, 1895.

106. *Bradstreet's*, October 28, 1882; *The South. A Journal of Southern and Southwestern Progress*, January 6, 1877.

107. Augusta *Chronicle and Constitutionalist*, June 30, 1878; but also see *Report of the Committee on Agriculture and Forestry on Conditions of Cotton Growers in the United States . . . Senate Report No. 986*. 53rd Cong., 3rd Ses. (Washington, 2 volumes, 1895).

108. *Commercial and Financial Chronicle*, November 21, 1874.

109. Department of State, *Commercial Relations of the United States for 1875*, 3, 750, 822-824; *1876*, 398, 463-465; *1877*, 381-382. New England Cotton Manufacturers Association, *Proceedings, No. 20, 1876*, 2, 51-54. *Commercial and Financial Chronicle*, January 1, 1876.

110. J. Coleman, "Report on the Agricultural Implements at the Philadelphia Centennial Exhibition," *Journal of the Royal Agricultural Society of England* (1877), 90-91.

111. As quoted by T. C. J. Whedbee, *The Port of Baltimore in the Making*, 89.

112. Garrett to J. S. Morgan, July 23, 1875: *Garrett Mss*.

113. *Railroad Gazette*, November 15, 1873.

114. Also see the New York *Tribune* report of December 11, 1874.

115. New York *Tribune*, March 27, 1875; *Commercial and Financial Chronicle*, December 4, 1875; and *Iron Age*, April 6, 1876.

116. See, for example, *L'Economiste Français*, 2 (October 7, 1876).

117. *Report of the Secretary of the Treasury for 1875*, xii; *Report of the Commissioner of Agriculture for 1876*, 164-166, 210, 271; and Grant, in Richardson, *Messages*, 9:4366.

118. Denver *Weekly Times*, July 5, 1876.

119. St. Louis *Republican*, January 2, 1875.

120. S. D. Carpenter, "Interest, Currency, and the Public Debt," speech of October 25, 1875: *Osborn Mss*.

121. E. M. Mack, "Life and Letters of William Morris Stewart," PhD Thesis, University of California, 1930, 110.

122. M. B. Hammond, "The Southern Farmer and the Cotton Question," *Political Science Quarterly* (September 1897), 470-472.

123. *Report of the Commissioner of Agriculture for 1876*, 167.

124. H. C. Carey, *Monetary Independence* (Philadelphia, 1875), 2.

125. *CR*, 4:1:1007-1008; 4:2:1009-1010.

126. New York State Chamber of Commerce to Congress, *NA* 46, S44A-H7.1.

127. *CR*, 4:7:67-90.

128. Cincinnati *Commercial*, July 8, 1876.

129. Michigan State Grange, *Journal of Proceedings for 1875*.

130. *CR*, 4:5:4561.

131. *Ibid.*, 4:5:4559, 4866.

132. *Ibid.*, 4:5:4562.

133. *Ibid.*, 4:2:197. Also see, for the market expansionist theme, *Senate Miscellaneous Document No. 132*. 44th Cong., 2nd Ses.

134. *CR*, 4:5:4562.

135. *Ibid.*, 4:4:4553.

136. *Ibid.*, 4:6:5080.

137. *Ibid.*, 4:6:5237.

138. J. W. Foster to B. Harrison, August 15, 1876: *Benjamin Harrison Papers*.

Chapter Eight

1. *Indiana Farmer*, October 24, 1891; *Michigan Farmer*, November 7, 1891. The bill did not pass.

2. Hayes, in Richardson, *Messages*, 9:4421-4423, 4428-4429. Also see W. K. Rogers (personal secretary to Hayes) to W. M. Evarts, December 8, 1877: *NA* 59. The letter reports the President "impressed with the importance" of the export activities of a trade association, and as wanting to give it "further encouragement and aid."

3. *Diary and Letters of Rutherford Birchard Hayes* (Columbus, 1922-1926), 3:402.

4. T. Donaldson to Hayes, February 18, 1877: *Rutherford Birchard Hayes Papers.*

5. Garfield, as quoted in C. L. Barrows, *William M. Evarts, Lawyer, Diplomat, States-man* (Chapel Hill, 1941), 313-314.

6. New York *Tribune,* July 17, 1877; S. Evarts (ed.), *Arguments and Speeches of William Maxwell Evarts* (New York, 1919), 3:396-397.

7. In addition to the statistical data cited earlier, consult Mintz, *Exports,* 7, 162-163, and Appendix A; P. A. Bruce, *The Rise of the New South* (Philadelphia, 1905), 51-52; and M. Jacobstein, *The Tobacco Industry in the United States* (Macmillan, 1927).

8. W. M. Evarts to T. Weed, July 27, 1877: *Thurlow Weed Papers.*

9. *Report on the Commercial Relations of the United States with Foreign Countries for the Year 1877. House Executive Document No. 102.* 45th Cong., 2nd Ses. (Washington, 1878), 52.

10. *Northwestern Miller,* August 3, 1877. On this fundamental point also see Barrows, *Evarts,* 375, 377, where he establishes the agreement of Hayes; B. Dyer, *The Public Career of William M. Evarts* (Berkeley, 1933), 234; and, the best study of all, the just-completed PhD thesis on Evarts by Gary Pennanen, University of Wisconsin. Also see New York *Tribune,* July 17, 1877; and E. H. Chapman to W. M. Evarts, November 7, 1877; *NA* 59, which establish public awareness.

11. *Commercial Relations for 1877,* 52; *Foreign Relations of the United States,* 1877, Appendix, 1-3.

12. Evarts, Circular on Trade Expansion of July 13, 1877: *NA* 59; Evarts to Bingham, June 21, 1877, *ibid.; Foreign Relations,* 1877, 2-3; and *Commercial Relations for 1878,* 5-6, 52-53; *1879,* 72-73.

13. Plunkett to Derby, September 8, 1877, No. 268, Foreign Office 5/1579: *Records of the British Foreign Office, Series 5, Volume 1579* (microfilm). See also *Commercial Relations for 1877,* 52.

14. E. W. Fox to Evarts, October 31, 1877: *NA* 59.

15. St. Louis *Evening Dispatch,* October 30, 1877.

16. *Commercial Relations for 1877,* 31.

17. Sedalia *Weekly Times,* March 14, 1878; also consult J. A. Leach, "Public Opinion and the Inflation Movement in Missouri, 1875-1879," *Missouri Historical Review* (1930), 122, 129, 134.

18. Sedalia *Daily Bazoo,* June 14, August 29, 1877.

19. *Colman's Rural World,* as recirculated by the Jefferson City *People's Tribune,* January 2, 1878.

20. As on February 22, 1877.

21. *Northwestern Miller,* July 13, 1877.

22. *Ibid.,* April 12, 1878.

23. Ridge, *Donnelly,* 98, 176-177; also consult the *Donnelly Mss.*

24. Augusta *Chronicle and Constitutionalist,* January 4, 1878.

25. Hutchinson, *McCormick,* 2:354-355; Chicago *Tribune,* March 5, 1877; and also see *Rural New Yorker,* July 12, 1879.

26. National Board of Trade, *Proceedings of the Annual Convention of 1877,* 175-176, 189-217.

27. Resolution of the Ohio Legislature, February 1878: *NA* 46, S45A-J5. Also see Augusta *Chronicle and Constitutionalist,* January 6, 1878.

28. J. H. Gallinger to C. Marseilles, November 19, 1898; as cited in H. W. Morgan, *William McKinley and His America* (Syracuse, 1963), 58.

29. Augusta *Chronicle and Constitutionalist,* January 5, 1878.

30. *Harper's Weekly,* April 13, 1878.

31. *Southern Planter and Farmer,* October 1877, November 1877.

32. Augusta *Chronicle and Constitutionalist,* January 1878.

33. *Ibid.,* January 5, 1878; and January 1, 12, 24, 1878.

34. *Reports of the Silver Commission of 1876. House Miscellaneous Report No. 396.* 49th Cong., 1st Ses. (Washington, 1887), 101-102, 109-110, 113, 131. The export orientation of the report was seen by N. A. Dunning, *The Philosophy of Price and Its Relation to Domestic Currency. National Watchman Economic Series* (Vol. I, No. 2., second edition, Washington, 1892), 179-182.

35. *Ibid.*, 134-135.

36. Blaine, speech of February 7, 1878, as reprinted in *Discussions*, 163-168.

37. L. Sage, *William Boyd Allison. A Study in Practical Politics* (Iowa City, 1856), 157; Hayes, *Diary*, 3:577; Seligman to Evarts, July 28, 1877: *William Maxwell Evarts Papers;* Belmont to Sherman, November 18, 19, 1877: *Sherman Mss.*

38. Roach, "Sectionalism," 510-511, provides an excellent analysis.

39. W. C. Stout to Hayes, April 23, 1877; W. H. Estel to Hayes, August 7, 1878: *Hayes Mss.*

40. See the account of a long interview with Hayes in Augusta *Chronicle and Constitutionalist*, January 8, 1878.

41. New York *Tribune*, January 29, February 8, 1879; Foster to Evarts, February 7, 1879: *NA* 59; Memorial from the California State Legislature, *NA* 46, S45A-H9.5.

42. D. A. Wells, "How Shall the Nation Regain Prosperity?" *North American Review* (November 1877), 544.

43. *Iron Age*, July 19, August 23, 1877; and see, as illustrative, A. Browder to Senator F. M. Cockrell, November 26, 1877; New Orleans Chamber of Commerce to Evarts, December 13, 1877; and Rep. W. W. Crapo (Massachusetts) to Evarts, October 16, 1877: all in *NA* 59.

44. *Commercial and Financial Chronicle*, February 24, May 19, 1877; Morgan Iron Works to Hayes, November 15, 1878: *Hayes Mss.;* Ostheimer Bros. to Evarts, July 3, 1877; Carey to Evarts, September 6, December 3, 1877; and Atkinson to Evarts, April 27, 1877: all in *NA* 59.

45. W. K. Rogers to Evarts, December 8, 1877: *NA* 59; and on the Samoan treaty see Kasson to Evarts, May 10, 1878: *Evarts Mss.* Also consult Plunkett to Derby, May 22, 1877: *Fo* 5/1577.

46. Washburn to Woodman, April 25, 1877: *Washburn Mss.*

47. A. Belmont to Sherman, November 18, 1877: *Sherman Mss.* But also consult Belmont to Sherman, May 8, 19, 1877; J. Seligman to Sherman, April 17, 1877: *Sherman Mss.* And see *The New York Times*, August 22, 1877; and *Bankers Magazine*, July 1877.

48. Chicago *Tribune*, April 28, 1877.

49. *American Farmer*, May 1877, June 1877, and September 1877.

50. Augusta *Chronicle and Constitutionalist*, June 12, 15, August 12, 1878.

51. *Economist*, June 23, 1879; *Rural New Yorker*, July 26, 1879. Also see *Consular Reports* No. 16 (February 1882), 201-206; No. 21 (July 1882), 411-415; *Rural New Yorker*, January 4, 1879; and J. B. Lawes, "Our Climate and Our Wheat Crops," *Journal of Royal Agricultural Society* (1880), 173-210.

52. Augusta *Chronicle and Constitutionalist*, June 15, 1878.

53. Letter to the editor, *Country Gentleman*, July 17, 1884.

54. Lipsey, *Price and Quantity*, 51, 77-78; M. Simon, "The United States Balance of Payments, 1861-1900," *Trends in the 19th Century*, 711; J. G. Williamson, *American Growth and the Balance of Payments, 1820-1913* (Chapel Hill, 1964), 33; R. C. Overton, *Burlington Route. A History of the Burlington Lines* (New York, 1965), 163.

55. B. L. Hoard to his grandmother, April 24, 1879: *Halbert Louis Hoard Papers.*

56. Davis, "California Breadstuffs," 530; J. Nommo, *The Proposed American Inter-Ocean Canal in Its Commercial Aspects. Treasury Department, August 7, 1880* (Washington, 1880), 20, 59; W. H. Dunwoody to Washburn, February 22, 1878: *William Hood Dunwoody Papers.*

57. *Farm and Factory*, May 18, 1877. Also consult *Northwestern Miller*, September 5, 1879; and C. A. Pillsbury, "American Flour," in C. Depew, *One Hundred Years of American Commerce* (New York, 1895), 1:270-272.

58. *Northwestern Miller*, August 24, 1877; Dunwoody to Washburn, February 22, 1878: *Dunwoody Mss.*

59. *Northwestern Miller*, June 14, 1878; St. Paul *Dispatch*, October 15, 1878.

60. *Report of the Commissioner of Agriculture for 1878*, 578-594.

61. *Consular Report*, No. 16 (February 1822), 201-206; Petition of Board of Trade of Elgin, Illinois, February 5, 1878: *NA* 46, S45A-H7.4; but see first the excellent study by Lampard, *Dairy.*

62. On leather, see *Commercial Relations for 1878*, 424.

63. See, for a typical report, *American Agriculturalist*, March 1879; *Prairie Farmer*,

February 9, June 15, 18, 1878; and *Report from the Select Committee on the Transportation and Sale of Meat Products. Senate Report 829.* 51st Cong., 1st Ses. (Washington, 1890), 3. The figures are from *Historical Statistics,* 546-547.

64. L. F. Swift, *The Yankee of the Yards. The Biography of Gustavus Franklin Swift* (Chicago, 1927), 24, 27, 63-64, 90-91, 109-110, 206-207.

65. N. F. McCormick to C. H. McCormick, Jr., June 1, 1879: *McCormick Mss.* Also see Hutchinson, *McCormick,* 2:643-645.

66. See the *Annual Report of the Interstate Commerce Commission for 1877,* and *1880.*

67. Garrett to Morgan, May 2, 1877: *Garrett Mss.*

68. Garrett to J. Walter, May 7, 1878: *ibid.*

69. Garrett to Walter, January 10, 1878: *ibid.*

70. *Manufacturers Record,* March 1, 1895.

71. Augusta *Chronicle and Constitutionalist,* January 4, 1878.

72. *Commercial Relations for 1881-1882,* 657, 668, 673.

73. Augusta *Chronicle and Constitutionalist,* June 30, 1878; February 14, 1880; G. W. Johnson, *The Making of a Southern Industrialist. A Biographical Study of Simpson Bobo Tanner* (Chapel Hill, 1952), 65-67.

74. *Commercial and Financial Chronicle,* September 15, 1877.

75. G. Atkinson to E. Atkinson, March 9, 1878: *Atkinson Mss.;* American Iron and Steel *Bulletin,* June 6, 1877; Knowlton, *Pepperell's Progress. History of a Cotton Textile Company, 1844-1945* (Cambridge, 1948), 191-198; and Clark, *History of Manufactures,* 2:413.

76. Consul to Berlin Foreign Office, December 30, 1878: in O. Stolberg-Wernigerode, *Germany and the United States During the Era of Bismarck* (Reading, 1937), 147.

77. *Report of the Commissioner of Agriculture for 1878,* 289.

78. *Rural New Yorker,* November 15, 1879; Augusta *Chronicle and Constitutionalist,* January 5, 1878; Indiana State Grange, *Journal of Proceedings for 1878; Report of the Commissioner of Agriculture for 1877,* and *1878;* and *Rural New Yorker,* February 8, 1879.

79. C. Adler, *Jacob H. Schiff. His Life and Letters* (Garden City, 1928), 1:29-30, 31-32.

80. *Annual Report of the Secretary of the Treasury for 1877,* xii, xli; *1878,* xvi-xvii, xxxiii; *1879,* xxx; Hayes, message of December 2, 1878, in Richardson, *Messages,* 9:4444, 4457.

81. F. H. Morse, "The American Export Trade," *International Review* (January 1879), 39-53.

82. Philadelphia *Enquirer,* as reprinted by *Northwestern Miller,* September 6, 1878.

83. J. P. Sheldon, "Report on the American and Canadian Meat Trade," *Journal of the Royal Agricultural Society of England* (1877), 307-308, for a graphic review by a Scot.

84. California *Patron,* February 1, 1879.

85. *Rural New Yorker,* February 1, 1879.

86. See, for example, State Granges of Texas and Arkansas, *Journal of Proceedings for 1877* and *1878;* and the National Grange, *Proceedings of the Session for 1878.*

87. *Commercial and Financial Chronicle,* January 18, 1879; State Grange of Texas, *Proceedings for 1877.* Also see the similar comment in *Southern Planter and Farmer* (October 1877).

88. Indiana State Grange, *Journal of Proceedings for 1878, 1879;* B. Victor, letter to the editor, *Rural New Yorker,* August 30, 1879; *American Farmer* (October 1877); S. N. Murray, "A History of Agriculture in the Valley of the Red River of the North, 1812 to 1920," PhD Thesis, University of Wisconsin, 1963, 234; Working, "Acreage and Production," 258; Speech by A. E. Stevenson, September 12, 1878: *Weller Mss.;* and J. A. Connally to Sen. R. Oglesby, February 9, 1878: in Unger, *Greenback Era,* 338, note 72.

89. Murray, "Agriculture in the Valley of the Red River," 234; St. Paul, Minnesota and Manitoba Railway, *The Land of the Golden Grain: North Dakota* (Chicago, 1883), 10-11.

90. Yankton *Press and Dakotian,* as quoted in Robinson, *Dakota,* 199. Also see Lamar, *Dakota Territory,* 206-207; A. H. Benton "Large Land Holdings in North Dakota," *Journal of Land and Utility Economics* (1925), 408-410.

91. Walla Walla *Statesman,* September 28, 1878; Colfax *Palouse,* February 21, 1879:

quoted in K. A. Murray, "The Movement for Statehood in Washington," *Pacific Northwest Quarterly* (1941), 373.

92.   Illinois Farmers' Association, *Proceedings of January 25, 1877*; S. Meyers, *The Hand-Workers of the Mississippi Valley. Their Power and Responsibility* (Chicago, 1875); Des Moines *Iowa Weekly People*, February 6, 1879; Augusta *Chronicle and Constitutionalist*, January 17, 1878; *Rural New Yorker*, June 14, 1879; and *Northwestern Miller*, August 2, 1878.

93.   C. F. Adams, *Railroads: Their Origin and Problems* (New York, 1878), 145, candidly recognized the substance of the case against the rails.

94.   Denver *Weekly Times*, January 2, 1878; H. D. Lloyd to Stone, September 23, December 20, 1879: *Henry Demarest Lloyd Papers*, referring to the impact of the Hepburn investigations in New York; *Rural New Yorker*, December 20, 1879.

95.   See, for example, the Proceedings of the Wyoming Stock Growers Association, April 2, 1877: *Wyoming Stock Growers Association Papers* (hereafter cited as *WSGA Mss.*).

96.   Remarks of Minnesota Worthy Master S. E. Adams, National Grange, *Journal of Proceedings of the Session for 1879*.

97.   St. Paul *Pioneer Press*, July 15, 1879. Also consult St. Paul *Dispatch*, June 24, August 5, 1878; St. Paul *Pioneer Press*, November 22, 1879; *Northwestern Miller*, June 22, 29, 1877; and R. L. Kramer, *The History of Export and Import Railroad Rates and Their Effect Upon the Foreign Trade of the United States* (Philadelphia, 1923), 20.

98.   J. J. Hill, "From Minnesota to the Sea," *World's Work* (December 1909), 12353.

99.   See *Rural New Yorker* for March 1879, when the editors dropped their earlier preference for state regulation.

100.   *Railroad Gazette*, June 14, August 9, October 4, 1878.

101.   Consult the petitions, resolutions, and letters in the following files in *NA* 233, HR 46A - H6.6; HR 47A - HR7; HR 46A - H8; HR 48A - H6.8; and *NA* 46, S48A - H23.

102.   *CR*, 8:1:99 - 101.

103.   *Ibid.* Also see *Bankers Magazine* (June 1882), 935.

104.   *Bradstreet's*, November 1, 1879; *Report of the Secretary of the Interior for 1879*, 62.

105.   National Grange, *Journal of Proceedings of the Session for 1877*; Wisconsin State Legislature, Memorials to Congress No. 7 and No. 8, 1877: *The Laws of Wisconsin for 1877* (Madison, 1877), 634 - 635; Texas State Grange, *Journal of Proceedings for 1878*; S. S. Watkins to Nance, February 23, 1879: *Albinus Nance Papers*; Glaab, *Kansas City*, 184 - 186.

106.   *CR*, 7:5:4643.

107.   Windom carried much of the burden of the battle. His main effort can be followed in *CR*, 7:5:4358 - 4367, 4440.

108.   *Tenth Census of the United States, 1880*, 3; *Agriculture*, 9.

109.   W. Trimble, "Historical Aspects of the Surplus Food Production of the United States, 1862 - 1902," *Annual Report of the American Historical Association for 1918* (Washington, 1921), 1:223 - 239, was the first to call attention to the foreign policy implications of the export boom. A convenient digest of European reaction and analysis appears in *Report of the Commissioner of Agriculture for 1883*, as part of "a special investigation . . . of the influence of American competition upon European agriculture" (p. 10). My own research in the relevant European sources, greatly aided by German and French colleagues, provides the basis for this analysis. Particularly helpful are *Annual Report of the Agriculture Department, Privy Council Office, on the Contagious Diseases, Inspection, and Transit of Animals*, which run from 1875 forward; the *Annales* of the French Senate; and the *Stenographische Berichte* for German discussions. There is a great deal of material available in the National Archives, and in various odd collections, and the citations are to such more accessible sources whenever possible.

110.   Gates, "Cattle Kings," 391, 394.

111.   Quoted by Alvord, "The Dairy Interests of the United States," in *Report of the Massachusetts Board of Agriculture for 1896*, 138. Also see Shelton, "American and Canadian Meat Trade," 295 - 296; and J. F. Tucker, "British Agriculture Under Protection and Free Trade, 1815 - 1895," PhD Thesis, University of Pennsylvania, 1957.

112.   London *Statist*, August 7, 1880.

113. *Bell's Messenger*, as quoted in *National Stockman*, September 15, 1885. Also consult London *Daily News*, September 19, 1879; and J. T. Critchell and J. Raymond, *A History of the Frozen Meat Trade* (London, 1912), 323.

114. London *Globe*, January 25, 1878. See also London *Miller*, September 5, 1879; *Rural New Yorker*, July 12, 1879; and C. P. Wright and J. S. Davis, "India As a Producer and Exporter of Wheat," *Wheat Studies* (July 1927), 381.

115. Letter to the editor, *Rural New Yorker*, August 16, 1879. Other examples of American awareness of the effect of their exports can be reviewed in the *National Livestock Journal*, June and November 1879, and in the items cited hereafter.

116. See Sheldon, "The State of Agriculture in England," *Journal of the American Agricultural Association* (1881), 53; also Tucker, "British Agriculture Under Protection and Free Trade," 118-120.

117. LeDuc, manuscript autobiography, 288-289: *William G. LeDuc Papers*. I have reversed the order of two clauses in the sentence. See also the excerpts of the British commission report in *Report of the Commissioner of Agriculture for 1883*, 336-337.

118. *Report of the Commissioner of Agriculture for 1883*.

119. German developments are reviewed in White to Evarts, July 3, 1879: *NA 59*; *Commercial Relations for 1878*; *Consular Reports, 1881*, 112, and *1883*, 102, 368-379; O. zu Stolberg-Wernigerode, *Germany and the United States of America During the Era of Bismarck*, translated by O. E. Lessing (Reading, 1937), 26, 140-141, 148-149, and *passim*; A. von Peez, *Die amerikanische Konkurrenz* (Vienna, 1881); G. Stolper, *German Economy, 1870-1940* (London, 1946); and A. S. von Waltershausen, *Das deutsche Einfuhrverbot amerikanischen Schweinfleisches* (Jena, 1884).

120. *Report of the Commissioner of Agriculture for 1883*, 337-342.

121. A. Ronna, *Essai sur l'Agriculture des États-unis d'Amérique: Le Blé aux États-unis d'Amérique, Production, Transports, Commerce* (Paris, 1880), 205, where he discusses the French government's study of the wheat crisis in terms of a conclusion that the American grain trade was "becoming the predominant element of the national prosperity and one of the real causes of the influence of the American Union on the rest of the world." Also see *Bradstreet's*, April 2, 1881.

122. See the candid historical evaluation of the Chicago Board of Trade, February 15, 1888, in *Counterfeit or Compounded Lard. House Report No. 3082*. 50th Cong. 1st Ses. (Washington, 1888), Appendix 13.

123. *Bradstreet's*, April 16, 1881.

124. Kasson to Evarts, March 4, 1878, January 11, 29, May 3, and September 2, 1879: all in *NA 59*.

125. Kasson to Evarts, May 3, 1879: *ibid.*

126. Fairchild to Blaine, July 16, 1881: *ibid.*

127. T. Wilson to J. Davis, December 4, 1882: *ibid.*; the Nantes Resolution can be seen in Gifford to Hitt, December 9, 1881: *ibid.* There is much material printed in *Report to Accompany Senate Resolution No. 345. Senate Report No. 551*. 48th Cong., 1st Ses. (Washington, 1884), and *House Executive Document No. 209*. 47th Cong., 1st Ses. (Washington, 1882). Also see *Consular Reports*, Vol. III (1881), 348-350; *ibid.*, No. 65 (1886), 195; and *New York Herald*, December 9, 19, 27, 1882, January 15, 1883. The major debate in Germany came on January 9, 1883.

128. A. D. Melvin, "The Federal Meat-Inspection Service," in *Twenty-third Annual Report of the Bureau of Animal Industry for the Year 1906* (Washington, 1908). One of the best secondary studies is H. Leech and J. C. Carroll, *Armour and His Times* (New York, 1938), which contains much useful material, as at 181.

129. The early phase of the battle can be followed in these accounts. Consult first the *National Livestock Journal* for March 1879, and then the issues of May 1879, April 1880, and October 1880; then see *Prairie Farmer*, August 3, October 26, November 2, 1878, and April 26, 1879; M. H. Smith to Garrett, May 29, 1879: *Garrett Mss.*; the yearly reports of the Commissioner of Agriculture; and the materials in the *LeDuc Mss.*

130. *Rural New Yorker*, February 15, 22, 1879; *American Agriculturalist*, January 1879; and *National Livestock Journal*, August and November 1879.

131. J. D. Squire and Co. to Evarts, May 17, 1879; Evarts to Marsh, and to Kasson, May 24, 1879: *NA 59*.

132. *House Executive Document No. 9*. 46th Cong., 3rd Ses. (Washington, 1880).

133.   A. Browder to Sen. F. M. Cockrell, November 26, 1877, sent on to Evarts: *NA* 59.

134.   Chamber of Commerce of New Orleans to Evarts, December 13, 1877: *ibid.*

135.   *Southern Planter and Farmer,* March 1877.

136.   A. O. Phelps, remarks of 1879, as quoted in J. C. Malin, *A Concern About Humanity* (Lawrence, 1964), 69.

137.   O. H. Kelley to LeDuc, January 28, 1877: *LeDuc Mss.*

138.   LeDuc's side of the argument can be followed in LeDuc to E. J. Rees, "Personal and Private," July 1879, and LeDuc to D. W. Akin, November 10, to W. Blend, November 23, 1879: all in *NA* 16; and in his manuscript "Autobiography," 226: *LeDuc Mss.*

139.   Petition for cabinet legislation from Illinois State Horticulture Society, January 28, 1878: *NA* 46, S45A-H1; *American Agriculturalist,* June 1879. Also see Texas State Grange, *Proceedings for 1877, 1878,* and *1879;* Augusta *Chronicle and Constitutionalist,* February 10, 1878; Indiana State Grange, *Journal of Proceedings for 1879;* and *Report of Special Commission on the State of Agriculture of the National Grange* (Washington, 1879).

140.   *Rural New Yorker,* February 8, 1879; *Report of the Commissioner of Agriculture for 1877,* 5; *Bradstreet's,* December 25, 1880.

141.   National Grange, *Journal of Proceedings for the Session of 1878.*

142.   *Rural New Yorker,* September 20, 1879.

143.   P. A. Chadbourne, "The Commercial Wealth of the United States," *Proceedings of the New England Cotton Manufacturers Association, 1879* (Boston, 1879).

144.   Lampard, *Dairy,* 124.

145.   International Dairy Fair Association to Evarts, November 11, December 4, 1879: *Evarts Mss.*

146.   Petition of Elgin, Illinois, Board of Trade, February 5, 1878: *NA* 46 S45A-H7.4; Resolution of the Richmond Chamber of Commerce, June 11, 1879: in *Franco-American Treaty of Commerce,* 60-61 (also *NA* 59).

147.   Texas State Grange, *Journal of Proceedings for 1878.*

148.   See McKinley's remarks of April 15, 1878; Resolution of the American Iron and Steel Association to Congress, February 12, 1878: *NA* 46, S45A-H7.3; and Wharton, *The Patriotism of Tariff Protection* (Philadelphia, 1878).

149.   The battle began in 1878, and the final stages can be followed in *CR,* 9:1:1055, 1237; 9:2:1730, 2103.

150.   See, for example, National Grange, *Journal of Proceedings for the Session of 1877; Northwestern Miller,* June 7, 1878; Augusta *Chronicle and Constitutionalist,* January 13, 15, 1878; Resolution of the Chicago Convention for the Promotion of American Commerce, October 20, 1878: *NA* 46, S45A-H23; Petition of the Merchants of St. Louis, April 14, 1879: *ibid.;* and *Northwestern Miller,* May 16, 23, 30, 1879.

151.   *Rural New Yorker,* January 11, 1879.

152.   Raleigh *Farmer and Mechanic,* February 21, 1878.

153.   *Rural New Yorker,* June 14, 1879; Indiana State Grange, *Journal of Proceedings for 1879;* National Grange, *Journal of Proceedings for the Session of 1879.*

154.   See, as illustrative, *Southern Planter and Farmer* (December 1877); F. P. Gower, president of the Philadelphia and Reading Railroad, to Evarts, January 15, 1878: *NA* 59; Chicago Board of Trade, resolution of May 27, 1879: *Franco-American Treaty of Commerce,* 56; Augusta *Chronicle and Constitutionalist,* March 22, October 9, 1879; *The Commerce of the North Pacific Coast. Speech by Senator John H. Mitchell of Oregon in the Senate. January 10, 1879* (Washington, 1879), 5-6, 27; *Northwestern Miller,* January 10, March 10, 1879; *National Live Stock Journal,* June 1879; and National Tanners and Hide Dealers Association to Evarts, October 30, 1877: *NA* 59.

155.   Morse, "The American Export Trade," *International Review* (January 1879), 39-53.

156.   *CR,* 7:3:2394; 8:2:1635-1636. Also see 8:3:2121-2122; and Morgan to Foster, September 7, 1878: *John W. Foster Papers.*

157.   On the decline, see *Commercial and Financial Chronicle,* March 20, 1880; and Clark, *History of Manufactures,* 2:406-407, 414-415.

158.   Augusta *Chronicle and Constitutionalist,* May 1, 1879.

159.   *The South* (April 1879); Augusta *Chronicle and Constitutionalist,* February 8, 1879; *Rural New Yorker,* February 22, 1879.

160. *International Monetary Conference Held in Paris, in August 1878. House Miscellaneous Document No. 396. Part 2.* 49th Cong., 1st Ses. (Washington, 1887); *Rural New Yorker*, July 12, 1879; Allison to Sherman, November 10, 1878, passed on to Hayes: *Hayes Mss.*; Jefferson City *People's Tribune*, May 21, 1879.

161. Logan to Sherman, July 19, 1879: *Sherman Mss.*

162. Speech of September 3, 1878, Minneapolis: reprinted in Blaine, *Discussions*, 199.

163. Richardson, *Messages*, 9:4461, 4522, 4530.

Chapter Nine

1. See, for example, the New York *Herald*, December 6, 1881.

2. R. W. Shufeldt, *The Relation of the Navy to the Commerce of the United States. March 23, 1878* (Washington, 1878), 13, 6-10. Also see J. D. J. Kelley, *The Question of Ships. The Navy and the Merchant Marine* (New York, 1884).

3. New York *Herald*, December 12, 1881.

4. *Bradstreet's*, August 16, 1884; National Grange, *Journal of Proceedings for the Session of 1886*, and *1881*.

5. Pennsylvania State Grange, *Journal of Proceedings for 1887*; Indiana State Grange, *ibid.*, *1882*.

6. *Breeder's Gazette*, June 5, 1884; Massachusetts State Grange, *Journal of Proceedings for 1883*.

7. National Grange, *Journal of Proceedings for the Session of 1880*; *American Agriculturalist*, August 1880.

8. *The New York Times*, December 3, 1882; Chicago *Tribune*, December 6, 1882, and March 16, 1883.

9. *CR*, 13:A:115-116.

10. *Ibid.*, 13:2:1553-1534.

11. *Ibid.*, 13:2:1564.

12. See, for example, N. M. Tilley, *The Bright Tobacco Industry, 1860-1920* (Chapel Hill, 1948), 327; New York *Journal of Commerce*, April 24, 1888; and North Carolina and Virginia Granges, *Journals of Proceedings for 1883*.

13. *CR*, 13:3:2105-2117.

14. *Ibid.*, 15:6:A:202; 14:4:A:75-77.

15. *Ibid.*, 13:2:1564.

16. *American Farmer*, October 1881.

17. *CR*, 15:6:A:209-211; 15:6:490.

18. C. B. Chess, letter to the editor, *Breeder's Gazette*, March 23, 1882.

19. London *Statist*, quoted by *Bradstreet's*, April 10, 1880.

20. J. Camsile to M. Marble, August 14, 1885: *Manton Marble Papers.*

21. *CR*, 13:3:2134; National Grange, *Journal of Proceedings for the Session of 1881.*

22. *CR*, 3:3:2131.

23. *Western Rural*, March 28, 1884.

24. H. D. Lloyd, "Some Dutch Notions," mss. copy, *Lloyd Mss.*

25. E. Atkinson, "The Railroad and the Farmer," *Journal of the American Agricultural Association*, 1:178-179.

26. J. F. Carr, "A Great Railway Builder," *The Outlook* (September 1907), 397.

27. Until all scholars are permitted to explore the *Hill Papers*, the full story of Hill's activities relating to foreign affairs must be pieced together from indirect evidence, and from his letters found in other collections and his published remarks. The following printed items proved of significant help to me: G. F. Parker, *Recollections of Grover Cleveland* (New York, 1909); J. G. Pyle, *The Life of James J. Hill* (Gardin City, 2 volumes, 1917); M. C. Blossom, "James J. Hill," *World's Work* (May 1901), 721-728; M. A. Severance, "A Great Railway Builder," *Outlook* (September 26, 1907), 391-398; M. A. Severance, "James J. Hill, A Builder of the Northwest," *Review of Reviews* (June 1900), 669-678. And the following items by Hill indicate clearly how much stress he placed on overseas market expansion: "History of Agriculture in Minnesota," *Collections of the Minnesota Historical Society* (1898), 8:275-290; "The Future of Our Oriental Trade," *World's Work* (August 1905), 6465-6467; "What We Must Do to Be Fed," *ibid.* (November 1909),1226-

1254; "From Minnesota to the Sea," *ibid.* (December 1909), 12338-12361; and "A Lost Opportunity on the Pacific," *ibid.* (January 1910), 12482-12498.

28. Hill, "History of Agriculture," 8:275-290.

29. Hill, remarks during the *Proceedings of the Waterways Convention, Superior, Wisconsin, August 7-8, 1889* (Minneapolis, 1889).

30. S. Fish to E. T. Jeffry, July 26, 1887: *Fish Mss.*

31. "Exportation of Agricultural Implements," *Report of the Commissioner of Agriculture for 1885*, 386-390; an excellent review of the trade.

32. These early activities are recounted by Lubin in *A New Political Issue. Protection to Staple Agriculture* (Sacramento, 1892), 1-3. Also see A. Hobson, "An American Pioneer in International Agriculture," *Journal of Farm Economics* (1932), 574-585.

33. See, for example, D. A. Wells, "Evils of the Tariff System," *North American Review* (September 1884), 276-277.

34. R. H. Edmonds, "Our Exports in Breadstuffs," *International Review* (November 1881), 462.

35. L. P. Brockett, *Our Western Empire: or the New West Beyond the Mississippi* (Philadelphia, 1882); *The American* (August 16 and 30, 1884).

36. M. M. Ballou, *Due South; or Cuba, Past and Present* (Boston, 1885).

37. Senate of the State of New York, *Testimony and Report of the Special Senate Committee Appointed to Investigate the System of Making Corners and Dealings in Futures* (Albany, 1882), 5-9, 603.

38. As examples, consult New York *Commercial Bulletin*, January 9, 1883; *Commercial and Financial Chronicle*, April 1, 1883; and *Bradstreet's*, December 25, 1880, January 8, 29, 1881, February 4, 1882, May 5, June 23, 1883.

39. New York *Tribune*, October 3, 1883; *Commercial and Financial Chronicle*, August 16, 1884; petition of the New York City Chamber of Commerce, December 28, 1884: *NA* 46.

40. *Bradstreet's*, February 21, 28, 1885.

41. See, for example, the testimony in *Senate Committee on Labor and Capital*, 2:87-121.

42. C. Schurz to T. C. Pound, September 15, 1888, and C. Schurz to C. Arco, 1889: *Speeches, Correspondence and Political Papers of Carl Schurz. Selected and Edited by F. Bancroft* (New York, 1913), Vols. 5, 6. I am indebted to Chester V. Easum for some very helpful suggestions in connection with Schurz.

43. *CR*, 13:3:2435-2438.

44. *Bradstreet's*, June 5, 1880, March 27, 1886; and *Bankers Magazine*, June 1882, and September 1880.

45. *Bankers Magazine*, September 1889.

46. *Commission to Central and South America*, 3.

47. Blaine to Garfield, February 16, 1881: Hamilton, *Blaine*, 502.

48. L. S. Sackville-West to Granville, December 28, 1881: P. Knaplund and C. M. Clewes, "Private Letters from the British Embassy in Washington to the Foreign Secretary Lord Granville, 1880-1885," *Report of the American Historical Association for 1941* (Washington, 1942), 1:161. Also see Sackville-West's analysis in "Report on Imports and Exports in the United States," Commercial No. 8 (1886): *Parliamentary Papers*, Vol. 67:2:151, in which he discusses the relationship between exports and the "conflict between the Western and Eastern states."

49. Milwaukee *Sentinel*, November 6, 1891.

50. *CR*, 13:3:2660-2667, esp. 2666-2667.

51. *Ibid.*, 14:2:1027.

52. Evarts to H. Hamlin, May 4, 1878: *NA* 46, Senate Foreign Relations Committee Files; Sargent's resolution of April 8, 1878; and Thompson to Shufeldt, October 29, 1878: *NA*, and also *Robert W. Shufeldt Papers*.

53. Blaine to Hitt, September 1, 1888: Hamilton, *Blaine*, 609-610 (but also see 503); Garfield on March 4, 1881: Richardson, *Messages*, 4600.

54. Blaine, as in *Chili-Peru. House Report No. 1790*. 47th Cong., 1st Ses. (Washington, 1882), 225; also see Hamilton, *Blaine*, 153-155; and *CR*, 7:5:4131-4134.

55. Arthur, Annual Message of December 6, 1881: *CR*, 13:1:23 ff.

56. The first quote from Frelinghuysen is from Frelinghuysen to Arthur, April 26, 1884; the evaluation in Adee to E. Root, longhand note of November 24, 1906: *NA* 59.

57. Arthur, Annual Message of December 6, 1881.

58. *Twenty-Fourth Annual Report of the Chamber of Commerce of the State of New York, 1881-1882* (New York, 1882), 13.

59. *Report of the Secretary of the Treasury for 1884*, x-xii, and continuing on to xxvii.

60. Arthur, Annual Message of December 1884: *Papers Relating to the Foreign Relations of the United States, 1884*, xiii, xix-xxi.

61. Bayard to Cleveland, December 22, 1886: *Bayard Mss.*; *Consular Reports No. 21* (January 1887), 117-118; Cleveland to Bayard, October 26, 1888: *Bayard Mss.*; Cleveland, Annual Message of December 6, 1886: Richardson, *Messages*, 5082-5112; and, on "Cleveland's willingness to manipulate foreign affairs for domestic votes," see C. S. Campbell, "The Dismissal of Lord Sackville-West," *Mississippi Valley Historical Review* (1958).

62. Thornton to Granville, May 5, 1880: Knaplund, "Letters," 93.

63. *Ibid.*, January 11, 1881: *ibid.*, 111.

64. *Ibid.*, March 22, 1881: *ibid.*, 122. Sackville-West to Granville, February 6, 1882: *ibid.*, 164.

65. Quoted in *American*, June 28, 1884.

66. *Northwestern Miller*, January 22, 1879; St. Paul *Pioneer Press*, January 29, 1881.

67. Kasson to Evarts, March 12, 1881; Kasson to Blaine, March 19, 1881; Mason to Hitt, June 22, 1881: all in *NA* 59. Also see *Bradstreet's*, March 5, 1881.

68. See, as typical of the foreign reports that became known through the agricultural and general press: Gerrish to Hay, March 9, 1881: *NA* 59; Taylor, *Chicago Board of Trade*, 2:620.

69. *Bradstreet's*, March 12, 1881; Blaine to Noyes, March 15, 17, 1881: *NA* 59; Thornton to Granville, March 7, 1881: Knaplund, "Letters," 120.

70. Cincinnati Chamber of Commerce to Blaine, March 5, 1881; Merchants Exchange of St. Louis to Blaine, March 7, 1881; J. O. Putnam to Blaine, March 9, 1881: all in *NA* 59.

71. S. Davis to Blaine, March 26, 1881; W. H. Davis to M. Scanlan, April 20, 1881; *NA* 59; Taylor, *Chicago Board of Trade*, 2:620.

72. Virginia petition of March 11, 1880: *NA* 46, Sen. 46A-H1.1; Chicago *Tribune*, April 26, 30, 1881.

73. Armour to Blaine, May 18, 1881: *NA* 59.

74. Hackberger and Co. to Blaine, May 18, April 21, 1881: *NA* 59; *Prairie Farmer*, March 12, December 3, 1881; Chicago *Tribune*, October 21, 1881.

75. Kasson to Blaine, March 12, 1881; Blaine to Lowell, March 17, 1881: *NA* 59.

76. See, for example, *Bradstreet's*, March 19, 1881.

77. Blaine to Noyes, June 8, 1881: *NA* 59.

78. Kasson to Blaine, March 12, 1881; Armour to Senator Logan for Blaine, December 15, 1881; Blaine to Morton, August 18, November 21, 1881: all in *NA* 59.

79. *Restrictions Upon the Exportation of Pork from the United States by the French Government. House of Representatives Executive Document No. 209*. 47th Cong., 1st Ses. (Washington, 1882).

80. Arthur, Annual Message of December 4, 1883: Richardson, *Messages*, 10:4758.

81. Morgan to Blaine, December 16, 1881: Hamilton, *Blaine*, 550.

82. On the cooperation, see *Bradstreet's*, December 3, 1881; and Blaine, "The Cotton-Goods Trade of the World, and the Share of the United States Therein," *Consular Report No. 12* (June 25, 1881); Atlanta *Constitution*, February 25, 1882. I am indebted to Patrick J. Hearden for his kindness in sharing his knowledge of this matter with me.

83. Atlanta *Constitution*, March 9, 1880, January 21, October 12, November 10, 1881; *Manufacturers Record*, February 14, June 19, July 25, 1880.

84. *Bradstreet's*, November 26, 1881; Boston *Journal*, as quoted in Atlanta *Constitution*, October 14, 1881. The best accounts are in the Atlanta *Constitution*: see, for example, October 6, 8, 10, 11, 12, 1881; and November 9, December 4, 1880. Also see M. Andres, "At the Atlanta Exposition," *Harper's Weekly* (November 2, 1895, to December 7, 1895), for a comparison. H. P. Hammett, "Manufacture of Cotton in the South," *Proceedings of State Agricultural and Mechanical Society of South Carolina and the State Grange, 1881*, 112-123, provides a good feel of contemporary ties between the two sectors of the economy. Also consult E. L. Jones, "Agricultural Origins of Industry," *Past and Present* (1968), 58-71, for an approach that is borne out in much of the materials I have investigated.

85. Blaine to Courly, November 19, 1881: *NA* 59.

86. Blaine to Morton, September 5, 1881: *ibid.*

87. Presidential statement of March 8, 1880: Richardson, *Messages*, 4537 - 4538.

88. *CR*, 7:2:1618 - 1622; and see J. Nimmo, *The Proposed American Inter-Ocean Canal in Its Commercial Aspects* (Washington, 1880), 128.

89. *House Miscellaneous Document No. 81*, 4 - 5, 7 - 8; and *The Clayton-Bulwer Treaty. House Report No. 1121*. 46th Cong., 2nd Ses. (Washington, 1880).

90. Rogers to Curtis, February 23, 1880: *Hayes Mss.*

91. Blaine to Lowell, June 24, 1881: *NA* 59.

92. Blaine, Statement of November 19, 1881: *ibid.*

93. *Chicago Weekly Magazine*, September 16, 1882. Also see Blaine to Morgan, June 16, 1881: *NA* 59.

94. A good example of Blaine's acknowledged strength in the West, and the concern it caused men oriented toward the conservative metropolitan wing of the party, is provided by J. F. Wilson to Allison, March 26, 1881: *Allison Mss.*

95. *Bradstreet's*, September 10, December 3, 1881, March 18, 1882.

96. See, for example, *CR*, 13:1:924, 978; Kasson's performance is at 13:2:1564.

97. Frelinghuysen to Windom, July 24, 1882: *NA* 59.

98. Early proposals for inspection can be followed in *Bradstreet's*, August 4, 1880; *American Agriculturalist*, June 1881; F. H. Mason, "The Opposition to American Meat in Europe," *Consular Reports No. 3* (1881), 192 - 197; and J. Low in *Breeder's Gazette*, December 15, 1881.

99. *Consular Reports No. 19* (1882), 21 - 28; and *No. 22* (1882), 542 - 545.

100. *Breeder's Gazette*, June 1, July 20, 1882; New York *Herald*, December 27, 1882.

101. Frelinghuysen to Sargent, February 10, 1883: *NA* 59.

102. Armour to Senator Logan for Frelinghuysen, March 1, 1883, enclosed in Frelinghuysen to Sargent, March 14, 1883: *NA* 59. Also see Frelinghuysen to Loring, July 30, 1883: *Frelinghuysen Papers.*

103. New York *Herald*, March 17, 1883; *Rural New Yorker*, March 31, 1883; and *Bradstreet's*, April 14, 1883.

104. Chicago *Tribune*, April 27, 1883; and see below.

105. Sargent to Frelinghuysen, January 1, 1883: *NA* 59; and see Wilson to Davis, December 4, 1882: *ibid.*, for a similar estimate at the time.

106. *Rural New Yorker*, June 9, 1883; *National Live Stock Journal*, September and November 1883; *Breeder's Gazette*, October 18, November 8, 1883. Also see *Rural New Yorker*, May 5, 12, 19, 1883, and *The New York Times*, September 13, 1883. A useful account appears in *Norddeutsche Allgemeine Zeitung*, April 27, 1883.

107. Arthur, Annual Message of December 4, 1883: Richardson, *Messages*, 10:4758, 4763.

108. J. B. Grinnell, letter to the editor, *Western Rural*, December 20, 1883, published in edition of January 5, 1884.

109. Chicago *Tribune*, December 23, 29, 31, 1883; *Rural New Yorker*, December 15, 1883.

110. *The New York Times*, February 28, March 31, April 13, 1881; Joint Resolution of Illinois Legislature, January 25, 1881: *NA* 46, Sen. 46A - H28 (and see others in the same file); Proceedings of a Convention of Agriculturalists, January 1882, Held at the Department of Agriculture: *NA* 16; *Breeder's Gazette*, April 17, 1884; *Rural New Yorker*, October 27, 1883; *Breeder's Gazette*, November 22, 1883; *National Live Stock Journal*, November 1883; *Rural New Yorker*, December 1, 1883.

111. Sturgis, Report for 1884: *WSGA Mss.*; *Rural New Yorker*, December 1, 1883; *National Live Stock Journal*, December 1883; *CR*, 15:1:402 - 405, 561; petitions and resolutions in *NA* 46, Sen. 48A - H1, and 233, HR48A - F6.2; Sturgis to S. W. Standout, March 13, 1884; E. R. Price to Sturgis, March 18, 1884; Sturgis to C. E. Fisher, April 12, 1884; Sturgis to G. W. Simpson, May 5, 1884; Simpson to Sturgis, May 10, 1884; T. J. Hand to Sturgis, May 10, 1884; Clay to Sturgis, May 26, 1884: all in *WSGA Mss.*; *Pleuro-Pneumonia Among Cattle. House Report No. 344*. 46th Cong., 3rd Ses. (Washington, 1884); *Breeder's Gazette*, January 24, 31, February 7, 14, March 13, April 6, 1884; *Country Gentleman*, June 26, 1884.

112. Topeka Board of Trade, petition of February 9, 1884: *NA* 233, HR48A - H6.10; *Western Rural*, February 23, 1884; the extensive materials in *NA* 46 and 233 Senate and

House; *Western Rural*, January 12, 19, 1884; and *CR*, 13:3:2731; 15:1:73, 243, 316-317, 402-404, 558-560.

113. H. White to C. Schurz, February 11, 1885: *Carl Schurz Papers*.

114. *Western Rural*, January 12, 19, February 9, 1884.

115. *Ibid.*, January 19, 1884.

116. *Rural New Yorker*, January 18, 1884.

117. See, for example, Frelinghuysen to Arthur, January 31, 1884: *NA* 59; it is also in *Importation of American Hog Products into Germany and France. House Executive Document No. 70.* 48th Cong., 1st Ses. (Washington, 1884), 1-6.

118. Frelinghuysen to J. H. Reagan, March 26, 1884: *NA* 233, HR48A-F6.1.

119. Frelinghuysen to J. F. Miller, March 26, 1884: *ibid.*

120. *CR*, 13:2:1553-1556; on the push for tobacco markets, see the materials in *NA* 59, and 233 HR46A-H9.1.

121. Indiana State Grange, *Journal of Proceedings for 1882*.

122. Texas State Grange, *ibid.*, *1880*.

123. Testimony of September 20, 1883: *Senate Committee on Labor and Capital*, 2:692-701.

124. *American*, October 25, 1884.

125. *CR*, 10:4:4015-4016 (Brown); 13:2:1553 (Ellis); and 15:6:A:490-491 (Ochiltree).

126. *Bradstreet's*, January 3, 1885.

127. National Grange, *Journal of Proceedings for the Session of 1881, 1884, 1887*. Also see Senate discussion of consular matters in 1887-1888.

128. W. E. Connelley, *The Life of Preston B. Plumb. A Pioneer of the Progressive Movement in America* (Chicago, 1913), 268, 280; and below.

129. *CR*, 15:6:5841-5849.

130. *Bankers Magazine* (December 1884); New York *Tribune*, October 8, 1883; *The New York Times*, December 3, 1883; *Bradstreet's*, January 19, 1884.

131. On the Cuban issue, see Texas State Grange, *Journal of Proceedings, 1880*; resolution of the Tennessee State Legislature to Frelinghuysen, March 26, 1883: *NA* 59; *Bradstreet's*, April 28, 1883; *National Tribune*, August 2, 14, 1883; Frelinghuysen's remarks of December 26, 1884; and *American*, December 6, 1884.

132. See, for example, Arthur's remarks of December 6, 1881: Richardson, *Messages*, 10:4631.

133. The basic published source is Department of State, *Congo Conference* (Washington, 1886), 166-167; but see also *A Report of Lieutenant Tount of a Journey on the River Congo. Senate Executive Document 77.* 49th Cong., 2nd Ses. (Washington, 1887), 33-36. I am indebted to Tom Terrill for materials below from the *Sanford Mss.*

134. Sanford to Davies, March 3, 1883: *Sanford Mss.* The quote from Stanley is in *Congo Conference*, 352-353.

135. A good account of the campaign is in Morgan to Sanford, February 5, 1885: *Sanford Mss.* Kasson also joined the effort; see Kasson to Frelinghuysen, October 15, 18, 1884, and Frelinghuysen to Kasson, October 17, 1884: *NA* 59.

136. Frelinghuysen to Arthur, January 29, 1885: *NA* 59.

137. *CR*, 24:1:561-562.

138. *Ibid.*, 14:4:A:33-34.

139. L. Barnes, "The Leavenworth Board of Trade," *Kansas Historical Quarterly* (1932), 360-378.

140. National Grange, *Journal of Proceedings for the Session of 1885*.

141. See, for example, the testimony of E. Sweet, June 10, 1884: *Ship Canal from the Great Lakes to the Navigable Waters of the Hudson River. House Report No. 423.* 54th Cong., 1st Ses. (Washington, 1896), Appendix F, 45.

142. An example of early pressure is C. Densing to Evarts, July 12, 1877: *NA* 59.

143. Blaine, Senate speech of June 5, 1878: in Blaine, *Discussions*, 186-193.

144. Blaine, Senate speech of January 29, 1879: also in W. S. Vail (ed.), *The Words of James G. Blaine on the Issues of the Day* (Boston, 1884), 145-151.

145. Algernon Paddock and Jay A. Hubbell were two such figures.

146. *Bradstreet's*, July 10, 1880.

147. *CR*, 14:1:934.

148. New York *Tribune*, October 8, 1883.

149. Oregon State Grange, *Journal of Proceedings for 1881, 1882;* and see *Report of Commissioners to Central and South America,* 6.

150. *CR,* 14:2:1080, 1077; for Blaine's speech of January 27, 1881, see Vail, *Blaine,* 156.

151. *CR,* 14:1:983, 977; 14:2:1078-1079. Other examples of the arguments advanced by spokesmen from agricultural states include 13:A:115-116; 14:1:929; 14:A:1020, 1029, 1115, 1125, 1749; and 14:4:A:131-132. Metropolitan spokesmen can be reviewed at 14:2:1025-1026, 1034, 1063, 1072; 14:4:A:3-5; and see the testimony of John Wanamaker, *Report of Commissioners to Central and South America,* 211. A revealing contemporary survey is one by Lieutenant J. D. Jerrold Kelley, *The Question of Ships. The Navy and the Merchant Marine* (New York, 1884). Plumb's remarks are in *CR,* 14:4:3692.

152. Hayes, Message of December 6, 1880: Richardson, *Messages,* 10:4565.

153. *Bradstreet's,* December 10, 1880.

154. This early (1879) exchange between Senators Blaine and Beck provides an excellent preview of the long argument: *CR,* 8:1:627-637.

155. Arthur, Message of December 6, 1881: Richardson, *Messages,* 10:4638.

156. *CR,* 13:4:3520-3526; 13:6:5528. Also see 13:6:5472-5473, 5652.

157. See *NA* 233 HR 48A-H19.2, and 16, Sen. 48A-H16.

158. St. Paul Chamber of Commerce, petition of January 28, 1884; Cincinnati Board of Trade, petition of May 8, 1884: *ibid.*

159. *CR,* 15:3:2763.

160. *Ibid.,* 15:2:1453-1454.

161. *Ibid.,* 14:2:1555.

162. *Ibid.,* 14:2:1115.

163. *Ibid.,* 15:3:2836-2839; and 15:2:1328-1340.

164. *Ibid.,* 13:6:5652.

165. *Ibid.,* 14:4:3099; 15:3:2763, 2799.

166. Shufeldt, *Senate Report . . . on the Construction of Additional Steel Vessels for the Navy, 1884. Senate Report No. 161.* 48th Cong., 1st Ses. (Washington, 1884), 19; Shufeldt, Report of the Naval Advisory Board, October 25, 1833, v.

167. *Ibid.,* 21; and see the report by Lieutenant Commander F. M. Barber, "The Navy, 1884," 67-69.

168. *Ibid.,* 9. Also see *Construction of Vessels of War for the Navy. House Report 653.* 47th Cong., 1st Ses. (Washington, 1882).

169. The House investigation, authorized on March 3, 1883, produced the *Report, Gun Foundry Board. House Executive Document No. 97.* 47th Cong., 1st Ses. (Washington, 1884).

170. *CR,* 14:2:1404.

171. *Ibid.,* 14:1:983; 13:6:5472-5473.

172. *Report on Additional Steel Vessels,* 1.

Chapter Ten

1. See Williams, *Contours of American History.*

2. See, for example, *Report of the Secretary of the Interior for 1877;* testimony of C. W. Elliott, a Nebraska stockman, in *House Select Committee on the General Depression in Labor and Business. House Miscellaneous Document No. 29.* 45th Cong., 3rd Ses. (Washington, 1879), 334; Des Moines *Iowa Weekly People,* February 6, 1879. The most specifically useful material on farm labor is: *Wages of Farm Labor in the United States. U.S.D.A. Division of Statistics. Miscellaneous Series Report No. 4* (Washington, 1892); G. K. Holmes, *Wages of Farm Labor. U.S.D.A. Bureau of Statistics. Bulletin No. 99* (Washington, 1912); L. F. Cox, "The American Agricultural Wage Earner, 1865-1900," *Agricultural History* (1948), 95-114; P. W. Gates, "Frontier Estate Builders and Farm Laborers," in W. D. Wyman and C. B. Kroeber, *The Frontier in Perspective* (Madison, 1957), 143-164; L. C. Gray, et al., "Farm Ownership and Tenancy," *U.S.D.A. Yearbook for 1923* (Washington, 1924), 507-600; W. E. Kearns, "The Farm Hand: An Unknown Quantity," *Arena* (November 1897), 661-672; and the vast number of references in the hearings and newspapers consulted. The literature on the public domain is almost as vast as the subject. The more gen-

eral items that helped me the most are as follows: *Senate Executive Document No. 181.* 48th Cong., 1st Ses. (Washington, 1884); *Senate Report No. 69.* 49th Cong., 1st Ses. (Washington, 1886); *Senate Executive Document No. 127.* 48th Cong., 1st Ses. (Washington, 1884); *Senate Executive Document No. 181.* 48th Cong., 1st Ses. (Washington, 1884); *House Report 1809.* 47th Cong., 1st Ses. (Washington, 1882); *House Miscellaneous Document No. 45.* 47th Cong., 2nd Ses. (Washington, 1884); *House Report 1325.* 48th Cong., 1st Ses. (Washington, 1884); *House Executive Document No. 119.* 48th Cong., 1st Ses. (Washington, 1884); *House Executive Document No. 30.* 49th Cong., 1st Ses. (Washington, 1886); C. L. Green, *The Administration of the Public Domain in South Dakota, South Dakota Historical Collections* (1940), 7 - 279; P. W. Gates, "Federal Land Policy in the South, 1866 - 1888," *Journal of Southern History* (1940), 303 - 330; P. W. Gates, "Land Policy and Tenancy in the Prairie States," *Journal of Economic History* (1941), 60 - 82; G. L. Anderson, "The Administration of Federal Land Laws in Western Kansas, 1880 - 1890: A Factor in Adjustment to a New Environment," *Kansas Historical Quarterly* (1952), 233 - 251; V. Carstensen (ed.), *The Public Lands. Studies in the History of the Public Domain* (Madison, 1963).

3. B. Moore, *Social Origins of Dictatorship and Democracy. Lord and Peasant in the Making of the Modern World* (Boston, 1966), offers a helpful discussion at this point; and W. B. Hesseltine, "Regions, Classes and Sections in American History," *Journal of Land and Public Utility Economics* (1944), 37 - 38, 42, contains an incisive analysis of the "imperialism of dominant groups" within American society.

4. Drache, *Day of the Bonanza,* 70 - 71, 10, 24 - 25, and 130, provides a good review of this image of the bonanzas.

5. Anon., "The Bonanza Farms of the West," *Atlantic Monthly* (January 1880), 33 - 44.

6. M. Frewen, *Melton Mowbray and Other Memories* (London, 1924), 122, 125. In addition to other materials cited below, see: A. W. Spring, "Powder River Live Stock Company," *The Colorado Magazine* (1951), 32 - 36; E. M. Richardson, "John Bull in the Cowmen's West: Moreton Frewen," *Montana* (1961), 37 - 45; and "Moreton Frewen and the Populist Revolt," *Annals of Wyoming* (1963), 155 - 173.

7. This account is based on materials in the *Frewen Papers* and the related materials in the Western History Manuscripts deposited in the University of Wyoming Library. A good introduction is H. O. Brayer, "The 76 Ranch on the Powder River," *Western Brand Book. Chicago Corrall* (1950), 73 - 80.

8. The details of these activities follow below.

9. On the early antimetropolitan feeling in Wyoming, see *Report of the Secretary of the Interior for 1880,* 76.

10. See Sheldon, "American and Canadian Meat Trade," 321 - 322, and below.

11. *Bradstreet's,* November 25, 1882; London *Times,* August 15, 1883. On nonagricultural investments, see O. O. Winther, "Promoting the American West in England, 1865 - 1900," *Journal of Economic History* (1956), 506 - 513; and R. W. Paul, *Mining Frontiers of the Far West, 1848 - 1880* (New York, 1963).

12. *North British Agriculturalist,* June 30, 1880.

13. *Bradstreet's,* February 19, 1881.

14. *Ibid.,* June 25, 1881.

15. *Ibid.,* July 22, 1882; J. S. Brisbin, *The Beef Bonanza; or How to Get Rich on the Plains* (Norman, 1959), 7, 36, 41 - 46, 191.

16. W. B. Grohman, "Cattle Ranches in the Far West," *Fortnightly Review* (1880), 441. Also see London *Economist,* February 3, 1883.

17. Mrs. L. L. Snowden to Land Commissioner, April 1, 1881: in *Letter from the Secretary of the Interior . . . on the Subject of Unauthorized Fencing of Public Lands, March 14, 1884. Senate Executive Document No. 127.* 48th Cong., 1st Ses. (Washington, 1886), 32.

18. F. E. Boyd to Land Commissioner, February 12, 1882: *ibid.,* 36 - 37.

19. *Ibid.,* 18.

20. *Ibid.,* 19.

21. *Ibid.,* 30.

22. See W. M. Pearce, *The Matador Land and Cattle Company* (Norman, 1964), 7, *passim;* H. O. Brayer, "The L 7 Ranches," *Annals of Wyoming* (1943), 5 - 36; and "More-

ton Frewen, Cattleman," *The Westerners Brand Book. Denver Corral* (1949), 1-18, in addition to the other works cited; and W. T. Jackson, "The Administration of Thomas Moonlight," *Annals of Wyoming* (1946), 139-162; and "Railroad Relations of the Wyoming Stock Growers Association, 1873-1890," *ibid.*, (1947), 3-24, in addition to his "Wyoming Stock Growers Association."

23. *Bradstreet's*, April 15, 1882.

24. J. D. Sargent to Land Commissioner, June 12, 1883; Kansas Petition of April 18, 1883; and G. W. Fairfield to Land Commissioner, November 26, 1883: all in *Secretary of the Interior . . . on the Subject of Unauthorized Fencing*.

25. Wyoming *Sentinel*, quoted in P. S. Wilson to Secretary Teller, January 4, 1883, *ibid.*; "Views of Thomas Sturgis, August 30, 1883," in *WSGA Mss.*; Cheyenne *Leader*, January 30, February 24, and August 24, 1883. Also see W. A. Hall to Land Commissioner, January 6, 1884, and J. L. McCowell to same, August 4, 1883: in *Secretary of the Interior . . . on the Subject of Unauthorized Fencing*, 31, 38; and *Rural New Yorker*, January 6, 20, March 24, 1883. The other materials that have proved most useful in connection with the movement against alien landholders are: *House Report No. 2308*. 48th Cong., 2nd Ses. (Washington, 1885); *House Report No. 1951*. 49th Cong., 1st Ses. (Washington, 1886); *House Report 3455*. 49th Cong., 1st Ses. (Washington, 1886); R. V. Clements, "The Farmers' Attitude Toward British Investment in American Industry," *Journal of Economic History* (1955), 151-159; Clements, "British Investment and American Legislative Restriction in the Trans-Mississippi West, 1880-1900," *Mississippi Valley Historical Review* (1955), 207-228; M. Rothstein, "A British Investment in Bonanza Farming, 1879-1910," *Agricultural History* (1959), 72-78; and M. Bronfenbrenner, "The Appeal of Confiscation in Economic Development," *Economic Development and Cultural Change* (April 1955), 201-218. The subject needs a full-length study.

26. Teller to Arthur, February 7, 1883: *Message from the President. . . . Setting Forth the Urgent Necessity of Stringent Measures for the Repression of the Rapidly Increasing Invasion and Violations of the Laws Relating to Public Lands. Senate Executive Document No. 61.* 47th Cong., 2nd Ses. (Washington, 1883), 1; Department of Interior, *Report of April 5, 1883* (Washington, 1883); *Report of the Secretary of the Interior for 1883*, xxxi-xxxii, 17; and *Letter from the Secretary of the Interior . . . on the Subject of Unauthorized Fencing*, 678.

27. See H. H. Dunham, *Government Handout: A Study in the Administration of the Public Lands, 1875-1891* (Ann Arbor, 1941), 296-297.

28. See, for example, *National Live Stock Journal*, April 1883; *Breeder's Gazette*, April 26, and June 21, 1883.

29. W. G. Moody, testimony of August 23, September 3, 1883: in *Senate Report on Labor and Capital*, 1:713-724, 969-979.

30. It reached 25.6 percent of all farmers in 1880: see L. C. Gray, et al., "Farm Ownership and Tenancy," *Yearbook of the United States Department of Agriculture, 1923* (Washington, 1924), 507-600.

31. National Grange, *Proceedings of the Session for 1884*.

32. J. A. Kasson, "The Monroe Declaration," *North American Review* (September 1881), 247-249. For the background, consult: *Geographical and Geological Surveys West of the Mississippi. House Report No. 612.* 43rd Cong., 1st Ses.; J. W. Powell, *Report on the Lands of the Arid Region of the United States* (Washington, 1878), esp. 22-45; and *CR*, 8:3:A:219-221, as a sample of the discussion.

33. *Report of the Secretary of the Interior for 1883*; and *Secretary of the Interior . . . on the Subject of Unauthorized Fencing of Public Lands*, 533-536.

34. *CR*, 14:1:986.

35. *Ibid.*, 14:2:1072.

36. H. P. Hammett, president of Piedmont Mills, letter to the editor, Atlanta *Constitution*, reprinted in *Manufacturers Record*, February 1, 1883.

37. *Western Rural*, January 5, 1884.

38. Remarks of February 28, 1884.

39. N. C. McFarland to Teller, May 15, 1884: *Letter from the Secretary of the Interior . . . Concerning Entries of Public Lands by . . . Foreign Corporations, May 29, 1884. Senate Executive Document No. 181.* 48th Cong., 1st Ses. (Washington, 1884), 3.

40. *CR*, 15:6:476-477.

41. *Bradstreet's*, October 11, 1884.

42. *Report from the Central and South American Commissioners. House Executive Document No. 226.* 48th Cong., 2nd Ses. Washington, 1885), 26, 3.

43. The de Mores adventure is recounted in L. M. Parker, "Medora and the Marquis de Mores," *Westerners Brand Book. Chicago Corral* (1950), 85-91; and A. O. Goplen, "The Career of the Marquis de Mores in the Badlands," *North Dakota History* (1946), 5-70.

44. Brayer, "When Dukes Went West," 68.

45. *Pall Mall Gazette*, March 15, 1864.

46. *North British Agriculturalist*, August 30, 1884; E. S. Bruce to Land Commissioner, July 23, 1883, November 8, 1883, and January 2, 1884: in *Secretary of the Interior . . . on Unauthorized Fencing of Public Lands*, 38-41, and also 84,; *Report of the General Land Office, 1884*, 16; *Unlawful Occupation of the Public Lands. House Report No. 1809.* 47th Cong., 1st Ses. (Washington, 1882); *Unlawful Fencing of Public Lands. House Executive Document No. 119.* 48th Cong., 1st Ses. (Washington, 1884); *Unlawful Occupancy of the Public Lands. House Report 1325.* 48th Cong., 1st Ses. (Washington, 1884); and *Letter from the Secretary of Interior . . . Concerning Entries of Public Lands by the Estes Park Company and Other Foreign Corporations. May 29, 1884. Senate Executive Document No. 181.* 48th Cong., 1st Ses. (Washington, 1884).

47. See, for example, the reports in the *Western Rural*, January 26, March 22, and June 14, 21, 1884; and J. Van der Zee, *The British in Iowa* (Iowa City, 1922).

48. *Rural New Yorker*, March 24, June 23, September 1, 1883. Also see *Senate Report on Labor and Capital*, testimony of J. K. Ingalls of New York, September 10, 1883.

49. *Unlawful Occupation of the Public Lands*, 1181-1182.

50. *CR*, 15:1:546-551. Also see 15:1:285, and 15:2:1351, 1960.

51. *Ibid.*, 4769-4783; and also Payson's report from the Committee on Public Lands, *Unlawful Occupancy of the Public Lands;* and *CR*, 15:4:3689-3690, 3779, and 4057.

52. Blaine, Letter of Acceptance, June 15, 1884; *Official Proceedings of the Republican National Conventions, 1884-1888* (Minneapolis, 1903); and K. H. Porter and D. B. Johnson (ed.), *National Party Platforms, 1840-1956* (Urbana, 1956), 72-74.

53. *Illinois State Journal*, October 1884.

54. *CR*, 16:1:861, 16:3:2027. Also see the *Report of the General Land Office for 1885*, esp. the report of inspector A. R. Green, November 3, 1884, 53.

55. *Ibid.*, 17.

56. *Western Rural*, March 21, 1885.

57. *Report of the General Land Office for 1885*, 11, 15-16, 48-49, 79; and see *ibid.*, for *1886*.

58. A useful review is the memo, "Unlawful Fencing," in the 1888 file of *William F. Vilas Papers*. Also see Richardson, *Messages*, 10:4892, 4894.

59. C. P. Wetzel to Dawes, May 15, 1885; E. Bodman to Dawes, October 15, 1885: *James William Dawes Papers; Bradstreet's*, August 15, 1885.

60. *Cheyenne Daily Sun*, February 27, 1877. Also see *National Stockman*, August 13, September 3, 1885.

61. F. R. B. Harrison to T. Sturgis, October 24, 1885: *WSGA Mss.*

62. Warren to W. A. Taylor, August 19, 1885: *Francis E. Warren Papers*.

63. A. E. Sheldon, *Land Systems and Land Policies in Nebraska* (Lincoln, 1936), 118-122, 140. There is a good review from Sparks's point of view in *Report of the General Land Office for 1886*.

64. R. S. Strahair to W. F. Vilas, April 12, 1888: *Vilas Mss.* Box No. 80 in the *Vilas Mss.* contains an excellent review of the trouble caused by the order. See, for example, the case of T. Kirkbride Hume, who was still struggling with the crisis in January 1889.

65. *Rooks County Record*, November 26, 1886; *Kirwin Independent*, January 6, 1887. Also see Kansas State Senate, Concurrent Resolution No. 7, February 3, 1886, *NA*, 46, Sen. 49A-H23.1; and *Rural New Yorker*, February 13, 1886.

66. *Report of the Secretary of the Interior for 1885*, 38.

67. H. George, "More About American Landlordism," *North American Review* (April 1886), 394. Also see T. P. Gill, "Landlordism in America," *ibid.* (January 1886); and H. C. Nixon, "Precursors of Turner in the Interpretation of the American Frontier," *South Atlantic Quarterly* (1929), 83-89.

68. On Atkinson, see his letter to the editor in *Bradstreet's*, June 26, 1886.

69. Warren to Thomas, November 13, 1886: *Warren Mss.;* also see E. M. Ricker to Vilas, March 24, 1888: *Vilas Mss.*

70. *Bradstreet's,* July 11, 1885.

71. T. Sturgis, President's Report to the WSGA for 1885: *WSGA Mss.* Also see *In the Senate of the United States in re The State and Territory of Dakota. Senate Report No. 15.* 49th Cong., 1st Ses. (Washington, 1886), 2.

72. *Rural New Yorker,* February 6, 1886.

73. See, as typical: *Western Rural,* January 30, February 27, 1886; New York *World,* May 23, 1885; New York *Herald,* April 17, 1886; A. J. Desmond, "America's Land Question," *North American Review* (February 1886), 153-158; *Report of the Secretary of the Treasury for 1885,* 45-46.

74. Oregon State Grange, *Journal of Proceedings for 1886; Western Rural,* April 3, 1886.

75. Chicago *Tribune,* clippings in *Richard J. Oglesby Papers.* Also see Schully to Koehule and Scapp, March 9, 1886; and Oglesby to Scully, March 9, 1886: *ibid.*

76. *Ownership of Real Estate in the Territories. House Report No. 3455.* 49th Cong., 1st Ses. (Washington, 1886), 3-4; *Report of the Secretary of the Interior for 1886,* 69; *In the Senate of the United States in re the Repeal of All Pre-Emption Laws. Senate Report No. 69.* 49th Cong., 1st Ses. (Washington, 1886); and the memo by E. A. Bowers, "The Territories, Fall 1888," in *Vilas Mss.*

77. *Land Titles to Aliens in the United States. House Report No. 2308.* 48th Cong., 2nd Ses. (Washington, 1885), 3-4; Several other members of the Congress also introduced alien land bills between December 1885 and mid-1886; see *CR,* 17:1:381, 427, 429-430. The other relevant hearings and reports are: *Aliens Owning Lands in the United States. House Report 1951.* 49th Cong., 1st Ses. (Washington, 1886); *To Amend the Alien Land Act. House Report No. 703.* 50th Cong., 1st Ses. (Washington, 1888); *Ownership of Real Estate in the Territories. House Report 954.* 50th Cong., 1st Ses. (Washington, 1888); *To Prohibit Aliens from Owning Land. House Report 1481.* 50th Cong., 1st Ses. (Washington, 1888); *To Amend the Alien Land Act. House Report 1140.* 51st Cong., 1st Ses. (Washington, 1890).

78. *CR,* 17:5:4380-4381. For the petitions, see *ibid.,* 17:6:6480; 17:7:6644-6645; and 17:9:496. They can be found in *NA* 46, and 233.

79. *CR,* 17:8:426-428.

80. *Ibid.,* June 7 (17:5:5379), and 24 (Senate), 1886.

81. *Ibid.,* 17:5:5108.

82. *Ibid.,* 17:8:7830-7834.

83. The final action, which culminated with the President's signature, can be followed in *CR,* 17:8:7954-7955, 8013-8014; 18L3:2319, 2435, 2439, 2470.

84. This campaign can be followed in *NA* 46, S50A-J25; *NA* 233, HR 50A-H25.3; *CR* 19:1:29, 235, 257, 317, 320, 363, 615 - 617, 984, 1041 - 1042, 1026, 1077 - 1079, et seq. through April 9, 1888; *Report of the Secretary of the Interior for 1887, and 1888;* and the materials cited in Note 77 above.

85. See Kansas Senate *Journal* and House *Journal* for 1887, 1889, and 1891; H. E. Socolofsky, "The Scully Land System in Marion County [Kansas]," *Kansas Historical Quarterly* (1950), 337-375; "William Scully: His Early Years in Illinois, 1850-1865," *Journal of the West* (1965), 41-55; and for Illinois, see *Annual Statutes, 1892,* House *Journal* for 1885, 1887, and 1891; and Senate *Journal* for 1887, 1891.

86. See, for example, *NA* 233, HR50-A-H25.3; *Bradstreet's,* September 7, October 22, 1887; *National Stockman,* December 20, 1888; and below.

87. Petition of Falls County, Texas, Alliance, December 24, 1887, *NA* 46, Sen. 50A-H30.21; Address of Macune, Alliance leader, in N. A. Dunning (ed.), *The Farmers' Alliance and Agricultural Digest* (Washington, 1891), 71; G. A. Bowen, "The Business Side of Farming and the Value of Organization," *Report of the Massachusetts Board of Agriculture for 1887,* 247-248, 253-255; Petitions from the citizens of Rockland, Maine, February 23, 1885: *NA* 233, HR 48A-H25.13; Denver *Republican,* February 21, 1887; *Nebraska State Journal,* February 2, 1887; *Public Opinion* (April-October 1887); Oregon State Grange, *Journal of Proceedings for 1887;* National Grange, *Journal of Proceedings for the Session of 1887.*

88. Iowa Legislature, Concurrent Resolution of April 3, 1888: *NA,* 233, HR 50A-H25.3.

89. Illinois House and Senate *Journals,* 1885.

90. Chicago *Tribune,* November 17, 1887.

91. *Report of the Secretary of the Interior for 1887*, 3.

92. J. J. Hill, remarks of August 1889: *Proceedings of the Waterways Convention, Superior, Wisconsin, August 7-9, 1889* (Superior, 1889).

Chapter Eleven

1. *Commercial and Financial Chronicle*, January 6, 1883; Taylor, *Chicago Board of Trade*, 2:635.

2. *Bradstreet's*, October 13, 20, December 29, 1883; testimony of C. A. Tripp, farmer of Butler, Missouri: *Senate Report on Labor and Capital*, 2:1393.

3. Lebergott, *Manpower in Economic Growth*, 179-180; *Western Rural*, May 24, 1884.

4. See the sources cited earlier on macroeconomic indicators.

5. R. F. Severson, "The American Manufacturing Frontier, 1870-1940," *Business History Review* (1960), 356-372.

6. *Western Rural*, March 10, 1898.

7. Smith, *Kansas*, 15.

8. Working, "Acreage and Production," 260-261.

9. Mintz, *Cyclical Fluctuations in Exports*, Appendix A.

10. L. E. Davis, "The Investment Market, 1870-1914: The Evolution of a National Market," *Journal of Economic History* (1965), 375.

11. *Western Rural*, May 10, 1884.

12. *Bradstreet's*, January 15, 1881; January 5, 1884.

13. Coleman to Hersey, April 2, 1886: *NA* 16, 94:285. Also see Nixon, "The Populist Movement in Iowa," *Iowa Journal of History and Politics* (1926), 13; and "The Economic Basis of the Populist Movement in Iowa," *ibid.* (1923), 373-396.

14. Barlow to Marble, June 15, 1885: *Marble Mss.*

15. *CR*, 19:6:5586.

16. *Rural New Yorker*, June 26, 1886.

17. *CR*, 17:1:427; also see testimony of F. D. Foster of Massachusetts, February 8, 1883: *Senate Report on Labor and Capital*, 1:51-52.

18. Sarah to Ellen, July 9, 1886: *John Sweet Donald Papers.*

19. Letter to the Editor, Iola, Kansas, *Register*, March 2, 1888.

20. R. Dawson to Dawes, February [?], 1886: *Dawes Mss.*

21. Fite, *Farmers Frontier*, 84.

22. S. S. Kuznets, et al., *Population Redistribution and Economic Growth, United States, 1870-1950. Volume II. Analyses of Economic Change* (Philadelphia, 1960), 146.

23. Petition of the Arkansas State Horticulture Society, February 26, 1886: *NA* 233, HR 49A-H2.6; Pennsylvania State Grange, *Journal of Proceedings for 1887*; St. Paul *Pioneer Press*, January 6, 1886; *Bradstreet's*, January 15, 1887.

24. Kenesaw County Farmers, petition received July 6, 1886: *NA* 46, S49A-H23; *Bradstreet's*, February 24, 1883; E. M. Lerner, "Southern Output and Agricultural Income, 1860-1880," *Agricultural History* (1959), 124; Woodward, *Origins of the New South*, 176; W. S. Morgan, *History of the Wheel and Alliance and the Impending Revolution* (Hardy, 1889), 296-297; Atlanta *Constitution*, January 26, 1881.

25. Delaware State Grange, *Journal of Proceedings for 1888*; *Bradstreet's*, April 28, 1880.

26. *CR*, 19:3:21-94; St. Paul *Pioneer Press*, June 8, 1887; and Citizens of Kent, Nebraska, to Governor A. Nance, February 25, 1880: *Nance Mss.*

27. I. L. Leonard, Secretary of the Oak Precinct, Nebraska, Alliance: *Western Rural*, January 16, 1886.

28. Kansas State Board of Agriculture, petition to Congress, February 1, 1886; and Burlington County petition of January 5, 1886: *NA* 46, S49A-H1.3; *CR*, 18:3:24-26.

29. Sturgis, Report of November 17, 1885: *WSGA Mss.*; J. Clay, "The Cheyenne Club," *ibid.*; Sturgis, *Address to the National Cattle Grower's Association* (Chicago, 1885); J. B. Grinnell, *Address to the Wyoming Stock Growers Association* (Cheyenne, 1885); Simpson to Sturgis, April 19, 1884; Hewitt to Sturgis, March 24, 1884; Clay to Sturgis, April 17, 1884; Plumb to Sturgis, April 28, 1884: all in *WSGA Mss.*; and *Breeder's Gazette*, April 10, 1884.

30. S. S., letter to the editor, *Western Rural*, February 16, 1884; M. George, *ibid.*, February 9, 1884.

31. *Ibid.*, February 23, 1884.

32. Based on Tontz's figures, "Memberships of General Farm Organizations," after reviewing the sources he cites and various other estimates in agricultural newspapers and journals, and in manuscript collections.

33. W. F. Brown, letter to the editor, *Country Gentleman*, November 20, 1884. Similar reports can be found on a regular basis in all newspapers dealing with agriculture, and in the annual reports of the state boards of agriculture.

34. *Bradstreet's*, April 11, 1885.

35. Nixon, "Populist Movement," 16; R. V. Scott, *The Agrarian Movement in Illinois: 1880-1890* (Urbana, 1962), 2; and, for a specific illustration, see J. L. Smith to T. Sturgis, March 29, 1887: *WSGA Mss.*

36. E. D. Stewart, "The Populist Party in Indiana," *Indiana Magazine of History* (1918), 337; R. V. Scott, "The Rise of the Farmers' Mutual Benefit Association in Illinois, 1883-1891," *Agricultural History* (1958), 44-55.

37. J. D. Hicks, *The Populist Revolt. A History of the Farmers Alliance and the Peoples Party* (Lincoln, 1961), 110.

38. H. Clevenger, "The Farmers Alliance in Missouri," *Missouri Historical Review* (1944), 35.

39. F. B. Zincke, *The Plough and the Dollar. Or The Englishman of a Century Hence* (London, 1883), 31.

40. Morgan, *Wheel and Alliance*, 620.

41. W. H. Hamilton, "Autobiography of a Cowman," *South Dakota Historical Collections* (1941), 19:477; W. E. Kearns, "The Farm Hand: An Unknown Quantity," *Arena* (November 1897), 661-672.

42. *Ibid.*, 667; *Western Rural*, January 10, 1885.

43. St. Paul *Pioneer Press*, January 27, 1885.

44. As quoted by W. T. K. Nugent, *The Tolerant Populists. Kansas Populism and Nativism* (Chicago, 1963), 97.

45. *American Non-Conformist*, May 31, 1888; *Western Rural*, January 3, 1885.

46. Macune, remarks during a Mississippi rally in 1888: in Dunning, *Alliance History*, 78-92; *Western Rural*, February 20, March 27, April 3, and September 25, 1886. The evidence abundantly supports the keen analysis of M. P. Rogin, *The Intellectuals and McCarthy: The Radical Specter* (Cambridge, 1967), an unusually fine study. Also see L. Fuller, "Colorado's Revolt Against Capitalism," *Mississippi Valley Historical Review* (1934), 344, 347, 349, 359 (and his full study as a PhD Thesis, University of Wisconsin, 1933).

47. *CR*, 15:6:A:374.

48. On local market emphasis, see New Hampshire State Grange, *Journal of Proceedings for 1876*; C. D. Wright to E. Atkinson, January 7, 1880; C. L. Flint to Atkinson, January 6, 1880; X. A. Willard to Atkinson, January 19, 1880; and P. C. Reynolds to Atkinson (via M. B. Anderson), February 23, 1880: all in E. Atkinson, *The Railroads of the United States: Their Effects on Falling Production in That Country and in Great Britain* (Boston, 1880), 6-7, 9-15.

49. S. L. Boardman to Atkinson, January 12, 1880: *Atkinson Mss.*; Massachusetts State Grange, *Journal of Proceedings for 1883*, et seq.

50. *Proceedings of the National Farm Alliance Seventh Annual Meeting: Minneapolis, October 4, 1887* (Minnesota, 1887).

51. *Message from the President of the United States . . . Relative to Commercial Agreements Made with Other Countries.* Senate Executive Document No. 119. 52nd Cong., 1st Ses. (Washington, 1892), Exhibit N, 139-151.

52. See *American Merchant Marine in the Foreign Trade.* House Report No. 1210. 51st Cong., 1st Ses. (Washington, 1890), 74; W. E. Curtis, *Trade and Transportation Between the United States and Spanish America* (Washington, 1889), 17-20; and *Consular Reports*, 1 (1880), 47-48.

53. *Report of the Commissioner of Agriculture for 1887*, 574. On tobacco, see: *Report of the Commissioner of Corporations on the Tobacco Industry. Part I* (Washington, 1909); *Consular Reports, Volume 20, Part II: Foreign Imports of American Tobacco* (Washington, 1900); B. W. Arnold, *History of the Tobacco Industry in Virginia from 1860 to 1894*

(Baltimore, 1897); G. K. Holmes, *The Tobacco Industry in the United States* (New York, 1907); W. W. Garner, et al., "History and Status of Tobacco Culture," *U.S.D.A. Yearbook for 1922* (Washington, 1923), 395-468; and M. Whitney and M. L. Floyd, "Growth of the Tobacco Industry," *U.S.D.A. Yearbook for 1899* (Washington, 1900), 429-440.

54. *Breeder's Gazette,* January 20, 1887.

55. *CR,* 11:1:744; Commissioner of Agriculture to E. W. Blatchford, January 7, 1884: *NA* 16; *Country Gentleman,* report on the National Convention of Stockmen in St. Louis, November 27, 1884; Gov. R. J. Oglesby, mss. copy of annual message of 1887: *Oglesby Mss.;* Dr. A. Ames, testimony of January 12, 1888, in *NA* 46, Sen. 50A-Fl; and see below.

56. *Adulteration of Food. House Report 199.* 46th Cong., 3rd Ses. (Washington, 1881), 5; Taylor, *Chicago Board of Trade,* 2:671-673; U.S.D.A., Division of Statistics. *Miscellaneous Series Report No. 5* (Washington, 1893), 93; *Report of the Bureau of Animal Industry for 1885, 1886, 1887.*

57. *Bradstreet's,* July 3, 1880, November 8, 1884.

58. C. P. Wright and J. S. Davis, "India As a Producer and Exporter of Wheat," *Wheat Studies* (July 1927), 317.

59. Mississippi State Grange, *Journal of Proceedings for 1884.*

60. *Western Rural,* February 6, 1886; *Prairie Farmer,* January 5, 1884; National Grange, *Journal of Proceedings for the Session of 1883.*

61. *Western Rural,* July 25, 1885.

62. G. S. Hubbard, *Recollections of Gordon S. Hubbard. An Address Before the Danville Old Settlers Association* (n.p., 1880); R. K. Slosson in *Western Rural,* August 15, 1885; and also H. Tuttle, *ibid.,* February 14, 1885.

63. W. B. Allison, mss. memo for speech: *William Boyd Allison Papers.* Also see *Western Rural,* March 14, 1885; *National Stockman,* May 28, 1885; and Chicago *Drovers Journal* for 1887.

64. Furnas to Dawes, May 21, July 24, 1884: *Dawes Mss.*

65. *CR,* 13:7:112; 15:3:2976.

66. *Ibid.,* 15:3:2897.

67. *Ibid.,* 17:4:1193-1194. Also 15:2:1480-1481.

68. On Kansas, see L. A. Fitz, "The Development of the Milling Industry in Kansas," *Kansas Historical Society Collections* (1912), 58-59. Statistics from Fossum, *Agrarian Movement in North Dakota,* 160; and H. Working, "Statistics of American Wheat Milling and Flour Disposition since 1879," *Wheat Studies* (December 1927), 101.

69. W. D. Washburn to Hale, June 22, 1884: *Washburn Mss.* Also see C. B. Kuhlmann, *The Development of the Flour Milling Industry in the United States* (Boston, 1929), 136.

70. Edgar Scrapbook, Volume 1: *William Crowell Edgar Papers.*

71. *Bradstreet's,* June 18, 1887; Davis, "California Breadstuffs," 532.

72. *Country Gentleman,* February 21, November 6, 1884; *Report from the Central and South American Commissioners,* 289-292; Farquhar to Wells, January 4, 1892: *Wells Mss.;* W. C. Mundt to McCormick, July 22, 1930: *McCormick Mss.; Consular Reports No. 48* (1884) and *No. 88* (January 1888); and Schoneberger's study of McCormick.

73. *Commercial and Financial Chronicle,* September 11, 1886; *Hearings before the House Ways and Means Committee on the Morrison Tariff Bill.* 48th Cong., 1st Ses. (Washington, 1884), 376-379; *Report from the Central and South American Commissioners,* 15; *The Cotton World,* September 17, 1877; Boston *Journal of Commerce,* July 4, 1885; *Manufacturers Record,* July 18, 1885.

74. *Manufacturers Record,* December 8, 1888; *Boston Journal of Commerce,* May 31, October 18, 1884; *Bradstreet's,* June 14, 1884; *Dixie,* December 1885 and August 1888; *Hearings on the Morrison Tariff,* 377 - 379; G. T. Winston, *A Builder of the New South. Being the Story of the Life Work of Daniel Augustus Tompkins* (New York, 1920), 126-127; and the thesis work of P. J. Hearden and G. G. Williamson.

75. Dunning, *Alliance History,* 50; *Report of the Central and South American Commissioners,* 50.

76. Atlanta *Constitution,* March 10, 1882.

77. Washington *Post,* December 30, 1884; *Hearings on the Morrison Tariff,* 379: *CR,* 13:3:2105-2107.

78. *Report of the Central and South American Commissioners,* 49, 183-184; Boston

Journal of Commerce, February 15, 1885; *Commercial and Financial Chronicle*, February 21, 1885.

79. *Bradstreet's*, September 5, 1885; Coleman to T. F. Bayard, May 17, 1886: *NA* 16; Richmond *Dispatch*, November 6, 1886; *Establishment of Export Tobacco Manufactories*. House Report 1141. 49th Cong., 1st Ses. (Washington, 1886), 1; *Consular Reports No. 97* (1888), 466-467.

80. New York *Journal of Commerce*, April 24, 1888; Tilley, *Bright Tobacco Industry*, 405; *Progressive Farmer*, April 9, 1889.

81. *Report of the Central and South American Commissioners*, 47-178. A good review of the early development of the export trade in canned goods is in *Bradstreet's*, December 4, 1880.

82. *Bradstreet's* April 21, 1880; D. A. Wells, "Revision of the Tariff," *Princeton Review* (November 1882), 347; and see Hewitt's remarks, *CR*, 13:3:2435-2436.

83. *Bankers Magazine* (April 1881), 754, 840.

84. *Bradstreet's*, February 9, May 3, November 15, 1884.

85. See, for example, the remarks of Ohio and Kentucky representatives: *CR*, 15:4:3552, 3667. Also S. J. Peelle (Indiana) to Kasson, July 11, 1888: *John Adam Kasson Papers*.

86. *Bradstreet's*, December 13, 1884, December 12, 1885. Also see *American Exporter* (February 1885), 12; and (July 1885), 1; Detroit *Tribune*, December 6, 1885; *The American*, July 5, October 18, November 22, 1884; New York Chamber of Commerce, petition of December 28, 1884: *NA* 46, Sen. 48A-H10; U. H. Crocker, *The Depression in Trade and the Wages of Labor* (Boston, 1886); *CR*, 18:1:636 (Boston Chamber of Commerce); and *Bradstreet's*, January 22, 1887.

87. *Bradstreet's*, January 7, 1888.

88. The best source for the final phases of the battle is *NA*, 46 and 233, for the 48th, 49th, and 50th congresses, where all the petitions and resolutions are on file.

89. T. B. Catron to S. B. Elkins, November 8, 1888: *Stephen B. Elkins Papers*. Also see R. E. Albright, "Politics and Public Opinion in the Western Statehood Movement of the 1880's," *Pacific Historical Review* (1934), 305; San Francisco *Chronicle*, November 11, 12, 14, 27, 1888.

90. Washington *Post*, December 12, 15, 1888.

91. Richardson, *Messages*, 10:4883; Morgan, *Alliance History*, 620; also see *The Nation*, January 14, 1886.

92. *Report of the Sixth Annual Session of the Farmers National Congress, St. Paul, Minnesota, August 25-30, 1886* (Indianapolis, 1886). And see *Bradstreet's*, May 22, 1886.

93. *Bradstreet's*, November 11, 1882, January 19, 1884 (letter from E. Atkinson). Also see W. D. Sheldon, *Populism in the Old Dominion. Virginia Farm Politics, 1885-1900* (Princeton, 1935).

94. Marble to A. J. Warner, February 24, 1885; D. Manning to Marble, April 29, 1885; Marble to Manning, May 3, 1885: all in *Manton Marble Papers*.

95. Manning to Marble, April 29, 1885; Bayard to Marble, April 30, 1885; Marble to Iddesleigh, July 30, 1885; Iddesleigh to Marble, July 22, 28, 1885; and Marble to Manning, August 8, 1885: *Marble Mss.*

96. Manning to Marble, September 6, 1885: *Marble Mss*. Also see Phelps to Bayard, "Confidential," October 20, 1885: *NA* 59.

97. Richardson, *Messages*, 8:344-346; *Report of the Secretary of the Treasury for 1885*, xxx, xxxv. Marble may even have written Cleveland's remarks on silver: see Marble to Cernuschi, October 31, 1885: *Marble Mss.*

98. Harrison to Michener, March 1, 1885: as quoted in H. J. Sievers, *Benjamin Harrison. Hoosier Statesman. From the Civil War to the White House, 1865-1888* (New York, 1959), 269.

99. *Western Rural*, November 21, 1885; also see August 15 and October 24, 1885.

100. *Bradstreet's*, September 25, May 29, 1886.

101. *Bradstreet's*, April 28, 1888; and see the Second Report of the English Royal Commission.

102. House of Commons, *Reports from Committees, Inspectors, and Others, 1888*, Volume 22:43, 49; Also see *Report of the Royal Commission on the Depression of Trade and Industry, 1886*; Robley, *The Monetary Problem*, 203, 236; Atkinson to T. Lyman, November 6, 1883: *Atkinson Mss.*; and *Consular Reports No. 87* (December 1887).

103. *The American*, July 11, September 19, 1885; *Western Rural*, May 1, 1886; S. Reed to J. Sherman, February 13, 1886: *Sherman Mss.*; and *CR*, 17:3:2182-2183.

104. *Bradstreet's*, April 10, November 13, 1886. The labors of Frewen and Bland can be followed in Frewen, *Memories*; Grenfell to Frewen, October 17, 1885, Bland to Frewen, September 9, 1886; I. C. Michaels to Frewen, November 6, 1886; L. S. Lathrop to Frewen, June 4, 1889: all in *Moreton Frewen Papers*; R. P. Bland, "The Restoration of Silver," *Forum* (November 1886); *Free Coinage of Silver. House Report No. 524. Part 2.* 49th Cong., 1st Ses. (Washington, 1886); and *Bradstreet's*, January 23, November 13, 1886.

105. *Free Coinage of Silver*, 6; Stewart to E. D. Stark, July 9, *Stewart Mss.*; *The Newspaper*, March 14, 1899; *Public Opinion* (August 25, 1888), 428; Indiana State Grange, *Proceedings for 1886*; Dunning, *Alliance History*, 41; Illinois State Grange, petition of March 29, 1886, and Memorial of International Bi-Metallic Coinage Association, 1886: *NA* 46, Sen. 49A-H1.3 and H9; *Western Rural*, February 13, March 6, 1886; *Farmers Review*, April 7, 1886; Oregon State Grange, *Journal of Proceedings for 1887*; and *Report of the Eighth Annual Farmers Congress, Topeka, Kansas, November 14-16, 1888* (Omaha, 1889).

106. See, in particular, the materials in *Arguments and Statements before the House Committee on Commerce* [on] *Certain Bills Proposing Congressional Regulation of Interstate Commerce. House Miscellaneous Document 55.* 47th Cong., 1st Ses. (Washington, 1882).

107. See *Hearings of the House Committee on Commerce on the Improvement of the Mississippi River. House Miscellaneous Document No. 56.* 47th Cong., 1st Ses. (Washington, 1882); *CR*, 13:3:2983-2988.

108. *House Committee on Commerce . . . Regulation of Interstate Commerce*, 43; Memorial from Illinois State Legislature to the House Committee on Mississippi River and Canal Improvements, *NA* 233, HR 48A-H26.2.

109. *Western Rural*, July 4, October 4, December 27, 1884; May 29, June 5, and November 20, 1886. Also see *Rural New Yorker*, March 10, 1883.

110. *American Farmer*, January 1881; Oregon State Grange, *Journal of Proceedings for 1882*. On the theory see A. Marshall, *Industry and Trade* (London, 1932), 742; and N. Rosenberg, "Some Institutional Aspects of *The Wealth of Nations*," Journal of Political Economy (1960), 557-570. I also found the following more general studies helpful: P. L. Berger and T. Luckmann, *The Social Construction of Reality* (Garden City, 1966); B. H. Hibbard, *Marketing Agricultural Products* (New York, 1922); J. A. Schumpeter, *History of Economic Analysis* (New York, 1954); V. P. Timoshenko, *The Role of Agricultural Fluctuations in the Business Cycle* (Ann Arbor, 1930); and W. Trimble, "Historical Aspects of the Surplus Food Production of the United States, 1862-1902," *Annual Report of the American Historical Association for 1918* (Washington, 1921). One of the most illuminating discussions of the time occurred between Governor W. Larrabee of Iowa and George S. Perkins, president of the Chicago, Burlington and Quincy Railroad. It can be followed in Perkins to Larrabee, July 18, 1887; Larrabee to Perkins, July 21, 1887; Perkins to Larrabee, August 5, 1887; Larrabee to Perkins, August 9, 1887; Perkins to Larrabee, August 16, 1887; and Larrabee to Perkins, December 19, 1887: *Chicago, Burlington and Quincy Collection*.

111. See, among the many examples, the testimony of the Worthy Masters of the Tennessee and California Granges in *Report of the Senate Select Committee on Interstate Commerce. With Appendix. Senate Report No. 46. Part 1.* 49th Cong., 1st Ses. (Washington, 1886), 1:A:111-113, 116-117; and *Hearings of the House Committee on Commerce on the Improvement of the Mississippi*, 13-14.

112. *Senate Select Committee on Interstate Commerce*, 1:A:73, 157-160; and esp. the testimony of Joseph Medill of the Chicago *Tribune* (from which the quotation is taken), *Senate Committee on Labor and Capital*, 2:965-967, 974, 988, 990, and also 970-971, 12000. On flour shipping and livestock growers' complaints, see the materials in the *Washburn, Davis, Dunwoody*, and *Edgar Mss.*, and the correspondence in the *WSGA Mss.* Also see *Bradstreet's*, February 20, 1886.

113. See the careful analysis of such matters by the Committee on Agriculture of the Massachusetts State Grange, *Journal of Proceedings for 1885*. On the profits, see R. C. Overton, *Burlington Route. A History of the Burlington Lines* (New York, 1965), 215. Then see *Bradstreet's*, October 25, 1884, January 10, 1885; and H. C. Farnsworth, "Decline and Recovery of Wheat Prices in the Nineties," *Wheat Studies* (June-July 1934), 289.

114. *The New York Times*, January 5, 1884; *Western Rural*, March 31, 1883.

115. See, for example, D. B. Henderson to Clarkson, January 5, 1885: *James S. Clarkson Papers;* and E. C. Brook, "The struggle for the adoption of the Interstate Commerce Commission, 1872 - 1887," PhD Thesis, University of Chicago, 1925, 193.

116. Cullom to H. D. Lloyd, December 18, 1886: *Lloyd Mss.*

117. See the first three reports of the Commission for the efforts to use the institution (III, 141-142, for example); and for the trouble over export rates (as in II, 692-695). The literature on railroad regulation is enormous. In addition to the materials already cited, those items that provided the most direct help for the period prior to the Populist movement are as follows: F. Andrews, *Railroads and Farming. U.S.D.A. Bureau of Statistics, Bullentin No. 100* (Washington, 1912); F. A. Dixon, *State Railroad Control with a History of Its Development in Iowa* (New York, 1896); J. F. Doster, *Alabama's First Railroad Commission, 1881-1885* (University of Alabama, 1949); H. E. Erdman, *The Farmers' Elevator Movement in Ohio* (Wooster, 1918); P. W. Gates, *The Illinois Central Railroad and Its Colonization Work* (Cambridge, 1934); W. F. Gephart, *Transportation and Industrial Development in the Middle West* (New York, 1909); A. T. Hadley, *Railroad Transportation: Its History and Its Laws* (New York, 1886); J. B. Hedges, *Henry Villard and the Railways of the Northwest* (New Haven, 1930); L. B. Irwin, *Pacific Railways and Nationalism in the Canadian-American Northwest, 1845-1873* (Philadelphia, 1939); G. Kolko, *Railroads and Regulations, 1877-1916* (Princeton, 1965); R. L. Kramer, *The History of Export and Import Railroad Rates and Their Effect Upon the Foreign Trade of the United States* (Philadelphia, 1923); R. A. Clemen, "Waterways in Livestock and Meat Trade," *American Economic Review* (1926), 640-652; A. W. Currie, "British Attitudes Towards Investment in North American Railroads," *Business History Review* (1960), 194-216; D. T. Gilchrist, "Albert Fink and the Pooling System," *ibid.* (1960), 24-49; C. A. Harper, "The Railroad and the Prairie," *Transactions of the Illinois State Historical Society* (1923), 102-110; J. B. Hedges, "The Colonization Work of the Northern Pacific Railroad," *Mississippi Valley Historical Review* (1926), 311-342; L. Jenks, "Britain and American Railroad Development," *Journal of Economic History* (1951), 375-388; S. N. Murray, "Railroads and the Agricultural Development of the Red River Valley of the North, 1870-1890," *Agricultural History* (1957), 57-66; J. B. Rae, "Commissioner Sparks and the Railroad Land Grants," *Mississippi Valley Historical Review* (1938), 211-230; O. N. Refsell, "The Farmers' Elevator Movement," *Journal of Political Economy* (1914), 872-895; C. J. Smith, "Early Development of Railroads in the Pacific Northwest," *Washington Historical Quarterly* (1922), 243-250; G. G. Tunnel, "The Diversion of the Flour and Grain Traffic from the Great Lakes to the Railroads," *Journal of Political Economy* (1897), 340-375. It may be useful to remind the reader that this is not primarily a study of railroad regulation, but rather a study that offers a new context for understanding the drive for regulation. Hence none of the secondary sources have been as helpful as the PhD work of Howard Schonberger; and the analysis here is based very largely on the primary materials.

118. *Progressive Farmer*, April 28, 1887.

119. Colorado State Grange, *Journal of Proceedings for 1888; Breeder's Gazette,* November 10, 1887.

120. G. F. Spin to Lamont, March 31, 1885: *Grover Cleveland Papers;* S. L. M. Barlow to Marble, February 26, 1885: *Marble Mss.*

121. Bayard to Wilson, May 16, 1885: *Thomas Bayard Papers.*

122. Foster to Gresham, September 28, October 26, 1884: *Walter Quintin Gresham Papers.*

123. G. K. Thorndike to Sen. Edmunds, December 29, 1884, January 19, 1885: *NA* 46 S48A-H10; Petition of New York Chamber of Commerce, December 28, 1884; Petition of New York Produce Exchange, December 29, 1884: *NA* 233 HR48A-H30.12; but see also the Western petitions and memorials in those files. The connection between Cuba and the Philippines was made by the Bath, Maine, Board of Trade, February 23, 1885.

124. "CUBA-ANNEX": *Cleveland Mss.*

125. Hewitt to Cleveland, March 29, 1885; S. M. Weed to Cleveland, April 18, 1885: *Cleveland Mss.*

126. Bayard to Cleveland, November 25, 1885: *ibid.*

127. W. R. Morrison to Marble, December 24, 1885: *Marble Mss.;* also see Frewen to W. H. Hulbert, November or December, 1885, passed on to Secretary of the Treasury

Manning: *Frewen Mss.*; and *Bradstreet's*, April 10, 1886. Also see Richardson, *Messages*, 10:4993.

128. For the continuing pressure on Cleveland, see: A. B. Farquhar (agricultural implements entrepreneur and important Pennsylvania Democrat) to Cleveland, March 8, 1886: *Cleveland Mss.*; Atlanta *Constitution*, September 30, 1887; Petitions from Fontoult, Minnesota, 1888: *NA* 46, S50A-J10.1. For the response, see Bayard to Curry, February 23, 1886: *NA* 59; Richardson, *Messages*, 11:5074-5075; and Bayard to Senator Call, August 29, 1888: *Bayard Mss.*

129. Naval appropriations for the Cleveland years were as follows (in millions): 1885, $14.98; 1886, $15.07; 1887, $16.50; and 1888, $25.77: *Naval Appropriations Bill. House Report 930.* 56th Cong., 1st Ses. (Washington, 1900), 20. The Administration's attitude can be reviewed in G. F. Parker, *Recollections of Grover Cleveland* (New York, 1909), 88, and the materials in the *Bayard, Cleveland,* and *Marble Mss.*, and in the William C. Whitney files in *NA* 80. Also see Bayard's earlier remarks in *CR*, 15:2:1456. On Venezuela consult Phelps to Bayard, October 30, 1886; Phelps to Lord Salisbury, February 8, 1887: *NA* 59; and Bayard to Wells, April 28, 1887: *Bayard Mss.*

130. There was no significant agrarian protest via petitions or memorials: see *NA* 46 and 233, S49A-H16, HR50A-H19.2. Much of the delay, as the Senate acknowledged, continued to arise from practical and technological difficulties rather than from ideological or political opposition. "The evidence we submit shows that no private or public establishment is prepared to furnish the heavy masses of metal for the guns. . . . They lack the experience that is needed for the immediate, perfect production of the steel best adapted for heavy guns and armor." *Report of the Select Committee on Ordnance and War Ships. Senate Report No. 90.* 49th Cong., 1st Ses. (Washington, 1886), xvii.

131. See, for example, the House Resolutions of February 8, December 11, 1883, January 7, 1884, January 26, 1886, February 23, 1886, and January 4, 1888; then consult *American Commerce and Arbitration. House Report No. 1648.* 49th Cong., 1st Ses. (Washington, 1886), 1-3, 9; *Bradstreet's*, April 11, 1885; A. D. Anderson to Cleveland, September 19, 1885: *Cleveland Mss.*; and Wells to W. C. P. Breckinridge, March 23, 1888: *William C. P. Breckinridge Papers.*

132. *CR*, 19:2:1655-1661.

133. Taylor, *Chicago Board of Trade*, 2:710; *Breeder's Gazette*, February 26, 1885; Sturgis to Coleman, April 24, 1885: *WSGA Mss.*; J. A. McShane to Dawes, May 13, 1885: *Dawes Mss.*; *Cr*, 16:3:2028.

134. *Address of Hon. Norman J. Coleman and Dr. D. E. Salmon before the Third National Convention of Stockmen, Chicago, November 17-18, 1885* (Washington, 1885); *Breeder's Gazette*, November 19, 1885; *Prairie Farmer*, November 28, 1885; and, on the general situation, see Brayer, "Range Country Troubles: 1885," *Westerner's Brand Book* (Denver, 1952), 171-185; and Cleveland's message of December 8, 1885, in Richardson, *Messages*, 10:4910-4912, 4916.

135. Frewen, *Memories*, 213-219; Sturgis to Frewen, June 20, August 8, 1884; H. M. Swift to Commission of British Agriculture (on to Frewen), September 3, 1884: *Frewen Mss.*; Sturgis, Annual Report for 1884: *WSGA Mss.*; Cheyenne *Democratic Leader*, August 24, 1884; and the studies by Osgood and Jackson.

136. *National Live Stock Journal* (March and June 1886); *Breeder's Gazette*, February 11, 1886; *Western Rural*, April 3, 1886.

137. *Breeder's Gazette*, July 1, 1886; *Western Rural*, August 14, 1886; *Rural New Yorker*, November 6, 1886. Also see the December 1886 issue of the *National Live Stock Journal*, which carries an excellent review of the demands for action.

138. *CR*, 17:2:1760; 17:3:2409; and see Chicago *Tribune*, February 26, 1886.

139. Bayard to Thompson, February 12, 1886: *NA* 59; Bayard to White, October 16, 1887: in C. C. Tansill, *The Foreign Policy of Thomas F. Bayard, 1885-1897* (New York 1940), 273; Report of J. B. Grinnell, 1884: *WSGA Mss.*

140. A. Larson, "The Winter of 1886-1887 in Wyoming," *Annals of Wyoming* (1942), 5-17; L. Atherton, *The Cattle Kings* (Bloomington, 1961), 154; M. Frink, *Cow Country Cavalcade* (Denver, 1954), 101.

141. Hesse to H. C. Plunkett, January 24, February 13, 1887: *Fred G. Hesse Papers.* The subsequent troubles can be followed in *Paririe Farmer*, April 9, June 27, 1887; Omaha *Bee*, February 2, 1888; Warren to J. H. Gray, December 20, 1888: *Warren Mss.*; and *Breeder's Gazette*, January 23, 1889.

142. Cleveland, message of February 16, 1887: Richardson, *Messages*, 11:5142.

143. *Breeder's Gazette*, February 1, 1888; Chicago *Tribune*, March 22, 1888; the petitions in *NA* 233, HR 50A-H10.4; Cleveland's special message of March 27, 1888: Richardson, *Messages*, 11:5197; *Message from the President . . . Relative to the Prevalence of Disease Among Animals in Europe*. Senate Executive Document No. 129. 50th Cong., 1st Ses. (Washington, 1888). An excellent account of this split in contained James B. Erlenborn's MA Thesis, University of Wisconsin. As an outline of the division, see *Report on the Transportation and Sale of Meat Products*. Senate Report No. 829. 51st Cong., 1st Ses. (Washington, 1890); *Breeder's Gazette*, July 4, 1888, January 23, February 15, 1889; October 22, 1890; February 11, June 2, and September 30, 1891; August 24, 1892; *National Stockman*, May 10, 1889, and March 6, 1890: and the files of the *Drovers Journal*, and the *Taylor County* (Texas) *News*.

144. *Western Rural*, August 28, 1886. On the role of the export push in changing attitudes, see: J. G. Gazley, *American Opinion of German Unification, 1848-1871* (New York, 1926); M. O. Kolbeck, *American Opinion on the Kulturkampf* (Washington, 1942); C. E. Schieber, *The Transformation of American Sentiment Toward Germany 1870-1914* (Boston, 1923); and below.

145. Tansill, *Bayard*, 28, and see the Western support in *CR*, 20:1492; 20:2:1119, 1283-1290, 1325, 1335-1337; and *Public Opinion* (January 26, 1889), 322.

146. *CR*, 14:2:1909. But also see *ibid.*, 14:2:1677-1750; 15:4:3550-3552; and *Report of the Secretary of the Treasury for 1885*, and *1886*.

147. *Bradstreet's*, February 3, 1883. On the fears, see J. Lyman to Chandler, September 20, 1884, White to Chandler, October 1, 1884, and Price to Chandler, October 10, 1884: all in *William E. Chandler Papers*. Then consult E. G. Hay to W. Barker, January 11, 1887: *Eugene Gano Hay Papers*; letters in *Bradstreet's*, July 1, June 24, 1882; *Report of the Tariff Commission of 1882*. House Miscellaneous Document No. 6, 47th Cong., 2nd Ses. (Washington, 2 volumes, 1882), 1:217, 229, 1075; 2:1493-1495, 1498; Massachusetts Grange, *Journal of Proceedings for 1883*; and *Western Rural*, April 12, 1884.

148. Hay to Swank, June 9, 1887: *E. G. Hay Mss.*; *Bradstreet's*, October 20, 1883.

149. The State Historical Society of the State of Wisconsin has a vast collection of Swank pamphlets, though they can be found in most libraries that preserve such materials. On McKinley, see *CR*, 15:6:A:137-138; and *Reduction of Tariff and Collection of the Revenue*. House Report 1620. 49th Cong., 1st Ses. (Washington, 1886), 17, 19.

150. Bayard to Phelps, November 21, 1887: *Bayard Mss.*

151. Horace S. Merrill, in *Bourbon Democracy of the Middle West, 1865-1896* (Baton Rouge, 1953), and in his biography of Vilas, has done much to delineate the outlook and dilemmas of these Westerners who identified with the metropolis, yet who had to survive in the agricultural sector of the political economy. See, for example, *Vilas*, 52-54, 78-79, 124-131, and 203-204.

152. Cleveland, message of December 6, 1887: Richardson, *Messages*, 11:5165-5170; and *Report of the Secretary of the Treasury for 1886*, li-lii.

153. On the Republican fears of just such a development, see Swank to Sherman, February 16, 1888: *Sherman Mss.*; and Spooner to Rusk, October 10, 1888: *Jeremiah M. Rusk Papers*.

154. W. Barker to W. Morrill, December 8, 1884: *Cleveland Mss.*

Chapter Twelve

1. Blaine, the "Paris Letter" of December 7, 1887.

2. *Western Rural*, December 25, 1886; Teller to Gresham, May 19, 1888: *Henry M. Teller Papers*; and Sage, *Allison*, 208-209.

3. See the materials in the *Rusk Mss.*

4. Warren to J. W. Meldrum, March 29, 1889: *Warren Mss.* Then see Harrison to Blaine, September 26, 1891: A. T. Volwiler, *The Correspondence Between Benjamin Harrison and James G. Blaine: 1882-1893* (Philadelphia, 1940).

5. *CR*, 18:1:634-635.

6. H. Clews to Sherman, August 24, 1888, Sherman to Clews, August 27, 1888: *Sherman Mss.*

7. *Breeder's Gazette*, August 8, 1888; speech in the House of May 15, 1879 (quoted

extensively by R. M. McElroy, *Levi Parsons Morton. Banker, Diplomat and Statesman* [New York, 1930], 87-88).

8.   Porter and Johnson, *National Party Platforms; Official Proceedings of the Republican National Convention, 1888* (Minneapolis, 1903), 108-112. Also see Sievers, *Harrison*, 266.

9.   Petition of Farmers Alliance of Nebraska, January 24, 1888: *NA* 233, HR 50A-H30.21; W. D. Hoard to H. C. Adams, August 15, 1888: *Henry Cullen Adams Papers;* Plumb to Harrison, July 3, 1888: *Harrison Mss.;* Medill to Allison, September 23, 1888: *Allison Mss.*

10.   Peele to Kasson, July 11, 1888: *Kasson Mss.*

11.   Harrison, remarks of July 31, 1888, and Letter of Acceptance of September 11, 1888: C. Hedges (ed.), *Speeches of Benjamin Harrison* (New York, 1892), 68, 114.

12.   Matt Quay, quoted in E. A. White, "The Republican Party in National Politics, 1888-1891," PhD Thesis, University of Wisconsin, 1941, 235.

13.   Sievers, *Harrison*, 371-406; White, "Republican Party," 240-249.

14.   For example, see L. T. Michener to S. Elkins, July 30, 1888: *Elkins Mss.*

15.   Blaine to Harrison, June 26, 1888: Volwiler, *Correspondence*, 28; H. S. Blaine Beale (ed.), *Letters of Mrs. James G. Blaine. Two Volumes* (New York, 1908), 2:211; Blaine to Phelps and Hitt, September 1, 1888: Hamilton, *Blaine*, 609-610; and Blaine to Reid, 1885: *Whitelaw Reid Papers.*

16.   Noble, remarks of May 1, 1889: *Proceedings of the Banquet of the Spanish-American Commercial Union, New York, May 1, 1889* (New York, 1889), 8-12.

17.   Quoted in Morgan, *Wheel and Alliance*, 33; J. W. Mackie, letter to the editor, *Pacific Rural Press*, January 13, 1889.

18.   Massachusetts State Grange, *Journal of Proceedings for 1889.* Also see *Bradstreet's*, June 8, 1889.

19.   W. W. Girton to T. C. Richmond, June 30, July 12, 1889: *Thomas C. Richmond Papers.*

20.   Warren to Carey, February 4, 1889: *Warren Mss.*

21.   *Pacific Rural Press*, January 12, 1889; S. G. Comstock to W. D. Washburn, May 14, 1889: *Davis Mss.*

22.   W. H. Ballou, "The West vs. the South," *Frank Leslie's Illustrated Newspaper*, November 23, 1889; *National Economist*, September 28, 1889.

23.   A. B. Shepperson, *Cotton Facts. A Compilation from Official and Reliable Sources of the Crops, Receipts, Exports, Stocks* (New York, 1890), 27; and see the testimony in *Report of the Industrial Commission on the Relations and Conditions of Capital and Labor*, 10:46-50.

24.   *Manufacturers Record*, August 10, 1889; *Bradstreet's* July 20, May 18, June 15, August 17, 1889.

25.   *Report of the Industrial Commission*, 14:529; *Bradstreet's*, May 31, 1890.

26.   Millers National Association to Blaine, August 15, 1889; Richmond, Virginia, Chamber of Commerce to Harrison, September 27, 1889: *NA* 43, Records of the Conference of American States.

27.   Blaine to Reid, June 11, July 8, 27, 1889: *NA* 59; *Breeder's Gazette*, November 27, December 18, 1889; Omaha Board of Trade to Blaine, September [?], 1889; and American Short Horn Breeder's Association to Blaine, November 30, 1889: *NA* 43.

28.   *Breeder's Gazette*, April 2, 1890, August 21, 1889.

29.   *Ibid.*, January 30, 1889.

30.   *Girard Herald*, March 16, 1889; *National Economist*, June 29, August 17, 1889; Oregon State Grange, *Journal of Proceedings for 1889.*

31.   Stewart to Harrison, February 5, 1889: *Stewart Mss.* E. M. Mack reproduces a good many significant Stewart letters in her thesis, "Life and Letters of William Morris Stewart, 1827-1909."

32.   Stewart to Windom, March 12, 1889; Stewart to W. A. A. Carsey, March 3, 1889: *ibid.*

33.   *Bradstreet's*, April 20, 1889.

34.   Stewart to Harrison, April 30, 1889: *Stewart Mss.*

35.   M. M. Este to Clarkson, May 8, 1889: *Clarkson Mss.*

36.   *Pacific Rural Press*, May 11, June 29, 1889. Also see Northern Alliance, *Journal of Proceedings for 1890.*

37.   *Breeder's Gazette*, September 25, 1889; J. G. Carlisle, "The Tariff and the Farmer,"

Forum (January 1890), 484; and see the 1890 Constitution of Wyoming, I, Section 30. Professor Barnes' biographical study of John G. Carlisle is one of the essential studies of this period.

38. *Bradstreet's*, September 7, 1889; National Farmers Congress, *Journal of Proceedings for 1889;* Connelley, *Plumb*, 317-318; Springfield *Republican*, clipping in 1889 folder of *William McKendree Springer Papers*, undated.

39. National Grange, *Journal of Proceedings for the Session of 1889*, and *1890*.

40. *National Economist*, March 30, October 12, 1889.

41. *Breeder's Gazette*, September 25, 1889; P. Armour, testimony before the Vest Committee, 1889.

42. New York State Grange, *Journal of Proceedings for 1889; Pacific Rural Press*, February 2, June 15, October 12, 1889.

43. *Pacific Rural Press*, August 3, 1889. The *Rural New Yorker*, May 17, 1890, carries a perceptive editorial on this split over methods and tactics.

44. *Breeder's Gazette*, February 27, April 8, 1889.

45. The Korean operation can be followed in F. H. Harrington, *God, Mammon, and the Japanese* (Madison, 1944).

46. See, for example, Harrison to Blaine, January 17, 1889: Volwiler, *Correspondence.*

47. As a typical warning, see the open letter from Steelle, *Farmer's Voice*, October 19, 1889; and the petitions for equal tariff protection in *NA* 46, S50A-J9.2.

48. Short Horn Breeder's Association, resolution of November 20, 1889: *NA* 46 S51A-J1.3; J. H. Pickrell, secretary of the same group, to Blaine, November 30, 1889; Omaha Board of Trade to Blaine, November 1, 1889; Produce Exchange of Chicago to Blaine, September 28, 1889; J. R. G. Pitkin to Blaine, July 3, 1889; J. F. Hanson to Blaine, July 30, 1889; Harrison to Blaine, July 30, 1889; F. G. Bingley to W. E. Curtiss, August 26, 1889: all in *NA* 43; *Pacific Rural Press*, September 14, November 2, 1889; and *Northwestern Miller*, July 12, 1889.

49. Milwaukee *Sentinel*, May 20, 1890; *Breeder's Gazette*, November 27, 1889, March 12, 1890; many of the petitions in *NA* 46, 233, are reprinted in *American Merchant Marine in the Foreign Trade. House Report 1210*. 51st Cong., 1st Ses. (Washington, 1890); *National Economist*, September 13, 1890.

50. *Bradstreet's*, October 5, 1889.

51. *Report of the Ninth Annual National Farmers Congress, Montgomery, Alabama, November 13-15, 1889* (Macedonia, 1890); National Grange, *Journal of Proceedings for the Session of 1889.*

52. W. A. Peffer, "The Farmer's Defensive Movement," *Forum* (December 1889), 464, 468.

53. *Proceedings of the Farmers and Laborers Union of America at St. Louis, December 3 to 7, 1889* (Washington, 1890); T. E. Watson, *Peoples Party Campaign Book* (author's edition, 1894), 111, "Report of the Committee on Demands, December 6, 1889."

54. *The Sub-Treasury System As proposed by the Farmers Alliance. Library of National Economist Extras. Volume I, Nos. 6 and 7, June and July 1891* (Washington, 1891), Chapters X, XII, especially 9-32; Macune's report to the St. Louis convention in Watson, *Campaign Book*, 111-117; New York *Mail and Express*, December 3, 1890; *Consular Report No. 109* (October 1889), 227-228, and *Rural New Yorker*, March 15, 1890, for typical reports on Russian projects that concerned the American farm businessmen. Also see *System of Sub-Treasuries. House Report No. 2143*. 52nd Cong., 1st Ses. (Washington, 1892); E. T. Peters, *Cooperative Credit Associations in Certain European Countries. U.S.D.A., Division of Statistics. Miscellaneous Series. Report No. 3* (Washington, 1892); J. D. Hicks, "The Sub-Treasury: A Forgotten Plan for the Relief of Agriculture," *Mississippi Valley Historical Review* (1928), 355-373; J. C. Malin, "The Farmers' Alliance Sub-Treasury Plan and European Precedents," *ibid.* (1944), 255-260; and C. C. Post, "The Sub-Treasury Plan," *Arena* (February 1892), 342-353.

55. H. Tracy, "The Sub-Treasury Plan," in Dunning, *Farmers Alliance*, 336-354.

56. *Pacific Rural Press*, May 30, July 4, August 1, 1891; then see *Rural New Yorker*, January 17, May 23, 1891; *National Economist*, February 4, 1891; and Post, "Sub-Treasury."

57. See the hundreds of petitions in *NA* 233, HR51A-H23.11 and *NA* 46, S51A-J1.3; those listed from twenty-four states in *CR*, 21: Index, 667; and, as typical, *Indiana Farmer*, May 24, 1890, *Kansas Farmer*, April 16, 1890.

58. *Country Gentleman*, April 21, 1890; *Rural New Yorker*, September 13, 1890 (editorial and article by F. Grundy).

59. *Pacific Rural Press*, April 5, 1890; petition from Delaware farmers, 1890, *NA 46*, S51A-J9.14; *Farm, Fireside and Stockman*, April 26, 1890; memorial from Farmers Mutal Benefit Association, March 19, 1890: *NA 233*, H51A-H5.1; and *National Stockman and Farm*, July 24, 1890.

60. Petition of Farmers of Minnehaha County, Minnesota, March 14, 1890: *NA 46*, S51A-J1.3.

61. *Country Gentleman*, October 16, 1890. Then see *Pacific Rural Press*, February 22, August 2, 1890; *Rural New Yorker*, March 1, 1890; *Country Gentleman*, May 15, 1890; J. E. Russell, *Speeches*, 37-38, 307, 343-347; and esp. the long discussion in *American Agriculturalist*, March and April 1890.

62. *Non-Conformist*, May 1, 1890; Michigan State Grange, petition of February 3, 1890: *NA 233*, HR51A-H5.1.

63. *National Stockman and Farm*, February 6, 1890; *Prairie Farmer*, May 24, 1890.

64. *American Agriculturalist*, May 1890; *Pacific Rural Press*, March 8, 1890; W. A. Peffer, petition of January 13, 1890: *NA 233*, H51A-H5.1; *Farm, Fireside and Stockman*, March 8, 1890; Cotner, *Hogg*, 74.

65. *National Economist*, March 1, 1890; Dunning, *Farmers Alliance*, 138-180.

66. *American Cultivator*, February 22, 1890; *Pacific Rural Press*, February 15, August 30, 1890; H. C. Adams, "Decoration Day Address, 1890": *Adams Mss.*; New York State Grange, *Journal of Proceedings for 1890*; and Cotner, *Hogg*, 81.

67. *Farmers Advocate*, April 16, 1890.

68. See Harrison's remarks in his last annual message of December 6, 1892: Richardson, *Messages*, 12:5763-5764. The most helpful materials beyond the manuscript sources have been: *Further Correspondence Relating to Diseases of Animals in the United States of America. Presented to both Houses of Parliament* (London, 1881); U.S.D.A., *Selected Correspondence Relating to the Export Trade of the United States in Live Stock and Meat Products. Report No. 53* (Washington, 1893); *House Executive Document No. 267, March 2, 1885*. 48th Cong., 2nd Ses. (Washington, 1885); *House Executive Document No. 159*. 48th Cong., 1st Ses. (Washington, 1884); *House Executive Document No. 35*. 47th Cong., 2nd Ses. (Washington, 1883); *House Executive Document No. 106*. 48th Cong., 1st Ses. (Washington, 1884); *House Executive Document No. 209*. 47th Cong., 1st Ses. (Washington, 1882); *Senate Executive Document No. 129*. 50th Cong., 1st Ses. (Washington, 1888); *Senate Report No. 596*. 50th Cong., 1st Ses. (Washington, 1888); *Senate Report No. 829*. 51st Cong., 1st Ses. (Washington, 1890), the Vest Committee Report; *Annual Reports, Together with Selected Correspondence . . . of Jeremiah M. Rusk, 1889-1892* (Washington, 1893); G. M. Gressley, *Bankers and Cattlemen* (New York, 1965); H. Hedges, *Economic Aspects of the Cattle Industry of the Nebraska Sand Hills* (Lincoln, 1928); G. K. Holmes, *Meat in Foreign Markets* (Washington, 1905); J. A. Hopkins, *Economic History of the Production of Beef Cattle in Iowa* (Iowa City, 1928); J. Nimmo, *Report in Regard to the Range and Ranch Cattle Business of the United States* (Washington, 1885); E. S. Osgood, *The Day of the Cattleman* (Chicago, 1957); H. E. Alvord, "The American Cattle Trade," *Journal of the Royal Agricultural Society of England* (1877), 356-374; H. C. Clark, "Meat Industries of the United States," *Annual Report of the Bureau of Animal Industry, 1887-1888*, 359-375; B. Duncan, "Protectionism and Pork: Whitelaw Reid as Diplomat: 1889-1891," *Agricultural History* (1959), 190-195; M. Frewen, "The Trans-Atlantic Cattle Trade," *Fortnightly Review* (1891), 713-724; J. L. Gignilliat, "Pigs, Politics, and Protection: The European Boycott of American Pork, 1879-1891," *Agricultural History* (1961), 3-12; F. R. Rutter, "Foreign Restrictions on American Meat," U.S.D.A., *Yearbook for 1906*, 247-264; D. E. Salmon, "The Federal Meat Inspection," U.S.D.A., *Yearbook for 1894*, 67-80; L. L. Snyder, "The American-German Pork Dispute, 1879-1891," *Journal of Modern History* (1945), 16-28; W. D. Zimmerman, "Live Cattle Export Trade Between United States and Great Britain, 1868-1885," *Agricultural History* (1962), 46-52; R. M. Packard, "The French Pork Prohibition in American Diplomacy, 1881-1891," PhD Thesis, Harvard University, 1954; and J. W. Whitaker, "The Rise and Development of Beef Cattle Feeding in Illinois and Iowa, 1840-1900," PhD Thesis, University of Wisconsin, 1965.

69. *Breeder's Gazette*, April 3, March 6, 1889.

70. See, for example, Reid to Harrison, Personal, January 24, 1890: *Reid Mss.*

71. Rusk, speech of September 18, 1889, St. Joseph, Missouri; J. M. Clark to Rusk, November 17, 1889: *Rusk Mss;* and Rusk to Blaine, November 2, 1889: *NA* 59.

72. *Breeder's Gazette*, January 29, 1890; *National Stockman and Farm*, January 30, 1890; *American Cultivator*, February 1, 1890; Rusk to E. H. Funston, February 3, 1890: *NA* 16; *CR*, 21:2:1193, 1716; 21:3:2070-2072; 21:4:3057-3058.

73. Sanders to Rusk, February 11, 1890: *Rusk Mss.; Breeder's Gazette*, February 12, 1890.

74. Rusk to Blaine, February 18, 1890: *NA* 16 and 59.

75. Blaine to Lincoln (and Rusk), March 4, 1890: *NA* 59.

76. Rusk, letter to the editor, *Breeder's Gazette*, March 19, 1890; Reid to Vignaud, April 3, 1890, Reid to Phelps, May 3, 1890: *Reid Mss.;* and *CR*, 21:3:2070-2072; 21:4:3056-3058 (the bill passed April 5, 1890); for the pressure see, for example, Star Alliance of Fillmore County, Nebraska, to the Senate, March 14, 1890, and *Breeder's Gazette*, February 19, March 19, and April 2, 1890.

77. Chicago *Tribune*, July 16, 1890; Comstock to Wellman, April 11, 1890: *Comstock Mss.;* New York *Tribune*, March 27, 28, 1890; and R. M. LaFollette, *Autobiography*, 49-50.

78. Chicago *Tribune*, March 31, 1890.

79. See the petitions from Nebraska, Kansas, Missouri, Virginia, Kentucky, and New Jersey in *NA* 233, HR51A-H23.2.

80. *Prairie Farmer*, March 15, May 3, 1890; Farmers Alliance of Leavenworth County, Kansas, petition of March 3, 1890: *NA* 46, S51A-J9.3; Union Alliance of Iowa to Allison, April 15, 1890: *Allison Mss.; Rural New Yorker*, April 12, May 3, June 14, 1890; *National Stockman*, May 1, 8, 15, 1890; *American Cultivator*, May 3, 1890.

81. *CR*, 21:3:2377-2378; also see 21:5:4576.

82. J. C. Dietz to Allison, January 25, 1890: *Allison Mss.*

83. Keyes to Spooner, March 14, 1890: *Elisha William Keyes Papers;* B. Johnson to Allison, March 19, 1890, and R. Donahue to Allison, May 27, 1890: *Allison Mss.*, which are clear warning letters.

84. *CR*, 20:2:1247; Reid to W. W. Phelps, May 3, 1890: *Reid Mss.*

85. E. S. Elliott to Gregory, April 9, 1890: *John Goadby Gregory Papers.*

86. Blaine to McKinley, April 10, 1890: Hamilton, *Blaine*, 683. On Hitt's report of May 1, 1890, see *Reciprocity Treaties. House Report No. 1827.* 51st Cong., 1st Ses. (Washington, 1890), 1.

87. Rusk to the New York *Daily Tribune*, April 21 (published April 23), 1890: *Rusk Mss.;* Reid to Phelps, May 3, 1890, Reid to Blaine, June 19, 20, 1890: all in *Reid Mss.*

88. *CR*, 21:5:4247-4254; and see McKinley's position as reported by L. L. Gage, *Memoirs* (Chicago, 1927), 90.

89. *CR*, 21:5:4257-4265.

90. Stewart to H. B. Kelly, March 11, 1890; Stewart to T. Nelson, E. C. Hardy, and W. Schmidt, April 15, 1890: *Stewart Mss.* Also see Comstock to J. W. Porter, May 20, 1890: *Comstock Mss.;* and W. Barker to Allison, September 16, 1890: *Allison Mss.*

91. The direct confrontation with the issue can be reviewed in the *Southern Mercury*, September 6, 1894, and March 14, 21, 28, 1895; Girard *Herald*, February 22, 1890, March 26, 1892; *American Cultivator*, March 8, 1890; *National Stockman*, June 26, 1890; Chicago *Tribune*, July 9, 1890; *Bradstreet's*, November 15, 1890; *Pacific Rural Press*, August 2, 1890; *Rural New Yorker*, February 28, April 11, July 25, 1891; the petitions in *NA* 46, S51A-F27, 51A-J9 and J26.1; and *CR*, 21:1:522, 753, 21:2:1077.

92. *CR*, 21:2:1135.

93. *Proceedings of the First National Silver Convention, St. Louis, November 26-28, 1889* (St. Louis, 1889).

94. Farmers of Hampstead County, Arkansas, petition of May 1, 1890: *NA* 233, HR51A-H5.1; J. B. Colgate to Allison, March 19, 1890: *Allison Mss.; CR*, 21:7:6454-6455. The thousands of petitions are in *NA* 46, S51A-K12 and J9.1; and *NA* 233, HR51A-H5.1. Typical press articles and accounts are *Pacific Rural Press*, August 17, 1889; *Prairie Farmer*, May 10, 1890; *Western Cultivator*, March 1, 1890; *Breeder's Gazette*, June 11, 1890; *Rural New Yorker*, July 19, 1890; *American Cultivator*, July 19, 1890; and *Country Gentleman*, October 2, 1890. Also see *House Report 1086.* 51st Cong., 1st Ses. (Washington, 1890); remarks by Rep. Lind of Minnesota, *CR*, 21:6:5692-5696; and "Lecture by Senator John C. Spooner, October 10, 1890": *Vilas Mss.*

95. Harrison to Blaine, August 15, 29, 1890; Blaine to Harrison, August 22, 1890: *Harrison Mss.;* Lodge to D. A. Gleason, December 15, 1890: *Henry Cabot Lodge Papers;* and Sherman to Clews, August 27, 1888, in answer to Clews to Sherman of August 24, 1888: *Sherman Mss.*

96. *International Monetary Conference Held at Brussels: Report . . . and Journal of the Sessions of November 22, 1892. Senate Executive Document 82.* 52nd Cong., 2nd Ses. (Washington, 1893), 164.

97. J. C. Borcham to Allison, July [?], 1890: *Allison Mss.;* J. H. Taylor to Sherman, September 15, 1890: *Sherman Mss.* Both collections contain letters of warning and protest.

98. On Harrison's role, see Harrison to Blaine, July 17, 23, 1890: in Volwiler, *Correspondence;* M. Dunnel to Harrison, July 24, 1890: *Harrison Mss.;* Harrison, message to the Congress of June 19, 1890: Richardson, *Messages,* 9:74; and New York *Evening Post,* May 7, 1891. On Blaine, see Blaine to McKinley, June 12, 1890: *NA* 233, HR51A-F41.2; Blaine to Frye, July 11, 1890: Hamilton, *Blaine,* 686; and *American Agriculturalist,* March 1893. On Foster, see *Proceedings of the Banquet of the Spanish American Commercial Union, May 1, 1889;* and *Boston Journal,* August 11, 1890.

99. Reid to McKinley, September 1, 1890: *Reid Mss.*

100. *Bradstreet's,* September 6, 1890. This long editorial, which also notes the importance of Hitt's work in the House, is an excellent review of the reciprocity fight. The hat episode is in New York *Tribune,* June 23, 1890.

101. *American Cultivator,* August 16, 1890; *Marine Journal,* August 30, 1890; Memphis *Commercial,* June 26, 1890.

102. *CR,* 219:9204-9207. The enthusiasm of Western farm businessmen is typified in Amboy, Illinois, *Journal,* June 25, 1890; *Prairie Farmer,* June 28, July 19, 1890; Chicago *Tribune,* July 24, September 12, 1890; New York *Tribune,* July 19, 26, August 28, 1890; *Nation,* August 7, 14, 1890; *Rural New Yorker,* August 16, 1890; Nebraska *State Journal,* September 24, 1890; *American Non-Conformist,* October 31, 1889; in the vast number of petitions in *NA* 46 and 233 (S51A-J9.6, J9.9, J10, and K15; and HR51A-F15.9); and in the debates in the Congress.

103. *Bradstreet's,* May 24, June 21, 1890; Blaine to Harrison, July 24, 1890: *Harrison Mss.; Our Day,* September 1890; C. R. Flint to Aldrich, September 21, 1890; Flint to W. E. Curtis, September 3, 1890: *James Franklin Aldrich Papers;* and *CR,* 21:9:9200-9207, 9514; 21:10:9603-9613, 9840, 9863-9864.

104. See *Bankers Magazine,* July, August, and September 1890; Baltimore *Herald,* June 29, 1890; Chicago *Tribune,* August 9, September 15, 1890; *Northwestern Miller,* September 5, 1890; *Dry Goods Economist,* February 8, 15, April 26, May 24, 1890; and petitions such as that of Indiana Millers to Blaine, October 27, 1890, in *NA* 43; and those of New York City and Buffalo merchants in *NA* 46, S51A-K15; and *Iron Age,* February 6, 1890.

105. Reid to Blaine, June 19, 1890: *NA* 59; Reid to Blaine, June 20, July 4, 1890; and Reid to Seckendorf, July 8, 1890; and materials in *Rusk Mss.* and *NA* 16.

106. Reid to Blaine, June 20, 1890: *Reid Mss.;* and see Reid to Elkins, September 1, 1890: *ibid.*

107. On the pressure, see Blaine to Reid, July 8, 27, 1889: *NA* 59; Chicago *Tribune,* August 1, 9, 22, 1890; *Breeder's Gazette,* August 20, October 1, December 10, 1890; *Pacific Rural Press,* August 23, 1890; Madison *Wisconsin Democrat,* August 28, 1890; *Iowa State Register,* August 31, 1890; Denver *Republican,* August 31, 1890; *Massachusetts Ploughman,* September 30, 1890; *American Cultivator,* September 27, 1890. Then see Reid to Blaine, July 4, 1890: *Reid Mss.*

108. Rusk to Crain, July 14, 1890: *NA* 16; Rusk to Blaine, July 23, 1890: *NA* 59; *Breeder's Gazette,* July 16, 1890; Reid to McKinley, September 1, 5, 1890: *Reid Mss.*

109. Comstock to H. C. Waite, June 8, August 18, 1890: *Comstock Mss.*

110. On the intraparty split see New York *Tribune,* July 27, 28, October 27, 1890; Pittsburgh *Dispatch,* October 26, 1890; and I. P. Brewer to Allison, November 17, 1890: *Allison Mss.;* along with Clarkson to Halford, November 20, 1890: *Harrison Mss.* But other useful items are Michener to Halford, August 25, 1890: *Harrison Mss.;* Treasury Department to Allison, September 1, 1890: *Allison Mss.; Breeder's Gazette,* September 10, 1890; Clarkson to Allison, September 13, 1890: *Allison Mss.;* and New York *Tribune,* September 17, 1890.

111. Comstock to D. C. Lightbourne, August 26, 1890 (in reply to a letter of August

22), and Comstock to Noyes Brothers and Cutler, September 1, 1890: *Comstock Mss.;* L. A. Leversen to W. E. Curtis, October 6, 1890: *NA* 43.

112. See J. D. Barnhart, "Rainfall and the Populist Party in Nebraska," *American Political Science Review* (1925), 534-536; and P. H. Argersinger, "Populists and Voting Behavior: the Kansas State Election of 1890," seminar essay done under the guidance of Al Bogue, University of Wisconsin, spring 1968, a very helpful study. I have consulted a great body of secondary literature on the Populists. For the most part, one is far better employed reading the published primary materials and contemporary accounts from 1887 to 1898. Save for a few studies, moreover, the earlier historical analyses are superior to the interpretations offered after 1950. A useful introduction to that debate is provided by N. Pollack, *The Populist Mind* (Indianapolis, 1967).

113. E. A. Oldham, "The Great Political Upheaval in the South," *Arena* (October 1890), 632. Also see *Bradstreet's,* November 8, 1890.

114. Stewart to G. T. Curtis, January 28, 1891: *Stewart Mss.;* Harrison to Reid, September 27, 1888: *Reid Mss.;* Hayes, *Diary,* entry of October 4, 1876; V. P. DeSantis, *Republicans Face the Southern Question—The New Departure Years, 1877-1897* (Baltimore, 1959), 195, 210.

115. Harrison to Cale, November 17, 1890: *Harrison Mss.;* Rusk to Payne, December 11, 1890; Rusk to Bennett, December 4, 1890, in *Rusk Mss.;* and I. C. Brewer to Allison, November 17, 1890: *Allison Mss.* Also see *Bradstreet's,* November 8, 29, 1890.

116. Michener to Halford, November 8, 1890; T. C. Platt to Harrison, March 2, 1891; Clarkson to Harrison, November 26, 1890: all in *Harrison Mss.*

117. Harrison, message of December 1, 1890: Richardson, *Messages,* 11:5542-5560.

118. A. L. Crosby, letter to the editor, *Rural New Yorker,* October 18, 1890; T. C. Platt to Harrison, March 2, 1891: *Harrison Mss.* Then review the *Journal of Commerce* beginning in January 1891, when it launched a steady coverage of Asian commerce.

119. The Ocala discussions and resolutions can be found in many newspapers (as *Pacific Rural Press,* December 6, 13, 1890) and in Dunning, *Farmers Alliance.* For samples of Populist and other reform views around the country in December 1890, see *Pacific Rural Press,* December 13, 1890; *Nation,* January 8, 1891; *National Economist,* January 24, 1891; *South American Journal,* February 28, 1891 (a poll on reciprocity, favored 2.5 to 1); and *The Demands of the Farmers. Governor Boies' Address of December 23, 1890; With Editorials from the Des Moines Leader:* Folder in *Weller Mss.*

120. *National Economist,* January 24, 1891; Boies. "Demands of the Farmers"; and *CR,* 23:3:2843-2844.

121. Subsequent quotes from the tour are taken from J. S. Shriver, *Through the South and West with the President* (New York, 1891). This quotation is from his message of April 7, 1891, to the Western States Convention, which informally launched the campaign. I have consulted the newspapers in the cities where Harrison spoke and consider the Shriver record accurate.

122. Harrison, August 1891: in Hedges, *Speeches,* 522, 540.

123. McKinley to Harrison, June 18, 1891: *Harrison Mss.*

124. Chandler to Harrison, June 18, 1891; Elkins to Harrison, August 11, 1891: *Harrison Mss.* Also see the speeches by Clarkson: Tacoma *Morning Globe,* July 27, 1891; *Iowa State Register,* July 22, 1891; and his lecture to the Republican League in Boston, April 23, 1891: all in *Rusk Mss.*

125. *Public Opinion,* October 31, 1891; *South American Journal,* February 27, 1892; *Iron Age,* November 22, 1891, January 21, 1892; *The Manufacturer,* January 30, 1892; Adler, *Schiff,* 473-476; *Rural New Yorker,* September 26, 1891.

126. A. Carnegie, "The McKinley Bill," *The Nineteenth Century* (June 1891), 1027-1036. On Carnegie's theory of "running full" and using the export market to absorb the costs, see T. J. McCormick, *China Market. America's Quest for Informal Empire, 1893-1901* (Chicago, 1967), 28.

127. See Harrison's message on Brazil, February 5, 1891: Richardson, *Messages,* 12:5576-5577; Blaine to Harrison, May 16, 1891: *Harrison Mss.*

128. Boston *Journal,* August 1, 1891; *CR,* 23:1:614-615. Also see President of the New York Board of Trade, March 11, 1891: *Rusk Mss.;* New York *Mail and Express,* June 27, 1891; *Bradstreet's,* July 25, 1891; *Dry Goods Economist,* September 26, October 3, 17, 1891; *Northwestern Miller,* October 16, 1891, and June 10, 1892. For the trade itself, see *Consular Reports No. 126* (March 1891), *No. 130* (July 1891), and *No. 164* (May 1894).

129. Fish to Fentness, March 26, 1892; Fish to Sen. McCreary, March 29, 1892; Fish

to Rep. J. F. Andrew, March 29, 1892; Fish to Wakeman, February 6, 1894; and Schreiber to Fish, April 28, 1891: all in *Fish* and *ICC Mss.*

130. Perkins to Nimmo, April 2, 1892; Perkins to T. M. Marquett, August 3, 1891; Perkins to W. C. Brown, May 26, 1891; and Perkins to Nimmo, February 9, 1891: all in *C. B. and Q. Mss.* On the contrast with Hill, discussed below, see the testimony of S. A. Thompson, February 1, 1892: *Ship Canal from the Great Lakes to the Navigable Waters of the Hudson River. House Report No. 423.* 54th Cong., 1st Ses. (Washington, 1896), Appendix A. The report is full of evidence on the concern with Asian markets.

131. *Rural New Yorker*, February 7, 1891; Kansas City *Times*, March 26, 1891.

132. *National Economist*, August 8, 1891.

133. Chicago *Tribune*, February 22, 1892.

134. *Report of the Proceedings of the Trans-Mississippi Congress at Omaha, Nebraska, October 19-22, 1891* (Omaha, 1892).

135. C. W. Davis, "Some Impending Changes," *Country Gentleman*, June 18, 25, 1891. Davis published in many journals and newspapers read by agricultural businessmen.

136. See, for example, Davis to Plumb, June 10, 1891, sent on to Rusk: *Rusk Mss.* On Noble, see his *Reports*, and the speech referred to in Note 16 above. Also see W. L. Merry's articles in *Forum*, November 1891 and February 1892.

137. On Democratic attacks, see *CR*, 23:2:2094-2095; 23:3:2103; and 23:4:3892. For the support, consult *Rural New Yorker*, February 14, April 4, 1891; Burlington, Iowa, *Hawkeye*, August 1, 1891; *Western Rural*, August 22, 1891; and National Grange, *Journal of Proceedings for the Session of 1891.*

138. *CR*, 23:5:4199-4214; *Western Rural*, July 30, 1892.

139. Rusk, "The Duty of the Hour," *North American Review* (April 1891), 423-430; Rusk, interview with New York *Herald*, printed March 23, 1892, *Rusk Mss.* Also see Rusk to Hatch, April 19, 1892; Rusk to H. C. Hansborough, May 3, 1892: *NA* 16.

140. There are good accounts of Murphy's activities in the New York *Tribune*, September 13, 1891; Milwaukee *Sentinel*, October 24, 1891; *Indiana Farmer*, October 24, 1891; *Michigan Farmer*, November 7, 1891; Chicago *Inter-Ocean*, June 10, 1892; and *Consular Reports*, Vol. 38: 232.

141. See Rusk, *Report of the Secretary of Agriculture for 1890*; Department of Agriculture, *Report on the Use of Maize (Indian Corn) in Europe and on the Possibilities of Its Expansion. Report No. 49* (Washington, 1891); Washington *Star*, May 21, 1892; and *Rural New Yorker*, December 26, 1891.

142. This has been reviewed by H. Borzo in an excellent article, "A Chapter in Iowa-Russian Relations," *Annals of Iowa* (1959), 561-596. His references guided my own research.

143. The activities of the flour millers can be followed in the *Edgar Mss.*; and in the *Northwestern Miller*, beginning December 4, 1891.

144. Harrison to Blaine, December 31, 1891: *Blaine Mss.*

145. Rusk to Henderson, February 25, 1892: *NA* 16.

146. Washington *Star*, December 26, 1891.

147. Phelps to Reid, March 19, 1891: *Reid Mss.* Also see Rusk to Harrison, March 16, 1891; Harrison to Blaine, May 27, 1891; Rusk to Blaine, February 10, 1892: *NA* 16 and 59; *Breeder's Gazette*, September 9, 1891; and Chicago *Tribune*, March 8, 1891.

148. Reid to Blaine, November 20, 1890; Reid to Foster, July 6, 1891: *Reid Mss.*; and Harrison to Blaine, August 1, 1891: *Harrison Mss.*

149. The Cincinnati meeting is conveniently reviewed in *National Economist*, May 30, 1891.

150. On the Peruvian base, see Harrison to Reid, October 21, 1891: *Reid Mss.*; Harrison to Blaine, October 1, 1891, December 31, 1891: *Blaine Mss.* On the preparations for war, see R. D. Evans, *A Sailor's Log* (New York, 1901), 277; and the materials in *NA* 80.

151. On early business advice, see Plumb to Tracy, July 29, 1891: *Tracy Mss.*

152. Blaine to Harrison, August 8, 10, 1891; Harrison to Blaine, September 18, October 14, 1891: Volwiler, *Correspondence*, and *Harrison Mss.*, and *NA* 59.

153. *Bradstreet's*, May 14, 1892. Also see Rear Admiral G. Brown to Tracy, July 29, 1890: *NA* 59.

154. *National Economist*, October 31, November 21, 1891.

155. On contemporary silver rhetoric, see: Bland, "What Shall the Ratio Be?" *North American Review* (July 1892), and in *Social Economist* (April 1892); Davis, "The Money

Question," *Arena* (April 1892), 543-555; Kyle's speech of May 3, 1892; *National Bulletin,* October 22, 1892; *Western Rural,* July 18, 1891; *Rural New Yorker,* September 12, 1891; the petitions in *NA* 46, S52A-J10; *Proceedings of the Second National Silver Convention, Washington, D. C., May 26-28, 1892* (Washington, 1892); T. A. Bland, *People's Party Shot and Shell* (Chicago, 1892).

156. Annual Message of December 9, 1891: Richardson, *Messages,* 12:5628-5630.

157. On these divisions, see *National Economist,* February 7, August 22, December 19, 1891; *Rural New Yorker,* December 12, 1891; *Farmers· Voice,* November 14, 1891; and J. S. Ferguson, "Agrarianism in Mississippi, 1871-1900. A Study in Non-Conformity," PhD Thesis, University of North Carolina, 1952, chapter XVI.

158. See *System of Sub-Treasuries. House Report 2143.* 52nd Cong., 1st Ses. (Washington, 1892).

159. Harrison, address of March 4, 1889: Richardson, *Messages,* 11:5445-5447; *Report of the Secretary of the Navy for 1889.*

160. A. T. Mahan, "The United States Looking Outward," *Atlantic Monthly* (December 1890), 816-824.

161. *CR,* 23:4:3861-3863.

162. J. W. Mackie, in *Pacific Rural Press,* July 18, 1891.

163. N. A. Dunning, *The Philosophy of Price and Its Relation to Domestic Currency* (Washington, 1892), 195.

164. Utopian novel, S. Crocker, *That Island. A Political Romance* (Kansas City, 1892), 123-124.

165. See, for example, *National Economist,* January 10, February 7, 14, 21, 1891.

166. *CR,* 23:2:1297. Also see the remarks of McKeighan of Nebraska, *ibid.,* 23:3:2436.

167. See, for example, the candid report on steel in J. W. Philip to Tracy, December 23, 1889: *Tracy Mss.;* and Harrison's similar review in his message of December 9, 1891: Richardson, *Messages,* 12:5635.

168. There are no such protests in the archives for the 51st and 52nd Congresses: see *NA* 46, 233.

169. *CR,* 21:4:3167; 23:2:1037; 23:4:3362-3363; *North Pacific Rural Spirit,* May 31, 1894.

170. *CR,* 23:7:6451.

171. See *Pacific Rural Press,* April 12, 1890, for a good expression of this attitude; and the *Rural New Yorker,* April 26, 1890, for a perceptive review of the split among farm businessmen.

172. *CR,* 23:6:5956.

173. *Ibid.,* 23:4:3108. On the Republican background of the Westerners, see *Christian Union,* June 25, 1891; and *Pacific Rural Press,* July 11, 1891.

174. *Rural New Yorker,* April 11, 1891; and see, for much illuminating detail, A. L. Diggs, *The Story of Jerry Simpson* (Wichita, 1908).

175. This summary is based on Simpson's speeches of April 8, 12, and May 7, 1892: *CR,* 23:4:3108-3114, 3230; and 23:5:4056-4057.

Chapter Thirteen

1. Cleveland to Vilas, August 17, 1890; E. B. Wall to Vilas, January 20, 1893: *Vilas Mss.;* and see Richmond *Dispatch,* June 21, 1891, for Southern opposition.

2. Cleveland to E. Anderson, February 10, 1891: in Parker, *Recollections,* 151; Cleveland to Vilas, January 28, 1891, August 13, 1892: *Vilas Mss.* Also see C. A. Towne, "The Reform Club's Feat of Unreason," *Arena* (July 1897), 27, 29.

3. Bayard to G. Gray, November 16, 1893: *Bayard Mss.*

4. *National Economist,* February 21, 1891; T. Watson, "The Negro Question in the South," *Arena* (October 1892), 541.

5. T. Watson, "Why the People's Party Should Elect the Next President," *Arena* (July 1892), 202.

6. *National Economist,* December 26, 1891: *Pacific Rural Press,* November 5, 1892. *Farmers Voice,* October 17, 1891.

8. N. Pollack, *The Populist Mind,* 59. The document is quoted from his collection, 60-66. Also see the St. Louis Platform of February 1892: *CR,* 23:4:3869.

9. *Southern Alliance Farmer,* July 5, 1892; Omaha *Public,* July 8, 1892.

10. *National Economist*, August 6, 1892; D. M. Robison, *Bob Taylor and the Agrarian Revolt in Tennessee* (Chapel Hill, 1935), 171; W. E. Fay, "Alliance Call for the Election of 1892," *Wisconsin Alliance Papers*.

11. *Literary Digest*, March 5, 1892; a random survey of metropolitan reaction to the St. Louis convention. Such judgments abounded throughout the campaign.

12. R. Q. Mills, "Reciprocity—Why Southward Only?" *Forum* (May 1891), 268-275.

13. T. F. Bayard, "Democratic Duty and Opportunity," *Forum* (June 1892), 419.

14. See New York *Herald*, June 9, 1892; *Rural New Yorker*, October 31, 1891; the Minneapolis and St. Paul press during the convention, and the biographies of McKinley for his efforts (aided by Hanna) to place himself in line for the nomination in 1896.

15. *Rural New Yorker*, October 31, 1891; *Nation*, February 19, 1891.

16. Boston *Journal of Commerce*, February 14, 1891; Comstock, "Notebook," data on Minnesota Republicans: *Comstock Mss.*; Beveridge, manuscript speech for campaign of 1892: *Albert J. Beveridge Papers*; G. F. Hoar, "Reasons for Republican Control," *Forum* (June 1892), 424-428; J. R. Hawley, "Mr. Harrison's Second Administration," *Forum* (July 1892), 650-661.

17. Porter and Johnson, *Platforms*, 93; also see *Western Rural*, August 6, 1892; and McKinley's account of Harrison's great emphasis on markets in *Tariff* (New York, 1896), 161-165.

18. Wall to Vilas, September 24, October 19, 1892: *Vilas Mss.*

19. Wall to Vilas, March 27, July 20, 1893; then see Wall to Vilas, September 8, November 30, 1892, and D. M. Dickinson to Wall, November 29, 1892: all in *Vilas Mss.*

20. S. R. Davis to Olney, March 23, 1893: *Richard Olney Papers*.

21. *National Economist*, February 4, 1893; *Indiana Farmer*, February 4, March 4, 1893.

22. *Pacific Rural Press*, February 4, 1893.

23. *Commercial Advertizer*, January 29, 1883.

24. Cleveland to Schurz, March 19, 1893; Schurz to Cleveland, July 27, 1893: *Schurz Mss.*

25. *Nebraska State Journal*, July 31, 1884; Morton to Perkins, January 13, 1887; and Morton to J. R. Dodge, March 22, 1893: *Morton Mss.*

26. Speech of September 22, 1859: *Morton Mss.*

27. Morton to Perkins, January 13, 1887: *Morton Mss.*

28. *Ibid.*; and see the following: J. S. Morton, "Some Financial Fallacies Among the Early Pioneers of Nebraska," *Proceedings and Collections of the Nebraska Historical Society* (1894-1895), 1:195-210; "Farmers, Fallacies, and Furrows," *Forum* (June 1894), 385-393; and "Social and Economic Progress: 1855-1897," *Proceedings and Collections* (1898), 2:83-87.

29. Morton to Martin, March 23, 1893; Morton to Weare, March 23, 1893: *Morton Mss.*; and *American Agriculturalist*, April 1893.

30. See, for example, Morton to J. C. Sibley, April 13, 1893; and T. J. Hudson to Morton, October 6, 1893: *NA* 16.

31. See Morton to W. S. Delano, May 20, 1893: *Morton Mss.*

32. *Manufacturers Record*, April 28, 1893; Morton to Delano, March 22, 1893: *Morton Mss.*; Morton to Gresham, April 7, 1893: *NA* 59; Gresham to Morton, July 15, 1893; Adee to Morton, July 27, 1893: *NA* 16.

33. Morton to Gresham, January 13, 27, 1894; Morton to H. W. Seymour, August 27, 1893: *Morton Mss.*

34. See, as typical, Morton to R. Ganz and Company of New York, June 29, 1893; Morton to Swift and Company, July 10, 1893; and Morton to Armour and Company, February 16, 1894; but also see, as typical, *Indiana Farmer*, July 8, 22, 1893; and *North Pacific Rural Spirit*, July 27, 1893. The letters are in *NA* 54.

35. Morton, Chicago speech of October 1893: *Morton Mss.*; also see Morton, "Farmers, Fallacies, and Furrows," 390-393; *Prairie Farmer*, October 21, 1893.

36. Massachusetts, Illinois, and Ohio State Granges, *Journal of Proceedings for 1893*; National Grange, *ibid.*; J. Trimble to Morton, December 7, 9, 1893; L. Rhone to Morton, December 20, 1893; A. C. Hedden to Morton, November 15, 1893: all in *NA* 16; and see *American Agriculturalist*, March 1894, for a good review of the situation.

37. J. H. Powers to Morton, January 6, 1894: *NA* 16; and sample such items as Morton to E. Buckman, January 9, 1894; Morton to Colorado Alliance, January 9, 1894; and Morton to H. L. Loucks, February 1, 1894: *Morton Mss.* They contain much of the man; and the incoming mail provides good insight into Alliance attitudes and arguments.

38. Sibley to Morton, February 19, 1894: *NA* 16; Morton to G. F. Nesbitt, March 9, 1894; Morton to Loucks, February 1, 1894: *Morton Mss.*

39. *Southern Mercury*, August 1, 1895; *National Economist*, February 11, 1893; *Prairie Farmer*, February 4, 18, 1893; *American Agriculturalist*, March 1893; and *Indiana Farmer*, January 21, and December 2, 1893. On silver, see Morton to H. Kountze, July 1, 1893; Morton to H. W. Yates, August 4, 1893; Morton to S. W. Chapman, August 5, 1893: *Morton Mss.*; and *Report of the Secretary of Agriculture for 1894*.

40. C. G. Dawes, *A Journal of the McKinley Years* (LaGrange, 1950), 28; Gordon, *Business Fluctuations*, 216.

41. See S. Rezneck, "Unemployment, Unrest and Relief in the United States During the Depression of 1893-1897," *Journal of Political Economy* (1953), 324-345; and C. Hoffman, "The Depression of the Nineties," *Journal of Economic History* (1956), 137-164, esp. 151, 149, 144-145 (Hoffman's thesis is worth reading for a more extended development); Lebergott, *Manpower in Economic Growth*, 522; and see R. Fels, *American Business Cycles, 1865-1897* (Chapel Hill, 1959), which is useful but not, on balance, as helpful as Gordon, Abramovitz, and others.

42. See, for example, the personal testimony in *Report of the Committee on Agriculture and Forestry on Conditions of Cotton Growers in the United States . . . and on Cotton Consumption and Production*. Senate Report No. 896. Two Volumes. 53rd Cong., 3rd Ses. (Washington, 1895: hereafter cited as *Cotton*), 1:280, 286, 308-309, 400. This is a very helpful and illuminating study.

43. New York, Ohio, Indiana State Granges, *Journal of Proceedings for 1893;* J. Hicks, *Populist Revolt*, 310; *Pacific Rural Spirit*, July 13, 1893; and *Agricultural Depression; Causes and Remedies. Report by Mr. Peffer, to the Senate Committee on Agriculture and Forestry, February 15, 1894. Senate Report 787*. 53rd Cong., 3rd Ses. (Washington, 1895: hereafter cited as *Peffer Report*), is an excellent source of material on conditions and on ideas for dealing with the depression. Also see *Biennial Report of the State Board of Land Commissioners to the Legislature of the State of Washington, 1894* (Olympia, 1894), 7; and C. W. Irish to Morton, March 21, December 27, 1894: *NA* 16; H. D. Fox to H. D. Fox, Jr., December 18, 1895: *Fox Mss.*

44. Sietz to H. E. Boen, January 21, 1894: *CR*, 26:10:1450; and see J. P. Steelle to Boen, January 24, 1894: *ibid.*

45. *Commercial and Financial Chronicle*, as quoted in O. M. W. Sprague, *History of Crises Under the National Banking System. Senate Document No. 538* (Washington, 1910), 202; *Bradstreet's*, December 30, 1893; and Dawes, *Journal*, 47.

46. W. H. Warren, *Report of the Thirteenth Annual Farmers National Congress, December 12-20, 1893* (Indianola, 1894).

47. Watson, *Peoples Party Campaign Book*, 12, 221, 92.

48. *CR*, 26:1:772-776.

49. *Ibid.*, 24:2:1526-1527; 26:A:370-377; Denver *Republican*, March 3, 1893; Illinois, California, Ohio, Massachusetts State Granges, *Journal of Proceedings for 1894; Kansas Farmer*, December 18, 1895; Agresti, *David Lubin. A Study in Practical Idealism* (Boston, 1922), 122; D. Lubin, *Farm Products Moved As Mail Matter at a Uniform Rate* (Sacramento, 1893); *Prairie Farmer*, February 11, August 19, 1893, June 24, 1894; *Western Swineherd*, February and July 1893; *Farm, Stock and Home*, January 15, February 15, 1893; *Indiana Farmer*, December 23, 1893; and *Iowa Homestead*, September 28, 1894. On implement firms, see *Farm Implement News*, esp. January 4, March 15, April 5, and June 14; and consult Schonberger, "McCormick," 91, 114. Also consult the petitions in *NA* 46, S53A-J3; *Rand McNally Banker's Monthly*, December 1894; and Davis, "California Breadstuffs," 533; *Manufacturers Record*, July 21, 1893, November 28, 1894; *National Economist*, March 4, 1893; J. D. Goldman to Sen. J. Z. George, November 8, 1893, and similar letters in *Cotton*, 1:410, and 2; *American Wool and Cotton Reporter*, July 27, 1893; *Peffer Report; Manufacturers Record*, November 11, December 2, 1892; January 6, 20, 1893; August 3, September 21, 1894; Cotner, *Hogg*, 311; and *Nicaragua Canal. House Report No. 226*. 53rd Cong., 2nd Ses. (Washington, 1893), 2.

50. The *Annual Reports* of the North Dakota Board of Railroad Commissioners, 1891-1896, provide considerable evidence on Hill's ideas and operations; Fish to Morgan, February 24, 1893; Fish to J. C. Welling (of Northern Pacific), August 3, 1893; Fish to Hill, August 3, 1893; and Fish to Cullom, December 15, 1894: all in *Fish Mss.* Also see Fish to Spelman, March 15, 1893; Fish to Peralta, November 17, 1893; and Fish to Wakeman, February 6, 1894.

51.   *The New York Times*, July 9, 15, 1893; and see W. A. Williams, "The Frontier Thesis and American Foreign Policy," *Pacific Historical Review* (1955), 379-395.

52.   Straus, speech of April 8, 1893; L. Hunt to Clarkson, August 28, 1894: *Clarkson Mss.;* Indianapolis *Journal*, June 29, 1893; and see J. R. Procter, "America's Battle for Commercial Supremacy," *Forum* (November 1893), 320-322.

53.   Significantly, Hill's article was reprinted in *Public Opinion*, May 17, 1894.

54.   Carnegie to Elkins, May 13, 1893: *Elkins Mss.;* Shaw, remarks in *Review of Reviews* (March 1893).

55.   *Bankers Magazine* (December 1893, October and March 1894).

56.   For background, see C. Foster, "The Financial Situation: II-The Brussels Conference Reviewed," *North American Review* (April 1893), 493-500; Barnes, *Carlisle;* Taylor, *Chicago Board of Trade*, 2:859; Carnegie to Cleveland, April 22, 1893, and to A. D. White, November 27, 1892: *Andrew Carnegie Papers.*

57.   Lynchburg, Virginia, *News*, April 28, 30, 1893.

58.   Belmont to Cleveland, June 26, 1893; Schiff to Cleveland, June 21, 1883: *Cleveland Mss.*

59.   See, for example, the July 1893 letters from F. P. Taylor (S. Carolina), L. B. Brown (Mississippi), J. L. Slayden (Texas), J. M. Hudson (Arkansas), and Allen-West Commission Company (Missouri), along with others, in *Cotton*, 1:299, 329, 353, 375, 409.

60.   Texas State Grange, *Journal of Proceedings for 1893.*

61.   Denver *Republican*, July 12, 13, 1893 (and see the remarks of E. R. Holden, a major smelter owner, *ibid.*, June 30, 1893); the petition of the Denver Chamber of Commerce and Board of Trade, July 28, 1893: *NA* 46, S53A-J9. Also see Denver *Republican*, July 1, 10, 1893; and *Rocky Mountain News*, July 24, 1893.

62.   Petition of Buffalo County, Nebraska, Farmers Alliance, July 14, 1893: *NA* 233, HR53A-H5.1; Oregon State Grange, *Journal of Proceedings for 1893; North Pacific Rural Spirit*, July 20, 1893; *American Agriculturalist*, April 1893. Also see *Farm, Stock and Home*, June 15, 1893.

63.   Hoar to Francis Walker, July 5, 1893: *Francis J. Walker Papers; The Carpenter*, June and August 1893, November 1895, July 1896; *Literary Digest*, August 26, 1893.

64.   Gresham to Schmitt, August 16, 1893: *Gresham Mss.;* also see D. B. Hill to Marble, August 14, 1893: *Marble Mss.;* Whitney to Gresham, August 1, 1893: *Gresham Mss.;* Clews to Cleveland, April 20, 1893: *Cleveland Mss.*

65.   Cleveland, message of August 8, 1893: Richardson, *Messages*, 12:5833-5836; Virginia Populist Platform, August 3, 1893: in W. D. Sheldon, *Populism in the Old Dominion. Virginia Farm Politics, 1885-1900* (Princeton, 1935), Appendix E; and see the petitions and memorials, such as the one from J. F. McQuay and others of Kentucky, September 9, 1893: *NA* 46, S53A-H51.

66.   *CR*, 25:1:403-407.

67.   *Ibid.*, 25:1:493, 576-577, 773-776.

68.   On the vote, see, for example, J. H. McDowell to Weller, August 29, 1893: *Weller Mss.; Indiana Farmer*, September 23, October 7, 1893.

69.   *Manufacturers Record*, March 11, 24, 1893; and petition of the Ladies of Utah, September 13, 1898: *NA* 233, HR53A-H5.1. This is an appropriate point to emphasize that this account is based upon a vast amount of primary evidence. The petitions and resolutions in HR53A-H5.1 and S53A-J1, J9, and J9.3 are almost numberless, and originated in every state. Alliance and Grange *Proceedings* are likewise full of the militant nationalistic expansionism. So are the individual manuscript collections. The articles and pamphlets are legion, but for a sample: G. C. Douglas, "Can the United States Restore the Bimetallic Standard of Money to the World," *Arena* (December 1893), 61-72; A. C. Fisk, "Does the Country Demand Free Coinage of Silver? Who Are in Favor, and Who Opposed, and Why?" *Arena* (June 1893), 57-69; W. H. Standish, "Seven Facts About Silver," *Arena* (September 1893), 418-429; "The Financial Problem the Supreme Political Question of the Hour," *Arena* (August 1893), 314-319; "The Impending Crisis," *Arena* (November 1896), 974-985; and Senator W. M. Stewart, "Monometallism Revolutionary and Destructive," *Arena* (August 1893), 277-285.

70.   *CR*, 25:1:1211-1217, 1230-1231; Stewart to C. P. Huntington, September 3, 1893: *Stewart Mss.; Arena* (September 1893), 417.

71.   *CR* (for Allen), 25:3:289-294; 25:3:296-315; 25:1:783-790; (for Peffer), 25:A:35-46.

72. *Ibid.*, 25:A:363; 25:A:170-189, 335.

73. Stewart to A. W. Thurman, November 4, 1893, to G. Colcord, November 5, 1893, and to W. A. Clark, April 24, 1894: *Stewart Mss.*

74. The evidence here is very great. See, for example, the following items in the *William Barker Papers:* Hoar to Barker, September 17, 1893; J. Sherman to Barker, October 24, 1893; Adams to Barker, December 6, 1893; Frye to Barker, December 4, 18, 1893; Lodge to Barker, April 17, 1894; and Chandler to Barker, March 7, 1895. Also see Adams to Lodge, May 6, 1894: *Lodge Mss.;* and Perkins to Hill, August 7, 1893, to Wolcott, August 11, 1893, to Jeffry, August 21, 1893, and "Memo of December 19, 1893": all in *C. B. and Q. Mss.* (along with Perkins to Manderson, February 25, 1895).

75. See *Cotton*, 2:12; and L. M. Keasby, "The New Sectionalism: A Western Warning to the East," *Forum* (January 1894), 576-587.

76. Santa Cruz Alliance, petition of March 5, 1894: *NA* 46, S53A-J9; *Southern Mercury*, April 12, 19, 1894; *People's Party Paper*, January 4, 1894. The editors of *Southern Mercury* did in this crisis generalize their assault upon the financiers of the metropolis into an attack on Jews. Having read a vast number of Populist papers, letters, and proceedings, it is my considered judgment that the incidence of anti-Semitism was very low. Those who maintain otherwise are unconvincing on two counts. First, they do not persuade one that they have done extensive research in the primary sources. Second, they do not conceptualize about the problem in a useful manner.

Jews did enjoy great power in European and American financial circles during this period. They further took great pride, as they had traditionally, in exercising that power. Hence to attack them for possessing and exercising that vast economic power is not *prima facie* evidence of anti-Semitism. To become such, it would have to be supported by proof of an exclusive assault on Jewish financiers, and of a general campaign against *all* Jews, whatever their wealth. The sources do not reveal such evidence. In a similar way, the rising opposition to immigration was due far less to any latent or overt racism than to the conclusions drawn from the analysis that established the end of the continental frontier.

77. *Indiana Farmer*, December 9, 1893.

78. Gresham to Ross, August 1, 1892; Gresham to Shimons, October 1, 1892: *Gresham Mss.;* B. O. Flower, "The Menace of Plutocracy," *Arena* (September 1892), 511; Cleveland *Herald*, October 2, 1892: Cleveland *Plain-Dealer*, October 4, 1893; *Indiana Farmer*, March 4, 1893; and *Review of Reviews*, March 1893.

79. Schurz, "Manifest Destiny," *Harper's* (October 1893), 737-746; Gresham to Schurz, October 6, 1893: *Gresham Mss.*

80. Gresham to I. Straus, January 6, 1894: *Gresham Mss.;* and W. Rockefeller to Gresham, January 4, 1894: *NA* 59 (which contains other such requests). Also see Mrs. Gresham, *The Life of Walter Quintin Gresham*, 2:778; and W. LaFeber, *The New Empire* (Cornell, 1963), 210 ff., for a useful account of the intervention.

81. Gresham to O. Straus, December 14, 1893: *Straus Mss.;* and Gresham to Thompson, January 10, 1894: *NA* 59.

82. There are many such letters in the *Hoar Mss.:* these are dated December 5, 6, and 7, 1893. Also see Harrison to Foster, May 1, 1893: *Foster Mss.;* J. R. Hawley to Reid, November 29, 1893: *Reid Mss.;* petitions from the State Legislature of Washington, February 25, 1893, and the San Francisco Chamber of Commerce, July 18, 1893:*NA* 46, S53A-J11.3; and *CR*, 26:2:1309-1313.

83. *Prairie Farmer*, November 25, 1893; *People's Party Paper*, December 29, 1893; then see, in sequence, the minority report on Hawaii, by Hitt, 8-9; Kyle in *CR*, 26:6:5129, 5193, 5369; Peffer, *ibid.*, 5434; and the vote on the Hitt resolution, February 6, 1894: *ibid.*, 26:2:1967-1970, where Populists Baker, Boen, Davis, Kem, McKeighan, and Simpson voted Aye. The motion lost 159 to 103, with 89 not voting.

84. See, for example, the remarks of Senators Turpie and Vest: *CR*, 26:1:523, 702-707; 26:2:1308.

85. *CR*, 26:2:1575-1578; Lodge to E. F. Atkins, June 18, 1894: *Lodge Mss.*

86. See *Violation of Armor Contracts. House Document No. 160.* 53rd Cong., 2nd Ses. (Washington, 1894); *People's Party Paper*, March 16, 23, 1894. Also see New York *Tribune*, March 2, 28, 29, 1894. A similar fight developed a bit later over collusion on prices: see *Prices of Armor for Naval Vessels* (Washington, 1896).

87. R. Q. Mills, "The Wilson Bill," *North American Review* (February 1894), 235-244. Also see Bryan in *C R*, 26:A:227-228.

88. Fish to J. F. Andrew, March 29, 1892: *Fish Mss.*

89. Atkinson to Carnegie, November 20, 1893: *Carnegie Mss.*

90. *Farm Implement News,* December 23, 1893; February 15, August 30, 1894; *Replies to Tariff Inquiries. Senate Report No. 424.* 53rd Cong., 2nd Ses. (Washington, 1894), 23, 37, 51; Butler to Cowhan, January 30, 1894: *McCormick Mss.;* petition of "workmen of Deering and Company," February 23, 1894: *NA* 46, S53A-J9.16 (and others in same file).

91. *CR,* 26:1:255; 26:2:1417-1422.

92. P. Voorheis to Peffer, July 24, 1893: *Peffer Report,* 112; *CR,* 26:1:796-798; *To Reduce Taxation, To Provide Revenue for the Government, and for Other Purposes. House Report No. 234.* 53rd Cong., 2nd Ses. (Washington, 1893), 45-52.

93. *Prairie Farmer,* November 18, 1893; *People's Party Paper,* January 12, 1894.

94. Frewen to Mrs. Frewen, April 10, 1894; Senators (33) to Frewen, April 23, 1894: *Frewen Mss.*

95. *CR,* 26:5:4527-4536.

96. *Ibid.,* 26:4:3936, 4016, 4104; 26:5:4295, 4309; 26:7:6197; *Nation,* March 15, 1894; *Prairie Farmer,* May 19, 1894.

97. *CR,* 26:6:5436.

98. Runyon to Gresham, February 20, 1894: *NA* 59; W. C. Ford to Bayard, July 22, 1893: *Bayard Mss.;* Memorandum from the German Embassy, July 16, 1894: *NA* 59.

99. *CR,* 26:4:3962-3993; Chicago *Record,* May 21, 1894. For Philadelphia Board of Trade, see *CR,* 26:5:4563.

100. *CR,* 26:7:6058-6060; also see the petitions at 26:6:5370; 26:7:6864.

101. *Ibid.,* 26:7:6330-6333; 26:5:5441; then see *North Pacific Rural Spirit,* January 4, February 22, April 5, 1894; *CR,* 26:5:4136-4137, 4628-4629; L. W. Nieman to Vilas, February 2, 1894, N. Brown to Vilas, March 10, 1894: *Vilas Mss.;* and the hundreds of petitions and resolutions, such as the Joint Resolution of the Senate and the House of the State of Iowa, March 1894, in *NA* 46 and 233, S53A-J9.16 and HR53A-H33.11.

102. Cleveland to T. C. Catchings, August 27, 1894: *Cleveland Mss.*

103. Watson, as quoted in C. Vann Woodward, *Tom Watson, Agrarian Rebel* (New York, 1955), 244; *Southern Mercury,* November 8, 1894. For other Populist views see *Peoples Call,* September 1, 1894; Virginia, Nevada, *Chronicle,* September 6, 1894; *Louisiana Populist,* September 9, 1894; and Watson, *Peoples Party Campaign Book.*

104. Susan Orcutt to L. D. Lewelling, June 29, 1894: quoted by Fite, *Farmers Frontier,* 129. Also see the reviews of the situation in *Prairie Farmer,* January 13, 1894; "A Bundle of Western Letters," *Review of Reviews* (July 1894); J. M. Thurston to Clarkson, August 29, 1894: *Clarkson Mss.;* and other agricultural press.

105. Watson, *Peoples Party Campaign Book,* 11; J. Lehlef to Vilas, March 15, 1894: *Vilas Mss.;* and T. B. Catron to Elkins, October 3, 1894: *Elkins Mss.*

106. W. E. Smythe, editor of *Irrigation Age,* in *Review of Reviews* (July 1894); and see *Clay Live Stock Report,* November 2, 1894; and *Farm Implement News,* October 11, 1894.

107. Clarkson, speech of May 10, 1893: in Sage, *Allison,* 256; and T. H. Carter to Clarkson, December 15, 1893: *Clarkson Mss.*

108. Indianapolis *Journal,* April 26, 1894; Cincinnati *Commercial Gazette,* June 7, 1894; Minneapolis *Tribune,* July 12, 1894; Chicago *Tribune,* May 6, 1894; and the superb review of the process by Scheidler, *Silver and Politics,* chapter IV, 93-118.

109. Detroit *Tribune,* June 4, 1894; Adams to M. Carey, December 21, 1893: *CR,* 26:3:2946.

110. Cameron to A. B. Humphrey, Secretary of the National Republican League, Denver, June 11, 1894: copy in *NA* 46, S53A.

111. Reed to Frewen, May 15, 1894; Lodge to Frewen, June 11, 1894; A. Higgins to Frewen, June 11, 1894: all in *Frewen Mss.;* "Silver and the Tariff at Washington," *Fortnightly Review* (May 1, 1894), 837-838; and Scheidler, *Silver and Politics,* 240.

112. Gresham to Dyer, May 2, 1894: *Gresham Mss.* Also see the most helpful memorandum of May 4, 1894 in the *John Bassett Moore Papers.*

113. Gresham to MacVeagh, May 7, 1894; and Gresham to Cooper, July 26, 1894: *Gresham Mss.*

114. *Maritime Canal Company of Nicaragua. House Report No. 1201.* 53rd Cong., 2nd Ses. (Washington, 1894), 1-4; *CR,* 26:1:561-562, 650-662, 1513-1518, 1526, 1529, and 1530; petitions in *NA* 233, HR53A-H14.2.

115. *CR,* 27:1:245-246, 347-351, 430-436; and see the petitions in *NA* 233, HR53A-H14.2.

116. Fish to R. D. Johnston, December 7, 1894: *IC Mss.*

117. Petition of Seattle Chamber of Commerce, January 3, 1895, and of San Diego Chamber of Commerce, December 25, 1894: *NA,* 46, S53A-K3; Resolutions of Commercial Club of St. Paul, January 30, 1895, and of Northwest Fruit Growers Association, February 8, 1895: *NA* 233, HR53A-H14.2; National Grange, *Journal of Proceedings for the Session of 1895;* and Grange petition of March 17, 1895: *NA* 46, S54A-J1; *CR,* 26:5:4629; 26:9:655, 657, 662, 669; 26:5:4900; New York State Grange, *Journal of Proceedings for 1894;* and the materials in Box 1 of the *Holcomb Mss.*

118. Deep Water Association, *Proceedings,* 35, 81-85; *Transactions of the California State Agricultural Society for 1894,* 35, 140, 149, 163-165, 169, 172, 186-187; *CR,* 26:10:1411-1412.

119. *Dixie,* July through December 1894.

120. Cincinnati *Commercial Gazette,* January 23, 1895.

121. *Southern Mercury,* May 17, 1894; Stewart to Sherman, April 15, 30, 1895: *Stewart Mss.*

122. W. H. Harvey, *The Great Debate; Coin's Financial School,* et al.

123. *CR,* 27:2:1136-1137, 1939; 27:2:977-981 (Allen begins on 971), 1277, 1329 ff.

124. *Ibid.,* 27:1:629. Also see the letter from "O.K." of Virginia to *People's Party Paper,* February 1, 1895; and the remarks of Senator Manderson of Nebraska, *CR,* 27:3:1980.

125. New York *Journal of Commerce,* July 28, 1894; *Commercial and Financial Chronicle,* August 18, 1894; Annual Message of 1894.

126. Parker, *Recollections,* 326.

127. *CR,* 27:3:2240-2243.

128. *Ibid.,* 27:3:2460-2461.

129. See the files in *NA* 233, HR53A-H23.1; *CR,* 27:4:3095; *People's Party Paper,* May 17, August 16, December 20, 1895. Also consult F. Emory to Bayard, May 28, 1895: *NA* 59; *U.S.D.A. Circular No. 5. The Treaty of Shimonoseki Between China and Japan of April 17, 1895, and Our Possibilities of Trade with Those Countries, October 16, 1895* (Washington, 1895); *Manufacturers Record,* April 19, May 31, 1895; Resolution of the New York Chamber of Commerce, 1895: in *Proceedings of the Trans-Mississippi Congress for 1899,* 34-36; and E. H. Knowlton, *Pepperell's Progress* (Cambridge, 1948), 197.

130. E. Uhl to Denby, June 8, 1895: *NA* 59.

131. See Morgan to Olney, March 6, 1895: *Olney Mss.; Public Opinion,* May 9, 1895; *Review of Reviews,* June 1895; New York *Tribune,* May 1, 2, 1895; the Memoranda dated March 22, 23/24 in the *Moore Mss.*

132. Cleveland to Bayard, February 12, 1895: *Cleveland Mss.*

133. *CR,* 27:2:1832-1834.

134. Lodge to C. K. Davis, April 9, 1895: *Davis Mss.*

135. Tansill, *Bayard,* 690, and his report of an interview with J. B. Moore, note 190, 708; Parker, *Recollections,* 195-196; G. L. Anderson, "General William J. Palmer, Anti-Imperialist," *The Colorado Magazine* (1945), 10-11; Cleveland to Bayard, December 29, 1895: *Cleveland* (and *Bayard*) *Mss.;* and below.

136. Detroit *Free Press,* May 10, 1895; Dickinson to Cleveland, May 15, 1895; and Cleveland to Dickinson, July 31, 1895: *Cleveland Mss.*

137. *People's Party Paper,* May 17, 24, 1895.

138. *CR,* 26:2:1574-1579 (Teller); and 26:6:5436 (Proctor).

139. *Ibid.,* 27:1:152, 577-578.

140. G. W. Auxier, "Middle Western Newspapers and the Spanish-American War, 1895-1898," *Mississippi Valley Historical Review* (1940), 524; *National Stockman,* July 18, September 24, 1895.

141. See, for example, the praise for Lodge in *People's Party Paper,* November 15, 1895.

142. Olney to Cleveland, September 25, 1895; Cleveland to Olney, September 29, 1895: *Cleveland Mss.*

143. Message of December 2, 1895: Richardson, *Messages,* 12:6061, 6068, 6085, 6087, 6088.

144. Parker, *Recollections,* 197-198.

145. Wilson, *Diary,* 4-5. Also see the wry comments of Secretary of Agriculture Mor-

ton, who opposed the message, in these letters: to E. Atkinson, December 18, 1895; to S. D. Elwood, December 21, 1895; to S. B. Evans, December 23, 1895; and to W. D. McHugh, December 23, 1895: all in *Morton Mss.*

146.   W. W. Cox to Morton, December 19, 1895 (and Morton's reply): *Morton Mss.*

147.   W. LaFeber, *New Empire*, 270 - 283, offers a helpful account of financial and industrial reactions. It can be supplemented with materials in *NA* 46, S54A - J12.1, J12.3; *NA* 233, HR54A - H11.5; and in the manuscript collections of Atkinson, Fish, etc. See, for example, Fish to J. Dunn, December 21, 1895: *IC Mss.*, in which Fish arranges to have his view of the effect of war—not unfavorable—planted in the Chicago *Tribune* and other newspapers.

148.   *Literary Digest*, January 4, 1896.

149.   *People's Party Paper*, June 28, July 12, December 27, 1895.

150.   *Southern Mercury*, December 19, 26, 1895; *Pacific Rural Press*, December 21, 1895.

151.   Stead to Lloyd, December 24, 1895; Lloyd to Morgan, and Lloyd to Pirie, December 30, 1895: all in *Lloyd Mss.*

152.   Bryan, remarks as newly elected president of the *Trans-Mississippi Commercial Convention, November 25 - 28, 1895: Official Proceedings* (Omaha, 1896), 130 - 131.

Chapter Fourteen

1.   *CR*, 28:1:36.

2.   *Ibid.*, 28:1:25.

3.   *Ibid.*, 28:1:294.

4.   *Ibid.*, 28:2:1448 - 1449.

5.   J. E. North to Allen, February 8, 1896: *Allen Mss.*

6.   See Allen's remarks of December 20, 1895: *CR*, 28:1:254; and Scheidler, "Silver and Politics," 222.

7.   *Farm, Field and Fireside*, February 8, January 4, 25, 1896.

8.   *National Stockman*, January 2, 1896.

9.   *Western Rural*, January 9, 30, February 20, March 5, 1896.

10.   *Rural New Yorker*, February 22, March 14, 1896.

11.   See, as typical of the overwhelming majority, the following items in *NA* 16 and 233, 54A - K5, J12.1. Topeka Philosophical Society, January 24, 1896; Citizens of Spokane, February 6, 1896; Bladen County, North Carolina, Alliance Chapter, January 30, 1896; Citizens of Des Moines, Iowa, December 4, 1895; Resolution of the National Grange, December 16, 1895; Indianapolis Board of Trade, January 13, 1896; Joshua Mattack of Mt. Holly, New York, February 13, 1896; Concurrent Resolution of Mississippi House and Senate, February 24, 1896; and Nebraska State Senate, January 12, 1897.

12.   *In the Senate of the United States . . . Mr. Morgan Submitted the Following Report on Hostilities in Cuba. Senate Report No. 141.* 54th Cong., 1st Ses. (Washington, 1896), 1 - 12.

13.   *CR*, 28:1:1065 - 1066; 28:2:1970 - 1972, 2066, 2241, 2249 - 2250, 2257.

14.   *The Cabinet Diary of William L. Wilson, 1896 - 1897.* Edited by Festus P. Summers (Chapel Hill, 1957), 25, 33, 35, 36.

15.   Lodge to Weld, December 19, 1896: *Lodge Mss.*

16.   Lodge to Taplin, December 21, 1896: *ibid.*

17.   See, for example, the petitions from the Milwaukee Chamber of Commerce, December 23, 1896; from the St. Louis Cotton Exchange, December 21, 1896: *NA* 46, S54A - K5; and *National Stockman*, March 12, 1896.

18.   *Farm, Field and Fireside*, March 14, 1896.

19.   *People's Party Paper*, January 17, 1896; and see *Southern Mercury*, March 19, 1896.

20.   *Belligerent Rights for Cuba. House Report No. 531.* 54th Cong., 1st Ses. (Washington, 1896), 1 - 4.

21.   *CR*, 28:3:2342 - 2343.

22.   *Ibid.*, 28:3:2347.

23.   See, for example, *Journal of Commerce*, March 2, 19, 1896; *Commercial Advertizer*, December 25, 1895; January 2, April 17, 25, 1896; and consult J. E. Wisan, *The Cuban Crisis As Reflected in the New York Press, 1895 - 1898* (New York, 1934).

24.   *CR*, 23:3:2719 - 2720, 2728.

25. Olney to de Lome, April 4, 1896: *NA* 59 (also *Olney Mss.*).

26. *Spanish Diplomatic Correspondence and Documents, 1896-1900: Presented to the Cortes by the Minister of State* (Washington, 1905: translation).

27. *Manufacturers Record*, November 20, 1896.

28. J. H. Tibbles to Allen, March 20, 1896: *Allen Mss.;* petitions to Senator Allen, May 1896: *NA* 46, S54A-J16.

29. New York State Grange, Pennsylvania State Grange, Illinois State Grange, and Kansas State Grange, *Journal of Proceedings for 1896.*

30. *National Stockman*, February 6, 1896; *Farm, Field and Fireside*, May 23, 1896. And New York State Grange, *Journal of Proceedings for 1896.*

31. *CR*, 28:5:4471-4472, 4474; 28:7:6195; and see F. B. Simkins, *Pitchfork Ben Tillman. South Carolinian* (Baton Rouge, 1944), 347-352.

32. *CR*, 28:5:4658.

33. *Farm, Field and Fireside*, February 15, 1896.

34. Atkinson to Morton, April 28, 1896: *NA* 16.

35. New York State Grange, *Journal of Proceedings for 1896;* Petitions from California, Oregon, Washington, Pennsylvania, and Ohio in *NA* 46, S54A-J1; *National Stockman*, January 9, 1896; *Manufacturers Record*, August 14, 1896; and petitions from Wisconsin in *NA* 233, HR54A-H32.3

36. *CR*, 28:1643; 29:1:157.

37. Simpkins, *Tillman*, 346-347.

38. Morton to J. P. Irish, March 14, 1896: *Morton Mss.*

39. Stewart to E. T. Winston, January 28, 1896: *Stewart Mss.*

40. Proceedings of the Iowa Alliance.

41. This should be established at this point in the reconstruction and analysis, but for 1896 see: *Farm, Field and Fireside*, January 11, April 11, and any random issue through November 1896; *Western Rural*, April 2, 1896; *North Pacific Rural Spirit*, April 10, May 15, 1896; *Country Gentleman*, February 6, 1896; and the petitions in *NA* 46, and 233, for the 54th Congress. The Balfour admission is in Balfour to Frewen, February 3, 1896: *Frewen Mss.* Frewen did not allow it to remain hidden there for later historians.

42. See, for example, *Manufacturers Record*, July 31, 1896.

43. *Progressive Farmer*, February 4, 1896.

44. M. Butler, "Why the South Wants Free Coinage of Silver," *Arena* (March 1896), 626, 629-632.

45. Lewiston, Idaho, *Tribune*, May 20, 1896.

46. Fowler to Davis, November 9, 1894: *Davis Mss.* Also see P. Cudmore to Davis, September 14, 1894: *ibid.*

47. See, for example, his "Notes on Reciprocity, 1895," which discusses the "vexatious" loss of the Cuban and German markets: *Davis Mss.*

48. *Northwestern Miller*, December 27, 1895; January 10, 17, 24, 1896; May 29, 1896.

49. *Ibid.*, February 21, March 6, 20, 1896.

50. *Farm, Field and Fireside*, January 25, 1896.

51. *Western Rural*, February 13, 1896 (also see February 6).

52. *National Stockman*, January 2, 1896; *Country Gentleman*, January 2, 1896 (and February 27 for the letter); *Western Rural*, February 27, 1896; *American Swineherd*, May 1896; and petitions from the National Live Stock Exchange, January 20, 1896: *NA* 46, S54A-J1.1.

53. *North Pacific Rural Spirit*, May 29, 1896; St. Paul *Pioneer Press*, January 5, 1896; and Brown, "Wool Manufacturers," 414.

54. *Rural New Yorker*, April 4, 1896.

55. *Northwestern Miller*, April 24, 1896.

56. *Northwestern Miller*, February 14, 1896; Elkins to Reid, March 10, 1896; and also see Reid to Mills, February 14, 1896: *Reid Mss.*

57. National Board of Trade, petition of January 30, 1896: *NA* 233, HR54A-H11.6; *Bradstreet's*, January 18, April 4, 1896. Also see A. Barnes, of the N.A.M., to K. W. Fishback, June 17, 1896; and Fishback to Barnes, June 15, 1896: *NA* 16.

58. *Manufacturers Record*, February 28, May 1, 8, 22, July 31, 1896. Boston *Journal of Commerce*, May 30, 1896; New England Cotton Manufacturing Association, *Transactions*, April 30, 1896; Tompkins, *The Future of Cotton Manufactures in the South* (Charlotte, 1896).

59. *Report of the Committee on Ways and Means Concerning Reciprocity and Com-*

mercial Treaties. House Report No. 2263. 54th Cong., 1st Ses. (Washington, 1896). The report was adopted in May 1896, clearly in time for the campaign. Also see related petitions and resolutions in *NA* 46, 233.

60. *Seventh Biennial Report of the Bureau of Labor, Census, and Industrial Statistics of the State of Wisconsin, 1895 - 1896* (Madison, 1896). The interviews were conducted *prior* to the election.

61. See, for example, the *Northwestern Miller*, November 13, 1896.

62. *Northwestern Miller*, June 26, 1896; and see F. B. Kellogg to Davis, February 18, 1896: *Davis Mss.*

63. McKinley to Reid, January 22, 1896: *Reid Mss.*

64. Dawes, *Journal*, 319; and on McKinley's political shrewdness, see P. W. Glad, *McKinley, Bryan and the People* (New York, 1964), the most perceptive short study of the issues and the campaign.

65. Wilson, *Diary*, 104; repeated remarks in Morton's correspondence: *Morton Mss.; Western Rural*, April 9, May 7, 1896.

66. Lodge to H. Lee, January 10, 1896: *Lodge Mss.;* Lodge to Frewen, January 17, 1896; Hoar to Frewen, November 28, 1896: *Frewen Mss.* Also see Clarkson to McMillan, October 5, 1896: *Clarkson Mss.*

67. E. O. Nicy to J. Sherman, May 14, 1896: *Sherman Mss.;* the Dawes *Journal* contains an excellent account of the fight against Eastern machines, and also in Illinois.

68. From the platform.

69. Address of the Silver Republicans of June 19, 1896. A convenient published version is in Bryan, *First Battle.*

70. Teller, Denver Policy Letter of July 1896; *Farm, Field and Fireside*, July 25, 1896; speech of October 3, in Detroit: *Literary Digest*, October 17, 1896.

71. *CR*, 26:9:A:223 - 233; and again see his speeches to the Trans-Mississippi Commercial Congress of 1895.

72. Chicago *Times-Herald*, March 14, 1896.

73. *People's Party Paper*, July 10, 1896.

74. Bryan, *First Battle*, 189 - 190; *Farm, Field and Fireside*, July 18, 1896.

75. It was "the most telling part" of the speech, observed *Farm, Field and Fireside*, July 18, 1896.

76. The record of the National Silver Party Convention can be followed in Bryan, *First Battle;* in Porter and Johnson, *Party Platforms;* and there is good coverage in *Farm, Field and Fireside*, August 1, 1896.

77. Porter and Johnson, *Platforms*, 104 - 106.

78. Bryan, as quoted in *Literary Digest*, July 25, 1896.

79. Wilson, *Diary*, 117.

80. Clarkson to Clawson, September 29, 1896: *Clarkson Mss.*

81. McKinley, *An Honest Dollar and a Chance to Earn It* (Akron, 1896).

82. *Farm, Field and Fireside*, June 27, 1896. Also see *Western Rural*, June 25, 1896.

83. *Public Opinion*, June 25, 1896.

84. T. B. Catron to Elkins, July 30, 1896: *Elkins Mss.* The Elkins, Clarkson, Allison, Dunwoody, and Davis collections have much on this early fear and anxiety. See also H. G. McMillan to Clarkson, September 5, 1896; S. B. Estes to Davis, July 13, 1896; and J. Washburn to Dunwoody, July 29, 1896, as illustrations.

85. Wilson, *Diary*, 129, 144.

86. McKinley to G. Miller, July 15, 1896; and McKinley to Fordyce, July 31, 1896: *McKinley Mss.*

87. Also see the analysis in H. Working and S. Hoos, "Wheat Futures Prices and Trading at Liverpool Since 1886," *Wheat Studies* (1938), 121 - 180.

88. Dunwoody to J. Wilson, August 19, 1896: *Dunwoody Mss.;* and see *National Stockman*, August 6, 1896; *Country Gentleman*, August 13, 20, 27, 1896.

89. *Prairie Farmer*, October 17, 1896.

90. Dunwoody to T. P. Beal, president of the Second National Bank of Boston, August 26, 1896; and C. C. G. Thorton to Dunwoody, August 28, 1896: *Dunwoody Mss.;* and see the interview with S. Fish in *Manufacturers Record*, October 16, 1896.

91. *Farm, Field and Fireside*, October 24, 1896.

92. Clarkson to McMillan, October 5, 1896: *Clarkson Mss.*

93. See von Marshall to Uhl, May 7, 1896: *NA* 59.

94. New York *Tribune*, August 27, 1896; *Bradstreet's*, August 29, 1896.

95. *National Stockman*, October 22, 29, 1896. Also see *Western Rural*, October 15, 1896; and *Northwestern Miller* October 23, 1896.

96. Platt to Morton, December 11, 1895: in McElroy, *Morton*, 291. Also see Clarkson to Fessenden, October 15, 1896: *Clarkson Mss.*; E. S. Goodrich to Davis, October 16, 1896: *Davis Mss.*; and F. O. Howe to Bryan, November 4, 1896: *William J. Bryan Papers*.

97. *Rural New Yorker*, November 14, 1896.

98. *Pacific Rural Press*, October 17, 1896; and see *North Pacific Rural Spirit*, October 23, 1896.

99. *Manufacturers Record*, October 23, 1896.

100. C. R. Van Hise to Mrs. Van Hise, September 24, 1896: *Charles Richard Van Hise Papers*.

101. Dunwoody to Thorton, October 20, 1896: *Dunwoody Mss.* Also see *Farmers Tribune*, October 28, 1896.

102. Minneapolis Speech, *First Battle*, 545-546. Also see the accounts in the Minneapolis and St. Paul press.

103. *Iowa State Register*, November 6, 1896.

Chapter Fifteen

1. W. W. Kimball, "War with Spain, 1896 . . ., June 1, 1896": NA 313.

2. H. Herbert to W. L. Wilson, October 27, 1896: *Cleveland Mss.*

3. Supreme Court of the United States, October term, 1903: *Transcript of Record, No. 277, Appeal from the Circuit Court of the United States for the District of Minnesota*, 1:667-670; *Manufacturers Record*, August 7, September 11, 18, 1896; Boston *Journal of Commerce*, December 12, 1896; *American Miller*, November 1, 1896, February 1, 1897; St. Louis *Globe Democrat*, December 26, 1896; J. B. Meikle, "American Mastery of the Pacific," *World's Work* (August 1905), 6468-6469; and also see *Manufacturers Record*, March 5, April 2, 1897.

4. The most detailed account of these maneuvers is provided by McCormick, *China Trade*; the Olney directive is Olney to Denby, December 13, 1896: *NA* 59. Also see *Age of Steel*, November 22, 1896; and *Rural New Yorker*, September 19, 1896. There is useful material in the *John R. Young Papers*, as well as in the more generally cited collections.

5. Wilson, *Diary*, 167. Also see *Farm, Field and Fireside*, November 21, 1896.

6. Cleveland, draft message for 1896: *Cleveland Mss.*; and in re the desire to have the issue settled, see materials in *Lodge, McKinley*, and *Roosevelt Mss.*

7. Cleveland, annual message as delivered on December 7, 1896: Richardson, *Messages*, 13:6146 ff.

8. Petition of Galveston, Texas, Alliance, December 21, 1896: *NA* 46, S54A-K5; Raleigh *News and Observer*, December 8, 1896; *Farm, Field and Fireside*, December 12, 1896; *CR*, 29:3:2172. For further pressure see *Farm, Field and Fireside*, January 2, 9, 1896; *Western Rural*, January 7, 28, 1896; and petition of citizens of Norwood, Stanley County, North Carolina, January 28, 1897: *NA* 233, HR55A-H6.3.

9. *National Cooperation Review*, January 9, 1897; *National Dry Goods Reporter*, December 19, 1896. Also consult *Bradstreet's*, December 26, 1896; and *Wall Street Journal*, February 9, 1897. *Manufacturers Record*, December 25, 1896; and see the issue of January 1, 1897, for a vast number of comments.

10. *Commercial and Financial Chronicle*, December 19, 1896, January 9, 1897; *Manufacturers Record*, January 1, 1897: "Pittsburgh Iron Executive" [Carnegie?], Union Boiler and Manufacturing Company, S. C. Forsaith Machine Company, National Specialty Manufacturing Company, and Milton Car Works; *Cement and Engineering News*, November 1896; and also see *Nation*, January 14, 1897.

11. *Wall Street Journal*, December 16, 1896; *Commercial and Financial Chronicle*, December 12, 1896.

12. Conversation between P.D. and K. Armour, as reported in Leech, *McKinley*, 292.

13. Fish to Dodge, March 24, 1897: *IC Mss.*; also his interview in *Manufacturers Record*, January 22, 1897.

14. *Manufacturers Record*, February 12, 1897.

15. Hay, as quoted by Leech, *McKinley*, 95.

16. Transcript of phone conversation between Gates and Hanna, February 22, 1897; and Hanna to Gates, March 19, 1897: *Aldrich Mss.* Also see the excellent description of McKinley in J. R. Mann to J. F. Aldrich, April 17, 1897: *ibid.*

17. Hanna, as quoted by Bristow, *Fraud and Politics*, 61.

18. See *Farm, Field and Fireside*, January 23, 1897.

19. Sherman to McKinley, February 15, 1897: *McKinley Mss.*

20. Wilson to G. T. Meggitt, March 26, 1897; Wilson to W. D. Hoard, April 8, 1897; and Wilson to L. H. Fallington, April 15, 1897: all in *NA* 16.

21. McKinley, inaugural address of March 4, 1897: Richardson, *Messages*, 6236-6241.

22. See, for example, *Farm Machinery*, June 8, 1897; *Mirror and Farmer*, June 10, 1897; petition of Farmers Institute of Lee Park, Nebraska, February 4, 1897: *NA* 46, S54A-J1.1; *Manufacturers Record*, July 9, 1897; *Bradstreet's*, July 10, 1897; and Lodge to Davis, September 10, 1897: *Lodge Mss.*

23. Thompson to McKinley, June 22, 1897: *McKinley Mss.*; Fish, interview in *Manufacturers Record*, July 9, 1897.

24. McKinley to C. W. Stone, February 13, 1897: *McKinley Mss.*; *The New York Times*, April 13, May 7, 8, 9, 1897; Wolcott to Chandler, November 13, 1896; Chandler to McKinley, December 17, 1896: *Chandler Mss.*; McKinley to Hay, June 27, 1897: *John Hay Papers.*

25. Wilson to Sherman, May 22, 1897; Sherman to Storer, June 5, 1897: *NA* 59; then see *Western Rural*, April 22, May 13, 1897; and the testimony in *Reciprocity Convention with France. Senate Document No. 225.* 56th Cong., 1st Ses. (Washington, 1900), 897.

26. *CR*, 30:2:1227; McCormick to Senator Davis, March 5, 1900: *Reciprocity with France*, 120; but also consult McCormick, *China Trade*, for a nice review of the debate.

27. *Memorial of the Clergymen of Philadelphia, February 22, 1897. Senate Document No. 60.* 55th Cong., 1st Ses. (Washington, 1897); Memorial by David Lubin on behalf of State Granges of California, Oregon, Illinois, Washington, Missouri, Virginia, and Pennsylvania of February 26, 1897; Memorial of the National Equitable Protection Association, March 2, 1897: all in *NA* 46, S54A-J1.1; the testimony and petitions in *Tariff Hearings Before the Ways and Means Committee, 1896-1897. House Document No. 338.* Two Volumes. 54th Cong., 2nd Ses. (Washington, 1897), 866-945; and *CR*, 29:3:2289; 30:1:447, 1240-1634; 30:1:1240-1242; 1603-1634.

28. Lodge to Lee, April 9, 1897: *Lodge Mss.*

29. *Farm, Stock and Home*, January 15, 1897; *Prairie Farmer*, March 27, July 31, 1897; *Farm, Field and Fireside*, April 3, 1897; petition of Farmers Institute of Lee Park, Nebraska, February 4, 1897: *NA* 46, S54A-J1.1; *CR*, 30:2:2539-2546, 2549-2565, et seq.; *Official Proceedings of the Ninth Session of the Trans-Mississippi Commercial Congress, Salt Lake City, July 14-17, 1897* (Salt Lake, 1897); *CR*, 30:2:2241 (Rep. J. D. Clardy of Kentucky); and *North Pacific Rural Spirit*, July 30, 1897.

30. *CR*, 30:1:43; *Washington Post*, April 5, 1897.

31. *CR*, 30:1:562, 615-621, 643-645, 656-660.

32. *Ibid.*, 30:1:684-694, 996, 1080; and 30:2:1192-1198; and Warren to H. G. Hay, June 6, 1897: *Warren Mss.* Also see the resolution of the Utah State Legislature of April 21, 1897: *NA* 46, S55A-H6.3; *Western Rural*, April 22, 1897; Marion Butler to Cooper, May 21, 1897, A. J. Bingham to Cooper, May 31, 1897 (and the Cooper speeches) in *Cooper Mss.*; and A. W. Dunn, *From Harrison to Harding, A Personal Narrative Covering a Third of a Century, 1888-1921* (New York, 1922), 326-237.

33. See, for example: Search to McKinley, April 1897: *McKinley Mss.*; the many circular letters of the N.A.M.; Boston *Journal of Commerce* (Southern edition), July 24, 1897; the releases of the Philadelphia Commercial Museum and Manufacturers Club; *Nation*, June 24, 1897; *Scientific American*, July 24, 1897; and Atkinson to Wells, June 9, 1897: *Wells Mss.*

34. This petition of April 13, 1897, and the others are in *NA* 46, S55A-K24. Also see J. F. Rusling to McKinley, June 18, 1897: *McKinley Mss.*

35. These quotations come from J. B. Moore's "Diary-Memoranda" (1897): *Moore Mss.*

36. *CR*, 30:1:946-947; *Farm, Field and Fireside*, May 29, 1897; Warren to Hay, June 6, 1897: *Warren Mss.*

37. *Western Rural*, May 27, July 29, 1897; *Farm, Field and Fireside*, May 22, June 5, 17, 26, 1897; and for metropolitan attitudes see the petitions in *NA* 16, S55A-J11.2.

38. L. F. Auga to Allen, May 17, 1897: *Allen Mss.*

39. *CR*, 30:2:1025-1026, 1201-1202.

40. Calhoun to Day, May 14, 1897: *Charles L. Kurtz Papers*; Calhoun, Reports of June 10 and 22, 1897: *NA* 59; *North Pacific Rural Spirit*, June 16, 1897.

41. Offner, *McKinley*, 142, note 7; *Western Rural*, July 1, 1897.

42. *Farm, Field and Fireside*, July 3, 1897; Sherman to Woodford, July 16, 1897: *NA* 59.

43. Lodge to Davis, August 10, 1897: *Lodge Mss.*

44. *Nation*, October 14, 1897; *Railroad World*, November 13, 1897; and *Wall Street Journal*, December 3, 1897.

45. Holls to A. D. White, September 3, 1897: *Holls Mss.* Also see T. Roosevelt to Lodge, September 15, 1897, and to F. V. Greene, September 15, 1897: *Theodore Roosevelt Papers.*

46. *Farm, Field and Fireside*, August 7, 28, October 12, 1897; *Nation*, September 23, 1897; *Milwaukee Union Signal*, September 25, 1897; *American Swineherd*, November 1897; Woodford to McKinley, September 3, 6, 1897: *McKinley Mss.*; Woodford to Sherman, September 20, 1897: *NA* 59.

47. See McCormick, *China Trade*; also Roosevelt to Lodge, September 21, 1897: *Roosevelt Mss.*; Leech, *McKinley*, 161.

48. *North Pacific Rural Spirit*, August 20, 1897; *Annual Session of the Farmers National Congress, St. Paul, August 31-September 6, 1897* (Chicago, 1897); the speech by Hill is a useful review of his long campaign. Also see A. Knox to Davis, August 3, 1897: *Davis Mss.*; and U.S.D.A., *Circular No. 17 of the Section on Foreign Markets, United States Wheat for Eastern Markets* (Washington, 1897); J. Brucker to Holls, October 19, 1897: *Holls Mss.*; New England Cotton Manufacturers Association, *Transactions of October 28, 1897*; *Commercial and Financial Chronicle*, December 25, 1897; New York *Journal of Commerce*, January 5, 1898.

49. Wilson to J. H. Gear, November 11, 1897: *NA* 16; *The New York Times*, November 5, 7, 9, 10, 11, 1897; Sherman to Woodford, November 20, 1897: *NA* 59.

50. *Farm, Field and Fireside*, October 30, November 13, 20, 1897; *Western Rural*, November 4, 11, 1897.

51. Day to Woodford, October 1, 1897: *NA* 59.

52. Woodford to McKinley, November 1897: as quoted in Offner, *McKinley*, 158.

53. Wilson to Sherman, November 6, 1897: *NA* 16, a typical protest and request for strong action.

54. *CR*, 31:1:3-5.

55. Roosevelt to Lodge, December 30, 1897: *Roosevelt Mss.*; Woodford to McKinley, December 26, 1897, and January 8, 1898: *NA* 59.

56. *Iron and Machinery World*, December 10, 1897; *Journal of Commerce*, December 29, 31, 1897; and below. Also see the ambivalence in *Commercial and Financial Chronicle* as early as November 6, 1897.

57. *CR*, 31:1:39-40; also see the remarks of Rep. John M. Allen of Mississippi.

58. *Sixty-Fourth Annual Report of the Philadelphia Board of Trade, 1897* (Philadelphia, 1897), 15.

59. These are taken from *Farm, Field and Fireside*, November 27, December 4, and 25, 1897, to show a line of thought in one typical paper. See the *Western Rural*, December 9, 1897, for comparison.

60. Davis to Kellogg, December 11, 27, 1897: *Davis Mss.* Also see New York *Tribune*, January 13, 1898; and Lodge to O'Meara, January 3, 1898: *Lodge Mss.*

61. G. F. Hoar, *Autobiography of Seventy Years* (New York, 1903), 2:306-308; Lodge to O'Meara, January 3, 1898: *Lodge Mss.*

62. Denby to Sherman, January 31, 1898: *NA* 59.

63. Memoranda, and other records in the files of the American Asiatic Association, courtesy of James Lorence; the New York Chamber of Commerce petition, January 28, 1898, can also be found in *NA* 59; and see *Asia* (1899), 34.

64. Lodge to H. White, January 31, 1898; White to Lodge, January 18, 1898; Lodge to O'Meara, January 3, 1898: *Lodge Mss.*; Warren to M. Nichols, February 22, 1898: *Warren Mss.*; *CR*, 31:1:426-427, 793-795, and 854-858.

65. Dawes, *Journal*, 139.

66. Lodge to White, January 31, 1898: *Lodge Mss.*

67. Resolution of the Legislature of Mississippi, January 17, 1898; and see the vast number of similar items in *NA* 46, S55A-J.1.

68. Holcomb to Barton, January 7, 1898: *Holcomb Mss.*; Governor Rogers to Barton,

January 31, 1898; Lee to Barton, February 4, 1898; Tanner to Barton, and proclamation of February 11, 1898: *NA* 59.

69.   Barton to Day, February 9, 1898: *NA* 59; Potter to Berry, January 30, 1898: *Holcomb Mss.*

70.   Memorial of January 1898 to McKinley from W. J. Wilcox and thirty-five other firms: *NA* 59.

71.   See the dispatches in *Consular Correspondence Respecting the Condition . . . in Cuba, the State of the War in that Island, and the Prospects of the Projected Autonomy. April 11, 1898. House Document No. 406.* 55th Cong., 2nd Ses. (Washington, 1898), 19, 52-53, et seq. They can also be found in *NA* 59.

72.   *CR,* 31:1:729, 767-770.

73.   *Western Rural,* January 20, 1898; *Nation,* January 27, 1898; Washington *Evening Star,* January 19, 21, 1898; Washington *Post,* January 20, 1898; and *CR,* 31:1:798.

74.   Gullon to Woodford, February 1, 1898; Woodford to McKinley, February 4, 7, 1898, and Woodford to McKinley, January 17, 28, 1898: *NA* 59.

75.   *Silver Knight-Watchman,* February 17, 1898. The variations can be seen in *CR,* 31:1:828-836, 854-858, 875, 892-893, 910-914, 947-948; 31:2:1083-1084, 1112-1113, 1135, 1210-1211, 1218, 1675-1676; 31:3:2048-2049; also see *Western Rural,* February 24, 1898; and the correspondence in the *Cooper Mss.*

76.   See the revealing speech by Rep. J. B. Clark of Missouri, including the remarks of J. A. Graham, managing editor of the St. Louis *Republic: CR,* 31:1:793-795. Also see *Western Rural,* February 3, 1898; *Manufacturers Record,* February 4, 1898; and the remarks of Rep. T. H. Tongue of Oregon, *CR,* 31:3:2235. *Southern Mercury,* January 6, 1898; and see the petitions in *NA* 46, S55A-J1; *CR,* 31:2:1578-1580; 31:3:2031-2034; *Western Rural,* March 17, 1898; Schurz, essay of March 19, in *Works,* 454-455; *Farm, Stock and Home,* April 15, 1898.

77.   *CR,* 31:1:700-704.

78.   There is an interesting letter from Crowninshield (Navy) to Lodge, September 9, 1898, discussing the episode. He was concerned lest it "might look a little too much as if the Administration or the Department, or both, had made up their minds that they were going to have a fight anyway whether Spain wanted it or not." He did not consider the issue of moving in Asia significant enough to deserve mention.

79.   Dingley, *Nelson Dingley,* 454; *CR,* 31:2:1770-1772; 31:3:2019-2022; and E. P. Andrus to Boardman, February 16, 1898: *Boardman Mss.*

80.   On the importance of April, see Woodford to McKinley, March 2, 1898: *NA* 59.

81.   Busbey, *Uncle Joe Cannon,* 186-190; Washington *Evening Star,* March 7, 8, 1898; Washington *Post,* March 8, 1898.

82.   McKinley's annual message of December 5, 1898: Richardson, *Messages,* 13:6307-6316, is a remarkably revealing public document. He spoke candidly on two crucial issues. One, that the March request for money was for "making instant provision for the possible and perhaps speedily probable emergency of war." Two, he acknowledged the clear intention to wage a two-front war to destroy "Spanish naval power in the Pacific Ocean and completely controlling the bay of Manila," *despite* the knowledge that the Spanish had assembled a "powerful squadron" in the Atlantic.

83.   *CR,* 31:4:3410-3413; and see 31:3:2069-2074; 31:4:3293; Washington *Evening Star,* March 29, 1898. Also *CR,* 31:4:3703; 31:5:4163; 31:3:2616, 2359-2360; 31:4:3255-3256, 3465-3466.

84.   *Silver Knight-Watchman,* March 3, 1898; *North Pacific Rural Spirit,* March 18, 1898; *Union Signal,* March 19, 1898; and see *Southern Mercury* throughout the period.

85.   *Prairie Farmer,* April 2, 1898; *Breeder's Gazette,* March 23, April 13, 1898; Colgate and Company to the Secretary of State, February 18, 1898: *NA* 59; *CR,* 31:3:2837-2841; and the speeches during the discussion of the $50 million appropriation, *CR,* 31:3:2602-2621; and 31:3:2554-2555, 2877-2879, 31:4:3213, 3220, 3249; and the materials in the *Boardman Mss.*

86.   *Wall Street Journal,* March 9, 1898; Fish to Welling, March 11, 1898: *IC Mss.*; Dodge to Alger, March 15, 1898, and Alger to Dodge, March 19, 1898: *Alger Mss.* Also see Reid to McKinley, March 8, 1898: *McKinley Mss.*

87.   *CR,* 31:3:2916-2919. Then see New York Chamber of Commerce petition, *CB,* 31:3:2866-2870. *Manufacturers Record,* February 18, March 16, 18, 1898; Fish to McKinley, March 10, 1898, Fish to Roosevelt, March 12, 1898, Fish to H. C. Leache, March 12,

1898, Fish to M. J. Sanders, March 17, 1898, Fish to A. Hogg, May 17, 1898, and Fish to R. H. Edmunds, May 17, 1898: all in *IC Mss.*

88. Resolution of January 31, 1898: *NA* 46, S55A-J11.1; Mosle to Day, February 9, 1898: *NA* 59; New York *Tribune*, February 10, 1898.

89. Morton to McKinley, March 20, 1898; McCook to McKinley, March 22, 1898; Lodge to McKinley, March 21, 1898; Reick to Young, March 25, 1898: *McKinley Mss.* Also see T. Beer, *Hanna,* 197-200; Washington *Post,* March 27, 1898; Washington *Evening Star,* April 6, 1898; *Western Rural,* March 24, 1898; *Literary Digest,* March 19, 1898.

90. See the petitions and resolutions beginning about March 25, 1898, in *NA* 233, HR55A-H6.3, and *NA* 46, S55A-J11.1.

91. See Cooper to Riel, April 21, 1898: *Cooper Mss.*; and Davidson to Boardman, April 9, 1898: *Boardman Mss.,* for two good accounts of these maneuvers. Then see Lodge to George [?], and Henry Lee, on April 4, 1898, and to John [?], April 15, 1898; *Lodge Mss.*

92. See the account of this cloud of telegrams dated April 4, in *The New York Times,* April 7, 1898.

93. *Southern Mercury,* April 14, May 5, 1898.

94. J. S. Woods, letter to the editor, *Southern Mercury,* July 21, 1898.

95. *Western Rural,* April 28, 1898; *Rural New Yorker,* April 23, 1898. Also see Oregon State Grange, *Journal of Proceedings for 1898;* and the remarks of Rep. Peters, *CR,* 31:5:4383.

Conclusion

1. McKinley's continuing skepticism of McCook's involvement in Cuba suggests this, as does even more his opposition to the hard-line colonial annexationists.

2. Warren to J. A. Breckous, April 13, 1898: *Warren Mss.*

3. *CR,* 31:4:3703, 3732, 4038, 4069; 31:A:279-281; and the materials in the *Jacob Calvin Cooper Papers.*

4. This analysis is based on the debates, materials in the *NA,* and the relevant manuscript collections.

5. J. W. Springer to W. M. Springer, April 3, 1898: *Springer Mss.*

6. *CR,* 31:7:6346-6347.

7. Petitions from Doniphan County, Kansas, March 15, 21; Nemaha County, Kansas, March 15, 1898; Grand Island, Nebraska (one of fifteen from Nebraska), March 1898: *NA* 233 and 16. The results of a postcard poll of other editors taken by the *Orange Judd Farmer* is also on file: they were against annexation "at present" because it would damage the beet-sugar businessmen. *CR,* 31:7:5988-5989.

8. *Western Rural,* May 26, 1898; *Manufacturers Record,* May 27, 1898; *Southern Mercury,* May 12, 1898; Wilson to McCoy, May 5, 1898: *NA* 16.

9. *Manufacturers Record,* again quoting the Chicago *Times-Herald,* July 8, 1898; *Farmers Review,* November 23, 1898; *Prairie Farmer,* June 23, 1900.

10. Hill, testimony: *Industrial Commission,* 6:130.

11. Fish, interview with *Manufacturers Record,* September 16, 1898; *Farm Implement News,* September 15, October 20, 1898; National Grange, *Journal of Proceedings for the Session of 1898.*

12. J. C. Hanley, testimony: *Industrial Commission,* 10:279.

13. *Manufacturers Record,* June 10, 1898. Also see the wealth of expansionist testimony by agriculturalists in *Industrial Commission,* 10, *passim.*

14. Letter to the editor, *Manufacturers Record,* July 15, 1898; Resolution of the Legislature of the State of Georgia, December 19, 1898: *NA* 233, HR55-H9.12; and letter to the editor, *Manufacturers Record,* September 16, 1898.

15. Tompkins, of course, provided a classic example of this integration into the metropolis. He had become the equal of Atkinson—if not, indeed, a more important figure. But see, as indicative, the excellent sampling of Southern and Northeastern business views in *Manufacturers Record,* June 17, 1898.

16. *Wallace's Farmer,* December 21, 1900.

17. Wilson to McCoy, May 5, 1898: *NA* 16. Italics added.

18. Wilson to N. M. Hubbard, May 27, 1898; Wilson to C. W. Dabney, June 1, 1898; Wilson to Hubbard, June 27, 1898: all in *NA* 16.

19. F. B. Thurber, "Wider Markets and How to Get Them," *Official Proceedings of the Trans-Mississippi Congress, 1899*, 33, 37-38.

20. *Western Rural*, May 26, 1898; letter to the editor, *Manufacturers Record*, July 15, 1898; Tompkins, as quoted in an extensive survey of businessmen, *ibid.*, June 17, 1898 (also see the remarks of James Orr).

21. *Western Rural*, June 9, 1898.

22. *Southern Mercury*, June 30, 1898; such early resistance is discussed by the *Rural New Yorker*, July 30, 1898; and is manifest in the *Western Rural*, July 7, 1898.

23. *Western Rural*, June 9, August 18, 1898.

24. Massachusetts State Grange, *Journal of Proceedings for 1898*; *Farmers Review*, November 16, 1898; *NR and FM*, January 12, February 9, 1899; *Western Rural*, December 8, 1898.

25. J. Weinstein, *The Corporate Ideal in the Liberal State, 1900-1918* (Boston, 1968).

26. Schurz, Saratoga paper of August 19, 1898: *Works*, 5:477-492; Schurz to McKinley, September 22, 1898: *ibid.*, 515-516; *Western Rural*, September 1, 1898; and see the poll of farmers in *NR and FM*, August 31, 1898.

27. Easley to J. H. Hammond, May 19, 1915: *John Jay Hammond Papers.*

28. McCormick, *China Trade*, 108; on the ambivalence after the May 11 decision, see Lodge to White, June 21, and September 12, 1898: *Lodge Mss.*; and McCormick, *ibid.*, 115-116.

29. Chicago *Times-Herald*, October 14, 1898; *Western Rural*, October 20, 1898.

30. Letter of ex-Governor W. A. MacCorkle, *Manufacturers Record*, September 16, 1898.

31. J. F. Hanson, of the Bibb Manufacturing Company of Macon, Georgia, in *Manufacturers Record*, June 17, 1898; but see the entire issue.

32. *Ibid.*, September 30, October 7, 1898 (quoting the Macon, Georgia, *Telegraph*); and the comments of Senator Allen, *CR*, 32:2:1480.

33. *CR*, 31:7:6702-6707; 32:2:1480-1484; and see Kyle's remarks as a member of the Industrial Commission; Joint Resolution of the Legislature of South Dakota, February 3, 1899: *NA* 46, S55A-J11.1. Bryan's position is well established, and Tillman explained his very similar outlook in the debates: "We only want enough of your territory to give us a harbor of refuge, a naval station, the right to protect you from outside interlopers, and to get such commercial advantage as you of right ought to give us": also quoted in Bryan, *The Second Battle* (Chicago, 1900), 410. Similar views can be sampled in *CR*, 32:1:1004-1008; 32:2:1221; 32:3:2408; and in petitions such as the one from the citizens of Dodgeville, Wisconsin, January 30, 1899: *NA* 46, S55A-J11.4, who advised "reserving full powers . . . to exercise a protectorate." Almost all the anti-annexationist petitions are printed postcards provided by the Anti-Imperialist League. Very few bear postmarks from agricultural regions.

34. *Farmers Review*, October 12, 1898; and see C. S. Campbell, *Special Business Interests and the Open Door Policy* (New Haven, 1951); and the thesis by Patrick Hearden.

35. This quotation is from Hanley's strong presentation of August 12, 1899, before Senator Kyle and other members of the Industrial Commission. But see all of Volume 10 for the extensive support for such a policy in Asia. Then sample such items as *Farmers Review*, October 17, 1900; *Minneapolis Journal*, September 24, 1900; *NR and FM*, March 23, 1899; *Prairie Farmer*, June 23, August 4, 1900; St. Louis *Post-Dispatch*, October 23, 1899; *Wallace's Farmer*, July 13, 1900; and the official *Proceedings* of the 1900 and 1901 Trans-Mississippi Commercial Conventions.

36. Senator McLaurin's speech is in *CR*, 33:3:2381-2385. The industry's campaign can be followed in Textile Manufacturers Association to Hay, January 3, 1899; Fall River Board of Trade to Hay, July 20, 1899: both in *NA* 59; in petitions of Southern Cotton Spinners Association of November 1899, and to Hay, January 9, 1900: *NA* 46, S56A-J12.6; in the *Tompkins Mss.*; and in *Manufacturers Record*, October 20, 1899; January 25, May 17, 19, June 17, 21, 28, July 5, and November 30, 1900. On Hill, see E. T. Chamberlain to G. B. Cortelyou, June 30, 1900: *McKinley Mss.*; and then consult G. Perkins, "Statement Upon Selling to Mr. Hill," *George Ward Holdrege Papers*; and G. W. Holdrege, *The Making of the Burlington* (Lincoln, 1921).

37. *Prairie Farmer*, August 4, 1900.

Index

About The Author

William Appleman Williams was born in Atlantic, Iowa, and educated at Kemper Military School, the U.S. Naval Academy, the University of Wisconsin, and the University of Leeds. He received his Ph.D. from the University of Wisconsin.

During World War II, Professor Williams served in the U.S. Navy as an executive officer in the Pacific theater. Since then he has taught at Washington and Jefferson College, Bard College, Ohio State University, the University of Oregon, and the University of Wisconsin. At present he is teaching at Oregon State University.

His books include: *American-Russian Relations, 1781-1947; The Shaping of American Diplomacy, 1750-1970; The Tragedy of American Diplomacy; The Contours of American History; The United States, Cuba and Castro; The Great Evasion: An Essay on the Contemporary Relevance of Karl Marx.* Professor Williams has also written many articles for popular and scholarly journals.

Professor Williams, his wife, and three of their five children make their home in Newport, Oregon.